MW01030336

A Shostakovich Casebook

Portrait of Shostakovich by Jeannette Brown

Russian Music Studies
Malcolm Hamrick Brown, Founding Editor

A Shostakovich Casebook

edited by
Malcolm Hamrick Brown

Indiana University Press
Bloomington and Indianapolis

This book is a publication of

Indiana University Press
601 North Morton Street
Bloomington, Indiana 47404-3797 USA

http://iupress.indiana.edu

Telephone orders	800-842-6796
Fax orders	812-855-7931
Orders by e-mail	iuporder@indiana.edu

The paper used in this publication meets the minimum requirements of American National Standard for Information Sciences—Permanence of Paper for Printed Library Materials, ANSI Z39.48-1984.

Manufactured in
the United States of America

Library of Congress Cataloging-in-Publication Data

A Shostakovich casebook / Malcolm Hamrick Brown, editor.
p. cm.—(Russian music studies)
Includes works originally published 1976–2002.
Includes bibliographical references and index.
ISBN 0–253–34364-X (cloth : alk. paper)
1. Shostakovich, Dmitrii Dmitrievich, 1906–1975.
2. Shostakovich, Dmitrii Dmitrievich, 1906–1975.
Testimony. I. Brown, Malcolm Hamrick. II. Series: Russian music studies (Bloomington, Ind.)
ML410.S53S46 2004
780'.92—dc22
2003017153

1 2 3 4 5 09 08 07 06 05 04

The crowd greedily reads confessions, memoirs, etc., because of its baseness it rejoices at the abasement of the high, at the weaknesses of the strong. It is in rapture at the disclosure of anything loathsome. "He is small like us; he is loathsome like us!" But you lie, you, scoundrels: he's small and he's loathsome, but not the way you are—differently.

—Pushkin, letter to Prince Vyazemsky

Contents

ACKNOWLEDGMENTS xi

NOTES ON TRANSLITERATION AND ON TRANSLATION xiii

Introduction 1

Part One

1. Shostakovich versus Volkov: Whose *Testimony*? (1980) 11
   Laurel E. Fay
2. Volkov's *Testimony* Reconsidered (2002) 22
   Laurel E. Fay

Part Two

3. A Side-by-Side Comparison of Texts from *Testimony* with Their Original Sources 69
4. A Pitiful Fake: About the So-Called "Memoirs" of D. D. Shostakovich (1979) 80
   Letter to the editor of *Literaturnaia gazeta*
5. The Bedbug (1979) 84
   Editorial in *Literaturnaia gazeta*, 14 November 1979, p. 8
6. The Official Dossier (1979) 90
   News item in *Literaturnaia gazeta*
7. Notes from the Soviet Archives on Volkov's *Testimony* (1995) 92
   Alla Bogdanova
8. An Episode in the Life of a Book: An Interview with Henry Orlov (2000) 97
   Ludmila Kovnatskaya
9. An Answer to Those Who Still Abuse Shostakovich (2000) 127
   Irina Shostakovich

10. On Solomon Volkov and *Testimony* (1988, 1997) 134
Boris Tishchenko

11. The Regime and Vulgarity (1999) 137
Elena Basner

12. Shostakovich's World Is Our World (1998) 142
Mstislav Rostropovich Talks with Manashir Yakubov

13. Shostakovich Remembered: Interviews with His Soviet Colleagues (1992) 150
Irina Nikolskaya

Part Three

14. A Link in the Chain: Reflections on Shostakovich and His Times (1976) 193
Henry Orlov

15. A Perspective on Soviet Musical Culture during the Lifetime of Shostakovich (1998) 216
Levon Hakobian

16. The Latest "New Shostakovich": Allan Ho and Dmitri Feofanov's *Shostakovich Reconsidered* (2000) 230
Levon Hakobian

17. Dialogues about Shostakovich: From the History of Russian Studies about Shostakovich (2002) 238
Ludmila Kovnatskaya

Part Four

18. Ian MacDonald's *The New Shostakovich* (1993) 257
Malcolm Hamrick Brown

19. Elizabeth Wilson's *Shostakovich: A Life Remembered* (1996) 265
Malcolm Hamrick Brown

20. A Response to Papers by Allan Ho and Dmitri Feofanov (1998) 269
David Fanning

21. Whose Shostakovich? (2000) 283
Gerard McBurney

22. The Shostakovich Variations (2000) 303
PAUL MITCHINSON

23. Shostakovich: A Brief Encounter and a Present Perspective (1996, 2002) 325
MALCOLM HAMRICK BROWN

24. Laurel Fay's *Shostakovich: A Life* (2000) 346
SIMON MORRISON

25. When Serious Music Mattered: On Shostakovich and Three Recent Books (2001) 360
RICHARD TARUSKIN

SELECTED BIBLIOGRAPHY 385

CONTRIBUTORS 391

INDEX 397

Acknowledgments

I acknowledge first of all the contributors whose scholarship made this volume possible. The reprinted works included here have been reviewed and corrected by their authors, and I very much appreciate the time this entailed.

My sincere gratitude to Levon Hakobian, Ludmila Kovnatskaya, and Sergei Lebedev for helping make contact with a number of the Russian contributors, as well as for providing critical service as authoritative informants about a variety of issues that arose in the process of putting the volume together.

Caryl Emerson read through the entire collection with an expert, discerning eye and shared comments and advice. Her professional generosity has much improved the finished book. She also called my attention to Pushkin's wonderfully ascerbic characterization of memoirs and confessions, which serves as a most appropriate epigraph for the volume.

I am much indebted to my darling and talented daughter, Jeannette, for the original drawing of Shostakovich that appears as the frontispiece of the *Casebook*, and to her husband, my gifted son-in-law, Paul Smedberg, who made an original computer painting from the drawing, which appears on the dust jacket.

In addition to writing the centerpiece article of the *Casebook*, "Volkov's *Testimony* Reconsidered" (chapter 2), Laurel Fay kindly provided translations for a number of the Russian-language articles and essays (identified in the notes to individual pieces) and, certainly as important, encouraged and supported the editor throughout the conception and realization of the project. Without her, it simply could not have happened.

My most cordial thanks to everyone!

Malcolm Hamrick Brown
Bloomington, January 2003

Notes on Transliteration and on Translation

Although the Library of Congress (LC) system of transliteration has generally been followed here (without the superscript arcs above the letters for those Cyrillic characters rendered by more than a single Latin character in the *strict* LC system), exceptions have been made in the case of Russian personal names, as well as the occasional other Russian proper name or title. These exceptions have been transliterated in a more "pronunciation friendly" style. The guiding principle was to find a spelling that would suggest to English speakers a pronunciation that would be recognizable to a Russian speaker. These "pronunciation friendly" transliterations have been applied consistently throughout the text, as well as in the reference notes, regardless of how they may have been transliterated in other contexts—including direct quotations and bibliographic references. But to facilitate searching in standardized databases, such as WorldCat, the primary entry in the index for these "pronunciation friendly" transliterations has been supplemented by the LC transliteration within square brackets. For example, the entry in the index for the name "Kremlyov, Yuli Anatolievich" is followed by "[Kremlëv, Iulii Anatol'evich]" and the title "Rayok" is followed by "[*Raëk*]."

With regard to the translation of Russian texts, the preferences of individual authors have been followed. This has occasionally resulted in somewhat different translations of the very same Russian text found in different articles in the *Casebook*.

A Shostakovich Casebook

Introduction

It matters that *Testimony*[1] is not exactly what Solomon Volkov has claimed it to be. Just as it matters that Anton Schindler's *Biographie von Ludwig van Beethoven* was written by an author shown to have forged entries in Beethoven's conversation books and even to have destroyed some of them. Scholars now know to treat with caution any anecdote about Beethoven related by Schindler as the sole eyewitness.

It matters even more, in the case of *Testimony*, because a book that *speaks in the voice* of a major twentieth-century composer casts a long shadow into the future. It matters, because knowing the difference between what is authentic and what is dubious not only informs the character of interpretations made today but also the relationship of present and future interpretations. And interpretation is the essence of the matter.

The earliest incentive for producing the present *Shostakovich Casebook* came from a colleague who teaches the standard "survey of twentieth-century music" for music majors. He took me aside one day in the hallway: "You know something? My students write term papers on Shostakovich *far* more than on any other twentieth-century composer. And they believe every word of *Testimony* and *Shostakovich Reconsidered.*[2] Why don't you put together a selection of writings that would give them a different perspective, especially including something from the Soviet or Russian point of view?"

It was not a bad idea. *Shostakovich Reconsidered* had already argued vehemently the case for Volkov's defense and for the absolute authenticity of *Testimony*. What was needed now was a casebook that would bring together in a single, concise source, in book form, selections from what was "already out there" but not always easily accessible—documents, articles, reviews, interviews, lectures.

The "Soviet or Russian point of view" indeed had not been made readily available because of language. What little had been translated had generally appeared in specialized journals. (In fairness to the authors of *Shostakovich Reconsidered*, their book provides examples of the "Soviet or Russian point of view" but only when it supports their arguments for the authenticity of *Testimony*. A range of contrary perspectives is not represented.)

With regard to Western specialists who raised basic questions about Volkov and *Testimony*, their primary venue had also been scholarly journals, literary magazines, and newspapers, which added an inconvenient step to the research process for students writing term papers. Even experienced scholars had occasionally been stymied by problems of access to a particular specialized journal. More problematical still, for researchers, were scholarly papers that were presented as public lectures.

Although these were all perfectly good reasons to put together a selection of materials that might give my colleague's students "a different perspective" on Shostakovich, I had not moved ahead with the project.

The decisive impetus came only when I learned from Laurel Fay that she had made an important new discovery and was writing what would become the focal point of the present volume—her article, "Volkov's *Testimony* Reconsidered."

Fay's much talked about but little read 1980 review, "Shostakovich versus Volkov: Whose *Testimony*?" would serve as the indispensable prologue to her new article. This early review, basic to an understanding of the reception history of *Testimony*, appeared in a specialized journal rarely seen by musicians and musicologists,[3] and had never been reprinted. Volkov's apologists claim that it set the belligerent tone for what would become the "Shostakovich Wars" in the late 1990s. Anyone interested in checking the accuracy of this claim can now verify Fay's approach for what it has been all along, both in her 1980 review and in her new "Volkov's *Testimony* Reconsidered"—restrained, factual, and skeptical in the best scholarly sense of the word (an approach also exemplified in her indispensable book, *Shostakovich: A Life*).[4] The reasons, then, are entirely obvious why Fay's two fundamental critical studies of *Testimony*—the one from 1980, the other from 2002—should occupy part 1 of the present Shostakovich casebook.

Part 2 provides the context for understanding not only Fay's critical evaluation of *Testimony* but also the background of the *Testimony* debate. All the documentary materials it includes represent "something from the Soviet or Russian point of view":

A "Side-by-Side Comparison of Texts from *Testimony* with Their Original Sources" reproduces the content of each of the eight pages of the *Testimony* typescript signed by Shostakovich (he signed but a single page from each of the book's eight chapters!) alongside the text as found in the original Soviet publications from which the *Testimony* typescript was copied.

"A Pitiful Fake" provides a complete translation of the 1979 letter from six of Shostakovich's students and close friends to the editor of the Soviet literary newspaper, *Literaturnaia gazeta,* denouncing *Testimony* as "lie . . . piled upon lie." An editorial accompanying the letter and published in the same issue of the newspaper mocks Volkov as a loathsome "bedbug," who feasts on the hallowed legacy of Shostakovich. The same issue of the newspaper offers an "Official Dossier" that recounts attempts by the Shostakovich family in late 1978—almost a year before the publication of *Testimony*—to find out from the publisher, Harper & Row in New York, the precise nature of Volkov's manuscript and to assert their legal rights as heirs to the composer's copyright.

Alla Bogdanova's "Notes from the Soviet Archives on Volkov's *Testimony,*" based on primary sources, supplements the historical account in the "Official Dossier" and reviews the initiatives taken by the Central Committee of the Communist Party of the Soviet Union to blunt criticism, should the purported "memoirs," when published, portray Shostakovich as a victim of the Soviet regime.

Émigré scholar Henry (Genrikh) Orlov was commissioned by Harper & Row in the latter half of 1979 to make a critical evaluation of the *Testimony* typescript, presumably for in-house use. Orlov had worked closely with Shostakovich, knew his idiosyncracies well, and was widely recognized as an authority on the composer's music, having published among other things the first book-length study devoted to the symphonies, *Simfonii Shostakovicha* [The symphonies of Shostakovich] (Leningrad: Muzgiz, 1961). The endorsement of *Testimony* by a prominent émigré Soviet specialist would certainly have bolstered the book's claim to authenticity. Orlov recounts the circumstances surrounding his commission from Harper & Row in a conversation with Ludmila Kovnatskaya, "An Episode in the Life of a Book: An Interview with Henry Orlov," and a copy of Orlov's original report to Harper & Row is included.

Irina Shostakovich, the composer's widow, has continually questioned the authenticity of *Testimony*, beginning with her oft-quoted statement in 1979, "Volkov saw Dmitrich three or maybe four times. . . . I don't see how he could have gathered enough material from Dmitrich for such a thick book."[5] Readers today may need a reminder that during the very period when Volkov says he was interviewing Shostakovich (1971–74), Irina scarcely left the composer's side. Increasingly infirm at the time, Shostakovich looked to his wife for help in the most ordinary routines of daily living. Irina's "Answer to Those Who Still Abuse Shostakovich," written in commemoration of the twenty-fifth anniversary of her husband's death, once again repudiates Volkov's version of events surrounding the genesis of *Testimony.*

Boris Tishchenko, one of Shostakovich's closest friends, as well as his student, likely drafted that 1979 letter-to-the-editor mentioned above, signed by the six close friends and students of Shostakovich. More than any of the signatories, Tishchenko had special reason to protest against *Testimony.* He was deeply implicated in the book's creation. Volkov had taken advantage of Tishchenko's ready access to the composer to arrange through him to speak in private with Shostakovich—a good turn Tishchenko has regretted since his earliest reading of *Testimony.* A concise but telling selection of Tishchenko's public comments on the subject can be sampled in "On Solomon Volkov and *Testimony*" (see also his interview with Irina Nikolskaya in chapter 13).

That oft-cited 1979 letter of protest from Shostakovich's students and friends has been dismissed out of hand, both by Cold War critics and Volkov's allies, as doubtlessly having been coerced by Soviet authorities. But the letter is passionately defended "as absolutely sincere" by Elena Basner, daughter of Veniamin Basner, a close friend of the composer and a signatory to the letter. Elena Basner's "The Regime and Vulgarity" recounts the events surrounding the writing of that 1979 letter and deplores the naïveté of radically revisionist views of Shostakovich inspired by *Testimony.*

In "Shostakovich's World Is Our World," Mstislav Rostropovich, dedicatee of Shostakovich's two cello concertos, reflects on his thirty-year friendship with the composer, telling his interlocutor, Manashir Yakubov, curator of the Shostakovich Family Archive, that he doubts the authenticity of the voice in *Testimony* when it speaks disdainfully about the creative imagination of Prokofiev.

Irina Nikolskaya's "Shostakovich Remembered" reports her conversations with seven of the composer's Soviet colleagues, each of whom enjoyed friendly relations, professional or personal, with Shostakovich over a period of years. All the interviewees voice an opinion about *Testimony.*

Part 3 of the casebook continues "something from the Soviet or Russian point of view" but, instead of the more documentary materials found in part 2, a sampling of scholarly work is presented here:

Henry Orlov's article, "A Link in the Chain: Reflections on Shostakovich and His Times," written the year after the composer's death, offers a cultural perspective informed by scholarly expertise and long personal experience within Shostakovich's immediate milieu. In style, Orlov pays homage to the Russian tradition of criticism as literary essay in the manner of belles lettres. Especially noteworthy, for readers of the Shostakovich casebook, is that in this 1976 article, written well in advance of *Testimony*, Orlov laments that Shostakovich neither left an autobiographical account of his life nor had in his circle an amanuensis-confidant, such as "Eckermann was to Goethe, or Robert Craft to Stravinsky, or Yastrebtsev to Rimsky-Korsakov."

Levon Hakobian, in contrast to Orlov, offers a distinctly post-Soviet "Perspective on Soviet Musical Culture during the Lifetime of Shostakovich"—one that should provide an important corrective to the simplistic view of musical life in the USSR as having been essentially polarized, with conformists on one side and dissidents (closeted or otherwise) on the other, the former incapable of creating artistically viable music, and the latter, although capable, having to struggle continuously against the harsh restraints of Socialist Realism to produce art works of any lasting value.

Hakobian's review, "The Latest 'New Shostakovich' " turns a penetrating post-Soviet eye on Allan Ho and Dmitri Feofanov's *Shostakovich Reconsidered*, suggesting that the book essentially misses the point about the role Shostakovich played in Soviet musical life.

Ludmila Kovnatskaya's "Dialogues about Shostakovich" turns to primary sources to shed new light on the reception history of Shostakovich's music in Soviet times. Two sets of letters provide the evidence, and two pairs of correspondents wrote them. One pair admired Shostakovich and his music; the other disdained both the composer and his music. Kovnatskaya's study discloses the sometimes curious and certainly contradictory consequences of how the changing reception history of Shostakovich's music played out in the professional lives of these pairs of correspondents.

A miscellany of articles, reviews, and lectures by Anglophone writers on Shostakovich comprise part 4 of the casebook. These reflect no unified theme but were selected to provide a sampling of writings by Western writers and musicologists who have remained skeptical about the relevance of *Testimony* to scholarly work on Shostakovich, and who therefore have been grouped together as exemplifying the "failures of modern musicology."[6] This selection of writings in a single location should allow interested readers to assess the validity of claims that these authors are professionally incompetent and practice "tabloid musicology."[7]

In a 1993 essay-review, the editor of the present volume discusses Ian MacDonald's *The New Shostakovich* (Boston: Northeastern University Press, 1990). Given the vehemence with which MacDonald nowadays defends Volkov and damns Laurel Fay, his 1990 judgment is worth remembering: "the detective work of Laurel Fay . . . has established beyond doubt that the [Volkov] book is a dishonest presentation" (p. 245).

Elizabeth Wilson's *Shostakovich: A Life Remembered* (Princeton, N.J.: Princeton University Press, 1994) is endorsed as a model of authentic memoirs in a brief review from 1996, also by the editor of the present volume. This collection of reminiscences by the composer's friends and colleagues—all firsthand witnesses to Shostakovich's life—stands in distinct contrast to Volkov's book.

David Fanning offers his invited response to papers read by Allan Ho and Dmitri Feofanov at the 1998 meeting of the American Musicological Society in Boston. These papers reflected the style and substance of their then recently published book, *Shostakovich Reconsidered*, which questioned the scholarship and professional ethics of Laurel Fay, Richard Taruskin, and the editor of the present volume. As reproduced in the *Casebook*, Fanning's response is preceded by a brief note from the volume editor and an "Author's Introduction to the Reader."

Gerard McBurney's insightful "Whose Shostakovich?" examines particular compositional characteristics of the composer's music, the origin of these characteristics in the historical milieu of Shostakovich's youth, and how the composer adapted them in his personal style. McBurney then suggests why the "listening experience" of such music offers so many opportunities for idiosyncratic interpretation.

Paul Mitchinson's "The Shostakovich Variations" offers the most comprehensive, thoroughly researched, and balanced account to date of what became known in the late 1990s as the "Shostakovich Wars."

The volume editor's "Shostakovich: A Brief Encounter and a Present Perspective" introduces a personal slant to the reception history of Shostakovich's music over a forty-year span and ends on a note of caution about simplistic interpretations of the meaning of the composer's music.

Simon Morrison's essay-review of Laurel Fay's *Shostakovich: A Life* (Oxford: Oxford University Press, 2000) not only rights the arrant bias evident in earlier reviews by Volkov's apologists but also makes a substantial original contribution to the critical literature on Shostakovich.

No one has argued more effectively and with more authority than Richard Taruskin against the whole-scale reinterpretation of Shostakovich's life and music on the basis of its supposed metaphorical or allegorical truth. In his extensive essay, "When Serious Music Mattered," Taruskin establishes the relevant historical and critical context before he reviews, with practiced expertise, three very recent books on Shostakovich.

Notes

1. Solomon Volkov, *Testimony: The Memoirs of Dmitri Shostakovich*, as related to and edited by Solomon Volkov, trans. Antonina W. Bouis (New York: Harper & Row, 1979).

2. Allan B. Ho and Dmitri Feofanov, *Shostakovich Reconsidered*, with an overture by Vladimir Ashkenazy ([London]: Toccata, 1998).

3. Laurel E. Fay, "Shostakovich versus Volkov: Whose *Testimony*?" *Russian Review* 39, no. 4 (October 1980): 484–93.

4. Laurel E. Fay, *Shostakovich: A Life* (Oxford: Oxford University Press, 2000).

5. Quoted by Craig R. Whitney, "Shostakovich Memoir a Shock to Kin," *New York Times*, 13 November 1979, p. C7.

6. This characterization has been the declared theme or subtext of a series of public presentations by the author-compilers of *Shostakovich Reconsidered*, starting with papers that either one or both presented at the AMS Midwest Chapter Program, fall 1997; AMS-Boston national program, fall 1998; AMS South-Central Chapter Program, spring 2000; and the International Shostakovich Symposium in Glasgow, Scotland, October 2000. It is also the subtext of the section titled "Selective Scholarship" in *Shostakovich Reconsidered* (pp. 242–55).

7. See the abstract of Allan B. Ho's paper "The *Testimony* Affair: Complacency, Cover-up, or Incompetence," presented at AMS-Boston, 31 October 1998. The characterization "tabloid musicology" was used in Dmitri Feofanov's paper "Shostakovich and the '*Testimony* Affair,' " delivered at the AMS Midwest Chapter Program in Chicago, 4 October 1997, a copy of which was given to the editor of the present volume by Mr. Feofanov.

Part One

1

Shostakovich versus Volkov

Whose *Testimony*? (1980)

LAUREL E. FAY

The recent publication in the West of an apparently "authorized" memoir by Dmitri Shostakovich[1] has created an uproar which extends well beyond the musical community. Rumors about the manuscript's existence and its startling revelations were in circulation for at least two years before the book's publication. Two months before its appearance, the *New York Times* published a tantalizing article, "Shostakovich Memoir, Smuggled Out, Is Due."[2] A section of the book, entitled "Improvising under Stalin's Baton," appeared in the *New York Times Magazine*[3] shortly before publication of the book itself in October 1979. The book was immediately reviewed by Harold Schonberg on the front page of the *New York Times Book Review*[4] and was indicated as an editors' choice and subsequently as one of the best books of 1979 by that newspaper.[5] Since that time *Testimony* has received a large number of reviews in publications ranging from *Time*, *Saturday Review*, and the *New Yorker* to the [London] *Times Literary Supplement*, the *New York Review of Books*, and others.[6]

What has attracted so much attention to this book? The Shostakovich of these memoirs, at the time of his death and for many years before by far the most prominent, honored, and respected composer in the Soviet Union, reveals here with unparalleled scorn and bitterness the fear and oppression that plagued his life. His attacks are not reserved for political figures alone but encompass prominent people in all walks of life, Soviet and non-Soviet. The book has been hailed as a persuasive indictment of Soviet cultural oppression.

That Shostakovich was directly affected during his lifetime by the vicissitudes of Soviet cultural politics is not news, but his extraordinary ability to weather the crises, and his creative drive in the face of criticism, have usually been interpreted as indicative of a fundamental adherence to the Communist party line and an acceptance of the "constructive" aesthetic guidance provided by the state. If this *Testimony* of Shostakovich is authentic, then it will certainly lead to some radical reevaluations not only of Shostakovich's life and music but of the history of Soviet musical and cultural life in general.

Needless to say, Soviet reaction to the publication has been swift and unambiguous. In a letter to the editor of *Literaturnaia gazeta*, six prominent Soviet composers, all former students and friends of Shostakovich, declare that Solomon Volkov is the actual author of the book which, they claim, "has nothing in common with the true reminiscences of D. D. Shostakovich."[7] Accompanying editorials savagely blast Volkov and trace the Soviets' unsuccessful legal attempts to block the publication of *Testimony*.[8] Tikhon Khrennikov, in a speech to the Sixth Congress of Composers of the USSR, branded the work as "that vile falsification, concocted by one of the renegades who have forsaken our country."[9] The immediate reaction of Irina Shostakovich, the composer's widow, was skeptical: "Volkov saw Dmitrich three or maybe four times. . . . He was never an intimate friend of the family—he never had dinner with us here, for instance. . . . *I don't see how he [Volkov] could have gathered enough material from Dmitrich for such a thick book* [emphasis added]."[10]

In previous reviews of *Testimony* in the West, two basic issues have come to the forefront. The first and most important one concerns the document's authenticity. The second, which presupposes the document *is* indeed authentic, questions the veracity of many statements contained therein. Most reviewers, unwilling or unable to focus on the first issue, have concentrated on the second, and many factual discrepancies, both in the text of *Testimony* and in Volkov's annotations, have been uncovered.[11] To mention only one not previously remarked upon, Shostakovich is quoted as saying in connection with his Fourth Symphony (1936):

> After all, for twenty-five years no one heard it and I had the manuscript. If I had disappeared, the authorities would have given it to someone for his "zeal." I even know who that person would have been and instead of being my Fourth, *it would have been the Second Symphony of a different composer.* (p. 212; emphasis added)

In his annotation to this passage, Volkov identifies the mysterious composer as Tikhon Khrennikov, the long-time head of the Composers Union and a conspicuous target of Shostakovich's abuse. Unacknowledged either in the text or in the footnote is the well-known fact that Khrennikov's *own* Second Symphony was begun in 1940, first performed in 1943, performed again in revision in 1944, and published by 1950. Obviously, something is not quite right. But in this case, as in many others, it is difficult to tell whether the discrepancy should be attributed to faulty memory or deliberate maliciousness on Shostakovich's part or to inept scholarship on Volkov's part. Despite the reservations raised by these flaws, as well as the wariness aroused by the tone and the occasional slangy translation of the memoirs, few Western critics have seen reason to dispute either the essential authenticity of the memoirs or Volkov's role as the "vehicle" for their transmission.

Let us turn then to the vital issue. The definition of authenticity in this case presumably boils down to the following: that *Testimony* faithfully and accurately reflects the information and opinions transmitted directly to Mr. Volkov by Shostakovich personally in an arrangement that the composer himself authorized for publication. Addressing the question of the authenticity of *Testimony* in a letter to the editor of *Books & Arts*, Peter Schaeffer laments:

> What I find alarming is not what the book . . . "discloses" about Shostakovich, improbable as it must read to the impartial observer, but that the scholarly atmosphere here in the United States is so poisoned that all traditional criteria for the objective evaluation of what in legal terms is hearsay are cheerfully thrown to the winds for the sake of acquiring yet another all-too-convenient piece of anti-Soviet propaganda and fouling the atmosphere of peaceful co-existence.[12]

Volkov's printed response to this letter is revealing:

> If the questions that Professor Schaeffer raised about the validity of *Testimony* were not purely rhetorical, he could easily find the answers in the book itself. These answers are contained in the lengthy preface; in the introduction, where letters from Shostakovich to me are quoted; in the photographs reproduced in the book, including those inscribed to me by the late composer; in the background note about me, appearing at the end of the book, listing my previous professional positions and publications.[13]

Professor Schaeffer's dismay that the authenticity of *Testimony* has yet to be subjected to a rigorous and objective evaluation deserves attention. Such an evaluation, however, is not something that can be accomplished easily. Shostakovich is dead. Obviously we cannot turn to him for verification. Volkov points us to the book itself. In his preface and introduction he describes the methods and circumstances which led to the publication of *Testimony*. It is a complicated process which, at crucial points, remains essentially unverifiable. For all practical purposes, the authenticity of the manuscript rests on two types of evidence. The first requires the tacit acceptance of Volkov's honesty and integrity. The second and more impressive piece of evidence is that each of the eight sections of the manuscript is headed[14] with the inscription "Read [*Chital*]. D. Shostakovich." According to the publishers of the book, the authenticity of the inscriptions has been verified by a handwriting expert. Before I continue, I should mention a third type of evidence, which, however illogically, has been used to adduce the memoir's authenticity. This is the fact that the Soviets have denounced the book. While such a denunciation might have been predictable, given the controversial and highly political nature of the book's contents, it simply does not follow that the book must therefore be authentic, as has been suggested.[15]

Simon Karlinsky has pointed out two passages in *Testimony* which are verbatim or near-verbatim reproductions of memoirs previously published by Shostakovich.[16] I have identified, so far, five additional extensive passages in the book which, likewise, are taken from previously published Soviet sources. The page reference in *Testimony* and the original sources for all seven passages are given in table 1.1.[17] As can be seen, the dates of the original sources range from 1932 to 1974. The subjects of the reminiscences include Musorgsky, Stravinsky, Meyerhold, Mayakovsky, and Chekhov.

Careful comparison of the original passages with their counterparts in *Testimony* indicates that some significant alterations have been made. In several instances, sentences which would date the reminiscences have been altered or removed from the variants in the book. In one, the sentence "I have been working on *Lady Macbeth* for around two and a half years" is transformed into "I worked on *Lady Macbeth* for almost three years" (p. 106). In another, the sentence "I am sincerely happy that the 100th anniversary of his [Chekhov's] birth is attracting to him anew the attention of all progressive humanity" is entirely omitted from the otherwise literal quote in *Testimony* (p. 178).

The average lengths of the quoted passages and the fidelity of their translations can be conveyed most effectively here by the juxtaposition of a representative passage from *Testimony* with a direct translation (my own) of its source:

Table 1.1 Correlation of Passages from "Testimony" with Previously Published Sources

Testimony	*Original Source*
32–33	[*D. Shostakovich*] in B. M. Yarustovsky, ed., *I.F. Stravinsky: stat'i i materialy* [I. F. Stravinsky: Articles and materials] (Moscow: Sovetskii kompozitor, 1973), pp. 7–8.
77–78	"Iz vospominanii" [From reminiscences], *Sovetskaia muzyka*, no. 3 (1974): 54.
106–107	"Tragediia-satira" [A tragedy-satire], *Sovetskoe iskusstvo*, 16 October 1932; reprinted in L. Danilevich, ed., *Dmitri Shostakovich* (Moscow: Sovetskii kompozitor, 1967), p. 13.
154–55	"Kak rozhdaetsia muzyka" [How is a musical concept born], *Literaturnaia gazeta*, 21 December 1965; reprinted in Danilevich, *Dmitri Shostakovich*, p. 36.
178–79	"Samyi blizkii" [One of my favorites], *Literaturnaia gazeta*, 28 January 1960; reprinted in Danilevich, *Dmitri Shostakovich*, pp. 34–35.
226–27	"Partitura opery" [The score of the opera], *Izvestiia*, 1 May 1941; reprinted in Danilevich, *Dmitri Shostakovich*, p. 14.
245–46	"Iz vospominanii o Mayakovskom" [From reminiscences about Mayakovsky], in *V. Mayakovsky v vospominaniiakh sovremennikov* [V. Mayakovsky as remembered by his contemporaries] (Moscow: Khudozhestvennaia literatura, 1963), p. 315.

Testimony, pp. 154–55	"Kak rozhdaetsia muzyka," from L. Danilevich, ed., *Dmitri Shostakovich* (Moscow: Sovetskii kompozitor, 1967), p. 36.
Is a musical concept born consciously or unconsciously? It's difficult to explain. The process of writing a new work is long and complicated. Sometimes you start writing and then change your mind. It doesn't always work out the way you thought it would. If it's not working, leave the composition the way it is—and try to avoid your earlier mistakes in the next one. That's my personal point of view, my manner of working. Perhaps it stems from a desire to do as	Is an idea born consciously or unconsciously? It's difficult to explain. The process of writing a new work is long and complicated. It happens like this: you begin to write and then you change your mind. It doesn't always turn out as it was conceived. If it turns out badly, let the work remain as it is—in the next I will try to avoid my earlier mistakes. That's my personal point of view. My manner of working. Perhaps it comes from a desire

much as possible. When I hear that a composer has eleven versions of one symphony, I think involuntarily, How [*sic*] many new works could he have composed in that time?

to do as much as possible. When I find out that a composer has made eleven versions of one symphony, I think involuntarily, how many new works might he have written in that time?

No, naturally I sometimes return to an old work; for instance, I made many changes in the score of my opera *Katerina Izmailova.*

No, of course I sometimes return to an old work. For instance, I corrected a great deal in the score of my opera "Katerina Izmailova." After all, nearly thirty years had passed since the days of its composition.

I wrote my Seventh Symphony, the "Leningrad," very quickly. I couldn't not write it. War was all around. I had to be with the people, I wanted to create the image of our country at war, capture it in music. From the first days of the war, I sat down at the piano and started work. I worked intensely. I wanted to write about our times, about my contemporaries who spared neither strength nor life in the name of Victory Over the Enemy.

I wrote my Seventh Symphony, the "Leningrad," very quickly. I couldn't not write it. War was all around. I had to be together with the people. I wanted to create the image of our country at war, to engrave it in music. From the first days of the war I sat down at the piano and began to work. I worked intensely. I wanted to write a work about our days, about my contemporaries who spared neither strength nor life in the name of victory over the enemy.

The only significant differences between the two passages occur in the elision of the first two paragraphs in the *Testimony* version and the omission from it of the sentence, "After all, nearly thirty years had passed since the days of its composition."[18]

None of this material "borrowed" from previously published sources could be considered controversial or inflammatory, though in a couple of instances it is contradicted in its transposed context by statements which follow in *Testimony.* Less than one page after he tells us: "From the first days of the war . . ." (cf. the complete quotation above) we read the following:

> The Seventh Symphony had been planned before the war and consequently it simply cannot be seen as a reaction to Hitler's attack. The "invasion theme" has nothing to do with the attack. I was thinking of other enemies of humanity when I composed the theme. (p. 155)

Subsequently Volkov quotes Shostakovich as explicitly equating these "enemies of humanity" with Stalin and his henchmen. Which explanation are we to believe?

In his preface Volkov tells us that "Shostakovich's manner of responding to questions was highly stylized. Some phrases had apparently been polished over many years" (p. xvii). Yet the sheer length of the identified quotations as well as their formalized language make it utterly inconceivable that the composer had memorized his previously published statements and then reproduced them exactly in his conversations with Volkov. But nowhere in his explanation of the book's genesis or methodology, nowhere in his documentation does Volkov acknowledge that some material in the book comes from previously published (and uncredited) sources. Indeed, Volkov states explicitly, "This is how we worked. We sat down at a table . . . then I began asking questions, which he answered briefly, and, at first, reluctantly. . . . I divided up the collected material into sustained sections . . . then I showed these sections to Shostakovich, who approved my work" (pp. xvi–xvii). Nowhere does Volkov suggest that any of his "collected material" for the book was obtained in any other way than from Shostakovich directly in private conversation. Is this unacknowledged "borrowing" from earlier publications how, in the words of Irina Shostakovich, "he could have gathered enough material . . . for such a thick book"?[19]

What is most disturbing about these borrowed reminiscences, however, is the fact that all seven occur at the beginning of chapters. While my request to view the original Russian manuscript has been refused by the publisher,[20] the implication which must be drawn from this coincidence is that the first pages of seven out of the eight chapters of *Testimony*, the pages on which Shostakovich's inscription "Read. D. Shostakovich" is alleged to appear, consist substantially, if not totally, of material which had already appeared in print under Shostakovich's name at the time of signing. The inevitable nagging questions must be asked. Is the manuscript which Shostakovich signed identical to the manuscript which has been translated and published as Shostakovich's *Testimony*? Is it possible that Volkov misrepresented the nature and contents of the book to Shostakovich just as he may be misrepresenting them to the reader?[21]

In light of these unsettling questions, a reexamination of the origin and transmission of *Testimony* is in order. Described as a "brilliant musicologist" on the dustcover of the book, Solomon Volkov was virtually unknown in the West when he emigrated to the United States in 1976. The documentation of his close relationship with the aging Shostakovich rests exclusively on his own "Testimony," though he freely quotes statements by and private letters from the composer to support his credibility. We must take this all on faith. Very little of what he claims can be verified objectively. For instance, he states that, while working on *Testimony*, Shostakovich would summon him "usually early in the morning, when the office was still empty" (p. xvii). In other words, there were no witnesses. Similarly, the conversations were recorded not on tape but in "notes in the short-hand that I had developed during my years as a journalist" (p. xvi). The resultant notes were arranged, by Volkov, into arbitrary but sustained sections which, presumably, Shostakovich read and signed. Obligingly, Volkov has provided an explanation for almost every possible objection that could be raised.

In examining Volkov's evidence, however, there are some indications that his own autobiography may be as misleading as the one he ascribes to Shostakovich. Volkov discusses, at length, the circumstances surrounding his production, in April 1968, of *Skripka Rotshil'da* [Rothschild's violin], a one-act opera by Veniamin Fleishman, a favorite student of Shostakovich who was killed during World War II. In his description of the events leading to the closing of the production—ostensibly on the charge of Zionism—Volkov strongly implies that this was the *first* and *only* performance of the work. He also states: "But the only thing available to researchers is the score, written from beginning to end in Shostakovich's characteristic nervous handwriting" (p. xiii). What he fails to mention is that Fleishman's opera had been performed at the Moscow Composers Union on 20 June 1960, had been broadcast on the radio in February 1962, had been favorably discussed in print,[22] and the piano score had been published, with a foreword by A. Livshits, in 1965.[23] Nevertheless, Volkov concludes: "For Shostakovich *Rothschild's Violin* represented unhealed guilt, pity, pride and anger: neither Fleishman nor his work was to be resurrected. The defeat brought us closer together" (p. xiv).

Included in Volkov's list of documentary evidence for the authenticity of *Testimony* are the photographs reproduced in the book. One picture in particular, reproduced in the frontispiece, assumes special significance. Volkov indicates that in November 1974 Shostakovich inscribed and presented him with this picture in order to facilitate acceptance of the manuscript in the West. The inscription reads: "To dear Solomon Moiseyevich Volkov in fond remembrance.[24] D. Shostakovich. 13 XI 1974. A reminder of our conversations about Glazunov, Zoshchenko, Meyerhold. D. S." Nothing about the picture itself or the inscription betrays any special degree of intimacy or conspiracy. The politely posed figures of Irina Shostakovich, Boris Tishchenko, Shostakovich, and Volkov, the use of Volkov's full name, and the specific wording (in Russian) of the inscription—all betoken a more formal relationship than the one we are expected to believe existed. And why are only three names mentioned? Shostakovich might have inscribed the picture in a manner both more personal and more pointed, "A reminder of our conversations," which would have implied much more as a document of authentication. The inscription could, in my view, as well be read as a *precise* reference to the limited content of their conversations and not a blanket acknowledgment.

Inevitably, the methodology of Volkov's *Testimony* must also be questioned. The unsystematic organization of the book effectively disguises the chronology of the reminiscences and obscures the question-answer context in which the reminiscences were evoked in the first place. Volkov admits: "I had to resort to trickery: at every convenient point I drew parallels, awakening associations, reminding him of people and events" (p. xiv). One can only wonder at the extent of the "trickery." Volkov also states: "He [Shostakovich] often contradicted himself. Then the true meaning of his words had to be guessed, extracted from a box with three false bottoms" (p. xvii). The only guarantee we are given that Volkov guessed correctly are the problematic inscriptions "Read. D. Shostakovich."

Many other perplexing questions are raised by the book. Knowing without a doubt that it could not be published in the Soviet Union, an assumption which subsequent events have decisively corroborated, why then did Volkov bother to make "several attempts . . . in that direction" (p. xviii)? Why would Shostakovich, while insisting that the manuscript be published only after his own death, callously disregard the ominous ramifications of its publication for his wife and family? Why did it take more than three years, after Volkov's emigration, to have the book translated and published?

It is clear that the authenticity of *Testimony* is very much in doubt. Volkov's questionable methodology and deficient scholarship do not inspire us to accept his version of the nature and content of the memoirs on faith. His assertion that the book itself is the evidence of its own authenticity is the product of circular reasoning. And Shostakovich's inscriptions on the manuscript, if they themselves are authentic, do not necessarily authenticate the version of the manuscript which has been presented to a naïve Western public. If Volkov has solid proof of the authenticity of these memoirs, in the form of original notes, letters from the composer, or other documents, he must be prepared to submit them to public scrutiny. Until such tangible proof is offered, we can only speculate about where the boundary lies between Shostakovich's authentic memoirs and Volkov's fertile imagination.

Editor's note: A copy of this review has been sent to Mr. Volkov with an invitation to respond to it in the pages of the *Russian Review.*

Notes

When this review article was first published in 1980, it established Laurel Fay as Solomon Volkov's most authoritative critic, a position she reaffirms in "Volkov's *Testimony* Reconsidered," written especially for the present volume (chapter 2). The original review-article "Shostakovich versus Volkov: Whose *Testimony*?" was published in the *Russian Review* 39, no. 4 (October 1980): 484–93, and is reprinted here with permission; typographical errors in the text originally published have been corrected. Portions of the review were presented originally in a paper entitled "Will the Real Dmitri Shostakovich Please Stand Up?" read at the Midwest Chapter of the American Musicological Society, Columbus, Ohio, on 12 April 1980.

1. Solomon Volkov, *Testimony: The Memoirs of Dmitri Shostakovich,* as related to and edited by Solomon Volkov, trans. Antonina W. Bouis (New York: Harper & Row, 1979).

2. Herbert Mitgang, "Shostakovich Memoir, Smuggled Out, Is Due," *New York Times,* 10 September 1979, p. C14.

3. "Improvising under Stalin's Baton," *New York Times Magazine,* 7 October 1979, pp. 122–23.

4. Harold C. Schonberg, "Words and Music under Stalin," *New York Times Book Review,* 21 October 1979, pp. 1, 46–47.

5. *New York Times Book Review,* 25 November 1979, p. 18.

6. Space is inadequate here to provide a complete list of reviews. Some of the most penetrating reviews and commentaries are listed in note 11.

7. V. Basner, M. Vainberg [Weinberg], K. Karaev, Yu. Levitin, B. Tishchenko, and K. Khachaturian, "Zhalkaia poddelka; pis'mo v redaktsiu *LG*" [A Pitiful fake; letter to the editor of *LG*], *Literaturnaia gazeta,* 14 November 1979, p. 8. Selection 4 in the present volume.

8. "Klop" [The bedbug] and "Ofitsial'noe dos'e" [The official dossier], *Literaturnaia gazeta,* 14 November 1979, p. 8. Selections 5 and 6 in the present volume.

9. Tikhon Khrennikov, "Muzyka prinadlezhit narodu" [Music belongs to the people], *Sovetskaia kul'tura,* 23 November 1979, p. 4.

10. Reported by Craig R. Whitney, "Shostakovich Memoir a Shock to Kin," *New York Times,* 13 November 1979, p. C7.

11. Noteworthy, in this respect, are Simon Karlinsky, "Our Destinies Are Bad," *The Nation,* 24 November 1979, pp. 533–36; Malcolm Brown, "Letters . . . Shostakovich," *New York Times Book Review,* 9 December 1979, p. 37; Oleg Prokofiev, "To the editor . . . Shostakovich's Memoirs," [London] *Times Literary Supplement,* 14 December 1979, p. 134; Robert Craft, "Notes from the Composer," *New York Review of Books,* 24 January 1980, pp. 9–12; Phillip Ramey, "The Shostakovich Memoirs: Do They Prove a Case?" *Ovation* 1, no. 1 (February 1980): 22–24, 76; George Steiner, "Books . . . Marche Funebre," *The New Yorker,* 24

March 1980, pp. 129–32; Galina Vishnevskaya interview with Bella Ezerskaia, "Trepet i muki aktyora: interv'iu s Galinoi Vishnevskoi" [The trembling and torments of an actor: Interview with Vishnevskaya], *Vremia i my*, no. 50 (1980): 160–61.

12. Peter Schaeffer, "Shostakovich's 'Testimony': The Whole Truth?" *Books & Arts*, 7 March 1980, p. 29.

13. Ibid.

14. The number and location of the inscriptions have been confirmed in a letter to the author, dated 9 July 1980, from *Testimony*'s editor Ann Harris.

15. S. Frederick Starr, "Private Anguish, Public Scorn," *Books & Arts*, 7 December 1979, p. 4.

16. Karlinsky, "Our Destinies Are Bad," p. 535. Despite his discovery of several problems in the absence of documentation in *Testimony*, Professor Karlinsky reasons that Volkov's "musicological expertise and his well-documented closeness to Shostakovich" leave no cause to doubt the authenticity of the manuscript. In fact, neither of these criteria has been demonstrated conclusively.

17. These do not exhaust the possibilities. Malcolm Brown has discovered a further example in *Testimony* (pp. 50–51), taken from D. D. Shostakovich, "Stranitsy vospominanii" [Pages from memoirs], in *Leningradskaia konservatoriia v vospominaniiakh* [Memoirs of the Leningrad Conservatory] (Leningrad: Muzgiz, 1962), pp. 125–26.

18. The examination of this and other passages quoted in *Testimony* should help to vindicate the translator, Antonina W. Bouis, from charges of incompetence.

19. See note 10.

20. Letter to the author, 9 July 1980.

21. Ironic, in this respect, is a note accompanying Volkov's article "Artistry as Dissent," *New York Times*, 16 April 1978, p. E19, in which the author was described as "working, at Columbia University, on a *biography* of Dmitri Shostakovich" (emphasis added). Was this book originally conceived as biographical?

22. G. Golovinsky, "S liubov'iu k cheloveku" [With love for a fellow man], *Sovetskaia muzyka*, no. 5 (1962): 28–34.

23. V. I. Fleishman, *Skripka Rotshil'da* [Rothschild's violin], arranged for voice and piano (Moscow: Muzyka, 1965).

24. "Dorogomu Solomonu Moiseevichu Volkovu na dobruiu pamiat'."

2

Volkov's *Testimony* Reconsidered (2002)

LAUREL E. FAY

Editor's note: Laurel Fay's reconsideration of *Testimony* comes in response to the book *Shostakovich Reconsidered* (Toccata, 1998) by Allan B. Ho and Dmitry Feofanov, vehement apologists for Solomon Volkov, who declare that Fay's 1980 review of *Testimony* "withers under cross-examination, revealing, at best, the author's naïveté of her subject matter and, at worst, her willingness to conceal and distort pertinent evidence" (*Shostakovich Reconsidered*, pp. 44–45).

Printed at the end of my 1980 review of *Testimony* was an invitation to Solomon Volkov to respond. On 22 October 1980, a few weeks prior to the review's publication, the editor of the *Russian Review*, Terence Emmons, sent Volkov a corrected proof of the review along with a formal invitation to reply. Volkov was promised that his response would be printed in the very next issue of the journal (January 1981). He never answered. But elsewhere he stated—and more than twenty years later he continues to affirm—the following three propositions:

a) that in compiling *Testimony* he employed no material from previously published sources;

b) that everything in *Testimony* was communicated to him by Shostakovich personally in conversation;

c) that he was not even acquainted with the previously published articles, extended passages of which are duplicated in his book.[1]

One of the articles duplicated in *Testimony*, Shostakovich's reminiscences of Vsevolod Meyerhold, was printed in *Sovetskaia muzyka* in 1974 and furnished with an introduction signed by "С. Волков" [S. Volkov] (fig. 2.1).[2] Since Solomon Volkov declares that he was unacquainted with the previously published articles duplicated in *Testimony*, are we to believe that two people by the name of "S. Volkov" were employed at *Sovetskaia muzyka* in 1974? Or that Solomon Volkov's name was affixed, without his having read the introduction, to something he did not write? Are we to believe that he did not bother to read the journal for which he worked, even when it included material pertinent to his ongoing collaboration with Shostakovich?[3] If he did not read it, how was he able to reproduce a passage that appears there, but *not* in *Testimony* (fig. 2.1, last paragraph on the page), in the interview he gave to an Italian journalist in the days immediately following Shostakovich's death?[4]

At the time I was researching my 1980 review, I asked to view the original Russian typescript of *Testimony*, but the editor of the book turned me down, which made it difficult to assess the full extent to which passages in *Testimony* duplicated their previously published Russian counterparts.[5] But after my review appeared I found a sample page of the "authorized" typescript of *Testimony* reproduced by way of visual illustration to another review.[6] The sample page shows Shostakovich's signature as it was inscribed, as Volkov says, on the first page of each of *Testimony*'s eight chapters (fig. 2.2). Between Shostakovich's signature and the typed Russian text, a second hand has inserted ГЛАВА ВТОРАЯ [CHAPTER TWO]. A stamped page number "040" appears in the upper right-hand corner.

This sample page contains the beginning of Shostakovich's reminiscences of Stravinsky. A comparison of the text on this page with that found in the text's original publication[7] (figs. 2.2 and 2.3) makes it clear immediately that not only is this a literal, word-for-word transcript of the original publication, but it also retains every single nuance of the original layout and punctuation. The passages are identical. (The single discrepancy between them is what appears to be an extra punctuation mark, a period after the comma in the sixteenth line of the *Testimony* typescript. The latter is obviously a typo that would be edited out of any publication.)

Before continuing, let us review how the collaboration between Shostakovich and Volkov is reported to have been carried out. Here is the method, as described by the editor in charge of publication, before *Testimony* appeared:

для Мейерхольда, пронесшего страстную любовь к музыке через всю жизнь.

После «Тристана» он поставил в Мариинском театре еще шесть опер, продолжая развивать и совершенствовать приемы, найденные в работе над Вагнером. Блистательной чредой проходят «Орфей» Глюка, «Электра» Р. Штрауса, «Каменный гость» Даргомыжского, вызывая волнение в публике и шум в прессе. И. Соллертинский дает следующее обобщенное описание мейерхольдовских музыкальных спектаклей: «Отсутствие натуралистической повадки и интонаций; вышелушивание всех элементов... бытовизма... статуарность поз; неторопливая ритмизованная пантомима, в пределе переходящая в танец; скульптурный, тщательно дозированный жест; ритм, угадываемый не только в движениях, но и в застывшей неподвижности; хор не дробится по мейнингенской выучке, не индивидуализируется, лишен натуралистической суетливости; он разбит на стилизованные скульптурные группы, лишь внезапно — в великолепном контрасте — приводимые в быстрое взволнованное движение, впрочем, ритмическое даже в беге. Таковы фурии в «Орфее», выбег рабов со светильниками в «Электре». В «Тристане» Мейерхольдом акцентируется внутренняя сила вагнеровского жеста...»

Музыка становится важнейшим элементом театральных поисков режиссера. Непрерывно, наподобие того, как это делалось в немом кинематографе, она звучала, например, в «Бубусе» (подробнее об этом говорится в заметках участника постановки Л. Арнштама); словесный материал пьесы трактовался как своего рода речитатив. Ритмическая организация мизансцен характерна для «Командарма 2». Существует целое исследование Э. Каплана о «партитуре» спектакля по «Ревизору». Примеры можно было бы умножать до бесконечности. Точнее, они охватили бы почти весь список опусов Мейерхольда.

Правда, опера надолго исчезла с творческого горизонта мастера. Он вернулся к ней позже, почти двадцать лет спустя, осуществив постановку «Пиковой дамы», а впоследствии начав работу над «Семеном Котко». Об этом периоде деятельности Мейерхольда рассказывают публикуемые ниже воспоминания Д. Шостаковича, А. Тышлера и Б. Покровского. Они написаны в 1972—1973 годах.

С. Волков

Д. Шостакович

ИЗ ВОСПОМИНАНИЙ

Первая моя встреча с Всеволодом Эмильевичем Мейерхольдом произошла в Ленинграде в 1928 году. Он позвонил мне по телефону и сказал: «С вами говорит Мейерхольд. Я хочу вас видеть. Если можете, приходите ко мне. Гостиница такая-то, номер такой-то». Я и пошел.

Всеволод Эмильевич пригласил меня работать у него в театре. В скором времени я поехал в Москву и стал служить в театре Мейерхольда по музыкальной части. В том же году я ушел оттуда, так как не нашел себе применения, которое удовлетворило бы и меня и Всеволода Эмильевича, хотя вообще мне было интересно. И самый большой интерес вызывали репетиции Мейерхольда, они захватывали.

Моя работа в театре, собственно, заключалась в том, что я играл на рояле. Скажем, если в «Ревизоре» в последнем акте актриса по ходу действия исполняла романс Глинки, то я надевал на себя фрачок, выходил на сцену как один из гостей и аккомпанировал актрисе. Играл я также в оркестре.

Жил я у Всеволода Эмильевича на Новинском бульваре, много работал, сочинял оперу «Нос». Как раз в это время на квартире у Всеволода Эмильевича случился большой пожар. В тот момент меня не было дома, он собрал мои рукописи и отдал мне их в полной сохранности. Это было удивительно, ведь могли сгореть его вещи, куда более ценные.

В 1929 году Всеволод Эмильевич опять позвонил мне по телефону в Ленинграде и пригласил к себе в гостиницу, где предложил написать музыку к комедии Маяковского «Клоп». Я сразу согласился и, пока сочинял, проигрывал отдельные фрагменты Всеволоду Эмильевичу. Он слушал и делал замечания. Помню, ему нравились эпизоды для трех баянистов. У него в театре было великолепное трио баянистов. Он интересно их использовал в спектакле.

Я видел многие постановки Мейерхольда — «Смерть Тарелкина», «Лес», «Мандат», «Бубус», «Ревизор», «Командарм 2», «Последний решительный», «33 обморока», «Дама с камелиями», «Пиковая дама», «Маскарад». Во время гастролей в Ленинграде видел я и несколько репетиций последнего его спектакля «Одна жизнь» по роману Н. Островского «Как закалялась сталь». Всеволод Эмильевич приглашал меня написать к этому спектаклю музыку, но тогда я не смог принять его предложение.

Мне чрезвычайно трудно сказать, какая из перечисленных работ произвела на меня наиболее сильное впечатление. Все было необыкновенно интересно. Однако, пожалуй, самым близким мне оказался «Ревизор», может быть потому, что в нем ощущалось какое-то соприкосновение с моей работой над оперой «Нос».

54

Figure 2.1. Excerpt from Shostakovich's Article in Issue No. 3 of *Sovetskaia muzyka*, 1974, p. 54

> Mr. Volkov describes the procedures for Shostakovich's and his work as follows: Shostakovich did not dictate to him. He would permit Volkov to ask questions, which he answered in short sentences. During these conversations, which lasted for about three years, Volkov took notes in a kind of personal shorthand he had developed during his years of work as a journalist. Gradually, he began to shape his notes into larger sections and chapters. He showed some of them to Shostakovich and he gave his approval. In the spring of 1974, Volkov began to organize the material into longer chapters. As soon as he had finished each chapter, he gave it to Shostakovich, who read it and as proof of his reading and approval, wrote at the head of each chapter "Read," followed by his signature, "Shostakovich." He deliberately chose to put the word *read* before his signature on each chapter in order to create a certain distance between himself and the text; and he decided also that the memoirs were not to be published until after his death.[8]

Volkov, in his preface to *Testimony*, amplifies the process:

> This is how we worked. We sat down at a table in his study, and he offered me a drink (which I always refused). Then I began asking questions, which he answered briefly and, at first, reluctantly. Sometimes I had to keep repeating the same question in different forms. Shostakovich needed time to warm up. . . . The mound of shorthand notes was growing. I read them over and over, trying to construct from the penciled scribbles the multifigured composition that I knew was there.
>
> I divided up the collected material into sustained sections, combined as seemed appropriate; then I showed these sections to Shostakovich, who approved my work. . . . Gradually, I shaped this great array of reminiscence into arbitrary parts and had them typed. Shostakovich read and signed each part.[9]

Keep in mind these two detailed accounts of how Volkov interviewed Shostakovich and then pieced together the composer's reminiscences to create a coherent text. And keep in mind as well the three propositions Volkov has affirmed for more than twenty years, which were reiterated at the outset of this article. This is the context in which Volkov asks us to accept the following as plausible:

a) that he was unfamiliar with the first major Soviet collection of materials about Stravinsky, published in 1973, which led off with Shostakovich's memoir of the Russian master;

b) that Shostakovich in this instance managed to convey to Volkov by means of his brief answers no fewer than 186 words that reproduced his earlier published statement on Stravinsky with perfect word-for-word accuracy;

c) that in fleshing out this passage from his own penciled scribbles, Volkov managed by accident to reproduce the opening section of the

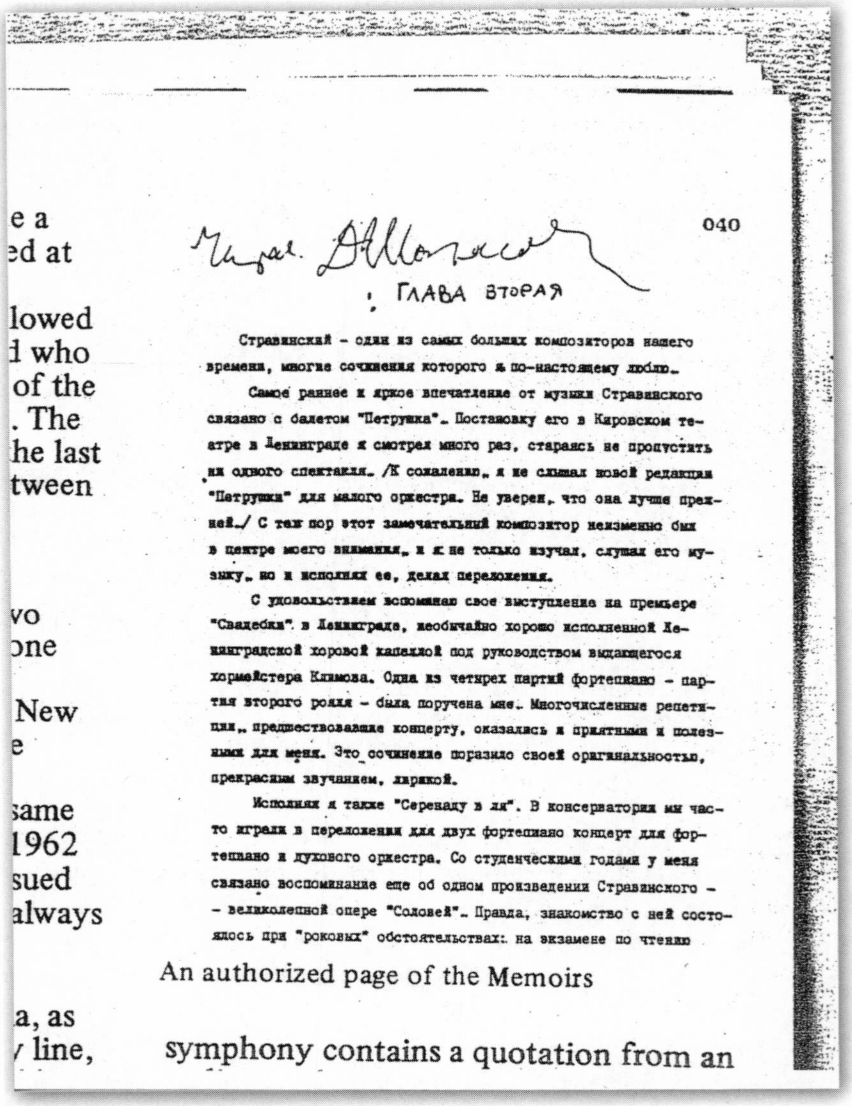

Читал. Д. Шостакович

040

ГЛАВА ВТОРАЯ

Стравинский – один из самых больших композиторов нашего времени, многие сочинения которого я по-настоящему люблю.

Самое раннее и яркое впечатление от музыки Стравинского связано с балетом "Петрушка". Постановку его в Кировском театре в Ленинграде я смотрел много раз, стараясь не пропустить ни одного спектакля. /К сожалению, я не слышал новой редакции "Петрушки" для малого оркестра. Не уверен, что она лучше прежней./ С тех пор этот замечательный композитор неизменно был в центре моего внимания, и я не только изучал, слушал его музыку, но и исполнял ее, делал переложения.

С удовольствием вспоминаю свое выступление на премьере "Свадебки" в Ленинграде, необычайно хорошо исполненной Ленинградской хоровой капеллой под руководством выдающегося хормейстера Климова. Одна из четырех партий фортепиано – партия второго рояля – была поручена мне. Многочисленные репетиции, предшествовавшие концерту, оказались и приятными и полезными для меня. Это сочинение поразило своей оригинальностью, прекрасным звучанием, лирикой.

Исполнял я также "Серенаду в ля". В консерватории мы часто играли в переложении для двух фортепиано концерт для фортепиано и духового оркестра. Со студенческими годами у меня связано воспоминание еще об одном произведении Стравинского – – великолепной опере "Соловей". Правда, знакомство с ней состоялось при "роковых" обстоятельствах: на экзамене по чтению

An authorized page of the Memoirs

symphony contains a quotation from an

Figure 2.2. Sample Page of the "Authorized" Typescript of *Testimony*, as Reproduced in Elmer Schönberger, "Dmitri Shostakovich's Memoirs: *Testimony*," *Key Notes* 10, No. 2 (1979): 57

Д. Шостакович

Стравинский — один из самых больших композиторов нашего времени, многие сочинения которого я по-настоящему люблю.

Самое раннее и яркое впечатление от музыки Стравинского связано с балетом «Петрушка». Постановку его в Кировском театре в Ленинграде я смотрел много раз, стараясь не пропустить ни одного спектакля. (К сожалению, я не слышал новой редакции «Петрушки» для малого оркестра. Не уверен, что она лучше прежней.) С тех пор этот замечательный композитор неизменно был в центре моего внимания, и я не только изучал, слушал его музыку, но и исполнял ее, делал переложения.

С удовольствием вспоминаю свое выступление на премьере «Свадебки» в Ленинграде, необычайно хорошо исполненной Ленинградской хоровой капеллой под руководством выдающегося хормейстера Климова. Одна из четырех партий фортепиано — партия второго рояля — была поручена мне. Многочисленные репетиции, предшествовавшие концерту, оказались и приятными и полезными для меня. Это сочинение поразило своей оригинальностью, прекрасным звучанием, лирикой.

Исполнял я также «Серенаду в *ля*». В консерватории мы часто играли в переложении для двух фортепиано концерт для фортепиано и духового оркестра. Со студенческими годами у меня связано воспоминание еще об одном произведении Стравинского — великолепной опере «Соловей». Правда, знакомство с ней состоялось при «роковых» обстоятельствах: на экзамене по чтению партитур. Пожалуй, это было несколько жестоко. Но, кажется, я справился с партитурой. Уже после этого я основательно изучил ее.

В свое время, вскоре же после издания, я сделал четырехручное переложение для фортепиано «Симфонии псалмов» Стравинского. Меньше всего мне удалась вторая часть: из-за обилия полифонии многое оказалось неисполнимым на фортепиано. Это, конечно, замечательное произведение. И все же я ощущаю в нем недостатки конструктивного

7

Figure 2.3. Excerpt from Shostakovich's Reminiscences of Stravinsky, Originally Published in L. S. Dyachkova, Comp., *I. F. Stravinsky: stat'i i materialy* [I. F. Stravinsky: Articles and materials], Ed. B. M. Yarustovsky (Moscow: Sovetskii kompozitor, 1973), p. 7

original publication, its punctuation and layout identical in every respect to the original;[10] and,

d) that this very same passage coincidentally ended up as one of the pages in *Testimony* which Shostakovich "authenticated" with the inscription "Read. D. Shostakovich."

The only page from the original typescript of *Testimony* to have been published up to now is the opening page of chapter 2, shown in figure 2.2.[11] But copies of a complete typescript have been in circulation over the years among some Russians living both within and outside the former Soviet Union, although the book itself has never been published in its original Russian language. Still unclear is how many of these circulating copies reproduce the original typescript bearing Shostakovich's "authenticating" signatures and how many might be retyped transcripts.[12] Individuals privileged to read these copies have not spoken for publication about the layout and physical characteristics of the typescript they read, only about what they believed to be the truth or falsehood of its contents. Neither has anyone among them acknowledged recognition that some passages in *Testimony* duplicated material already published in the Soviet Union during Shostakovich's lifetime nor an awareness that this duplicated material was located on the very pages of the *Testimony* typescript "authenticated" by the composer's signatures.

After a copy of the Russian typescript came into the possession of the Shostakovich Family Archive in Moscow, I was given my first opportunity, in September 2000, to examine what is, to all appearances, a photocopy of the original Russian typescript of *Testimony.*

The document in Moscow is an unbound, single-sided photocopy made on 8½ × 11 inch white stock (the U.S. standard). It would appear to have been made in the United States at the time Volkov was seeking a publisher for his work. He is reported to have shared copies of the typescript with prominent émigré cultural figures who might assist him in making contacts with publishers.[13] Although it is entirely possible that the Moscow typescript is not a first-generation copy of the original, the text is entirely legible throughout, as are Shostakovich's inscriptions.

The text is typed, apparently using the same typewriter throughout, but with a few emendations and deletions—as well as some reorganization—effected by hand. It is divided into eight chapters, corresponding exactly to the number and ordering of chapters in the English-language publication of *Testimony.* Sinkage on the first pages of each of the chapters—with the exception of chapters 3 and 7, discussed below—provided the space in which Shostakovich might conveniently sign his name. The typescript exhibits a double set of page numbers. Each chapter is paginated individually, counting from 1, in the same typeface as the text, with the numbers located in the top center of the page, although no typed number appears on the first page because of the sinkage at the top. The typed numbering commences, therefore, with page 2 of each chapter. After all the chapters had been arranged in final order, the pages first to last were then stamped in the upper right-hand corner of each page with sequential numbering, extending from 001 to 404; the stamped page number is in a larger typeface entirely different from the typeface of the text and the typed chapter pagination.[14]

Several features of the photocopied typescript in the Shostakovich Family Archive lead me to conclude that it is indeed an exact copy of the *Testimony* typescript used in making the published English translation, rather than an interim version or a retyped copy:

a) The facsimile of page 040 of the "authorized text of *Testimony*" published in 1979 (shown in fig. 2.2 and discussed above) is an exact duplicate of the same page 040 of the Moscow typescript, identical in every respect down to the redundant punctuation mark.

b) All Shostakovich's signatures visible on the Moscow typescript conform exactly to those reproduced from the authorized text and placed above typeset pages in the German and Finnish editions of *Testimony* and are associated with the same chapters.[15]

c) In his outside reader's report, commissioned by Harper & Row for the stated purpose of establishing the authenticity of Volkov's text before publication, Henry Orlov cites material that appears on more than a dozen pages of the original Russian typescript of *Testimony*, all of which coincides precisely with what appears on the same pages of the Moscow typescript.[16]

d) A word-by-word comparison of the complete text of the Moscow typescript with the published English translation of *Testimony* corroborates the latter as a faithful, competent translation of this more than four-hundred-page text. Handwritten insertions and deletions in the Moscow typescript correspond exactly to the English text.[17]

When I wrote my 1980 review I had only the English translation of suspect passages in *Testimony* to compare to their original Russian-language sources, allowing only a rough assessment of the similarities and differences between them. A comparison of the passages *in the same language* yields much more telling results. Chapter 2, devoted to Stravinsky, is not the only one that opens with a verbatim transcript of previously published material.

The first page of chapter 8—Shostakovich's visa visible at the top—duplicates exactly the first 231 words of one of Shostakovich's published reminiscences of Mayakovsky, retaining every detail of its punctuation and layout.[18] Likewise, the first pages of chapters 5 and 6—each with Shostakovich's visa—are verbatim transcripts of previously published texts, 180 and 183 words, respectively, that retain the original punctuation and layout, with the exception that in each instance a single sentence has been removed. That these deletions occurred after typing is evidenced on the photocopied pages of the Moscow typescript by obvious gaps, into which the missing text fitted; just below these gaps one can see horizontal shadow lines, suggesting that the missing text has been pasted over with some sort of correction tape.[19] In each instance the deleted sentence makes a temporal reference that would allow a reader to infer the date when the reminiscences were originally produced. On the first page of chapter 6, the missing sentence reads, "I am sincerely happy that the 100th anniversary of his [Chekhov's] birth is attracting anew to him the attention of all progressive humanity."[20]

The sentence missing from the first page of chapter 5 (p. 211 of the Moscow typescript; see fig. 2.4, following line 15), reads, "After all, nearly thirty years had passed since the days of its [Katerina Izmailova's] composition."[21] This was the page that I juxtaposed (in my own translation) with the English text of *Testimony* in my 1980 review. Since I did not have access at that time to the original Russian text of *Testimony*, I erred on the side of caution and allowed for the possibility of minor discrepancies between them. But comparison with the Moscow typescript confirms that the two passages are identical in all respects, except for the deleted sentence.

Although the opening sentence and the beginning of the second sentence in chapter 4 (p. 145 of the Moscow typescript) have been modified to obscure the fact that, as originally published, these remarks clearly dated the composer's reminiscences about the opera *Ledi Makbet Mtsenskogo uezda* [Lady Macbeth of the Mtsensk District op. 29 (1930–32)] to the early 1930s, when the opera was still in progress, the text that follows for the rest of the page duplicates verbatim 178 words from the published Russian source.

Turning to the first pages of both chapter 3 (p. 106) and chapter 7 (p. 326) in the Moscow typescript, no Shostakovich inscription can be seen at the top of either page. This is explained by the fact that both pages show evidence of several lines of text having been pasted in at the

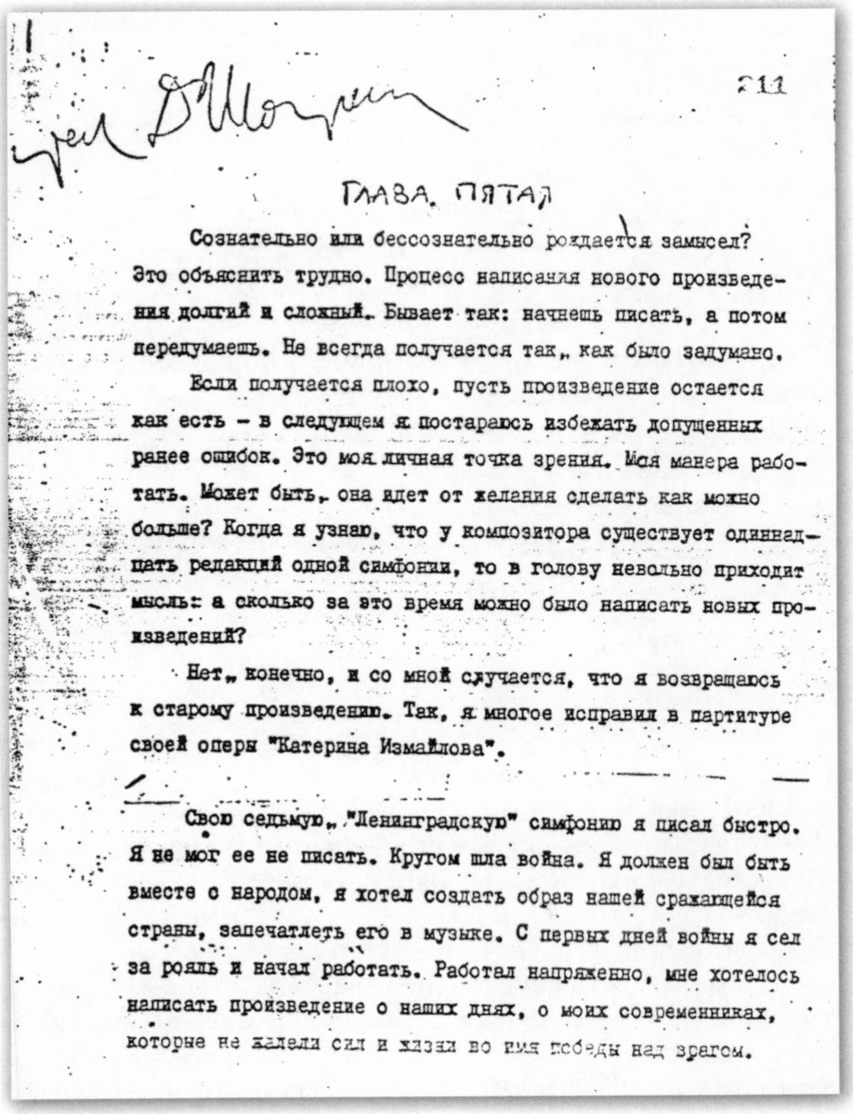

Д. Шостакович

211

ГЛАВА ПЯТАЯ

Сознательно или бессознательно рождается замысел? Это объяснить трудно. Процесс написания нового произведения долгий и сложный. Бывает так: начнешь писать, а потом передумаешь. Не всегда получается так, как было задумано.

Если получается плохо, пусть произведение остается как есть – в следующем я постараюсь избежать допущенных ранее ошибок. Это моя личная точка зрения. Моя манера работать. Может быть, она идет от желания сделать как можно больше? Когда я узнаю, что у композитора существует одиннадцать редакций одной симфонии, то в голову невольно приходит мысль: а сколько за это время можно было написать новых произведений?

Нет, конечно, и со мной случается, что я возвращаюсь к старому произведению. Так, я многое исправил в партитуре своей оперы "Катерина Измайлова".

Свою седьмую, "Ленинградскую" симфонию я писал быстро. Я не мог ее не писать. Кругом шла война. Я должен был быть вместе с народом, я хотел создать образ нашей сражающейся страны, запечатлеть его в музыке. С первых дней войны я сел за рояль и начал работать. Работал напряженно, мне хотелось написать произведение о наших днях, о моих современниках, которые не жалели сил и жизни во имя победы над врагом.

Figure 2.4. Page 211 of the Moscow Typescript

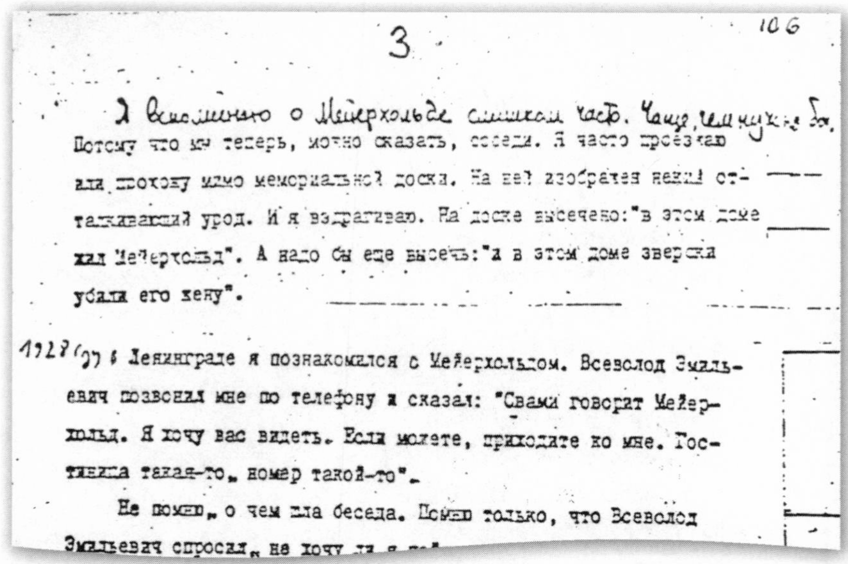

3 106

Я вспоминаю о Мейерхольде слишком часто. Чаще, чем нужно бы.
Потому что мы теперь, можно сказать, соседи. Я часто проезжаю или прохожу мимо мемориальной доски. На ней изображен некий отталкивающий урод. И я вздрагиваю. На доске высечено: "в этом доме жил Мейерхольд". А надо бы еще высечь: "и в этом доме зверски убили его жену".

1928 (27) В Ленинграде я познакомился с Мейерхольдом. Всеволод Эмильевич позвонил мне по телефону и сказал: "Свами говорит Мейерхольд. Я хочу вас видеть. Если можете, приходите ко мне. Гостиница такая-то, номер такой-то".

Не помню, о чем шла беседа. Помню только, что Всеволод Эмильевич спросил, не хочу

Figure 2.5. Page 106 of the Moscow Typescript

top, out of pitch and alignment with the rest of the text on the page. The added text fills in the space normally made by the sinkage noted earlier at the start of each new chapter—the space where the composer always affixed his visa, "Read. D. Shostakovich."[22]

In the case of chapter 3, the derivation of the grafted text becomes readily apparent. Above the five lines of text pasted in at the start of the chapter, presumably obscuring Shostakovich's visa, the opening line has been written in by hand, and not the hand of the composer: "I think of Meyerhold too frequently, more frequently than I should."[23] Two pages later, on page 108, the identical sentence is found again, this time typed, above a gap and a horizontal shadow line—likely a narrow strip of correction tape (figs. 2.5 and 2.6). (This redundancy was edited out of the published English translation.) Further, each of the first three pages of this chapter, pages 106 to 108, reveals signs of having been cut and pasted to accommodate the shifting of lines of text from page 108 to page 106. No typed page number appears on any of the pages (we would expect it to have been omitted on the first page but to appear in the top center of pages 107 and 108), because the original typed number has been cov-

108

Может быть, это один из самых больших секретов нашей жизни. Старики этого секрета не знали. Потому они всё потеряли. Остается надеяться, что молодежь будет счастливее.

Я вспоминаю о Мейерхольде слишком часто. Чаще, чем нужно бы.

Мейерхольд любил элегантно одеваться. И любил окружать себя красивыми вещами: картины, фарфор, хрусталь и прочее. Но все это не может идти ни в какое сравнение со страстью к роскоши Зинаиды Николаевны.

Райх была женщина очень красивая. Может быть, немного тяжеловатая. Это особенно было заметно на сцене. По сцене Зинаида Николаевна двигалась наредкость неуклюже.

Райх свою красоту

Figure 2.6. Page 108 of the Moscow Typescript

ered over by the cutting and pasting. Neither does a stamped page number appear in the upper right-hand corner, for the same reason. Hand numbering has been substituted.[24]

To sum up, the evidence makes it clear that the opening paragraph of chapter 3, including what Ho and Feofanov (p. 211) characterize as a "flagrantly 'inflammatory' " comment about the brutal murder of Meyerhold's wife (a comment that would have been unthinkable in a Soviet source during the composer's lifetime), was not originally found on the first page of this chapter of *Testimony* but on the third page, where no authenticating inscription by Shostakovich is to be found.

The first page of chapter 3 differs in yet another respect from all others at the beginnings of chapters. Although the rest of the text, following the opening paragraph, bears an unmistakable relationship to the reminiscence published in *Sovetskaia muzyka* in 1974—and none of this material is sensational or "inflammatory"—it is much less literal in its replication of text than all the other chapter beginnings in the *Testimony* typescript. Sentences have been rephrased, rearranged, or shortened. None of this, however, has affected the overall relationship of the two texts, which essentially correspond. When one recalls that this is the very reminiscence of Meyerhold already published under the byline of S. Volkov during Shostakovich's lifetime and that it was presumably based on notes Volkov made during an interview with the composer,[25] the minor differences between the earlier published text and the text as it appears in *Testimony* might be interpreted as reasonable editorial license exercised by a journalist in republishing his old interview in a new context. Nevertheless, the passage draws attention to itself by its uniqueness in the *Testimony* typescript.

At the time of my 1980 review of *Testimony* I was able to identify the published sources for the first pages of seven of the eight chapters. But I could not find a source for the first page of chapter 1. Neither did I ever expect to find one. My examination of the Moscow copy of the *Testimony* typescript, however, has finally provided the answer to this lingering conundrum. As Ho and Feofanov have pointed out, this opening page contains flagrantly inflammatory statements that would have been inconceivable in a Soviet publication, such as the following examples: "Others will write about us. And naturally they'll lie through their teeth—but that's their business" and "Looking back, I see nothing but ruins, only mountains of corpses. And I do not want to build new Potemkin villages on these ruins."[26] Ho and Feofanov—who claim to have seen the signed pages of the original typescript of *Testimony*—emphasize that this text appears on a page of the typescript that was signed by Shostakovich, thus precluding the conclusion that Volkov submitted only innocuous, previously published material for authentication.[27] For more than twenty years, Volkov, his publisher, and his defenders have all maintained that Shostakovich's signature appears on the first page of chapter 1 of the original typescript, as well as on all the following first pages of chapters, and nowhere else.[28]

The claim is false. The first four pages of the Moscow typescript of *Testimony* (figs. 2.7–2.10) flatly contradict it. The Russian text on these opening pages corresponds fully to the beginning of chapter 1 of the published English translation of *Testimony*. All four pages display two sets of pagination similar to what has been described earlier. But typed internal numbering is not visible on any of the first three of these pages. Instead, page number "1" is entered by hand in the top center of the first page, and underneath appears the handwritten ГЛАВА ПЕРВАЯ [CHAPTER ONE], which has been marked through. Stamped page number "001" is placed in the top right-hand corner. On the page fol-

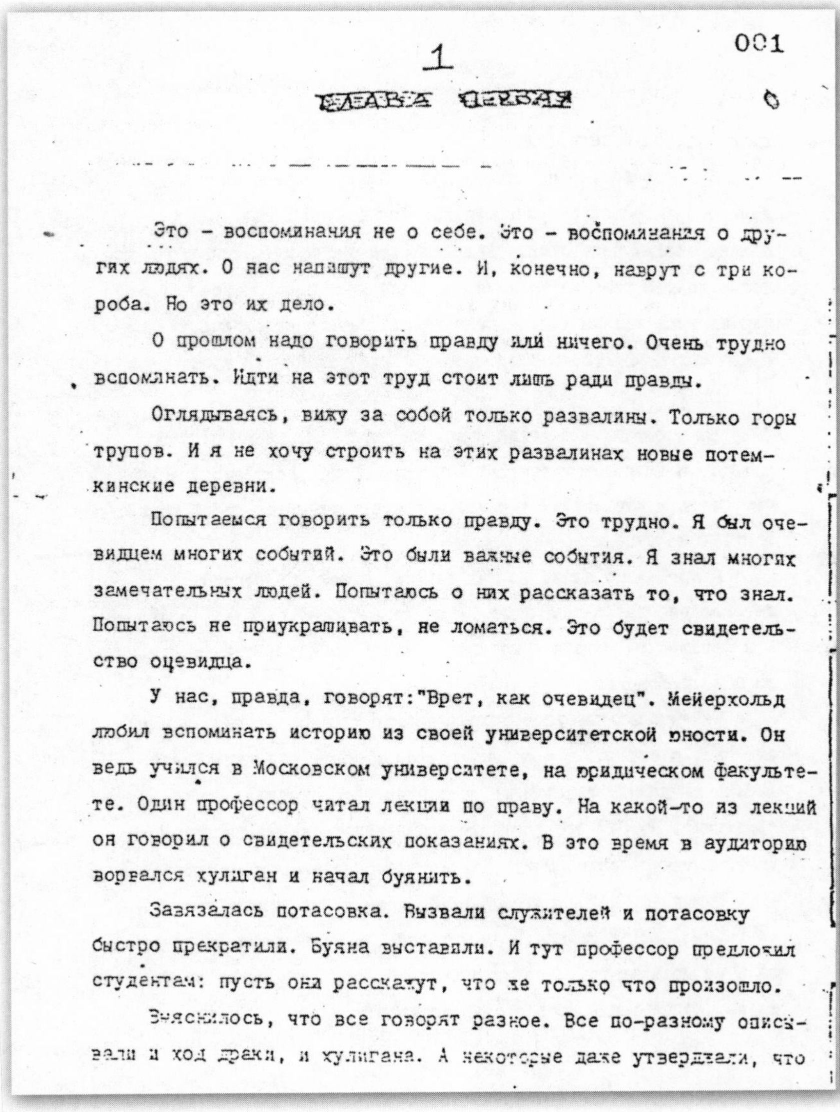

1 001

ГЛАВА ПЕРВАЯ

Это - воспоминания не о себе. Это - воспоминания о других людях. О нас напишут другие. И, конечно, наврут с три короба. Но это их дело.

О прошлом надо говорить правду или ничего. Очень трудно вспоминать. Идти на этот труд стоит лишь ради правды.

Оглядываясь, вижу за собой только развалины. Только горы трупов. И я не хочу строить на этих развалинах новые потемкинские деревни.

Попытаемся говорить только правду. Это трудно. Я был очевидцем многих событий. Это были важные события. Я знал многих замечательных людей. Попытаюсь о них рассказать то, что знал. Попытаюсь не приукрашивать, не ломаться. Это будет свидетельство очевидца.

У нас, правда, говорят:"Врет, как очевидец". Мейерхольд любил вспоминать историю из своей университетской юности. Он ведь учился в Московском университете, на юридическом факультете. Один профессор читал лекции по праву. На какой-то из лекций он говорил о свидетельских показаниях. В это время в аудиторию ворвался хулиган и начал буянить.

Завязалась потасовка. Вызвали служителей и потасовку быстро прекратили. Буяна выставили. И тут профессор предложил студентам: пусть они расскажут, что же только что произошло.

Выяснилось, что все говорят разное. Все по-разному описывали и ход драки, и хулигана. А некоторые даже утверждали, что

Figure 2.7. Page 001 of the Moscow Typescript

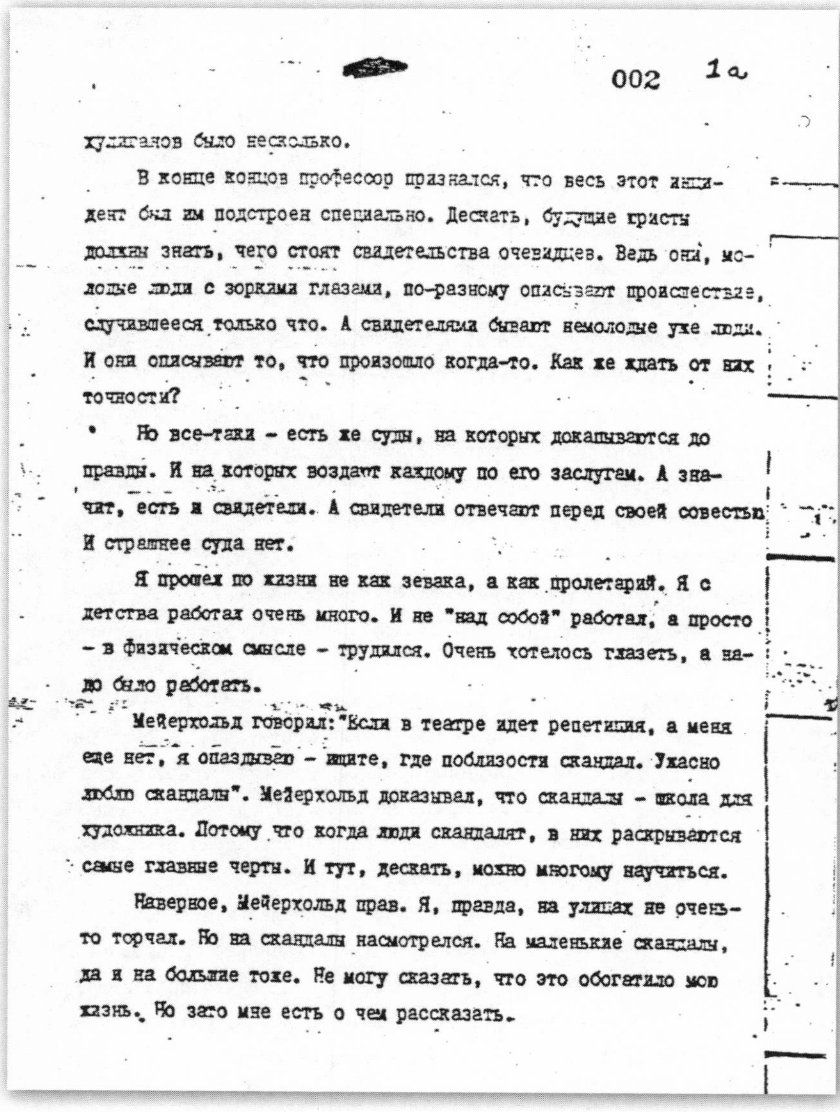

002 1a

хулиганов было несколько.

В конце концов профессор признался, что весь этот инцидент был им подстроен специально. Дескать, будущие юристы должны знать, чего стоят свидетельства очевидцев. Ведь они, молодые люди с зоркими глазами, по-разному описывают происшествие, случившееся только что. А свидетелями бывают немолодые уже люди. И они описывают то, что произошло когда-то. Как же ждать от них точности?

Но все-таки - есть же суды, на которых докапываются до правды. И на которых воздают каждому по его заслугам. А значит, есть и свидетели. А свидетели отвечают перед своей совестью. И страшнее суда нет.

Я прошел по жизни не как зевака, а как пролетарий. Я с детства работал очень много. И не "над собой" работал, а просто - в физическом смысле - трудился. Очень хотелось глазеть, а надо было работать.

Мейерхольд говорил: "Если в театре идет репетиция, а меня еще нет, я опаздываю - ищите, где поблизости скандал. Ужасно люблю скандалы". Мейерхольд доказывал, что скандалы - школа для художника. Потому что когда люди скандалят, в них раскрываются самые главные черты. И тут, дескать, можно многому научиться.

Наверное, Мейерхольд прав. Я, правда, на улицах не очень-то торчал. Но на скандалы насмотрелся. На маленькие скандалы, да и на большие тоже. Не могу сказать, что это обогатило мою жизнь. Но зато мне есть о чем рассказать.

Figure 2.8. Page 002 of the Moscow Typescript

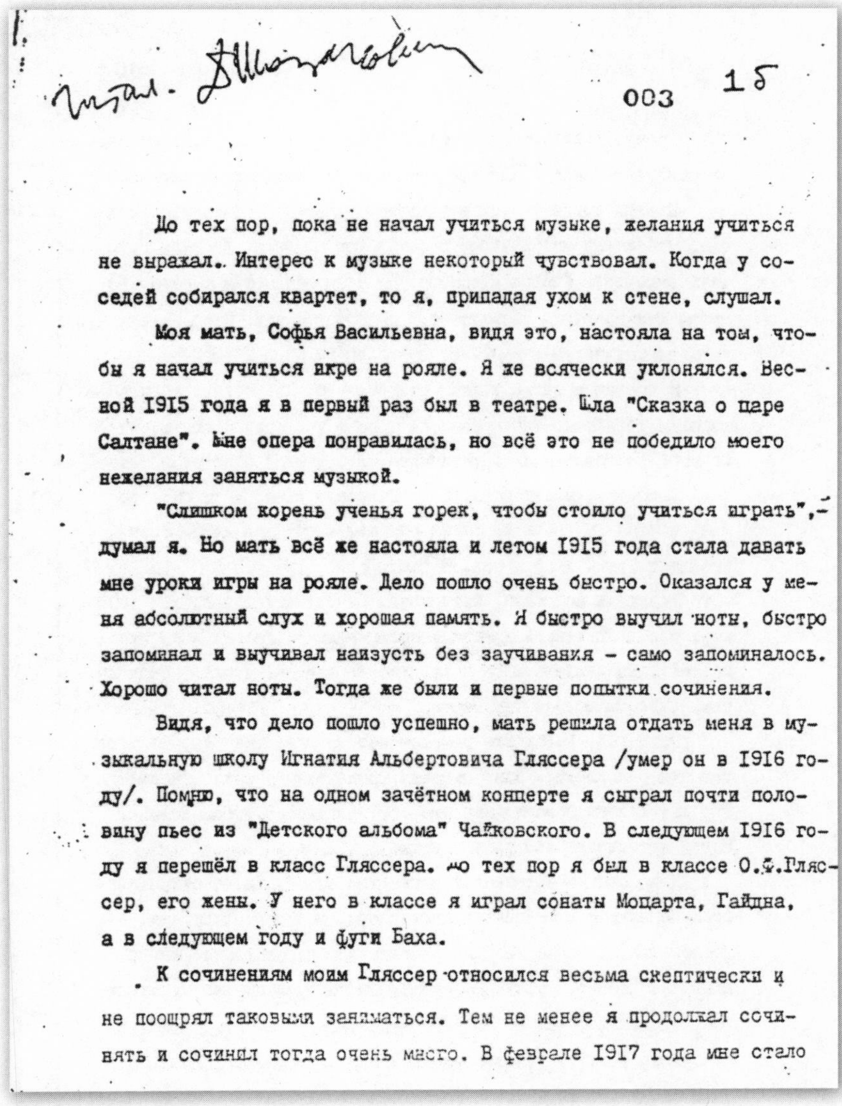

Читал. Д. Шостакович

003 1б

До тех пор, пока не начал учиться музыке, желания учиться не выражал. Интерес к музыке некоторый чувствовал. Когда у соседей собирался квартет, то я, припадая ухом к стене, слушал.

Моя мать, Софья Васильевна, видя это, настояла на том, чтобы я начал учиться икре на рояле. Я же всячески уклонялся. Весной 1915 года я в первый раз был в театре. Шла "Сказка о царе Салтане". Мне опера понравилась, но всё это не победило моего нежелания заняться музыкой.

"Слишком корень ученья горек, чтобы стоило учиться играть",- думал я. Но мать всё же настояла и летом 1915 года стала давать мне уроки игры на рояле. Дело пошло очень быстро. Оказался у меня абсолютный слух и хорошая память. Я быстро выучил ноты, быстро запоминал и выучивал наизусть без заучивания - само запоминалось. Хорошо читал ноты. Тогда же были и первые попытки сочинения.

Видя, что дело пошло успешно, мать решила отдать меня в музыкальную школу Игнатия Альбертовича Гляссера /умер он в 1916 году/. Помню, что на одном зачётном концерте я сыграл почти половину пьес из "Детского альбома" Чайковского. В следующем 1916 году я перешёл в класс Гляссера. До тех пор я был в классе О.Ф.Гляссер, его жены. У него в классе я играл сонаты Моцарта, Гайдна, а в следующем году и фуги Баха.

К сочинениям моим Гляссер относился весьма скептически и не поощрял таковыми заниматься. Тем не менее я продолжал сочинять и сочинил тогда очень много. В феврале 1917 года мне стало

Figure 2.9. Page 003 of the Moscow Typescript

- 2 - 004

неинтересно ходить к Гляссеру. Он был человек скучный, но весьма самоуверенный. А мне его поучения уже казались смешными.

Я ведь тогда учился в училище Шидловской. Уверенности в том, что стану музыкантом, в семье еще не было. Из меня готовили инженера. Учился я хорошо. По всем предметам хорошо. Но потом музыка стала занимать все больше времени. Отец думал, что из меня получится ученый. Но не вышло из меня ученого.

Я всегда и везде учился старательно. Мне хотелось быть хорошим учеником. Мне нравилось хорошо учиться. Я люблю, чтобы со мной разговаривали с уважением. Это у меня с детства такое.

Потому я, может быть, и от Гляссера ушел. Мать была против, а я настоял на своем. Я такие решения сразу принимаю. Решил, что не пойду - и не пошел. И все.

Родители мои были, безусловно, интеллигенты. И, как таковые, обладали тонкой душевной организацией. Любили искусство, красоту. Изобразительное искусство любили. К музыке, между прочим, имелось особое тяготение.

Отец пел. Цыганские романсы пел. Всякие тма "Ах, не тебя так пылко я люблю". Или "Отцвели хризантемы в саду". Волшебная музыка, сильно помогло мне это обстоятельство впоследствии. Когда я таперствовал по киношкам.

Я от своего интереса к цыганским промансам не открещиваюсь. Не вижу в этом ничего постыдного. В отличие, скажем, от Прокофьева. Который изображал священное негодование, когда слышал подобную музыку. Наверное, он получил лучшее музыкальное воспитание, чем я. Но зато я не сноб.

Мать училась в Петербургской консерватории. У Розановой училась, у той же дамы, к которой впоследствии и меня привела.

Figure 2.10. Page 004 of the Moscow Typescript

lowing, stamped number "002" appears in the same position, and to its right and slightly higher a handwritten "1a" has been entered. (Where the internal typed page number would normally appear, in the top center, something has been blotted out.)

Only on the third page does one finally encounter the composer's familiar visa, "Читал. Д. Шостакович" [Read. D. Shostakovich], inscribed starting at the top left of the page within the space made by a sinkage characteristic of chapter beginnings noted elsewhere in the typescript. Stamped number "003" occupies its usual position at the top right of the page, and, further to the right and slightly above, the number "1b" has been entered by hand.

The page following, the fourth, exhibits the stamped "004" placed as usual, but in the top center appears a typewritten "-2-," in the familiar typeface seen throughout the *Testimony* typescript. From here on, the numbers internal to the chapter are typed in that same familiar typeface, and they proceed in normal sequence to the end of the chapter. Similarly, the stamped numbering also continues normally. No further alterations appear.

And what is the text that appears beneath the composer's visa on page 1b (003)? Like all the other texts on signed pages, it is a verbatim transcript of a previously published memoir, in this case a statement Shostakovich penned in 1927 but published only in the September 1966 issue of *Sovetskaia muzyka*, on the occasion of his sixtieth birthday: "I had not expressed a desire to study music before I began taking lessons, although I had some interest in music and listened ear to the wall when a quartet met at the neighbors," and so on, for a total of 238 exactly quoted words.[29] The sinkage at the top of this page, typical of that found at the beginnings of other chapters, along with the presence of Shostakovich's inscription, show that this was originally the first page of what became the first chapter of the published book and that the two "inflammatory" pages preceding it—hand-numbered "1" and "1a" respectively—were slotted in after Shostakovich's signature of approval had been obtained. If Ho and Feofanov actually examined the typescript, as they claim, then they have knowingly and deliberately misrepresented its contents and appearance in an attempt to deceive their readers.

In sum, *all* the pages of *Testimony* signed by Shostakovich are analogous. They all consist of word-for-word (or, in one case, slightly paraphrased) quotation of material published in the Soviet Union before Shostakovich's death in 1975. All the signed pages contain uncontroversial subject matter. In seven cases out of eight, they reproduce exactly the layout and punctuation of their original published sources. Furthermore, the quoted material on these signed pages is confined to and precisely circumscribed by the length of a single typed page of the Russian text. In every case, the direct quotation ceases abruptly—even breaking off in mid-sentence—the moment one turns to the next page.[30] Beyond the first page the texts diverge, sometimes radically. Take, for example, chapter 2 of the *Testimony* typescript—the reminiscence about Stravinsky (fig. 2.2)—where a single word on the second page provides the pivot, after which the text veers off in tone and content from the original Russian publication. The total length of the verbatim transcript of previously published material, in other words, extends only one word longer than a single typed page. In the most striking divergence, the Shostakovich of *Testimony* questions Stravinsky's "Russianness":

> It's another question as to how Russian a composer Stravinsky is. He was probably right not to return to Russia. His concept of morality is European. I can see that clearly from his memoirs—everything he says about his parents and colleagues is European. This approach is foreign to me.
>
> And Stravinsky's idea of the role of music is also purely European, primarily French. . . .
>
> When Stravinsky came to visit us, he came as a foreigner. It was even strange to think that we were born near each other, I in Petersburg and he not far from it.[31]

In the partially quoted statement published in 1973, Shostakovich displays no such skepticism:

> I consider Stravinsky to be a truly Russian composer. The Russian spirit is ineradicable in the heart of this real, genuinely great, multifaceted talent, born on Russian soil and bound to it by blood.[32]

Ho and Feofanov found several research psychologists who were prepared to testify—based presumably on information the authors provided them—that Shostakovich was probably capable of repeating substantial passages of his own words verbatim. Beyond establishing this as a hypothesis, however, Ho and Feofanov produce no evidence that Shostakovich ever repeated such large chunks of his own statements word-for-word in conversation. Indeed, the style of the duplicated passages contrasts with all known recollections or descriptions of his speech habits.

In speaking, Shostakovich often manifested nervous mannerisms, the spasmodic repetition of words or short phrases as well as common verbal "tics"—"you know" [понимаете], for instance. If, however, he had been prone to self-quotation at such length and on such a grammatically polished formal scale as found in the passages quoted in *Testimony*, other examples of this practice might have been expected to turn up elsewhere. Yet no examples remotely comparable have surfaced, despite all the new information and resources made available to researchers in the past twenty-odd years.

True, Shostakovich had a phenomenal musical memory, and he was famous for being able to quote long stretches from the works of his favorite authors. He was also a storyteller with a repertory of staples many remember hearing more than once. Still, the ability to commit to memory and reproduce music or literary texts does not inevitably translate into the desire or propensity to repeat one's own statements verbatim.

No evidence has been produced to demonstrate that Shostakovich ever repeated one of his stories exactly the same way twice. Rather, the opposite has been shown. Daniel Zhitomirsky recalls the celebration after the première of the composer's Ninth Symphony in 1945, when Shostakovich entertained his guests brilliantly with a yarn about a Moscow musicologist and a rubber object of an intimate nature:

> But the crux of the matter was not in the topic of the story itself. D. D. had composed extempore a stunningly witty "scherzo." And when he finished, everyone asked for an encore. He complied with the request and retold the story from its very beginning, but with virtuosic variations.[33]

"With virtuosic variations"—that, surely, is the mark of a genuine storyteller, not literal fidelity to a script.

A similar situation occurs in letters Shostakovich wrote describing the same circumstance to different friends. On 11 February 1960, while in the hospital, Shostakovich addressed letters to Lev Lebedinsky in Moscow and Isaak Glikman in Leningrad. The main substance of both letters is the same: the composer's ironic reflections occasioned by reading a Soviet novel of the 1920s, *Natalia Tarpova* by Sergei Semyonov. With two addressees living in different cities and unlikely to compare notes, here was a perfect opportunity for Shostakovich to repeat himself were he so inclined. Yet, even though the tone and content of the two letters correspond, no more than a few words of literal repetition, here and there, can be found. Indeed, far from repeating himself, Shostakovich seems to have gone out of his way to find different ways to say the same thing, as becomes apparent in a comparison of the opening paragraphs of the two letters:

> [To Glikman]
> I am in the hospital where they plan to treat my right hand. I'm very bored. It's truly boring to spend time in the hospital since I'm completely healthy. Last time I was cheered by the hope that they might cure my hand. Now I don't have an iota of hope.[34]

> [To Lebedinsky]
> I'm bored to death. I'm completely healthy, so my stay in the hospital doesn't cheer me up. The hope for a cure relieved my first stay, but this time nothing relieves it.[35]

Attempting to offer a plausible hypothesis to explain why so much "borrowed" material ended up appearing at the beginnings of chapters on the very pages signed by Shostakovich, Ho and Feofanov suggest that Shostakovich may have exercised authorial control without Volkov being aware of it.[36] They even raise the possibility that the passages quoted from Shostakovich's reminiscences of Stravinsky and Meyerhold, published in 1973 and 1974, respectively, might have been recycled *from Testimony* and not the other way around, since Volkov says that his collaboration was ongoing at the time.[37] But let us remember that Volkov also says that he did not become aware of any of these publications until 1980, after the appearance of my review, and he says, in addition, that he made no copies of the typescript of *Testimony* at the time he was collaborating with Shostakovich.[38] If we accept Ho and Feofanov's explanations, we must be prepared to believe that Shostakovich himself surreptitiously copied Volkov's transcribed texts without informing him, and then arranged for their publication.

We must also believe that Shostakovich himself contrived to keep his previously published statements substantially intact, despite Volkov's description of how the composer responded during their collaboration: the brief, at first reluctant answers, the short sentences, the rephrasing of questions. We must believe that Shostakovich's statements somehow survived the process Volkov described—the latter's transcribing, arranging, and rearranging into "arbitrary" parts of his shorthand notes—and then were restored, word-for-word, punctuation, paragraphs and all, to occupy the exact space of a single typed page.

Ho and Feofanov offer no explanation as to why Shostakovich might have felt compelled in the first place to locate such innocuous material on these single typed pages. Even had he wanted to convey exactly the same sense, why might he have been motivated to repeat his already published statements verbatim in an otherwise candid memoir? And how could all of this have been accomplished without raising any suspicion in Volkov's mind or leaving a trace on the finished typescript?

Volkov has suggested that the noncommittal, formulaic inscription, "Read. D. Shostakovich," was devised by the composer to create a certain distance between himself and the text, in the event that it was published during his lifetime or should pressure be brought to bear by the KGB.[39] Ho and Feofanov report that one of Volkov's former colleagues and a deputy editor of *Sovetskaia muzyka*, Liana Genina, has confirmed that "Read. Shostakovich" was an authentic formula used by the composer.[40] But Ho and Feofanov elected not to report Genina's complete statement:

> Yes, it was his all-purpose signature: just "Read," and no evaluation whatever. Except when authors who were real pains in the neck got to him and then the signature changed to "Print [Печатать]. Shostakovich."[41]

In other words, the form his inscription took on the particular pages of *Testimony* was not something especially devised, as Volkov suggested, but the composer's standard and entirely routine visa.

Shostakovich made no secret of the fact that he was a "signer." His readiness to sign documents without reading them was well known. He told Flora Litvinova, "When somebody starts pestering me, I have only one thought in mind—get rid of him as quickly as possible, and to achieve that I am prepared to sign anything!"[42] Galina Shostakovich, the composer's daughter, observed in 1995 with respect to *Testimony* that "Shostakovich did sign some stupid articles about inconsequential subjects without reading them, but he would not have signed something this big and important without reading it."[43] It is hard to disagree with Galina that *Testimony* turned out to be something big and important enough that Shostakovich really should have read it before signing. But only Solomon Volkov can vouch for Shostakovich's full and witting partnership in the production of the book that was published four years after his death as his *Testimony*. When he signed those few pages of inconsequential quotations from his previously published articles, Shostakovich may well have had no inkling of how big and important Volkov's book would become, or even what kind of book it would be. The presence of his signature and stock formula above recycled passages (and *only* recycled passages) in the *Testimony* typescript provides no warranty that Shostakovich had either read the entire typescript or understood its true purpose.

❧

The notion that *Testimony* might not be exactly what Volkov claimed—that it might represent something other than Shostakovich's own reminiscences, carefully vetted and knowingly authorized for publication—met with significant resistance in the 1980s and 1990s. Even after considering the evidence provided in my 1980 review, many Western scholars continued to quote from the book, albeit with perfunctory caveats. Most journalists, musical annotators, and critics were happy to rely on it as a faithful, straightforward dissemination of Shostakovich's words and views.

To be sure, the "voice" in *Testimony* may well reflect the composer's personal views more faithfully than anything published before 1979, as many émigrés have confirmed. Kirill Kondrashin, for instance, vouched for the image of Shostakovich that emerged from Volkov's book:

> It was with the greatest agitation that I read Shostakovich's memoirs, prepared by Solomon Volkov. Much of what comes as a surprise to the Western reader was not a surprise for me. I knew many things and guessed many others; but there were new things in it even for me, things that made me look at some of his works differently.[44]

Other émigrés and Westerners who had known the composer less well—and sometimes not at all—echoed Kondrashin's opinion.

On the other hand, the Shostakovich rendered by Volkov in *Testimony* proved unrecognizable to Galina Vishnevskaya, someone whose closeness to Shostakovich in his later years few would challenge. In a 1980 interview she repudiated Volkov's book in no uncertain terms:

> I read this book in manuscript in the Russian language, in Paris. It made a strange impression on me. To me it appeared to be a collection of stories more or less well known to the musical world at large. If this book had been written representing Solomon Volkov as the author, I would have perceived it completely differently. But Volkov placed these stories in Shostakovich's mouth and in doing so he debased and misrepresented Shostakovich's spiritual makeup. I personally knew a completely different person, not the one who emerges from the pages of this book.[45]

Vishnevskaya went on to publish her own memoirs, *Galina*, in 1984.[46] They contain a vivid portrait of the Shostakovich she and her husband, Mstislav Rostropovich, befriended over many years. The Shostakovich who emerges from the pages of Vishnevskaya's memoirs is a complex, contradictory personality, no less disaffected in many respects than Volkov's protagonist. A number of Western commentators, insensitive to differences in nuance and unaware of Vishnevskaya's stated opinion, have erroneously adduced her memoirs in support of the authenticity of *Testimony*.

In contrast to Vishnevskaya's close creative rapport with the composer, Vladimir Ashkenazy has stated that he met Shostakovich only "two or three times" before he left the Soviet Union at the age of twenty-six in 1963, once when he played Shostakovich's Piano Trio op. 67 and a couple of times casually at concerts: "I shook his hand, I think. But I never met him properly."[47] Notwithstanding this admission that he hardly knew the composer and the fact that he had long been living in the West by the time Volkov began his meetings with Shostakovich in 1971, Ashkenazy has been a staunch advocate of *Testimony* ("When I read *Testimony*, there was no question in my mind that the real Shostakovich was here in this book. All that we knew about him was now confirmed in print") and an equally obdurate foe of its critics.[48]

Some prominent émigrés apparently found the sensationalism and scandal surrounding *Testimony* distasteful. In the months after its appearance, Mstislav Rostropovich pointedly declined to discuss Volkov's book in public at all, whether to endorse or to denounce it. He began to voice an opinion publicly only many years later, and then in oblique terms, as in the following comments published in 1986, 1998, and 1994, respectively:

> Shostakovich maintained, ostensibly, that Prokofiev orchestrated poorly. According to Volkov, what didn't Shostakovich say! His "memoirs" are full of exaggerations of the kind friends make in private, but never write down. Possibly his friends were too gossipy and Volkov made use of them. But Shostakovich would never have taken such a risk; he was too afraid that his children would be deprived of everything.[49]

> When I read the rubbish written by Solomon Volkov, I must say I was deeply surprised to find him making out that Shostakovich had put his own signature to the pages. For example, on Dmitri Dmitrievich's attitude to Prokofiev, I heard him say many times: "He's a composer of genius. This is a work of genius!"[50]

> Contrary to what is written in Solomon Volkov's *Testimony*, Dmitri Dmitrievich worshipped Stravinsky and considered the Symphony of Psalms to be one of the most brilliant works in existence.

> I have to say that I consider the Volkov book is not a balanced account. It is like a series of anecdotes; or rather, as basically everything that is stated there is true,

one might say a series of "interesting little stories." Shostakovich was a man who, for the sake of a good story, could go so far as to invent a tale.[51]

Rostropovich's seeming ambivalence about *Testimony*—and on the rare occasions when he has addressed it, his focus on specific errors of fact rather than on its fundamental authenticity—has emboldened the book's supporters to enlist him among their ranks.[52] With the suave finesse of a publicity sound bite, the subordinate phrase "basically everything that is stated there is true" is extracted from the substantially more complicated sense conveyed by Rostropovich in the complete quotation. The outspokenly pro-*Testimony* manifesto, *Shostakovich Reconsidered*, presents Rostropovich as if he were a current contributor to the volume. But appearances are deceiving. The interview with Rostropovich published there, on the subject of Rostropovich's relationships with Shostakovich and Prokofiev, was in fact conducted by Volkov in 1978, a year before *Testimony* was published. (In retrospect, it might seem curious that no mention whatsoever is made in this 1978 interview of the sensational soon-to-be-published "authorized" memoirs of Shostakovich.) Repackaged and touched up with introductory and concluding comments, along with a new title, this twenty-year-old interview reappears fully reincarnated in the 1998 *Shostakovich Reconsidered*.[53]

While Maxim Shostakovich was still living behind the Iron Curtain, his opposition to *Testimony* was readily discounted in the West as having been coerced by Soviet authorities. The startling news that he had defected, with his son, in April 1981, sparked renewed interest in his "true" opinion of his father's supposed memoirs. At his first press conference in Washington, D.C., on 23 April 1981, Maxim responded:

> I know Volkov's book, and I made a statement about it in Moscow. The thing is, in my opinion the book consists of two parts. The first deals with Shostakovich's attitude as a [Soviet] citizen towards what was going on in the years Volkov describes, something that was well known back home, even if it wasn't to be found in print. Even here, one encounters lots of mistakes and inaccuracies. To write about Dmitri Shostakovich, about the questions he pondered, or about the people who were close to him, it should be all or nothing at all. It should not be hearsay about what he said at dinner or among friends or in conversation with students. . . . Unfortunately the book amounts to a compilation of exactly this sort of hearsay. . . . And many outstanding composers and musicians, whom he loved and respected, are presented in some sort of bad light.
>
> But the main thing—and this is obvious and very important—is that Volkov interviewed Dmitri Shostakovich as a representative of *Sovetskaia muzyka*, where he worked as a journalist in those years. It is difficult to imagine that Dmitri

> Shostakovich would have wanted everything that found its way into [Volkov's] book published in the pages of *Sovetskaia muzyka.* As far as I'm concerned, this explains my attitude to this book sufficiently.[54]

In a lengthy interview conducted shortly afterward in New York, Maxim was even more categorical:

> They are not my father's memoirs. It is a book by Solomon Wolkow [*sic*]. Mr. Wolkow must explain how this book came about. . . . It is a book about my father rather than by him. The journalist Wolkow interviewed my father four, or six, times for the magazine *Soviet Music.* He got this interview authorised. Can you imagine that such critical statements as were later published in the book could ever have been made for a Soviet magazine? Wolkow probably slotted numerous pages between the unnumbered pages of the interview. It's easily done. . . .[55]

And in a 1982 interview with Alexander Abramov, Maxim alluded to people besides his father who had found voice in *Testimony:*

> —Was Dmitri Dmitrievich really like the person represented in Volkov's book?
>
> —True, he met with my father a few times, and their conversations are reflected in the book. The political tendency, the political opinions of my father are represented correctly. But, on top of this, various hearsay and testimonials that did not originate with my father found their way into the book. I know who the originator was, but I won't talk about it now. In your articles on Shostakovich [i.e., Abramov's articles], what is your own and what is my father's is obvious, but in Volkov's book, it is difficult to distinguish what is Shostakovich and what is Volkov.[56]

Over the years Maxim has occasionally mitigated his public criticism of *Testimony*, granting that the book is broadly accurate in its description of the political circumstances of Shostakovich's life and the spiritual torment he endured, but without retreating from his earlier stand that *Testimony* is a book *about* rather than *by* his father—a book rife with factual errors, misrepresentations, and rumor:

> —In your opinion, do Solomon Volkov's memoirs contain a truthful portrait of your father?
>
> —No! I've reiterated this many times! This is his [Volkov's] book about Shostakovich. Volkov has described the political situation of my father's surroundings with great reliability, but when he resurrects in his memory Shostakovich's attitude to other composers and conductors—to Toscanini, for example, or Prokofiev—he reports inaccurate information. If one wants to sketch the profile of musicians with prominent names, then one must not content oneself with extracting a single phrase out of context. . . .
>
> — . . . that would be tendentious, inaccurate?

—Unquestionably. Here is an example for you regarding Tchaikovsky. I remember that Shostakovich might tell me at breakfast that he despised Tchaikovsky's development sections, then maintain something different at lunch, and at dinner sum up to the effect that never was there anything more beautiful than "The Queen of Spades."[57]

Maxim gave a comparable assessment to the British musicologist David Fanning, who asked him in 1991 if his attitude toward *Testimony* had changed in any way:

> No, I would still say it's a book about my father, not by him. The conversations about Glazunov, Meyerhold, Zoshchenko are one thing. But it also contains rumours, and sometimes false rumours. It's a collection of different things—real documentary fact and rumour. But what's more important is that when we take this book in our hands we can imagine what this composer's life was like in this particular political situation—how difficult, how awful it was under the Stalin regime. Other things may be right or wrong, for instance regarding my father's relations with Prokofiev, with Stravinsky, his opinions on Tchaikovsky, Toscanini—not everything is the truth. But I never tried to take this book and say page by page what is wrong, what is right. Maybe I need to do it.[58]

In sum, Maxim's perceived about-face in his views coupled with the display of amicable sociability toward Volkov in various public arenas in recent years—as well as his endorsement of Ian MacDonald's *Testimony*-based *The New Shostakovich*[59]—have blinded *Testimony*'s supporters to the fact that Maxim always refers to it as a book by Solomon Volkov and never as "my father's memoirs."

For all the doubts that several of the composer's intimates have raised, as have cautious scholars, about Solomon Volkov's integrity and the authenticity of what he marketed as the memoirs of Shostakovich, the sales and exposure of *Testimony* did not suffer from the controversy. Appearing as it did shortly before the Soviet invasion of Afghanistan at the final crest of Cold War tensions—a time when the eventual end of the Cold War and the demise of the Soviet Empire were as yet entirely unforeseen—*Testimony* fell on extremely fertile ground. Viewed from any perspective, Shostakovich was a towering figure in twentieth-century world culture. And he was much too good and much too important a composer for the West ever to digest easily that he was a true believer in communism and the Soviet system. That these memoirs might not be completely genuine proved a minor inconvenience. They gave voice to what many desperately wanted to hear, what many already claimed to hear unmistakably in the composer's music. Or close enough. Many embraced the artful dodge of the "essential" truth of *Testimony*, a convenient fiction that could be invoked at the discretion of the believer to override any misgivings about the literal truth.

If *Testimony* was first and foremost a political bombshell, at least part of its fallout was musical. Its appearance helped reinvigorate interest in Shostakovich's music in the West at a time when rankling dissatisfactions with the post–World War II supremacy enjoyed by "serialism" and the academic musical avant-garde had reached the point of rupture. Performers and audiences alike were ready and eager to seize any opportunity to explore and champion more accessible, more obviously communicative music, music with recognizable links to the venerable traditions of the past. Shostakovich's music provided a perfect catalyst for the reassessment of values.

When glasnost finally gave Soviets the opportunity not so much to read *Testimony* (many of those in Russian musical circles had long had access to photocopies circulating covertly) as to discuss it openly and candidly, the reactions exhibited the same emotional intensity, the same divisions that had manifested themselves earlier in the West. Musicologist Daniel Zhitomirsky, for example, accepted its authenticity without question, recognizing in the book a portrait of the composer that tallied closely with his own memories of him in the early 1960s.[60] And Lev Lebedinsky, who had enjoyed Shostakovich's friendship in the 1950s and 1960s, was adamant in his support of *Testimony:*

> I regard this book as one of the most important publications devoted to the composer, and its authenticity does not raise any questions. I am ready to put my signature under every word of this book. It is the truth about Shostakovich.
>
> *You observed Shostakovich's life closely did you not?*
>
> Yes, I met with D. D. very often and it seemed to me that he was candid with me. Many of our conversations found their reflection in Volkov's book. (With this phrase it is as if my interlocutor alludes to his participation and assistance in the creation of S. Volkov's book. Compiler's remark.)[61]

The compiler's aside in parentheses—by Irina Nikolskaya, who interviewed Lebedinsky—is remarkable. Evidently she understood the tone of Lebedinsky's comment as intimating that he had helped Volkov compile *Testimony*.

Volkov himself, toward the end of his preface to *Testimony*, thanks "my distant friend who must remain nameless—without your constant involvement and encouragement, this book would not exist" (p. xviii).

The identity of the mysterious helper did not remain a secret for long. After Boris Tishchenko's signature appeared among those condemning *Testimony* in the Soviet press, Volkov bemoaned the perceived betrayal:

> Without the help of my friend I would never have completed that work. He was Shostakovich's pupil, the favorite one. He realized how important it was for the aging master to have a chance to shout the truth about himself to the world before he died. He did everything he could to make this possible.[62]

That Tishchenko was close to Shostakovich, and in a position to exploit his access to the composer to further Volkov's cause, is unquestionable. The precise nature of the indispensable service or services Tishchenko rendered to Volkov remains unclear.

Volkov's effort to discredit Tishchenko took a distinctly snide tone when he accused his former friend of selling out, of turning from a staunch nonconformist into a "Soviet composer laureate" solely to acquire official titles and prizes.[63] But the ad hominem character of this attack went largely unnoticed. What attracted more attention was Tishchenko's steadfast refusal to reverse his position, even after glasnost offered a golden opportunity. At a press conference in 1988, Tishchenko was handed a question about *Testimony:*

> The writer of the note asks how I respond to this book today.
>
> Today, just as yesterday, I respond negatively to any kind of falsification. I can swear that this book is a falsification, my hand on the Bible. I was present during Shostakovich's conversation with the author. Shostakovich had said to me: "You see, he insists on these meetings, please attend them." So I attended. What Shostakovich said could be put into the thinnest notebook, whereas what came out abroad comprises some four hundred pages. Before his departure [from the USSR], the author swore that he would leave me a copy of the notes he had taken during his conversation with Shostakovich. But he never did.
>
> The book contains an enormous collection of outlandish stories about Shostakovich. For instance, monstrous pronouncements about Meyerhold's family and disparaging words about Akhmatova are attributed to Shostakovich. After my article in *Literaturnaia gazeta,* the Composers' Union received a telegram addressed to me: "Congratulations on your joining the ranks of Soviet composers. S. Volkov." I answered: "I go the way of those who compose symphonies, not those who write pseudo memoirs. Next time we meet, let's discuss the matter like real men."[64]

Once again Volkov countered with allegations of conformism and cowardice, this time in his 1995 book, *St. Petersburg: A Cultural History.* Volkov asserted that "undoubtedly Tishchenko's fear of open confrontation with the authorities" prompted him to reject opportunities for his *Re-*

quiem (to Akhmatova's poem) to be performed in the West, because this "would lead to a loss of the privileges he enjoyed."[65] Tishchenko then rejoined in the postscript to the publication in 1997 of Shostakovich's letters to himself:

> Another far more cynical event . . . Dmitri Dmitrievich's untimely passing meted out to the world was a commercial venture pushed through by an adept hanger-on of a musical journalist by the name of Volkov. Having removed himself a safe distance, he published his notes of the conversations which—in response to his numerous, insistent requests—I had once upon a time arranged for him to have with Shostakovich, not without encountering the latter's resistance. D. D. agreed only on the condition that I would be present during their conversations. And I, on the condition that a copy of the notes would be given to me. Of course, I received no such copy, and the modest, restrained reminiscences about the years of his childhood and youth ballooned into a very hefty volume fleshed out with third-person stories and shameless self-promotion. Dmitri Dmitrievich was presented as such a malicious dissident. The poorly disguised impatience with which the author awaited D. D.'s death is something I won't forget. . . .
>
> Questions about these "memoirs" hound me to this day. I have developed a short, pithy formulaic answer: this isn't Shostakovich's memoirs, nor even a book by Volkov about Shostakovich, but a book by Volkov about Volkov.[66]

If we are to believe Volkov, the intercession of Tishchenko with Shostakovich was necessary only to overcome the composer's jitters about working on his memoirs.[67] In his preface to *Testimony* and elsewhere, Volkov traces a long history of dealings with the composer, starting in 1960, when he was introduced to Shostakovich after publishing an early review of the Eighth Quartet.[68] Contacts continued with the organization of a festival of Shostakovich's music in Leningrad, the staging of a short-lived production of the opera *Rothschild's Violin* by Shostakovich's student Veniamin Fleishman ("The defeat brought us closer together,"[69] says Volkov), and finally with the composer's preface to Volkov's book on young Leningrad composers (which included Tishchenko). On the book's publication in 1971, "Shostakovich's preface had been cut severely, and it dealt only with the present—there were no reminiscences," Volkov tells the reader of *Testimony*. "This was the final powerful impetus for him to give the world his version of the events that had unfolded around him in the course of half a century."[70] Volkov concedes that Tishchenko was present at the first of his meetings with Shostakovich in 1971 but denies that he was present at any more of their meetings, although Volkov acknowledges that Tishchenko knew that work on the memoirs was continuing and he occasionally acted as a go-between.[71] If

Volkov's first meeting with Shostakovich took place in Repino, as can be inferred from a note Tishchenko wrote him at the time,[72] then Tishchenko was also present during at least one further meeting between the two: The frontispiece photo in *Testimony*—which pictures the seated figures of the composer's wife, Irina, Tishchenko, Shostakovich, and Volkov—was snapped inside Shostakovich's Moscow apartment.

No one has questioned that Volkov met with Shostakovich or that the purpose of their meetings was to record the composer's reminiscences. The composer himself wrote in his own hand on the frontispiece photo mentioned above, "In memory of conversations about Glazunov, Zoshchenko, Meyerhold." But the number of times they met remains a matter of heated debate. In extended conversations with the authors of *Shostakovich Reconsidered*, Volkov mentions "dozens" of meetings with Shostakovich between 1971 and 1974.[73] This was news, since Volkov had not earlier calculated the number of interviews or the range of their dates, either in *Testimony* or anywhere else.

Twenty years ago Irina Shostakovich, the composer's widow (his third wife), told reporters that Volkov had met with her husband "three or maybe four times."[74] She holds to this estimate to the present day and continues to express disbelief in the authenticity of *Testimony*.[75] Bear in mind that throughout the period from 1971, when Volkov supposedly began his collaboration with Shostakovich, until the composer's death in 1975, the chronically ill Shostakovich was heavily dependent on Irina. She was his constant companion and helpmeet. His grown children, Maxim and Galina, had long been living independently, with families of their own, and neither was at home to help or witness their father's interaction with Volkov. During these years Shostakovich required Irina's assistance for the most trivial of tasks—to button his buttons, to put on his coat. It is difficult to believe that her husband would have concealed "dozens" of meetings with Volkov or that he *could* have done so. Yet she abides by her earliest estimate that Volkov met with her husband only a few times to prepare an article, or articles, for *Sovetskaia muzyka*.

Volkov, in his book *St. Petersburg: A Cultural History*, cites several of his interviews with Shostakovich, providing the year and location for each. He refers once to a 1972 conversation in Moscow. Four notes relate to a conversation in Repino that year, but with no indication about how many meetings might have been involved. One conversation in Moscow in 1973 is cited, and another in 1974.[76] Notably none of these citations provides information that duplicates material found in *Testimony*. Such precision in identifying particular meetings at which Shostakovich conveyed specific information—more than twenty years after the interviews took place—strongly suggests that Volkov kept capable records.[77] Were he more disposed to resolve the inconsistencies, and lay to rest the persistent doubts, he might provide solid evidence to back up his claim about the provenance of *Testimony*, rather than expecting his version of events to be accepted on faith. Perhaps he could provide a precise tally that documents the dates and locations of his "dozens" of meetings with Shostakovich.

Volkov has alleged that the objections of Shostakovich's widow to *Testimony* were prompted by the KGB,[78] and that she and others close to the composer may have been motivated by fear of losing their status:

> The members of Shostakovich's inner circle, including his immediate family, were placed in an awkward situation by the publication of *Testimony*, which could have affected their official standing and real privileges (dachas, perks, etc.). They also faced a moral dilemma, because they could not imitate Shostakovich—go along with the authorities outwardly but be a hidden dissident. *Testimony* denied them of a moral fig leaf. Shostakovich had had his say, but what about them? Their position as conformists was revealed. And today, their main motivation, besides quite understandable jealousy, is the defense of their own position.[79]

Beyond the unsettling implication that Shostakovich perpetrated *Testimony* with callous disregard for the consequences to those nearest and dearest to him (having directed that it be published *only* after his death), Volkov's allegation raises yet another unexamined question: Who owns the copyright to Shostakovich's "memoirs"?

During the months prior to *Testimony*'s publication, repeated requests for clarification from the Soviet All-Union Copyright Agency (VAAP) were rebuffed on the grounds that "Shostakovich's heirs have no rights to this work and their permission is not required to publish."[80] Who, then, does own the copyright to Shostakovich's "memoirs"? None other than Solomon Volkov himself.[81] Consequently, another question deserves an answer. How does a music journalist who represents himself as no more than a faithful scribe, the mouthpiece for Shostakovich's reflections, come to be the sole copyright owner and financial beneficiary of these memoirs, with no rights or benefits accruing to the composer's legal heirs as recognized by international law?[82]

Tishchenko and the composer's widow are, to all appearances, the only two people actually to have been present during meetings between Volkov and Shostakovich. In an attempt to neutralize their firm conviction regarding the limited extent of the composer's interactions with his amanuensis, Volkov's defenders point to the recently published reminiscences of Flora Litvinova. Litvinova became acquainted with the composer and his family when all were evacuated to Kuibyshev in 1941. Although Litvinova's primary friendship was with Shostakovich's first wife, Nina Vasilievna Varzar, she remained on good social terms with the composer until the end of his life. The following passage in her reminiscences was penned in the late 1980s:

> I read Solomon Volkov's book. Unfortunately, a long time ago and in English. I must admit that most of the stories retold by Volkov we also heard from Shostakovich. Dmitri Dmitrievich liked, especially when somewhat inebriated, to shoot the breeze, hyperbolising them [his tales], sharpening them, and, of course, making some of them up.
>
> One more thing—in the last years of his life we met rarely, and not for long, or accidentally. And once, at such a meeting, Dmitri Dmitrievich said: "You know, Flora, I met a wonderful young man—a Leningrad musicologist (he did not tell me his name—F. L.). This young man knows my music better than I do. Somewhere, he dug everything up, even my juvenilia." I saw that this thorough study of his music pleased Shostakovich immensely. "We now meet constantly, and I tell him everything I remember about my works and myself. He writes it down, and at a subsequent meeting I look it over."[83]

Litvinova dates her final conversation with Shostakovich to 1970 or 1971, placing it after the composer had returned from treatment at Ilizarov's clinic in Kurgan. She further identifies the location as the Creative Retreat [*dom tvorchestva*] in Ruza and recalls that the Fourteenth Symphony figured among the topics of conversation.

Shostakovich made three trips to Kurgan, two in 1970 and one in 1971. That the Fourteenth Symphony figured in his last conversation with Litvinova suggests late 1970 or early 1971 as the likeliest period when their final meeting took place. On his return from his last trip to Kurgan in late June 1971, Shostakovich went immediately to the Creative Retreat in Repino, where he completed his Fifteenth Symphony on 29 July 1971. Had his final conversation with Litvinova in Ruza taken place after this, it seems reasonable that his newest work would have provided a more topical subject of conversation than his two-year-old Fourteenth Symphony.

Volkov has acknowledged that his collaboration with Shostakovich did not begin until 1971. All indications point to a first meeting—attended by Tishchenko—that took place in Repino in July of that year, that is, most likely after Litvinova's final conversation with Shostakovich.

Placed in the context of the chronological particulars enumerated above, Flora Litvinova's reminiscences appear less compelling as a source of reliable documentary evidence.

Elena Basner, daughter of composer Veniamin Basner, one of the six composers whose signature appeared under the 1979 letter in *Literaturnaia gazeta* denouncing *Testimony*,[84] has taken issue with the assumption that her father might have affixed his signature under duress, without having read *Testimony*.[85] She asserts firsthand knowledge that her father, along with Boris Tishchenko and Moisei Weinberg—the latter her father's close friend—had familiarized themselves with Volkov's book and sincerely repudiated it. They signed the letter to *Literaturnaia gazeta* of their own free will.[86]

Similarly, Faradzh Karaev, son of Kara Karaev, another of the signatories, rejects the explanation proffered by Rodion Shchedrin—and accepted uncritically in *Shostakovich Reconsidered* (pp. 64, 119)—that his father was coerced into signing the letter under threat that he would be kicked out of the hospital where he was undergoing treatment for a heart condition. Faradzh, himself a composer who studied with his father and was close to him, informed me that his father read *Testimony* in German translation—a language he read fluently—and told his family that "Mitya couldn't have written this, let alone allowed its publication. It is clearly a fabrication."[87] As in the Basner household, the topic came up more than once in family conversations. Kara Karaev also recorded unflattering comments in his diaries, which are now in his son's possession. Karaev was indeed in the hospital when he signed the letter to *Literaturnaia gazeta*, but his son is certain that Karaev, too, signed the letter of his own volition, after due, informed consideration.

The presumption that men and women of conscience in the Soviet Union would, and could, only sign such letters under duress is fundamentally untenable. No fewer than three, and quite possibly all six, of the signatories to the letter denouncing *Testimony* signed their names precisely in order to bear witness to their honest convictions. By the same token, the invocation of the "KGB connection" in the debate over the authenticity of *Testimony* is a red herring but one that taps into a rich vein of lingering Cold War stereotypes. We now know that Shostakovich's inscriptions on the typescript of *Testimony* were not, as Volkov advertised, a formula deliberately devised by the composer to distance himself should the KGB become involved. And, despite the fact that many people knew that Volkov was meeting with Shostakovich during the time when the interviews were taking place, the first evidence of any

KGB "interest" in *Testimony* dates from 1976,[88] when Volkov was seeking to emigrate from the Soviet Union. If *Testimony* is authentic—that is, if it is indeed Shostakovich's own reminiscences carefully vetted and authorized by him for publication—then it must have existed as a finished typescript before 9 August 1975, the date of Shostakovich's death.[89] That the KGB may later have attempted—unsuccessfully, as it turned out—to prevent the publication of *Testimony* has no bearing on the question of its authenticity.

❦

What follows are extracts from two letters Shostakovich wrote in 1959. They were official, business letters, the first addressed to Yuri Keldysh, the editor-in-chief of *Sovetskaia muzyka*, the second to Yuli Kremlyov, a member of the journal's editorial board, of which Shostakovich himself was a member. The letters were written to protest the publication, in the June 1959 issue of the journal, of impresario Sol Hurok's reminiscences about Alexander Glazunov,[90] specifically concerning questionable financial transactions that allegedly took place during Glazunov's tour to America in 1929. (In the memoir Hurok describes how friends and admirers had padded the meager conducting fees paid to Glazunov during his tour and contributed seven to eight thousand dollars to a fund that was presented to him in the guise of performance "royalties.") Shostakovich's first letter is dated 24 June 1959:

> These memoirs cast a shadow on the irreproachable figure of the great Russian composer. I knew Glazunov passably well, personally, and I cannot imagine Alexander Konstantinovich taking money without the firm conviction that the money was due him. His fastidiousness in financial matters was well known.
>
> It is impossible to read without being offended how Ossip Gabrilowitsch forked over 500 dollars, Frederick Stock 8,000 dollars, and that Glazunov took this money. . . . Sol Hurok's reminiscences about Glazunov with hand outstretched to take alms ought not to have been published. Everyone knows that Schubert died of syphilis. But there is no need to publish a corresponding "scholarly" study about it. Musorgsky died from excessive drinking. There is no need to write articles and studies about that either, just as the shameless portrait of Musorgsky by Repin should not be widely disseminated. It seems to me that the situation is sufficiently clear. I consider the publication of Sol Hurok's reminiscences about Glazunov a serious mistake for which I am also to blame, since evidently I let them slip by before they were printed.[91]

The circumstance addressed here most probably was one of those not unusual instances when Shostakovich had signed off without bothering to read the material. What *is* unusual is his taking the trouble to make his principled objection known, and his determination to rectify his oversight. He requested, formally, that his letter be published in the next issue of *Sovetskaia muzyka.* Still concerned to make his point, Shostakovich felt obliged to amplify in a follow-up letter to Kremlyov, dated 3 July 1959:

> It seems to me you misunderstood my main point, which consists in the following: We, heirs of the great composers of the past, strive to find out more about their lives and work. For that reason the enormous interest in various types of reminiscences and memoir literature is not accidental. I firmly believe, however, that only those facts that characterize the composer most vividly as an artist, or as a personality, ought to be reported. I do not contest the facts reported by Sol Hurok. But why was it necessary to communicate them to the reader? All the more so, since Glazunov was an exceptionally fastidious person, and only some sort of extraordinary circumstances could have impelled him to accept a financial handout from American musicians.[92]

Shostakovich then reiterated his request that his original letter be published in the journal. But his request was refused, and his letter went unpublished. Other members of the editorial board evidently perceived nothing offensive in Hurok's memoir.[93]

Is the author of these letters the same person who dictated and authorized the publication of *Testimony*, a book whose expansive and comparatively affectionate portrait of Glazunov nevertheless dwells cruelly on Glazunov's human weaknesses, his drinking problem, his dependencies, his infantilism? Is the man who challenged the right to report facts if they do not contribute to a constructive appreciation of artistic or personal achievement, and who felt shame for allowing it to occur on the pages of *Sovetskaia muzyka*, the same person who, twelve years later, produced a book rife with petty and spiteful gossip, with barely a warm or generous word to say about anyone who had crossed his path, and, moreover, made sure he would not be around to accept responsibility for it?

Where does all this leave us? It leaves me with the ever more firm conviction that *Testimony* is not a literary testament willingly bequeathed to us by Shostakovich, much less the "Bible" for Shostakovich studies, as it has been hailed.[94] At best, *Testimony* is a simulated monologue, a montage stripped of its original interrogatory and temporal context, by an unproven ghostwriter[95] who has repeatedly professed ignorance of the basic published materials by and about the composer, and who has admitted to having resorted to guesswork.[96]

At worst, *Testimony* is a fraud. Perhaps Volkov thought he was doing the world a favor by packaging and marketing the famous composer's "memoirs" in a fashion that catered to Cold War sensibilities,[97] but the very existence of the book reflects a crude betrayal of its subject's principles and ideals. The Cold War is over. While *Testimony* may have jump-started the revival of interest in the composer's music in the West, it may finally prove to be the single biggest impediment to an understanding and appreciation of the complex circumstances of Shostakovich's life, of his accomplishments and greatness, and of the terrible sacrifices he was obliged to make to achieve them.

Notes

Significant portions of this article were originally published in Russian as "Vozvrashaias' k 'Svidetel'stvu' " [*Testimony* revisited], in *Shostakovich: mezhdu mgnoveniem i vechnost'iu* [Shostakovich: Between now and eternity], comp. L. Kovnatskaya (St. Petersburg: Kompozitor, 2000), pp. 762–88. Additional material was developed for a series of lectures presented at American and Canadian universities in 2000 and 2001. For their assistance in shaping the final text, I would like to thank Malcolm Hamrick Brown, Ludmila Kovnatskaya, Irina Shostakovich, Kathleen Moretto Spencer, and Richard Taruskin.

1. This was reconfirmed in the vigorous defense of the authenticity of Volkov's book in Allan B. Ho and Dmitri Feofanov, *Shostakovich Reconsidered* ([London]: Toccata, 1998); see "Shostakovich's *Testimony:* Reply to an Unjust Criticism," p. 212. Subsequent page references to Ho and Feofanov refer to this book. In an interview conducted after the publication of Ho and Feofanov's study, Volkov claimed never to have heard of the original sources of any of the material reproduced in *Testimony:* " 'No, no,' he insists over the phone, 'if I did I wouldn't have included it of course.' " See Paul Mitchinson, "The Shostakovich Variations," *Lingua franca* 10, no. 4 (May–June 2000): 49. A revised and updated version of this article is included in the present volume (chapter 22).

2. *Sovetskaia muzyka,* no. 3 (1974): 54. Although aware of the source, Ho and Feofanov failed to mention the connection to Volkov.

3. Evidently this may be precisely what Volkov expects us to believe. Asked to explain the apparent anomaly in this issue of *Sovetskaia muzyka,* Volkov responded: "I can assure you that there wasn't a single staffer who would read the current issue of the magazine in its entirety. Material dealing with Shostakovich was appearing in almost every issue" (Mitchinson, "The Shostakovich Variations," p. 49; chapter 22, p. 308 in the present volume).

4. Carlo Benedetti, "Dimitri Sciostakovic di fronte ai fatti della vita e dell'arte," *l'Unità,* 20 August 1975, p. 7.

5. Letter from Ann Harris to the author dated 9 July 1980. Ms. Harris informed me that the "original Russian manuscript is in safekeeping and therefore not available for inspection."

6. Elmer Schönberger, "Dmitri Shostakovich's Memoirs: *Testimony*," *Key Notes* 10, no. 2 (1979): 57. The article was first published in the weekly *Vrij Nederland*, 10 November 1979.

7. L. S. Dyachkova, comp., *I. F. Stravinsky: stat'i i materialy* [I. F. Stravinsky: Articles and materials], ed. B. Yarustovsky (Moscow: Sovetskii kompozitor, 1973), p. 7. By his own admission, in addition to this volume, Volkov must also have been ignorant of the fundamental collection *Dmitri Shostakovich*, ed. L. Danilevich (Moscow: Sovetskii kompozitor, 1967), where four of the other quoted passages identified in my review had been recently reprinted, as well as of several other standard sources for Shostakovich studies. The improbability of such a claim may be less apparent to the Western reader unfamiliar with the highly centralized world of Soviet musicological publishing.

8. Letter from Ann Harris to Henry Orlov dated 9 April 1979; this description is duplicated in her subsequent letter to him dated 26 August 1979 (see chapter 8 in the present volume).

9. Solomon Volkov, *Testimony: The Memoirs of Dmitri Shostakovich*, as related to and edited by Solomon Volkov, trans. Antonina W. Bouis (New York: Harper & Row, 1979), pp. xvi–xvii.

10. Ho and Feofanov, incidentally, shrug off this coincidence, with the comment that "duplicating the exact punctuation is not as difficult as Western minds might think, given the strict rules for the use of commas, etc., in Russian" (p. 199 n. 323). They cite no authority for this claim. I have shown these two juxtaposed passages to some two dozen native speakers and professors of Russian. Taking into consideration the conditions Volkov described, not one of them believed that there was even a remote possibility that the text and punctuation could have been duplicated by accident. All believed it had been copied.

11. Although Ho and Feofanov include an appendix of photos and facsimiles of documents in their book (pp. 300–311), their omission of anything from the typescript of *Testimony* is conspicuous.

12. A partial transcript has been posted on a Russian website: <http://uic.nnov.ru/~bis/dsch.html>, accessed 25 June 2003.

13. Irina Shostakovich, in conversation with the author, 18 September 2000.

14. On the opening page of chapter 2 reproduced as figure 2.2, for example, there is a single number ("040") in the upper right-hand corner of the page. The page that succeeds it contains a typed "-2-" in the top middle and a stamped "041" in the upper right-hand corner of the page, marking it as page 2 of chapter 2 and page 41 of the complete typescript. Ho and Feofanov (p. 210) identify the authorized Russian typescript as a "404-page manuscript." In fact, although the numbering terminates at 404, the Moscow typescript actually contains 405 pages; in a substantial re-editing and rearrangement of material in chapter 7 that obviously took place after the sequential numbering had been stamped—a process that necessitated the renumbering of many pages by hand—the last two pages of that chapter have been renumbered 356 and 356a. Chapter 8 commences on page 357.

15. Notwithstanding this convergence, Ho and Feofanov's inference (p. 215) that the presence and location of facsimiles of Shostakovich's signatures in these editions furnish evidence of the authenticity of the Russian source text is an obvious fallacy.

16. For Orlov's report, dated 28 August 1979, see chapter 8 in the present volume.

17. Although changes were made, inevitably, during the course of translating and publishing, most of them are quite minor. Overwhelmingly they concern the clarification or elimination of literary and topical references that would be less familiar or recognizable to a non-Russian reader than to a native speaker. In other words, most of the changes can be classified as reasonable and justifiable editorial emendations.

18. "Iz vospominanii o Mayakovskom" [Reminiscences of Mayakovsky], in *V. Mayakovsky v vospominaniiakh sovremennikov* [V. Mayakovsky in the reminiscences of his contemporaries], ed. V. V. Grigorenko et al. (Moscow: Gosudarstvennoe izdatel'stvo khudozhestvennoi literatury, 1963), p. 315.

19. What cannot be determined with any certainty from the photocopied typescript is whether Shostakovich's signatures at the top of these pages were affixed before or after the text had been altered.

20. The one-hundredth anniversary of Chekhov's birth was in 1960.

21. "Ved' so dnia eë sozdaniia proshlo okolo tritsati let." Nearly forty years had passed since its composition by the time Volkov began his conversations with Shostakovich.

22. Two facsimiles of unique Shostakovich visas—not duplicates of any of the six found in the Moscow typescript—are reproduced at the head of chapters 3 and 7 in the German and Finnish editions of *Testimony*. See *Zeugenaussage: Die Memoiren des Dmitrij Schostakowitsch*, aufgezeichnet und herausgegeben von Solomon Volkow, trans. Heddy Pross-Weerth (Hamburg: Knaus, 1979), pp. 104, 245; *Dmitri Šostakovitšin muistelmat*, Koonnut Solomon Volkov, Venäjänkielisestä käsikirjoituksesta Suomentanut Seppo Heikinheimo (Helsinki: Helsingissä Otava, 1980), pp. 109, 264.

23. "Ia vspominaiu o Meyerkhol'de slishkom chasto. Chashche, chem nuzhno by."

24. Normal chapter and manuscript numbering resumes on page 109.

25. The one indication we have from the composer about the extent and scope of any "collaboration" with Volkov is the postscript to his inscription on the frontispiece photo in *Testimony:* "In memory of conversations about Glazunov, Zoshchenko, Meyerhold. D. Sh."

26. Volkov, *Testimony*, p. 3.

27. Ho and Feofanov, p. 211. On page 217 n. 378, the authors—whose study was based on "unprecedented" access to Volkov's personal archive and more than one hundred hours of face-to-face and phone conversations with him—include themselves among a select group of people "who have examined pages of the manuscript signed by Shostakovich."

28. In his reader's report for Harper & Row, Henry Orlov wrote that "except for the inscription by his [Shostakovich's] hand at the head of each of the eight chapters, the manuscript bears no traces of his handwriting, no alterations or even slight corrections" (see chapter 8 in the present volume). When shown photocopies of the signed typescript pages in March 2001, Orlov admitted that he had not paid any attention to the actual number or location of the signatures during the limited time made available to him to consider the manuscript back in 1979; both letters

to him from Ann Harris had located the composer's inscriptions "at the head of each chapter." My personal examination of the Moscow typescript confirms Orlov's observation that, with the exception of the signatures, it contains no other traces of Shostakovich's handwriting.

29. D. Shostakovich, "Avtobiografiia" [Autobiography], *Sovetskaia muzyka*, no. 9 (1966): 24–25; the translation follows that of *Testimony*, p. 4. Ho and Feofanov (p. 212) acknowledge that a passage from this source is reproduced on an "interior" page of *Testimony*, without acknowledging that it was here, and not on the first page of the chapter, that Shostakovich's signature appears. The only alterations to the passage in the *Testimony* typescript are the spelling out of first names and patronymics instead of the initials found in the original. In addition, the death date of Gliasser is erroneously given as "1916" in the Moscow typescript, instead of 1925. This typo was corrected in the published text of *Testimony*.

30. As one turns from page 003 to 004 (see figs. 2.9 and 2.10), for example, the verbatim quotation breaks off abruptly in mid-sentence. Whereas the sentence spanning the page turn in the *Testimony* typescript reads, "V fevrale 1917 goda mne stalo // neinteresno khodit' k Gliasseru"; in the original publication it reads as "V fevrale 1917 goda mne stalo//skuchno zanitmat'sia u Gliassera."

31. Volkov, *Testimony*, pp. 33–34.

32. Dyachkova, *I. F. Stravinsky: stat'i i materialy*, p. 8.

33. Daniel Zhitomirsky, "Shostakovich," *Muzykal'naia akademiia*, no. 3 (1993): 28; translation from Ho and Feofanov, p. 466.

34. *Pis'ma k drugu: Pis'ma D. D. Shostakovicha k I. D. Glikmanu* [Letters to a friend: The letters of Dmitri Shostakovich to Isaak Glikman], ed. and with commentary by Isaak Davydovich Glikman (Moscow: Izdatel'stvo "DSCH"; St. Petersburg: Kompozitor, 1993), p. 151.

35. "Dusha i maska: pis'ma D. D. Shostakovicha k L. N. Lebedinskomu" [Soul and mask: The letters of Shostakovich to Lebedinsky], *Muzykal'naia zhizn'*, nos. 23–24 (1993): 12.

36. Ho and Feofanov, p. 212.

37. Ibid., p. 213 n. 360.

38. Solomon Volkov, "Zdes' chelovek sgorel" [A man burned out here], *Muzykal'naia akademiia*, no. 3 (1992): 4; translated in Ho and Feofanov, p. 321.

39. Volkov, "Zdes' chelovek sgorel," p. 4; translated in Ho and Feofanov, p. 320. See also Ann Harris letters to Henry Orlov in the present volume, chapter 8.

40. L. Genina, "Razbeg pered propast'iu" [A running start before the abyss], *Muzykal'naia akademiia*, no. 3 (1992): 13; cited in Ho and Feofanov, pp. 215–16.

41. Ibid.

42. Quoted in Elizabeth Wilson, *Shostakovich: A Life Remembered* (Princeton, N.J.: Princeton University Press, 1994), p. 162. Similar admissions can be found in many other sources.

43. Quoted in Ho and Feofanov, p. 83.

44. Comments at the symposium "The Interior Shostakovich," Bucknell University, Lewisburg, Pennsylvania, 9 September 1980, translated by A. Bouis. See *DSCH* (autumn 1991): 35. Kondrashin's own memoirs, including his reminiscences of Shostakovich, were published posthumously: V. Razhnikov, *Kirill Kondrashin*

rasskazyvaet o muzyke i zhizni [Kondrashin speaks about music and life] (Moscow: Sovetskii kompozitor, 1989).

45. Bella Ezerskaia, "Trepet i muki aktyora: interv'iu s Galinoi Vishnevskoi" [The trembling and torments of an actor: Interview with Galina Vishnevskaya], *Vremia i my*, no. 50 (1980): 160–61.

46. Galina Vishnevskaya, *Galina: A Russian Story* (New York: Harcourt Brace Jovanovich, 1984).

47. *DSCH* 20 (spring 1992): 4.

48. Ashkenazy supplied the "Overture" to Ho and Feofanov's *Shostakovich Reconsidered*, pp. 9–11. See also "Papa, what if they hang you for this?" *Financial Times Weekend*, 5–6 August 2000, p. viii.

49. Originally published in *Le Monde*, 28 November 1986; translated as "Iz vospominanii M. L. Rostropovicha" [From M. L. Rostropovich's reminiscences], in *Sergei Prokofiev 1891–1991: dnevnik, pis'ma, besedy, vospominaniia* [Sergei Prokofiev 1891–1991: Diary, letters, conversations, reminiscences], comp. M. E. Tarakanov (Moscow: Sovetskii kompozitor, 1991), p. 256.

50. "Shostakovich's World Is Our World: Manashir Yakubov Talks to Mstislav Rostropovich," *Shostakovich 1906–1975*, program booklet for the Barbican Centre series (19 February–28 October 1998), p. 19; reprinted in the present volume; see chapter 12.

51. Wilson, *Shostakovich: A Life Remembered*, pp. 187–88.

52. See, for instance, Ho and Feofanov, pp. 217, 297.

53. Solomon Volkov, "Tradition Returns: Rostropovich's Symbolism," in Ho and Feofanov, pp. 359–72. By misidentifying the original publication date of this interview, Ho and Feofanov suggest that the interview itself took place more than a decade later than its actual date of 1978. They cite a *reprint* publication from 1990, with no reference to the original publication: "Vozvrashchenie traditsii: simvolika Rostropovicha" [Tradition returns: Rostropovich's symbolism], *Znamia*, no. 1 (1990): 220–26. But the interview was, in fact, first published in 1982 as "O Sergee Sergeeviche i Dmitri Dmitrieviche: interv'iu s Mstislavom Rostropovichem" [About Sergei Sergeevich and Dmitri Dmitrievich: Interview with Mstislav Rostropovich], *Chast' rechi: al'manakh literatury i iskusstva*, nos. 2–3 (1981–82): 254–62. This 1982 publication names Volkov as the copyright holder, which means that re-publication of the interview by Feofanov and Ho would have required neither Rostropovich's knowledge or consent. An English translation different from that used by Ho and Feofanov was published in 1987: "A Conversation with Mstislav Rostropovich," *Keynote* [New York] 11, no. 1 (March 1987): 8–12. This translation gives the actual date of Volkov's interview with Rostropovich as 1978.

54. Transcribed and translated from a tape of the press conference.

55. "Shostakovich: Why I Fled from Russia," interview with Norbert Kuchinke and Felix Schmidt, *Sunday Times* [London], 17 May 1981, p. 35.

56. "Maxim Shostakovich o svoyom ottse: interv'iu Alexandra Abramova" [Maxim Shostakovich about his father: An interview by Alexander Abramov], *Vremia i my*, no. 69 (1982): 180–81.

57. "Prénom Maxime," *Le Monde de la Musique*, no. 118 (January 1989): xv; translated here from the Russian text by L. Hrabovsky in *Sovetskaia muzyka*, no.

9 (1989): 56. See also David Hendricks, "Maxim Shostakovich," *Ovation* 5, no. 5 (June 1984): 12, 14.

58. "Always a Great Composer, Not a Papa: Maxim Shostakovich Talks to David Fanning about performing Dmitri Shostakovich," *Gramophone*, no. 5 (1991): 1992. More recently Maxim pinpointed just such an anomalous passage in *Testimony*. Referring to one of its most sensational "revelations" (p. 141), that of his father's Tenth Symphony (specifically the second movement) as a portrait of Stalin, Maxim told an interviewer: "That is an example of a rumor. . . . I think some musicologists set this idea forth. Others repeated it. I don't think of it that way. Father never said it was a portrait of Stalin." See Chris Pasles, "Was He or Wasn't He?" *Los Angeles Times/Calendar*, 29 November 1998, p. 74.

59. Maxim's blurb on the dust jacket of *The New Shostakovich* (Boston: Northeastern University Press, 1990) declares it "one of the best books about Dmitri Shostakovich that I have read."

60. Daniel Zhitomirsky, "Shostakovich ofitsial'nyi i podlinnyi; stat'ia pervaia" [Shostakovich official and genuine], *Daugava*, no. 3 (1990): 92. Zhitomirsky quotes here in reverse translation from the German edition of *Testimony*.

61. *Melos*, nos. 4–5 (1993): 78. Although the journal was published in English, the translations were problematical, sometimes inaccurate. The translation of the passage as given here has been corrected to conform more accurately to the transcript of the original interview in Russian. This and the other interviews are reprinted in the present volume in chapter 13.

62. Solomon Volkov, "Rekviem po drugu," *Novoe russkoe slovo*, 12 April 1980, p. 6; published in English as "Requiem for a Friend," *Ovation*, no. 1/6 (July 1980): 14.

63. Ibid. In 1978 Tishchenko won the State Prize of the RSFSR and was awarded the title "Honored Artist of the RSFSR." The Russian and English versions of "Requiem for a Friend" vary somewhat. Tishchenko's transition from staunch nonconformist into composer laureate is found in the English version. In the Russian version, the synonymy of Tishchenko and Judas is invoked by means of a quote from Pushkin's "Imitation of the Italian" [*Podrazhanie italiianskomu*] of 1836. Volkov's disposition to slander people unable to defend themselves has been remarked upon by Levon Hakobian in *Music of the Soviet Age, 1917–1987* (Stockholm: Melos Music Literature Kantat HB, 1998), p. 56 n. 91; as well as in Hakobian's review of Ho and Feofanov's *Shostakovich Reconsidered*, "Ocherednoi 'Novyi Shostakovich' " ["The latest 'new Shostakovich' "], *Muzykal'naia akademiia*, no. 2 (2000): 134 n. 4. Chapter 16 in the present volume is a translation of Hakobian's review.

64. Boris Tishchenko, "Velikie khudozhniki" [Great artists], *Sovetskaia kul'tura*, 15 October 1988, p. 8; translated as "Briefly on Important Issues," in *Music in the USSR* (July–September 1989), p. 35. The translation used here has been corrected, with reference to the Russian original, by Malcolm Brown. See chapter 10 in the present volume.

65. Solomon Volkov, *St. Petersburg: A Cultural History* (New York: Free Press, 1995), p. 487.

66. *Pis'ma Dmitriia Dmitrievicha Shostakovicha Borisu Tishchenko: s kommentariiami i vospominaniiami adresata* [Letters from Dmitri Dmitrievich Shostakovich to

Boris Tishchenko: With commentaries and reminiscences of the addressee] (St. Petersburg: Kompozitor, 1997), pp. 48–49.

67. Solomon Volkov, "Universal Messages: Reflections in Conversation with Günter Wolter," *Tempo*, no. 200 (1997): 15.

68. S. Volkov, "*Novyi kvartet D. Shostakovicha*" [Shostakovich's new quartet], *Smena*, 7 October 1960, p. 3. Volkov has remarked about Shostakovich's music: "I always intuitively felt in his music a protest against the regime. This is what I tried to express, as much as was possible, in that Leningrad newspaper, in my review of the Eighth Quartet when I was sixteen. He knew that and was grateful to me" (Volkov, "*Zdes' chelovek sgorel*," p. 6; quoted in Ho and Feofanov, p. 329). Yet surely Volkov is flattering himself about the penetrating insights in his schoolboy review—replete with such clichés as "the problems disturbing progressive humanity," "the cruel and meaningless machine of war," and "let there never again be wars"—and about the significance this review by a sixteen-year-old could have held for Shostakovich.

69. Volkov, *Testimony*, p. xiv.

70. Ibid., p. xv.

71. Ho and Feofanov, p. 70.

72. Ibid., pp. 72, 306.

73. Ibid., pp. 43, 70, 73.

74. Craig R. Whitney, "Shostakovich Memoir a Shock to Kin," *New York Times*, 13 November 1979, p. C7.

75. See Irina Shostakovich, "An Answer to Those Who Still Abuse Shostakovich," *New York Times*, 20 August 2000, pp. AR 27, 31; chapter 9 in the present volume is a reprint of this article.

76. Volkov, *St. Petersburg: A Cultural History*, pp. 555, 571, 574.

77. In an October 1998 interview, nonetheless, Volkov vouched that "for security reasons" his notes were never preserved. See Edward Rothstein, "Sly Dissident or a Soviet Tool? A Musical War," *New York Times*, 17 October 1998, p. B9.

78. Solomon Volkov, "Letters: Shostakovich—A Response," *New York Times*, 27 August 2000, p. AR2.

79. Quoted in Ho and Feofanov, p. 60 n. 51. See also Solomon Volkov, "Shostakovich's Testimony," *Moscow News*, no. 34 (30 August 2000): 11.

80. Letters dated 6 December 1978 and 2 February 1979 and signed by Edward Miller, vice president and general counsel of Harper & Row; see "*Ofitsial'noe dos'e*" [The official dossier], *Literaturnaia gazeta*, 14 November 1979, p. 8; article 6 in the present volume is a translation of this news item.

81. Volkov, *Testimony*, p. vi. While Ho and Feofanov (p. 216 n. 373) assert—on the basis of a conversation with Volkov—that his publisher controls the world rights to the material, they also confirm that Volkov himself owns the copyright of *Testimony*.

82. Shostakovich's legal heirs are his widow, Irina Shostakovich, and his two children, Maxim and Galina.

83. Flora Litvinova, "*Vspominaia Shostakovicha*" [Remembering Shostakovich], *Znamia*, no. 12 (December 1996): 168–69; translated in Ho and Feofanov, p. 251. Although Litvinova's memoir was originally written for—and first published by—

Elizabeth Wilson in her volume *Shostakovich: A Life Remembered*, Wilson edited this passage out of the English-language publication.

84. "*Zhalkaia poddelka: O tak nazyvaemykh 'memuarakh' D. D. Shostakovicha*" [A pitiful fake: About the So-Called "Memoirs" of Shostakovich], *Literaturnaia gazeta*, no. 46 (14 November 1979): 8; chapter 4 in the present volume is a translation of this letter to the editor.

85. Without investigating the circumstances behind this particular letter, Ho and Feofanov fall back on the sweeping generalization that "denunciations were a common practice in the Soviet Union, and often the signers neither read nor agreed with that which they had 'endorsed' " (*Shostakovich Reconsidered*, p. 64). They suggest that the authors of this letter "had not actually read that which they were criticizing" (p. 66).

86. Elena Basner, "*Vlast' i poshlost'*" [The regime and vulgarity], *Izvestiia*, 8 July 1999, p. 5; chapter 11 in the present volume is a translation of this letter to the editor.

87. In conversation with the author, Moscow, 12 May 1999.

88. Ho and Feofanov, p. 48.

89. When interviewed by an Italian journalist in the days after Shostakovich's death, Volkov revealed that he had worked with the composer on his memoirs, entitled *Testimony*. The interview was published under a photo inscribed to Volkov by Shostakovich (subsequently reproduced as the frontispiece of *Testimony*) and was generously illustrated with direct quotations of the composer's statements. The comments about Meyerhold and Zoshchenko (both mentioned in the photo's inscription) closely resemble material subsequently published in *Testimony*. But the overwhelming majority of the quotations in the interview bear no resemblance, either in substance or in tone, to anything found in the published text of *Testimony*. What appears here are professional, not political, observations. They deal, for instance, with the composer's attitude to creativity and the creative process—with an extended reference to the theory of literary critic Yuri Tynianov—to rules and tradition, humor, the nature of stereotypes and cultural fashions. Who decided to exclude all this from the composer's memoirs, and when? See Carlo Benedetti, "Dimitri Sciostakovic di fronte ai fatti della vita e dell'arte," *l'Unità*, 20 August 1975, p. 7.

90. "Patriarkh russkoi muzyki" [The patriarch of Russian music], *Sovetskaia muzyka*, no. 6 (1959): 138–40; this was a translation of an extract from *Impresario: A Memoir by S. Hurok*, in collaboration with Ruth Goode (New York, 1946), pp. 147–52.

91. I. Bobykina, ed., *Dmitri Shostakovich v pismakh i dokumentakh* [Shostakovich in letters and documents] (Moscow: RIF "Antikva," 2000), pp. 421–22.

92. KR RIII, f. 79, op. 1, ed. khr. 550, l. 3r&v. I am deeply grateful to Ludmila Kovnatskaya for alerting me to the existence of this letter, and to Olga Dansker and Galina Kopytova for providing the Russian text.

93. See Bobykina, *Dmitri Shostakovich v pismakh i dokumentakh*, p. 423 n. 6.

94. See, for example, Vladimir Zak, "Shostakovich's Idioms," in Ho and Feofanov, p. 503.

95. The title of an article by Solomon Volkov, published in the Soviet journal

Ogonyok (no. 7 [February 1991]: 9), bears the title "Priznanie pisatel'ia-prizraka" [The confession of a ghostwriter].

96. "He often contradicted himself. Then the true meaning of his words had to be guessed, extracted from a box with three false bottoms" (Volkov, *Testimony*, p. xvii).

97. Interviewed by Stephen Johnson in 1998, Volkov reminded listeners: "The tenor of the book [*Testimony*] was mainly political, as you remember" ("Brave Words, Brave Music," produced by Derek Drescher, broadcast on BBC Radio 3, 16 August 1998).

Part Two

3

A Side-by-Side Comparison of Texts from *Testimony* with Their Original Sources

The left-hand column below corresponds to the published text of *Testimony* (which replicates the Moscow typescript of *Testimony*). The right-hand column corresponds to the texts in the original Russian sources. Columns have been aligned to facilitate comparison, which introduces some abnormal spacing in the text, but underscores the extent of recycling in *Testimony*. All eight chapters of the book are represented here. (May the reader be reminded that Shostakovich's signature was affixed *only* on the pages of recycled text shown here, and nowhere else in the typescript.)

Chapter 1, pp. 4–5, Solomon Volkov, *Testimony: The Memoirs of Dmitri Shostakovich*, as related to and edited by Solomon Volkov, trans. Antonina W. Bouis (New York: Harper & Row, 1979) [Moscow typescript, p. 003]:	D. Shostakovich, "Avtobiografiia" [Autobiography], *Sovetskaia muzyka*, no. 9 (September 1966): p. 24:
I had not expressed a desire to study music before I began taking lessons, although I had some interest in music and listened ear to the wall when a quartet met at the neighbors'.	I had not expressed a desire to study music before I began taking lessons, although I had some interest in music and listened ear to the wall when a quartet met at the neighbors'.
My mother, Sofia Vasilievna, saw this and insisted that I begin learning the piano, but I hedged. In the spring of 1915 I attended the theater for the first time and saw *The Legend of Tsar Saltan*. I	My mother, S. V. Shostakovich, saw this and insisted that I begin learning the piano, but I hedged. In the spring of 1915 I attended the theater for the first time and saw *The Legend of Tsar Saltan*. I

liked the opera, but it still wasn't enough to overcome my unwillingness to study music.

The root of study is too bitter to make learning to play worthwhile, I thought. But mother had her way and in the summer of 1915 began giving me lessons. Things moved very quickly, I turned out to have absolute pitch and a good memory. I learned the notes quickly, and I memorized easily, without repetition—it came on its own. I read music fluently and made my first attempts at composing then too.

Seeing that things were going well, Mother decided to send me to the music school of Ignatiy Albertovich Gliasser (he died in 1925 [1916*]). I remember that at one recital I played almost half the pieces in Tchaikovsky's *Children's Album.* The next year, 1916, I was promoted into Gliasser's class.

Before that, I had been studying with his wife, O. F. Gliasser. In his class I played sonatas by Mozart and Haydn, and the following year, Bach's fugues.

Gliasser treated my composing quite skeptically and didn't encourage me. Nevertheless, I continued composing and wrote a lot then. By February 1917 I
//
[Moscow typescript, p. 004]:
lost all interest in studying with Gliasser. He was a very self-confident but dull man. And his lectures already seemed ridiculous to me.

[*The date given in the Moscow typescript is an obvious error.]

liked the opera, but it still wasn't enough to overcome my unwillingness to study music.

The root of study is too bitter to make learning to play worthwhile, I thought. But mother had her way and in the summer of 1915 began giving me lessons. Things moved very quickly, I turned out to have absolute pitch and a good memory. I learned the notes quickly, and I memorized easily, without repetition—it came on its own. I read music fluently and made my first attempts at composing then too.

Seeing that things were going well, Mother decided to send me to the music school of I. A. Gliasser (he died in 1925). I remember that at one recital I played almost half the pieces in Tchaikovsky's *Children's Album.* The next year, 1916, I was promoted into I. A. Gliasser's class.

Before that, I had been studying with his wife, O. F. Gliasser. In his class I played sonatas by Mozart and Haydn, and the following year, Bach's fugues.

Gliasser treated my composing quite skeptically and didn't encourage me. Nevertheless, I continued composing and wrote a lot then. By February 1917 I

became bored studying with Gliasser. Then my Mother decided to present me and my sister to A. A. Rozanova, the professor at the Leningrad Conservatory with whom she herself had studied at one time.

Chapter 2, pp. 32–33, *Testimony* [Moscow typescript, p. 040]:

Stravinsky is one of the greatest composers of our times and I truly love many of his works. My earliest and most vivid impression of Stravinsky's music is related to the ballet *Petrushka.* I saw the Kirov Theater of Leningrad production many times, and I tried never to miss a performance. (Unfortunately, I haven't heard the new edition of *Petrushka* for smaller orchestra. I'm not sure that it is better than the earlier one.) Since then this marvelous composer invariably has been at the center of my attention, and I not only studied and listened to his music, but I played it and I made my own transcriptions as well.

I recall with pleasure my performance in the première of *Les Noces* in Leningrad, extraordinarily well performed by the Leningrad Choir under the direction of the outstanding choirmaster Klimov. One of the four piano parts—the second piano—was entrusted to me. The numerous rehearsals turned out to be both pleasant and beneficial for me. The work amazed everyone by its originality, sonority, and lyricism.

I also performed the *Serenade in A.* At the Conservatory we often played the piano concerto transcribed for two pianos. My student days hold another memory of a work by Stravinsky—the excellent opera *The Nightingale.* Of course, my acquaintance with it was made under "fatal" circumstances: during an exam on reading

I. F. Stravinsky: Stat'i i materialy [I. F. Stravinsky: Articles and materials], comp. L. S. Dyachkova, ed. B. M. Yarustovsky (Moscow: Sovetskii kompozitor, 1973), p. 7.

Stravinsky is one of the greatest composers of our times and I truly love many of his works. My earliest and most vivid impression of Stravinsky's music is related to the ballet *Petrushka.* I saw the Kirov Theater of Leningrad production many times, and I tried never to miss a performance. (Unfortunately, I haven't heard the new edition of *Petrushka* for smaller orchestra. I'm not sure that it is better than the earlier one.) Since then this marvelous composer invariably has been at the center of my attention, and I not only studied and listened to his music, but I played it and I made my own transcriptions as well.

I recall with pleasure my performance in the première of *Les Noces* in Leningrad, extraordinarily well performed by the Leningrad Choir under the direction of the outstanding choirmaster Klimov. One of the four piano parts—the second piano—was entrusted to me. The numerous rehearsals turned out to be both pleasant and beneficial for me. The work amazed everyone by its originality, sonority, and lyricism.

I also performed the *Serenade in A.* At the Conservatory we often played the piano concerto transcribed for two pianos. My student days hold another memory of a work by Stravinsky—the excellent opera *The Nightingale.* Of course, my acquaintance with it was made under "fatal" circumstances: during an exam on reading scores. You might say it was

//
[Moscow typescript, p. 041]:
scores. I'm a little angry with the opera for that. It was like the Spanish Inquisition—a cruel sight. But I managed somehow and conquered *The Nightingale.*

rather brutal. But, it seems, I managed to deal with the score. Subsequently, I studied it thoroughly.

❧

Chapter 3, pp. 77–78, *Testimony* [Moscow typescript, pp. 106–107]:

D. Shostakovich, "Iz vospominanii" [From my recollections], *Sovetskaia muzyka*, no. 3 (March 1974): 54 [see Fay, "Volkov's *Testimony* Reconsidered," chapter 2 in this volume, for an explanation as to why the parallel texts are not always identical in this instance]:

I think of Meyerhold too frequently, more frequently than I should, because we are now neighbors of sorts. I often walk or drive past the memorial plaque that depicts a repulsive monster and I shudder. The engraving says: "In this house lived Meyerhold." They should add, "And in this house his wife was brutally murdered."

I met Meyerhold in Leningrad in 1928. Vsevolod Emilievich called me on the telephone and said, "This is Meyerhold speaking. I want to see you. If you can, come to me. Hotel So-and-so, room such-and-such."

My first meeting with Vsevolod Emilievich Meyerhold took place in Leningrad in 1928. He called me on the telephone and said: "This is Meyerhold speaking. I want to see you. If you can, come to me. Hotel So-and-so, room such-and-such." And I went.

I don't remember what we talked about. I only remember that Vsevolod Emilievich asked me if I would like to join his theater. I agreed immediately and a short time later I went to Moscow and began working in the Theater of Meyerhold in a musical capacity.

Vsevolod Emilievich invited me to work in the theater with him. I agreed immediately and a short time later I went to Moscow and began serving in the Theater of Meyerhold in a musical capacity.

But I left the same year: it involved too much technical work. I couldn't find a niche for myself that satisfied both of us, even though it was very interesting to be part of the theater. Most fascinating were Meyerhold's rehearsals. Watching him prepare his new plays was enthralling, exciting.

I left the same year,
because I couldn't find a niche for myself that satisfied both of us, even though it was interesting.
Most interesting were Meyerhold's rehearsals; they were enthralling.

My work in the theater, basically, was playing the piano. Say, if an actress in *The Inspector General* was called upon to sing a romance by Glinka, I donned tailcoat, went on as one of the guests, and sat down at the piano. I also played in the orchestra.	My work in the theater, basically, was playing the piano. Say, if an actress in the last act of *The Inspector General* was called upon to sing a romance by Glinka, I donned a tailcoat, went on stage as one of the guests, and accompanied the actress. I also played in the orchestra.
I lived at Vsevolod Emilievich's apartment on Novinsky Boulevard. In the evenings we often spoke of creating a musical drama. I was working hard then on my opera, *The Nose*. Once there was a big fire at Vsevolod Emilievich's apartment.	I lived at Vsevolod Emilievich's apartment on Novinsky Boulevard. I was working hard on my opera, *The Nose*. Once there was a big fire at Vsevolod Emilievich's apartment.
// [Moscow typescript, p. 107]:	
I wasn't home at the time, but Meyerhold grabbed my music and handed it to me perfectly intact. My score survived thanks to him—a magnificent deed, for he had things much more valuable than my manuscript.	I wasn't home at the time, but he collected my music and handed it to me perfectly intact. It was amazing, since much more valuable things of his might have burned.
But everything ended well; I don't think that his property was heavily damaged either. If it had been, he would have had to answer to his wife, Zinaida Nikolayevna Raikh.	In 1929 Vsevolod Emilievich called me on the telephone again and invited me to his Leningrad hotel, where he suggested I write music for Mayakovsky's comedy, *The Bedbug*.

❦

Chapter 4, pp. 106–107, *Testimony* [Moscow typescript, p. 145]:	D. Shostakovich, "Tragediia-satira" [A tragedy-satire], *Sovetskoe iskusstvo*, 16 October 1932; reprinted in L. Danilevich, ed., *Dmitri Shostakovich* (Moscow: Sovetskii kompozitor, 1967), p. 13.
I worked on *Lady Macbeth* for almost three years. I had announced a trilogy	I have been working on *Lady Macbeth* for almost two and a half years. *Lady Macbeth* is the first part of a planned tril-
dedicated to the position of women in various eras in Russia. The plot of *Lady Macbeth of Mtsensk District* is taken from the story of the same name by Ni-	ogy dedicated to the position of women in various eras in Russia. The plot of *Lady Macbeth of the Mtsensk District* is taken from the story of the same name

kolai Leskov. The story amazes the reader with its unusual vividness and depth, and in terms of being the most truthful and tragic portrayal of the destiny of a talented, smart, and outstanding woman, "dying in the nightmarish conditions of prerevolutionary Russia," as they say, this story, in my opinion, is one of the best.

by Nikolai Leskov. The story amazes the reader with its unusual vividness and depth, and in terms of being the most truthful and tragic portrayal of the destiny of a talented, smart, and outstanding woman, "dying in the nightmarish conditions of prerevolutionary Russia," as they say, this story, in my opinion, is one of the best.

Maxim Gorky once said: "We must study. We must learn about our country, her past, present, and future"; and Leskov's story serves this purpose. [It is an unbelievably powerful depiction of one of the dismal epochs of prerevolutionary Russia.*] *Lady Macbeth* is a true treasure trove for a composer, with its vividly drawn characters and dramatic conflicts—I was attracted by it. Alexander Germanovich Preis, a young Leningrad playwright, worked out the libretto with me. It followed Leskov almost in its entirety, with the exception of the third act, which for greater social impact deviates slightly from the original. We introduced a scene at the police station and left out the murder of Ekaterina Lvovna's nephew.
[*This sentence is present in the Moscow typescript but was edited out of the published translation of *Testimony*.]

Maxim Gorky once said: "We must study. We must learn about our country, her past, present, and future"; and Leskov's story serves this purpose. It is an unbelievably powerful depiction of one of the dismal epochs of prerevolutionary Russia. *Lady Macbeth* is a true treasure trove for a composer, with its vividly drawn characters and dramatic conflicts—I was attracted by it.
A. G. Preis, a young Leningrad playwright, worked out the libretto with me. It followed Leskov almost in its entirety, with the exception of the third act, which for greater social impact deviates slightly from the original. We introduced a scene at the police station and left out the murder of Ekaterina Lvovna's nephew.

I resolved the opera in a tragic vein. I would say that *Lady Macbeth* could be called a tragic-satiric opera. Despite the fact that Ekaterina Lvovna is a murderer, //
[Moscow typescript, p. 146]:
she is not a lost human being. She is tormented by her conscience, she thinks about the people she killed. I feel empathy for her.

I resolved the opera in a tragic vein. I would say that *Lady Macbeth* could be called a tragic-satiric opera. Despite the fact that Ekaterina Lvovna is a murderer of her husband and father-in-law

I nevertheless feel empathy for her.

Chapter 5, pp. 154–55, *Testimony* [Moscow typescript, p. 211]:

Is a musical concept born consciously or unconsciously? It's difficult to explain. The process of writing a new work is long and complicated. Sometimes you start writing and then change your mind. It doesn't always work out the way you thought it would. If it's not working, leave the composition the way it is—and try to avoid your earlier mistakes in the next one. That's my personal point of view, my manner of working. Perhaps it stems from a desire to do as much as possible. When I hear that a composer has eleven versions of one symphony, I think involuntarily, How [*sic*] many new works could he have composed in that time?

No, naturally I sometimes return to an old work; for instance, I made many changes in the score of my opera, *Katerina Izmailova.*

I wrote my Seventh Symphony, the "Leningrad," very quickly. I couldn't not write it. War was all around. I had to be with the people. I wanted to create the image of our country at war, capture it in music. From the first days of the war, I sat down at the piano and started work. I worked intensely. I wanted to write about our time, about my contemporaries who spared neither strength nor life in the name of Victory Over the Enemy.

D. Shostakovich, "Kak rozhdaetsia muzyka" [How music is born], *Literaturnaia gazeta,* 21 December 1965; reprinted in Danilevich, *Dmitri Shostakovich,* p. 36:

Is a musical concept born consciously or unconsciously? It's difficult to explain. The process of writing a new work is long and complicated. Sometimes you start writing and then change your mind. It doesn't always work out the way you thought it would. If it's not working, leave the composition the way it is—and try to avoid your earlier mistakes in the next one. That's my personal point of view, my manner of working. Perhaps it stems from a desire to do as much as possible. When I hear that a composer has eleven versions of one symphony, I think involuntarily, How many new works could he have composed in that time?

No, naturally I sometimes return to an old work; for instance, I made many changes in the score of my opera *Katerina Izmailova.* After all, nearly thirty years had passed since the days of its composition.

I wrote my Seventh Symphony, the "Leningrad," very quickly. I couldn't not write it. War was all around. I had to be with the people. I wanted to create the image of our country at war, capture it in music. From the first days of the war, I sat down at the piano and started work. I worked intensely. I wanted to write about our time, about my contemporaries who spared neither strength nor life in the name of Victory Over the Enemy.

//

[Moscow typescript, p. 212]:

I've heard so much nonsense about the Seventh and Eighth Symphonies. It's amazing how long-lived these stupidities are. I'm astounded sometimes by how lazy people are when it comes to thinking.

In breaks from work, I used to go outside and look with pain and pride at my beloved city. There it stood, scorched by fires, having endured all the suffering of war. Leningrad was fighting back with courage.

Chapter 6, pp. 178–79, *Testimony* [Moscow typescript, p. 250]:

D. Shostakovich, "Samyi blizkii" [One of my favorites], *Literaturnaia gazeta*, 28 January 1960; reprinted in Danilevich, *Dmitri Shostakovich*, pp. 34–35:

I really love Chekhov, he's one of my favorite writers. I read and reread not only his stories and plays, but his notes and letters.

I really love Chekhov, he's one of my favorite writers. I read and reread not only his stories and plays, but his notes and letters. I am sincerely happy that the 100th anniversary of his birth is attracting anew to him the attention of all progressive humanity.

Of course, I'm no literary historian and I can't give a proper assessment of the work of the great Russian writer, who I feel has not been thoroughly studied and certainly not always correctly understood. But if I were suddenly expected to write a dissertation on an author, I would choose Chekhov, that's how close an affinity I feel for him. Reading him, I sometimes recognize myself; I feel that anyone in Chekhov's place would react exactly as he did in confronting life.

Of course, I'm no literary historian and I can't give a proper assessment of the work of the great Russian writer, who I feel has not been thoroughly studied and certainly not always correctly understood. But if I were suddenly expected to write a dissertation on an author, I would choose Chekhov, that's how close an affinity I feel for him. Reading him, I sometimes recognize myself; I feel that anyone in Chekhov's place would react exactly as he did in confronting life.

Chekhov's entire life is a model of purity and modesty—and not a modesty for show, but an inner modesty. That's probably why I'm not a fan of certain memorial editions that can only be described as a spoonful of pitch in a barrel of honey. In particular, I'm quite sorry that the correspondence between Anton Pavlovich and his wife was ever published; it's so intimate that most of it

Chekhov's entire life is a model of purity and modesty—and not a modesty for show, but an inner modesty. That's probably why I'm not a fan of certain memorial editions that can only be described as a spoonful of pitch in a barrel of honey. In particular, I'm quite sorry that the correspondence between Anton Pavlovich and his wife was ever published; it's so intimate that most of it

should not be seen in print. I'm saying this with respect for the strictness with which the writer approached his work. He did not publish his works until he brought them
//
[Moscow typescript, p. 251]:
to the level that he considered at least decent. On the other hand, when you read Chekhov's letters you gain a better understanding of his fiction; therefore I am ambivalent on the question.

should not be seen in print. I'm saying this with respect for the strictness with which the writer approached his work. He did not publish his works until he brought them to perfection.

Chekhov's biography was one of the noblest and most upright. I admire his life's attainment—the trip to Sakhalin, the impulse to see everything with his own eyes, to understand and feel it himself.

❦

Chapter 7, pp. 226–27, *Testimony*
[Moscow typescript, p. 326]:

Musorgsky and I have a "special relationship." He was an entire academy for me—of human relations, politics, and art. I didn't study him with only my eyes and ears, for that's not enough for a composer or any professional. (That holds for the other arts as well. Think how many great painters spend years slaving over copies without seeing anything shameful in it.)

Almost simultaneously with the creation of my piano* quintet, I was busy on a new edition of his opera, *Boris Godunov.* I had to look through the score, smooth out a few wrinkles in the harmonization and some unfortunate and pretentious bits of orchestration, and change a few discrete progressions. A number of instruments had been added to the orchestration that had never been used by either Musorgsky or Rimsky-Korsakov, who edited *Boris.*
[*The word "piano" is absent in the Moscow typescript.]

D. Shostakovich, "Partitura opery" [The score of an opera], *Izvestiia,* 1 May 1941; reprinted in Danilevich, *Dmitri Shostakovich,* pp. 14–15:

Almost simultaneously with the creation of my quintet, I was busy on a new edition of his opera, *Boris Godunov.* I had to look through the score, smooth out a few wrinkles in the harmonization and some unfortunate and pretentious bits of orchestration, and change a few discrete progressions. A number of instruments had been added to the orchestration that had never been used by either Musorgsky or Rimsky-Korsakov, who edited *Boris.* I revere Musorgsky, I consider him one of the greatest Russian composers.

To penetrate as deeply as possible into the original creative conception of this genius composer, to reveal his conception and convey it to listeners was my task.

Musorgsky had made many changes and corrections on the advice of Stasov, Rimsky-Korsakov, and others, and then Korsakov made quite a few changes on his own. Korsakov's edition of *Boris Godunov* reflects the ideology, ideas, and artistry of the last century. You can't help respecting the enormous amount of work done by him. But I wanted to edit the opera in a different way.

Musorgsky had made many changes and corrections on the advice of V. Stasov, N. Rimsky-Korsakov, and others, and then N. Korsakov made quite a few changes on his own. Korsakov's edition of *Boris Godunov* reflects the ideology, ideas, and artistry of the last century. You can't help respecting the enormous amount of work done by him. But I wanted to edit the opera in a different way, to express in it, in so far as possible, the character of the Soviet era. I wanted a greater symphonic development, I wanted the orchestra to do more than simply accompany the singers.

I wanted a greater symphonic development, I wanted the orchestra to do more than simply accompany the singers.

Rimsky-Korsakov was despotic and tried to make the score submit to his own style, rewriting a lot and adding his own music. I changed only a few bars and rewrote very little.
//
[Moscow typescript, p. 327]:
But certain things did have to be changed. The scene in the forest outside Kromy had to be given a worthy spot. Musorgsky had orchestrated it like a student afraid of failing an exam. Falteringly and badly. I did it over.

Rimsky-Korsakov was despotic and tried to make the score submit to his own style, rewriting a lot and adding his own music. I changed only a few bars and rewrote very little.

In Musorgsky's score the bell-ringing and the coronation at the beginning of the opera, and the polonaise in the Polish act, sounded very badly. And yet these are scenes of enormous symphonic tension!

Chapter 8, pp. 245–46, *Testimony* [Moscow typescript, p. 357]:

D. Shostakovich, "Iz vospominanii o Mayakovskom" [Reminiscences of Mayakovsky], *V. Mayakovsky v vospominaniiakh sovremennikov* [V. Mayakovsky in the reminiscences of his contemporaries], ed. V. V. Grigorenko et al. (Moscow: Gosudarstvennoe izdatel'stvo khudozhestvennoi literatury, 1963), pp. 315–16:

I became fascinated by Mayakovsky's poetry at an early age. There's a book called *Everything Written by Vladimir Mayakovsky*, printed on bad paper in 1919. That was my introduction to the poet. I was very young then, barely thirteen, but I had friends, young literary men, who were great fans of Mayakovsky, and they were happy to explain the more difficult parts of the book that I liked so much. In the years that followed, I tried never to miss a single one of his appearances in Leningrad. I went to his readings with my writer friends and we listened with great interest and enthusiasm.

My favorite poem of his was "Kindness to Horses," and I still like it and consider it one of his best works. In my youth, I was impressed by "A Cloud in Trousers" and I liked "Spine Flute" and many other poems. I tried to set some of his poems to music, but I couldn't do it. I must say that setting poetry to music is very difficult, particularly for me, since even now I can hear his readings and I would want the music to reflect his intonations as he read his own work.

In early 1929, Vsevolod Emilievich Meyerhold, who was producing *The Bedbug*, asked me to write the music for the play. I took on the project with pleasure. I naïvely thought that Mayakovsky in real life

//

[Moscow typescript, p. 358]:

would be just as he was in his poems. Naturally, I didn't expect him to be wearing his Futuristic yellow shirt and I didn't think that he would have a flower drawn on his cheek. That kind of foolishness in the new political climate could have done him only harm.

I became fascinated by Mayakovsky's poetry at an early age. There's a book called *Everything Written by Vladimir Mayakovsky*, printed on bad paper in 1919. That was my introduction to the poet. I was very young then, barely thirteen, but I had friends, young literary men, who were great fans of Mayakovsky, and they were happy to explain the more difficult parts of the book that I liked so much. In the years that followed, I tried never to miss a single one of his appearances in Leningrad. I went to his readings with my writer friends and we listened with great interest and enthusiasm.

My favorite poem of his was "Kindness to Horses," and I still like it and consider it one of his best works. In my youth, I was impressed by "A Cloud in Trousers" and I liked "Spine Flute" and many other poems. I tried to set some of his poems to music, but I couldn't do it. I must say that setting poetry to music is very difficult, particularly for me, since even now I can hear his readings and I would want the music to reflect his intonations as he read his own work.

In early 1929, Vsevolod Emilievich Meyerhold, who was producing *The Bedbug*, asked me to write the music for the play. I took on the project with pleasure. I naïvely thought that Mayakovsky in real life would be just as he was in his writings: a tribune, a brilliant witty orator. When I met him at one of the rehearsals, he amazed me with his gentleness, courtesy, quite simply with his breeding. He turned out to be a pleasant, attentive person who liked to listen more than to speak.

4

A Pitiful Fake: About the So-Called "Memoirs" of D. D. Shostakovich (1979)

LETTER TO THE EDITOR OF *Literaturnaia gazeta*

[A note from the editor of *Literaturnaia gazeta:* We are publishing below a letter from composers who were not only students of D. D. Shostakovich at various times but also individuals who were close to him. All prominent figures in Soviet music, their works are well known to Soviet and foreign listeners. V. E. Basner and M. S. Weinberg are both Honored Artists of the RSFSR. K. A. Karaev is a Peoples' Artist of the USSR, a laureate of the Lenin and State Prizes of the USSR, a Hero of Socialist Labor, and a member of the Academy of Sciences of the Azerbaijan SSR. Yu. A. Levitin is an Honored Artist of the RSFSR and a laureate of the USSR State Prize. B. I. Tishchenko is an Honored Artist of the RSFSR and a laureate of the RSFSR Prize. K. S. Khachaturian is an Honored Artist of the RSFSR and a laureate of the USSR State Prize.[1]]

[*To the editor:*] It was with distress and indignation that we became acquainted with the book published by Harper & Row in New York City under the guise of D. D. Shostakovich's "memoirs."

Zhalkaia poddelka: O tak nazyvaemykh "memuarakh" D. D. Shostakovicha" [A pitiful fake: About the so-called "memoirs" of D. D. Shostakovich], *Literaturnaia gazeta,* 14 November 1979, p. 8. Laurel Fay kindly provided the translation used here.

The illustrious and stalwart image of our great contemporary, the outstanding composer Dmitri Shostakovich, has been sullied by the hands of a certain Solomon Volkov.

It is absolutely clear to us, students of Shostakovich and people who knew him intimately and continually associated with him, that the book has little in common with Dmitri Shostakovich's actual reminiscences. The real author of this book, S. Volkov, has invented much of it, very much indeed.

Even Dmitri Dmitrievich's genuine comments, many of which are well known and have been published more than once, are presented in a manner that distorts and falsifies the meaning of his words.

Knowing Dmitri Dmitrievich's incredible tact and politeness, one cannot even imagine him as the author of all those crude words and scathing descriptions of great composers, musicians, writers—Soviet and foreign—in which the book abounds. The figure of the true author of these "memoirs" emerges from all these fabrications, a malicious renegade who set himself the goal of reducing the image of the great composer to his own pitiful level.

We remember how steadfastly modest and reserved Dmitri Dmitrievich was in everything concerning his compositions. One can only stare openmouthed at the explications and wordy interpretations of the "contents" of his music found in this book, ostensibly stemming from the composer himself.

Much is said in the book about the criticisms leveled at D. D. Shostakovich.

Indeed, the article "Sumbur vmesto muzyki" [A muddle instead of music], in which one of the best operas of the twentieth century, *Ledi Makbet Mtsenskogo uezda* [Lady Macbeth of the Mtsensk District] (*Katerina Izmailova*), was severely and unfairly criticized; the article "Baletnaia fal'sh" [Balletic falsity], and especially the criticisms of 1948, "accusing" D. D. Shostakovich and other composers of formalism, gave rise to many bitter feelings on the part of Dmitri Dmitrievich. We know, however, that this fragile, easily wounded man was possessed of iron fortitude. He endured the unfounded accusations courageously, and time and time again confirmed his rightness and his greatness in his music.

But the main thing, which is well known, is that a resolution of the Central Committee of the Communist Party of the Soviet Union, adopted in 1958, revoked the accusations of formalism against the whole group of composers, declaring the accusations unfair and unfounded.

We do not intend to dwell on all the distortions of D. D. Shostakovich's ideas contained in these so-called memoirs, however easy this might be, or on all the juggling of facts and the heaps of lies. People who knew our teacher will recognize all too starkly the compiler's monstrous attempt to draw some sort of "alternative" image of Shostakovich. Lie is piled upon lie. The composer's exceptional compassion, his sincere generosity in everything, his good-heartedness—which was continually sensed not just by us, his students, but also by a host of other musicians and cultural figures, Soviet and foreign—all are replaced, in Volkov's writings, by a mass of defamatory inventions about the composer's embitterment and constant petty irascibility. It is as if these determined the whole framework of Shostakovich's thoughts and feelings, ostensibly deriving from an intense enmity toward everyone and everything surrounding him in our society.

This sinister transformation was necessary, in the final analysis, in order to try to distance Shostakovich from Soviet music, and Soviet music from Shostakovich. The cynicism is all the more disgusting in that all of Dmitri Dmitrievich's life and work, from his first compositions to his last, are associated with the revolutionary history of our country and its present-day life. Through his creative work and his civic activities, Dmitri Dmitrievich, with uncommon commitment, rendered invaluable assistance to the younger generation of Russian-Soviet composers, to the country's national musical schools, and to tens and hundreds of its talented representatives.

By his example, D. D. Shostakovich taught people to be good, honest, and decent in their relations with others, to be uncompromising toward duplicity and falsehood. His legacy is sacred not only to us, his students, but to everyone who knew Dmitri Dmitrievich, who experienced firsthand the magnetic appeal of his enormous, infinitely noble personality.

How grotesque that the disgusting attempt to erase all this has been ascribed to the composer himself by means of a forgery.

We are aware that the family of the late Dmitri Dmitrievich, when they heard that the book was being prepared for publication, approached the publisher on more than one occasion with a request to be sent a copy of the manuscript. The family's request, however, was rejected by the American publisher, who evidently understood that their acquaintance with the manuscript would lead to a speedy exposure of the forgery.

Unfortunately a number of publishers and magazines abroad are picking up this shameful concoction with the fruitless aim of discrediting our nation, Soviet culture, and one of its finest representatives, D. D. Shostakovich.

But no lie invented by the soiled hands of schemers and rogues can distort the noble image of a great composer and ardent patriot of his motherland. To promulgate an "alternative" image of Shostakovich's music and his whole life is a hopeless endeavor. The music itself refutes all such attempts by purveyors of falsehood.

V. Basner, M. Weinberg, K. Karaev, Yu. Levitin,
B. Tishchenko, K. Khachaturian

Note

1. The surnames, as spelled in Cyrillic, are listed in alphabetical order both here and at the end of the letter to the editor: Veniamin Efimovich Basner (1925–1996); Moisei [Mieczysław] Samuilovich Vainberg [Weinberg] (1919–1996); Kara Abul'fazogly Karaev (1918–1982); Yuri Abramovich Levitin (1912–1993); Boris Ivanovich Tishchenko (b. 1939–); and Karen Surenovich Khachaturian (b. 1920–).

5

The Bedbug (1979)

EDITORIAL IN *Literaturnaia gazeta*, 14 NOVEMBER 1979, P. 8

So, then, just what is this publication that bills itself as *Testimony: The Memoirs of Dmitri Shostakovich,* and then, in smaller letters, "as related to and edited by Solomon Volkov"? In other words, "memoirs" that have been "related," and which, moreover, have been "edited" not by the "teller" but by the "listener." Let us keep this in mind.

The book begins with an introduction by Volkov himself from which it is apparent that this turncoat, who swapped the Soviet Union several years ago for the United States of America, became so infatuated with Dmitri Shostakovich when he was but a sixteen-year-old (the composer was then fifty-four) that he became a sort of "confessor," a "confidant of secrets," and the biographer of the celebrated composer.

If we take at face value the stunning myth about the "spiritual kinship" of Shostakovich with this pretentious, half-educated person operating in the field of musicology, then it follows that we ought to believe what the great musician ostensibly "confessed" to the bedbug that

---

The editor's selection of a title for the editorial, "The Bedbug," is an obvious pun on Vladimir Mayakovsky's "magical comedy"—the play *Klop* [The bedbug], for which Shostakovich composed appropriately high-spirited incidental music, opus 19 (1929). Laurel Fay kindly provided the English translation used here.

attached itself to him. At any rate, that is evidently what Volkov and the American publisher of these "memoirs," Harper & Row, are counting on.

What did Shostakovich confess to this bedbug who published the "memoirs" in the composer's name and modestly made his own name scarce from the first page onward (out of sight in a crack, one might say), conducting the entire ensuing narrative as if it had been written from first word to last by the composer himself?

First of all, that he (Shostakovich) was always alien to Soviet society. That he could not stand it, and, consequently, he lived a double life all his years. That he wrote music for people he despised. That he proclaimed his devotion a hundred times over to a people and a social system he hated. And that he did not even in the least regard his famed Seventh Symphony as an indictment of fascism.

If we are to believe Volkov, then the Shostakovich his contemporaries knew as a modest, restrained, and benevolent person was a misanthrope and a malcontent who defamed his colleagues with unconcealed spite. As created by the contemptible imagination of a philistine turncoat, this man allows himself to cast slurs upon Sergei Prokofiev and Reinhold Glière, Vladimir Mayakovsky and Evgeny Mravinsky, all whose friendship and collaboration Shostakovich cherished and about which he spoke on many occasions. With equal bitterness, Volkov's "Shostakovich" also has his say about Stanislavsky, Romain Rolland, Bernard Shaw, and Leon Feuchtwangler.

Does the above, perhaps, suffice for an image of Shostakovich as an embittered misanthrope—the portrait Volkov libelously depicted?

Dmitri Shostakovich was never such a person.

True, his creative fate at times proved difficult.

Shostakovich blazed new trails in music, in some sense outstripping his time. His music was not appreciated and accepted by everyone. Let us just say that in 1936, when that vicious, crude article about his opera *Ledi Makbet Mtsenskogo uezda* [Lady Macbeth of the Mtsensk District], appeared, it might have driven anybody into depression, not just Shostakovich, although him more than others. One can suppose that the unjustly insulted composer uttered the harshest words on this situation.

But to imagine that a man who hated his society and reviled the finest masters of its culture could accept (with gratitude from the bottom of his heart, about which he spoke many times) the tribute of recognition by that very society (and those masters!), could join the Communist Party, give of his time (and give of it, by all accounts, wholeheartedly) to the duties of a deputy and other civic responsibilities, to imagine such is impossible for an honest person.

But one need not try to imagine it, because Volkov draws Shostakovich in his own image, as an anti-Soviet and a double-dealer. Such is the "conception" that reveals itself from the very first pages and fills the entire book with rancid venom.

It is symptomatic that, even in America, the appearance of the "memoirs" was accompanied not only by the customary sensational propaganda but also, on this occasion, by a dose of well-founded doubt.

Harold Schonberg—the music critic of the *New York Times*—poses the reasonable question: "Are the words *really* Shostakovich's? The question arises because we in the West are automatically suspicious of mysterious Soviet manuscripts that have to be taken on faith." Schonberg continues, "In the preface and introduction to this book, Mr. Volkov goes into detail about the genesis and history of the Shostakovich memoirs. But we have to take his word for it, and that will not satisfy most musicologists and historians, a surly lot who demand proof."

Even the BBC confessed later, "One cannot say that everyone here has accepted on faith Volkov's declaration that he simply wrote down and edited Shostakovich's reminiscences. So, at present, it is hard to say how much in the published memoirs is Shostakovich himself, and how much is Volkov."

One would have thought the matter clear. The little book [*knizhonka*] got published, but confidence in it is scant, and it stirs up dissatisfaction and annoyance. Well then, write off your direct costs and propaganda losses, gentlemen, and let us forget about this foul-smelling incident.

Nothing of the kind! The thirst for an anti-Soviet scandal has overcome the arguments of reason. Radio, magazines, and a number of publishers have joined the ideological diversion. One seriously doubts that they will abruptly alter their tone.

Mr. Schonberg reassures himself: "Yet there is no good reason to disbelieve Mr. Volkov's account, and certainly there is nothing in the book that is incompatible with what we know, or have read about, or have been told about Shostakovich." There you have it: "nothing . . . incompatible."

But, gentlemen, have you read the following statement Shostakovich made on the eve of the Second Congress of Soviet Composers in 1957: "We have the invaluable collective experience of the entire multinational Soviet composers' community, the experience of a long-term struggle for a musical culture of high intentions, great ethical ideas, and great truth, for art developed under the banner of Socialist Realism. This experience assumes exceptional significance not only for our music but for musicians the world over."

So, if one is to believe Volkov, once Shostakovich had pronounced these words and returned home, the great master began to hurl abuse at that experience and to denounce his colleagues one after the other.

Gentlemen, have you read Shostakovich's article in *Literaturnaia gazeta* of 21 December 1965, in which he wrote: "The composer must have the support of his audience. To work, to compose without it is inconceivable. I remember the great honor I felt at the festival in Gorky, where almost fifty of my works were performed. Festivals, composers' concerts, and musical premières are regularly held in Gorky. And yet it is just a city like so many others." To suppose that, after this, the composer haughtily disparaged his Soviet listeners is to suppose the most insulting, preposterous hypothesis about a great artist, who worked for his people, for his socialist culture.

Gentlemen, have you read Shostakovich's last article, almost his spiritual testament, "Muzyka i vremia" [Music and the times], published in the journal *Kommunist* in May 1975? Shostakovich reminisced: "There were four years of war, four years of a fight to the death against fascism. Thinking back on them today, I am struck over and over again by how rich, how intensive the spiritual life of our society was, notwithstanding the burdens and deprivations of wartime. At its foundation lay the highest morality and humanism. It was these very qualities that determined the point of every Soviet man at the front or at the rear. Our people conquered the enemy not only by force of arms, by heroic effort, but also by their great spirituality. In truth, 'rectifying death with death,' they defended their socialist motherland, they stood up for the historical course begun under Lenin's leadership." So what happened then? Shostakovich pronounced these words, and an hour later he made his "confession" to Volkov, lambasting everyone and everything.

What is the point here? Who benefits from an image deflated by a malicious philistine to his own level? The secret is revealed in the very same issue of the *New York Times:* "Shostakovich was a great talent ruined by the system under which he was working." There you have it. It all comes down to the socialist system.

You lie, gentlemen! His huge talent consisted of accomplishments acknowledged the world over.

During his lifetime Shostakovich was elected honorary member of the Swedish Royal Academy of Music, the Italian Santa Cecilia Academy of Arts, the Serbian Academy of Arts and Sciences, the French Order of Arts and Letters, the English Royal Academy of Music, the National Institute of Arts and Letters (USA). He received an honorary doctorate from Northwestern University (USA). The composer always accepted such recognition on behalf of himself as a representative of Soviet culture. Hence, when he received the International Peace Prize, he declared: "This high award obliges me to fight always for peace and friendship among nations, so as always to be worthy of the high award presented to me today, and so as always to fulfill with honor the high calling of a son of the great Soviet people."

You say the system "ruined" his talent, gentlemen? But an unprejudiced approach always affirmed the deep connection between Shostakovich's work and this system, Soviet society, the people. Here, for example, is what renowned French cultural figures wrote about Shostakovich.

The composer André Jolivet: "He creates in an enormous, very musical country—and this assures enormous advantages—and consequently his work became its symbol."

The writer Jean-Richard Bloch: "Yes, Shostakovich's subsoil is utterly special, it is a country for giants. The smallest step in it is measured in *versts*, the ordinary scale is changed, altered, transformed accordingly into some sort of new standard. In truth, the music is for a sixth part of our planet. This is a land of *bogatyrs*, whether they be scholars, engineers, soldiers, or artists."

Thus have spoken masters of Western culture. It turns out that Shostakovich perceived what they said (as well as what was said by Bernard Shaw and Romain Rolland) as his just due, but what about later? Later he assured Volkov that all these people were liars.

The Soviet system, Soviet society, having rejected all that was unjust in evaluating the composer's work, bestowed upon the artist its highest recognition and love. His great creations entered the spiritual treasure house of our people. His quests for innovation, which stood opposed to the lack of spirituality in Western "avant-gardism," enriched the musical art of the contemporary world and opened new horizons for the development of the mighty realistic tradition. The performance of Shostakovich's works—which by their merits have become the classics of socialist culture—has been and is now greeted with enthusiasm by listeners everywhere. The great composer symphonist has experienced the most valuable and important thing for an artist—the impassioned recognition of his entire life's creative mission and the gratitude of people for what he created—an art of great revolutionary thought and profound humanity.

Shostakovich was awarded the titles "Hero of Socialist Labor" and "Peoples' Artist of the USSR." The Lenin Prize and State Prizes were conferred upon him. For many years he served as a secretary of the Union of Composers of the USSR. He headed the Union of Composers of the Russian Federation. He was a member of the Soviet Committee for the Defense of Peace and a deputy to four Supreme Soviets of the USSR. The composer accepted every acknowledgment of this nationwide recognition with a feeling of sincere gratitude and high responsibility. He promised "henceforth never to stint on effort, in order to justify the people's trust" (from an election speech), and he kept to his word religiously. He was gladly nominated to responsible posts, and he gladly accepted the honor and responsibility.

This is the consummate artist, Communist, and citizen depicted by Volkov as some kind of "petty demon" in the mode of Sologub's gymnasium instructor, Peredonov, whose greatest delight when he returned home was to fall into a disgusting orgy of spitting on everyone and everything. What else can this be other than a vain attempt not only to defile the memory of a great composer but also to slander the people whose culture nurtured him, the people he created for.

The publishers claim that on Volkov's "composition" they found notations made by Shostakovich, "I have read." But for someone who has perverted Shostakovich's entire life, it would not be difficult to do something similar with the composer's "visas." Volkov's dirty fingerprints—this is what would be easy to find on the pages of Volkov's manuscript! And they are bound to be genuine.

6

The Official Dossier (1979)

NEWS ITEM IN *Literaturnaia gazeta*

The letter from the students of Shostakovich, published on this page, reports that the composer's family approached the American publisher with urgent requests to be allowed to examine the manuscript of *Testimony*.

Published here is the official documentation.

On 29 November 1978 the legal department of the All-Union Copyright Agency (*Vsesoiuznoe agenstvo avtorskikh prav: VAAP*) advised the publisher Harper & Row in New York that Irina Antonovna Shostakovich, the composer's widow, had authorized VAAP to represent her legal rights by requesting the text of the manuscript, since "the publisher had not approached her in conjunction with the publication of the manuscript, and its nature was unknown to her."

On 13 December of the same year the composer's widow, son, and daughter appealed to the vice president of Harper & Row, Robert E. Bench: "Once again we confirm the need to receive promptly from you information about the book. . . . We would hope that, having undertaken this publication, you are conscious of your responsibility in matters related to the protection of Dmitri Shostakovich's name and copyright."

"Ofitsial'noe dos'e" [The official dossier], *Literaturnaia gazeta*, 14 November 1979, p. 8. Laurel Fay kindly provided the English translation used here.

In a teletype message, dated 2 February 1979, Edward A. Miller, vice president and general counsel of Harper & Row (citing his earlier response of 6 December 1978, which VAAP did not receive) declared: "Shostakovich's heirs have no rights at all to this work, and their permission is not required to publish it." (?!) [*sic*]

Understandably such a discourteous response did not satisfy the Soviet side. On 21 February 1979 VAAP notified the publisher that, based on the company's response, it was unclear whether Harper & Row was preparing to publish some sort of "memoirs" by Shostakovich himself or a book about him by another author. "If you intend to identify Dmitri Shostakovich as the author of the forthcoming book, then the claims of his heirs remain in force."

On 1 June 1979 the composer's family protested once more against the publication of any works whatever by Shostakovich without their prior written consent. "We are not aware that D. Shostakovich gave his consent to anyone to publish his materials posthumously."

A copy of the letter was sent to VAAP. In connection with this, the assistant chairman of VAAP's directorate, Yu. Rudakov, wrote, on 5 June, to Miller: "The copyright of an author's words—which are, as is well known, among the property subject to copyright—pass after the author's death to his heirs. . . . Without the consent of the heirs of D. Shostakovich, the publisher has no right to publish the work in question."

No answer to this communication was received.

Evidently even the American publisher does not believe in the authenticity of the "memoirs," or else Harper & Row would have refrained from its unauthorized publication, if only for legal considerations. Unfortunately the publisher was guided by other considerations, far removed from a sense of respect for the memory of a great composer.

7

Notes from the Soviet Archives on Volkov's *Testimony* (1995)

ALLA BOGDANOVA

Preserved in the archives of the Central Committee of the Communist Party of the Soviet Union (CPSU) are several documents that preceded the publication of Solomon Volkov's book of memoirs. Among these documents is one entitled "Transcript of a Conversation with Irina Antonovna Shostakovich, the Composer's Widow, in the Offices of the All-Union Copyright Agency (VAAP)," along with a copy of a letter from the composer's family members to the vice president of Harper & Row Publishing House. These two documents add little, strictly speaking, to the sensational story of the publication of Volkov's memoirs. But they recount at length how Shostakovich "spoke about his own life story in conversations with the Soviet musicologist Solomon Maseevich [*sic*] Volkov, who had come forward as a representative of the journal *Sovetskaia muzyka*."

We read the following in the transcript report of the conversation:

> Irina Antonovna Shostakovich was asked why she had not at the time approached VAAP in order to avert ahead of time an undesirable publication

---

This is an extract from Bogdanova's book *Muzyka i vlast' (poststalinskii period)* [Music and the regime (the post-Stalinist period)] (Moscow: "Nasledie," 1995), pp. 373–77.

abroad; she answered, "Everybody concerned knew about the conversations, including the journal *Sovetskaia muzyka*."

To the question, did the widow intend now to authorize VAAP to take steps to avert release, in the United States, of a book that might damage the memory of the great composer, I. A. Shostakovich responded, "For the moment I do not see any reason for concern. After all, the book may well contain only Dmitri Dmitrievich's autobiographical commentary, in which case there is no reason to object. We would only like to be convinced that the American publisher would not add anything to the composer's remarks."

. . . In conclusion, I. A. Shostakovich observed that, in her opinion, the fears of VAAP were unfounded because information about the life and work of D. Shostakovich was well known to the entire world and a new book could not, in principle, reveal anything unexpected. (Dated 22 November 1978)

Following this meeting with Irina Shostakovich, P. Gavrilov, head of the Legal Services Department of VAAP, sent a telegram to the American publisher with a request, on behalf of the composer's lawful heirs, to send the text of D. D. Shostakovich's manuscript to VAAP "so that the heirs can familiarize themselves with it and arrive at a relevant decision" (dated 29 November 1978).

On 13 December 1978 the members of Shostakovich's family—Irina Shostakovich, Galina Shostakovich, and Maxim Shostakovich—sent the following letter to Robert Bench, vice president of Harper & Row (a copy of the letter is also preserved in the files of the Central Committee of the CPSU):

We would hope that, having undertaken this publication, you are conscious of your responsibility in matters related to the protection of Dmitri Shostakovich's name and copyright.

Most interesting about these letters is the sequel, the instantaneous reaction of the Party's Central Committee to the possible attempt by S. Volkov to portray Shostakovich as a composer who had been unjustly criticized and victimized, and who would have been inclined to oppose the Soviet regime. A document appeared on the *very day following* the dispatch of the letter from Shostakovich's family to the publisher. This document is preserved in the archive of Minutes of the Cultural Department of the Party's Central Committee, dated 14 December 1978, and titled, "Concerning Measures for Propagandizing and Preserving D. D. Shostakovich's Creative Legacy."

Our concern is prompted by information in hand that the [American] publisher intends to ascribe an anti-Soviet character to the publication.

In response to this concern, the Minutes then enumerate everything that was being done to immortalize the memory of D. D. Shostakovich:

> In November 1975 the Central Committee adopted a resolution on immortalizing the memory of D. D. Shostakovich. The composer's name was conferred on the Leningrad Philharmonic Orchestra and also on one of the ships of the Baltic Naval Fleet, [1] . . . for example. Matters were resolved concerning provision for the composer's widow, Irina Antonovna Shostakovich. . . . Initiatives were set in motion to propagandize Shostakovich's creative work. The composer's compositions have been included in a cycle of subscription concerts by the nation's philharmonic societies and other concert organizations. His works are continually being performed here by soloists and performing ensembles, as well as during tours abroad. In this connection, his compositions dedicated to historical revolutionary and contemporary themes are being given substantial attention. The Leningrad Philharmonic Orchestra, for example, opens its concert season every year with a performance of Shostakovich's Seventh Symphony, "The Leningrad."

After having enumerated yet another series of initiatives, the authors of the Minutes continue:

> The USSR Ministry of Culture and the USSR Union of Composers recommend taking measures, together with other organizations, to expose the provocative venture by the American publisher Harper & Row.
>
> At the present time the All-Union Copyright Agency (VAAP), at the request of D. D. Shostakovich's lawful heirs, has demanded that the publisher provide an explanation. In case the American publisher refuses to discuss the matter with VAAP and releases the "memoirs," which distort Shostakovich's civic and creative personality, it is intended, through Soviet and foreign information agencies, to describe the publication as an anti-Soviet forgery that discredits the name of a great composer. . . .
>
> Without awaiting further developments in the situation, it is intended to take additional measures to familiarize Soviet and Western society with the truthful political and creative views and pronouncements of D. D. Shostakovich throughout his entire life.[a]

Among other documentation for this, the Cultural Department and V. Shauro (following whose signature the Minutes were issued) mention two audiotaped speeches of Shostakovich: "Included in them are pronouncements about Soviet music, about the patriotic and social vocation of Soviet composers, and about the worldwide priority of our musical school. In his comments about England,[2] the composer makes a critical observation about the way of life of the capitalist world and emphasizes the advantages of the Soviet system."

These and several other of the composer's pronouncements have been designated for wider use in counter-propaganda, radio broadcasts, and also as gramophone recordings for distribution in this country and abroad. (Dated 14 December 1978)

As is well known, the "Memoirs" produced quite an uproar, which has only now subsided, after having created good publicity for the author, even though Volkov's book essentially contains nothing that might not have been learned about the composer earlier.

What is so eminently worthwhile in recalling this history is quite simply to have it serve as a reminder of just how "the powers that be" went about forming an "OPINION [*sic*]," as Rostropovich so accurately put it in his letter about Solzhenitsyn.[b]

Notes

1. This is erroneous as it was a ship belonging to the Odessa Fleet.
2. The reference here is to an audiotape recording of Shostakovich's comments about his trip to the Edinburgh Festival in 1962.

Editor's Notes

Bogdanova's critical and, to some extent, tendentious discussion of music and the Soviet regime during the post-Stalinist years grew out of her access to the Archives of the Central Committee of the Communist Party of the Soviet Union. Generously furnished with extended direct quotations from primary sources, as well as a substantial number of photocopies of complete documents, her book represents the sole study of its kind known to the editor at the time the present volume was in preparation.

a. In the wake of this plan to publicize Shostakovich's political and creative statements throughout the span of his public life, the following important collection was published: *D. Shostakovich o vremeni i o sebe 1926–1975* [D. Shostakovich about himself and the times, 1926–1975], comp. M. Iakovlev, ed. G. Pribegina (Moscow: Sovetskii kompozitor, 1980). This chronological selection of materials signed by the composer (along with a listing of the original sources from which the selected materials were drawn) appeared very early in 1980, quite soon after the appearance of Volkov's *Testimony*. It is the most comprehensive single collection available of Shostakovich's public statements, all of which Shostakovich presumably authorized in advance of their original publication.

b. The reference here is to the "Open Letter" of 31 October 1970 from Mstislav Rostropovich addressed to the editors of the newspapers *Pravda*, *Izvestiia*, *Literaturnaia gazeta*, and *Sovetskaia kul'tura*, but which was not published by any of the Soviet newspapers; it was subsequently leaked to the Western news media and printed abroad. An English translation of the letter can be found in *Galina: A Russian Story*, the memoirs of the renowned soprano and Rostropovich's wife, Galina Vishnevskaya (New York: Harcourt Brace Jovanovich, 1984), pp. 488–91. In the letter, Rostropovich complains vociferously about the continuing repressive cultural situation in his homeland, where works of art were still being banned on the grounds that "there is an opinion that this is not to be recommended." He then writes, "OPINION has prevented my compatriots from seeing Tarkovsky's film, *Andrei Rublev* [Andrei Rubliov] . . . OPINION . . . stopped the publication of Solzhenitsyn's *Cancer Ward* [Rakovyi korpus] . . . [and] I know that my letter will certainly be followed by the appearance of an OPINION about me as well" (pp. 490–91).

8

An Episode in the Life of a Book

An Interview with Henry Orlov (2000)

LUDMILA KOVNATSKAYA

Research devoted to an artist's creative work continues and elaborates the life of the artwork, whereas an artist's memoirs reflect to a far greater degree his or her personal life—details about events and experiences. The latter attracts incomparably more engaged attention, in terms of sociological interest, than does a scholarly study. The book *Testimony: The Memoirs of Dmitri Shostakovich*, "as related to and edited by Solomon Volkov," confirms this statement.[1]

When these memoirs first came to light, the forefront of attention from a sociological perspective was occupied by two gigantic and opposing waves of reaction—official critical denunciation, initiated and supported by the KGB, and sensational critical acclaim in the West. On reading the memoirs, critics and apologists alike experienced a shock. Discussion in the USSR centered on the authenticity of the manuscript and the tales, stories, and anecdotes contained in it, whereas, in the West, discussion focused on the life of Soviet intellectuals as depicted in the

---

Ludmila Kovnatskaya, "Epizod iz zhizni knigi: Interv'iu s Genrikhom Orlovym" [An episode in the life of a book: An interview with Genrikh/Henry Orlov], *Shostakovich: Mezhdu mgnoveniem i vechnost'iu* [Shostakovich: Between now and eternity], ed. and comp. L. G. Kovnatskaya [St. Petersburg: Kompozitor, 2000], pp. 17–38. Published here by permission, for the first time in English translation.

document. In the West the publication of *Testimony* coincided with an ever increasing appreciation of Shostakovich's music and admiration for him as an individual. Having stirred up interest in the composer's personality, the book enlarged the mythological aura already surrounding the name "Dmitri Shostakovich." I think it is reasonable to say, from our present perspective, that *Testimony* has become part of a worldwide cultural process and a formative factor in the public's conscious perception of the composer's personality, far more than any other book about Shostakovich, primarily on the strength of the book's ready accessibility to a vast audience. The impact of the memoirs here in Russia, the composer's home country, was more constrained, given that the original Russian text of the book had not been published; its reception here was also somewhat reserved—associated most probably with a certain defensiveness toward the inevitable pain of being obliged once again to traverse Shostakovich's extremely difficult life and to relive it with him.

Here in the composer's homeland, up to the present time, *Testimony* is rarely mentioned, no substantial commentaries have been published,[2] and the book has not been subject to systematic investigation. Meanwhile, in the world at large, especially among professionals, the book is often cited and serves as a subject for debate, not only in general discussions but also in more specialized ones. Now, two decades after the book's publication, the heated arguments in the West about its authenticity have flared up again with renewed intensity, and a number of our countrymen and former compatriots, representing different generations, have assumed active roles. Some among Shostakovich's contemporaries, who had been acquainted with the master, recognized his "voice" from the tales they had heard him tell, his intonation, and his idiosyncratic manner of speaking and expressing himself; others had no such impression of the "voice" in the "Memoirs."

Some Western scholars have made textual analyses of *Testimony*, raising important issues relevant to establishing its authenticity. This sort of analysis, carried out competently and objectively, results in an informed conclusion, as evidenced in the two articles by Laurel Fay contained in the present volume (chapters 1 and 2).

In light of the fundamental question of authenticity, not just of the finished book but of the manuscript itself (the rough drafts and the final version), factual information—about the history of the book's creation, the editorial procedures involved, and the eventual process of its publication—is not only vital and urgent but also crucial to both sides in the debate. Biographers and scholars who are prepared to use *Testimony* in their work are not likely to remain indifferent to one episode in the life of this book, namely, an event that occurred before the book's publication involving an expert's examination and evaluation of the manuscript. It is precisely this episode that is considered here.

Having decided to publish *Testimony* as the sensational memoirs of Shostakovich, the publishing house of Harper & Row invited the composer's fellow countryman Genrikh [Henry] Alexandrovich Orlov, someone who himself had collected memoirs from Shostakovich, to examine the manuscript and render an opinion. For those who may not be familiar with Orlov's name and his research, allow me to introduce him briefly.

Professor Henry Orlov, Doctor of Arts History, is an outstanding figure among Russian scholars, musicologists, and historians of culture. His monograph, *Simfonii Shostakovicha* [The symphonies of Shostakovich] (Leningrad: Muzgiz, 1961), remains, to the present day, more than three decades after its publication, one of the best books in any language about Shostakovich's symphonies. In his influential *Russkii sovetskii simfonizm* [Russian Soviet symphonism] (Moscow: Muzyka, 1966), Orlov developed a fundamental research methodology for studying the genre of the symphony, which numerous scholars who have written on the symphony have widely adopted in the years following. Orlov's fundamental work on the philosophy of music, *Drevo muzyki* [The tree of music] (Washington, D.C.: H. A. Frager, 1992; St. Petersburg: Sovetskii kompozitor, 1992), includes a foreword written by the eminent Russian musicologist Mikhail Semyonovich Druskin about Orlov, perhaps his most brilliant student:

> Orlov is attracted by the unfamiliar, the not yet studied, at the same time as he offers nontraditional conclusions about the familiar. His individual style reveals a penchant for constructing generalized conceptions, for audacious flights of scholarly fantasy, for concentrated argument sometimes sharpened by the polemical, and a superb literary style, at once logically rigorous and metaphorically imaginative. These qualities have favored the successful development of a new area of interest in Russian musicology, of which Orlov can rightly count himself the originator. The range of problems comprised is suggested by the titles of his articles: "Psikhologicheskie mekhanizmy muykal'nogo vospriiatiia" [The psychological mechanisms of musical perception] (1963); "Khudozhestvennaia kul'tura i tekhnicheskii progress" [Artistic culture and technical progress] (1969); "Semantika muzyki" [The semantics of music] (1973); "Vremennye kharakteristiki muzykal'nogo opyta" [The temporal characteristics of musical experience] (1974); "Strukturnye funktsii vremeni v muzyke" [The structural functions of time in music] (1974); and others. But the more deeply Orlov plumbed the scholarly

> depths he elected to explore, the sharper his conflict with dogmatic ideology became. An inevitable rupture was brewing. When the publisher rejected the manuscript of his research entitled "Vremia i prostranstvo muzyki" [Time and space in music], Orlov decided to emigrate from the Soviet Union.[3]

Over a period of six years in the United States Orlov served as Visiting Professor at Cornell University, Harvard University, and Wesleyan University. Disillusioned with the American system of higher education in the humanities, he abandoned his career as a university professor and gave up teaching altogether. He is currently a publisher (under the name of H. A. Frager) and a translator of works in philosophy and arts history.

Orlov reluctantly recalled his dealings with the publisher Harper & Row and deliberated about which documentary materials from his personal archive he would place at my disposal. The documents he selected are presented here in chronological order, accompanied by Orlov's responses to questions I asked during the course of several conversations in April 1995 in Washington, D.C., and in July 1998 in Prague, the Czech Republic.

L. K. Do you know whose idea it was to ask *you specifically* to give an opinion about the manuscript of the book?

H. O. I can only offer my supposition. I think that the initiative for my being commissioned to review it originated with none other than Solomon Volkov. In any case, when I was considering the conditions of the review as presented in the very first letter, Ann Harris, the volume editor and senior editor at the publishing house, told me that posting the letter had been delayed for three days so that Volkov and his attorneys could work out the text. For this reason, I presume that the person who initiated the commission was Volkov.

L. K. We have this first letter at hand?

H. O. Yes, the letter of 9 April 1979. The conditions as laid out therein were too absurd to accept. And I refused.

[transcription of letter follows]

April 9, 1979

Mr. Henry Orlov
52 Davis Avenue
Brookline, Massachusetts 02146

Dear Mr. Orlov:

The purpose of this letter is to give you some background information about the manuscript of TESTIMONY: THE MEMOIRS OF DMITRI SHOSTAKOVICH, as related to and edited by Solomon Volkov, which we have asked you to review; and also to outline the nature of and terms for this review.

Mr. Volkov describes the procedures for Shostakovich's and his work as follows: Shostakovich did not dictate to him. He would permit Volkov to ask questions, which he answered in short sentences. During these conversations, which lasted for about three years, Volkov took notes in a kind of personal shorthand he had developed during his years of work as a journalist. Gradually, he began to shape his notes into larger sections and chapters. He showed some of them to Shostakovich and he gave his approval. In the spring of 1974, Volkov began to organize the material into longer chapters. As soon as he had finished each chapter, he gave it to Shostakovich, who read it and as proof of his reading and approval, wrote at the head of each chapter the word "Read," followed by his signature, "Shostakovich." He deliberately chose to put the word "read" before his signature on each chapter in order to create a certain distance between himself and the text; and he decided also that the memoirs were not to be published until after his death.

We are requesting that you review the manuscript, and based upon that review—as well as your own knowledge and experience of the events and people described in the manuscript—tell us in writing whether or not you can express an opinion as to its authenticity; and if you can express such an opinion, to state the basis for it.

The terms under which this reading will take place are that it will be reviewed in our offices at 10 East 53rd Street, New York, N.Y.: and that in order to preserve the confidentiality of the memoirs, the manuscript must be read in the presence either of myself or my editorial assistant. Any notes that you may make while reviewing it will have to remain in our possession except while you are reading it or preparing your opinion. In order that you have access to these notes while preparing that opinion, I or my editorial assistant will be present during that process as well. When you have completed it, you will give us the written opinion and your notes. Confidentiality requires that you not retain any copies of the opinion, the notes, or the manuscript.

For the same reasons of confidentiality, we must ask that you agree not to disclose any information about the manuscript without our prior written permission.

Mr. Volkov has been provided a copy of this letter so that he is aware of the basis on which you will review the manuscript.

With good wishes,

Yours sincerely,
[signed] Ann Harris

L. K. I must admit that such phrases as "in order that you have access to these notes" (i.e., that you yourself should have access to your own notes) or "I or my editorial assistant will be present during that

1817

Harper & Row, Publishers, Inc.

New York Hagerstown San Francisco London

Ann Harris
Senior Editor

10 East 53d Street, New York, New York 10022

April 9, 1979

Mr. Henry Orlov
52 Davis Avenue
Brookline, Massachusetts 02146

Dear Mr. Orlov:

The purpose of this letter is to give you some background information about the manuscript of TESTIMONY: THE MEMOIRS OF DMITRI SHOSTAKOVICH, as related to and edited by Solomon Volkov, which we have asked you to review; and also to outline the nature of and terms for this review.

Mr. Volkov describes the procedures for Shostakovich's and his work as follows: Shostakovich did not dictate to him. He would permit Volkov to ask questions, which he answered in short sentences. During these conversations, which lasted for about three years, Volkov took notes in a kind of personal shorthand he had developed during his years of work as a journalist. Gradually, he began to shape his notes into larger sections and chapters. He showed some of them to Shostakovich and he gave his approval. In the spring of 1974, Volkov began to organize the material into longer chapters. As soon as he had finished each chapter, he gave it to Shostakovich, who read it and as proof of his reading and approval, wrote at the head of each chapter the word "Read," followed by his signature, "Shostakovich." He deliberately chose to put the word "read" before his signature on each chapter in order to create a certain distance between himself and the text; and he decided also that the memoirs were not to be published until after his death.

We are requesting that you review the manuscript, and based upon that review -- as well as your own knowledge and experience of the events and people described in the manuscript -- tell us in writing whether or not you can express an opinion as to its authenticity; and if you can express such an opinion, to state the basis for it.

The terms under which this reading will take place are that itwill be reviewed in our offices at 10 East 53rd Street, New York, N.Y.: and that in order to preserve the confidentiality of the memoirs, the manuscript must be read in the presence either of myself or my editorial assistant. Any notes that you may make while reviewing it will have to remain in our possession except while you are reading it or preparing your opinion. In order that you have access to these notes while preparing that opinion, I or my editorial assistant will be present during that process as well. When you have completed it, you will give us the written opinion and your notes. Confidentiality requires that you not retain any copies of the opinion, the notes, or the manuscript.

For the same reasons of confidentiality, we must ask that you agree not to disclose any information about the manuscript without our prior written permission.

Mr. Volkov has been provided with a copy of this letter so that he is aware of the basis on which you will review the manuscript.

With good wishes,

Yours sincerely,

Ann Harris

Harper & Row, Publishers, Inc. Cable: Harpsam Phone: 212-593-7000

Figure 8.1. Photocopy of the First Letter, Dated 9 April 1979, from Ann Harris, Senior Editor, Harper & Row, Addressed to Henry Orlov, Concerning Solomon Volkov's Manuscript

process as well" (in what capacity? as a witness? as a supervisor?)—such phrases convey the impression that the letter was prepared by some high-level governmental agency charged to protect the memoirs of a spy who holds top-secret clearance.

What was the attitude toward such a procedure by the officials in charge of offering the commission on behalf of the publisher? What did you sense—was it the customary procedure for them?

H. O. I think that the case fell somewhat outside the publisher's usual practices—I mean not so much the reviewing process itself, but the specific conditions worked out for the reviewer. When I realized the extraordinarily strict conditions of non-disclosure, of not even being able to keep for myself my own notes about the manuscript, of having to write the review only on the publisher's premises in the presence of the editor, of my obligation to keep quiet about the contents of the book until its publication and to keep quiet about my opinion of it to the end of my days—I phoned Volkov and, as best I remember, half-jokingly asked him what was going on with such ridiculous conditions as were laid out in the publisher's letter, did he really not trust me? Volkov responded to my question in an official tone of voice: "That is the publisher's policy." Naturally I could not accept the conditions as offered and turned down the review. Ann Harris commented that were she in my shoes, she would have done the same thing.

Four and a half months later, on 26 August 1979, I received a repeat letter of commission, in which for the first time the conditions offered me were substantially moderated. The first three paragraphs repeated verbatim the first letter, but the paragraphs following took a different line:

[transcription of letter follows]

August 26, 1979

> . . .
>
> The manuscript is to be reviewed by you in my presence in order to preserve the confidentiality of its contents. You may take such notes during your reading of the manuscript as are necessary to enable you to prepare your report on its authenticity. Mr. Volkov would prefer that these notes be taken in English rather than in Russian, but if this will hamper you in the preparation of your report, Russian can be used.
>
> You agree to provide us with your written report on the manuscript as promptly as possible. It is understood that Harper & Row shall own all rights to this report; and that you will not publish or otherwise disclose any portion of it without our express written consent. Upon receipt of the report, we will pay you the sum of

$500 in full consideration of your services in reviewing the manuscript and preparing your report.

Because of the sensitive nature of the Memoirs and their origins, we ask that you agree not to inform anyone outside of your immediate family of the fact that you have reviewed the manuscript at our request. We also request that you not disclose or discuss the contents of the manuscript without our written permission or until such time as the book itself appears.

We are most grateful for your willingness to review the manuscript, and would appreciate your confirming your agreement to the terms of review enumerated in this latter by signing a copy of the letter in the place indicated below.

Yours sincerely,
Ann Harris

ACCEPTED AND AGREED TO:

____

Henry Orlov

L. K. You remember, of course, the procedure for reviewing in the Soviet Union and the types of reviews in those years: an internal or external reader, and a "dissenting" reader, anonymous or not. What type of review did this one remind you of?

H. O. All in all, it seemed like a routine internal editorial review. Not anonymous, since I signed it. The only thing unusual was the munificence with which I was paid for my work—more accurately, for my vow of silence.

L. K. What happened after you received the second letter?

H. O. It's hard to reconstruct a precise sequence of events now, some twenty years later. The second letter is dated 26 August 1979, while my report is dated 28 August. I agreed to the new terms in a phone conversation with Ann Harris, and the next day she brought the manuscript by hand to Boston, together with the contract, which I then signed immediately. I had to read the four-hundred-page manuscript in a few hours, because Ann Harris was obliged to take it back to New York that same afternoon.

L. K. Tell us, please, what was the *mise en scène* during those hours when you were preparing to write the review?

H. O. I went off by myself with the manuscript, while Ann Harris and Mirra[4] talked and drank coffee. I later joined them. The weather had turned warm, and we were sitting on the front porch of the house.

1817

Harper & Row, Publishers, Inc.

New York Hagerstown San Francisco London

Ann Harris
Senior Editor

10 East 53d Street, New York, New York 10022

August 26, 1979

Mr. Henry Orlov
52 Davis Avenue
Brookline, Massachusetts 02146

Dear Mr. Orlov:

The purpose of this letter is to give you some background information about the manuscript of TESTIMONY: THE MEMOIRS OF DMITRI SHOSTAKOVICH, as related to and edited by Solomon Volkov which we have asked you to review; and also to outline the nature of and terms for this review.

Mr. Volkov describes the procedures for Shostakovich's and his work as follows: Shostakovich did not dictate to him. He would permit Volkov to ask questions, which he answered in characteristically short sentences. During these conversations, which increased in frequency and lasted for about three years, Volkov took notes in a kind of personal shorthand he had developed during his years of work as a journalist. Gradually, he began to shape his notes into larger sections and chapters. He showed some of these to Shostakovich and he gave his approval. In the spring of 1974 Volkov began to organize the material into longer sections. As soon as he had finished each section and it was typed, he gave it to Shostakovich, who read it and as proof of his reading and approval, wrote at the head of each chapter the word "Read," followed by his signature, "Shostakovich." He deliberately chose to put the word "read" before his signature on each chapter in order to create a certain distance between himself and the text; and he decided also that the memoirs were not to be published until after his death.

We are requesting that you review the manuscript, and based on that review -- as well as your own knowledge and experience of the events and people described in the manuscript -- tell us in writing whether or not you can express an opinion as to its authenticity; and, if you can express such an opinion, to give us the basis for it.

The manuscript is to be reviewed by you in my presence in order to preserve the confidentiality of its contents. You may take such notes during your reading of the manuscript as are necessary to enable you to prepare your report on its authenticity. Mr. Volkov would prefer that these notes be taken in English rather than in Russian, but if this will hamper you in the preparation of your report, Russian can be used.

Harper & Row, Publishers, Inc. Cable: Harpsam Phone: 212-593-7000

Figure 8.2. Photocopy of Letter Dated 26 August 1979 from Ann Harris to Henry Orlov

Harper & Row, Publishers

-2-

You agree to provide us with your written report on the manuscript as promptly as possible. It is understood that Harper & Row shall own all rights to this report; and that you will not publish or otherwise disclose any portion of it without our express written consent. Upon receipt of the report, we will pay you the sum of $500 in full consideration of your services in reviewing the manuscript and preparing your report.

Because of the sensitive nature of the Memoirs and their origins, we ask that you agree not to inform anyone outside of your immediate family of the fact that you have reviewed the manuscript at our request. We also request that you not disclose or discuss the contents of the manuscript without our written permission or until such time as the book itself appears.

We are most grateful for your willingness to review the manuscript, and would appreciate your confirming your agreement to the terms of review enumerated in this letter by signing a copy of the letter in the place indicated below.

Yours sincerely,

Ann Harris

ACCEPTED AND AGREED TO:

____
Henry Orlov

Figure 8.2. continued

L. K. Might your review have hindered in any way the publication of Volkov's manuscript?

H. O. During the four hours I spent studying the manuscript and thinking about the report to come, I felt conflicted. On one hand, much in the manuscript struck me as antipathetic, but, on the other, I did not want to undercut the book's prospects for publication. Therefore, during a break, I asked Ann Harris, who was waiting patiently for me to finish the job, "What influence might this review have on the future of the book?" To which she replied quite simply: "None whatsoever, because in two weeks the book will come out in Europe in five languages."[5] At that, I heaved a sigh of relief.

[transcription of Orlov's review follows]

TESTIMONY: THE MEMOIRS OF DMITRI SHOSTAKOVICH[a]
by Solomon Volkov

Reviewed by Henry F. Orlov
[*NB: typographical errors, misspellings, and non-idiomatic expressions as in original*]

The manuscript's title makes one stumble. As far as I know, in the vast literature of the kind, this is going to be the first book of memoirs written in the first person singular, which have been neither written nor dictated by the memorialist. In the letter of commission to me, the work is described as the outcome of elaborations on the materials that had been obtained in the form of "characteristically short sentences" with which Shostakovich answered to the questions Mr Volkov was permitted to ask. As Mr Volkov informs, he did not put Shostakovich's words on paper as they were spoken, but instead he took notes "in a kind of personal shorthand" and then "shaped" the notes into larger sections and chapters. Unfortunately, there are no traces left in the manuscript as to what kind of questions he asked and what Shostakovich's answers precisely were. Giving Mr Volkov full credit as a faithful and conscientious interpreter, one still has to face the fact: the firsthand quality of evidence, most valuable in memoirs, is patently missing from his version of Shostakovich's testimonies. It just cannot be taken as the testimony, likewise no court would have taken as the witness' testimony what even a closest and best-informed friend of his would have to say on his behalf.

What we are dealing with is, clearly, Mr. Volkov's own original literary work based eventually on Shostakovich's statements and remarks. With regard to such a work, authenticity is a rather ambiguous criterion. It can be considered not before the questions are answered as to what kind of material the manuscript contains and what the possible impact on the reader it may have.

The work is obviously not on music and those interested in Shostakovich the composer in particular or in Soviet musical culture in general would find here but few, if any, precise and reliable facts which they had not already come across one way or other: no documents quoted or referred to, very few dates given, most of the names omitted, rumors and hearsay rampant. The aged and ailed composer was speaking entirely from his memory whose precision leaves much more to worry about than that of the editor. Here is one example. It says (p. 212) that the stupid musicologists have repeated for 30 years that opinion on the 7th and 8th as "war symphonies:"

> The 7th was conceived before the war. And, consequently, it simply could not appear as a response to the Hitler's invasion. The "theme of invasion" is in no way related with the invasion. It was the mankind's enemies of a very different sort whom I thought about when the theme had already been composed.

However, one page earlier Shostakovich supposedly says of the same symphony:

> I merely could not help writing it. The war was going on around. I had to stay close to my people, I wanted to create an image of the country in battle, to fix it in music . . . to write a work about our days, about my contemporaries who . . . etc.*

Which of the two mutually contradictory statements should the reader take as authentic one?

Being read closely, the manuscript reveals many such discrepancies in the repetitive discussions of certain subjects, persons, and events. And this renders my warning to the eventual reader almost superfluous: not to take anything as authentically Shostakovich's and thus to create a distance between oneself and the text not unlike that Shostakovich himself preferred to maintain by signing not the manuscript but the word "read" which means no more than it means.

Significantly enough that, except for the inscription by his hand at the head of each of the eight chapters, the manuscript bears no traces of his handwriting, no alternations or even slight corrections. It would be neive to assume that Shostakovich agreed with every word written on his behalf by Mr Volkov. He of course could not have agreed with every word in my book-manuscript that I asked him to read in 1960, and yet I received it back with a thank but with no suggestions or remarks. (He did ask me to make some cuts though, which I shall describe later) Throughout the later part of his life he was very consistent in abstaining from all kinds of share, interaction, and participation. He would not argue with his critics, nor would he correct the officially inspired articles written by others, that he was made to sign as "the author" for publication in the Party press. He was consistent in creating a distance between himself and the word both about his and authorized by him. He was known to collect clips of everything printed about him, specifically with accusation and condemnations, which he considered as stupid as the most favorable reviews. It'd take a psychologist or psychiatrist to decide whether the nature of his withdrawal and detachment was arrogance, stoicism, or masochism.

What is beyond doubt, however, and what had been known to some informed people is that during his last years Shostakovich was a cripple, psychologically as well as physically. He was by no means alone to suffer from all sorts of humiliation and frustration, to see his close friends betray him or disappear, to fear for his own freedom and life, to be sadistically manipulated by the system, and used against his will, creed, and conscience. Since he stood high, close to the top, and was enormously gifted, dangerously influential, and world-wide known, he was abused and must have suffered more than others. That he actually was loyal and instrumental to the system he despised and hated made him hate and despise himself. Yet, the others, he must have thought, were no better (see, for instance—p. 284—the bitter and self-justifying assaults on the "free liberals"—Andre Malraux, Feuchtwanger, Bernard Shaw, Romain Rolland—for their friendliness to Stalinism), and to those people he was intolerant and pitiless. However, he was not too kind to those either who, like Zoshchenko, Akhmatova, and Yudina, managed to live more independent lives, to be stronger committed to their moral standards and less helpful to the state. It seems that his psychological condition was getting worse over the last years of his life. In 1960 he asked me not to quote from the statements that he had either signed and published or publicly read in 1937, 1948 and sometime later, which were imposed on him with threats or solicited by friends: "I showed lack of courage, was faint-hearted," he explained. In Mr Volkov's version, however, one finds not a single word of such self-criticism or admission of fault or weakness.

This helps understand why the manuscript, as is promissed in the beginning, deals to a great extent with other people and much less with Shostakovich's own life and work. Its tone and mood vacillate between all shades of grumbling, exasperation, contempt, anger, jealousness, irony, petty cavil, and mean hints—with regard to "others"—and pitiful boastfulness with regard to himself (see pp. 93, 129, 193, 201–1, 371); spared are only Borodin, Mussorgsky, and Glazunov who are treated rather sympathetically, the latter two partly on the common basis of alcoholic addiction, though (which, however, Shostakovich merely bragged of rather than shared).

In some portions, the intonation of the manuscript sounds quite familiar; one hears the peculiarly Shostakovich's voice and way of speaking with abrupt, scrambled phrases sprinkled with acid wits, which is how the "short sentences" at the root of the manuscript might well have sounded. The 406-page monologue put in the composer's mouth, as it were, is something very different. It is styled throughout in an acrimonious, often base language, including the large portions contributed by Mr Volkov in which he rephrases in the vernacular some of the published autobiographical materials.**

Now and then, the rather insignificant, often anecdotic story is prefaced by sluggish and waterish rumifications and moralizations. It seems equally doubtful that a man of taste and intellect could seriously and passionately compare Stalin and Toscanini as dictators (p. 29), or draw an elaborate parallel between Stalin's era and the historical situation of Boris Godunov (pp. 335–8), or discuss Stravinsky's music in proverbially non-professional terms of "like" or "dislike" (p. 40), or go into a long and amateurish reasoning on meaning in music and its social importance (p. 340–1).

Here and there, one shrugs at misquotations*** or factual mistakes****. We shall perhaps never know whether those and other blunders affecting both content and style result from errors of the composer's memory and slips of the tongue of from Mr Volkov's slips of the pen and literary faults. The former can but be commented on; the latter should have been thoroughly and carefully edited—if only there would have existed a way to tell one from the other.

The sharpness and peculiar coloring of Shostakovich's manner of speech could not suffice as the guide-line for such a massive and intensely personal monologue. In order to maintain the chosen style, Mr. Volkov had to stylize the image of the speaker himself. That was a bold and risky aspiration, and a difficult literary task—far beyond the responsibilities of a humble and cautious interpreter he would like to appear. As a result, Shostakovich appears on stage in the make-up of a misanthropic and morally degraded lumpen-intellectual, hostile and disagreeable to the entire world, seeing nothing around him but the ignoble and vile, and inclined to annoying home-bred philosophizing—a version of the character Dostoevsky portrayed in the Notes from the Underground: "I am a sick man. . . . A vicious man. Unattractive, that is. I think, my liver must be out of order."[6]

The fiction writer is free to invent whatever he likes. The trouble, however, is that "Shostakovich" is not the name of a fictitious character. Even though the traits with which Mr Volkov endowed his literary hero are not totally alien to Shostkaovich's personality, the latter cannot be reduced to the image created by the Testimony. What may deem authentic on the small scale thus turns out on the large scale to be a gross mispresentation.

The English-speaking reader, laymen and scholars alike, have had so far little access to an adquate knowledge and comprehension of Shostakovich's complex musical career and legacy, life, background, personality, psychology, and extremely involved environment. His fullest and truest Testimony is in the music he wrote, not in the careless remarks that the old, terminally ill, and psychologically disturbed man could have made shortly before he died physically, even if those remarks were preserved with word-to-word fidelity. I doubt that the literary work by Mr Volkov would bring the reader any closer to the difficult and delicate subject, or contribute to a deeper understanding of what made Shostakovich Shostakovich. I fear, on the contrary, that its content and style would rather reinforce the widespread opinion about Shostakovich's music as being stylistically obsolete but mostly displeasing.

In the page 250, Mr Volkov relates Shostakovich saying: "It is deplorable that the correspondence between A. P. Chekov and his wife was published, so intimate a correspondence that one would not like to see it printed."[7] This directly applies to the present manuscript.

[signed] Henry Orlov
August 28, 1979

*Here and elsewhere, the translations from the Russian are mine (H[enry].O[rlov].)

**See, for ex. pp. 6–7 the recollections on the childhood borrowed from the composer's "Dumy o proydennom puti" [Meditations on the path traveled] (Soviet Music 1956. Incidentally, it is hard to comprehend, pp. 7–8, how the sight of the children allegedly killed by the police in 1905 could impress Shostakovich not yet born at that time.

***Hamlet, p. 115; Fadeiev's diary, p. 258; Rimsky-Korsakov's reply to Diaghilev's invitation, p. 177; etc.

****The score of Chaikovsky opera Voyevoda destroyed by fire in the opera-house was restored from the parts in 1946 by Yuri Kochurov, not by Lamm, p. 165; "The Nose" was excluded from the repertoire after an inspired "protest of the workers" in a Leningrad newspaper, not because of too many rehearsals, p. 130.

[end of transcription] [See fig. 8.3.]

L. K. What position did you occupy then, and, so far as you know, what about Solomon Volkov?

TESTIMONY: THE MEMOIRS OF DMITRY SHOSTAKOVICH
by Solomon Volkov

Reviewed by Henry F. Orlov

The manuscript's title makes one stumble. As far as I know, in the vast literature of the kind, this is going to be the first book of memoirs written in the first person singular, which have been neither written nor dictated by the memorialist. In the letter of commission to me, the work is described as the outcome of elaborations on the materials that had been obtained in the form of "characteristically short sentences" with which Shostakovich answered to the questions Mr Volkov was permitted to ask. As Mr Volkov informs, he did not put Shostakovich's words on paper as they were spoken, but instead he took notes "in a kind of personal shorthand" and then "shaped" the notes into larger sections and chapters. Unfortunately, there are no traces left in the manuscript as to what kind of questions he asked and what Shostakovich's answers precisely were. Giving Mr Volkov full credit as a faithful and conscientious interpreter, one still has to face the fact: the firsthand quality of evidence, most valuable in memoirs, is patently missing from his version of Shostakovich's testimonies. It just cannot be taken as the testimony, likewise no court would have taken as the witness' testimony what even a closest and best-informed friend of his would have to say on his behalf.

What we are dealing with is, clearly, Mr Volkov's own original literary work based eventually on Shostakovich's statements and remarks. With regard to such a work, authenticity is a rather ambiguous criterion. It can be considered not before the questions are answered as to what kind of material the manuscript contains and what the possible impact on the reader it may have.

The work is obviously not on music and those interested in Shostakovich the composer in particular or in Soviet musical culture in general would find here but few, if any, precise and

Figure 8.3. Photocopy of Henry Orlov's Original Report

2

reliable facts which they had not already come across one way or other: no documents quoted or referred to, very few dates given, most of the names omitted, rumors and hearsay rampant. The aged and ailed composer was speaking entirely from his memory whose precision leaves much more to worry about than that of the editor. Here is one exapple. It says (p. 212) that the stupid musicologists have repeated for 30 years the opinion on the 7th and 8th as 'war symphonies:"

> The 7th was conceived before the war. And, consequently, it simply could not appear as a response to the Hitler's invasion. The "theme of invasion" is in no way related with the invasion. It was the mankind's enemies of a very different sort whom I thought about when the theme had already been composed.

However, one page earlier Shostakovich supposedly says of the same symphony:

> I merely could not help writing it. The war was going on around. I had to stay close to my people, I wanted to create an image of the country in battle, to fix it in music. . . to write a work about our days, about my contemporaries who. . . etc. *

Whis of the two mutually contradictory statements should the reader take as authentic one?

Being read closely, the manuscript reveals many such discrepancies in the repetitive discussions of certain subjects, persons, and events. And this renders my warning to the eventual reader almost superfluous: not to take anything as authentically Shostakovich's and thus to create a distance between oneself and the text not unlike that Shostakovich himself preferred to maintain by signing not the manuscript but the word "read" which means no more than it means.

* Here and elsewhere, the translations from the Russian are mine (H.O.)

Figure 8.3. continued

3 3

Significantly enough that, except for the inscription by his hand at the head of each of the eight chapters, the manuscript bears no traces of his handwriting, no alterations or even slight corrections. It would be neive to assume that Shostakovich agreed with every word written on his behalf by Mr Volkov. He of course could not have agreed with every word in my book-manuscript that I asked him to read in 1960, and yet I received it back with a thank but with no suggestions or remarks. (He did ask me to make some cuts though, which I shall describe later) Throughout the later part of his life he was very consistent in abstaining from all kinds of share, interaction, and participation. He would not argue with his critics, nor would he correct the officially inspired articles written by others, that he was made to sign as "the author" for publication in the Party press. He was consistent in creating a distance between himself and the word both about him and authorized by him. He was known to collect clips of everything printed about him, specifically with accusation and condemnations, which he considered as stupid as the most favorable reviews. It'd take a psychologist or psychiatrist to decide whether the nature of his withdrawal and detachment was arrogance, stoicism, or masochism.

What is beyond doubt, however, and what had been known to some informed people is that during his last years Shostakovich was a cripple, psychologically as well as physically. He was by no means alone to suffer from all sorts of humiliation and frustration, to see his close friends betray him or disappear, to fear for his own freedom and life, to be sadistically manipulated by the system, and used against his will, creed, and conscience. Since he stood high, close to the top, and was enormously gifted, dangerously influential, and world-wide known, he was abused and must have suffered more than others. That he actually was loyal and instrumental to the system he despised and hated made him hate and despise himself. Yet, the others, he must have thought, were no better (see, for instance--p. 284-- the bitter and self-justifying

Figure 8.3. continued

4

assaults on the "free liberals"--Andre Malraux, Feuchtwanger, Bernard Shaw, Romain Rolland--for their friendliness to Stalinism), and to those people he was intolerant and pitiless. However, he was not too kind to those either who, like Zoshchenko, Akhmatova, and Yudina, managed to live more independent lives, to be stronger committed to their moral standards and less helpful to the state. It seems that his psychological condition was getting worse over the last years of his life. In 1960 he asked me not to quote from the statements that he had either signed and published or publicly read in 1937, 1948 and sometime later, which were imposed on him with threats or solicited by friends: "I showed lack of courage, was faint-hearted," he explained. In Mr Volkov's version, however, one finds not a single word of such self-criticism or admission of fault or weakness.

This helps understand why the manuscript, as is promissed in the beginning, deals to a great extent with other people and much less with Shostakovich's own life and work. Its tone and mood vacillate between all shades of grumbling, exasperation, contempt, anger, jealousness, irony, petty cavil, and mean hints --with regard to "others"-- and pitiful boastfulness with regard to himself (see pp. 93, 129, 193, 201-2, 371); spared are only Borodin, Mussorgsky, and Glazunov who are treated rather sympathetically, the latter two partly on a common basis of alcoholic addiction, though (which, however, Shostakovich merely bragged of rather than shared).

In some portions, the intonation of the manuscript sounds quite familiar; one hears the peculiarly Shostakovich's voice and way of speaking with abrupt, scrambled phrases sprinkled with acid wits, which is how the "short sentences" at the root of the manuscript might well have sounded. The 406-page monologue put in the composer's mouth, as it were, is something very different. It is styled throughout in an acrimonious, often base language, including the large portions contributed by Mr Volkov in which he rephrases in the vernacular some of the published auto-

Figure 8.3. continued

5

biographical materials.*

Now and then, the rather insignificant, often anecdotic story is prefaced by sluggish and waterish rumifications and moralizations. It seems equally doubtful that a man of taste and intellect could seriously and passionately compare Stalin and Toscanini as dictators (p. 29), or draw an elaborate parallel between Stalin's era and the historical situation of Boris Godunov (pp. 335-8), or discuss Stravinsky's music in proverbially non-professional terms of "like" or "dislike" (p. 40), or go into a long and amateurish reasoning on meaning in music and its social importance (p. 340-1).

Here and there, one shrugs at misquotations** or factual mistakes***. We shall perhaps never know whether those and other blunders affecting both content and style result from errors of the composer's memory and slips of the tongue of from Mr Volkov's slips of the pen and literary faults. The former can but be commented on; the latter should have been thoroughly and carefully edited--if only there would have existed a way to tell one from the other.

The sharpness and peculiar coloring of Shostakovich's manner of speech could not suffice as the guide-line for such a massive and intensely personal monologue. In order to maintain the chosen style, Mr Volkov had to stylize the image of the speaker himself. That was a bold and risky aspiration, and a difficult literary task--far beyond the responsibilities of a humble and cautious interpreter he would like to appear. As a result,

* See, for ex. pp. 6-7 the recollections on the childhood borrowed from the composer's "Dumy o proydennom puti" (Soviet Music 1956. Incidentally, it is hard to comprehend, pp. 7-8, how the sight of the children allegedly killed by the police in 1905 could impress Shostakovich not yet born at that time.

** Hamlet, p. 115; Fadeiev's diary, p. 258; Rimsky-Korsakov's reply to Diaghilev's invitation, p. 177; etc.

*** The score of Chaikovsky opera Voyevoda destroyed by fire in the opera-house was restored from the parts in 1946 by Yuri Kochurov, not by Lamm, p. 165; "The Nose" was excluded from the repertoire after an inspired "protest of the workers" in a Leningrad newspaper, not because of too many rehearsals, p.130.

Figure 8.3. continued

6

Shostakovich appears on stage in the make-up of a misanthropic and morally degraded lumpen-intellectual, hostile and disagreeable to the entire world, seeing nothing around him but the ignoble and vile, and inclined to annoying home-bred philosophizing--a version of the character Dostoevsky portrayed in the Notes from the Underground: "I am a sick man... A vicious man. Unattractive, that is. I think, my liver must be out of order."

The fiction writer is free to invent whatever he likes. The trouble, however, is that "Shostakovich" is not the name of a fictitious character. Even though the traits with which Mr Volkov endowed his literary hero are not totally alien to Shostakovich's personality, the latter cannot be reduced to the image created by the Testimony. What may deem authentic on the small scale thus turns out on the large scale to be a gross mispresentation.

The English-speaking reader, laymen and scholars alike, have had so far little access to an adequate knowledge and comprehension of Shostakovich's complex musical career and legacy, life, background, personality, psychology, and extremely involved environment. His fullest and truest testimony is in the music he wrote, not in the careless remarks that the old, terminally ill, and psychologically disturbed man could have made shortly before he died physically, even if those remarks were preserved with word-to-word fidelity. I doubt that the literary work by Mr Volkov would bring the reader any closer to the difficult and delicate subject, or contribute to a deeper understanding of what made Shostakovich Shostakovich. I fear, on the contrary, that its content and style would rather reinforce the widespread opinion about Shostakovich's music as being stylistically obsolete but mostly displeasing.

In the page 250, Mr Volkov relates Shostakovich saying: "It is deplorable that the correspondence between A.P.Chekov and his wife was published, so imtimate a correspondence that one would not like to see it printed." This directly applies to the present manuscript.

August 28, 1979

Henry Orlov

Figure 8.3. continued

H. O. At that time, in the period April through August 1979, I already knew I would be working at Wesleyan University, where I would start in September. As for Volkov, so far as I know he was not working anywhere, not receiving a salary, and was apparently staking everything on publication of his book.

L. K. Don't you imagine that in picking you as the reviewer, they had in mind your university connection in America? Besides that, of course, you are the author of a wonderful book about the Shostakovich symphonies, in which you were able to convey to the reader a sense of the composer's tragic fate (let's not forget the ideological situation during the 1960s in the Soviet Union, when your book was published!), and you are a person who saw Shostakovich quite often, knew him and had a firsthand impression of him as a living personality.

H. O. I think that my academic situation played no part at all in this case. Besides, the publisher was obviously unaware of my forthcoming university appointment. I also do not think that my reputation as the author of a book and articles about Shostakovich was known to the publisher or that this had any bearing on the situation. The only thing that mattered was Solomon Volkov's taking the initiative, and he wanted to neutralize what he thought might be an opponent or a dangerous reviewer.

L. K. In other words, you are suggesting that he was fearful that a person who had been a witness to the fate of the composer and his works and who, moreover, was a Shostakovich specialist might come out in the press with a critical review or present material evidence capable of raising questions about the authenticity of *Testimony*?

H. O. Yes, that's exactly what I think. Although I must confess I have not had the slightest inclination to publish anything critical about the book. Once I had become acquainted with the manuscript, I tried to distance myself from this not very reputable enterprise.

L. K. Why are you convinced that Volkov expected a negative review from you? Perhaps just the opposite. Perhaps he expected you of all people to give this "dissident" book a positive review, and that's why he advanced your candidacy as a reviewer.

H. O. Out of the question. I was an academic researcher who specialized in Shostakovich's creative legacy, while Volkov was readying publication of sensational pseudo-memoirs. The two of us had absolutely nothing in common, and he certainly understood that.

L. K. I am holding in my hand a photograph and letters (including copies of yours) that establish that you and Volkov were on friendly terms before you received the initial letter of commission. The two of you exchanged news about your lives. It might have been expected that anything *but* mention of this publication would be in these letters. But yes, there is indeed a brief conversation about it: Volkov expresses concern that not all the material will arrive on time, and he "might be obliged to tinker around" with the book for maybe another two years (letter of 23 September 1976). In the same letter Volkov informs you that a certain publisher is interested in "the idea of Shostakovich's memoirs," as Volkov puts it, but that they asked him the name of someone who lives in the West who already knew about the existence of these memoirs while still in Russia, and Volkov says he mentioned your name as the most prominent Shostakovich specialist, adding that, should you object to this, he would immediately "take back" his words. Later on, in a letter of 10 October 1976, you express support for him, stating your willingness to write an introduction for the book. Volkov is shocked. He says he never even dreamed of the possibility of getting an introduction from Orlov (letter of 25 October 1976).

In other words, the two of you seem to be speaking about the same thing, but, in reality, about different things: you about an introduction or preface to the book, and he, quite obviously, about an introduction guaranteeing the book's authenticity (Volkov having already given your name to the publisher). Don't you think that the idea got transformed in Volkov's mind from an unrealized introduction into a commission for you to review the manuscript?

H. O. I question if it is worthwhile to attempt to reconstruct Volkov's tactics! I have the suspicion that the April proposal was put together by Volkov's lawyer on the assumption that I would refuse, because at that moment a negative review could have raised the publisher's doubts about the manuscript's authenticity. But by the end of August, when the book was already at the printers and nothing could stop its publication, the terms of the outside review could be relaxed without any risk. It seems clear that the only reason for commissioning a review that would be worth nothing to anybody was to buy my silence.

L. K. When did you actually first learn about a book of Shostakovich's memoirs?

H. O. I learned about Volkov's plan, in general terms, without any details, during my final weeks in the Soviet Union. I remember that, on 17 January 1976, after hiking to all the chancelleries and ministries involved in validating documents, I arrived at Anatoly Naiman's[b] place, where, somewhat later, Volkov also turned up. Volkov arrived after a meeting at the Union of Composers with Khrennikov who, in the presence of Irina Antonovna Shostakovich, demanded in extremely harsh language that he "put the manuscript on the table," threatening him that otherwise he would never leave the Soviet Union. Volkov was frantic. He answered, according to him, by saying that he was quite simply unable to put the manuscript on the table because it had already been sent abroad.

Afterward, two or three months later, my wife and I met Volkov and his wife, Marianna, in Rome, visited museums and enjoyed ourselves. Later Volkov turned up in New York, but I was already in Ithaca [at Cornell University]. The composer Sergei Ussachevsky[c] phoned me there and questioned me about my knowledge of Volkov and his manuscript. Then and there, I said I was willing to write an introduction to it.

A year later, in 1978, Volkov and I met in Boston, where he gave two lectures at Harvard. I was his interpreter, intermediary, and guide, and our association was entirely friendly. Volkov was even then very much in a state of consternation, because all parts of the manuscript had still not arrived. As he described it, they were arriving through various channels. He held onto these pieces of the manuscript with a passion, not letting any of them out of his hands, saying that he was surrounded by "capitalist sharks." He said that he had become more of a Marxist than he had been in the past, and that if he left the manuscript with some publisher, somebody would surely make off with it.

L. K. Did you two ever discuss the contents of the manuscript or discuss together even a single episode from the future *Testimony*?

H. O. No. Volkov never said a thing about its contents or showed me a single line of text from the manuscript. He quite consistently maintained his policy of silence not only about the contents of the manuscript but also about the circumstances of its preparation and his work on it—only afterward did I learn about all this, while reading his foreword to the Russian original, and even before that, from the letter of commission, in which the process of the work was described thoroughly and in detail.

L. K. Explain to me, please, why "Mr. Volkov would prefer that these notes be taken in English rather than in Russian." What was going on here?

H. O. Probably he was not confident of his English and wanted the lawyers, who prepared the text of the agreement with me and represented his interests, to be able to study in minute detail the text of my review, as well as my preparatory notes.

L. K. You knew, of course, that a number of newspaper and journal articles signed by Shostakovich had not actually been written by him. Tell me, what were you expecting, knowing that in a moment the memoirs of Shostakovich would be in your hands? You say in your review what you found, but what did you not find?

H. O. I knew that beginning about 1937 a number of articles signed with the name Shostakovich had not been written by him but prompted from above and signed by him because of his insufficient force of character, but I presumed that the memoirs related by Shostakovich to Volkov would possess a different character (I speak about this in my review). I was far from thinking that Volkov would take advantage of the name of Shostakovich, as others had done. I thought that every one of Shostakovich's words was precious, and the idea never occurred to me that his words might somehow be distorted, switched around, falsified. I had the highest expectations for these memoirs; this is why I had even offered my services in writing an introduction.

L. K. Today, after more than twenty years since you resettled in the United States, when nearly two decades separates you from the moment when you wrote your review, how would you at the present time, distant from this past history, assess the situation in which you found yourself back then?

H. O. All of it now belongs to the past. I recognize that it was an attempt to catch me in a mousetrap—an attempt that failed, however, because of my own gullibility.

L. K. Are you referring to your broadcast interview on BBC, which we also heard in Russia? Why, despite the publisher's ban on your speaking about the book, did your voice nevertheless resound through the airways?

H. O. My gullibility wasn't the only factor, but also a breach of professional ethics on the part of the BBC correspondent, Mr. Vladimir Kozlovsky, who telephoned and asked me what I thought about the book. He and I had been acquainted. I thought he was asking me unofficially and made no attempt to hide my opinion, which, as had already been explained to me, could in no way change the fate of the book. But Kozlovsky, as it turned out, taped our conversation and then broadcast it.

L. K. And how, as a matter of fact, did Mr. Kozlovsky find out that you might have an opinion about the manuscript? Who pointed him toward you? Did he say anything about this?

H. O. I don't know how he found out, and I don't remember now what he said in asking me about the book. I do remember, however, that it was a private conversation, not an interview. (Incidentally, it would be interesting for me to listen to that tape again, now.)

L. K. Did the broadcast occur before or after publication of the book?

H. O. I don't remember when Kozlovsky phoned. Judging by the fact that the letter from the publisher was written in August, and the book was supposed to be published in two weeks, i.e., it was already typeset and printed for all practical purposes, so it must have been September. That the broadcasting of my opinion changed nothing, and had no bearing on the fate of the book, was confirmed by later events.

L. K. Were there any repercussions on either side of the Atlantic from your radio broadcast, and, if so, what exactly were they?

H. O. The most curious repercussion occurred in the Soviet Union, and, what's more, it involved repeating my broadcast opinion (I won't swear to the accuracy of this): at the Sixth Congress of Soviet Composers, in November 1979, Khrennikov felt obliged to comment on the recently published "memoirs of Shostakovich as related to Volkov" and called the work "slanderous," adding: "even the renegade Orlov could not bear it," evidently having in mind my involuntary interview on BBC.[8] As for repercussions on this side of the ocean, one could scarcely anticipate any, since Americans did not listen to BBC broadcasts to Russia, and only Harper & Row knew about the existence of my review.

L. K. In one of our conversations, you mentioned Maxim Shostakovich's reaction.

H. O. Yes, I was told that when Maxim Shostakovich, after having emigrated from the Soviet Union with his son, Dmitri, stepped off the ramp at the airport in New York, he was asked immediately what he thought about his father's memoirs in Volkov's version. He said that in his view the book was put together from hearsay and anecdotes, and that he was in complete agreement with the opinion Mr. Orlov expressed about the book.

L. K. Are you taking into account that this statement might have been made under duress? Consider the complexities of the situation in which Shostakovich's son found himself, both for him personally and for his entire family, having made the difficult decision to emigrate in a period when every case of emigration was subject to discussion by the authorities and, in such a case as his, also by the international press! Would you be interested to know Maxim Dmitrievich's opinion now?

H. O. Hardly any statement of opinion he might have made at the time about the book, be it positive or negative, could have endangered him or anybody else. The matter was insignificant in comparison with Shostakovich's son having departed the Soviet Union for permanent residency abroad! Concerning his position today, I confess I don't concern myself either with the fate of Volkov's book or with opinions about it, because for me these opinions would change nothing.

L. K. Even if you are removed from current polemics surrounding the "Memoirs," you surely know about the existence of Allan Ho and Dmitri Feofanov's book, *Shostakovich Reconsidered*,[9] whose authors attempt to prove the authenticity of Volkov's work and do everything possible to make short shrift of the arguments of the work's critics.

H. O. I have not read Ho and Feofanov's book and know about it only from Ian MacDonald's essay-review on the subject [see Allan Ho's website, where MacDonald's essay-review is posted: http://www.siue.edu/~aho/musov/fay/fayrev6.html—L.K.]. Without getting into details, let me say that the furious attacks on their critics by those who support the Volkov "Memoirs" remind me of one of the spectacles loved by Americans—mud-wrestling.

The arguments of the defenders of the "Memoirs" abound in juggled facts, polemical exaggerations, quotations out of context, intentional misreadings, inability to reason things out, and plain conjecture. But the critics also make assertions that are not always above reproach, which opens them to attacks by the demagogues.

The specter of the KGB and the Soviet Communist Party still haunts Volkov's defenders, who seem blinded by the "discovery" that Shostakovich was at odds with the Soviet regime, so they attempt to portray him as an out-and-out dissident. But he was neither a dissident nor a faithful servant of the Party and government. In some sense, often depending on the circumstance, he was either one or the other. His character, his behavior, his situation, and the role he played in both the musical and public life of the USSR were all pathologically ambivalent, which precludes a one-sided assessment. This is why Volkov's "Memoirs" are a falsification, when all is said and done, despite the fact that they reproduce Shostakovich's bilious tone and brusque intonation quite believably, as well as repeat a number of the well-known tales he himself told.

L. K. At the end of your review, you mention the perception, widespread in the seventies, of Shostakovich's music as stylistically outmoded. Such a judgment appears to be rather odd now, when his music has gained admirers throughout the world, and interest in him as a composer has grown steadily. But I, too, remember that period, the Western critics then, and the cultural situation at the time. I am reminded, as a point of comparison, of a passage from Lillian Libman's book about Stravinsky that recounts how American university students and many young orchestral musicians saluted Robert Craft and honored him as an expert in the field of avant-garde music, but not at all as Stravinsky's associate.[10] What sort of impression did you have at that period, based on your association with students and colleagues; what did they know about Shostakovich, how well and how much of his music did they know, and were they interested in him as a personality?

H. O. I did not teach Russian and Soviet music either at Cornell or at Harvard, so Shostakovich's name came up rarely. True, at Cornell I tried to acquaint my students with the Eighth Symphony and, in response, saw blank stares and puzzled faces: the music said nothing to them. Only after I related the circumstances under which the symphony was composed, the motivation for the work, the composer's conception of it, then played it for them again, only then did they respond in a manner that exhibited somewhat more comprehension.

I should say, in general, that my impression at the end of the seventies and beginning of the eighties was of Shostakovich being viewed in the States as if through the wrong end of binoculars. Other major European composers were perceived similarly—Schoenberg, Webern, and the late Stravinsky. At that time, interest in Shostakovich's music was negligible, or so it seemed to me, and his music was performed much less often than, say, the music of Prokofiev. It is impossible to appreciate Shostakovich's music without having the "key" to it; one must know a great deal about the circumstances of its composition and know how to decipher its secret meaning. I have to say, generally speaking, that in the States at the time an extremely naïve if not actually disrespectful attitude toward Shostakovich prevailed. Patricia Blake, who reviewed *Testimony* in the weekly news magazine *Time*,[11] admitted that Volkov's book had been an astonishing revelation to her, that before reading it she had considered Shostakovich to be a Soviet composer in the full sense of the word, a pet of the regime, and that she had never even suspected that he might have felt internal conflicts, much less conflicts with the regime, but that now she understood that Shostakovich had been an unhappy man who lived in dissent with himself.

L. K. Does this not mean that *Testimony* fulfilled some sort of historical mission?

H. O. The appearance of Volkov's book almost twenty years ago unarguably created a fairly big surge of interest in Shostakovich among various groups associated with music in the States. However, to speak even then about its "historical mission" would have been premature at best. Sensational revelations and exposés pop up time and again in the American book market, and they're quickly forgotten. Sensation with a touch of scandal is a sure-fire recipe for immediate fame and quick money here in the States. I do not presume to judge how seriously anyone today takes Shostakovich's portrait against the backdrop of Soviet reality as painted by Volkov. His book could not have been a revelation even then to English-language reader-specialists familiar with, say, Boris Schwarz's capital study[12] in which the musical life of the USSR and the situation of people involved in culture and art is abundantly documented and described "from within." The single perceptible trace left today by Volkov's book can be found in the absurd debates between its supporters and its critics whom the former see as the heirs of the KGB.

L. K. Henry, in any serious work on Shostakovich in any language, but especially in Russian, be they academic theses or scholarly articles and books, your name surfaces as a Shostakovich specialist, and one of the most interesting up to the present. Your book *The Symphonies of Shostakovich*, is regarded as not only a triumph of talent over standardized Soviet thinking but also a perspicacious commentary on the composer's works. As a consequence of this, you are continually invited to participate in conferences dedicated to Shostakovich, and attempts are made repeatedly to attract you back to work in this area. For instance, Dr. Rosamund Bartlett, the organizer of the outstanding conference at the University of Michigan in 1994,[d] which featured performances by the Borodin Quartet and special exhibitions devoted to Shostakovich, consulted me during the planning of the conference about how you might be invited and agree to come and give a talk. In St. Petersburg we also attempted to interest you in our conference, "Shostakovich in a Changing World" (1994). Although I anticipated ahead of time your answer to our inquiry, we nevertheless made the attempt, hoping you might agree, but you refused. Please explain why.

H. O. The reason for my refusal was entirely personal and, in any case, had nothing whatever to do with my feelings about Shostakovich.

Thirteen years ago, after finishing work on the English version of *The Tree of Music*, I put a period at the end of my career as a musicologist, having decided that forty years devoted to musicology was quite enough and that now it was time to do something else. This decision was, to some extent, inescapable: I perceived a complete incompatibility between my understanding of the ideas and aims of musicology and the understanding that prevailed in American universities, and among publishers and journals. This is why I now desist from any attempts at reincarnating myself as a musicologist, even as a Shostakovich specialist.

L. K. In other words, your experience in reviewing *Testimony* has no connection at all with your refusal.

H. O. Not the slightest. The review was written when I was still active as a musicologist. But now, it is nothing more than a document from my archive.

L. K. I am grateful to you, Henry, for this conversation and for allowing me to publish these documents from your archive—the letters and the review. I hope that they will be of interest to readers of this volume. Thank you!

November 1997–August 1998.

Notes

1. Solomon Volkov, *Testimony: The Memoirs of Dmitri Shostakovich*, as related to and edited by Solomon Volkov, trans. Antonina W. Bouis (New York: Harper & Row, 1979).

2. The exceptions are two interviews with Solomon Volkov: Galina Drubachevskaia, "Zdes' chelovek sgorel" [A man burned out here], *Muzykal'naia akademiia*, no. 3 (1992): 3–12; and Lili Pann, "Muzyka prosvechivaet cheloveka naskvoz' " [Music illuminates the man through and through], *Literaturnaia gazeta*, 2 July 1997, p. 14.

3. M. I. Druskin, foreword to *Drevo muzyki* [The tree of music] by Gennrikh [Henry] Orlov (Washington, D.C.: H. A. Frager, 1992; St. Petersburg: Sovetskii kompozitor, 1992), p. vi.

4. Mirra [*sic*] Meilakh, then wife of Orlov.

5. *Testimony* was published within two months, on 31 October 1979.

6. F. M. Dostoevskii, *Sobranie sochinenii* [Collected works], ed. L. P. Grossman et al., 10 vols., vol. 4: *Proizvedeniia, 1846–59* [Works, 1846–59] (*Zapiski iz podpolia* [Notes from the underground]) (Moscow: Gosudarstvennoe izdatel'stvo khudozhestvennoi literatury, 1956), p. 133.

7. D. Shostakovich, "Samyi blizkii" [One of my favorites], *Literaturnaia gazeta*, 28 January 1960; reprinted in L. Danilevich, *Dmitri Shostakovich* (Moscow: Sovetskii kompozitor, 1967), p. 35.

8. This remark is not documented in the records of the Sixth Congress of Soviet Composers, 20–26 November 1979; perhaps it was a "comment from the hall."

9. Allan B. Ho and Dmitry Feofanov, *Shostakovich Reconsidered*, with an overture by Vladimir Ashkenazy ([London]: Toccata, 1998).

10. Lillian Libman, *And Music at the Close: Stravinsky's Last Years. A Personal Memoir* (New York: Norton, 1972), p. 123 and passim.

11. Patricia Blake, "Music Was His Final Refuge," *Time*, 29 October 1979, pp. 114–X9.

12. Boris Schwarz, *Music and Musical Life in Soviet Russia, 1917–1970* (London: Barrie & Jenkins, 1972; New York: Norton, 1972); reprinted and enlarged, *Music and Musical Life in Soviet Russia, 1917–1981* (Bloomington: Indiana University Press, 1983).

Editor's Notes

a. The text printed here replicates Orlov's original typewritten text, as can be seen by comparing it with the photocopy of the original report reproduced in fig. 8.3; typographical errors, misspellings, and non-idiomatic expressions *have not been corrected.* Only Orlov's internal notes, identified by asterisks (*, **, etc.) have been transposed and reproduced at the end of the complete printed text, instead of at the bottom of individual pages, as in the original typed report.

b. Anatoly Naiman (b. 1935?) is a Leningrad poet, essayist, and literary figure who was a friend of fellow poets Joseph Brodsky and Evgeny Rein; at one time Naiman was Anna Akhmatova's private secretary.

c. Orlov refers to composer "Sergei" Ussachevsky, but the composer in question is almost certainly the Russian-born American composer Vladimir Ussachevsky, one of the founders of the Columbia-Princeton Electronic Music Center.

d. The conference referred to is Shostakovich: The Man and His Age, 1906–1975, University of Michigan, 25–30 January 1994.

9

An Answer to Those Who Still Abuse Shostakovich (2000)

IRINA SHOSTAKOVICH

The *New York Times* printed the following preface to Irina Shostakovich's article:

Irina Shostakovich is the widow of Dmitri Shostakovich. They married in 1962, and she was his third wife. The following are her reflections, translated by Irina Roberts, on her husband's life and posthumous reputation.

Dmitri Shostakovich was born in 1906. He enjoyed early success as a composer, but his relations with the Soviet regime deteriorated. In 1936, his opera *Ledi Makbet Mtsenskogo uezda* [Lady Macbeth of the Mtsensk District] op. 29 (1930–32) was condemned in *Pravda* as "muddle instead of music," and he was denounced by friends and colleagues. His Fifth Symphony restored his standing in 1937. In 1948 he was denounced

---

First published in the *New York Times*, Sunday, 20 August 2000, pp. AR 27 and 31. Abridged versions of the article appeared earlier in the Russian-language newspaper *Moskovskie novosti*, 8–14 August 2000, p. 15; and the next day, 9 August 2000, it was printed by the newspaper's English-language affiliate, *Moscow News*, 9–15 August 2000, p. 11, in that paper's own translation. The *New York Times* version is reprinted here by permission of the *New York Times* and the author.

again, with others, for "formalist" tendencies and forced to recant. Though the climate of repression relaxed somewhat after the death of Stalin in 1953, recriminations persisted, and Shostakovich bore the marks of trauma to the end of his life.

In 1973, he was named as a signatory to a letter denouncing the dissident Russian physicist Andrei Sakharov. Earlier, he had been named as a signatory to a statement demanding the release of the Greek composer Mikis Theodorakis, who was imprisoned by Greece's right-wing regime from 1967 to 1970.

Mrs. Shostakovich refers to Leo Arnshtam, a film director, and Isaak Glikman, a drama critic and historian. Both were friends of Shostakovich's throughout his lifetime. Lev Lebedinsky, a musicologist, befriended Shostakovich in the 1950s.

The book to which she refers, *Testimony: The Memoirs of Dmitri Shostakovich*, as related to and edited by Solomon Volkov, was published in 1979 by Harper & Row and has since been the subject of a lively controversy over its authenticity.

Moscow

Dmitri Shostakovich died twenty-five years ago this month. Since then, his music has been alive and has gained in popularity; the number of his fans has risen in leaps and bounds, and his music has found its way into the hearts of people in many different countries. At present, young performers are taking the place of Shostakovich's deceased contemporaries and lending their skills and talent to the art of performing his music.

Shostakovich was loved and recognized in the music world ever since his youth; that music world tried to protect and shelter him from the wrath of his persecutors during the more difficult times, even when it was dangerous and the forces were unequal. By defending him, people who themselves were oppressed and scared were defending their own human dignity and their right to create. Only very few of them had the courage to protest openly, but most musicians persistently rebuffed all the attacks, mockery, and incitement mounted against him. Of course, there were also rabid persecutors who were eager to please and expected to benefit from such persecution, as well as born informers and those who were simply easily persuaded and not very bright.

Dmitri Shostakovich was as defenseless as the rest of us, but he had much more to lose. He had to worry about the future of his work, which was treated shamelessly. Consequently, he considered it more important than anything else to be worthy of his talent and to develop it, evading his enemies and misleading them whenever possible. In the process, he managed to help many other people, protecting and supporting them, and for this he is remembered with gratitude.

But not by everyone. Even now some people nurse grievances and feel offended that he did not help promote them, even though it seemed to them he could have.

Then there are those who believe they are as talented as he was but think that he was far too cunning and smart, and that they were innocent and defenseless; that he prevented them from making it to the top by the mere fact of his existence.

There was yet another category: young people with progressive views, who have aged by now, who tried to push Shostakovich forward and force him to present their ideas in a way they themselves were too cowardly to do. Furthermore, they were prepared to follow him, hide behind him, while striving to achieve their most ambitious goals.

Everyone who knew the Soviet way of life has his or her own ideas about it, but it needs a lot of courage to defend your ideas personally and not use someone else as a shield.

But now Dmitri Shostakovich is gone, and anything goes. The time has come to exploit his name, even to the point of abusing and humiliating his memory. Things are easier now, and people have found their voices. The dead are defenseless.

They are now recalling what happened and what didn't and, by attributing various scandalous remarks to the great composer, are finding it easy to settle old scores, to appropriate his ideas and pass them off as their own.

Then, too, by collecting true and false testimonies from his aging contemporaries and putting them through the grinder, people can create any picture they wish and documentarily "prove" that Shostakovich had no talent, that he was cunning and knew how to cheat, that he was weak and dishonest. But it is also possible to prove the opposite.

The story of his life has been turned into a battlefield. Of course, everything and everyone is pulled into the line of fire. They shout obscenities on the Internet, publish articles, and write books and plays about Shostakovich; someone even went to the trouble of composing an opera about him.

These people were and are still trying, but failing, to establish their right to possess him. And it does not matter whether they shout from the reactionary positions of party ideology or act under the avant-garde flag; the Right and the Left meet in the end.

Among them are some of his talented pupils who were professionally unsuccessful, envious colleagues, and music critics who are interested in scandal above all else. Although they do not know or understand the historical evidence involved, they are not ashamed to repeat any lies and pass them off as established facts.

I take the liberty of claiming that people who have no morals, which are vital in all human relations, will never understand Shostakovich and his music. Ask yourself before you accuse someone else: how would you have behaved at such a difficult time and in such difficult circumstances?

The only consolation is that no one can ever hurt or upset Dmitri Shostakovich again, and time will eventually set everything right.

Volkov and Testimony

During interviews, I am often asked about the veracity of the book *Testimony* by Solomon Volkov, published as Shostakovich's memoirs. Here is what I think.

Mr. Volkov worked for the magazine *Sovetskaia muzyka*, where Shostakovich was a member of the editorial board. As a favor to Boris Tishchenko, his pupil and colleague, Shostakovich agreed to be interviewed by Mr. Volkov, whom he knew little about, for an article to be published in *Sovetskaia muzyka*. There were three interviews; each lasted two to two and a half hours, no longer, since Shostakovich grew tired of extensive chat and lost interest in conversation. Two of the interviews were held in the presence of Mr. Tishchenko. The interviews were not taped.

Mr. Volkov arrived at the second interview with a camera (Mr. Volkov's wife, a professional photographer, always took pictures of Mr. Volkov with anyone who might become useful in the future) and asked Mr. Tishchenko and me to take pictures "as a keepsake." He brought a photograph to the third interview and asked Shostakovich to sign it. Shostakovich wrote his usual words: "To dear Solomon Maseyevich [*sic*] Volkov, in fond remembrance. D. Shostakovich 13.XI.1974." Then, as if sensing something amiss, he asked for the photograph back and, according to Mr. Volkov himself, added: "In memory of our talks on Glazunov, Zoshchenko and Meyerhold. D. Sh."

That was a list of the topics covered during the interviews. It shows that the conversation was about music and literary life in prewar Leningrad (now St. Petersburg) and nothing more. Some time later,

Mr. Volkov brought Shostakovich a typed version of their conversations and asked him to sign every page at the bottom.[a] It was a thin sheaf of papers, and Shostakovich, presuming he would see the proof sheets, did not read them. I came into Shostakovich's study as he was standing at his desk signing those pages without reading them. Mr. Volkov took the pages and left.

I asked Shostakovich why he had been signing every page, as it seemed unusual. He replied that Mr. Volkov had told him about some new censorship rules according to which the publishers would not accept his material without a signature. I later learned that Mr. Volkov had already applied for an exit visa to leave the country and was planning to use that material as soon as he was abroad.

Soon after that, Shostakovich died, and Mr. Volkov put his plans into further action.

Mr. Volkov had told a lot of people about those pages, boasting his journalist's luck. This threatened to complicate his exit. It seems that he managed to contrive an audience with Enrico Berlinguer, secretary of the Italian Communist Party, who happened to be visiting Moscow, showed him the photograph signed by Shostakovich, and complained that he, Mr. Volkov, a friend of Shostakovich, was not allowed to leave the country for political reasons. In any case, an article about Mr. Volkov appeared in the Italian Communist newspaper *L'Unita*.[b] Apparently, it did the trick.

I met Mr. Volkov at a concert and asked him to come and see me (but without his wife, as he had wanted) and leave me a copy of the material he had, which was unauthorized (since it had never been read by Shostakovich). Mr. Volkov replied that the material had already been sent abroad, and if Mr. Volkov were not allowed to leave, the material would be published with additions. He soon left the country, and I never saw him again.

Later on, I read in a booklet that came with the phonograph record of the opera *Ledi Makbet Mtsenskogo uezda* [Lady Macbeth of the Mtsensk District] conducted by Mstislav Rostropovich, which was released abroad, that Mr. Volkov was Shostakovich's assistant with whom he had written his memoirs. Elsewhere I read that when Shostakovich was at home alone, he would phone Mr. Volkov and they would see each other in secret.

Only someone with rich fantasy could invent something like that; it was not true, if only because at that time Shostakovich was very ill and was never left on his own. And we lived outside Moscow at the dacha.

There was no opportunity for secret meetings. Mr. Volkov's name is nowhere to be found in Shostakovich's correspondence of the time, in his letters to Isaak Glikman, for example.

Mr. Volkov found a publisher in the United States, and the advertising campaign began. Extracts from the book appeared in a German magazine and reached Russia, where at that time there was state monopoly on intellectual property. The Soviet copyright agency VAAP asked for verification of Shostakovich's signature. American experts confirmed its authenticity. The book was published. Each chapter of the book was preceded by words written in Shostakovich's hand: "Have read. Shostakovich."

I can vouch that this was how Shostakovich signed articles by different authors planned for publication. Such material was regularly delivered to him from *Sovetskaia muzyka* magazine for review, then the material was returned to the editorial department, where Mr. Volkov was employed. Unfortunately, the American experts, who did not speak Russian, were unable and certainly had no need to correlate Shostakovich's words with the contents of the text.

As for the additions, Mr. Volkov himself told me that he had spoken to a lot of different people about Shostakovich, in particular to Lev Lebedinsky, who later became an inaccurate memoirist and with whom Shostakovich had ended all relations a long time before. A friend of Shostakovich's, Leo Arnshtam, a cinema director, saw Mr. Volkov at his request, and Arnshtam later regretted it. A story about a telephone conversation with Stalin was written from his words. All this was included in the book as though it were coming from Shostakovich himself.

The book was translated into many languages and published in a number of countries, except Russia. Mr. Volkov at first claimed that the American publishers were against the Russian edition, then that the royalties in Russia were not high enough, then that those offering to publish it in Russia were crooks, and, finally, that he had sold his manuscript to a private archive and it was not available anymore. Retranslation into Russian relieves the author of responsibility and permits new liberties.

Other "Signatures"

Dmitri Shostakovich was accused of signing a letter from the intelligentsia against the academician Andrei Sakharov published in 1973 in *Pravda.* Yes, Shostakovich's name is among those signatories, but he never signed the letter. On the morning of the day in question, I answered a multitude of phone calls from *Pravda*, first saying that Shostakovich was out, then saying he was at the dacha. When they said they were going to send a car to the dacha, we simply went out and did not come back until evening when the issue of the paper was already in print. Nevertheless, Shostakovich's name appeared among the signatories.

Some time ago we tried to obtain the original letter, but *Pravda* refused us, while admitting "there was such a practice at that time." But I know it without being told. The same thing had happened earlier with a letter in support of Mikis Theodorakis. At that time Shostakovich was in the hospital. There was no use questioning the signature after it had already happened.

Editor's Notes

a. The pages of the *Testimony* typescript on which Shostakovich affixed his signature were signed at the top. See Fay, "Volkov's *Testimony* Reconsidered," chapter 2 of the present volume.

b. The Italian newspaper *La Stampa* is named here in Irina Shostakovich's article as printed in the *New York Times*, but someone at the *New York Times* made this error, not Mrs. Shostakovich. The earlier Russian-language text of Mrs. Shostakovich's article reads simply, "An article about Mr. Volkov, with the very same photograph, appeared in the Italian Communist Party newspaper. That did the trick." The specific name of the Party newspaper is not mentioned at all (Irina Shostakovich, a letter, "Miortvye bezzashchitny?" [Are the dead defenseless?], *Moskovskie novosti*, 8–14 August 2000, p. 11). The English-language translation of the text, published the next day in the Russian newspaper's affiliate, *Moscow News*, reads, "The Italian Communist daily *L'Unita* published a feature on Volkov with the same photograph. That did the trick" (Irina Shostakovich, "The Dead Are Defenseless?" *Moscow News*, 9–15 August 2000, p. 11).

10

On Solomon Volkov and *Testimony* (1988, 1997)

BORIS TISHCHENKO

From an interview with Boris Tishchenko published in *Sovetskaia kul'tura,* 15 October 1988[a]

I have been handed a question regarding the book published in the West about D. D. Shostakovich, its author being Solomon Volkov. The writer of the note asks how I respond to this book today.

Today, just as yesterday, I respond negatively to any sort of falsification. I can swear that this book is a falsification, my hand on the Bible. I was present during Shostakovich's conversation with the author. Shostakovich had said to me, "You see, he insists on these meetings, please attend them." So I attended. What Shostakovich said could be put into the thinnest notebook, whereas what came out abroad comprises some four hundred pages. Before his departure [from the USSR], the author swore that he would leave me a copy of the notes he had taken during his conversation with Shostakovich. But he never did.

The book contains an enormous collection of outlandish stories [*rosskazni*] about Shostakovich. For instance, monstrous pronouncements about Meyerhold's family and disparaging words about Akhmatova are attributed to Shostakovich.

After my article in *Literaturnaia gazeta*,[b] the Composers Union received a telegram addressed to me: "Congratulations on your joining the ranks of Soviet Composers. S. Volkov." I answered: "I go the way of those who compose symphonies, not those who write pseudo memoirs. Next time we meet, let's discuss the matter like real men."

Comments on Volkov from Tishchenko's commentary to *The Letters of Dmitri Dmitrievich Shostakovich to Boris Tishchenko* (1997)[c]

Another far more cynical event presented to the world by Dmitri Dmitrievich's premature death . . . was the commercial enterprise rushed through by that efficient journalist and music hanger-on named Volkov. Removed to a safe distance, he published notes made during conversations with Shostakovich, which, after numerous and insistent requests I had facilitated in due time, but not without resistance from D.D. The latter agreed only on the condition that I be present during these conversations. And I agreed only on the condition that a copy of the notes be provided to me. Naturally I received no such copy. Meanwhile, the modest and reserved reminiscences about years of childhood and youth got puffed up into a very plump volume, padded with third-hand stories and shameless self-promotion. Dmitri Dmitrievich is represented as some sort of malicious dissident. I will never forget the author's poorly concealed impatience for D.D.'s death. The whole affair caused Irina Antonovna much unpleasantness ("If you want to play havoc, play it with your *own* hands; is this anything other than setting Shostakovich out in front of you like a shield?" she observed). And Maxim as well. He got so fed up with the endless quizzing and querying that he mimeographed copies of his opinion and passed them around to anybody who wanted them, including me. He says pointedly, "the book includes plenty from its true author, Solomon Volkov, which he pulled together from hearsay and conversations with third parties, elaborated and interpreted in his own style, but then placed into the mouth of Shostakovich. A big part of these memoirs amounts to a retelling of tales heard from other individuals presented as if they had been heard from Shostakovich himself."

"Where did this 'hanger-on' come from?" asked Maxim. "I never saw him at our dinner table."

Questions about these "memoirs" continue to plague me to the present day, so I have worked out a short and pithy formulaic answer: These are not the memoirs of Shostakovich, not even a book by Volkov about Shostakovich, but a book by Volkov about Volkov.

Editor's Notes

a. "Velikie Khudozhniki" [Great artists], an interview with Boris Tishchenko, *Sovetskaia kul'tura*, 15 October 1988, p. 8.

b. Tishchenko is referring to the letter to the editor headlined "*Zhalkaia poddelka*" [A pitiful fake], which he and five other students and friends of Shostakovich signed, published in *Literaturnaia gazeta*, 14 November 1979, p. 8. Selection 4 in the present volume is a reprint of the letter.

c. *Pis'ma Dmitria Dmitrievicha Shostakovicha Borisu Tishchenko* [The letters of Dmitri Dmitrievich Shostakovich to Boris Tishchenko], with the addressee's commentary and reminiscences (St. Petersburg: Kompozitor, 1997), pp. 48–49.

11

The Regime and Vulgarity (1999)

ELENA BASNER

This letter is prompted by the publication in *Izvestiia* (13 May 1999) of the article by Alexander Zhurbin, "Sledstvie zakoncheno—ne zabud'te!" [The inquest is ended—don't forget it!], an interview with the authors of the new book about Shostakovich [*Shostakovich Reconsidered*], the text of which amounts to an apologia for Solomon Volkov's book [*Testimony*].

I will not deny that I felt very receptive toward this publication, if only because it touched on people exceedingly dear to me: my father, Veniamin Basner, my father's closest friend, Moisei Weinberg, and, of course, Dmitri Dmitrievich Shostakovich himself. I am hard-pressed here to find words that can express the true nature of the high regard for Dmitri Dmitrievich held by my father and the composer's numerous students and friends. Suffice it to say that for me, as best as I can remember my feelings at the time, he was (and he remains) the embodiment of all that is most worthy and noble in humankind, and his music may well be the greatest artistic revelation of the twentieth century. I do not know what Papa might have done after reading this publication—maybe he would simply have been upset. But since both he and Moisei

---

"Vlast' i poshlost' " [The regime and vulgarity] appeared as a letter to the editor, *Izvestiia*, 8 June 1999, p. 5.

Samuilovich Weinberg are no longer able to make a statement about the matter, I myself have decided to comment on a number of points raised in the article.

I shall begin with a concrete example, obviously not the most important one for the interviewer but paramount for me. Speaking about the letter in *Literaturnaia gazeta*,[a] Mr. Zhurbin asserts that none of the signers of the letter "had at that moment read the book, and five of them even admitted that they had signed the letter under duress." I can declare that this is not true. A representative of Tikhon Nikolaevich Khrennikov, who was president of the Composers Union at the time, arrived at my father's place and spent the entire day reading Volkov's book aloud to him and Boris Ivanovich Tishchenko, translating as he read "from the page." I myself was present and clearly recall their reaction to the book. They were indignant.

Later on, when they sent me a copy of Volkov's book at my request, Papa and I often talked about it. What most aroused his indignation was that Volkov placed all sorts of anecdotes and tales that had made the rounds among musicians into the mouth of Shostakovich. Dmitri Dmitrievich, who frankly could not stand anecdotes in general, is transformed into some sort of viperous, rancorous old man who knows "something bad about everybody"; it is hard to imagine anything more antithetical to Shostakovich!

I shall not touch on the factual side of the issue, which Boris Ivanovich Tishchenko and, of course, Irina Antonovna Shostakovich are more knowledgeable about than anyone (the former having personally introduced Solomon Volkov to Dmitri Dmitrievich after Volkov's numerous requests). I wholly and completely believe them; in other words, I am convinced that the "confessions" of Shostakovich are smoke and mirrors, a hoax pure and simple.

A more complicated matter: I might have liked Volkov's book had it been written in the third-person narrative, not the first. It might have been a very good and honest book. But let us agree that it is one thing to write *about* a person and quite another to have the person say whatever *you* want him to say. Volkov certainly understood that as merely the author of the latest monograph on Shostakovich he would not be nearly as interesting as the "person who published the authentic Testimony" of Shostakovich himself.

I want to bring up yet another point that I heard from my father. "Have you ever thought about why Volkov will never agree to publishing his book in Russian?" he asked me, back in those glorious years of Perestroika. "Because anybody who has heard Dmitri Dmitrievich's living voice even once would realize right away that it is a forgery. The book works only in translation." And it is true. Shostakovich's speech was so expressive, pungent, and idiosyncratic (with a stress on the second syllable) that to imitate it is practically impossible. I understood this when I read Galina Vishnevskaya's memoirs. I had mixed feelings about them, but on the page where she describes how Shostakovich took part in an exam on Marxism-Leninism she draws an absolutely living portrait of him. It is clear right away that the story is really his, with his inimitable "delo ko shcham, ko shcham" [it was time for *shchi* (cabbage soup), for *shchi*], "ei by na travku, ponimaete" [she ought to be outside on the grass, understand] (unfortunately, Vishnevskaya's book is not at hand and I am quoting from memory, but I can even see Dmitri Dmitrievich at that moment, as if he were alive, nervously wringing his hands).[b] Volkov could never imitate that. But in translation, of course, all this is smoothed out.

In a word, turning back to where I started: Papa, Weinberg, and Tishchenko were absolutely sincere in their rejection of Volkov's book and his behavior (although I think Boris Ivanovich Tishchenko, if he so wishes, can express his own perspective on the subject). And I fail to understand the arithmetical law that supports an alleged admission by five of the six signers of the letter.[c] As for any pressure exerted on them, it is absolutely out of the question, based on what I know. Still, the tendency toward a cliché is enshrined in human nature: if "stagnation is abloom"[d] and if there is a collective letter from those years, it must mean that the "signatories" of the letter acted contrary to their conscience and their sense of honor! Believe me, this is not what happened here.

I have a few more words to say in closing. Given a phenomenon such as Shostakovich, I feel sorry for those people—musicians and nonmusicians—for whom the most important question is whether he was "pro-Soviet" or "anti-Soviet." (For some odd reason, the episode with [Joseph] Brodsky described by Dovlatov comes to mind: "If Yevtushenko is against collective farms, then I'm *for* them," as well as the phrase, "After the Communists, I hate *most of all* the anti-Communists!") I am sorry for those who are told that "the finale of Shostakovich's Fifth Symphony is not a hymn to the triumph of good over evil but, in fact, the opposite" and that "the scherzo of the Tenth Symphony was conceived as a musical portrait of Stalin!"[e] What a primitive, protozoan level of understanding! And how vulgar.

Very likely I started to write this letter just to say that what is most unbearable in our life nowadays is vulgarity—thick, fetid vulgarity gurgling all around. Now they are even trying to pour it over one who, not being a fighter against the regime, resisted vulgarity in all its forms with the very essence of his being. This is unworthy. It insults not only the memory of a great musician but also those who love his music. The scherzo of the Tenth Symphony is a work of genius and will always be a protest against vulgarity, as all of Shostakovich's music is.

I should have liked very much to maintain a dispassionate tone here, but, since it appears I am unable to do so, I shall close my letter with the following: I feel sorry for everyone involved—for Volkov, for Zhurbin, and for those poor naïve Americans—for whom this new bit of a book was so obviously intended: just think, to believe for so many years that "Shostakovich loved the Soviet regime" and suddenly to discover that "Shostakovich did not love the Soviet regime" (exactly so, even grammatically!). Well, if you take all this seriously as scientific fact, I can only repeat yet again, I feel very sorry for you all.

Respectfully,
Elena Basner

Editor's Notes

Elena Basner is the daughter of the composer Veniamin Basner, who was a close friend of Shostakovich. In her letter to the editor of *Izvestiia*, translated here, Basner disputes the claim that her father and the five other friends and former students of Shostakovich, who signed the 1979 letter calling *Testimony* a "pitiful fake," were forced to sign. See note c below.

a. Basner has in mind "Zhalkaia poddelka" [A pitiful fake], *Literaturnaia gazeta*, 14 November 1979, p. 8. A translation of this letter is included in chapter 4 of the present volume.

b. In her memoirs Vishnevskaya provides the complete context for the comments quoted by Basner, which the latter found so utterly characteristic of Shostakovich. Vishnevskaya recalls, "Shostakovich liked to tell how he monitored exams on the history of the Communist Party being taken by students at the Moscow Conservatory (that was before he was fired in 1948)," and she recounts an anecdote Shostakovich related: "My job was to sit there quietly while the professor who taught the course administered the exam to each student. Well, I sat there for several hours, until the last students were finishing—it was time for cabbage soup [*delo ko shcham*, i.e., it was late and time for a bite to eat]. It was spring, the birds were chirping outside, the sun was pouring through the window, and I noticed one girl sitting there suffering. What anguish was in her eyes! She probably didn't know a thing. I thought: what a pretty girl, no doubt a singer, and there she is suffering, you know, inside the classroom, when she ought to be outside on the grass, on the grass, understand! [*ei by na travku, na travku, ponimaete*]." Quoted, with the editor's corrections of the translated text, from Vishnevskaya's memoirs, *Galina*, translated by Guy Daniels (New York: Harcourt Brace Jovanovich, 1984), pp. 239–40.

c. In reference to the claim that five had "admitted that they had signed the letter under duress," when this author knows firsthand of three who did *not* sign under duress.

d. In reference to the period of so-called stagnation under Brezhnev.

e. See *Testimony*, pp. 183 and 141, and *Shostakovich Reconsidered*, pp. 165 and 168.

12

Shostakovich's World Is Our World (1998)

MSTISLAV ROSTROPOVICH TALKS WITH
MANASHIR YAKUBOV

M.Y. During the year that marked Shostakovich's ninetieth anniversary [1996], you revived *Ledi Makbet Mtsenskogo uezda* [Lady Macbeth of the Mtsensk District] in its original form in Petersburg and Moscow, and you then arranged a Russian festival of Shostakovich's work according to a program that he himself had drawn up with you years ago (after, in fact, the first big festival of his music held in England). It has now become clear that this has been as much a century for music as a century for literature. It has given us many wonderful composers. In Russian music alone, there are Scriabin and Rachmaninoff and Prokofiev. . . . Yet you have chosen Shostakovich once again for another big festival. Why? Why does the work of a composer who was working during the middle years of the century in a totalitarian society which was alien and incom-

---

Taken from the *Programme Book* for the London Symphony Orchestra's "*Shostakovich 1906–1975*" series, 19 February–28 October 1998. Translation by Jenefer Coates and Andrew Huth. The London Symphony Orchestra (LSO) holds the copyright for the English translation of the interview. Reprinted by permission of the LSO.

Figure 12.1. Shostakovich and Rostropovich at the Time of the Premiere of the Second Concerto for Cello and Orchestra, 25 September 1966

prehensible to most people elsewhere still manage to excite not only his own fellow-countrymen but the whole world as well?

M.R. It seems to me that if you consider historical developments in, say, the nineteenth century or even earlier, then liberation from tyranny was evidently beginning to occur in many countries throughout the world. A new, more democratic way of life was starting to emerge. . . .

In the twentieth century, maybe as a result of the First World War, certain intellectual ideas began to ferment. Perhaps they had started even before that time, after all Shostakovich wrote *The Year 1905* [Symphony No. 11 in G Minor op. 103 (1957)] and we should trust to his judgment, because it was he who gave emotional meaning, and described in a musical language that could be understood without an interpreter, the entire history of the Soviet Union and Russia. The intellectual ideas prompted the poor to push—I can't find a more exact word—to agitate, in the simplest of terms, for the same rewards as the rich. But neither work nor talent came into account. The slogan was quite simple: "We are all equal." And Lenin simplified it still further: "Grab back from the grabbers!" As a result, one-sixth of the Earth's surface suffered terrible tragedy—with starvation, cannibalism, concentration camps, mass executions, and so on.

. . . The plague of communism swept like a hurricane through a whole lot of countries, not only in Europe but also in Asia, Africa, South America. Totalitarianism—in its different variants—did not affect Russia alone. But I always believed that someone would eventually emerge in literature or painting whose work would convey the horrors and nightmares of our own age, in much the same way that Goya managed to capture life in Spain during his own time.

Our era did not produce a painter of comparable caliber, but it did produce a composer, and this was one who lived through it all and expressed it all with genius, and who depicted the tragedy of this worldwide process, furthermore, not from the outside, like an observer, but from the inside. You see, this idea of equality, of equal happiness for everyone, was very simple and a great temptation. Many believed that a new era, an era of real freedom, a new way of life, would begin or had already begun after the Revolution and that everything was going to start afresh. That was the way it was advertised. And it is interesting to note that many people with great gifts and high intelligence were completely taken in by it. I might mention here that, when he was young, Dmitri Dmitrievich, whom I admire most profoundly, was also taken in, just as were—in some respects—Kandinsky and Meyerhold and such different poets as Blok and Mayakovsky. . . .

M.Y. There was great enthusiasm—many people got carried away.

M.R. They certainly did! I think even I might have been attracted as well!

But then it quickly became clear that it was only forms of terror that were new. New forms of art were not needed, and they were soon put in their place. When Meyerhold warned: "Watch out, we are about to let mediocrity rule in the arts, don't throw the baby out with the bathwater," he ended up paying with his own life for saying so. It was a total catastrophe and people went underground, they withdrew inside themselves. Shostakovich also withdrew and went underground. But some people could not manage it, they were unable to make the necessary switch. And the Bolsheviks deported whole groups of philosophers and religious thinkers, who were sent not into internal exile but into real exile. This, too, was one of the great human tragedies of the twentieth century.

That is why the figure of Shostakovich is so important, for he personifies an entire epoch in the life of this planet, and not only for those who lived in totalitarian countries. Otherwise people throughout the whole world would not listen to his music so much.

M.Y. You knew Shostakovich not only as a composer but also in a personal capacity—first as a student at the Conservatory, then as a performer of his works, and, later on, when you became friends.

M.R. Yes, I joined his orchestration class in 1943, and we were parted in 1974 when I left Russia.

M.Y. So you knew him for more than thirty years. What would you say were his essential qualities?

M.R. A whole book could be written about that, about our studying, our meetings, and our conversations. . . . But I would say his most essential quality was his deep humanity toward everything—in life, in his relationships, and in his art.

When I was a student I was not exactly shy with him, but I never dared to be too familiar, or pester him. I was full of admiration but I was afraid of taking up his time. You know, I think he had some sort of biological mechanism rather like a fish has radar which helps it sense obstacles some way off in the water, because somehow or other he could sense other people's attitudes toward him. I was always amazed that even if we had not seen each other for a long time (after I had stopped studying), he never forgot to wish me a happy birthday, or a happy New Year.

In the summer of 1959 he gave me the score of the First Cello Concerto [in E-flat Major op. 107 (1959)], and, five days later, I went with my accompanist, Alexander Dedyukhin, to Shostakovich's dacha in Komarovo, in order to play it to him. When I asked: "Dmitri Dmitrievich, could we possibly play for you?" he answered: "I'll get you a music-stand, Slava." It was one of the greatest moments in my life to be able to say: "I don't need one!" and when I said those words, I felt my spirits soar up to the skies. His eyes grew wide, of course, but he did not fetch the stand. I played the whole thing from memory. It went well. I had never studied so much before in the whole of my life. He had handed me the manuscript only in the evening of the 1st of August, and I worked for ten hours on the 2nd, and ten hours on the 3rd. But on the 4th, I could not take so much, so I only worked for eight hours then, and I did another eight on the 5th—and then, finally, on the 6th, I went to see him. And in spite of everything, it came out well! . . . When I said to him "I don't need one!" he gave me such a look, that for the sake of that look alone, it would have been worth working for another fifty hours.

I played for him three times altogether on that occasion. Isaak Davidovich Glikman came over to hear me the third time—Shostakovich had called him up. But the trouble was that Glikman had said, "I can't get there for at least forty-five minutes," so while we were waiting, out came a bottle of vodka, and, of course, we passed the time very nicely polishing it off between us. Glikman duly arrived and Dmitri Dmitrievich, feeling very merry and still glowing over my double performance, settled himself down. . . . This time it was for Glikman. What did I play? Well, I seem to remember it was a concerto, but . . . by Saint-Saëns. Dedyukhin, however, played from the score that still lay before him—by Shostakovich. Glikman looked somewhat shocked, but had, it seems, no grounds for criticism, and said not a word.

When it was over, I said: "I have to go home. I'll take the '*Strela*' " ["*Krasnaia Strela*," or the "Red Arrow," the express train between Moscow and Leningrad] and Dmitri Dmitrievich said, "I must see you off." So he came with me from his dacha to Leningrad. As we were walking through the old railway station building, I caught the way he looked at everything. Though it was summertime, the weather was still not yet hot, and there were enormous numbers of people either asleep or just lying around next to one another on the cold tiles of the floor. The look on his face was so full of compassion, the sight of it all made him wince. He did not notice me observing him but at that moment I realized, seeing him so moved by what was, after all, such an everyday sight, the extent to which he felt for other people. This was his true self.

I must say I would never have played the cello as I do had I not studied with Shostakovich. In truth, I got much more from him than from my cello teacher [Semyon Matveevich Kozolupov, 1884–1961]. My teacher did show me certain cello strokes which I changed in the course of time, and he taught me certain techniques . . . But he was a great lover of such outstanding contemporary composers as Dotzauer, Popper, Piatti, and others of similar ilk. Once, when we were discussing *Lady Macbeth of Mtsensk*, he said: "Our young composers have forgotten about melody. They make their music into some sort of obstacle race."

After I had conducted Prokofiev's *Voina i mir* [War and peace] at the Bolshoi Theater [in 1969], Shostakovich wrote a review for the newspaper *Sovetskoe isskusstvo*, but publication was held up for some time. I, of course, knew nothing about it. But suddenly he rang me up: "Slava, can you pop over, I'd like to see you." When I arrived, he said: "I have written this article, but it has not been published and maybe it never will be, but I'd still like you to have it." And he handed me the manuscript. He gave me that manuscript to make it absolutely clear that he had written it himself—perhaps because he usually dictated his articles or maybe somebody else wrote them for him. But in this case, every single word was written in his own hand. The article, which did appear about three weeks later, said: "Prokofiev's *War and Peace* is an opera of genius."

When I read the rubbish written by Solomon Volkov [*Testimony: The Memoirs of Shostakovich*], I must say I was deeply surprised to find him claiming that Shostakovich had put his own signature to the pages. For example, on Dmitri Dmitrievich's attitude to Prokofiev: I heard him say many times: "He's a composer of genius, this is a work of genius!" And Shostakovich once even stated in an interview that the impulse for writing his First Cello Concerto sprang from Prokofiev's *Sinfonia Concertante* for cello and orchestra. It always delighted him. Whenever I was playing the *Sinfonia Concertante* in Moscow, Shostakovich would always come along if he was in town, and he never missed a single concert.

Quite often I played with the Moscow Philharmonic Orchestra, where there was a percussionist who had lost a leg during the Patriotic War [World War II]. He did not always wear his artificial limb. Sometimes he would simply tuck up his empty trouser leg and stand on his one good leg in order to hit that last stroke, which, after I have been twirling around on the cello like someone right up high in the tent at the circus, has the effect of bringing everything, with a single blow, to a sudden halt. Dmitri Dmitrievich, when he used to come to my dressing room afterward, was always so impressed by this: "Wonderful, it was so wonderful! And that final stroke, which smashes everything down and brings it all to an end. . . . And on top of it all, that man up there on his one leg banging on the kettledrum with such force!" The whole picture so excited and inspired him that in his First Concerto, instead of one single blow, he has seven blows on the kettledrum!

He also remarked apropos [of] Prokofiev's *Sinfonia Concertante:* "How wonderful the cello sounds with the celesta!" There is just such a passage in the finale, when the main theme drops to a slow tempo for the cello while the celesta plays ornamental passages. And similarly, at the end of the second movement in Shostakovich's First Concerto, when I am playing on the cello, the string harmonics and celesta play along with me as well. So there are things in his First Concerto which I know for sure he took from Prokofiev, because Shostakovich, in full admiration, pointed them out to me himself. To suggest antagonism toward Prokofiev is sheer nonsense, in my view. Quite simply, they composed completely, diametrically, different music because they were musically gifted in diametrically different ways.

I also know about Sergei Sergeevich's attitude toward Shostakovich—although he rarely, very rarely, mentioned it. Much more often, it was Shostakovich who expressed his respect for Prokofiev. Prokofiev only found one fault with Dmitri Dmitrievich. He would say: "You know, Slava, I must say Shostakovich's *gifts for melody* could be a bit richer." But both of them, of course, were geniuses.

M.Y. And what do you remember about the important premières of non-cello music?

M.R. Well, the Eighth Symphony, first of all. That gave me the greatest shock of my entire life. I attended the Moscow première. I had already been his student at the Conservatory. I had been with him for rehearsals—yet I could never believe that that man sitting there was the very same one who had composed it. I could never believe it! Even though he was my teacher and I'd already got to know him quite well, I found it incredible, impossible to believe!

And now whenever I have a chance to hear or conduct the Eighth Symphony, I never fail to be impressed by the depth and power of the music and the genius of its creator. It reflects all the complexity of modern man in the modern world. We hardly know ourselves; we never have time to get to know ourselves. We act, and in acting quickly and thinking quickly, we never have time to stop and analyze ourselves. This is all the more the case today. Everything is getting more and more complicated and it's speeding up. In order to understand life at its deepest, you need tremendous intellectual strength. That is what Shostakovich had.

I always thought Shostakovich knew everything there was to know about mankind. When I was young, I was quite scared of his learning. Unlike many others, he knew not only what he liked but also what he did not like. Everything he came across was grist for the mill of his intellect. He had an immense "appetite" and superb "powers of understanding." The breadth of his perception is demonstrated by the great range of literature he draws from: from Shakespeare and Krylov, Dolmatovsky and Dostoevsky, Burns and Gogol, Pushkin and satirical texts from *Krokodil* ["The Crocodile," the Soviet humor magazine], Lermontov and Yevtushenko, Rilke, Kuechelbecker, Raleigh, Sasha Chorny, Apollinaire, Tsvetaeva, Marshak, Leskov, Japanese, Spanish and Jewish poetry, Blok and Michelangelo.

And similarly he draws in the whole of life—from disappointment and tragic conflict to interludes of happiness and hope. Yet, despite confronting the most dreadful aspects of human existence, descending into the dark abyss of sorrows and disaster, Shostakovich's art still remains utterly human.

Shostakovich's world is our world. For many decades my own life was inextricably part of that world, and has continued to be so, even now. To have lived at the same time as Shostakovich is a source of great joy. To have been involved in his creative life has been an immense responsibility. And to play his music has been the greatest happiness.

13

Shostakovich Remembered

Interviews with His Soviet Colleagues (1992)

IRINA NIKOLSKAYA

People in the West do not necessarily understand the complex, diverse, and contradictory circumstances that developed around Shostakovich in the USSR, and in Russian cultural life, during the period of the composer's lifetime. The extent to which he actively participated in or resisted participation in public life, civic or musical, his reaction to persecution and repression (the first wave of which crested in 1936, the second in 1948), the degree to which his creative stance depended on particular life experiences or political exigencies—none of this is as clear as it might seem to be at first glance and surely requires further careful investigation. Solomon Volkov's *Testimony* has promoted a certain one-sided perspective on Shostakovich's personality and art, although the book undoubtedly played a role in attracting attention in the West to

---

First published in the journal *melos*, nos. 4–5 (summer 1993) ("Special Issue on Dmitri Shostakovich"): 65–87. As published in *melos*, Irina Nikolskaya's interviews, in English translation, appeared under the general heading, "Dmitri Shostakovich. Part II." Vahid Salehieh, editor of *melos* and director of the publishing house Kantat HB, most generously provided the editor of the present volume with a copy of Nikolskaya's original Russian typescript of the interviews. This typescript serves as the basis for the English translation published here. Mr. Salehieh and Ms. Nikolskaya have given their permission to re-publish the interviews in the present volume. The interviews took place July through December 1992.

one of the greatest Russian composers of the twentieth century. It is hoped that the interviews offered here will provide a more realistic and multidimensional image of the composer.

Certain key subjects have continually surfaced in my conversations with individuals who knew Shostakovich in one way or another and were familiar with his personality and artistic intentions. One issue, which has been interpreted quite differently here in Russia than abroad, is whether the accusation of "formalism" influenced his creative work. Most musicians in our country believe that the ideological persecution he experienced had no significant influence either on his music or his creative ideas, with the possible exception of such conciliatory works as *Pesn' o lesakh* [Song of the forests] op. 81 (1949). Boris Tishchenko, Shostakovich's student, and his contemporaries Ivan Martynov and Lev Lebedinsky have consistently affirmed their belief that even had Shostakovich enjoyed complete creative freedom, he would very probably not have wanted to make radical changes in his musical language; neither would he have become an avant-garde composer as the concept was understood in the 1950s and 1960s. Given the artistic climate during the composer's last years, small wonder that Shostakovich expressed particular admiration for Benjamin Britten's traditionalist musical language.

I asked everyone I interviewed about Solomon Volkov's book, and the responses ranged all the way from utter rejection to wholehearted vindication. Much in *Testimony* has been called into question. One would be hard-pressed to disagree with Volkov's opponents who say that the portrait he paints of Shostakovich depicts a great composer in decline. Volkov himself understands this and has stated, "People change, sometimes radically—and not necessarily for the better, but in other ways. A person is different at different stages of life, at different times of day, and at different hours of the day, throughout his lifetime."[1] A contrary, idealized portrait of the composer would be equally vulnerable to dispute.

The interviews that follow disclose not only disagreements but also many noteworthy agreements. Certain works are evaluated in much the same way (e.g., the Eighth, Tenth, Eleventh, and Thirteenth symphonies). Likewise, the fundamental humanism of Shostakovich's creative legacy, his creative rapport with his epoch, and his moral, artistic, and human qualities are unanimously appreciated. All the interviewees regard Shostakovich as a central, tragic figure in Russian art of the twentieth century—perhaps the most profound Russian composer of our time, and certainly comparable, psychologically, to Dostoevsky. Now let us turn to the words of my interlocutors:

Marina Dmitrievna Sabinina (1917–2000). Doctor of Arts History and author of *Shostakovich-simfonist* [Shostakovich the symphonist] (Moscow: Muzyka, 1976), 475 pp.

I.N. I would like to hear about your recollections of Shostakovich.

M.S. I became acquainted with Shostakovich in an extremely difficult period of his life, very soon after the notorious Resolution of the Party Central Committee in 1948. Later, sometime in the mid-1950s, he told me about the whole experience with amazing good humor. A good sense of humor, generally speaking, had long been an integral part of his personality.

I.N. You mean to tell me that he understood the utter absurdity of the situation, the Party declaring war on "formalism" in art and demanding all Soviet artists to conform totally to the ideals of Socialist Realism—a concept that was a mystery to everybody?

M.S. No doubt about it! He completely understood the whole outrageous comedy, the farce of everything that happened. And he cocked a sarcastic eye at it, somehow managing to rise above the events of our "Soviet reality."[a] He said to me,

> When all that "song-and-dance" started—the meetings of the Party Central Committee, the barrage of mud-slinging in the press—I got out of Moscow as fast as I could, to compose. My First Violin Concerto was in full swing at the time, and I was completely preoccupied. Moscow was nothing but continuous interruption. My friends called to sympathize. My enemies called to mock me some more. Even common Soviet citizens rang up because they believed what they read in the papers: I was the leading formalist, so I must be an "enemy of the people." In short, it was impossible to live, so I got away to Uzkoe, the academy's "creative retreat," where I managed to finish up the concerto. Think about this: one afternoon I popped into the poolroom to watch some of the other residents playing pool. While I stood there watching the game, not saying a word, I heard some music playing over the loudspeaker. Suddenly one of the players got irate: "They publish the Party's special Resolution. They rave against the formalists. But those formalists simply will not give up! Just listen to that racket coming over the radio!" He then brusquely switched it off. Let me tell you, Marina Dmitrievna, I was on cloud nine from sheer delight! It was Tchaikovsky's Sixth Symphony!

I remember another chat with Dmitri Dmitrievich around the time we first met. One evening, I was sitting in the foyer outside the Small Hall at the Moscow Conservatory waiting for a friend, when Shostakovich walked up. He was also waiting for somebody. "May I sit here next to you?" he asked. "Let's wait together!" A bit later, a meeting of the

Academic Council ended, and a line of distinguished professors, the council members, their decorum even then very much intact, started filing past us toward the cloakroom. As they walked by, Dmitri Dmitrievich lampooned each one in an apt and humorous verbal "portrait." This was the winter of 1949–50, and that very council had only recently dismissed him from the Moscow Conservatory because of the scandal. He'd been humiliated and harassed, but he still retained enough spirit to laugh, feel mischievous, and make ironic jokes. His sense of humor was inborn, an organic part of his character, and for many years it served as a protective covering for him.

I.N. But what about the tragic element in his creative work?

M.S. No doubt Shostakovich was a tragic figure, both as a human being in the context of his time and as an artist (not unlike his idol Musorgsky). The tragic component is made all the more prominent by those delightfully cheerful, clever, carefree, life-affirming images that predominate in a number of his prewar compositions, for instance, the Piano Concerto No. 1 in C Minor with solo trumpet op. 35 (1933) and the First String Quartet in C Major op. 49 (1938). Unfortunately, however, Shostakovich gradually lost his sunny, mischievous humor, his ability to enjoy life, because of his illnesses, as well as the suffocating social-political atmosphere. And also, certainly, because of the compromises he made as an artist, which had to have been bitter and humiliating for him. Just consider the music he composed for such appallingly offensive and hypocritical films as *Vstrecha na El'be* [Meeting at the Elba], *Padenie Berlina* [The fall of Berlin], and *Nezabyvaemyi 1919* [The unforgettable year 1919]. He had to force himself to compose music for these films, so it couldn't have been any good. But this was the period when, for all practical purposes, his music was not being played at all. He had no money to live on, yet he had to support not only his family in Moscow but also his mother and sisters in Leningrad. Film music provided his main income.

I don't know if an official document forbidding performances of Shostakovich's music was ever issued after the 1948 Party Resolution. More likely the performing organizations and philharmonic societies simply received oral "recommendations" amounting to a ban. I remember in June 1949 inviting a small group of [Moscow] Conservatory friends to my place to listen to works by our favorite composer; it was a deliberate act of protest against the state policy. Shostakovich's student Karen Khachaturian brought along the manuscript of the songs *Iz evreiskoi narodnoi poesii* [From Jewish folk poetry, op. 79 (1948)], which we hadn't yet heard. We thoroughly enjoyed singing and playing them. Heinrich Neuhaus, who lived in my building, was a part of the group. He had come along as soon as he heard about the reason for our gathering. [Neuhaus was a renowned pianist and the teacher of Sviatoslav Richter and Emil Gilels, among other notables.—I.N.] In addition, the young players in the Moscow Philharmonic Quartet (later named the Borodin Quartet) played for us Shostakovich's Third String Quartet in F Major op. 73 (1946). The group had just recently formed. They played the quartet twice, the second time as an encore! (To me, the Third Quartet is one of his most beautiful and profoundly tragic chamber music works.) Our night of music making ended only at the crack of dawn, and still we could scarcely pull ourselves away from Shostakovich's music.

During the 1950s, when I was working for the journal *Sovetskaia muzyka*, I had various occasions to see how kindly Shostakovich responded to people who needed his help. Sometimes he found himself doing things that were not especially agreeable to him personally. But this was a characteristic feature of his personality; he had to struggle, sometimes, with contradictory impulses.

I.N. Are you perhaps also thinking about his decision to join the Communist Party?

M.S. That's a long story. He applied for Party membership in the autumn of 1960. I'll tell you briefly about one circumstance that I am convinced prompted his decision.

In the summer of 1956, when Shostakovich was a member of the editorial board of *Sovetskaia muzyka*, the journal was threatened with mayhem. Four of the more aggressive and orthodox members of the board sent a letter to the Party Central Committee warning that the journal had fallen into the "swamp of formalism and cosmopolitanism" and had "abandoned the Party line." The letter urgently demanded that the journal's "delinquent" leadership be dismissed.

What incited the furious anger of the finger-pointers was Lev Lebedinsky's positive review of Shostakovich's Eighth Symphony, among other things. Evgeny Mravinsky had just conducted the symphony in Moscow. At that period, the Eighth was regarded in the "halls of power" as ideologically suspect, pacifist, and very nearly anti-Soviet.

The fate of the journal was to be decided at a meeting of the Central Committee, and only Party members were invited to participate. Shostakovich, not being a Party member, was not invited. Emil Gilels attended, of course, but when he sensed the highly charged atmosphere, he excused himself immediately, complaining of a pain in his heart. Nobody else was left to stand up and defend the journal. And a year later the journal's entire editorial team was fired.

Dmitri Dmitrievich understood that if he held Party membership, it would allow him to play a more active and influential role in musical affairs. He had a very strong streak of civic-mindedness, along with an urge to defend the innocent and to do what is right.

I.N. And what was Shostakovich like in the 1970s when Volkov talked with him?

M.S. Gloomy, reserved, and unsociable. Completely different than he'd been in the 1940s, 1950s, and 1960s. I met him only occasionally at concerts; he was thin, limping, leaning on a cane. Volkov says in the preface to his book that Dmitri Dmitrievich considered him to be "the most intelligent man of the new generation" [p. xvi]. My acquaintance with this "most intelligent" individual was rather cursory and superficial, but I found him, as a human being, to be not very likeable, extremely conceited, rude, and, excuse me, ill mannered.

In the 1970s Shostakovich was afflicted by a succession of incurable diseases. Physical suffering, fear of death, and the burden of the ordeals he had lived through did their bloody business, affecting his psyche and influencing what he said to Solomon Volkov and what Volkov wrote down. I do not believe, however, that everything Volkov published came from Shostakovich's mouth. Some of it was taken from other publications; some of it Volkov could have heard from Shostakovich's students. Irina Antonovna, the composer's widow, swears that Volkov was neither a frequent guest at their place nor spent enough time with Dmitri Dmitrievich to produce the entire book.

Shostakovich's terribly despondent mood at the time is eloquently expressed in his unrealized plan to compose operas based on Chekhov's *Chornyi monakh* [The black monk] and *Palata No. 6* [Ward No. 6]. Regarding those strangely detailed descriptions of sadism and mad, nightmarishly depraved inclinations—I completely believe Volkov heard them from Shostakovich. Volkov could not have made that up. Here was the former soccer fan, now terrified of crowds, afraid of people watching him from behind his back, imagining their hands reaching out to him.

I.N. Since you wrote a widely known book about the Shostakovich symphonies, I would be interested to have your perspective on the curious proximity of such vastly different works as the Twelfth and Thirteenth symphonies.

M.S. Shostakovich was obliged to compromise more than once, particularly during the latter half of the 1940s and the beginning of the

1950s. I have in mind those egregious film scores mentioned earlier, that jingoistic cantata *Nad rodinoi nashei solntse siiaet* [The sun shines over our motherland] (1952), and the oratorio *Pesn' o lesakh* [Song of the forests] (1949), all of which reveal very little in common with Shostakovich's authentic style. Clichés worked out in scoring films migrated into the Twelfth Symphony. The work should not be performed very often, in my opinion, if only out of respect for the memory of a great composer.

As early as the 1930s, Shostakovich had been "encouraged" to compose a "Lenin" symphony. He had dedicated the Eleventh, "The Year 1905" ("*1905 god*," 1956–57) to the First Russian Revolution, so, after it, they turned the screws on him still more insistently: he really needed to commemorate the events of "Great October" and the monumental figure of Lenin. Finally Shostakovich gave in. And, as I've been told, he turned out that insipid, flabby, watered-down score of the Twelfth Symphony, "The Year 1917" ("*1917 god*," 1959–61), in about two weeks. The Eleventh, as you know, still contains material worthy of true creative inspiration, material capable of stirring the imagination toward allegorical symbolism. The third movement, for example, which depicts the slaughter of peaceful demonstrators in 1905, can also be associated with Soviet mass executions and Stalinist repression. The first movement, with its melodies of prerevolutionary songs about tsarist penal camps and exiles also brings to mind the victims of Stalinist Gulags and the millions who perished in concentration camps and prisons.

The Twelfth Symphony was intended to glorify October, but the musical symbology there was absolutely unsuitable. It was Shostakovich's most bitter compromise. While the films and cantatas are thankfully long forgotten, the Twelfth, alas, remains in his list of symphonies and appears on the programs of ceremonial jubilee festivals.

But Shostakovich always sought revenge for his compromises. The trivial vulgarity of the Twelfth was followed by the Thirteenth, "*Babyi Yar*" (1962), the most transparent and sincerely revealing of them all. Perhaps it resembles more a placard than a symphony in the Beethoven-Mahler-Shostakovich sense, given that it draws attention to some of Russia's most acute moral and social problems, placed in the context of much superb music, of course. The Thirteenth was very brave for those times. They dropped it from the repertoire, for good reason, but then resurrected it a few years later, only with an expurgated, toned-down text. The following stanza appears in "*Babyi yar*"[2]—the Yevtushenko poem set by Shostakovich as the first movement of the symphony:

Mne kazhetsia seichas—ia iudei.	I feel now that I am a Jew.
Vot ia bredu po drevnemu Egiptu.	Here am I, wandering through ancient Egypt.
A vot ia, na kreste raspiatyi, gibnu,	Here am I, pinioned on a cross, dying,
i do sikh por na mne—sledy gvozdei	and the marks of nails still scar my flesh.

Shostakovich's music, with its labored struggle upward, as if stifled by the dense chromaticism, reflects magnificently the tragic imagery of the text. But the character of this music is not at all compatible with the revised text, which is awkward and incongruous:

Ia zdes' stoiu, kak budto u krinitsy,	I stand here as if at a wellspring,
daiushchei veru v nashe bratstvo mne.	which nourishes my faith in our brotherhood.
Zdes' russkie lezhat i ukraintsy,	Here lie Russians and Ukrainians,
lezhat s evreiami v odnoi zemle.	together with Jews, in a common earth.

May God forgive Evgeny Yevtushenko! He's a talented poet who spoiled his own verses and ruined the harmonious union of text and music in the hope of protecting the symphony from the wrath of anti-Semite Party bonzes.

I.N. And why did Mravinsky refuse to conduct this symphony? I remember Kirill Kondrashin conducting.[b]

M.S. I don't know. I know only that relations between Mravinsky and Dmitri Dmitrievich grew chilly during his last years. It is a complicated question. Both had problematic personalities, especially in old age. But Mravinsky deserves sincere gratitude for his loving promotion, and exceptionally careful preparation, of so many premières of Shostakovich's best works. For instance, in preparing the première of the First Violin Concerto op. 77 (1947–48), with Oistrakh as soloist, Mravinsky called for nineteen full orchestra rehearsals!

I.N. Tell me, please, were you able to publish everything you wanted to say in your book about Shostakovich, or were you compelled not to, because of political considerations?

M.S. Naturally I had to throw whole passages into the trash can, otherwise the book would not have been published. I had wanted to reveal truthfully the tragedy of a genius, broken and trampled by crude, uncouth nonentities, a genius who was obliged to buy the right to be himself at the cost of certain compromises. But to speak straightforwardly was impossible. So, against my will, I resorted to hints, allusions, and innuendos. I had to tone down my sharply negative critique of the Twelfth Symphony. At that time, no one dared to criticize it.

I.N. What, in your opinion, accounts for the difference in the perception of Shostakovich's music here in Russia and abroad? What is it that we are able to discern and they are unable to?

M.S. Understandably we sense in his music many more subtexts relevant to both public events and matters of public concern, but also to society's moral and ethical concerns, which are even more important. Foreigners are simply not in a position to identify with all the dramatic events through which we as a people have lived, so they tend to interpret Shostakovich's music as "pure" music, isolated from its social-historical context. Some French colleagues once told me that they did not particularly like Shostakovich's symphonies, which were too weighty and too long for them, too much like Mahler, whom the French also do not regard highly. My French colleagues were right that the Shostakovich symphonies remind one of Mahler. There is a similar concentration of moral and philosophical energy, a similar poignancy in musical discourse, and even the style sometimes suggests Mahler. Consider the Fourth Symphony, for example.

I.N. What is the source of Shostakovich's predilection for Jewish folklore?

M.S. Indeed he had such a predilection. It first appeared in the Piano Trio op. 67 no. 2 (1944), long before the song cycle *Iz evreiskoi narodnoi poesii* [From Jewish folk poetry]. The Piano Trio is dedicated to the memory of his closest friend, Ivan Sollertinsky, a brilliantly gifted musicologist, and it was completed soon after Sollertinsky's death. The finale, based specifically on Jewish melodic-rhythmic motifs, unfolds in a succession of astonishing and horribly grotesque musical images. Why? This question was raised at the scholarly conference devoted to Shostakovich held in Cologne in 1985. I responded by reminding the conferees that at the very time Shostakovich was composing the Trio, hundreds of thousands of Jews were being murdered in gas chambers, cremated in ovens, and executed by firing squads in Nazi concentration camps. Shostakovich, being a man of the highest moral standards and one who possessed an exceptionally acute sense of personal responsibility, could not fail to respond to these monstrous atrocities except by a passionate cry of protest. He would continue responding later on as well (remember the Thirteenth Symphony!), because he despised anti-Semitism with the furious hatred of a true Russian *intelligent*.[c]

❦

Israel Vladimirovich Nestyev (1911–1993). Doctor of Arts History and professor at the Moscow Conservatory; served in the Soviet armed forces during the Great Patriotic War, 1941–45.

I.N. Did you know Shostakovich well?

I.V.N. I had the pleasure of meeting with Dmitri Dmitrievich Shostakovich many times, and I was often present at performances of his music when he himself would demonstrate new works to his colleagues. I'll never forget the day, in autumn 1941, when Dmitri Dmitrievich played the first movement of his new Seventh Symphony, which would later be called the "Leningrad" Symphony op. 60 (1941). He had just arrived in Moscow from the Leningrad blockade. The demonstration took place in the editorial boardroom of the newspaper *Sovetskoe iskusstvo.* Before he started, I remember, Shostakovich warned us, a bit self-deprecatingly, about the resemblance of the "invasion episode" in the symphony's first movement to Ravel's *Bolero.* These two works, as you know, make use of a similar compositional device—a succession of thematic variations unfolds over a snare-drum *ostinato.* The music of the Seventh Symphony, of course, suggests a completely different meaning than that of the Ravel. Shostakovich takes a monotonous Prussian march, sets it in the style of the most banal music-hall tune, then relentlessly and ingeniously turns it into a grotesque thematic parody that implicitly, and with enormous force, stigmatizes the nonentity of German Nazism.

I also remember some of the prewar premières of Shostakovich's music, for instance, the first performance of his wonderful Piano Quintet op. 57 (1940), played by the Beethoven Quartet with Shostakovich himself at the piano. Many people in the audience were taken aback at the time by the unusually sharp and contradictory thematic juxtapositions: the self-consciously "learned-style" polyphony in some movements (the Prelude, the Fugue, and the wonderful Intermezzo), together with the rather frivolous, dance-hall rhythms of the finale. This unfamiliar mix of disparate thematic topics struck some listeners as quite objectionable, despite the fact that paradoxical contrasts such as this illustrate one of Shostakovich's most important discoveries—a method very much in line with the creative practices of Gustav Mahler, Shostakovich's ideal.

Already at that time Shostakovich demonstrated in his music a knack for "combining what was uncombinable," an approach later to be described by Russian musicologists as "polystylistics." In Russian music today, composers often combine ultramodern devices with old-fashioned ones, the complicated with the simple or even the hackneyed. The fact is that stylistic features associated with today's "post-modernism" appeared long ago in Shostakovich's music. He had no compunctions about using stridently grotesque combinations of style elements borrowed from the Baroque (Bach and Handel) with those borrowed from Romanticism (Mahler), sometimes also including elements from music of the sort you might hear on the street, including the most trite and commonplace. Shostakovich once admitted that when he saw people smiling at his concerts, he felt tremendous satisfaction. His works often juxtapose tragedy and merciless sarcasm, the latter aimed at philistinism, vulgarity, and inhumanity.

I.N. Has your perspective on Shostakovich's music changed over the years?

I.V.N. Almost twenty years have passed since Shostakovich left us. Certainly during his lifetime he enjoyed enormous prestige among intellectuals [the *intelligentsia*],[d] despite all the attacks by the Stalinist regime. During those years, he sometimes composed works *à l'occasion*, works with a certain measure of "officialese." His Twelfth Symphony is such an example, in my opinion, and the least successful of all his symphonies. But his finest tragic scores undoubtedly belong at the summit of world music. The *Largo* of the Fifth Symphony op. 47 (1937), for instance, I now perceive to be a requiem for the millions of innocent victims of the Stalinist regime. Let me remind you that this symphony appeared in 1937 at the height of the "Ezhov terror,"[e] when, at Stalin's behest, masses of blameless people were executed, including some of Shostakovich's closest friends. He suffered deeply. In those years, no other artist, whatever the field—no painter, playwright, or film director—could even think of protesting against the Stalinist terror through his art. Only instrumental music, with its own distinctive methods of expressive generalization, had the power to communicate the terrible truth of that time.

I.N. What do you remember about Shostakovich's relations with the regime?

I.V.N. Shostakovich's life turned out tragically. In early 1936 the then all-powerful Stalin attended a performance of the opera *Ledi Makbet Mtsenskogo uezda* [Lady Macbeth of the Mtsensk District] on the second stage of Moscow's Bolshoi Theater. The production was not particularly successful. (Yet before this, superb performances of the opera, in both Leningrad and Moscow, had received enthusiastic reviews in the press.) Stalin utterly rejected the opera, harshly denouncing it as "muddle instead of music."

I.N. Are those Stalin's actual words?[f]

I.V.N. Yes, there's evidence that those were his words. Immediately afterward, the notorious article "*Sumbur vmesto muzyki*" [A muddle instead of music] was published in *Pravda*, in effect ravaging Shostakovich's music. It was a painful trauma for the composer. Over some months Shostakovich suffered from depression and never again, after 1936, produced another opera (although he was undoubtedly a born dramatist). *Lady Macbeth of the Mtsensk District* (or *Katerina Izmailova*), which was a remarkable opera, was officially banned and only revived in Russia after Stalin's death. From that time on, the composer preferred to speak his mind through purely instrumental music, which was much less dangerous for his relationship with the powers that be.

I.N. Yet, all the same, Stalin managed to take advantage of Shostakovich's international fame for his own political purposes.

I.V.N. Yes, to some extent he did. In 1949, according to reports, Stalin unexpectedly phoned Shostakovich and asked him to travel to the United States as a delegate to the Congress for World Peace. Dmitri Dmitrievich was astonished to hear Stalin's voice on the phone. After speaking about the Congress, the Leader added, "We have criticized you, but we criticized you because *we love you.*" At almost exactly the same time, in a conversation with the theater director V. I. Nemirovich-Danchenko, Stalin expressed his opinion about Shostakovich: "He's probably a very talented individual, but much too much in the 'Meyerhold' mold." Stalin, of course, was referring to the renowned Russian avant-garde theater director Vsevolod Meyerhold, who was arrested by the NKVD [later renamed the KGB] in the late 1930s and shot as an "enemy of the people."

I.N. Were you ever a witness to any critical attacks on Shostakovich?

I.V.N. I was indeed, and more than once. I remember a discussion about his Twenty-Four Preludes and Fugues for Piano op. 87 (1950–51). Those musicians inclined toward officialdom harshly criticized this superb cycle, but such people as the pianist Maria Yudina and the composers Nikolai Peiko and Georgy Sviridov, among others, defended it. I was astonished by Shostakovich's remarkable forbearance, as he listened to the remarks directed at him. He never objected, never complained about those who insulted him, and certainly he never protested to the authorities in charge, as did other composers. Unlike them, he generally appeared bewildered by praise, and the exaggerated enthusiasm of ladies simply annoyed him.

If Dmitri Dmitrievich himself took the floor at a public hearing to criticize one of his colleagues, he never failed to reveal his natural tact and, besides that, his general manner revealed just how uncomfortable he actually felt.

I.N. What do you think about Solomon Volkov's book about Shostakovich?

I.V.N. As you know, this book supposedly presents Shostakovich's point of view. And it must certainly include some genuine conversations between this particular musicologist and the composer. But, over and above this, I am convinced that Dmitri Dmitrievich as I knew him would never have approved publication of certain passages in the book. For example, the book includes attacks on the conductor Evgeny Mravinsky, to whom Shostakovich was indebted for many of his artistic successes. Shostakovich was scrupulously conscientious and exceptionally compassionate in his dealings with people; he would never have allowed himself to subject his former friend to a public "lashing." Perhaps at tea he might have said something or other about how Mravinsky upset him, but he would never have permitted it to be published.

❧

Valentin Alexandrovich Berlinsky (b. 1925). Cellist of the Borodin Quartet; the only member who has played with the quartet from the time of its founding in 1946 until the present.

I.N. The performances of Shostakovich's string quartets by the world-renowned Borodin Quartet have not only been widely acclaimed but have also been acknowledged to have set a certain standard for their interpretation. Which of the ensemble's meetings with Dmitri Dmitrievich do you remember?

V.B. I remember many of them. One was at the very first festival of Shostakovich's music in Gorky [1962]. Shostakovich, who was already quite ill, appeared with us for the last time as pianist, in his Piano Quintet op. 57 (1940). After that, we always got in touch with him each time he completed a new quartet. These contacts, in fact, had become a tradition from the time our ensemble was formed. We eventually played all the Shostakovich quartets, but the Third was the first one we played in public. We had heard the well-known Beethoven Quartet play the first two Shostakovich quartets when the players were our teachers at the Moscow Conservatory.[g] They were the ones who encouraged us, while we were still students, to start our own quartet ensemble. The "Borodins" never played a Shostakovich quartet publicly without first asking the composer to comment on our interpretation. (I have kept a number of his letters. In one of them he raves about our interpretation and sends best wishes for future performances.)

I.N. What was the nature of his comments?

V.B. They mostly concerned errors in the printed notation, less often in the tempo. In fact, as I said, Dmitri Dmitrievich made all sorts of corrections during our quartet rehearsals. This was the case up until the time of the last quartets, the Thirteenth, Fourteenth, and Fifteenth, which we were never able to play for him.

The first time the future members of the Borodin Quartet got together was when we were all still students, in 1945 to be precise: Rostislav Dubinsky, first violin; Nina Barshai, second violin; Rudolf Barshai, viola; and myself, cello. I remember very well how we readied ourselves to play Shostakovich's First Quartet for the composer. He agreed to come listen to us at 9:00 A.M. I started downstairs to meet him and saw him already coming up the stairs, puffing. It was barely a minute past nine, but he started apologizing for being late. Everybody knew about Shostakovich's scrupulous exactitude and punctuality. He absolutely could not stand any sort of tardiness! I think he inculcated this trait in a great many people who associated with him, including me.

We took Shostakovich into a classroom and started readying ourselves to play the quartet, when Shostakovich said, "What a shame. I forgot to bring the score with me! But all the same, I'll try to play some parts of it from memory to give you an idea about tempos." (He composed the First Quartet op. 49 in 1938, you know.) Whereupon Dmitri Dmitrievich went to the piano and, still standing, played the work from beginning to end. That was the first encounter of the future Borodin Quartet with Shostakovich.

I.N. He evidently sensed the creative potential of the young ensemble and felt sympathetic toward it from the start.

V.B. That certainly seems to have been the case, because when we invited him to play his Piano Quintet with us, he accepted with pleasure.

I also remember an amusing incident connected with our playing the Third Quartet for him. At the beginning of the piece a typical accompaniment figure appears in the cello part, with the indication *arco*—to be played with the bow. During rehearsal we had decided that I would play it *pizzicato*, that is, to pluck the string, which seemed to sound better to us. When Dmitri Dmitrievich came to hear us, I managed to play only a single note *pizzicato* before he stopped us and turned to me, "It is marked *arco* there." "Yes, Dmitri Dmitrievich," I answered, "but we played through the quartet and it seems to us that *pizzicato* would be better here." Shostakovich answered immediately in his characteristic manner, "Yes, yes, it would be better. But please play it *arco* anyway!" He didn't like to argue, but he was very stubborn and always insisted on his own way.

I have to say that on the whole Shostakovich had a phenomenal command of writing for the string quartet; everything in his quartets falls "under the fingers." Few composers today can compete with him in this regard. I would even say he sensed the "soul" of the quartet. Even Beethoven wrote less gratefully for this combination. Pianists who play his music are also surprised by the exceptional pianistic qualities of Shostakovich's piano works.

I.N. Do you think that the fifteen string quartets represent the full range of Shostakovich's creative evolution? Is it possible to gain a comprehensive impression of him as a composer solely on the basis of the fifteen quartets?

V.B. Definitely! His ethics, aesthetics, and style are all distilled in the quartets, along with his personality; it, too, is somehow totally expressed in the quartets.

I.N. What is it in Shostakovich's creative legacy that means the most to you personally?

V.B. That is a rather deep and serious question.

I.N. Your perspective as a performer interests me. Surely some particular element must have impressed and attracted you immediately, and more than anything else, when you and the other members of the Borodin Quartet became familiar with a new work by Shostakovich. Performers in general must sense a composer's emotional world both subtly and profoundly.

V.B. I can only speak about my personal feelings, although, in many respects, I think my colleagues in the quartet shared my impressions.

This is how I see Shostakovich's creative evolution: his music developed along a line of ever intensifying drama, I would even say tragedy. His quartets have much in common with Beethoven's in terms of their profound creative conception. But all the finales in Dmitri Dmitrievich's quartets are tragic in character, unlike those of Beethoven. And I think I know why. Beethoven, more often than not, arrives at a life-affirmative finale, despite all the conflicts and collisions, all that is lived through beforehand in the music's unfolding. Beethoven was a person who believed deeply in, and looked toward, some brightness on the other side of life. But Dmitri Dmitrievich was an atheist and could not see anything beyond human existence. Shostakovich was afraid of death. He could not envision an exodus from human suffering. You understand, of course, this is my subjective opinion.

I.N. Have attitudes toward Shostakovich's works changed or at least ameliorated over the years?

V.B. Certainly attitudes have ameliorated. And it has not only been a matter of time but also a drawn-out process of comprehending Shostakovich's art. This latter process, in fact, can be identified in the attitudes abroad, among concert organizers in various countries of the world, toward Shostakovich's music. Earlier, when our quartet was invited for concert tours, the organizers were not very willing for us to include Shostakovich's quartets in our concert programs, preferring instead the Russian classics. But nowadays we can play Shostakovich as much as we like, in practically any country.

The Borodin Quartet, at one time or another, recorded all fifteen Shostakovich quartets for the Soviet record company Melodiya, which sold these recordings to various foreign companies without saying a word about it to us. But discussion is now going on with several of the foreign companies about putting all our recordings together in an anthology comprising the entire collection, which I hope will be done.

I.N. Have you had an opportunity to read Solomon Volkov's much talked about book? It continues to stir up controversy here in Russia. I would be interested to hear what you have to say about it.

V.B. I don't agree with either the opponents or the advocates of the [illegible] ere in between. But my own view [illegible] l prejudice: I do not like memoirs [illegible] I would insist that we do not have [illegible] body else's dirty linen and expose [illegible] of day, especially when speaking [illegible] of the weaknesses in Dmitri Dmi- [illegible] us the right to judge and condemn [illegible]

[illegible] ut memoirs in general and about [illegible] eve that it contains certain things [illegible] s that correct?

[illegible] n, an author's subjective point of [illegible] moirs, even distorts them to some [illegible] f memoirs by Rostislav Dubinsky, [illegible] n Quartet, which he published in the United States after his emigration.[h] The book contains, to put it mildly, a number of inaccuracies. For instance, he writes that several of Alfred Schnittke's works were banned from performance in the 1960s and 1970s; but they were not actually banned; rather, they were "not recommended" for performance. This is not the same thing. In fact, the Borodin Quartet went right ahead and played these works. "Recommendations" of this sort could come from the USSR Ministry of Culture, from the Cultural Department of the CPSU[i] Central Committee, and from the USSR Union of Composers. "Banned," however, probably sounded a lot more exciting to Western publishers than "not recommended," and so Dubinsky gave in.

The situation was quite different in the 1930s and 1940s when Shostakovich's music was not being performed at all (my mention of the 1940s is prompted by the Party Resolution of 1948). This earlier ban remained in force for several years; performance was officially forbidden. Schnittke's music, however, was not forbidden; it was simply not welcomed. That Schnittke, like Gubaidulina and Denisov, remained on the outside of official musical life is another issue. Their music was excluded from the major concert venues, and they encountered enormous difficulties trying to organize performances of their works. But despite all this, their music was still performed and well known among musicians, as well as among a sizable group of the liberal intelligentsia.

Elsewhere in his book, Dubinsky writes about anti-Semitism. It is absolutely true, of course, that a "state sponsored anti-Semitism" existed in our country. But to attribute every repression solely to anti-Semitism is also inaccurate. Just consider the brilliant conducting career of Rudolf Barshai, not to mention many other examples among performances. As a Jew myself, I never sensed anti-Semitism in our musical circles.[j] Shostakovich, too, in fact, harshly condemned anti-Semitism.

Dmitri Dmitrievich certainly had his weaknesses as a human being, I'll say again. He just could not take any pressure on himself and consequently would try to escape it as quickly as possible. As a result, he would sign any kind of "appeal" or "protest" shoved under his nose by the Party Central Committee, "without looking" at it. In fact, they would continue "pressing" him until he signed. This is how his name appeared on a document condemning the scientist Andrei Sakharov and what Sakharov was trying to do. It's a joke to think that Shostakovich would have condemned Sakharov. But Sakharov was a fighter, whereas Shostakovich was never a fighter in his life. Still, both were geniuses and the finest representatives of our country. How can one possibly judge or condemn

Shostakovich on the basis of "facts" such as this, if such can indeed be called facts? This is why I do not like memoirs and put no faith in them.

❦

Ivan Ivanovich Martynov (b. 1908). Musicologist; awarded a state citation as "Honored Arts Professional of the Russian Federation"; active for many years in the Union of Composers of the USSR and the Union of Composers of the Russian Federation.

I.N. You were very much involved in our country's musical life for many years and closely involved with the works of Shostakovich. What are your most vivid memories of Dmitri Dmitrievich?

I.M. I have lots of memories of him. He exemplified the highest ethical and moral standards, and I've never had greater admiration or respect for anyone. But for this talk, I want to focus on circumstances associated with the opera *Ledi Makbet Mtsenskogo uezda* [Lady Macbeth of the Mtsensk District] and the Eighth Symphony op. 65 (1943). Let me tell you about what I personally witnessed.

By the beginning of the 1930s Shostakovich's name had already attracted considerable attention among young musicians in Moscow. We knew his First Symphony op. 10 (1924–25) and the suites from the ballets *Bolt* [The bolt] and *Zolotoi vek* [The golden age]. I have to admit that the latter two works, with their flamboyant orchestration, grotesquerie, and so on, appealed to us more than the symphony. But at that time Shostakovich was not yet "Composer No. 1" for us. We were still fascinated by Scriabin, and Prokofiev was all the fashion.

Then, after a while, the opera *Ledi Makbet* [Lady Macbeth] appeared and turned a lot of our thinking around, forcing us to see Shostakovich as one of the major composers of the twentieth century. First, the opera was a great success in Leningrad, and then later in Moscow's Nemirovich-Danchenko Theater—a production I had the good fortune to see, which was also enormously successful. Sitting in the first row were Antonina Nezhdanova, the legendary Russian soprano, and Nikolai Golovanov, conductor at the Bolshoi Theater. These two musicians "of the old school" stood up and clapped their hands along with everybody else.

Then a second production of the opera opened in Moscow at the Bolshoi's filial theater, a devastating review followed in *Pravda*, and *Ledi Makbet* was immediately banned from the repertoire and the vocal score withdrawn from sale. Additional abusive articles followed, and the opera was harshly censured at a meeting organized by the Union of Composers.

All who spoke at the meeting had to tune their remarks in harmony with the Party Resolution. Nobody dared to contradict the opinion of the Party Central Committee. Nevertheless, a handful of musicians found ways to say something good about the opera along with their criticisms, so the condemnation was not unanimous. I believe many musicians even at the time were able to grasp the opera's enormous artistic importance.

Shostakovich's Fifth Symphony appeared soon afterward, and the regime's attitude toward the composer changed radically. Those in power viewed the symphony as Shostakovich's rehabilitation. All the same, a few members of the Russian Association of Proletarian Musicians (RAPM) even found reason to attack the symphony.[k]

Ledi Makbet, renamed *Katerina Izmailova*, was restored to the stage only in the early 1960s.[l] The idea for doing so had developed somewhere "on high" but was accompanied by a certain reluctance, so it was decided to turn the matter over for discussion at the Composers Union. I was present on the occasion. Shostakovich and the composer Moisei Weinberg, each seated at a piano, played through the entire opera, first to last. Afterward, Tikhon Khrennikov[m] opened the floor and called for discussion. Then suddenly, without waiting for comments, he exclaimed, "But what is there to discuss? This work represents the best musical memory of our youth. All of us have tolerated too much error and injustice." And so began the opera's eventual revival, and its success was furthered by Galina Vishnevskaya's unforgettable Katerina. As I see it, the power of Shostakovich's creative genius inevitably triumphed over whatever ideological impediments were dreamed up.

Now on to the Eighth Symphony, which was also subjected to a dire fate. The Seventh Symphony, "The Leningrad" op. 60 (1941), had made an enormous impression both here and abroad, from the time of its first performance in 1942. So when it became known in early 1943 that Shostakovich had completed an Eighth Symphony, everybody was convinced it would be something like the Seventh. The first formal hearing of the music, with the composer at the piano, took place at the Commission on Art Affairs (now the Ministry of Culture) on a hot summer afternoon, the humidity stifling despite all the windows being wide open. The symphony lasted more than an hour. After Shostakovich finished playing, confusion reigned in the office of the Chairman of the Commission. Nobody said a word. The Seventh Symphony had been accessible and filled with an almost graphic musical imagery, while the musical language of the Eighth was complex and philosophical. This was a Shostakovich unwilling to make the slightest concession. Then the unexpected happened. Dmitri Dmitrievich suddenly announced, "My dear friends! This is complicated music and clearly you've not understood all of it or figured it out. So I'll play the whole thing again." And he did, the entire symphony. This time a few people even praised it.

The symphony's première took place on 2 November 1943. Attracted by the popularity of the Seventh Symphony, the top brass were sitting in the front row. They didn't react badly to the work. Two days later, on 4 November 1943, my positive review appeared in the newspaper *Vecherniaia Moskva.* But then, nothing more was said about it. The symphony was given the "silent treatment." About two months passed before the decidedly "cool" or sharply critical commentaries started to appear. No decision had been made at this point to "muzzle" Shostakovich, but all the same the symphony could not be accepted; it was simply much too far removed from the accepted idea of Socialist Realism, which required a hale and hearty character and a dependably optimistic finale.

The Eighth Symphony is one of the composer's most tragic works. I personally find in it much in common with Musorgsky's *Pesni i pliaski smerti* [Songs and dances of death]. This symphony epitomizes all the drama and sorrow of its epoch. I remember attending a magnificent performance conducted by Mravinsky in Leningrad. During the concert someone in the audience experienced pain in his heart and fainted. That was in 1947. A year later, when Shostakovich was once again being persecuted, this incident was cited as evidence that Shostakovich's music could bring on a heart attack. In short, attempts were continually being made to discredit the Eighth Symphony. When the Czechs invited Mravinsky to conduct the symphony at the Prague Spring Festival in 1957, all kinds of pressure was put on him to refuse, because the Eighth Symphony was not considered worthy of representing Soviet culture. The work was nevertheless performed at the Prague Spring and enjoyed phenomenal success.

I.N. And what can you tell us about Shostakovich's activity as First Secretary of the Composers Union of the Russian Federation?[n]

I.M. No one expected that Shostakovich would be elected First Secretary. I took part in the meeting of the Secretariat of the Russian Composers Union when the election was scheduled. Shostakovich was nominated by Khrennikov, which clearly confirmed that his candidacy had been approved from "on high." Following his election, Shostakovich went right to work and announced that the Secretariat would meet twice a week, the first time to deal with organizational questions and the second to listen to music (previously the Secretariat had met only twice a month). This arrangement continued for two or three years, with only slight cutbacks in the number of meetings. Over this period we listened to an enormous amount of contemporary Soviet music. Shostakovich instituted an "iron" discipline and would not allow anyone to arrive even a minute late, although, truth be known, none of us had previously considered tardiness to be a mortal sin. Dmitri Dmitrievich was something of a pedant. Besides that, he expected the members of the union's Board of Directors to travel around the country and familiarize themselves with composers' works on location. This not only significantly promoted creativity in the provinces, but it also encouraged a new sense of unity among composers throughout the Russian Federation.

Dmitri Dmitrievich could not tolerate boorishness and incivility toward anyone. I remember one occasion when we were traveling together in the Russian Federation. Our group was scheduled to meet with a local leader about some creative problem. The fellow in charge shook Shostakovich's hand and, without a glance at anyone else, said, "Well, let's get down to work." At that, Shostakovich replied, "No indeed. We're not about to get down to work. You've greeted me, but there are eight other people here. Say hello to everyone, or we're all leaving immediately." So the local bigwig was obliged to go all around shaking hands and saying, "How do you do?" He'd probably never had to do anything like that before, given his sense of self-importance. This incident revealed another aspect of Shostakovich's character: he carried the whole thing off without the slightest ostentation. Shostakovich's involvement in this sort of active social service continued until about 1967 or 1968.

Let me conclude my comments with another revealing anecdote about Shostakovich's character. I don't remember how it happened, but he and I ended up together in a group attending a dress rehearsal of the Moiseev Dance Company. The program included a charming little genre scene called "Sunday." The plot was as follows: a housemaid and a cook in their pretty Sunday dresses are receiving guests, a telegraph operator and a janitor. They all dance a quadrille. The girls act coquettishly. The telegraph operator puts on a courtly manner to woo the housemaid. In short, the scene was quite amusing. Everybody laughed and everybody liked it. Only Dmitri Dmitrievich sat in gloomy silence. Then he jumped up and declared, "That number ought to be struck from the program. Why are you all laughing at those poor people who just happened to end up in that social situation? You remind me of the boys who threw spitballs at Akaky Akakievich in Gogol's story *Shinel'* [The overcoat]." Needless to say, the idea hadn't entered anyone else's mind. But Shostakovich had taken the scene seriously. It was typical of him to defend the "unimportant" folk, very much in the tradition of Gogol, Dostoevsky, and Chekhov.

❦

Lev Nikolaevich Lebedinsky (1904–1992). Musicologist; member of the Communist Party from 1919; a leading member of the Russian Association of Proletarian Musicians from 1923 to 1932.

I.N. I would be interested to hear what you think about Solomon Volkov's book, which supposedly represents the memoirs of our great composer?

L.L. I consider this book to be one of the most important publications devoted to the composer. Its authenticity is beyond question. I am prepared to sign my name under every word in the book. It is the truth about Shostakovich.

I.N. You were able to observe Shostakovich's life up close?

L.L. Yes, I met with Dmitri Dmitrievich quite often and I think he was candid with me. Many of my conversations with him are reflected in Volkov's book.° The book came as a big surprise here in our country because our social-political system had interpreted Shostakovich's creative work from an utterly different perspective. Dmitri Dmitrievich had been obliged to hide the true meaning of his symphonies. But he shared his creative conceptions with me, and there are many examples.

I.N. Has your own attitude toward Shostakovich's work changed over the years?

L.L. No, my attitude hasn't changed at all. I think Shostakovich was a fighter.

I.N. What do you mean by that?

L.L. It has been said that Shostakovich was not enough of a social activist in our country, but this is fundamentally untrue. He inflicted powerful blows on the Stalinist regime, although, of course, the majority of his listeners did not realize it.

I.N. Can you illustrate your point?

L.L. Take the Eighth and Tenth symphonies. These works powerfully depict the white heat of a dramatic struggle. Shostakovich was speaking out forcefully in these works, but from behind a transparent mask, so to speak. He was obliged to shield himself from retaliation by composing pure instrumental music.

I.N. But how do you explain Symphony No. 11, "The Year 1905," dedicated to the first Russian revolution, and Symphony No. 12, "The Year 1917," dedicated to Lenin?

V.B. Dmitri Dmitrievich himself said that the Eleventh Symphony speaks not so much about the past as about the present. For me, the Eleventh Symphony conveys an image of a "Stalinist prison." It denounces Stalinism, metaphorically, and therefore I believe it continues the fundamental ethical-conceptual line that extends throughout all the Shostakovich symphonies.

As for the Twelfth Symphony, it follows that same line but in another way. For me, this so-called "Lenin" Symphony amounts to a debunking of Leninism. The symphony even contains something like a typical soliloquy that seems to parody Lenin's style of speaking. The next symphony, the Thirteenth, voices Shostakovich's protest against Stalinist anti-Semitism. In fact, I do not believe that Shostakovich ever deviated from this fundamental line in his symphonies. Already in the First Symphony I hear sounds of alarm, the premonitions of a terrible future. These recur again and again in the later symphonies, from the Fourth on.

The Fifteenth Symphony is autobiographical. The quotation from Rossini's *William Tell* symbolizes Shostakovich's youthful strivings, his sincere feelings about the social and political ideals of that period in his life. But this topic is gradually displaced, and the image of death begins to play the primary role—indeed, the central role—in the composer's Fourteenth and Fifteenth symphonies. Genius that he was, Shostakovich felt death approaching. No wonder the Fifteenth was his last symphony.[p]

I.N. What do you know about the history of Shostakovich's relationship with Evgeny Mravinsky?

L.L. Dmitri Dmitrievich made known his opinion that Mravinsky's interpretations were deficient in depth.

I.N. What can you say about Shostakovich as a personality?

L.L. I continue to hold the highest regard for Shostakovich. True, we had some disagreements about his attitude toward Boris Pasternak, Alexander Solzhenitsyn, and Andrei Sakharov, which he expressed in print,[q] but these disagreements could not sever the bonds that united us, above all, our shared sense of being confined in a "Stalinist prison."

As a human being, Shostakovich was charming, spontaneous, and witty. He loved good company with whom he could also enjoy a few drinks.

I.N. But his relationship with some of his composer-colleagues did not always turn out to be friendly.

L.L. Quite true. He did not get along well with Prokofiev and spoke about him rather harshly, although he acknowledged Prokofiev's great talent. He did not feel close to Stravinsky as a composer, but this should come as no surprise, of course, given that the two represented such different trends in Russian music. Shostakovich remained a committed realist, whereas Stravinsky kept to the creative stance of a *miriskusnik*—an heir to the *Mir iskusstva*, or World of Art movement, to Sergei Diaghilev's aesthetic and artistic philosophy.

I.N. How did Shostakovich view himself in life and in art?

L.L. He viewed himself as a tragic figure. And he was certainly that. Moreover, those who do not hear this in his music have not yet grasped the most important element in his work. He valued this feeling in himself, the feeling of perpetual sorrow for those who had perished, a feeling he never lost. This suggests an analogy with the poetry of Anna Akhmatova, particularly with her *Rekviem* [Requiem]. Of course, there are other sides to his creative legacy—satire, irony, sarcasm—but the most important aspect is tragedy.

❦

Boris Ivanovich Tishchenko (b. 1930). Noted St. Petersburg composer and professor at the St. Petersburg Conservatory; named Honored Artist of the Russian Federation and People's Artist of the Russian Federation. A close family friend of Shostakovich, he studied composition with him from 1962 to 1965.

I.N. How would you describe the role Shostakovich played in your creative life?

B.T. I would say that Shostakovich sustained my will to live. His music, and his very existence, gave meaning to my life. Shostakovich's greatness as a human being was no less than his greatness as a composer. His relationship with people, with his colleagues, was founded in mutual trust and respect. Since his death, I have experienced the influence of his music even more deeply and more powerfully. For me, the art of Shostakovich is a phenomenon of cosmic magnitude.

I.N. What music did Shostakovich feel passionate about?

B.T. His great admiration of Mahler is well known, but at some point in the late 1960s or early 1970s he remarked, "I used to think that Mahler was the best composer of all times and peoples, but now I think Bach is better." On another occasion he said that Stravinsky was the most outstanding twentieth-century composer. He deeply respected Britten, whose music was akin to his. As for composers of the past, he especially appreciated Haydn, Mozart, and Beethoven.

I.N. What Soviet music did he like?

B.T. He singled out in particular works of Galina Ustvolskaya, Alexander Lokshin, and Mechislav [Moisei] Weinberg. He loved to exchange opinions about the latest works of his students and colleagues, and about his own works as well.

I.N. Don't you agree that a number of his contemporaries were and have remained under his strong influence? For instance, Weinberg?

B.T. Influence, absolutely. But it would be inaccurate to call any of these composers epigones. Don't forget the saying, "The Chinese look the same only from a distance!" While we're on the subject, I'd also say that the influence was mutual.

Shostakovich was always an indefatigable listener to music. He often listened in the rooms of the Secretariat of the Russian Composers Union. And he listened to all kinds of music. He used to say, "I'm omnivorous. I love all music, from Bach to Offenbach."

I.N. What interested Dmitri Dmitrievich besides music?

B.T. Lots. He was an avid reader, read a great deal and often recommended one book or another: "Be sure to read this," he would say. Besides that, he himself had a literary gift. Indeed, even his personal letters are chefs d'oeuvre both in conception and style. He was coauthor of his operas *Nos* [The nose] and *Ledi Makbet Mtsenskogo uezda* [Lady Macbeth of the Mtsensk District]. He himself wrote the libretto of his satirical anti-Stalinist *Peepshow, Antiformalisticheskii rayok* [The antiformalist peepshow].[r] During his last years he planned new operas: *Tikhii Don* [The quiet Don], after Sholokhov, and *Chornyi monakh* [The black monk], after Chekhov.

I.N. What do you think about Solomon Volkov's book?

B.T. I consider it unethical to mention that name in a conversation about Shostakovich.

I.N. Do you know why relations between Shostakovich and Mravinsky cooled? Mravinsky, of course, conducted many premières of Shostakovich's works.

B.T. No, I don't. And I don't rely on secondhand information. I do know that Dmitri Dmitrievich greatly appreciated Mravinsky's interpretations. I was reminded of this yet again in 1972, when I was sitting next to Shostakovich at a rehearsal of the Fifteenth Symphony in the Great Hall of the Leningrad Philharmonic.

I.N. Do you think that the harassment and persecution Shostakovich endured in the 1930s and 1940s harmed his work?

B.T. I think the attacks inflicted more damage on his health than on his work. We know Shostakovich had three heart attacks, the last coinciding with the onset of his cancer. Medical research has shown that cancer can be caused by psychological factors. . . . All the same, in his music Shostakovich never ceased to be a powerful personality.

❧

Manashir Yakubov (b. 1936). Doctor of Arts History; Honorary Member of the International Shostakovich Society (London) and Honorary Member of the Japanese Shostakovich Society; since 1981, curator of the Shostakovich Family Archive.

I.N. Do you sense any change in the evaluation of Shostakovich's works in our society today? What is your own perspective on this? In short, have there been any particular developments?

M.Y. I should say so, especially now in these troubled times. But *how* attitudes have changed is another matter. When society is divided into factions and various groups emerge, each in its own way wants to lay claim to Shostakovich. Some representatives of the more liberal ideological factions speak of Shostakovich as their forebear, while other, more conservative groups argue with them and try to prove that Shostakovich was an iron-clad Socialist Realist who wrote songs about Stalin, composed the cantata *Nad rodinoi nashei soltse siiaet* [The sun shines over our motherland] (also called *Kommunisticheskoi partii—slava!* [Glory to the Communist Party]), *Pesn' o lesakh* [The song of the forests]; won six Stalin prizes, composed a symphony about Lenin (the Twelfth, "The Year 1917"), and wrote the choral cycle *Vernost'* [Loyalty] to poems by Evgeny Dolmatovsky, and so on. Meanwhile, representatives of still other opposing ideological camps announce that Shostakovich is really *their* Shostakovich.

Even a "museum movement" exists among some radical "left" composers, who declare that Shostakovich is a classic and ought to be relegated to a museum. A fine-looking portrait of him ought to be painted—no doubt something resembling an icon—which can then be dusted off and displayed on appropriate jubilees. This particular tendency, to invalidate Shostakovich's music for today, seems to me utterly wrongheaded. Indeed, the ongoing struggle that rages around his name proves the continuing validity of Shostakovich's art.

Some people declare that Shostakovich was a closet dissident. Lev

Lebedinsky holds to this viewpoint and has claimed insistently that Shostakovich's Twelfth Symphony is a "debunking of Marxism-Leninism." Time was, however, when Lebedinsky thought differently and staunchly defended Marxist-Leninist ideals (it's not by chance that, once upon a time, his main publications dealt with the Eleventh Symphony, "The Year 1905," and similar Shostakovich works on themes of the Revolution).[s] The late Daniel Zhitomirsky, in his time, also "made" Shostakovich into a purely Soviet artist. But, more recently, both Lebedinsky and Zhitomirsky have tried to portray Dmitri Dmitrievich as a person living in internal exile, one who totally rejected the existing system and repudiated everything Soviet. But let us not forget that a number of works Shostakovich composed are as clear as crystal with respect to their ideological content. And not just those mentioned above, which were often composed "under pressure," but also those composed from the heart, works he felt inspired to compose. Take, for instance, the Second Symphony, "Dedicated to October," which exemplifies art inspired by the Revolution, both in its ideological orientation and in its title. This symphony, as a work of art, however, does not fit the pigeonhole of Socialist Realism. No wonder it was condemned and not performed for decades.

As I see it, Shostakovich was a true "living classic." This is what I mean by that: a "living classic" can never be fitted into the confines of a prevailing ideology, even within a totalitarian system. Shostakovich embodied the best qualities of the Russian character. He was a "Russian man" in the full, multifaceted sense of the word. Hence the living Shostakovich united within himself many different traits of character and ways of thinking and feeling, at different periods of his life, at the very same time, including that of being an "internal exile" (like so many other members of the intelligentsia). But at the same time he was also still a patriot and held onto a belief in some of the ideals of the Revolution.

I.N. In light of what you have said, can you imagine Symphonies No. 11, 12, 13, and 14 as belonging to the same conceptual line, notwithstanding their diametrically different ideological orientations?

M.Y. No problem at all to imagine it, since they were all composed by a person who was living in our "Soviet reality"[t]—a reality far more complicated than any of the patterns into which the Communists, on the one side, or the avant-gardists, on the other, have tried to fit Shostakovich. We were obliged to accommodate to that kind of life, and we were obliged to pay a price for true art. Of course, accommodation could be made in different ways. Some people became murderers; others, who wanted to live, became their victims. This is why Osip Mandelshtam first wrote such anti-Stalinist verses as "We live as ourselves in disguise, not feeling the ground under our feet," but later he composed poems eulogizing Stalin. The same thing happened with the poets Anna Akhmatova and Boris Pasternak, and the composers Prokofiev and Shostakovich. Didn't Prokofiev suffer from a split personality? Wasn't he obliged to hide both his religious beliefs and his hatred of the Bolsheviks? That was life. That is why we find such complicated, contradictory conceptual lines in the creative work of our great artists—lines that intermingle conflicting elements: the elevated and the ignoble, the horrifying and the humorous.

It is entirely possible that, when he was composing his Eleventh Symphony, Shostakovich had in mind not only the Revolution of 1905 but also the expectation that listeners would also hear more generalized metaphors of violence and human suffering, not just what the Communist ideologues wanted them to hear. Incidentally I even think that the Twelfth Symphony manifests high artistic values. People have forgotten a very important statement Shostakovich made in a radio interview. He called attention to the fact that he viewed the Eleventh and Twelfth symphonies as a diptych and wanted them to be performed one after the other in a single concert. I related this to the conductor Genady Rozhdestvensky, and afterward Rozhdestvensky twice arranged such performances abroad. In his opinion these symphonies, played together, sound much more convincing.

I.N. There is one question I am asking everyone: What do you think about Solomon Volkov's book? Here in our country reactions have ranged all the way from total rejection and condemnation to total vindication.

M.Y. The book has not yet been published in Russia, and it has become increasingly clear that it will not be. The publisher responsible for releasing the book has supposedly vetoed publication of the Russian original. This is the story Volkov tells in the newspaper *Nezavisimaia gazeta.* It didn't surprise me. Every edition of the book that I've seen shows that Volkov himself owns the copyright, not some publisher.

I.N. Why do you think Volkov doesn't want to publish the original?

M.Y. Volkov is afraid of it. He's afraid of being exposed, because the book is only partially authentic. Volkov himself told me that he met with Shostakovich only three times. It isn't possible to produce a book this size after only three meetings. Specialists in the West have repeatedly pointed out some rather obvious instances of falsification in the book. Laurel E. Fay has even written an article about it. And Henry Orlov, the eminent ex-Soviet musicologist and Shostakovich expert, has expressed his opinion of the book quite clearly. Orlov is well known to have been personally and closely associated with Shostakovich for many years, in contrast to Solomon Volkov, who had to beg Boris Tishchenko to introduce him to Shostakovich. The foreword to Volkov's book about young Leningrad composers served as the pretext, since Shostakovich's students were to be included among them. Dmitri Dmitrievich never refused such requests and eventually agreed to say a few words. After that, Volkov managed to get Shostakovich talking, not about himself but about his contemporaries who were subject to repression. Volkov personally told me all this. This topic always greatly upset Dmitri Dmitrievich—the fates of Vsevolod Meyerhold, Mikhail Zoshchenko, the composer Alexander Glazunov. No wonder the cautious Shostakovich wrote on the back of the photo he gave Volkov that it was a reminder of their talks about Meyerhold, Zoshchenko, and Glazunov, or something like that (the photo is reproduced in Volkov's book along with Shostakovich's inscription on the back of the photo).[u] Shostakovich wanted to make it clear that there were no other talks. Considering what happened, no wonder Shostakovich thought it necessary to list exactly the people about whom he and Volkov spoke.

If the book were published here in Russia, it would become clear immediately which texts are genuine and which are not. Volkov made use of many texts published during Dmitri Dmitrievich's lifetime, sometimes after appropriate paraphrasing, when a particular text suited his purpose.

If Volkov weren't afraid of being exposed, he could become the center of a new sensation even now. But this would entail his confessing what in the book is genuine and what he himself introduced or wrote on the basis of stories told to him by informants in Moscow and Leningrad—informants such as that very same Lev Lebedinsky, whom I mentioned earlier, or Leo Arnshtam, among others. But I do not believe Volkov is man enough to make such a confession.

Concerning the contents of the book, I think only a poorly informed reader could take some of the material at face value. For instance, take the episode about how Tikhon Khrennikov became general secretary of the USSR Union of Composers. Nobody knows how this actually happened, since the incident, as described, took place between Stalin and his personal secretary, Poskrebyshev, who was Stalin's devoted slave—so devoted, in fact, that when the "Leader of the People" ordered the arrest of Poskrebyshev's wife, he did not protest. It is hardly possible that Poskrebyshev would have told anyone in the world about his talk with Stalin concerning Khrennikov's appointment. In short, the whole scene is nothing more than a pseudo-historical yarn—very effective, calculated for the philistine sensibilities of a mass audience, but absolutely far-fetched, and all the more far-fetched that Shostakovich would have communicated this to Volkov.

Volkov can be "caught in the act" in connection with other matters in the book as well. For instance, consider the episode about Alban Berg's coming to Leningrad in 1927 for the première of his opera *Wozzeck.* Volkov describes in detail how Shostakovich did not miss a single performance, how Berg was received in Leningrad, how a dinner was arranged in Berg's honor, and so on. Then comes a curious passage in which Shostakovich speaks about Berg's departure, but in the words of Alexander Pushkin from Pushkin's "little tragedy," *Motsart i Sal'eri* [Mozart and Salieri]. Salieri speaks these words at his parting from Mozart, subsequent to his having slipped poison into Mozart's wine. (Volkov, by the way, fails to mention that the words come from Pushkin.) As presented by Volkov, Shostakovich bids farewell to Berg, one of his idols, in the words of Salieri! Dmitri Dmitrievich had an astonishing knowledge of Russian literature, especially Pushkin and Gogol, and he would never have played the fool in this manner.

Let me repeat: Until Volkov's book is published in Russian, it is impossible even to contemplate a serious textual analysis. Otherwise, Volkov can always say, "My book has been translated incorrectly!" The translation of subtleties and shadings leads inevitably to deviations in meaning, and a textual analysis aimed at establishing the text's authenticity would necessarily focus on subtleties and shadings. This is why, I believe, Volkov will never agree to publish this book in Russian, much less in a facsimile edition of his original manuscript.[v]

I.N. Some of the individuals I've interviewed doubt that Shostakovich could possibly have referred to Mravinsky in the manner reported in Volkov's book.

M.Y. This, unfortunately, is exactly the sort of problem I was talking about. As soon as we start to analyze the non-Russian text, we step on a slippery slope, because the translation itself can always be blamed. For example, Khrennikov is said to have become Stalin's "house dog" [*tsepnaia sobaka;* literally, a dog on a chain]. However, no such expression exists in German; but there is *Bluthund,* which is not at all the same thing.[w] As it happens, a translation of the German edition of the book was read to poor Khrennikov, who flew into an indescribable rage [in

German, *Bluthund* refers to the pedigree dog, the bloodhound, but figuratively to a bloodthirsty man, *ein blutgieriger Mensch*].

Still another matter is raised, this one psychological in nature, by Volkov monopolizing our communication, as it were, with Shostakovich. People close to the composer's age, who moved within some of the same circles as he did, believe they knew him quite well and that he could never have said certain things Volkov reported. But they are in a precarious position. Shostakovich could well have said something to Volkov that he never said to anyone else in his circle. One can be prompted to say one thing or another, depending on the circumstances and on the particular individual with whom one is speaking.

Still others, who knew the composer intimately, believe that the book actually does include matters that Dmitri Dmitrievich told Volkov, or possibly could have told him, but that Volkov reported them in a very deceptive manner. For my part, I have yet another explanation that lies altogether elsewhere. I believe that Volkov's source was a bitter and spiteful individual, someone such as Lev Lebedinsky. Volkov could very well have heard from Lebedinsky exactly the sort of statements that he attributes to Shostakovich in his book.

I.N. And what do you know about the sad finale of Shostakovich's friendship with Mravinsky?

M.Y. First of all, it was not a finale but an episode. The finale was not the same. The nature of the episode can be deduced from the performance history of Shostakovich's works.

I.N. Are you thinking of the Thirteenth Symphony?

M.Y. Not only of that but also of an earlier period in their acquaintance when Mravinsky also stopped conducting the premières of Shostakovich's orchestral works. Let me elaborate. Relations between Shostakovich and Mravinsky have always been idealized, which is not unusual, given the general tendency to idealize. Our contemporaries had the impression that theirs was an ideal creative friendship. But, as I see it, their relationship was not without problems from the very beginning. Anyone who carefully reads through Shostakovich's article about Mravinsky will feel it. To be specific, you can read there in black and white that Mravinsky's painstaking queries and scrupulous method of working on a score irritated Shostakovich and drove him to wit's end.[x] Of course, he did express appreciation for the purely technical excellence of Mravinsky's performances. Had their partnership been truly ideal, how can one explain that more than half the Shostakovich symphonies are missing from

Mravinsky's performance record? He never conducted the Second, Third, Fourth, Thirteenth, and Fourteenth symphonies, or any number of the composer's orchestral works. Mravinsky's affiliation with Shostakovich was "selective," depending on whether he liked or understood a particular work. Some things he never accepted.

Their relations were severed with the Thirteenth Symphony.[y] When Shostakovich completed the symphony, he proposed that Boris Gmyrya, whom he admired very much, should sing the bass solo and that Mravinsky should conduct. Shostakovich went first to Gmyrya and played the entire symphony for him. Gmyrya, who felt great affection for the composer, nevertheless hesitated. He felt that he was in a problematic situation, because during the war he happened to be in territory occupied by the Germans and had appeared in concerts there. Apparently this had long been forgotten. Later on, he had even been awarded the Order of Lenin. Still his situation was delicate, and he had to be careful. Gmyrya did some further checking around with officials at the Party Committee of the City of Kiev, and as soon as they became acquainted with the text of *Babyi Yar*, as well as with the other movements of the symphony, they "recommended," to put it mildly, that Gmyrya not perform in the symphony. Gmyrya explained all this straightforwardly and candidly to Shostakovich. The latter did not take offense and continued his friendly relations with Gmyrya.

Why am I telling you all this? I wish to draw a clear distinction between the conduct of Gmyrya and that of Mravinsky.

After his meetings with Gmyrya, Shostakovich traveled to Leningrad to show Mravinsky the score. This happened at the beginning of the summer. Mravinsky promised to learn the symphony over the summer, and the première was planned for autumn. But that fall, when the date of the première had to be set, Mravinsky claimed that, when he left Leningrad for vacation, he had forgotten to take the score with him, and now he didn't have time to learn it before the première. Dmitri Dmitrievich could not forgive Mravinsky for this, at least not right away. As you know, Kirill Kondrashin conducted the première.

This is all I know about why there was a rift between Shostakovich and Mravinsky, which lasted for several years. Eventually, however, the passage of time put the affair in perspective. Mravinsky continued to conduct Shostakovich's music. He performed the Fifteenth Symphony during Shostakovich's lifetime and even recorded it twice, if I'm not mistaken. Still and all, the earlier relationship between the composer and the conductor was never fully restored. In fact, after the situation with the Thirteenth Symphony, Shostakovich did not offer Mravinsky the premières of either the Fourteenth or the Fifteenth.

I.N. How did it happen that you became associated with the Shostakovich Family Archive? What kind of archive is it, and what exactly do you do there?

M.Y. I became acquainted with Shostakovich around 1969. For three years, from the end of 1967 to the beginning of 1971, I was working for the Lenin Prize Committee, and Shostakovich was a member of the Committee's Music Section; this gave me the opportunity to interact with him more or less regularly. He was maniacally punctual and always arrived at meetings of the Music Section before anyone else. I knew this and made a point of arriving even earlier. We would talk about various things, but that's another story. I had already published a few articles about Shostakovich's music by then, and he evidently liked them, as I learned later from Dmitri Dmitrievich's widow.

When Melodiya, the recording company, released a record of Shostakovich's song cycle on texts by Michelangelo, in which direct references are made to the fate of Alexander Solzhenitsyn, many musicologists were apprehensive and refused to write anything about the cycle.[z] I received a telegram from Shostakovich asking me to write the liner notes for the recording, which provided yet another opportunity for us to get together.

After Dmitri Dmitrievich's death, at my first meeting with Irina Antonovna, I offered to help sort out his papers. Over the next ten years I wrote the prefaces to twenty-five of the volumes in Shostakovich's *Collected Works*,[aa] not one of which is credited to me. This entailed an enormous amount of work researching archival sources, and every bit of it was published anonymously.

I.N. Why?

M.Y. Because the director of the Muzyka publishing house received information that I was a dissident and might emigrate and go to Israel. I have the page proof with the listing of scholars who worked on the *Collected Works*, and my name has been crossed out. During my employment with the edition, Irina Antonovna proposed that I also work on Dmitri Dmitrievich's materials at her apartment, where Shostakovich had lived. And I did so for quite a number of years.

The collection is rather substantial, comprising manuscripts, concert programs and posters, literary materials, and letters addressed to Shostakovich, along with copies of his answers to the letters. This archive also comprises Shostakovich's personal library, which is priceless: it includes editions of his music that he himself signed, sometimes with notated corrections to the score; his personal collection of music and books, including rarities with autograph dedications from famous writers; and books Dmitri Dmitrievich used. For example, there is the collection of Jewish folk songs from which he selected the texts for his well-known song cycle *Iz evreiskoi narodnoi poesii* [From Jewish folk poetry] op. 79, as well as books of verses by Evgeny Yevtushenko, Marina Tsvetaeva, Wilhelm Küchelbecker, and others. In the course of my work, I naturally also had to familiarize myself with the state archival collections containing Shostakovich materials, particularly those in the Russian State Archive of Literature and Art (formerly the *Tsentral'nyi gosudarstvennyi arkhiv literatury i iskusstva*) and the Glinka State Museum (*Gosudarstvennyi muzykal'nyi muzei im. Glinki*).

At the present time I am writing scholarly studies based on archival materials. By way of example, I'll mention two of the most important ones thus far. The first, "The Musical and Literary Sources of Shostakovich's *Antiformalist Peepshow*,"[bb] entails a thorough analysis of the libretto and its several sources (this part of the study might be regarded as essentially documentary in character). The music is also analyzed thoroughly, revealing numerous quotations both obvious and oblique. The date of the work's conception is also established.

I.N. What date did you discover?

M.Y. The first movement of *Peepshow*, with Edinitsyn and Dvoikin (before the appearance of Troikin) was composed in 1948, which I demonstrate entirely from the evidence of the extant autographs; in other words, everything before the episode where they dance the *lezginka*, inclusive. Lebedinsky didn't know about these autographs and spread the rumor that he was the author of the libretto.[cc]

The second project, based exclusively on the archives, is a facsimile edition of Shostakovich's Seventh Symphony. I am editor of this publication and author of the scholarly commentary, in connection with which I also decipher fragments of the symphony's rough drafts. The rough drafts are dated and stand as irrefutable evidence that the symphony was composed after the start of the Great Patriotic War. The great Japanese publishing house, Zen-On Music Company Limited, published the facsimile edition in September 1992. The publication was conceived in honor of the company's Fiftieth Jubilee. The foreword is printed in Russian, Japanese, English, and German.[dd]

I.N. What are your plans for the future?

M.Y. I've started writing a book about the opera *Ledi Makbet Mtsen-*

skogo uezda [Lady Macbeth of the Mtsensk District], since the archives contain much valuable material associated with the history of the work's composition, the persecution of Shostakovich after its production, the second version of the opera titled *Katerina Izmailova,* and so on. I am also gradually collecting material for another book temporarily entitled, "Shostakovich's Manuscripts." I envision this book as perhaps being more for the general reader than the scholar. In the book I'll tell the story of my search for manuscripts and my discovery of previously unknown works by Shostakovich, as well as of their first performances. I will also touch on purely musicological matters.

Despite the widespread impression that Shostakovich never made changes in his finished works, he occasionally did make changes and some of them were quite significant. In this regard, a comparison of *Lady Macbeth* with *Katerina Izmailova* reveals much of interest. In some respects, they are different operas. The very conception of the opera is radically changed in the second version, with corresponding changes in both libretto and music. It is a fallacy to believe that, in response to criticism, Shostakovich deleted all the "spiky" parts of the score and lowered the tessitura of the voice parts. In some sections just the opposite is true, for instance, in the scene of Katerina's suicide he raised the tessitura still higher. The manuscript evidence of his work on the second version of the opera refutes the popular notion that he was a "broken" man and simply capitulated. They certainly wanted to subjugate his will, but they couldn't do it.

I.N. Let us hope that your books will contribute to revealing the historical truth about Shostakovich and that his art will be appreciated anew.

M.Y. The documents themselves will eventually be published, and it is harder to argue with documents than with opinions. People's ideas are "perishable goods." This is why I prefer to rely on documentary materials.

Notes

1. Solomon Volkov, "Zdes' chelovek sgorel" [A man burned out here], *Muzykal'naia akademiia,* no. 3 (1992): 8.

2. Babyi Yar is the place-name of a ravine near Kiev where Hitler's fascist invaders conducted mass executions of Jews.

Editor's Notes

a. "Soviet reality," or *sovetskaia deistvitel'nost'*, is a stock phrase in the lexicon of Soviet-era sociopolitical jargon.

b. Nikolskaya asks several of her interviewees about Shostakovich's relations with Mravinsky, sometimes pointing out that Mravinsky did not conduct the première performance of the controversial Thirteenth Symphony. With regard to the latter, my colleague, Michael Parrish, director of the library of the Indiana University School of Business and School of Public and Environmental Affairs, kindly called my attention to the following letter to the editor of the British journal *Gramophone:*

> In his review of Shostakovich Symphonies (*Gramophone*, November 1994, p. 84), David Gutman writes of "Mravinsky's politically motivated refusal to undertake the première of the Thirteenth in 1962." I suppose one of the sources of this information is *Kirill Kondrashin rasskazyvaet o muzyke i zhizni* [Kirill Kondrashin talks about music and (his) life], in conversation with Vladimir Razhnikov (Moscow: Sovetskii kompozitor, 1989). However, as far as I can gather from Alexandra Mikhailovna Vavilina-Mravinskaya (the conductor's widow) and some members of the Leningrad Philharmonic Orchestra, Mravinsky devoted himself solely to music and was not concerned with political issues.
>
> The story Mrs. Mravinsky (formerly Principal Flautist of the Leningrad PO [Philharmonic Orchestra] and currently Professor at the St. Petersburg Conservatory) told us at a party in Tokyo this October [1994] is as follows. When Shostakovich brought the score of his new Thirteenth Symphony to Mravinsky, the conductor's second wife, Inna (a close friend of Vavilina, his third wife), was seriously ill with cancer, and Mravinsky's circumstances were very difficult. Some say that relations between Shostakovich and Mravinsky were bad at that time, but this is not true. The reason why Mravinsky did not première this symphony is that he simply could not do so, although he tried. The score on which he made notes for the performance supports this story, which is related also in an article by N. Kozhevnikova (*Sovetskaia kul'tura*, 8 June 1991).
>
> [signed] Kenzoh Amoh,
> Tokyo, Japan
> [*Gramophone*, December 1994, p. 8]

c. The connotations of the noun *intelligent*, as it is understood by Russians of the Soviet and post-Soviet periods, embraces attributes associated in English with the noun *intellectual* but must not be confused with it. The Russian concept is far richer in connotations, among them an active commitment to social justice, a determination always to take a critical view of reality, a desire to perpetuate the intellectual and ethical principles exemplified in prerevolutionary Russian art and literature, and a resolve to be a "keeper" of a richer, *specifically Russian* intellectual heritage that, during Soviet times, was assiduously controlled, and often censored, by officialdom.

d. See note c above.

e. Nikolai Ezhov, then head of the NKVD (later, the KGB), was the principal overseer of the Great Purges in the period from 1937 to 1938.

f. Whether or not these were Stalin's words, who actually wrote the notorious *Pravda* editorial remains a mystery. See Laurel Fay's comments on the matter in her *Shostakovich*, p. 304 n. 67.

g. Shostakovich's Third String Quartet in F Major op. 73 was composed in 1946, the same year as the founding of the Borodin Quartet ensemble. The "Beethovens" gave the work's première performance that same year, on 16 December, in Moscow. Although Berlinsky speaks only of the "Beethovens" performing Shostakovich's First and Second quartets, it seems highly likely that some of the "Borodins," all four of whom were still students at the Conservatory, would have been present for such a notable occasion as the première performance of Shostakovich's Third String Quartet. For information about the première performances of all fifteen of the Shostakovich quartets, see Fay, *Shostakovich*, pp. 359–60.

h. Rostislav Dubinsky, "founder of the Borodin Quartet" [from the book's dust jacket], *Stormy Applause: Making Music in a Worker's State* (New York: Hill and Wang, 1989).

i. CPSU is the Communist Party of the Soviet Union.

j. Dubinsky writes in his memoirs, "In our quartet all four of us were Jewish, though the cellist, Valentin Berlinsky, was Jewish only on his father's side. His passport said he was Russian. That was his choice, because in the postwar Soviet Union the word 'Jew' had become somewhat taboo. Free of the stigma of being branded a Jew, Berlinsky, who had been a member of the Young Communist League, the Komsomol, joined the Communist Party. This gave him a noticeable advantage over the rest of us" (*Stormy Applause*, pp. 8–9).

k. Either Martynov's memory failed him here or he intended to say "former" members of the RAPM tried to mount an attack on the Fifth Symphony. The RAPM had been dissolved some five years before the Fifth Symphony (along with *all* proletarian organizations in literature and the arts), by the Party's Resolution of 23 April 1932, "On the Reconstruction of Literary and Artistic Organizations," which had put an end to the so-called proletarian phase in Soviet arts history.

l. The name of the "lady" in Shostakovich's *Lady Macbeth* op. 29 is Katerina Izmailova, and, in fact, the 1934 production at Moscow's Nemirovich-Danchenko Theater had run under the title *Katerina Izmailova*, at exactly the same time as the première production was still running in Leningrad's Maly Opera Theater under the title *Ledi Makbet Mtsenskogo uezda* [Lady Macbeth of the Mtsensk District]. Revising the opera in the period from 1954 to 1963, Shostakovich decided, perhaps for political reasons, to use the title *Katerina Izmailova*. When the revisions were completed, he appended a new opus number, op. 114 (see Manashir Yakubov's comments about the composer's revisions on page 184 of the interviews printed here. The Stanislavsky Nemirovich-Danchenko Theater in Moscow staged the revised version of the opera in an "unofficial" première on 26 December 1962 and in an "official" première on 8 January 1963. See Fay, *Shostakovich*, pp. 75, 194, 197, 237–39.

m. Tikhon Nikolaevich Khrennikov (b. 1913), a composer, was tapped by the Party Central Committee (reportedly approved by Stalin himself) to assume leadership of the Union of Composers of the USSR in 1948. He held this position throughout the remaining fifty-one-year existence of the Soviet Union, holding a succession of titles: General Secretary (1948–57), First Secretary (1957–90), and, finally, Executive Secretary and President (1990–91). After the demise of the USSR it was widely believed that Khrennikov would be voted out of office by the successor Union of Composers of the newly declared Russian Federation of the Commonwealth of Independent States, but in fact the union's membership has continued to support him in a leadership position (2002).

n. The Composers Union of the Russian Soviet Federal Socialist Republic, as distinct from the umbrella organization, the Composers Union of the entire country, that is, the Composers Union of the Union of Soviet Socialist Republics.

o. A handwritten note by Irina Nikolskaya in the typescript of her 1992 interview with Lebedinsky reads, "My interlocutor, in saying this, seems to suggest that he had a hand in helping Volkov put his book together."

p. Lebedinsky's statement in Russian is no less vague and ambiguous than the English translation: "Kak chelovek genial'nyi, on chuvstvoval priblizhenie smerti, nedarom 15-ia stala poslednei ego simfoniei."

q. Lebedinsky is disingenuous to suggest, in this curiously phrased remark, that he disagreed privately with Shostakovich about the composer's compliance with the Party line in opposing political dissidence. Lebedinsky himself, a Party member since 1919, *never* openly supported such politically controversial figures as Pasternak, Solzhenitsyn, or Sakharov or, for that matter, any other politically suspect person or cause. Yet Lebedinsky's remark here seems intent on representing himself as a true dissident.

The point should also be made that, notwithstanding Lebedinsky's listing of the names Pasternak, Solzhenitsyn, and Sakharov, no evidence supports the suggestion that Shostakovich's signature appeared on any published document criticizing Pasternak, who was awarded the Nobel Prize for Literature in 1958 for his novel, *Doktor Zhivago* [Doctor Zhivago]. Pasternak declined the honor but was nevertheless expelled from the Union of Writers of the USSR that same year. In the case of Solzhenitsyn, Shostakovich signed a petition requesting an apartment in Moscow for the writer but "could not support his defiant public exhibition of political dissidence" (see Fay, *Shostakovich*, pp. 269–70); still, no *published* criticism of Solzhenitsyn appeared over Shostakovich's signature. Only in the case of Sakharov can we find Shostakovich's name, perhaps "attached" by someone other than himself, on a published document condemning the scientist's "anti-Soviet" political position; Shostakovich's name, along with the names of eleven other musicians, appeared at the end of an indignant letter to *Pravda* in August 1973, claiming that Sakharov "disgraces the calling of a citizen" (see Fay, *Shostakovich*, p. 278).

r. Shostakovich's title pays homage to Musorgsky's *The Peepshow* or *Rayok* [*Raëk*], a work that lampoons the enemies of "The Five" (the "Mighty Little Handful" or *Moguchaia kuchka*). The word *rayok* has often been translated as "peepshow," one of its conventional meanings in the nineteenth and early-twentieth centuries, referring to a box containing a series of rolled-up pictures that could be viewed through a small opening as they were scrolled past by turning a hand crank. The Russian word was also used for a "puppet show," as well as for comic or satirical theatrical sketches, or scenes, usually in measured rhythmic speech, recalling the style and spirit of popular literature (see Vladimir Dal', *Tolkovyi slovar' Velikoruskago Iazyka* [Interpretive dictionary of the great Russian language], 2nd ed., corrected and enlarged [St. Petersburg: M. O. Vol'f, 1882; repr. Moscow: Russkii iazyk, 1982]; D. N. Ushakov, ed., *Tolkovyi slovar' russkogo iazyka* [Interpretive dictionary of the Russian language] [Moscow: Gosudarstvennoe izdatel'stvo inostrannykh i natsional'nykh slovarei, 1939], s.v. *Rai*). The root word *rai* literally means "paradise"; hence the basic meaning of *rayok* in English is something like "little paradise" (English, not rich in diminutives, offers limited possibilities). While Shostakovich surely had in mind, first of all, a humorous vocal sketch similar in approach to Musorgsky's *Rayok*, we cannot be certain that he was aware of the other connotations of the word, such as "peepshow" or "puppet show," as exemplified in Stravinsky's *Petrushka* (see *Entsiklopedicheskii slovar' Granat* [The Granat encyclopedic dictionary] [repr. Moscow: Ridel, 1999], s.v. Rai). He likely did know the long-time use of the term in reference to the highest gallery in a theater, "little paradise/heaven," as it were (a more appealing image than the American "peanut gallery").

s. Lebedinsky's Soviet-era ideological orthodoxy can be sampled in his brochure *Sed'maia i odinnadtsataia simfonii D. Shostakovicha* [The Seventh and Eleventh Symphonies of D. Shostakovich], published in the series *V pomoshch' slushateliam narodnykh universitetov kul'tury: Besedy o muzyke* [Aids to listeners at people's universities of culture: Conversations about music] (Moscow: Sovetskii kompozitor, 1960).

t. See note a above.

u. The photo is reproduced as the frontispiece in the first English edition of *Testimony* (New York: Harper & Row, 1979), p. [iii], and the inscription from the back of the photo, reproduced below the picture in the book, reads, "To dear Solomon Maseevich [*sic*] Volkov in fond remembrance. D. Shostakovich. 13 XI 1974. A reminder of our talks about Glazunov, Zoshchenko, Meyerhold. D.S."

v. A handwritten note by Irina Nikolskaya in the typescript of her 1992 interview with Yakubov reads, "The journal *Muzykal'naia akademiia* plans to publish Volkov's book in 1993, possibly in installments." Reference is then made to L. Genina, "Razbeg pered propast'iu" [A running start before the abyss], *Muzykal'naia akademiia*, no. 3 (1992): 13, where one reads, "there is the hope, that in 1993 you may possibly read for the first time in Russian, on the pages of our journal [i.e., *Muzykal'naia akademiia*], or a supplement to the journal, the book [i.e., *Testimony*] that has already gone half 'round the world." But publication in Russian did not happen in 1993 and has not happened yet (2002).

w. Yakubov refers here to the text as translated in the German edition of *Testimony*. The English text at the same spot refers to Khrennikov as "one of the wolfhounds" of Stalin (p. 138).

x. Laurel Fay writes, "Mravinsky prepared the Fifth Symphony with a fastidiousness that alarmed even the composer. . . . What the composer remembered as a veritable inquisition, Mravinsky recalled as his own frustrating attempt to enlist the author's help in order to interpret his intentions correctly" (*Shostakovich*, p. 101).

y. Irina Nikolskaya adds a note at this point in her typescript to say that Yakubov's account of the falling out between Shostakovich and Mravinsky "is confirmed by Kirill Kondrashin in conversation with Vladimir Razhnikov," *Kirill Kondrashin rasskazyvaet o muzyke i zhizni* [Kiril Kondrashin talks about music and life] (Moscow: Sovetskii kompozitor, 1989), p. 187; but see note b above.

z. *Suita na stikhi Mikelandzhelo Buonarroti* [Suite on Texts of Michelangelo Buonarroti] op. 145, for bass and piano (1974), and op. 145a, for bass and orchestra (1975).

aa. D. Shostakovich, *Collected Works in Forty-Two Volumes/Sobranie sochinenii v soroka dvukh tomakh* (Moscow: Muzyka, 1979–87), editorial notes in Russian and English.

bb. The score of the *Antiformalist Peepshow*, edited by Yakubov and with his detailed commentary, has been published: *Antiformalisticheskii raëk*, a political satire for reader, four bass soloists, and mixed chorus (SATB), with piano accompaniment (Moscow: Isdatel'stvo "DSCH," 1995).

cc. Nikolskaya's typescript includes a note saying, "This date does not always figure in performances abroad of the *Antiformalist Peepshow*. At the 1990 Warsaw Autumn Festival, the date was given as 1957." Publicity in advance of the surprise American première of the work in January 1989 assigns the date of composition to "around 1960" and identifies Lev N. Lebedinsky, "a poet [*sic*] who was imprisoned by Stalin," as the compiler/arranger of the libretto (see John Rockwell, "Rostropovich to Conduct Première of Unpublished Shostakovich Work," *New York Times*, 11 January 1989, p. C17; Joseph McLellan, "The NSO's Surprise Shostakovich," *Washington Post*, 11 January 1989, pp. C1, C10; Allan Kozin, "Shostakovich Première," *New York Times*, 17 January 1989, p. C16).

The names of the three characters in *Peepshow*, Edinitsyn, Dvoikin, and Troikin (who was added later), can be translated as "Number One," "Number Two," and "Number Three," and they represent Stalin, Andrei Zhdanov (who took the initiative in mounting the attack on "formalism" in music and the other arts), and Dmitri Shepilov (the editor of *Pravda*). The words themselves evoke the grades students receive in Russian schools: *edinitsa* is a "one," the lowest mark a student can receive; *dvoika* is "two"; and *troika*, "three," is unsatisfactory but passing.

dd. Dmitri Shostakovich, *Symphony No. 7 "Leningrad" Op. 60 (1941)*, facsimile edition of the manuscript, with a commentary by Manashir Yakubov (Tokyo: Zen-On Music Company Limited, 1992).

Part Three

14

A Link in the Chain

Reflections on Shostakovich and His Times (1976)

HENRY ORLOV

Shostakovich died on 9 August 1975. The sad news swept the free world in a matter of hours, but it took two days for Soviet citizens to be informed of the event. Brezhnev and the members of the Politburo were the first to sign the official obituary, followed by musicians, composers, and dozens of others. All the familiar clichés were packed into it: "Faithful son of the Communist Party, renowned public figure, artist-citizen who devoted all his life to . . ." It was as if Shostakovich had already envisioned the scene two years earlier, when he set Marina Tsvetaeva's verse to music:[a]

Net, bil baraban pered smutnym polkom,	Yea, a drum tapped a tribute 'fore uneasy ranks,
Kogda my vozhdia khoronili:	When our leader we laid to his rest.
To zuby tsarevy nad miortvym pevtsom	'Twas the tsar's clicking teeth drumming out
Pochiotnuiu drob' vyvodili.	A tattoo o'er the poet, asleep in his grave.
Takoi uzh pochiot chto blizhaishim druz'iam	Such honor as this, that his closest of friends
Net mesta. V izglav'e, v iznozh'e,	Had no place. At head and at feet,
I sprava i sleva—ruchishchi po shvam,	At right and at left, arms stiff at attention,
Zhandarmskie grudi i rozhi.	The mugs and the chests of the guards.
Ne divno li—i na tishaishem iz lozh	What wonder, that now on this quietest of beds,
Prebyt' podnadzornym mal'chishkoi?	The fellow's still under surveillance?

Na chto-to, na chto-to, na chto-to pokhozh	It looks like . . . looks like . . . like some kind of
Pochiot sei, pochiotno—da slishkom!	Honor, this honor, . . . but honor too much!
Gliadi, mol, strana, kak, molve vopreki,	"Behold, how despite all the rumors," 'twas said,
Monarkh o poete pechiotsia! . . .	"The monarch attends to the poet!" . . .

Today, this sounds almost like a direct challenge. But who would have thought that a poem about Pushkin—courted, even in death, by the tsar—would turn out to be such a time bomb!

The fates of the two, Pushkin's and Shostakovich's, are strangely similar. Pushkin, however, did not have to borrow or paraphrase the words of others, whereas, for Shostakovich, this device became indispensable, as the safe way to convey his true thoughts. Direct or disguised quotations—poetic and musical, allusions to his own works and the works of others, ellipses and hints—had developed over the decades into a special method of self-expression, a covert language that he used with extraordinary inventiveness.

❧

It is needless to repeat the well-known truisms about Shostakovich's power and magnitude as a musician. And yet to live in and by music, to treat it only as a natural language of sound, pregnant with unfathomable resources of beauty and harmony, was not his primary goal: beauty, harmony, and originality had become the properties of cryptic messages, a source of aesthetic satisfaction even for those unaware of his "notes in a bottle." Thus many of his admirers in the West, who were captivated by the richness and force of Shostakovich's discourse, failed to understand that what they heard was passionate *speech*. Even in Russia these qualities played a dual role, allowing Shostakovich to utter forbidden truths while at the same time providing others an opportunity to perceive those heart-rending confessions and agonized thoughts as pure music. Many high-ranking listeners pretended to be uncomprehending aesthetes.

The composer skillfully facilitated this mutually convenient myopia. He always found an acceptable pretext, suggesting the possibility of loyal interpretation. Otherwise, how could he have responded to the Soviet reprisal in 1956 against the Hungarian rebels, with its roaring tanks and thundering guns, except through the songs of prerevolutionary Russian rebels and prisoners, the image of a country in chains? And what if he had not entitled his Eleventh Symphony "The Year 1905" and timed its appearance to the fortieth anniversary of the Soviet Union? Shostakovich excelled in making gestures of reassurance to the prison guards while surreptitiously releasing his true thoughts to the world outside.

He was, indeed, an artist-citizen, a thinker, philosopher, pamphleteer, poet, and preacher in music, who lived by the hardships and hopes of this world, who strove to understand, explain, shock, revile, and support. Where, then, does one find his credo expressed, his beliefs articulated? Perhaps in the numerous articles signed with his name, the public speeches delivered with his voice? To suppose this to be the case would be far too naïve. Future scholars will have to decide which of those articles and speeches reflected his true beliefs and which were prompted by the weighty argument, "It must be thus," and then sheathed in the ideas of others or written entirely in their hands, like his widely quoted, "My creative answer," in response to the humiliating *Pravda* editorials in 1936 and the penitent speech at the First Congress of Soviet Composers in 1948 (Shostakovich himself admitted to the present writer, "I was fainthearted in both instances"). He did not protest against being used.

"It must be thus." Those of the Soviet intelligentsia were all too familiar with this magic formula, which more than once compelled Shostakovich to act as if he were on the side of his communist guardians and tutors. Not surprisingly he, who had just been declared "Formalist No. 1," was named a delegate in 1949 to the international Cultural and Scientific Congress for World Peace in the United States, in order to recount personally how wise the Party and the Soviet government had been in their fatherly concern for the welfare of Soviet music.

Only the articles and notes published before 1937 raise no doubts about Shostakovich's authorship. Both their substance and style recall his music—angular, prickly, sincere without reservation, aggressive, and direct. Later, one no longer hears his inimitable manner of speaking, the ideas are smoothed out, balanced carefully, the statements almost impersonal in tone.

The literary legacies of writers and poets, artists and musicians, especially great ones, are truly indispensable for an understanding of their times, lives, and personalities. Musicians, both past and present, from the modest to the greatest, have left behind an enormous body of writings that reflects their experiences, perspectives, and attitudes toward various aspects of life. Shostakovich would have had a lot to tell about himself and his work. But one will look in vain for his name among the authors of numerous chronicles, memoirs, diaries, collections of articles, speeches, and reviews. He chose unnatural silence over dangerous sincerity. He was reserved even with his closest longtime friends. And none among them turned out to be what Eckermann was to Goethe, or Robert Craft to Stravinsky, or Yastrebtsev to Rimsky-Korsakov. Among the people who knew him best, all that memory preserved were anecdotal stories—an intimate folklore, of sorts—told and retold time and again, embellished with his idiosyncratic mannerisms, fragments of his ideas and opinions, often distorted and quoted out of context.

Even so, Shostakovich's contemporaries managed to sense his true personality, character, and way of thinking. In his homeland his very name came to be surrounded by a halo. During the darkest days of Stalinism he seemed to represent the conscience of the nation. In the West his figure evoked interest and sympathy among millions.

It is no simple matter to define what in Shostakovich attracted people of such vastly different cultures, upbringings, lifestyles, and worldviews. "Shostakovich was a musical genius!" That he was. But why not Prokofiev, a musician no less gifted, highly acclaimed, and better known in the West, why did he not become an icon like Shostakovich? "Shostakovich expressed himself to the fullest in his music." Certainly he did—where else? Still, let us not forget that his music is seldom "pretty" and very far from "easy listening." His major works impress with the power of a shock, and demand highly emotional participation and intellectual effort, for which comparatively few listeners are prepared. Not many are able and ready to enter the complex, uneasy, frightful world of his music. Yet Shostakovich lived in the minds even of those who neither understood nor liked him, nor ever heard his music.

❦

He was often called an "honest musician." Few of his fellow composers were deemed worthy of such a description. The words were used so frequently that they ceased to seem strange. But when did being honest become an aesthetic characteristic? Yet precisely this word holds the clue. Despite forced concessions and compromises, under a host of watchful eyes, Shostakovich managed to remain honest in his music. His music was a testament in which, through the patchwork of covers, musical metaphors, and cleverly suggested allusions, the author's personality and convictions were clearly perceived. His music was also a sermon because he, like Dostoevsky, Musorgsky, Chekhov, and Mahler, could not help but feel the pain of human suffering, could not help but try to open his compatriots' eyes on themselves and their true situation, to make them think for themselves and shake off their complacency, to try to raise their sense of dignity and civic duty. In a country where the machine of totalitarianism had turned human society into a trembling herd, honesty was a rare commodity, more precious than daily bread.

Even to the least sophisticated listeners, the general tone of Shostakovich's music—serious, harsh, and dramatic—sounded as a refutation of the myth, "life has become better and more joyful," which the tyrant had invented and common folks believed in. In a country cut off from the community of world cultures and traditions, and beguiled into viewing the past as filled with outmoded prejudices and the present as drowning in the miasma of degeneration and spiritual decay, Shostakovich's music recalled the spiritual riches and vitality of true art, of the great old masters, and also conveyed the nervous pulse of contemporary life, which Shostakovich had already captured in his early works and which still endured, notwithstanding strict sanitary controls over the cultural fodder approved for consumption in Soviet society.

In a country where "the great and only true doctrine" monopolized truth and logic itself, Shostakovich stirred minds, offered his own worldview, prompted questions and the search for answers. In the twentieth-century version of tribal society bedazzled by the light of the only "great personality, the leader, teacher, friend," Shostakovich dared to be a personality in his own right and to emit a light of his own. The cult of the father figure was an obligatory official ritual, the product of brainwashing, a form of mass hysteria. The light emitted by Shostakovich's music shone as a beacon to those trying to survive on the dark ocean of lies and stupidity. He did not aspire to play such a dangerous role, but he could not help doing so simply by being himself.

Those born and brought up in a free society can hardly comprehend what it takes to remain honest in a police state or imagine themselves in the place of someone whose very thought of liberty puts freedom or life at stake. Shostakovich was obliged to be especially cautious. He was left untouched by the devastating purges of the 1930s only by a freak of fate. People disappeared for no reason, and he, still young and not all that highly reputed as a musician, had already built up a solid "criminal record"—the scathing *Pravda* editorials of 1936 (following which, a newspaper in Ukraine warned: "Composer Shostakovich, a known enemy of the people, has arrived in Kiev"); his friendship with the emigré Evgeny Zamyatin, his collaboration with Vsevolod Meyerhold and the painter Nikolai Radlov, both of whom were soon arrested, his close family ties with one of the Red Army's top commanders, Mikhail Tukhachevsky, later executed, not to mention his many lesser-known friends and acquaintances who were eventually swallowed by the blind terror.

The machine kept grinding up its victims to the accompaniment of the weighty "It must be thus," the sad stifled queries, "Can it be true that he, too . . . ?" and the bloodthirsty chorus of eminent Soviet public figures calling in the newspapers for "a dog's death to the dogs!" Shostakovich's name never appeared among the signatories of such collective appeals.

❧

Let us try to understand what it takes to be honest under the Damocles sword of fear, when even a look, a gesture, or a casual remark could be fatal. "A careless word is not a bird; once released, it can never be recaptured!" So goes a Russian proverb with sinister overtones. Censorship did its job and served, in a sense, as a guardian angel to writers by eliminating careless words. Yet every deleted word left a trace in the secret dossiers.

Even more terrifying was the unofficial censorship—the unremitting vigilance of countless enthusiastic volunteers who, on the slightest pretext, were ready to send a signal about the "unhealthy attitudes," "suspicious actions," or "ideological mistakes" on the part of their coworkers and neighbors. Sometimes the signals were sent through the press or at open meetings, thereby swaying public opinion; but more often they were sent through the channels of secret informants who, like metastases, pervaded the entire body of society.

Omnipresent supervision over every step—be it in literature, journalism, science, poetry, music, or any other art—and the fear of being exposed and denounced represented only the outer aspect of the situation. An individual still capable of thinking independently lived in a state of chronic inner doubleness. Alone with his thoughts, he was terrified by the fear of alienation from his compatriots, of losing contact with them. In a society that always voted unanimously, any truly personal thought carried the frightening taste of apostasy, the threat of misunderstanding and disaster.

The situation of the intelligentsia—the *social mid-stratum,* as it was termed in the USSR—was especially difficult. A uniquely Russian phenomenon, the Soviet intelligentsia inherited and lived by the values and ideas of those prerevolutionary Russians who saw their historic mission as serving the public good—the People, the Truth, the Ideal of a better, more reasonable and just society.

A most interesting phenomenon is that the revolutionaries who protested and rebelled against the old order of tsarist Russia had been brought up and formed by that very order. Calling for freedom, they themselves were far from free. They struggled not to dethrone but to replace authority. Rejecting the system and rationale of enslavement, they wholeheartedly embraced an opposing ideology: no matter if it was political or religious, reformist or revolutionary, pro-Western or Slavophile, terrorist ploys or guerrilla actions, the revolutionaries served their cause selflessly, sacrificially. Even convinced atheists served with religious fervor, eagerly suffering in the name of their cause, prepared to become "victims on the altar of freedom."

It was nothing other than self-negation. They believed in ideas more than in themselves. In the name of an idea they were prepared to reject their own feelings, which were perceived as too subjective, unreliable, and unstable, whereas the idea was magnificent, its logic powerful, simple, self-evident.

The authority of an idea is preferable to that of power only if the idea does not ascend to power. Embodied in a state system, depersonalized and idolized, an idea breeds the most inhuman, intolerant, and violent forms of totalitarianism. It not only defines a new political and social order but also dictates what its subjects must think and how they must act.

The ideas that led to the October coup and those which, in subsequent decades, became the banner of protest against the inhumanity of the victorious regime, sprang from the same root. The new martyrs surely had difficulty comprehending that it was their own and their predecessors' aspirations, labors, and sacrifices that had created and supported the blind monster devouring its creators and their children alike.

❦

An unusual destiny awaited Shostakovich. Unlike many fellow artists he did not have to struggle for fame. From the day in 1926 when the nineteen-year-old youth made his debut with the First Symphony op. 10 (1924–25) and continuing throughout the next half-century, he was a focal point at home and in the West, both as a musician and a personality.

The nature of his talent became obvious at once. Despite clear musical influences from Prokofiev, Scriabin, Tchaikovsky, and Wagner, reviewers did not consider reproaching him for imitation, so organically did he blend different ideas and colorations into his solidly constructed compositions. Shostakovich was an eclectic in the best sense of the word, choosing not to adopt only one approach but selecting and harmonizing the best of many. Aspiring to capture and reflect his time, he, like Bach, Mozart, Mahler, and Britten, fused many different trends and idioms, unconcerned with the purity of his *own individual style*. A diversity of sources, combined with freedom from aesthetic dogmatism, remained his lifelong signature.

The First Symphony only partially demonstrated the young composer's predilections and potential. With all the seriousness of his age, he tested himself in the realm of conceptual symphonic drama, soaring on the wings of symbolic images that had nothing in common with events, emotions, and colors of the first post-October years. Let us not forget, however, that the composer's very earliest, still juvenile pieces were written at a time when adults were talking about world war and the protests on the streets of Petrograd.

Childhood impressions themselves could hardly have determined the composer's future, yet they helped him to recognize his connection with his past—particularly with his grandfather, who had been exiled to Siberia for antigovernment activities. It would be a mistake to suppose that ideological pressure alone made Shostakovich turn periodically to revolutionary themes and ideas, to images of heroes and martyrs fighting for freedom. The subject itself had strongly attracted him, though it was not a dominating theme. Indeed, some of his works that related to the Revolution annoyed the vigilantes who oversaw the "ideological and aesthetic purity of Soviet art."

The new graduate of the Leningrad Conservatory made his first moves during the latter half of the 1920s. The scene burst with temptations and discoveries for the young, impressionable musician. After a decade of isolation, contacts with European art were being reestablished: concert halls and theaters resounded with the music of Stravinsky, Honegger, Hindemith, and Schoenberg, the operas of Berg and Křenek, the symphonies of Mahler. Shostakovich studied feverishly, absorbing new compositional techniques, experimenting in different styles, developing his own idioms. For Shostakovich, those years were decisive in forming his creative mind, inculcating in him a sense of the times and the new social conditions.

During the five short years in the 1920s that were to become known as "the golden age," the search for fresh, revolutionary approaches in the arts was understood not merely as a possibility but as an obligation, a civic duty. "October" became the slogan of innovation in all areas of life and culture. Not only did it inspire ordinary citizens who were involved in educating the masses throughout the country, it also motivated such notables as Meyerhold and Tairov in theater, Mayakovsky in poetry, and Eisenstein in cinema, to name but a few. Shostakovich, too, drew inspiration from this slogan. All were stimulated to revolutionize their art but also to reach beyond art, as their ultimate goal was the renewal of life: breaking the shackles of submission and slavish thinking, denouncing ingrained habits of obsequiousness, triteness, vulgarity, and exposing the deceits of Philistine complacency and blind mob instinct. They saw themselves as gravediggers of the past, sanitation workers of the present, builders of the future. Their art was not an end in itself but a means to the future they envisioned.

Shostakovich sought to be in the thick of life, to participate fully in an immediate, practical, and useful way. He did not dodge any kind of work and willingly wrote music for propaganda shows and musicals on topical subjects, just like Mayakovsky, who did not spare his talent in rhyming texts for commercial advertisements, political posters, or placards promoting good health and hygiene. New colors and musical idioms invaded Shostakovich's music. He parodied the rhythms and melodies of Offenbach operettas, dance hall tunes, circus shows, vulgar songs, and trashy ditties, which he used alongside burlesqued quotations from Beethoven, Bach, Haydn, and Weber. And he treated this diverse material, with its rapidly changing styles and characters, in a manner not unlike cinematographic montage—a possible extension of his work as a pianist in silent movie theaters. His ballets, *The Bolt* (1930–31) and *The Golden Age* (1929–30), his opera *The Nose* (1927–28), and his Concerto for Piano, Trumpet, and String Orchestra (1933) abound in such contrasts, amuse by their exaggeration to the point of caricature, and sparkle with joyous humor and acerbic irony.

A number of years passed before the composer turned such material into a language of dark parables, although, even earlier, his *grotesquerie* flickered with cold, frightfully soulless, irrationally mechanical images. Only for rare short moments, the musician's real face—serious and sensitive—emerged out of the kaleidoscopic images. Later he would often speak through his music about himself. Intensely dramatic and personal contemplations would become an important ingredient of his symphonies and chamber music. But, for now, he was fulfilling the "social command" by listening to the voices of his time, peering into and capturing the fleeting images of turbulent contemporary life, and, like a street artist, hurrying to come up with hastily sketched portraits.

Two large-scale compositions belong to this period: Symphony No. 2 in B Major op. 14, "To October" (1927); and Symphony No. 3 in E-flat Major op. 20, "The First of May" (1929). Both were commissioned, of course, but were in no way forced on the composer. Both fulfilled the requisites of propaganda art and solidified his reputation as a "revolutionary composer." The young Shostakovich could hardly remain indifferent to celebrations of the revolutionary "honeymoon," with their genuine mass enthusiasm, their contagious sight and sound. He created two murals for orchestra and chorus, depicting, in one, a political rally with rousing speeches igniting the crowd and, in the other, a holiday celebration with an assortment of youthful songs and marches. Such cheerful colors shone even more brightly in a song composed for the film *Vstrechnyi* [The counterplan] (1932), in which eager factory workers volunteer to produce more than the state plan required. The song, however, had little to do with matters of productivity; rather, the text spoke of welcoming the dawn of a new day in the life of the country. It gained immediate and unprecedented popularity. Ten years later, fitted with a new text, the song was reborn as the jubilant "Song of the United Nations Organization," just recently founded.[b]

During the 1920s, and even later, very few artists managed to keep cool heads amid the vapors of universal exultation, to perceive in the midst of the Revolution's "honeymoon" the terrifying future that was approaching. The feverish chase after today's headlines, the surrender to "civic duties," the waste of talent in "service to society" brought many to ruin. Shostakovich, however, soon became disillusioned. As early as 1931 he published an article bluntly denouncing the preponderance of hackwork and opportunism in propaganda art and declared that nearly everything he had composed during the preceding five years had no artistic value. He now faced an acute need to restore the health of his creative personality, to distance himself from the trivial tasks he had so conscientiously tried to accomplish, and to explore the newly acquired wealth of musical idioms he had mastered. During those earlier years not only had his compositional technique developed, but he himself had also matured intellectually and emotionally, and his perception of reality, its contradictions, conflicts, and problems, had deepened. He stood at the threshold of new discoveries.

❦

The composer's decisive step soon brought impressive results. In 1932 he completed the opera *Ledi Makbet Mtsenskogo uezda* [Lady Macbeth of the Mtsensk District] (*Katerina Izmailova*), and in 1936 the score of the Fourth Symphony was soon to be performed. One-fifth of his career had passed and numerous works lay ahead that would multiply his fame, but never again would we see the vistas that opened from these twin peaks he had achieved. For the first time in post-October Russia, a great opera and a great symphony appeared. Both startle by their grasp of life at the core, their insight into the eternal problem of human existence. Both are shockingly tragic—quite unexpected from a composer well known for musical pranks, witticisms, and sense of humor. Perhaps most important, both works show Shostakovich at the summit of inner creative freedom and reveal his true face as a composer. Today one can only guess how the rest of his career and his musical legacy would have transpired had he been allowed to develop without obstacles.

An independent worldview directly contradicted official ideology, especially at a time when the tide of purges was rising. For two years *Lady Macbeth* had filled Leningrad's Malyi Opera Theater to capacity, until an editorial in *Pravda* "unjustly defamed" the work (in the identical words the same newspaper would publish twenty years later!). The opera was promptly banned and publicly condemned by fellow musicians who only the previous day had eulogized it. Consigned to limbo for a quarter of a century, the opera was repeatedly condemned as a shameful stain on Soviet music. To avoid a similar rebuff, Shostakovich canceled the première of the Fourth Symphony op. 43 (1934–36), already in rehearsal by the Leningrad Philharmonic Orchestra. This work, too, sank into oblivion, to be remembered as another of Shostakovich's "ideological" blunders.

This double blow was all the more painful in that it was delivered by the "fatherly hand" of the Party and the government of the working class, whom Shostakovich had so recently been serving in good faith and in whose name he had even reproached more cynical colleagues. There can be little doubt of his sincerity in the "October" and "First of May" symphonies; nor later, when he informed the readers of *Sovetskaia kul'tura* about his plans for a grand cantata, *From Marx to Our Days*, for voices and orchestra on texts related to revolutionary movements in the West and in Russia; nor still later, in 1938 and 1940, when he spoke of his work on a "Lenin symphony" that was conceived as early as 1924, during the period of national mourning after Lenin's death. None of this should be understood as deceptive, as false assurance of loyalty. Shostakovich honestly wanted to create a musical monument to the Great Leader of the October Revolution, but he failed. The idea he had entertained for forty years resulted in the stillborn Twelfth Symphony op. 112 ("The Year 1917" [1959–61])—a pale illustration of the events of October 1917.

For years Shostakovich had studied the musical and poetic folklore of the Revolution, which nurtured his imagination. In the 1930s he had willingly, and not without eagerness, composed music for films on revolutionary subjects, including, among others, *The Man with a Gun* op. 53 (1938) and the "Maxim" trilogy—*Maxim's Youth (The Bolshevik)* op. 41 (1934), *Maxim's Return* op. 45 (1936–37), and *The Vyborg District* op. 50

(1938). *The Ten Poems on Texts by Revolutionary Poets of the Late-Nineteenth and Early-Twentieth Centuries* op. 88, for *a cappella* chorus, composed in 1951, cannot be explained away simply as an attempt at rehabilitation after the new blow received in 1948. The revolutionary songs heard and treated in a monumental way in the Eleventh Symphony ("The Year 1905" [1956–57]) were aimed directly at prison guards, gendarmes, and tyrants, who had never been absent from Russian life but who, only after the Revolution, had finally acquired the power and arrogance to feel themselves masters at home and in control of the fate of the world.

Although the ideals of the Revolution had been transformed into a morbid reality, Shostakovich long remained faithful to them. He shared the mind-set of those naïve idealists who, in the words of a poignant saying, "were locked up while waiting, and then, their waiting rewarded, were locked up again," and who honestly believed themselves to be victims of mistakes. The dogma of revolution, its "scientific" predictions and "universal truth," had bewitched them.

Shostakovich entered a new phase after 1936, when the symphony became the dominant means for communicating his thoughts. During the following fourteen years he composed six symphonies, the Fifth through the Tenth. In one symphony after another he "created worlds," like Mahler. Yet, unlike Mahler's symphony-confessions—and his own Fourth Symphony—Shostakovich's new creations were now protected by the armor of a conceptual frame. Each is unique, musically speaking, but all of them rest on a thoroughly thought-out foundation of inner relationships, not purely musical but musically embodied concepts and ideas that support the imposing formal structure.

Shostakovich himself declared the rationalized basis of his creative approach: "With me, a programmatic concept always precedes composition."[c] These words can be taken as truthful, even if they were written in 1951, when all "pure" music was considered "formalistic." He never put his programs to words, except for occasional suggestive titles, but an undisclosed program was always present—a complex dynamic system of all-important philosophical antitheses: the collective and the individual, harmony and chaos, man and nature, compassion and violence, joy and sorrow, life and death.

❧

Shostakovich was a born composer for the theater. But the fate of two ballets and two operas,[d] written within the span of only five years, had turned out to be deplorable (although for different reasons). Still, having turned to the symphony, he continued to think as a composer for the theater. In his hands, these purely instrumental compositions became musical dramas. Each exhibits a succession of stages organized around a central event, very much like a dramatic play: from prologue and initial conflict, through complication and contrasting "scenes," to cataclysmic culmination, denouement, and epilogue. This is in no sense abstract music. Generalized concepts become vivid personages and situations. The composer skillfully brings them to life, endows them with characteristic colors, intonations, gestures, and "manners." In this crowd of thematic "personages" placed in a succession of kaleidoscopic "scenes"—the pathos of tragedy and the buffoonery of the marketplace, the heroic and the grotesque, the mundane and the irrational, irony and lyricism, the infernal and the bucolic—coexist and clash.

Precisely by constructing his symphonies on rationalized concepts, Shostakovich succeeded in delaying the decay of this classical form in the twentieth century. He treated the symphony as a "model of the world" and believed strongly in its revelatory and redemptive power. Herein, perhaps, lies the secret of the magnetic attraction Shostakovich's symphonies of the 1930s and 1940s exerted both in his homeland, where official ideology dulled the mind with loony dogmas and demagogical "ideals," and in the West, where the tribulations of two world wars and economic crises had stripped away Victorian innocence, leaving a sense of bewilderment and helplessness in the face of incomprehensible and hostile chaos. Shostakovich's symphonies intimated solutions, instilled hope, and offered a bird's-eye view of the world.

The Left in the West especially welcomed such a view. Not surprisingly, the Fifth Symphony (1937), with the monolithic pace of its finale, became a symbol of international solidarity in the struggle against fascism and was hailed by the French and Italian Communist Parties. Millions of people among the Allies opposing Hitler acclaimed the Seventh Symphony, the "Leningrad" Symphony (1941), and the Eighth (1943). The two latter symphonies reflect, from different angles, the struggle between humanitarian values and destructive forces unbridled—the Seventh in a style of heroic reportage, the Eighth in a more symbolic, almost surrealistic manner.

The events of World War II served but to catalyze these symphonies in the composer's creative imagination. The conflicts and struggles they portray are universal. They bring to mind not simply battles between competing armies but the forces operating in any society and within every human soul. Without recourse to words, Shostakovich's music presents his ideas as living, full-blooded entities and expresses them with eloquence inaccessible in words.

The composer's great service to his country, his contribution to the fight against fascism, did not protect him from retribution. He broke ranks, became too famous, and took too many liberties as a composer. In 1948 he, among others, was accused of "formalism" at a time when ideological "mistakes" were nearly identical with political ones, and official criticism amounted to a guilty verdict without the right of appeal.

Shostakovich did not fall silent when the symphony was tabooed as a means of creative self-realization. He continued to compose, although his First Violin Concerto (1947–48), the Twenty-Four Preludes and Fugues (1950–51), and the song cycle *Iz evreiskoi narodnoi poesii* [From Jewish folk poetry] (1948) remained unknown outside a circle of his closest friends. Meanwhile, he presented to the public festive overtures, pieces for children, and the pompously infantile oratorio *The Song of the Forests* (1949), as well as patriotic cantatas such as *Our Song* (1950; for bass, mixed chorus, and piano), *March of the Defenders of Peace* (?1950; for tenor, chorus, and piano), and *Nad rodinoi nashei solntse siiaet* [The sun shines over our motherland] (1952; for boys' choir, chorus, and orchestra). He did so not only to remain an active composer and to rehabilitate himself but also to make a living. When life is deprived of meaning, work becomes the meaning of life—a narcotic against adversities and a tonic for one's dignity and self-respect. Shostakovich may well have said, on his own behalf and for many of his Soviet colleagues, "I compose, therefore I still *am*."

After a long intermission, and the very same year as Stalin's death, Shostakovich returned to the symphony: The Tenth (1953) concluded the symphonic period of his career, making him both the conscience and model of moral stoicism for those of his compatriots still spiritually alive. What was simply music for Western listeners was something immeasurably more important for people living in a country that was hermetically sealed, enclosed in an atmosphere choked by lies, hypocrisy, and fear—for them it was a symbol of human dignity.

A time of change arrived with "The Thaw." Crimes of the preceding quarter-century were hurriedly explained away by blaming the "cult of personality," while the Party remained at a safe distance, as if the execution of millions had been Stalin's private affair. A new political course was solemnly proclaimed, steered toward the restoration of Leninist norms for the Party leadership, as if the creator of the Cheka[e] and the ideologue of mass terror had been someone other than the founder of the Soviet state. Beria was executed, and, although his place did not remain vacant, repression ebbed. Those who survived the persecution returned from prisons and camps. Citizens were called on to speak their minds openly, without fear. Although the encouraging gestures seemed not to be entirely convincing, the field had been partially cleared of mines. Past events could be recalled, with some reservations, and debate about the present and future gave birth to the dissident movement, which took its first timid steps under the slogan, "Pay heed to your own Constitution!" Still, the ideological war against the "rotten West" did not end. On the contrary, a new general offensive on that front was just beginning. But cracks in the Iron Curtain were evident. For the first time in many years it was possible to become acquainted with selected works of contemporary art from abroad; one could make independent discoveries, pick and choose, and become informed.

In the context of these changes, Shostakovich's symphonies were seen and heard differently. Their rich meaning, conveyed without words, and the austere taciturnity surrounding their conception now seemed abstract. By the end of the 1950s most of Shostakovich's followers and imitators had gone their own ways. The composer himself must have felt compelled to give his ideas and convictions more direct and immediate expression. He was only fifty-five years old, but at pains to find a new direction, a path to self-realization under new conditions. The final two decades of his life speak of some uncertainty.

Willing to believe that "The Thaw" foretold an approaching spring, Shostakovich discarded the armor of symphonic generalities. He now wanted to speak of particular events, to dispose of allegories, to give things their proper names. The polemical word became his main tool. The old Shostakovich—the satirist, pamphleteer, and orator—was reborn in order once again to scathe ugliness and injustice.

His new direction led to the Thirteenth Symphony (1962), in which the composer, to use his own words, addressed "the problem of civic morality."[f] He found sentiments that responded to his own ideas in the poetry of the young Yevtushenko, whose poems spoke about the shame of anti-Semitism, about humor as the invincible foe of tyrants, about the martyrdom of Russian women, the baseness of opportunism, and the glory of devotion to truth and freedom from fear. The poem entitled "Fears" (Mov. 5) had the feeling of a declaration. It alone of the entire cycle was written especially for the symphony at the composer's request:

Umiraiut v Rossii strakhi,
slovno prizraki prezhnikh let...
Ia ikh pomniu vo vlasti i sile
pri dvore torzhestvuiushchei Izhi.
Strakhi vsiudu, kak teni, skol'zili...
Gde molchat' by—krichat' priuchali,
I molchat'—gde by nado krichat'...
Tainyi strakh pered ch'im-to donosom,
tainyi strakh pered stukom v dver'...

Fears are dying out in Russia,
like the wraiths of yesteryear...
I recall them strong and potent
at the Court of Lies Triumphant.
Fears all 'round like shades were lurking...
When we should have silent kept,
they made us scream,
and when we should have screamed,
they kept us silent...
The silent fear of anonymous accusation,
the fear to hear a knocking at the door...

Strakhi novye vizhu, svetleia:
strakh neiskrennim byt' so stranoi,
strakh nepravdoi unizit' idei,
chto iavliaiutsia pravdoi samoi...

I see new fears a-dawning:
the fear of betraying one's country,
of falsely defaming ideas
that manifest self-evident truths...

I kogda ia pishu eti stroki
i poroiu nevol'no speshu,
to pishu ikh v edinstvennom strakhe,
Chto ne v polnuiu silu pishu.

And even as I write these lines,
at times unwittingly rushing,
I write them obsessed by the singular fear
that my words possess less than full force.

This valiant affirmation, jointly declared by Shostakovich and Yevtushenko, was made too soon, its optimism premature. Fear and lies were not yet ready to die in Russia. Life remained as before, and still "No monument stood over *Babyi Yar*" (Mov. 1, Sym. 13). Opportunists and demagogues continued to prosper. And the authors of courageous declarations again had to choose their words with utmost care, retreat to reticence, and resort to their mastery of Aesopian language. Even though the musical-poetical declaration by Yevtushenko and Shostakovich had been carefully tuned in unison with Khrushchev's revelations at the Twentieth Party Congress and to its official resolutions, the declaration turned out to be much too liberal. The poet was obliged to make a new, more politically correct version of his poems, and the Thirteenth Symphony—having been performed, despite stumbling blocks—was treated badly by the press and long remained unpublished.

"You may not be a poet, but a citizen you must be" (Nekrasov, *Poet and Citizen* [*Poet i grazhdanin*], 1856). When civic virtues are being preached, the quality of the poetry is of little consequence. Like many other readers, Shostakovich closed his eyes to the narcissism and affectation of Yevtushenko's poems; he placed his talent at their service, put them on a pedestal, and set them to inspiring music. For Shostakovich, this was not a sacrifice. He was prepared to serve civic values at any cost.

Shostakovich returned to the theater to compose an operetta, *Moscow*,

Cheryomushki op. 105 [*Mosvka cheryomushki*] (1957–58), that pokes fun at everyday misadventures, fools, and scoundrels. He wrote songs, *Satires* [*Satiry*] op. 109 (1960), to the verses of Sasha Chorny, with the cautious subtitle, "Little Pictures from the Past" [*Kartinki proshlogo*] that deride the many faces of vulgarity and banality. He did not hesitate to lampoon triteness by setting to music lines from letters to the editor of *Crocodile* (*Krokodil* 24 [30 August 1965]), the official Soviet magazine of satire—the very symbol and quintessence of Soviet Philistinism (Five Romances op. 121 [1965]). If high art is powerless against the "statesmanship" of brutes, lackeys, and enthusiastic idiots, then he will speak to them in their own language, mixing high art and the commonplace, as in his youth, attacking the enemy on his own ground: if aesthetics stands in the way, then so much the worse for aesthetics.

❧

There was something obsessive in all this—morbid, bitter, and hopeless. Even the composer's humor started to sound this way. On the eve of his sixtieth birthday, he composed a work that calls for a psychological rather than a musical analysis. The title reads, *Preface to the Complete Edition of My Works and a Brief Reflection apropos of this Preface* [*Predislovie k polnomu sobraniiu moikh sochinenii i kratkoe razmyshlenie po povodu etogo predisloviia*], for bass and piano, with words and music by Dmitri Shostakovich. Listed as op. 123 (1966), the work was performed at a concert for which the composer paid with a heart attack. In the *Preface*, he paraphrased, in first person singular, Pushkin's epigram, *The Story of a Versifier* [*Istoriia stikhotvortsa*]:

Vnimaiu ia privychnym ukhom svist,	With accustomed ear I catch a tweet,
Maraiu ia edinym dukhom list;	Scribble in a sweep a single sheet;
Potom vsemu terzaiu svetu slukh;	Then torture all around who hear the hash;
Potom pechtaius', i v Letu—bukh!	Then off to press, and into Lethe splash!

And in the section called *Brief Reflection* [*Kratkoe razmyshlenie*] he extended his self-characterization to "many, many other composers," and then concluded with a detailed listing of all his honorifics and titles. It is as difficult to understand this act of public self-humiliation and self-torture as it is to understand why, four years later, he composed the *March of the Soviet Militia* op. 139 [*Marsh sovetskoi militsii*] (1970) for a competition initiated by the Ministry of Internal Affairs (MVD), and then, as the winner, posed for a photo standing next to the MVD minister

Nikolai Shchelokov, the spiritual heir of Count Benckendorff, chief of the tsar's notorious "Third Section" during Pushkin's time.

The Thirteenth Symphony was followed by the vocal-symphonic Poem for bass, chorus, and orchestra, *The Execution of Stepan Razin* op. 119 [*Kazn' Stepana Razina*] (1964), again to texts by Yevtushenko. On the surface this is a narrative about the leader of a peasant uprising, about his love of freedom and self-sacrifice. In fact, the emphasis is shifted. The peasant hero is about to die under an executioner's ax, before the eyes of an excited, maliciously curious and jeering crowd of onlookers:

Vy vsegda pliuete, liudi,	Ah, people, you always spit
v tekh, kto khochet vam dobra.	on those who wish you well.

But unexpectedly something changes in the hero's last moments,

Ploshchad' chto-to poniala,	The square had understood something,
ploshchad' shapki sniala.	the square removed their hats.
I skvoz' ryla, riashki, khari	And past the snouts and ugly mugs
tseloval'nikov, menial,	of publicans and money-changers,
slovno bliki sredi khmari,	like spots of light amidst the clouds,
Sten'ka litsa uvidal.	Stenka caught sight of faces,
Byli v litsakh dal' i vys'...	eyes far off and fathomless...
Stoit vsio sterpet' besslIozno	'Tis worthwhile to suffer dry-eyed,
byt' na dybe-kolese,	to bear the pain of the rack,
esli rano ili pozdno	if sooner or later,
prorastaiut litsa grozno	faces grow threatening
u bezlikikh na litse.	on those who had been faceless.

That Shostakovich composed his Poem specifically for the sake of setting the words above cannot be doubted. He pointedly asked the present writer to emphasize their importance in an article being prepared for the composer's sixtieth birthday. They expressed his hope that sacrifice is not in vain, that the hero, if not in life then perhaps in death, will succeed in awakening the lethargic souls of his fellow citizens.

This theme would become crucial in his works after 1960. It recurs in different guises and takes on a distinctly autobiographical significance. The creator of monumental symphonic canvases started to focus more on chamber music—string quartets and vocal cycles. The one who had pondered the fate of the world, who had preached *urbi et orbi*, now began to confront his most secret thoughts—about himself and about death—and allowed us to eavesdrop.

The last eight string quartets and the sonatas for violin and viola represent a musical diary of his final fifteen years. Indeed, the Eighth Quartet (1960) amounts to a musical autobiography of sorts, using direct and indirect quotations—from the First Symphony and *Lady Macbeth*, through the Second Piano Trio and the Eighth Symphony, to the Cello Concerto, the Eleventh Symphony (Mov. 3, "Eternal Memory" [*Vechnaia pamiat'*], quoting the melodies of the old revolutionary songs, "You fell a victim" [*Vy zhertvoiu pali*] and "Tormented by grievous bondage" [*Zamuchen tiazhioloi nevolei*]). The composer thus revisits the milestones of his life and, in the end, arrives at a mournful conclusion.

The Eighth Quartet and other later works offer listeners many opportunities to admire the beauty of the music, the richness of its subdued colors, and to appreciate the harmony of its form, its depth of expression, as well as to draw parallels with Beethoven's late quartets—but only if one can bear the suffocating atmosphere of weary apathy, the numbness of a lonely soul troubled by ghosts, the feelings that dominate these "poems" about dying.

Against this background, the Fourteenth Symphony op. 135 (1969) reflects the composer's preoccupation during the last years of his life. He was barely living, rather, slowly dying—physically, because of irreversibly deteriorating health, and spiritually, since few bygone passions remained. With characteristic skill in selecting poetic texts, he spoke through the words of Guillaume Apollinaire (translated by M. Kudinov) in the symphony's central movement, "In Santé Prison" (Mov. 7):

A nebo! Luchshe ne smotret'—	And the sky! Better not look—
Ia nebu zdes' ne rad . . .	it brings me no joy here . . .
Den' konchilsia. Lampa nad golovoiu	Day has ended. A lamp above my head
gorit, okruzhionnaia t'moi.	burns, surrounded by darkness.
Vsio tikho.	All is quiet.
Nas v kamere tol'ko dvoe:	Only two of us in the cell:
Ia i rassudok moi.	I and my reason.
[Apollinaire, translated by M. Kudinov]	[Translated from Kudinov's Russian]

Le ciel est bleu comme une chaine
dans une fosse
Le jour s'en va voici que brûle
une lampe dans la prison.
Nous sommes seuls dans me cellule
belle clarté chère raison.
[Guillaume Apollinaire]

Reviewers tried in vain to interpret the Fourteenth Symphony as a moral and social condemnation of violence. But in the symphony Shostakovich focuses not on violence itself but on the consequences of violence. The critics pointed, to no avail, to the composer's words about Musorgsky's *Songs and Dances of Death* [*Pesni i pliaski smerti*] as the prototype for this symphony. Nowhere, however, does the symphony come close to the Christian motif[g] of *memento mori* that so fascinated Musorgsky, to those symbols of death whose presence place man's life and actions in the perspective of Faith and Light Eternal. The Fourteenth Symphony is devoid of this light. Death is the end of everything, a senseless nothing, a black pit of nonbeing whose mouth gapes horribly before us. This anti-requiem speaks not so much of death itself as of the endless agonies of the dying and empathy for all those being killed, spiritually mortified, or who commit suicide.

Here, too, the word occupies center stage; the music only supports, comments on, and intensifies the meaning and the emotional undercurrents. Shostakovich composed the symphony for the sake of the words. In it, he speaks about himself and his fate through the masterfully selected, surrealistic texts.

Before "The Lorelei" (Mov. 3) throws herself into the Rhine, she declares,

Zhizn' mne v tiagost', episkop,
  i prokliat moi vsor.
Kto vzglianul na menia,
  svoi prochiol prigovor . . .
Serdtse tak isstradalos,
mchto dolzhna umeret' ia.
[Apollinaire, translated by M. Kudinov]

Life is a burden to me, Lord Bishop,
  and my gaze accursed.
Whoever has looked at me,
  has divined his doom . . .
My heart has suffered so,
  that I must die.
[Translated from Kudinov's Russian]

Je suis lasse de vivre
  et mes yeux son maudits.
Ceux qui m'ont regardée
  évêque ont péri . . .
Mon coeur me fait si mal
  il faut bien que je meure.
[Apollinaire, based on Brentano]

"The Suicide" (Mov. 4) speaks about suffering that endures even from beyond the grave:

Tri lilii, tri lilii, lilii tri
    na mogile moei bez kresta . . .
rastiot iz rany odna . . .
Drugaia iz serdtsa rastiot moego,
    chto tak sil'no stradaet
    na lozhe chervivom;
a tret'ia korniami mne rot
    razryvaet.
Oni na mogile moei odinoko rastut,
    i pusta
vokrug nikh zemlia, i, kak zhizn' moia,
    prokliata ikh krasota.
[Apollinaire, translated by Kudinov]
	Three lilies, three lilies, lilies three
	    grow on my grave, without a cross . . .
	One grows from my wound . . .
	Another grows from my heart,
	    which suffers so much
	    on this verminous bed;
	while the third lacerates my mouth
	    with its roots.
	Alone they grow on my grave,
	    and barren is
	the land around them; like my life,
	    their beauty is accursed.
	[Translated from Kudinov's Russian]

Trois grands lys Troi grands lys
    sur ma tombe sans crois . . .
L'un sort de ma plaie . . .
L'autre sort de mon coeur
    qui souffre sur la couche
    où le rongent les vers.
L'autre sort de ma bouche.
Sur ma tombe écartée ils se dressent
    tous troi
Tout seuls tout seuls et maudits
    comme moi je crois.
[Apollinaire]

The voice of resolute protest is heard only once in the symphony: Apollinaire's "Reply of the Zaporozhean Cossacks to the Sultan of Constantinople" [*Otvet zaporozhskikh kazakov konstantionopol'skomu sultanu;* Kudinov's translation of *Réponse des cosaques de zaporogues au sultan de Constantinople*] (Mov. 8) is a veritable emotional explosion, overflowing with hate and brutal verbal abuse. This, as well as all the other poems in the symphony, was perceived as sharply dissonant in 1970—a time when Lenin's centenary was busily being celebrated in the Soviet Union.

Shostakovich's earlier dramatic conceptions had always included catharsis. Even the cold, hollow, and cruel world of the Fourteenth Symphony contains this essential element. But here, emotional release is accomplished in a particular manner. The overall dispirited picture is mitigated only in Küchelbecker's apostrophe to the poet, "O, Delvig, Delvig!"[h] (Mov. 9), and in Rainer Maria Rilke's "The Death of the Poet" [*Smert' poeta;* T. Silman's translation of *Der Tod des Dichters*] (Mov. 10). This was not deliverance by purification through suffering, by surmounting tragedy, or by courageous acceptance of destiny, as had been characteristic before in Shostakovich. Instead, this was mourning over an artist who had perished, an artist whose aspirations had been lofty and noble.

The final lines of "O, Delvig, Delvig!" voiced a theme that would become the principal motif in Shostakovich's compositions during his last years, enciphered in the instrumental works, expressed allegorically in the vocal ones:

Tak ne umriot i nash soiuz,	Thus our bond, free, joyful, and proud,
svobodnyi, radostnyi i gordyi!	shall not die!
I v schast'e i v neschast'e tviordyi,	And in happiness and in sorrow it stands firm,
soiuz liubimtsev vechnykh muz!	the bond of lovers of the eternal Muses!

This lingering, uncertain hope for immortality in the arts—the only justification for a mutilated life—glows like a smoldering coal amid the ashes of a burned-out ruin.

Editor's Notes

Henry Orlov's article, having been completed in 1976, the year after Shostakovich's death and three years before the publication of Volkov's *Testimony*, represents a perspective entirely free of the controversy surrounding *Testimony*. Efim Etkind commissioned the article for a collection to be entitled *Kontrakul'tura* [The counterculture] but the book failed to materialize, and Orlov's article collected dust. Ten years later Mark Popovsky, editor of the journal *Strana i mir* (Munich) convinced the author to prepare a revised version, which was published in the journal under the title "Pri dvore torzhestvuiushchei lzhi" [At the court of lies triumphant], no. 3 (1986): 62–75. A substantially abridged version of that article was then published under the title, "Zveno v tsepi" [A link in the chain], in the periodical *Sovetskaia kul'tura* (4 May 1989), p. 5. This abridged version also appeared, in translation, as "A Link in the Chain," in the English-language quarterly newsletter *Music in the USSR* (January–March 1990): 37–41, published by VOAP [Vsesoiuznoe obshchestvo avtorskikh prav (The All-Union Society for the Protection of Authors' Rights)], Goskonzert, and the Union of Soviet Composers. The complete 1986 version was subsequently reprinted twice, under the title "Pri dvore torzhestvuiushchei lzhi" [At the court of lies triumphant], in the journal *Iskusstvo Leningrada*, no. 4 (1989): 58–69, and in the book *D. D. Shostakovich: sbornik statei k 90-letiiu so dnia rozhdeniia* [D. D. Shostakovich: A collection of articles on the 90th anniversary of his birth], comp. L. Kovnatskaya (St. Petersburg: Kompozitor, 1996), pp. 8–28. The English translation published here restores Orlov's *original* 1976 article in order to underscore his thoughts in that period immediately following the composer's death and before *Testimony*, when the author's recollections of the political and musical scene in the Soviet Union, as well as his memory of his own personal interviews with Shostakovich, remained vivid in his mind. The author himself has kindly provided the English translation.

a. Here and elsewhere the volume editor has rendered the Russian poetic texts into English.

b. Shostakovich's "Song of the Counterplan" was arranged with a new text by Harold J. Rome and published in English in 1942, under the title "The United Nations," and was intended to be a World War II rallying anthem for the Allied nations. The United Nations Organization was not founded until 1945. Because of the English title that Harold Rome gave to Shostakovich's song, it "has been widely misinterpreted as a hymn for the international organization." See Laurel E. Fay, *Shostakovich: A Life* (Oxford: Oxford University Press, 2000), pp. 72, 302 n. 17.

c. As quoted in *D. Shostakovich o vremeni i o sebe* [D. Shostakovich about the times and himself], comp. M. Iakovlev, ed. G. Pribegina (Moscow: Sovetskii kompozitor, 1980), p. 146; reprinted from *Sovetskaia muzyka*, no. 5 (1951).

d. The ballets were *Zolotoi vek* [The golden age] op. 22 (1929–30), and *Bolt* [The bolt] op. 27 (1930–31); and the operas were *Nos* [The nose] op. 15 (1927–28), and *Ledi Makbet Mtsenskogo uezda* [Lady Macbeth of the Mtsensk District] op. 29 (1930–32).

e. The Cheka or *ЧК* (Chrezvychainaia Komissiia po bor'be s kontrrevoliutsiei, sabotazhem i spekuliatsiei = The extraordinary commission for the struggle with counterrevolution and sabotage) was the Soviet Security Agency from 1918 until 1922—the primary apparatus of the so-called Red Terror.

f. "In the Thirteenth Symphony I specifically addressed the problem of civic morality" (Shostakovich, as quoted in M. Sabinina, *Shostakovich simfonist: Dramaturgiia, estetika, stil'* [Shostakovich the symphonist: Dramaturgy, aesthetics, style] [Moscow: Muzyka, 1976], p. 369).

g. Some scholars who have closely studied Musorgsky's life and works would argue that the *Songs and Dances of Death* reflect more Paganism than Christianity, with an admixture of shamanistic devils from further East.

h. The poets Anton Antonovich Delvig (1798–1831) and Wilhelm Karlovich Küchelbecker (1797–1846) were educated, along with Pushkin, at the renowned Lycée of Tsarskoe Selo, where all three became close friends and imbibed a common liberalism that viewed autocracy and serfdom as Russia's twin evils. Küchelbecker was eventually exiled to Siberia as a consequence of his involvement in the abortive Decembrist coup d'état of 1825, which had attempted to thwart the official oath of allegiance to the new monarch, Nikolai I. Küchelbecker's life in Siberia was one of abject poverty; he died there of tuberculosis in 1846 at the age of forty-nine. His friend, Pushkin, had been killed in a duel in 1837, and Delvig had died at the premature age of thirty-three. Küchelbecker's elegy, "O Delvig, Delvig!" is a cri de coeur for final redemption of lives lost in the pursuit of valiant ideals:

Bessmertie ravno udel i smelykh vdokhnovennykh del i sladostnovo pesnopeniia!	Immortality is equally the reward of bold inspiring deeds and of sweet song!

15

A Perspective on Soviet Musical Culture during the Lifetime of Shostakovich (1998)

LEVON HAKOBIAN

Current inhabitants of what constitutes the former Soviet Union are familiar with the fact that during the entire seventy-odd years of communist rule, the prosperous West remained generally unaware of and indifferent to what we experienced spiritually.

It seems that a shared perception among people in the West has elaborated a distinctly dark image of life under the Hammer and Sickle, listing its major constituents in one breath: the GULAG, the KGB, a militaristic euphoria, hard drinking, a bureaucracy in splendor and working people in misery, empty shops and endless lines, the dismal faces of passers-by in the streets, and bombastic propaganda about the regime's successes. According to this stock classification, only two categories of humankind in Soviet society were worthy of attention: the cowardly,

---

Originally published as the introduction and the introductory commentary to the chapter "The Rise of Shostakovich," in Hakobian's *Music of the Soviet Age, 1917–1987* (Stockholm: Melos Music Literature Kantat HB, 1998), pp. 9–15, 56–62, respectively. Reprinted with permission of the author and the publisher. The text, as printed here, has been revised in accordance with idiomatic usage and American spelling conventions.

cruel, corrupt communist elite, on the one side, and, on the other, the courageous handful of dissidents. As for the rest of the population, they were automatically considered an amorphous and sterile mass of silent conformists. The typology of artistic creativity was supposed to correspond generally to the same fundamental dualism: the stillborn art of Socialist Realism, favored by the communist government and intended to serve the ideological necessities of the regime, had its exact antithesis in a dissident art whose principal aim was to defy the regime and to unmask its abominations. It has been tacitly presumed that the average person of the Soviet age, having been deprived of a legally available, digestible spiritual and intellectual food, was thus compelled to consume, on the sly, the achievements of native dissidents or Western intellects, or else to float passively in the emptiness deliberately created around him by the Kremlin's captains of ideological warfare.

Such a scheme, to be completely accurate, obviously would depend on a purely theoretical Orwellian outlook. It overlooks the existence of a highly specific and rich spiritual atmosphere elaborated by several generations of "conformists"—that is, properly speaking, by the common efforts of the majority of the country's intellectuals and creative people—a spiritual atmosphere that represents one of the most powerful realities of the Soviet epoch and, *sub specie aeternitatis*, may be regarded as an achievement of utmost importance (however unintentional!) by the communist regime. In the domain of arts and letters, the atmosphere in question revealed itself through a mighty current of independent creation free from "politics" directly expressed (of whatever coloration, dissident or Marxist–Leninist–Stalinist)—a current that proved itself capable of surviving all the changes in the Party's general line and that showed the first signs of abating only in the mid-1980s, with the beginning of unexpected freedom and total "early capitalistic" commercialization.

The artistic trend under consideration—or, to put it more precisely, this trend of independent creation with rather indistinct boundaries which turned out to be powerful enough to penetrate all kinds of arts and letters—existed in a complex interrelationship with the officially approved worldview. Moreover, it had few points of contact with social satire or direct protest against the ruling dogmas. Thus it can hardly be referred to as the antithesis of official art in any strict sense. Still, no artist lived in a vacuum; nobody could risk turning himself off from the notorious and omnipresent Soviet "doublethink." Artists, with rare exceptions, preferred to be good "conformists" in their social behavior. Even so, the atmosphere of the epoch thrust on them certain specific demands. As a result, the best artistic creation of the Soviet epoch stands as a peculiar commentary on the officially imposed *Weltanschauung*, realized not so much on the level of straightforward criticism and direct negation as on a deeper gnosiological and ontological analysis. The basis for such an analysis consists in a special psychological quality, which generally being highly characteristic of the psychology of an intellectual raised under the pressure of the Soviet State, has not yet obtained an appropriate terminological label. To my mind, the quality in question might be called "existentialism"—though, of course, not existentialism in the conventional philosophical sense but rather an elemental phenomenon belonging in the realm of the collective unconscious and representing an indispensable counterbalance to the pure materialism of the standard Marxist-Leninist worldview.

This kind of "existentialism" deserves special attention. The homeland of the Karamazov brothers has never been short of "thinkers" eagerly speculating, over a glass of vodka, about the deepest and most complex problems of human existence. Indeed, from the earliest days of the communist domination of Russia, a common topic for debate has been whether this national disposition to homebred "philosophy" led to the state of public mind that resulted in the 1917 Revolution. Be that as it may, this Revolution, having swept almost all true philosophers out of the country (or having thrown them into concentration camps), and having nothing to put in their place but the wretched, plainly atheistic doctrine of so-called dialectical and historical materialism, provided an extremely powerful impetus to the process of further substituting a native philosophy for the professional one.

No wonder that, under the conditions of a repressive state, "private" thoughts should be centered especially on the paramount subjects of existentialist philosophy: the tragic splitting of the human soul between good and evil, the impossibility of reaching complete mutual understanding with one's fellow man, and the search for self-identity in an alien and absurd world. Paraphrasing Mayakovsky's verse, "We didn't study dialectics according to Hegel," one might assert that the Soviet people identified with and experienced the depths of existential philosophy directly, without the mediation of Heidegger, Jaspers, Camus, or Sartre. The perpetual presence in the everyday life of every Soviet citizen of tempting, existential Evil served as the most efficient means for training the instinct for existential choice. The average Soviet individual was compelled to make such a choice on virtually every level of relations with the external world.

The essence of a Soviet individual's elemental existentialism could scarcely be perceptible to those who had no idea of such typically Soviet phenomena as the *stukach* (a "knocker" or "rapper"; a snitch, informer, or stool-pigeon who works on behalf of the political police), the *vintik* (a "cog" or "little screw"; a term Stalin himself used to define a good Soviet citizen who functions honestly as a cog in the well-oiled state machinery), or the *zhlob* (vernacular, a "lout" or "slob"; designating the alter ego of a *vintik:* an inflated nonentity, ruthlessly elbowing his fellow citizens in order to snatch his share of the good things in life). It is very important to keep in mind that virtually any more or less valuable work of art created on the territory of the former USSR belongs to the pen, brush, or chisel of a potential or real victim of *stukach*es, surrounded by hostile *zhlob*s, while resisting the humiliating status of *vintik*.

It is equally important to consider that *stukach*es, *vintik*s, and *zhlob*s had elaborated their own substitute for arts and letters that entered into complex and often ambivalent relationships of reciprocal influence with the more respectable forms of artistic creation. All this contributed, in an indirect if psychologically understandable way, to the development of the highly specific "existentialist" spirit that emanates from the best of the artistic production of the Soviet age and unaccountably stirs the minds of sensitive listeners, readers, and spectators. Moreover, this happens even if the latter are not fully aware of the art's social and psychological essence and, as seems to occur quite often, even if they fail to differentiate it from a deliberate, though perhaps more or less disguised, critique of the prevailing social order. Naturally official ideology, having at its disposal a special equivalent of the doctrine of *privatio boni* (according to which Evil, as a self-contained ontological entity, could not exist in communist society), was highly intolerant of any manifestation of such an intellectual and spiritual deviation.

The history of arts and letters in the Soviet state represents a huge martyrology not only of creators but also of tortured and condemned works, including even those that had nothing in common with risky political matters. Fortunately the art of music, owing to its abstract nature—especially in comparison with the word-related arts, and even with the imitative arts—seems to have enjoyed a privileged position. As the outstanding prose writer Andrei Platonov (1899–1951) put it, "Music is definitively prohibited literature when it starts to mumble; out of this—out of what had been definitively prohibited—a great and independent art was born."[1]

True, music experienced the spiteful Party documents of 1936 and

1948, and the persecutions of "formalist" musicians from the 1930s to the 1950s and of the "avant-gardists" in the 1960s and 1970s. On the other hand, no significant composer perished in the GULAG under Stalin, very few left the country under Brezhnev, and almost no one under any general secretary was forcibly expelled from the Union of Composers. (Expulsions from the "creative unions," as generally practiced in the USSR, represented an extremely severe punishment that implied the absolute impossibility of legal professional activity within the country.) Consequently the proportion of forbidden or "not recommended" musical works (i.e., "not recommended" for public performance or publication) turned out to be more modest than that of banned books, as well as that of prohibited films, theater performances, paintings, and sculpture (no wonder that repressions against literature should be especially cruel, since the Russian people traditionally believed in the transforming power of the word).

Having reached its "optimal" state, so to speak, during the years of Brezhnev's "stagnation," the system of relatively mild suppression created around music a sufficiently strong force field that, independent of its inventors, acted as an efficient filter for real talent and prevented the most powerful from falling into futility. Such a system was mild enough to circumvent excessively cruel actions that could have resulted in unnatural, if not tragic, interruption of a composer's career. A similar system also furthered the development of the performing arts, as well as the art of European-style musical composition in the empire's remote dependencies; in some of the latter, this led to fairly impressive results.

In short, if there were one single credible realm in which the Party provided the favorable conditions for artistic creativity proclaimed in Soviet propaganda, that realm was music.[2] For this reason, the musical culture of the Soviet Empire provides unique testimony about one of the most somber and absurd pages in world history viewed from the inside and at the same time somewhat "at a distance," thanks to the mediating nature inherent par excellence in music. In certain of its finest manifestations, music achieved a striking synthesis of modern technical means of composition mingled with elements of a truly Soviet "existentialist" mentality. Western critics are accustomed to drawing attention to the first component in this duality, gladly pointing out that the "Russians" have assimilated sophisticated Western "tricks"—with a considerable delay and, frequently, in a somewhat coarse manner. But the second component usually either passes unnoticed or, being generally alien to Western minds, is misinterpreted. As a consequence, the musical culture of the Soviet age is perhaps all too often treated as something not devoid of a certain quasi-exotic interest but as having only marginal significance in the wider context of major twentieth-century trends. And it is precisely the "Sovietness" of this musical culture that to this day still seems to impede its appreciation on its own merits by the outside world—precisely its "Sovietness," with its deeper existential content that is more than purely musical, and certainly not its occasional distasteful dash of Socialist Realism. Here we may appropriately recall Evgeny Yevtushenko's famous line, "A poet in Russia is more than a poet,"[a] the term *poet* being fully applicable, of course, to musicians as well.

If the outside world has failed to appreciate Soviet musical culture on its own merits, a corresponding reaction of reciprocal misunderstanding of modernist artistic production coming from the prosperous West has also frequently been observed here, even in the most nonconformist artistic circles of the USSR. Such a reaction was, and still is, expressed mainly in the characteristic formula of the arrogance of the oppressed and humiliated: "If only we had their troubles!" [*Nam by ikh zaboty*!].[3]

The musical culture of the Soviet age had its unquestionable leader, Dmitri Shostakovich, whose heritage, as a whole, can be considered the most genuine, deep, and authentic embodiment of the spiritual and psychological milieu of his epoch. Of course, as far as Shostakovich is concerned, it would be unfair to speak about any form of underestimation. His music is sufficiently appreciated throughout the world to satisfy our self-respect, if not to forget the somewhat negligent attitude displayed by that same world toward some of Shostakovich's talented confreres. The key to the adequate critical interpretation of Shostakovich's musical legacy seems, however, not yet to have been found. As one prominent scholar in the field has pointed out, "The persistent misinterpretation of Shostakovich's music is arguably the most grotesque cultural scandal of our time—not because it has caused his music to be devalued (he has long been deemed one of the century's half-dozen great composers), but because it allowed it to become highly rated for entirely the wrong reasons."[4] With regard to the very same scholar's own attempt to propose a "just" interpretation of Shostakovich, I shall return in a moment, since his approach raises an issue requiring discussion.[5] At this point I should merely like to add that in the cultural history of our times there was yet another, no less "grotesque" though quite "silent" scandal, when the great musical world virtually overlooked the splendid heyday of Soviet music from the 1960s to the 1980s, that is, in the very middle of the seemingly dismal Brezhnev era.[6] These two "scandals" already give sufficient reason for continuing the work initiated by Boris Schwarz,[7] author of the best-known book on Soviet music, and to write a new critical survey of music under the Hammer and Sickle. Additionally the "avant-garde" of the 1920s warrants more attention, as do Prokofiev's last two decades, Khachaturian, the best of Sviridov, as well as the worthy contributions of numerous unclassifiable artists of several generations.

Finally, Socialist Realism, which should not be painted in one color, deserves an evenhanded assessment. To sum up, there was an immense musical culture that proved capable of engendering something of value even in the most somber years of 1948 to 1953. This culture may well serve, *urbi et orbi*, as striking evidence of the human spirit's wonderful capacity to derive profit even from the most inauspicious conditions.

❧

Nowadays, no discussion of Shostakovich suffices without reference to the notorious *Testimony* compiled by the composer's alleged amanuensis, Solomon Volkov. I do not presume that I myself am competent enough to explicate what in *Testimony* was really meant and what was added, if not falsified, by Volkov.[8] I make bold merely to assert that the book in which the figure of the composer is adjusted, so to speak, to the mediocre intellectual and professional level of the compiler, represents no interest regarding the understanding of either Shostakovich's personality or his art.

Indeed, all the noise once raised by Shostakovich's memoirs—generally "positive" in the West and decidedly "negative" in the USSR—was essentially conditioned by two quite trivial factors:

(a) Shostakovich allowed himself some sharply critical, even hostile, remarks about various well-known persons who had been considered to be his good colleagues if not his close friends;

(b) Shostakovich hated Stalin and Stalinism, and was not fond of the Soviet regime in general.

The first of these factors amounts to petty gossip, of interest only to lay readers, not to serious musicians. The second is even more trivial, because Shostakovich's attitude toward Stalin did not differ from that of any other more or less intelligent Soviet citizen. By the late 1960s and 1970s, all possible illusions about Stalin and Stalinism (including the latter's disguised Brezhnevian version) had been thoroughly dispelled. Apart from the most inveterate natural-born *stukach*es, *zhlob*s, and dumb *vintik*s, only narrow-minded and detached Western intellectual leaders of the Jean-Paul Sartre type could see in Stalin and his companions anything but a gang of criminals. Soviet propaganda succeeded in swindling foreigners but not the native people. Only those who were and are completely unaware of Soviet reality could be mistaken on this subject.

Even in those times when Shostakovich enjoyed supreme official favor, Party functionaries undoubtedly did not believe the great musician to be a man of their circle. All the ritual exchange of compliments between him and the Soviet power structure during his last twenty years[9] was nothing more than a game in the style of routine Soviet "doublethink," carried out according to firmly established and universally recognized rules. The "unanimous" criticism of *Testimony* in the Soviet press, too, was a game of a similar kind. The changed tone in recent pronouncements by a number of Russian musicians and critics[10] clearly shows the worth of such "unanimity."

Nonetheless, the revelations of *Testimony* have given rise to some farfetched attempts to reinterpret Shostakovich's musical legacy. The worst of these may well be that the confessions of Volkov's interlocutor have been widely accepted as embodying some "essential truth" about the genuine meaning of Shostakovich's musical and human message. The partisans of this notion confuse two decidedly *not* synonymous issues, a belief in the authenticity of *Testimony* and an uncritical, literal reading of what Shostakovich is reported to have said to his interlocutor about the anti-Stalinist and anti-Soviet symbolism of his major scores. One need not be an expert in modern semantics to realize that no musical symbol can be translated adequately into verbal language (at least in the case of a genuinely worthwhile artistic creation, as distinct from something like *The Franco-Prussian War*—that curious musical work that Dostoevsky described in chapter 5 of his novel *Besy* [*The Devils;* also translated as *The Possessed*]). Therefore, when Shostakovich discusses, or alludes to, the disguised "dissident" content of his works, this must be treated as a casual self-description, not as something related to deeper "essential truths." The "essential truth" of any credible artwork lies in a realm that has little in common with the political convictions of its creator. Even the most righteous protest against tyranny will be of no lasting value unless supported by some mysterious force inexplicable in rational terms. All this sounds quite axiomatic. But the partisans of a "new" view of Shostakovich (i.e., one influenced by *Testimony*), in their eager desire to find in him a disguised anti-Soviet ideologist and critic of the totalitarian system, seem to overlook consideration even of such obvious things as this.

I shall not discuss here Solomon Volkov's original contribution to the science of "Shostakovich-ology," which consists mainly in introducing the label *yurodivy* as a key word characterizing Shostakovich's role in Soviet society. In Russia, the *yurodivy*—"God's fool"—was a kind of holy fool allowed by tyrants to utter certain forbidden truths. Volkov's pretension that this term designates the very nature of Shostakovich's personality is as derisive as the obsolete view of him as a good loyal Communist and an orthodox representative of the Soviet artistic establishment.[11] Neither perspective warrants discussion. All the same, Volkov's oversimplification has turned out to be very attractive, even for some of the better-qualified scholars. Accordingly, the British writer Ian MacDonald carried out a large-scale project of reinterpreting Shostakovich's oeuvre in the light of *Testimony*.[12]

MacDonald's book is not short of attacks on those critics and performers who are interested "in beauty rather than truth, form rather than being, the score rather than the mind behind it"[13]—every second member of these pairs of opposites being related, evidently, to Shostakovich's constant desire to express his attitude toward the regime and its abominations, as if this were the final, the most profound depth of his art. Taking the confessions of *Testimony*'s hero as his point of departure, MacDonald shows a rich imagination in speculating about how the composer reflected in music his own presumed reactions to the events of political and social life around him.[14] True, some of MacDonald's observations are not lacking in insight. For instance, he has aptly pointed out the special role played in Shostakovich's music by the two-note dominant-tonic progression, although when he ascribes to it the function of symbolizing the person of the dictator [i.e., Stalin], this seems to be a weak interpretation. It would be more plausible to associate it with a generalized idea of aggressive triviality or inflated primitiveness. Further, when MacDonald identifies duple rhythms/meters with Stalin and triple ones with "the people," this seems still more doubtful, since the body of Shostakovich's scores, taken as a whole, offers no sufficient corroboration. Needless to say, the composer's own explanations and comments about himself as quoted in *Testimony* are taken in their literal sense, which sometimes leads to rather comic results. For instance, proceeding from the affirmation of *Testimony*'s hero that the second movement of the Tenth Symphony represents a musical portrait of Stalin,[15] MacDonald draws a fantastic image of the "Georgian gopak" whose aggressive 2/4 rhythms symbolize the very nature of the enraged tyrant.[16] I find it hard to believe that MacDonald

(a) is unaware that the gopak is not a Georgian dance but a Ukrainian one;

(b) is unaware of the absence of any specifically Georgian (as well as, incidentally, any Ukrainian) trait in the piece in question; and

(c) supposes the desire to portray Stalin in music to be Shostakovich's ultima ratio for composing such a movement.

The same writer's analogous assertions concerning many other scores by Shostakovich seem to be equally ill grounded and dubious. True, MacDonald proved to be perspicacious enough to discern the presence of an element of irony in the background of Shostakovich's published articles, speeches, and remarks about himself. This discovery cannot be dismissed as trivial, especially when one considers that at the time MacDonald was writing his book he could not have been familiar with Shostakovich's letters to Isaak Glikman, in which the composer was infinitely more "himself" than in his conversations with Volkov.[17] Still, it is a pity that Westerners need Volkov to realize that the "true" Shostakovich was strikingly different from his outward, artificially maintained "persona." Soviet people had always been fully aware of this. No wonder the avant-garde musicians of the 1960s and 1970s, being, in general, highly sensitive to any manifestation of civic conformism, nevertheless saw Shostakovich as a moral authority and forgave him all his "compromises," including those which, frankly speaking, seem rather unforgivable (such as his signing, along with Khachaturian, Sviridov, and Shchedrin, a shameful letter against Andrei Sakharov).[18]

In most other respects, the portrait of Shostakovich that MacDonald presents is equally unconvincing. It is, indeed, sheer primitivism to reduce the whole message of this great artist to a two-dimensional "stereo signal"—the tragic versus the satiric—to see in his scores something like a series of musical "feuilletons,"[19] more or less immediately reflecting the course of events in his country, but to overlook almost completely the presence in them of some deeper dimension, responsible for their eternal, timeless value. MacDonald's "two-dimensional" "new Shostakovich" is an uninteresting, dull person, bearing similarities paradoxically to Romain Rolland's Beethoven—the same type of man, fully absorbed in his own unhappiness, his own bile (in the case of Shostakovich, disguised in what, in Russian, was called ironically *grazhdanskaia skorb'*, or "civic grief"). Is it truly possible to imagine that an artist of genius could have such a shallow spiritual life?

"*Yurodivy*," "Charlie Chaplin á la Russe," "singer of social masochism," "slave and prisoner of an anti-human political system," "anti-hero"—recent papers on Shostakovich abound in labels denoting what one might call his "shadowy" side, as if the authors had set out to neutralize a different set of labels, those that had been applied to the same composer in official appraisals during the years he was still a singer of the heroic deeds of the Soviet people, a "loyal son of the Communist Party," and a privileged member of the Soviet establishment. To prolong the game of labeling—a quite futile game, in fact—one could consider Shostakovich a belated representative of the Karamazov family for whom what was most important was to "resolve an idea" (*mysl' razreshit'*) and who, for the sake of this, did not hesitate to enter into a direct dialogue with the forces of evil. Anyway, as explanation or justification for Shostakovich being "two-faced," all such labels amount to mere metaphors having little genuine usefulness. A much better (although, perhaps, also far from exhaustive) characterization of this type of artistic and social conduct might be provided by an old Russian proverb quoted by one of Shostakovich's favorite authors, Nikolai Leskov: "Be faithful in your friendship and loyal in your service, but keep the 'finger' in your pocket" ["Druzhba druzhboi, i sluzhba sluzhboi, a za pazukhoi shish"].[b] Millions of people, the flower of the nation, lived according to this principle—quite typical of the "fellow traveler"[c]—without much bothering about its ethical aspect, vacillating between fairly understandable and conscious conformism and an awareness of being constantly faced with something alien, objectionable, and sinister. Although the presence of this ugly "thing"—exteriorized in the repressive regime—prevented them from "giving the finger" overtly, it nevertheless engendered an extraordinarily rich psychological background for every kind of reflection on the ultimate and most profound metaphysical questions. If the best artistic production created under the Soviet regime indeed possesses some depth and greatness, it is attributable precisely to this uniquely inspiring background, and certainly *not* to the petty desire of artists to "give the finger" to Soviet power, to communism, to Stalin, or to some other embodiment of ontological Evil. As MacDonald and many other contemporary writers would have it, Shostakovich was concerned not so much with creating artistic values or "resolving ideas," as with "giving the finger" on every suitable occasion. Such a vision of Shostakovich is indeed relatively "new," but it seems far too vulgar to be accepted uncritically.

Notes

1. Andrei Platonov, *Dereviannoe rastenie: iz zapisnykh knizhek* [A wooden plant: From notebooks] (Moscow: Pravda, 1990), p. 31, as quoted in the interesting essay on the phenomenon of "Sovietness" in music by Ludmila Bakshi, "Popytka prosh-

chaniia: Neskol'ko tezisov o muzyke totalitarnoi epokhi" [An attempt at leave-taking: Some theses about music of the totalitarian epoch], *Muzykal'naia akademiia*, no. 1 (1992): 40–46.

2. Cf., however: "Far from caring for Russian music, the Soviet Communist Party has, since 1917, done a very conscientious job of all but destroying it" (Ian MacDonald, *The New Shostakovich* [Boston: Northeastern University Press, 1990], p. 257). This is an obvious oversimplification. In reality, the Soviet Communist Party was trying very conscientiously to adapt Russian music (as well as non-Russian music, incidentally) to its specific needs, and partly succeeded. The "by-products" of this continual and bothersome "job" turned out so unexpectedly remarkable, however, that they outweigh all its negative consequences.

3. Cf. the categorical declaration by Solzhenitsyn, "If the twentieth century has any lesson for mankind, it is we who will teach the West, not the West us," as quoted in MacDonald, *The New Shostakovich*, p. 263.

4. Ibid., p. 258.

5. See Levon Hakobian, "The Latest 'New Shostakovich': Allan Ho and Dmitri Feofanov's *Shostakovich Reconsidered* (2000)," chapter 16 of the present volume.

6. Cf. the utterly naïve "Notes on the Soviet Avant-garde," by Joel Sachs, written as recently as the early 1980s, in *Russian and Soviet Music: Essays for Boris Schwarz*, ed. Malcolm Hamrick Brown, Russian Music Studies (Ann Arbor: University of Michigan Research Press, 1984), pp. 287–307.

7. Boris Schwarz, *Music and Musical Life in Soviet Russia, 1917–1981*, enlarged ed. (Bloomington: Indiana University Press, 1983).

8. That Volkov does not hesitate to slander those who are unable to defend themselves compels us to take anything he says with reserve (see his "Zdes' chelovek sgorel" [A man burned out here], *Muzykal'naia akademiia*, no. 3 [1992]: 3–12).

9. The body of Shostakovich's pronouncements, forming his "hagiographic" portrait from the orthodox Soviet point of view, is carefully collected in the Soviet "answer" to Volkov's publication, D. Shostakovich, *O vremeni i o sebe* [About the times and about myself], comp. M. Iakovlev, ed. G. Pribegina (Moscow: Sovetskii kompozitor, 1980); published in English as Dmitri Shostakovich, *About Himself and His Times*, comp. L. Grigoryev and Ya. Platek, trans. Angus and Neilian Roxburgh (Moscow: Progress, 1981).

10. Cf., for instance, Liana Genina's "Razbeg pered propast'iu" [A running start before the abyss], *Muzykal'naia akademiia*, no. 3 (1992): 13; and idem, "Ot redaktsii" [From the editor], *Sovetskaia muzyka*, no. 3 (1980): 33–34. Cf. also Irina Nikolskaya's selection of interviews with Russian musicians, selection 13 in the present volume.

11. Here, it must be pointed out that the Western press of the "pre-Volkov" era indeed abounded in astonishing if not directly stupid commentaries on Shostakovich's music. Even such a competent and, in many instances, fairly acute critic as Gerald Abraham had considered the Fifth Symphony—this encyclopedia of human suffering—"merely dull," denying Shostakovich a melodic gift (Gerald Abraham, *Eight Soviet Composers* [London: Oxford University Press, 1943], pp. 28–29). And another highly esteemed critic, Claude Rostand, accused Shostakovich

of "platitude" and allowed himself to scoff at Shostakovich's "political, economic, and patriotic cantatas" (as quoted in Jacques Di Vanni, *1953–1983: Trente ans de musique soviétique* [Arles: Actes Sud, 1987], p. 23). Reading these and similar specimens of nonsense (still others, also from important musical authorities of the Western world, are quoted by Karen Kopp, *Form und Gehalt der Symphonien des Dmitrij Schostakowitsch* [Bonn: Verlag für Musikwissenschaft, 1990], pp. 11–12), one cannot help recalling what Lermontov said on one occasion: "[The West] could not comprehend our glory." Against such a background, even Volkov's wretched "revelations" can produce an impression of something valuable.

12. MacDonald, *The New Shostakovich*.

13. Ibid., 259.

14. Regarding such stubborn resolve to find the explicit programmatic content of virtually any piece of music, one is unexpectedly reminded of the attitude of conservative Soviet musicologists Yuli Anatolievich Kremlyov and Josif Yakovlevich Ryzhkin, the authors of rather grotesque papers that followed a similar methodological approach in treating works by Beethoven and other composers (cf., for instance, Ryzhkin's "Siuzhetnaia dramaturgiia betkhovenskogo simfonizma" [The topical dramaturgy of Beethoven's symphonism], in *Betkhoven: sbornik statei* [Beethoven: A collection of articles], comp. and ed. N. L. Fishman, 2 vols. [Moscow: Muzyka, 1971–72], 2:101–60.

15. Solomon Volkov, *Testimony: The Memoirs of Dmitri Shostakovich*, as related to and edited by Solomon Volkov, trans. Antonina W. Bouis (New York: Harper & Row, 1979), p. 141.

16. MacDonald, *The New Shostakovich*, p. 206.

17. *Pis'ma k drugu: Dmitri Shostakovich—Isaaku Glikmanu* [Letters to a friend: Dmitri Shostakovich to Isaak Glikman] (Moscow: DSCH, 1993). Although, on the other hand, Gerald Abraham in fact had already noticed something of the sort in Shostakovich's Third Symphony. As early as 1943, Abraham proved shrewd enough to suspect that if something were "wrong" with this seemingly cheerful Komsomol Third Symphony, it was conditioned not so much by a lack of inspiration on the part of the composer but by some other enigmatic factor: "One cannot help feeling that the composer is playing a part. He is by nature a wit (or a humorist), and wits do not make good hymn writers. He tries to be Marxian, but fantastic Gogolian humour keeps breaking in" (Abraham, *Eight Soviet Composers*, p. 18).

18. This letter was published in *Pravda* on 3 September 1973.

19. MacDonald, *The New Shostakovich*, p. 171.

Editor's Notes

a. "Poèt v Rossii—bol'she, chem poet," the first line of the introductory poem, "Molitva pered poèmoi" [A prayer before the poem], to his extended cycle, *Bratskaia GES* [The Bratsk Hydro-Electric Power Station].

b. Leskov's addendum, "a za pazukhoi shish" (literally, "but keep a fig in the bosom") gives the Russian saying a rather vulgar comic twist, meaning to keep it out of sight. In American practice, the middle "finger" is extended upward, and the thumb and other fingers are folded into the hand. Russians make a fist with the thumb sticking up between the index and middle fingers. When an American gives someone the "finger," the implication of this aggressively obscene gesture generally needs no further comment. The Russian "fig," on the other hand, as in Leskov's humorous phrase, implies a viciously joyous rejection of something expected: "You're not about to get anything out of me!"

c. "Fellow traveler"—a direct translation of the Russian word *poputchik*—a person who more or less supported the cause of the Communist Party but who was not a member.

16

The Latest "New Shostakovich"

Allan Ho and Dmitri Feofanov's *Shostakovich Reconsidered* (2000)

LEVON HAKOBIAN

A large part of the book *Shostakovich Reconsidered* comprises articles and materials by various authors, including some translated from Russian and already familiar to our readers. The compilers and editors of this work are the pianist and lawyer Dmitri Feofanov and the musicologist Allan Ho; they themselves have written the extensive opening section. As a source of new information about Shostakovich, the book offers little of interest, although as a peripheral artifact of musical life it has a certain curiosity. For this reason, a few words devoted to it are in order.

The title page of the book mentions only two names; but the structure and content of the material found inside provide every reason to consider that, in actuality, Feofanov and Ho had another equally involved coauthor working with them. This was Ian MacDonald, a British journalist

---

Translated from Levon Hakobian, "Ocherednoi 'Novyi Shostakovich' " [The latest "new Shostakovich"], *Muzykal'naia akademiia*, no. 2 (2000): 133–35. The author renders his Armenian surname as "Hakobian" in the Latin alphabet. In the Library of Congress transliteration, it would be "*Akopian.*" The author approved the English translation printed here. Permission to reprint was also granted by Yu. S. Korev, editor in chief of *Muzykal'naia akademiia.*

and author of the book *The New Shostakovich* (Boston: Northeastern University Press, 1990). The book under review includes a number of MacDonald's articles that continue and develop ideas first presented in *The New Shostakovich*. Moreover, Feofanov and Ho frequently cite MacDonald in their text.

Shostakovich, in MacDonald's interpretation, is, first and foremost, a closet dissident, a thorough and assiduous chronicler of and sarcastic commentator on all the most important events that took place in his country. Clearly such a view of Shostakovich was formed under the decisive influence of the notorious *Testimony* (New York: Harper & Row, 1979), as related to and edited by Solomon Volkov, which, according to MacDonald, contains a certain "essential truth" about the creative work of our composer. Having taken the outspoken hero of *Testimony* as his point of departure, MacDonald interprets Shostakovich's entire oeuvre as one gigantic insult directed at the hated communist regime.

Feofanov and Ho's "reconsidered" Shostakovich is exactly the same personality as MacDonald's "new Shostakovich." In other words, the title of the new book does not correspond to its content. If perhaps MacDonald's Shostakovich of 1990 was to some extent new at the time,[1] then by now such an interpretation of the composer has become commonplace. In publications here and abroad during the past decade there is no more hackneyed a subject than that of Shostakovich-the-dissident, and many commentators, homegrown and Western, have occupied themselves with nothing more out of the ordinary than searching through Shostakovich's scores for secret signs of Aesopian language and subtexts that smack of anti-Soviet criticism and social commentary. The Shostakovich now presented to us as "reconsidered" is nothing more than worn and threadbare merchandize repackaged in slightly fresh wrapping.

The overriding intention of the book's authors is to prove the authenticity of *Testimony* irrevocably, once and for all. The first part of the book (the section written by Feofanov and Ho) is constructed on the model of a courtroom trial: quoted material, facts, testimonial evidence, and the like, are called up and subjected to thorough cross-examination intended to convince those who doubt that the book published by Volkov contains the genuine thoughts and words of the composer. Another important postulate is likewise proven irrefutably: Shostakovich did not love the Soviet regime. Frankly I cannot imagine that serious contemporary people could be interested in reaching a verdict on a question that's not worth a hill of beans.[a]

From the point of view of judicial norms, in accordance with which any and all doubts must be decided in favor of the accused, the authenticity of *Testimony* has for a long time needed no further proof: virtually everything in the book has been confirmed one way or another by information from other independent sources. The issue is not the authenticity of Shostakovich's memoirs but that the book, truth be told, is rather crude and jejune. The Israeli musicologist Joachim Braun, cited by Feofanov and Ho, accurately characterizes the book as a collection of "lobby gossip." Even the sun has spots: that Shostakovich had a penchant for gossip is not extraordinary. Neither was Stravinsky in his "dialogues"[b] above reproach in this regard. Stravinsky was just luckier with his interlocutor. Robert Craft continually kept the intellectual level of the conversation on a high plane; as a consequence, Stravinsky emerges from the pages of the "dialogues" as a profound, significant, and charismatic human being. The Shostakovich of *Testimony*, on the other hand, adapting to the far more limited intellectual and professional level of his interlocutor, emerges as repetitive, superficial, and entirely devoid of charisma.[2] Volkov's hero is Shostakovich if not "on a chamber pot [na sudne]"[c] then in his underwear.[3] As expected, the general public finds such a Shostakovich more lovable than the one who composes operas and symphonies; this is why *Testimony* enjoyed such great commercial success. But *Shostakovich Reconsidered* has only a peripheral relationship to Shostakovich the creative musician. No wonder it is almost never cited in serious analytical studies (i.e., scholarly studies, as distinct from memoirs or popular accounts).[4] In regard to the latter, a "certificate of authenticity" in the form of Feofanov and Ho's zealously realized book will change nothing.

Even less understandable is why energy was needlessly wasted on proving Shostakovich's lack of love for the communist regime. We know all too well that, on the whole, the attitude of any thinking Soviet citizen toward the regime was virtually identical. In this way Shostakovich was no different from millions of his fellow citizens of all classes and social strata whose lives were built according to the principle formulated by Leskov long before 1917: "Be faithful in your friendship and loyal in your service, but keep the 'finger' in your pocket" ["Druzhba druzhboi, i sluzhba sluzhboi, a za pazukhoi shish"].[d] In this regard, Westerners who never experienced the delights of life under the Soviet regime are well served by the parables of George Orwell and Kurt Vonnegut, which clearly illustrate how and why it is possible to loathe and despise a totalitarian regime at the same time as one faithfully and truthfully serves it, even occupying a rather high position within its system. It is amusing that one of the most important leitmotifs of *Shostakovich Reconsidered* consists in the refutation of the thesis advanced by the American scholar Richard Taruskin: "Shostakovich was, obviously, a most loyal musical son of Soviet Russia."[e] Vladimir Ashkenazy, in his preface, makes the author of this assessment a shameful example, and MacDonald (in his article "The Academic Misrepresentation of Shostakovich") utterly annihilates him, expressing doubts about his professional competence. Other specialists on Shostakovich who do not hear the anti-Soviet "premise" in the composer's music, in the opinion of MacDonald, also catch hell—Malcolm Brown and Laurel Fay, first of all.

The humor in the situation consists not so much in the fact that MacDonald, from the viewpoint of professional competence, is far more vulnerable than the scholars he names, but in the fact that the subject under discussion is fabricated, in the full sense of the word, out of whole cloth. Shostakovich was not only "a most loyal musical son of Soviet Russia." (Of course he was, and to deny this, as it applies to Shostakovich before 1936—and that is exactly the period to which Taruskin refers—is absurd to say the least.) But he was also someone who sincerely hated the regime. He was not only a victim of the regime; but he was also one of its pillars. His music served not only as a banner of nonconformity but also as one of the few undeniably worthwhile items of Soviet export—along with weapons, the ballet, and hockey. To speak about Shostakovich only as a victim and a dissident is to proclaim an impoverished and hypocritical half-truth.

The composer's music as such is given relatively little attention on the pages of *Shostakovich Reconsidered.* A poorly informed reader might get the impression that our subject wrote no work more remarkable than the *Antiformalisticheskii rayok* [The antiformalist peepshow]. In the course of the book, other hackneyed topics, already stuck in our teeth too long, are discussed yet again in greater or lesser detail: the anti-Stalinist subtext of the "invasion themes" in the Seventh and Twelfth symphonies; the Eleventh's allusion to the 1956 Hungarian Uprising; the anti-Soviet gist of the Fifth's Coda; and the like. Everything that makes Shostakovich's music something more than a " 'finger' in the pocket," that is to say, everything that makes it art, remains far outside the covers of this book.

I should like to call attention to another matter. In substantiating their thesis about Shostakovich's aversion for the regime, the authors of the book cite, by way of example, his disdainful pronouncements about the RAPM (The Russian Association of Proletarian Musicians) and about the creative work of the leading Proletarian composer of the 1920s, Alexander Davidenko.[5] Yet, in this connection, the authors remain mum about one curious fact. At a certain moment, evidently soon after the war, Lev Nikolaevich Lebedinsky (1904–92) made an appearance in Shostakovich's intimate circle. Lebedinsky, a former Cheka[f] agent and a Party member from 1919, was the long-time boss of the RAPM; he was also Davidenko's friend and first biographer. Lebedinsky's articles and reminiscences about Shostakovich, written in a later period after the composer's death, are frequently cited in *Shostakovich Reconsidered* as if they were primary sources that ought to be trusted without question—no doubt because, in these later publications, Lebedinsky represents himself as an advocate for the authenticity of *Testimony* and as a confirmed enemy of communism. In spite of all this, Lebedinsky's way of thinking could not have differed more strikingly during his earlier days as a young and energetic leader of the RAPM. His main articles from 1928 through 1931, published in the official RAPM journal, *Proletarskii muzykant* [The proletarian musician], remind one of spiteful and crude political denunciations. They are conspicuous in their maliciousness, even in comparison with similar music-critical "produce" from that period by other members of the RAPM. Lebedinsky's articles call to mind yet again the policeman Nebaba from Ilf and Petrov's *Zolotoi telyonok* [The golden calf], as well as Bulgakov's Latunsky and Shvonder.[g]

Such hostility toward Stalinism by a former member of the RAPM is understandable: the "Shvonders," if they managed to escape destruction, had been thrust to the distant fringe of social survival during Stalin's years of omnipotence. Those among them who survived until Khrushchev and Brezhnev became witnesses to the utter discredit of ideas to which they had genuflected in their youth—ideas embodied in the music of Davidenko in particular. In the 1960s, very probably under Lebedinsky's influence, Shostakovich made two at first glance strange but altogether symbolic gestures, taking into account the prevailing sociological situation at the time. First, he arranged two of Davidenko's revolutionary choruses and published them as his opus 124.[6] Then later he wrote (or, in any case, he signed) a foreword to a collection of articles about Davidenko.[h] Keeping in mind these and other later homages that Shostakovich paid to the revolutionary "romanticism" of his youth[7] (about which MacDonald and company remain studiously silent, resolutely excluding them from their conception of a "new" or "reconsidered" Shostakovich), an intriguing question arises about the true nature of the composer's celebrated anti-Soviet sentiments. What was the greater part of it, a noble and justifiable hatred of Bolshevism or a querulous hostility toward the Sharikovs[i] who, once having acceded to power, debased the noble ideals that long ago had promised so much? Feofanov and Ho's book offers no answer to this question.

Notes

1. True, as portrayed by MacDonald, he was one-dimensional and unmusical, but that is already another issue. I offered my own opinion of MacDonald's book in my article "Zapadnye avtory o Shostakoviche: obzor i kommentarii" [Western authors on Shostakovich: A survey and commentary], *Shostakovichu posviashchaetsia: sbornik statei k 90-letiiu kompozitora (1906–1996)* [Dedicated to Shostakovich: A collection of articles for the composer's 90th anniversary (1906–1996)], comp. Elena Borisovna Dolinskaya (Moscow: Kompozitor, 1997), pp. 17–26.

2. Volkov's persistent attempt to lower a conversation to the intellectual level of crude scullery blather is demonstrated quite eloquently in his recently published dialogues with Joseph Brodsky, *Conversations with Joseph Brodsky* (New York: Free Press, 1998).

3. In the interview with Volkov, "Zdes' chelovek sgorel" [A man burned out here], published in the journal *Muzykal'naia akademiia*, no. 3 (1992): 3–12 (which is reprinted in *Shostakovich Reconsidered*, the book under review here), Volkov rather candidly explains his professional credo: he sees himself as a person whose mission is to present to the public the private lives of famous people. That this profession, in his view, involves little in common with the ethics of a gentleman is strikingly confirmed by those places in the interview where Volkov slanders the memory of people who never compromised themselves in the slightest. [Among others, perhaps, Hakobian undoubtedly had the distinguished violinist Oleg Moiseevich Kagan in mind when he wrote these words.—Ed.]

4. In fact, the same is true of *The New Shostakovich* by Ian MacDonald. The latter has been seriously offended by this circumstance, which one can verify on MacDonald's personal Internet site, "Shostakovichiana," where, for several years now, scarcely restraining his vocabulary, he has carried on a passionate dispute with those scholars from the academic community who underestimate the importance of his work.

5. Pronouncements of this sort figure, in particular, in Shostakovich's letters from 1931 to the composer Vissarion Shebalin [1902–1963] (published in Sofia Khentova's *V mire Shostakovicha* [In Shostakovich's world] [Moscow: Kompozitor, 1996] p. 129). [In his original review, Hakobian mistakenly identified the title of Khentova's book as *Vokrug Shostakovicha* (In Shostakovich's circle).—Ed.]

6. Shostakovich clearly wanted to give this work a certain weight, in as much as he provided it with an opus number. Note, in this regard, that his orchestration of Musorgsky's *Pesni i pliaski smerti* [Songs and dances of death], completed at the very same time, was left without an opus number.

7. Such later homages include the Eleventh Symphony, "The Year 1905" op. 103 (1956–57)—a belated realization of the RAPM idea of a symphony based on revolutionary songs—the Symphonic Poem *Oktiabr'* [October] op. 131 (1967) and

the choral cycle *Vernost'* [Loyalty], eight ballads for unaccompanied male chorus (1970).

Editor's Notes

a. Hakobian invokes the Russian idiom "vyedennogo iaitsa ne stoit," which literally means "not worth an empty eggshell."

b. This is a reference to the series of autobiographical conversations between Stravinsky and Robert Craft, which were collected and published in six books, four published by Doubleday (Garden City, N.Y.)—*Conversations with Igor Stravinsky* (1959), *Memories and Commentaries* (1960), *Expositions and Developments* (1962), and *Dialogues and a Diary* (1963); and two published by Knopf (New York)—*Themes and Episodes* (1966) and *Retrospectives and Conclusions* (1969).

c. Hakobian's complete sentence, "Volkov's hero is Shostakovich if not 'on a chamber pot [*na sudne*]' then in his underwear," invokes Alexander Pushkin's letter of November 1825 to his friend Prince Vyazemsky, à propos of the loss of Byron's diaries. With characteristic passion, Pushkin writes:

> Why do you regret the loss of Byron's notes? The devil with them! Thank God they are lost. He made his confession in his verses, in spite of himself, carried away with the rapture of poetry. In cool prose . . . he would have been caught in the act, just as Rousseau was caught in the act—and spite and slander would have triumphed once again. Leave curiosity to the crowd and be at one with Genius. . . . We know Byron well enough. We have seen him on the throne of glory; we have seen him in his coffin in the midst of Greece's rising from the dead. Why should you want to see him on a chamber pot? The crowd greedily reads confessions, memoirs, etc., because in its baseness it rejoices at the abasement of the high, at the weaknesses of the strong. It is in rapture at the disclosure of anything loathsome. "He is small like us; he is loathsome like us!" You are lying, you scoundrels: he's small and he's loathsome, but not the way you are—differently. (*The Letters of Alexander Pushkin*, translated, with preface, introduction, and notes, by J. Thomas Shaw [Madison: University of Wisconsin Press, 1967], pp. 263–64)

The final passage has been used as the epigraph for the present volume.

d. See chapter 15, editor's note b, in this volume.

e. I have deliberately translated this "quotation" back into English from Hakobian's Russian paraphrase, which is *not* an exact rendering of Taruskin's original English statement describing Shostakovich as "perhaps Soviet Russia's most loyal musical son" ("The Opera and the Dictator," *The New Republic* [20 March 1989], p. 40).

f. Lebedinsky's association with the Cheka is confirmed in his short c.v., published in the journal *Muzykal'naia nov'*, no. 8 (1924): 21. At that time people would not hesitate to parade such biographical details, unlike the tendency nowadays to conceal them. For a description of the Cheka, see chapter 14, editor's note e, in this volume.

g. The character Semyon Vasilievich Nebaba, is fleetingly identified in Ilf and Petrov's satirical story *Zolotoi telyonok* [The golden calf] (1931), as a corrupt cop who took bribes for protection from a beggar pretending to be blind but who, after the Revolution, becomes a *music critic*! Latunsky is a spiteful literary critic from Bulgakov's *Master i Margarita* [The master and Margarita] (1939). The same author's novella *Sobach'e sertse* [The heart of a dog] (1925), if interpreted as an allegory of Soviet life in the 1920s, depicts the character Shvonder as a type of narrow Bolshevik dogmatist and stool pigeon, something of a Leninist-Trotskyite, who belongs to a class that would eventually be all but exterminated during the Stalinist purges.

h. The book in question is *Alexander Davidenko: vospominaniia, stat'i, materialy* [Alexander Davidenko: Recollections, articles, materials], comp. Nikolai Avksentievich Martynov (Leningrad: Muzyka, 1968). Although Shostakovich's contribution to the book is entitled "Vmesto predisloviia" [In place of a foreword], it is in fact the only "foreword" in the book and appears on pages 3 to 5, immediately after the brief acknowledgments from the compiler.

i. This is another reference to Bulgakov's *Heart of a Dog*. Sharik is the mongrel dog transformed into Sharikov, the homunculus who possesses both the mentality of a dog and the criminal past associated with the human organs transplanted into him by Dr. Preobrazhensky. Interpreted as political allegory, Sharikov can be seen as a premonitory image of Stalin; hence Hakobian's reference to "the Sharikovs" invokes the heirs of Stalin who ruled Soviet Russia during Shostakovich's lifetime.

17

Dialogues about Shostakovich

From the History of Russian Studies about Shostakovich (2002)

LUDMILA KOVNATSKAYA

The main material for my report comes from two sets of letters. The correspondents engaged in conversation are Russian music scholars and critics of the Soviet period: on the one side, they are Alexander Naumovich Dolzhansky (1908–1966) and Victor Petrovich Bobrovsky (1906–1979),[1] and, on the other, Yuli Anatolievich Kremlyov (1908–1971) and Sergei Vasilievich Aksiuk (1901–1994).[2] To what extent the phrases "on the one side" and "on the other" should be understood here not as conventional and formulaic but as substantive will shortly become obvious to those familiar with the political and ideological nature of Soviet musical and musicological life. For everyone else, I trust it will become clear in a moment.

"In every conversation between two people there are six interlocutors: each one as he *is* (known only to God), each as he seems to himself, and each as he seems to his confrere, and all of them are unalike," so notes Mikhail Gasparov on the nature of the dialogue.[3] Such an astute observation can be extrapolated, of course, to include letter writing as a form of written conversation, like diaries or marginal notes, which also represent an indirect form of dialogue. The fine point, I would suggest, consists in the distance between "I" and the images reflected in the virtual mirror of "I, as I seem to myself" and "I, as I seem to the other." The conversationalist, correspondent, or diarist, whose conscience experiences the pressure of a divided psyche and whose social behavior is contradictory, views these images as profoundly dissimilar and distant from one another. The one whose principles are firm, and whose behavior is determined by these principles, views the three images within a single spectrum of notions. For a third person, an integrated, whole person, the differences between the images are minuscule and can fuse together almost without "seams and gaps." Any corrections, whether of sociopsychological or ideological or affective attributes, fit quite well within Gasparov's psychogenic model. The characters of my story fit into this model as well.

It is well known that the prominent Soviet scholars, the theorists Alexander Dolzhansky and Victor Bobrovsky, Shostakovich's contemporaries, were insightful researchers as well as discerning experts and admirers of the music (and the persona) of Shostakovich. Their theories originated in their analyses of his music. Such, for instance, was Dolzhansky's theory of the fugue[4]—which has widespread theoretical significance—and his modal theory[5] (including the Alexandrian modal-pentachord),[6] which interprets the degrees of the twelve-tone scale as a diatonic phenomenon.[7] The same can be said about the functional theory of musical form developed by Bobrovsky—which he regarded as a self-contained system with variable combinations and changeability of functions—one of the most basic concepts in contemporary music theory.[8]

It is very difficult to describe these two remarkable people in such a brief article.[9] I should just mention that Bobrovsky—whose father was arrested while in exile, then repatriated, condemned, and executed in Soviet Russia[10]—was one of the musicians most loyal to Shostakovich. In her article about Bobrovsky, Evgeniya Chigaryova speaks about him in these words: "As a person with a 'troubled conscience,' Bobrovsky worried about everything that was happening then in our country. He suffered from being forced to remain silent, from being unable to tell the 'whole truth' in his published works (this especially concerned his writings about Shostakovich). And then he started keeping a journal, not at all of a personal nature, which he entitled 'O samom vazhnom' [About what is most important],[11] together with his personal reflections, 'Shostakovich v moei zhizni' [Shostakovich in my life],[12] both published posthumously."[13]

Turning to Dolzhansky, his character was completely in accord with the root of his last name (*dolg*, or "duty"). He was even unafraid to raise his voice publicly in defense of Shostakovich during the course of the campaign of 1948–49.[14] He saw his action and the position he took as an expression of duty. The result was not long in making itself felt: disparagement of his work, and of himself personally, formed the constant backdrop of his life.[15]

According to the current clichés in discussions about Shostakovich, Dolzhansky and Bobrovsky might be called closet dissidents. They did not belong to the Soviet *nomenklatura* (i.e., the elite named to their positions by organs of the Party), they did not hold important official posts, and they did not serve the system demonstratively and with zeal. As musicians, they both responded to the language of Shostakovich's music, the multivalence of its meanings. And they developed their own "Aesopian language" in analyzing his music—its modal nature, its compositional peculiarities, the origins of its techniques, and the methods the composer followed in realizing his ideas. People of my generation read the scholarly writings of Dolzhansky and Bobrovsky not only for the sake of their remarkable professional mastery but also for the spiritual messages communicated by means of the "working language" of our profession. Their articles demonstrated that the structural analysis of music, which was incomprehensible to the controlling authorities and therefore suspect, was capable of revealing profound artistic meaning.[16] Their works established that fundamental scholarship can be based on the artistic creativity of today. During the years when Soviet historical and aesthetic musicology was primarily servile, *theorists* became the conduits of free thought and innovative ideas. And that is why the music of Shostakovich nurtured more than one generation of brilliant scholar-theorists and, over the decades, attracted younger adherents.[17]

The published correspondence of Dolzhansky and Bobrovsky, friendly and collegial (I recommend it to interested readers), dates from the 1960s—the years of the premières of the Twelfth and Thirteenth symphonies, the Ninth, Tenth, and Eleventh string quartets, and the memorable first performance of the Fourth Symphony and the revival of *Ledi Makbet Mtsenskogo uezda* [Lady Macbeth of the Mtsensk District] (under the title *Katerina Izmailova*). Neither the Eleventh Symphony nor, especially, the Twelfth was a favorite work by their favorite composer. "Oh, how I'd like to hear a non-programmatic symphony by him!" writes Bobrovsky. "But there doesn't seem to be one in the offing."[18]

Bobrovsky and Dolzhansky thought of themselves as members of a "brotherhood-in-Shostakovich," as it might have been called in the nineteenth century. "Dear friend Shostakovichian," Dolzhansky addresses

Bobrovsky on one occasion.[19] Disagreements and arguments that cropped up between them had the character of ideal creative discussions and constructive criticism. In other words, these were individuals close in spirit.

The next two characters in my story of dialogues about Shostakovich, Sergei Aksiuk and Yuli Kremlyov, were also spiritually close. The first, a music critic and composer, was a Party functionary. During the years under consideration, he was editor in chief of the publishing house Sovestkii kompozitor, a *nomenklatura* position. He was also secretary of the board of the USSR Union of Composers in Moscow. As a composer, Aksiuk was all but unknown even in professional circles, let alone among the broad public. His compositions were performed at the House of Composers on the occasion of his jubilees. Had he not been a Party bigwig, he could scarcely have expected to be feted with concerts devoted to his works. The speeches and articles of Aksiuk the critic, collected in a modest volume,[20] were tied to events in the nation's life associated with the Communist Party.

Yuli Kremlyov, an Honored Artist of the RSFSR and Doctor of Arts, headed the Music Department at the Research Institute of Theater, Music, and Cinematography in Leningrad.[21] That, too, was an appointed position; candidates had to be approved by the higher authorities, making it a *nomenklatura* post. But, at the same time, Kremlyov was also one of the country's most prominent scholars and was exceptionally productive, with numerous publications. His three-volume study *Russkaia mysl' o muzyke* [Russian thought about music][22] and a series of monographs on turn-of-the-century French composers (Debussy, Massenet, Saint-Saëns),[23] as well as his many articles and speeches,[24] were widely used as required textbooks in the higher music schools of the country. In his scholarly work, Kremlyov revealed himself to be a loyal son of the regime, attesting to the ideological principles of the communist system, something to which all his works without exception bear witness. Among other things, he was indignant about the "ideological neutrality of young people," as well as about such contemporaneous developments as, for instance, the publication of Schoenberg's music, which just began in the USSR at that time, and preparations in the works for a concert of Stravinsky's music.[25]

Like Dolzhansky and Bobrovsky, Kremlyov and Aksiuk also corresponded about Shostakovich—this was around the time of the première of the Tenth Symphony and the heated debate that followed (the symphony was first performed on 17 December 1953). Both opposed not just that particular composition but were against all Shostakovich's creative work. Kremlyov was fierce and uncompromising. Aksiuk was sometimes more tolerant than his correspondent, but, on the whole, was just as uncompromising and vigilant.[26] Although Shostakovich's name is not mentioned at all in the introductions to the collections of Kremlyov's articles, he wrote a few pieces specifically devoted to him.[27] Kremlyov became especially "famous" for his essay on the Tenth Symphony, which appeared as a review of the première—a "fame" based largely on his sharply critical comments about the new symphony, made during the famous three-day discussion of the work at the Union of Composers in Moscow some months after the symphony's première in Leningrad. Kremlyov's prevailing attitude toward the creative output of the country's leading composer can be inferred from a passage in an article he wrote about Sviridov's *Pateticheskaia oratoriia* [Oratorio patètico]: "How gratifying it would be, for instance, if Shostakovich were to continue and develop the line in his creative work set forth in his oratorio, *Pesn' o lesakh* [Song of the forests]."[28]

As for Aksiuk, he viewed Shostakovich as a socially and ideologically harmful artist who thrived thanks to a double standard: "Shostakovich swears by the names of Musorgsky and Tchaikovsky, and, in Leningrad, he breeds modernist apprentices in his Leningrad circle and indulges them to the utmost. It is all disgusting. And there is no assurance that it will soon 'pass.' On the contrary, 'this' will broaden and deepen. But all the same, we must 'wear the stone away' drop by drop."[29] Elsewhere Aksiuk writes in solidarity with Kremlyov:

> Your opponents (mine, too) . . . consider anybody who contradicts them a reactionary. . . . Incidentally, let us pose the question: just who are these "opponents"? Well, of course, they're the "highbrow" musicologists. . . . As you certainly know and feel, there is a bias in editorial circles, and to a great extent in musicological ones as well, a bias against your position of ruling out Shostakovich as the crowning achievement of Soviet music and of rejecting a rapprochement between, and a knitting together of, realism and modernism.[30]

The opinions exchanged in these two sets of correspondence are based on well-grounded listening experiences and on practical activities involving each of the four participants as critics and publicists. But their perspectives are rooted in different areas of musicology: Kremlyov's and Aksiuk's in ideologically charged aesthetics, and Bobrovsky's and Dolzhansky's in theoretical analysis. Comparing the two dialogues seems appropriate, given their similarity in tone—sincere, mutually trusting.

We believe what we read, because the letters correspond, and are even identical, to the published works of these authors.

The correspondents conducted dialogues in which the "word with a sideward glance" [*slovo s ogliadkoi*] was a rare visitor, whereas the "penetrated word" [*proniknovennoe slovo*]—both Bakhtin's expressions—was customary. What follows is an example of the former, a "word with a sideward glance." The sinister shadow of the regime, which fell, as a rule, across any dialogue between Soviet citizens, here extends into a conversation between Dolzhansky and Bobrovsky. Bobrovsky discovers at the end of Dolzhansky's book on Shostakovich's 24 Preludes and Fugues a passage about the content of that cycle being emblematic of the theme of war and peace, in the embodiment of which this "remarkable master of Socialist Realism . . . achieved something that not a single composer from a bourgeois country could have achieved."[31] Dolzhansky admits to Bobrovsky (in confidence) that the paragraph was written at the publisher's insistence. But he betrays no embarrassment or protest in his confession, writing instead that he considers "these lines to be useful for the propaganda of Sh[ostakovich]'s music."[32] This is but one of a myriad of examples of ideological adaptation to conditions.

Let us focus now on the Tenth Symphony. During the mid-1950s, as everyone knows, this symphony engendered one of the most fiery and intractable ideological discussions in musical circles.[33] A variety of analytic sketches and observations about the Tenth are scattered throughout Bobrovsky's and Dolzhansky's writings, but in only one case do they constitute an independent article.[34] The Tenth presented them with material rich in possibilities for analysis and for stylistic generalizations. They treasured it as one of Shostakovich's symphonic masterpieces, and a masterpiece of all European music.

Kremlyov, on the other hand, defined his attitude about the Tenth as follows: "Shostakovich's Tenth Symphony has its apologists and its foes. As always, there are also those who are indifferent."[35] One cannot bring oneself to regard Kremlyov as an apologist or as one of the indifferent, so that leaves a foe, albeit one who recognized the Tenth as a phenomenon.

On what grounds, then, does Kremlyov incriminate the symphony and its author? In accordance with the practice of Marxist-Leninist aesthetics, Kremlyov interprets the correlation of form and content as a dialectical opposition, thus content divorced from form becomes for him the object of a separate, so to speak "formless," investigation. The absurdity of such an approach by Kremlyov is exposed in all its shamelessness, to wit, the world of this music is alien to him, he cannot accept it emotionally, and therefore the more brilliant and inspiring the composer's mastery, all the worse it is, because it masks the depraved content.

I had the opportunity to examine Kremlyov's copy of the program book from the première of Shostakovich's Tenth Symphony in the Great Hall of the Leningrad Philharmonic (Thursday, 17 December, and Friday, 18 December 1953. The Republic's Honored Collective, the Philharmonic Symphony Orchestra, conducted by Evgeny Mravinsky). Poor Yuli Anatolievich Kremlyov! What he was obliged to endure during a concert that other listeners found profoundly moving! He noted down his immediate impressions of the music in the margins alongside the printed program notes by the well-known critic Yulian Vainkop. At times Kremlyov's comments are amazingly precise but monstrously distorted by his inferences. I reproduce his handwritten text in full:

1st movement
Incredibly gloomy themes. The low register is almost inaudible. Many chorale-like sonorities. Polyphony. Suddenly a melancholy waltz.
Middle [section]—wild cacophony, thundering and false.
End—the tweeting of a flute out of perceptible range. A train whistle. Funereal tolling.

2nd movement
Wild tempo. Infernal din, whistling, drums. You're at the point of going mad. A terrifying trombone solo *prestissimo*. Everything horribly gloomy. Instruments not used idiomatically. Images of a veritable front-line battle intrude. Terrifying music. Decay, cynicism, the howl of a maniac.

3rd movement
On the whole the great art of a master. Especially the polyphony. Form very tight. A master of the orchestra. A theme in Eastern style, with a little drum. In 3rd movement, much mockery on timbres. Solos of all sorts for this. Things then sink into "nothingness." Suddenly the mocking "laughter" of oboes, the disintegration of an idea. Separated sounds. The East in the style of Khodzha-Einatov.[36] Disgusting inhuman noise. In general a mass of *ff*. 3 bass drums, apparently. Phrases: the sputtering of timpani, the mocking squeak of the violin, separate notes in horns. Ends with the cheeping of a flute outside the tonality. Savage falsity alongside beautiful phrases.

4th movement
The oboe sounds so vile it's hard to recognize. The East again? How gloomy everything is. The bassoon openly intones the funeral service. Everything is somehow separated. Now it fades away, now it disintegrates entirely into specks. Then a deafening blow, a wild leap. Again a rupture into "nothingness," a squeak, a rustling. And it's like that the entire symphony. Aha! Things have started to

perk up. The wild ruckus of a Fl[ute] and violins *pp*. Geometry, combination of musical figures. Flutes squealing the whole time. Ravings. And this is "lively and merry" music?! Some kind of dance theme tears into the squealing of the flutes. The din intensifies. The cynical merriment of the entire orchestra dominated by blows on the drum and flutes wailing and squealing. Suddenly everything stops. Nothingness. Medieval gloom, the groans of tormented monks marching in a crypt. A bassoon laughs. A wallop. Cacophony throughout the entire orchestra. Foxtrot rhythm, a tavern. A fl[ute] squeals, trombones bawl on the highest possible notes.

What a bunch of solos!!

In complete conformity with the postulates of Socialist-Realist aesthetics, Kremlyov identifies himself with the average, democratic listener, one from the so-called broad circle of listeners, and he is convinced that Shostakovich's symphony has been "undone" by the professionals. Placing professionalism over and against dilettantism was an approach saturated with the antagonism of class struggle. In ideological and aesthetic polemics the method was risk free.

In the collection *Materials of the Second All-Union Congress of Soviet Composers*,[37] Kremlyov's speech is missing, like those of the other non-principal speakers. The newspaper *Sovetskaia kul'tura* contains an account of it,[38] but we are able to examine the original manuscript, where Kremlyov writes:

> My neighbors in the apartment next door are members of a family of workers. They don't like jazz or low-grade entertainment. They like classical music—Beethoven, Glinka, Tchaikovsky, Chopin. They grasp Soviet literature with ease, and Soviet painting (including even those artists who were branded "formalists," for instance, Alexander Deineka and Vladimir Favorsky). They love much in Soviet music: songs and related genres, a number of the works of Tikhon Khrennikov, Ivan Dzerzhinsky, Aram Khachaturian. But when, for instance, Shostakovich's Violin Concerto is played on the radio, they ask with great bitterness, with great pain and anxiety: Why, oh why do they write such music?
>
> Well then, should one blame these listeners? No, one should blame our music, which is extraordinarily *distant* from the spiritual needs of listeners and which, under the guise of sophistication, cultivates vagueness, lack of clarity, subjectivity.[39]

Both Kremlyov's analysis of the Tenth Symphony in the margins of his Leningrad Philharmonic program book and his article about the work make for interesting reading: his excellent ear and rich associative memory continuously inform him about the semantically saturated content of the symphony; his immediate reactions focus precisely on the world of emotions that lay behind Shostakovich's music. But he was unwilling to accept its nonclassical structure, the absence of classical melody, syntax, and formal articulation, and, as a consequence, his understanding/misunderstanding of the work is characterized by such expressions as "undifferentiated flow," "chaos," and "uncertainty." He feared an ambiguity of meanings ("the themes are emotionally undefined," "the imagery is vague"). Something that "remains unclear," as he put it, frightens him.[40]

The paramount question for Kremlyov was the clarity of the music's content, or perhaps, more accurately, its monosemantic conceptual meaning. In his speech at the Second Congress of Composers, he says: "If D. Shostakovich's Tenth Symphony truly reveals reality in its revolutionary development and shows us the roots of the future, then what awaits us in the future? Such vague, uncertain feelings as these?"[41]

The finale of Shostakovich's Tenth Symphony—as we know, the finale was a general problem and, at the same time, a phantom problem in Soviet symphonic writing—was unconvincing, according to Kremlyov, as a consequence of the one-sided content of the work as a whole. And his words of conclusion sounded a warning "signal" about the ideological depravity of Shostakovich's symphony.

One might think that Kremlyov's stance in his article, one identical to that which the Party and government demanded from Soviet artists and critics, would not land him in trouble. But life in the USSR was diverse and illogical, and Kremlyov was obliged to struggle for three years in order to publish his critical article on Shostakovich's Tenth Symphony. Representatives of the Soviet *nomenklatura* (particularly V. F. Kukharsky)[42] were among those on whom its fate depended. It was published in the April 1957 issue of *Sovetskaia muzyka*, yet, on 5 March 1957, Israel Nestyev sent the author the objections of the editorial board and a summary of the minutes from their meeting. Allow me to quote two opinions. "Kukharsky: I am also critical of the Tenth Symphony. . . . [But] the way the article is written will create an undesirable resonance (in view of the fervently dithyrambic statements of the defenders of the symphony). [S. S.] Skrebkov:[43] The article may become a 'tasty morsel' for the bourgeois yellow press abroad. Once again there will be an outcry about 'the persecution of Shostakovich.' "[44] Either of these opinions might well have been a statement of conviction or a maneuver—a clumsy attempt "to defend Shostakovich."

Later on in Nestyev's letter the following comment appears: "Shostakovich himself spoke on behalf of publishing the article."[45] This very circumstance gave Kremlyov a reason to appeal to Shostakovich the following year requesting the composer to defend his critical article about the Eleventh Symphony from the symphony's admirers.[46] Their written exchange follows:

12 February 1958 [Leningrad]

Dear Dmitri Dmitrievich!

I have written a critical article about your Eleventh Symphony. This article was earmarked for issue no. 2 of the journal *Sovetskaia muzyka* of this year. Then it was postponed to issue no. 3. I have just found out that they are contemplating postponing publication of the article again. I find such suppression of criticism and of the free exchange of opinions unfair,* and hope that, as a member of the editorial board, you will take all due measures to publish my article as planned in the third issue of the journal.

Best regards,
Yu. Kremlyov

*By the way, I didn't object when the journal published favorable evaluations of your latest symphony [i.e., the Eleventh]. Fairness demands that other views be aired too.[47]

14 February 1958, Moscow

Dear Yuri[48] Anatolievich!

As a member of the editorial board of *Sovetskaia muzyka*, I do not consider it possible to take part in discussions of those articles which concern me personally, or my compositions, whether these articles are positive or negative. This has always been my position and this is how it will remain in the future.

D. Shostakovich[49]

23 February 1958 [Leningrad]

Dear Dmitri Dmitrievich!

I have received your postcard and am amazed by it. I did not ask you to "take part in discussions" of my article on your Eleventh Symphony. I only expressed the hope that you, as a member of the editorial board of *Sovetskaia muzyka*, would take measures to ensure that my article is published in the third issue as scheduled. . . . That was the reason I wrote to you, hoping that you would assist in establishing fairness in the exchange of free opinions.

Once someone told me that you had spoken on behalf of publishing my article on your Tenth Symphony. I don't know what motivated you then, but one way or another I was led to assume that you would act in a similar manner now. Unfortunately I was mistaken in my hopes. Therefore I can only apologize for the inconvenience I have caused.

Best regards,
Kremlyov[50]

8 March 1958, Moscow

[From a letter of Yu. V. Keldysh to Yu. A. Kremlyov:]

At the meeting of the editorial board on 24 February I read aloud your telegram demanding the publication of your article on Shostakovich's Eleventh Symphony. Nevertheless, the majority of the board members continued to object categorically to publication of the article. Only Shostakovich took quite a different position. Although he did not attend the meeting, he later communicated to us his request that the article be published.[51]

This written exchange demonstrates strikingly the change in the alignment of social forces and energy flows that raged around Shostakovich and his symphony. The collisions within the Soviet macro-world are reflected as if in a distorting mirror in this micro-world: here, to the inexperienced eye, Kremlyov appears to be the dissident, with all the consequences that follow from such a situation. Writing to two young correspondents about his relations with newspapers and journals in connection with his evaluation of the music of Shostakovich and the composer's role in Soviet culture, Kremlyov says: "Unfortunately, you are mistaken in thinking that the account of the discussion printed in *Sovetskaia muzyka* is accurate. My speech, for one, was not only significantly abridged (although it had been in writing) but abridged tendentiously, at the expense of deliberately weakening the persuasiveness and thoroughness of my arguments."[52]

With his accustomed impartiality, Kremlyov struggled against the privileged: "But the special position of D. Shostakovich, S. Prokofiev, A. Khachaturian, and, recently, G. Sviridov, continues. They are the objects of a cult. 'Excuse us, we do criticize them!'—or so says the editorial board [meaning the editorial board of *Sovetskaia muzyka*.—L.K.]. Well, what of it? In some naïve cults it is permissible even to hack to pieces the god, the idol. But they are gods all the same."[53]

Kremlyov puts his finger here on one of the important features of the social status of the most prominent Soviet artists, who were at one and the same time cruelly criticized but also extolled, persecuted but also privileged. This stratagem of ambivalence, which governed an artist's position, was played out depending on the ideological state of affairs in society at the moment.

By the end of the fifties, it had become clear to Shostakovich's opponents that "to criticize him and other musical monstrosities at the present time means to start a war without soldiers, and, who knows, the criticism may backfire on the one doing the criticizing," as one of Kremlyov's correspondents wrote him.[54] And, in truth, the specifically ideological slant of Kremlyov's critical writings, not only about Shostakovich but also about other outstanding twentieth-century composers, backfired on him, and certain of his critical turns of phrase, in the form of ideological clichés, entered the repertoire of musicological folklore.[55]

The attentive reader of the correspondence between Bobrovsky and Dolzhansky will discover that the publication of their writings about Shostakovich was also sometimes delayed or withdrawn as a result of arbitrary rulings by individuals on editorial boards and in the censorship apparatus. However, neither Bobrovsky nor Dolzhansky bothered Shostakovich with requests to intervene on his behalf. At the same time, scholarship (just like scholarly truth)—which, in ideal circumstances, does not require martyrdom of its practitioners—could not protect them from the aggressiveness of politically and ideologically engaged journalism.

In 1964 Bobrovsky wrote to Dolzhansky: "Dear Alexander Naumovich, I am happy that I can argue with you freely. How good it is."[56] Let us take a moment to remember what a dream that seemed to be in those years, the very possibility of arguing with your colleagues, answering only to scholarship and to one's own conscience; not having to bear ideological responsibility for one's documented scholarly opinion, for constructive criticism; not being immediately and predictably slandered, persecuted, tormented, fired, made ill, and the like, as was the rule at the time in dealing with the scholarly community, with those whose works exemplified genuine scholarly achievement. From our present perspective, it is obvious that this situation did not become obsolete even in the following decades (up to the end of the 1990s). Moreover, I think it is crystal clear that such a situation is not intrinsic to "one country taken separately" (to put an ironic twist on the slogan of the Leader of the Proletariat, "socialism in one country taken separately"). In other words, it is not a specifically Soviet manifestation.

In the story I have told, the muddle and confusion existing among groups of people who seemed to be ideological opposites exposed the existential tyranny and depravity typical of—but not only of—the Soviet regime. Bobrovsky had this in mind when he wrote: "He [Shostakovich] could not disregard the inner deception of our existence; the pain he experienced for us all, for our spiritual impurity, for the daily desecration of the truth, this was what summoned his muse to life."[57]

Notes

Editor's note: Marina Slavina and Laurel Fay kindly provided the translation used here.

1. See "Perepiska V. P. Bobrovskogo i A. N. Dolzhanskogo o Shostakoviche" [The correspondence of V. P. Bobrovsky and A. N. Dolzhansky about Shostakovich], edited, and with commentary, by Olesia Bobrik and Evgeniya Chigaryova, in *D. Shostakovich: mezhdu mgnoveniem i vechnost'iu. Dokumenty, materialy, stat'i* [D. Shostakovich: Between now and eternity], ed. Ludmila Kovnatskaya (St. Petersburg: Kompozitor, 2000), pp. 546–98. Hereafter, "Perepiska."

2. Published here for the first time. Olga Lvovna Dansker, my esteemed colleague in the Manuscript Division at the Russian Institute for the History of the Arts, has my heartfelt gratitude for furnishing me with the material of this correspondence.

3. M. L. Gasparov, *Zapisi i vypiski* [Notes and extracts] (Moscow: Novoe literaturnoe obozrenie, 2000), p. 235.

4. A. Dolzhansky, "Otnositel'no fugi" [Regarding the fugue], *Sovetskaia muzyka*, no. 4 (1959): 94–102; see also his *24 Preliudii i fugi D. Shostakovicha* [D. Shostakovich's 24 Preludes and Fugues] (Leningrad: Sovetskii kompozitor, 1963; 2nd rev. ed., 1970). The theory has been thoroughly analyzed by K. I. Yuzhak; cf. K. Yuzhak, "Shostakovich Dolzhanskogo: opus 87, izmeniaiushchiisia vo vremeni" [Dolzhansky's Shostakovich: opus 87, Changing over time], in *D. D. Shostakovich: Sbornik statei k 90-letiiu so dnia rozhdeniia* [D. D. Shostakovich: A collection of articles dedicated to the 90th anniversary of his birth], ed. Ludmila Kovnatskaya (St. Petersburg: Kompozitor, 1996), pp. 194–227.

5. Dolzhansky, "O ladovoi osnove sochinenii Shostakovicha" [On the modal basis of Shostakovich's works], *Sovetskaia muzyka*, no. 4 (1947): 65–74.

6. Dolzhansky, "Alexanderiiskii pentakhord v muzyke Shostakovicha" [The Alexandrian pentachord in the music of Shostakovich], in A. Dolzhansky, *Izbrannye stat'i* [Selected articles] (Leningrad: Muzyka, 1973), pp. 86–120.

7. Bobrovsky, "Nauchnoe tvorchestvo A. N. Dolzhanskogo" [Dolzhansky's

scholarly work], in Dolzhansky, *Izbrannye stat'i* [Selected articles] (Leningrad: Muzyka, 1973), pp. 3–20.

8. In a letter dated 25 February 1964, concerning his labor of many years on the changeability of functions in musical form, Bobrovsky informed Dolzhansky: "I discovered them while analyzing Shostakovich, and now I am applying them to other phenomena, in particular to Chopin" ("Perepiska," p. 574).

9. I was fortunate to have been a student in Dolzhansky's class on polyphony at the Leningrad Conservatory. I visited his home many times. I observed and heard Bobrovsky lecture at the Institute of Fine Arts, especially in 1976–77.

10. See Evgeniya Chigaryova, "Razbiraia semeinye arkhivy . . ." [Sorting through the family archive . . .] *Russkaia mysl'*, no. 4323, 22–28 June 2000, p. 12.

11. V. Bobrovsky, "O samom vazhnom" [About what is most important], *Muzykal'naia akademiia*, no. 1 (1997): 6–20.

12. V. Bobrovsky, "Shostakovich v moei zhizni: lichnye zametki" [Shostakovich in my life: Personal notes], *Sovetskaia muzyka*, no. 9 (1991): 23–30.

13. Chigaryova, "Razbiraia semeinye arkhivy . . . ," p. 12.

14. Evidence for this can be found in the discussion that took place at the Leningrad Union of Composers and at the Leningrad Conservatory regarding Mikhail Ivanovich Chulaki's paper about the Resolution of the Central Committee of the Communist Party of 10 February 1948 on Vano Muradeli's opera *Velikaia druzhba* [The great friendship] (see Tsentral'nyi Gosudarsvennyi Arkhiv Literatury i Iskusstva in St. Petersburg [hereafter, TsGALI SPb], *f.* 348 [*f.* = *fond* = collection], *op.* 1 [*op.* = *opis'* [inventory], *d.* 77 [*d.* = *delo* = file], *ll.* 47 [*ll.* = *listy* = pages] and following; *d.* 78, *ll.* 97 and following; and TsGALI SPb, *f.* 298, *op.* 4, *d.* 611, *ll.* 10–11).

15. See, for instance, his letter dated 1 April 1966; "Perepiska," pp. 596–98.

16. On this issue, see V. Bobrovsky, "Po povodu stat'i 'Vyshe uroven' teoreticheskoi nauki' " [Concerning the article "Raise the level of theoretical science"], *Sovetskaia muzyka*, no. 8 (1966): 49.

17. In this context, I should also mention the late Lev Abramovich Mazel' (1907–2000).

18. See "Perepiska," p. 574 (letter dated 25 February 1964).

19. See "Perepiska," p. 580 (letter dated 29 February 1964).

20. S. V. Aksiuk, *O muzyke: stat'i i retsenzii* [About music: Articles and reviews] (Moscow: Sovetskii kompozitor, 1980).

21. Formerly and currently known as the Russian Institute (Zubovsky) for the History of the Arts.

22. Yu. Kremlyov, *Russkaia mysl' o muzyke: ocherki istorii russkoi muzykal'noi kritiki i estetiki v XIX veke* [Russian thought on music: Essays in the history of Russian music criticism and aesthetics of the 19th century], vol. 1, 1825–60; vol. 2, 1861–80; vol. 3, 1881–94 (Leningrad: Gosudarstvennoe Muzykal'noe Izdatel'stvo, 1954, 1958, 1960).

23. *Klod Debiussi* [Claude Debussy] (Moscow: Muzyka, 1965); *Zhiul' Massne* [Jules Massenet] (Moscow: Sovetskii kompozitor, 1969); *Kamil' Sen-Sans* [Camille Saint-Saëns] (Moscow: Sovetskii kompozitor, 1970).

24. Yu. Kremlyov, *Izbrannye stat'i i vystupleniia* [Selected articles and speeches] (Moscow: Sovetskii kompozitor, 1959).

25. Yu. Kremlyov, "Po povodu stat'i A. Nikolaeva" [Concerning the article by A. Nikolaev], *Sovetskaia muzyka*, no. 10 (1957): 93.

26. An excerpt from Aksiuk's letter to Kremlyov, dated 27 May 1966, pays witness to this, evidently in response to accusations of having craftily indulged the "modernists," Aksiuk remarks: "still, Prokofiev and Shostakovich aren't exactly s.o.b.s [*kuritsyny syny;* literally, sons of chickens, a euphemistic version of *sukin syn*, or son of a bitch]" Kabinet rukopisei Rossiiskogo instituta istorii iskusstv (hereafter, KR RIII) [Manuscript Division of the Russian Institute of the History of the Arts], *f.* 79, *op.* 1, *ed. khr.* 316 [*ed. khr.* = *edinitsa khraneniia* = storage unit], *ll.* 56, 56 *verso.*

27. In Kremlyov's comprehensive list of works only two articles are devoted entirely to Shostakovich, and a third is devoted partially to him. These are, respectively, "Violonchel'nye sonaty Yu. Kochurova i D. Shostakovicha" [The cello sonatas of Kochurov and Shostakovich], *Sovetskaia muzyka*, no. 11 (1935): 60–68; "Strunnyi kvartet Shostakovicha" [Shostakovich's string quartet], *Sovetskaia muzyka*, no. 11 (1939): 46–52; and "O Desiatoi simfonii D. Shostakovicha" [On Shostakovich's Tenth Symphony], *Sovetskaia muzyka*, no. 4 (1957): 74–84.

28. Yu. Kremlyov, "O 'Pateticheskoi oratorii' G. Sviridova" [About Sviridov's *Oratorio patètico*], in Kremlyov, *Izbrannye stat'i* (Leningrad: Muzyka, 1976), p. 176.

29. From an undated letter to Kremlyov; KR RIII, *f.* 79, *ed. khr.* 316, *l.* 48 *verso*, 49.

30. From a letter to Kremlyov dated 9 September 1965; KR RIII, *f.* 79, *ed. khr.* 316, *l.* 47.

31. See "Perepiska," pp. 574–75.

32. See "Perepiska," pp. 576–77.

33. See, for example, the exchange of opinions in the article-report "Znachitel'noe iavlenie sovetskoi muzyki (Diskussiia o Desiatoi simfonii D. Shostakovicha)" [A significant occurrence in Soviet music (A discussion about D. Shostakovich's Tenth Symphony], published in *Sovetskaia muzyka*, no. 6 (1954): 119–34.

34. Dolzhansky devoted one article to the Tenth Symphony, "Ob odnoi teme iz Desiatoi simfonii" [About one theme from the Tenth Symphony], which deals with the subordinate flute theme in the first movement. The article, in the context of an intertextual discussion, demonstrates the enormous power of the "intonational drama" and how it relates to the composer's greatest achievements and the innate significance of this particular symphony. See A. Dolzhansky, "Iz nabliudenii nad stilem Shostakovicha" [From observations on Shostakovich's style], in *Cherty stilia D. Shostakovicha* [D. Shostakovich's style traits], ed. L. G. Berger (Moscow: Sovetskii kompozitor, 1962), pp. 75–83.

35. See "Desiataia simfoniia D. Shostakovicha" ["Shostakovich's Tenth Symphony"], in Kremlyov, *Izbrannye stat'i i vystupleniia*, p. 66.

36. Leon Alexandrovich Khodzha-Einatov (1904–54), Soviet composer born in Tiflis, studied in Yerevan, Armenia, and was an Honored Artist of the Armenian Soviet Socialist Republic.

37. *Materialy vtoporo vsesoiuznogo s"ezda sovetskikh kompozitorov Composers* (Moscow, 1958).

38. *Sovetskaia kul'tura*, 2 April 1957, p. 4.

39. KR RIII, *f.* 79, *op.* 1, *ed. khr.* 51, *l.* 2.

40. The third movement only seems to him the most attractive "thanks to its characteristic of comparative clarity"; cf. Kremlyov, "Desiataia simfoniia," p. 74.

41. KR RIII, *f.* 79, *op.* 1, *ed. khr.* 51, *l.* 15.

42. Vasily Feodosievich Kukharsky (1918–95), a musicologist-functionary associated with the Party Central Committee and later with the USSR Ministry of Culture.

43. Sergei Sergeevich Skrebkov (1905–87), a music theorist, Honored Artist of the Russian Soviet Federated Socialist Republic, taught at the Moscow Conservatory, widely known as a published scholar and researcher.

44. KR RIII, *f.* 79, *op.* 1, *ed. khr.* 456, *l.* 22–22 *verso.*

45. Ibid.

46. In contrast to his article criticizing the Tenth Symphony, Kremlyov's critique of the Eleventh went unpublished both during his lifetime as well as in the posthumous collections of his articles. It has not turned up in Kremlyov's personal archive (KR RIII, *f.* 79), which is surprising since he usually duly filed away copies of his articles and speeches.

47. KR RIII, *f.* 79, *op.* 1, *ed. khr.* 278, *l.* 4.

48. Shostakovich mistakenly writes Kremlyov's given name as *Yury*, instead of *Yuli.*

49. KR RIII, *f.* 79, *op.* 1, *ed. khr.* 550, *l.* 1.

50. Ibid., *ed. khr.* 278, *l.* 1.

51. Ibid., *ed. khr.* 405, *l.* 1. Nonetheless, Kremlyov's article on Shostakovich's Eleventh Symphony was not published. See note 46 above.

52. Fragment of a letter from Kremlyov, dated 11 November 1954, to two like-minded young men, Anatoly Volkov from Kharkov—who had graduated from the Kharkov Conservatory that year, from the departments of Violin and Music History-Theory, and was now employed by the Voroshilovgrad Philharmonic—and Leonid Batkin—who was finishing up in the History Department of Kharkov State University (KR RIII, *f.* 79, *op.* 1, *ed. khr.* 148, *l.* 1). Kremlyov's letter to Volkov and Batkin is attached to the typescript of their article "*Za vysokuiu ideinost' iskusstva (ob odnoi strannoi simfonii)*" [In support of high ideological content in art (about one strange symphony)] (KR RIII, *f.* 79, *op.* 1, *ed. khr.* 325, *l.* 1).

53. Ibid., *ed. khr.* 51, *l.* 19.

54. Letter from the Kiev musicologist and composer Valerian Danilovich Dovzhenko, dated 10 October 1959 (ibid., *ed. khr.* 375, *l.* 40 *verso*).

55. In particular the book *Ocherki tvorchestva i estetiki Novoi venskoi shkoly* [Essays on the compositions and aesthetics of the New Viennese School] (Leningrad: Muzyka, 1970).

56. See "Perepiska," p. 584.

57. Bobrovsky, "Shostakovich v moei zhizni: lichnye zametki," p. 24.

Part Four

18

Ian Macdonald's *The New Shostakovich* (1993)

MALCOLM HAMRICK BROWN

According to the publisher's puff on the dust jacket, Ian MacDonald's *New Shostakovich* is the first important biographical work on the composer to take Solomon Volkov's *Testimony* into account (*Testimony: The Memoirs of Dmitri Shostakovich*, as related to and edited by Solomon Volkov [New York: Harper & Row, 1979]).[1] MacDonald argues that Shostakovich's music cannot be grasped as pure music in isolation from its political-cultural framework. He therefore makes it his task to attempt a reconstruction of that framework, into which he places the familiar facts of Shostakovich's life but reinterpreted through the new perspective introduced in Volkov's *Testimony.* The result is a book shot through by a fundamental and pervasive flaw—MacDonald's insufficiency of judgment, or of scholarly conscience, vis-à-vis Volkov.

At the very beginning of his book (pp. 3–4), MacDonald reviews the critical debate about the authenticity of *Testimony* that arose in the immediate aftermath of the book's publication in 1979, and he acknowledges that musicologist Laurel Fay proved conclusively that Volkov lied about how he put *Testimony* together ("Shostakovich versus Volkov: Whose *Testimony*?" *The Russian Review* 39, no. 4 [October 1980]: 84–93]). But this is evidently not good enough for MacDonald, who declares that the "truth and value" of *Testimony* can only be gauged by collating and cross-referencing its claims with "the Testimony of Shostakovich's contemporaries" and the evidence of "Shostakovich's music itself" (p. 14). Thereupon follows a re-viewing of Shostakovich's biography through the distorting lens of *Testimony*, accompanied by MacDonald's own idiosyncratic "analyses" of the music, which he treats virtually as hard evidence, equivalent in weight to the authentic memoirs and scholarly studies also invoked along the way to bolster his interpretations.

Some 240 pages later, following an ostensibly evenhanded process of collating and cross-referencing the known facts with the circumstantial evidence, MacDonald sums up his study with a rhetorical flourish that supplies the title for his book: "Is the new Shostakovich the real Shostakovich?" It is no surprise when he answers himself in the affirmative: "Of course" (p. 244). But still skittish about having finally laid his neck on the line—following his earlier feints and starts, stringing all the way back to the beginning of his book—MacDonald demurs yet again on the very next page, conceding once more that "the detective work of Laurel Fay . . . has established beyond doubt that the [Volkov] book is a dishonest presentation" (p. 245).

What is going on here? If MacDonald has known all along that Volkov lied about how *Testimony* was put together, why would he make his own book scarcely more than an elaborate gloss, a "musical" *vita parodia*, as it were, on Volkov's Shostakovich? The answer would seem to be that the Shostakovich of *Testimony* provides MacDonald with an altogether convenient biographical framework on which to hang his own bizarrely literalist interpretations of Shostakovich's music. As for Laurel Fay's compelling demonstration that *Testimony* was fraudulently represented to the public, MacDonald finds it convenient to embrace the conceit that although "Volkov may have to some extent misrepresented his material, . . . its essential truth . . . [is] altogether beyond doubt" (p. 264). "Essential truth"? What casuistry.

MacDonald thus warms over what he knows to be Volkov's tainted fare and dishes it up in a fricassee of bona fide memoirs (Ilya Ehrenburg, Nadezhda Mandelstam, Eugenia Ginzburg), reliable accounts (Roy Medvedev, Alexander Solzhenitsyn, Czesław Miłosz), and real scholarship (Adam Ulam, Robert Conquest, Gleb Struve), and then seasons his casserole with the likes of the following "interpretation" of the third movement of Shostakovich's Fourth Symphony (a piece MacDonald believes to be the "musical dramatization of Shostakovich's humiliation at the Composers Union conference"):

> A little strutting promenade for bassoons and giggling piccolo leads us into the hall where thrumming harps call the conference to order. A wan waltz (the composer?) enters and sits dejectedly while flute and piccolo trill the opening remarks in a mood of schoolboy hilarity soon dispelled by three table-thrumping chords across the full orchestra. (p. 115)

Such an "interpretation" amounts to nothing more than a caricature that impoverishes the very nature of art by suggesting that the creative stimulus for an artwork is identical with its artistic realization. Even might it be proven that a specific incident in Shostakovich's life prompted the composition of the musical episode under discussion (and MacDonald does not prove it in this case or in any other), how demeaning of the composer's creative aspirations to propose that he reconceptualizes a life experience in musical terms so precise that they retain the empirical specificity of the original incident. So much for the artistic universality of Shostakovich's music.

❦

Maxim Shostakovich, the composer's son, has complained about *Testimony* from the time he defected to the West in 1981: "These are not my father's memoirs. This is a book by Solomon Volkov. Mr. Volkov should reveal how the book was written."[2] Eight years later, in France, Maxim was still insisting on the same point in his response to the question, "Do Volkov's memoirs paint an accurate portrait of your father?"

> No! I have repeated this many times! That is a book about Shostakovich [i.e., not the "memoirs of Shostakovich"—M.H.B.]. Volkov describes the political situation around my father with much truthfulness, but when he cites Shostakovich's attitude toward other composers and conductors, such as Toscanini or Prokofiev, he reports the matter inaccurately. If one hopes to capture the personality of one of the great names in music, one must not content oneself with extracting a single phrase. . . . Here's an example relative to Tchaikovsky. I remember how Shostakovich would say to me at breakfast that he detested Tchaikovsky's developments, then assert something else at lunch and conclude at dinner that there was nothing more beautiful than the *Queen of Spades*.[3]

Given Maxim Shostakovich's long-standing and outspoken skepticism about Volkov, what a surprise to pick up MacDonald's book and find the jacket blurb, "I highly recommend Ian MacDonald's THE NEW SHOSTAKOVICH. It is one of the best books about Dmitri Shostakovich that I have read," credited to Maxim Shostakovich. How could Maxim have been duped into endorsing MacDonald's book, given the latter's flagrant dependence on Volkov? To suggest an answer, let us take a second look at what Volkov accomplishes in *Testimony*.

Solomon Volkov is a writer who has a way with words and a novelist's feel for time and place. *Testimony* accurately captures the texture and tone of musical life in the Soviet Union during the Shostakovich era, if we are to believe a number of former Soviet musicians, all of whom authenticate this aspect of Volkov's book from the perspective of personal experience—among them Mstislav Rostropovich, Rostislav Dubinsky, Lazar Gosman, and also Maxim Shostakovich, as illustrated by the quotation above.

This, then, is the crux of the matter. Those who experienced firsthand the stern political vicissitudes of Soviet musical life, especially during the grimmest decades of Stalinist intimidation, who felt muzzled for years, fearful of voicing even the mildest protest openly, desire desperately that the world should know and truly *believe* just how terrible things really were. Volkov, with his undeniable gifts as a raconteur, succeeded in conjuring up those terrible realities and giving them emotional force by association with Shostakovich, who has long been characterized as a tragic figure in Western writing on Soviet music. So what if Volkov *did* fudge about how he put *Testimony* together? So what if his Shostakovich stories might be twice- or thrice-told tales borrowed from a communal repository of anecdotes and yarns shared among the master's inner circle of colleagues, students, and friends, perhaps "improved," wittingly or unwittingly, in the process of retelling, then passed along to persons on the outside? Volkov may have misrepresented *Testimony*, but what clearly matters much more to many a former Soviet musician is that Volkov's book exposes before the world some "essential truth" (as MacDonald might put it) about Soviet musical life. This, for them, is justification enough to avert their eyes from the evidence of Volkov's dishonest presentation, even to wink at his patently fraudulent claim that Shostakovich dictated the whole of *Testimony*.

If "essential truth," then, is the issue, just how much of this precious commodity relevant to the composer himself can MacDonald extract from Volkov's cobbled together "memoirs of Shostakovich"? Henry (Genrikh) Orlov, a close associate of the composer's who emigrated from the Soviet Union to the United States in 1976, has this to say in his reflections written about Shostakovich from exile but published in the Soviet Union after the reforms of perestroika:

> He was reserved and introverted, even with his closest, long-time friends. There was no [Johann] Eckerman, no Robert Craft, not even a [Vasily] Yastrebstev

among them.[4] Everything preserved in the memories of the people who knew him and passed along by word of mouth amounts to chance—anecdotal episodes, fragmentary thoughts, opinions taken out of context—and fails to embody the *essence of his personality* [emphasis added]. Fused together, these fragments create a one-dimensional cartoon-like image, such as that produced by Solomon Volkov, the author of the memoirs published in the West, in spite of Volkov's attempt to portray Shostakovich talking and to stylize his specific and well-known mannerisms of speech.[5]

It is the "one-dimensional cartoon-like image" of Volkov's Shostakovich that also troubles the composer's son, Maxim, as he makes clear in his complaint, "If one hopes to capture the personality of one of the great names in music, one must not content oneself with extracting a single phrase." Yet Maxim has allowed his family name to be co-opted for commerce in behalf of MacDonald's book. Perhaps, however, this can be explained by a son's devotion to the memory of a beleaguered father. MacDonald's *New Shostakovich*, after all, does not linger over what was for Maxim a particularly distressing aspect of Shostakovich-via-Volkov—the composer's often ill-spirited and caustic evaluation of his fellow composers and other musicians. Instead of this (but still following Volkov's lead), MacDonald dwells more on Shostakovich as throttled hero who finds voice for his dissidence only through the eloquence of his music. This perspective must arouse great sympathy in Maxim, however much he may realize in his heart of hearts that such a characterization deserves numerous and complex qualifications—such qualifications as have begun to appear in Russian publications since the advent of perestroika and the collapse of the Soviet Union.

Responding recently to the protestation, "But even Shostakovich was secretary of the RSFSR Union of Composers," composer Edison Denisov offered one such qualification of the Shostakovich character:

They made him secretary of the Russian Union of Composers, because they needed his name for cover! And Shostakovich understood that very well. He took a fairly cynical position. He played along with the game. We were friends. I'm obliged to him for a lot. . . . But I believe there were things he did not have to do. He did not have to sign the letter against Solzhenitsyn or to sign those infamous articles in *Pravda*. He was in some ways a weak person. Sometimes he showed courage. Sometimes he went along with those gangsters. Of course, he was under enormous pressure. As a matter of fact, once—it was in Sverdlovsk—he got sick and asked me to stay with him. All night long he talked about himself, sounding the refrain, "I've been a coward all my life."[6]

Numerous questions remain unanswered about why Shostakovich decided to join the Communist Party only in 1960. This was the period of the so-called Thaw in Soviet life, following Khrushchev's revelations of the crimes of Stalin's cult of personality at the Twentieth Party Congress in 1956. Few former Soviet musicians who lived through that period believe that Shostakovich, in his position as leading Soviet composer, was compelled to apply for Party membership. Grigory Frid, himself a well-established Party member in 1960 but today an outspoken critic of the past and composer of what would surely not have been counted a Party-line opera, *The Diary of Anne Frank* [*Dnevnik Anny Frank*], recalls the occasion of Shostakovich's acceptance into the Party:

> I remember his speech, which I listened to with a feeling of profound pain. He the greatest of composers, nervously, stumbling over his words, begged the Party to have faith in him and promised to write a new symphony, which would be his response to our faith in him.[7]

Another recent memoirist makes this telling observation:

> After Shostakovich joined the Party he turned into an obedient instrument of the Party apparatus, fulfilling all the demands of its bureaucrats. He would propose, during elections at the Union of Composers, to reject supplemental lists of candidates, he would sign any sort of document for the newspapers. It is not easy to understand this. . . . Shostakovich could not fail to have comprehended the unworthiness of his conduct.[8]

As more of Shostakovich's contemporaries speak out and as reliable documentary information becomes available, the "real" Shostakovich is likely to emerge as both a sometime closet dissident and a sometime collaborator. His "deeper intentions" (MacDonald's phrase) in such works as, for example, the Seventh Symphony—if a convincing methodology can be devised for illuminating them!—are likely to be no less ambiguous and contradictory than the following two passages MacDonald quotes from Volkov's Shostakovich:

> The Seventh Symphony had been planned before the war and consequently it simply cannot be seen as a reaction to Hitler's attack.[9]

> I couldn't not write it [the Seventh Symphony]. War was all around. I had to be with the people, I wanted to create the image of our country at war, capture it in music.[10]

MacDonald hastens to explain the contradiction by pointing out that the second of the two statements comes from one of the plagiarized sections of *Testimony.* In MacDonald's view, the plagiarized passage has less validity, presumably since it was cleared for publication by the Soviet authorities, whereas the phrase attributed to Shostakovich by Volkov, whose reportage MacDonald has admitted to being fraudulent, should nonetheless be accepted as closer to the "essential truth." Might I offer the possibility that Shostakovich could well have made *both* statements—if, indeed, he made either of them—and both in complete sincerity?

MacDonald seems not to know that creative artists like common folk routinely wear masks appropriate to the occasion, disguising parts of a "whole" personality, not always with the intention to deceive so much as to facilitate. However much Shostakovich may have despised the regime under which he was fated to fulfill the whole of his productive life and to whatever extent hatred of that regime may have fueled the fires of inspiration, he was surely much more than a simpleton, a Holy Fool, a Russian *yurodivy* lamenting the "essential truth" about that regime in his music. Such a characterization, which Volkov introduced and MacDonald embraced, smacks more of hagiography than responsible biography. But then, a responsible scholar eschews on principle data known to be skewed, no matter how attractive it may appear in support of one or another pet hypothesis. Ian MacDonald, however, is a music journalist, and his *New Shostakovich* will undoubtedly provide belated program annotators and hurried writers of record liner notes with grist to spare in turning out "creative" explications of Shostakovich's music for decades to come.

Notes

1. Ian MacDonald, *The New Shostakovich* (Boston: Northeastern University Press, 1990). Brown's essay-review was originally published in *Notes* 49, no. 3 (March 1993): 956–61. This review article was winner of the Music Library Association's Eva Judd O'Meara Award for the best review published in *Notes* during 1993.

2. Quoted from an interview of 23 April 1981 for "Radio Liberty," Washington, D.C.; my translation.

3. An interview by Patrick Szersnovicz and Grégory Thomas in *Le monde de la musique*, no. 118 (January 1989), suppl.: xv.

4. Eckerman, Craft, and Yastrebstev were, respectively, the interlocutors of Goethe, Stravinsky, and Rimsky-Korsakov.

5. Genrikh Orlov, "Dmitriĭ Shostakovich: Zveno v tsepi" (Dmitri Shostakovich: A link in the chain), *Sovetskaia kul'tura*, 4 May 1989, p. 5.

6. Denisov quoted by Evgeny Bilkis, *Nezavisimaia gazeta*, 28 March 1992, p. 7.

7. Grigory Frid, "Vozrozhdenia zavisit ot nas" [The rebirth depends on us), *Sovetskaia muzyka*, no. 8 (August 1989): 9.

8. Victor Bobrovsky, "Shostakovich v moei zhizni; Lichnye zametki" [Shostakovich in my life: Personal observations], *Sovetskaia muzyka*, no. 9 (September 1991): 28.

9. Volkov, *Testimony*, p. 155; quoted in MacDonald, *The New Shostakovich*, p. 155 [*sic*].

10. Ibid., p. 154; quoted in MacDonald, *The New Shostakovich*, p. 155.

19

Elizabeth Wilson's *Shostakovich: A Life Remembered* (1996)

MALCOLM HAMRICK BROWN

This is a remarkable book, filled with remarkable revelations, unforgettable stories, and poignant images. Just glance through the episodes previewed below for a sampling of the densely textured memories that Elizabeth Wilson has woven into her extraordinary documentary biography.[1]

Recounting his obligatory yet shameful public confession of 1948, Shostakovich exclaims, "Yes, I humiliated myself, I read out what was taken to be 'my own' speech. I read like the most paltry wretch, a parasite, a puppet, a cut-out paper doll on a string!!" He shrieks out the last phrase, repeating it like a frenzied maniac (pp. 294–95).

Friends of the composer are excitedly sharing impressions of the Picasso exhibition in Moscow, when Shostakovich suddenly barks, "Don't speak to me of him, he's a bastard." Silence. "Yes, Picasso, that bastard, hails Soviet power and our communist system at a time when his followers here are persecuted, hounded, and not allowed to work." Someone objects, "But your followers are also hounded and persecuted." Abashed, he responds, "Well, yes, I too am a bastard, coward and so on, but I'm living in a prison, and . . . frightened for my children and for myself. But he's living in freedom, he doesn't have to tell lies. . . . And Picasso's revolting dove of peace! How I hate it! I despise the slavery of ideas as much as I despise physical slavery" (pp. 271–72).

Shostakovich addresses the audience at the "closed" première in 1969 of his Fourteenth Symphony—an homage to Musorgsky's *Songs and Dances of Death* [*Pesni i pliaski smerti*]. "Death is terrifying, there is nothing beyond it. I don't believe in life beyond the grave," he declares, and ends his remarks with the suggestion that one should hope only to die with a clear conscience, "so that one need not be ashamed of oneself." The symphony begins, and during an intensely quiet passage midway through, Pavel Apostolov, a notorious official persecutor of Shostakovich in 1948, whose black deeds and vulnerable conscience are well known to many in the audience, suffers a heart attack and dies (p. 418).

In 1971 the celebrated English composer Benjamin Britten hears Shostakovich's Thirteenth String Quartet in a private audition arranged by the composer. It would be their last personal meeting. Britten, shaken by the somber, requiem-like music of the quartet, impulsively grabs Shostakovich's hands and kisses them (p. 439).

Aged beyond his years by 1973, compromised by life's vicissitudes, Shostakovich signs a letter in *Pravda* denouncing Andrei Sakharov. Soviet intellectuals feel betrayed. Shortly thereafter, Shostakovich dutifully puts in an appearance at the audition of a new work by avant-garde Soviet composer Edison Denisov. He takes a seat at the very end of a row in the middle of the hall. All and sundry have to pass by him to get to their seats. When Yuri Lyubimov, the eminent director and founder of Moscow's controversial Taganka Theater, starts by, Shostakovich stands up to greet him. It is difficult for Shostakovich to rise (by that period he could hardly walk and then only with the aid of a stick). Struggling to his feet he turns to Lyubimov with hand outstretched. But Lyubimov looks him in the eye and demonstratively moves on by, without acknowledging the composer. Shostakovich goes white. Asked later how he could do such a thing, Lyubimov answers, "After Shostakovich signed that letter against Sakharov and Solzhenitsyn I can't shake his hand" (pp. 432–33. But see Irina Shostakovich, selection 9, this volume, pp. 132–33).

Wilson was motivated to take on this project by the conviction that "now is the time, while some key witnesses are still alive, to try and tap living memory" (p. xi). She set about to interview everyone whom she could identify who might have had some significant association with Shostakovich, exempting only the composer's widow, and his son and daughter, believing "that it would be ridiculous to ask any of them for a short memoir when each could write a book on the subject" (p. xiii). About thirty or so original memoirs were eventually collected, on tape or in written form. Add to this, interviews with individuals who preferred not to speak on record but who nevertheless provided "deep insight into the background and context of [the] subject" (p. xii). Finally, Wilson culled a mass of sources already published—reminiscences, letters, documents—finding some seventy-five worthy secondary references to supplement her original material. She then arranged the memoir and documents to produce a sequential biography, knitting together the first-person accounts with essential historical and social commentary, along with appropriate introductions to the speakers whose memoirs constitute the bulk of the text.

The work is not without faults, but these recede into insignificance when viewed in the perspective of Wilson's estimable accomplishment. I therefore demur at discussing defect, preferring instead to focus attention on the book's overriding importance as a document. Simply put, it is indispensable for anyone interested in Shostakovich, or in Soviet culture and society generally.

The complicated, often contradictory, yet full-blooded personality who emerges out of the cumulative impressions gained from reading these memoirs is a far cry from the one-dimensional, "cut-out paper doll" encountered in such a work as Solomon Volkov's much-discussed *Testimony*, the purported "memoirs of Dmitri Shostakovich" (New York: Harper & Row, 1979), a book that any serious scholar ought by now to know is indelibly tainted with still unanswered questions about how it was put together. Wilson's assembled memoirs not only resurrect a thoroughly human and believable Shostakovich, they also situate him in a network of intricately woven and often deeply moving personal histories.

Comparatively little is said about the composer's music output, certainly little of technical substance, but these memoirs constitute a *sokrovishche*—a treasure trove—of private perspectives on the Aesopian "meaning" of Shostakovich's music for his Soviet contemporaries. After reading again and again about how Shostakovich's music spoke solace to Soviet listeners, scholars and performing musicians alike will surely find themselves confronting the most vexing questions posed by contemporary critical interpretation and musical exegetics.

I have studied Soviet music for some forty years. No other book exposes so much of the personal tissue of Soviet musical life as this one. It is truly remarkable.

Note

1. Elizabeth Wilson, *Shostakovich: A Life Remembered* (Princeton, N.J.: Princeton University Press, 1994). The review was published in *Slavic and East European Journal* 40, no. 1 (spring 1996): 192–93. The version printed here has been minimally revised.

20

A Response to Papers by Allan Ho and Dmitri Feofanov (1998)

DAVID FANNING

At the annual meeting of the American Musicological Society in 1998, Allan Ho and Dmitri Feofanov read papers respectively titled, "The *Testimony* Affair: Complacency, Cover-Up, or Incompetence" and "Shostakovich the Anti-Communist: Confirming *Testimony.*" The papers were planned to advertise Ho and Feofanov's recently published book, *Shostakovich Reconsidered,* and to publicize the book's thesis: "For whatever reason—complacency, a desire to cover up material to protect personal egos and professional reputations, or even incompetence—the leading American scholars of Shostakovich's life and music have failed to report evidence that corroborates *Testimony* and vindicates Volkov."[a]

British musicologist David Fanning was invited to present his "Comments at the Panel, 31 October 1998," as a formal response to the papers by Ho and Feofanov. Fanning's "Comments" are reproduced below, immediately following his "Author's Introduction to the Reader."

Author's Introduction to the Reader

What Shostakovich said and wrote, what he meant by what he said and wrote, and what he meant by the music he composed are all fascinating and important issues. But there are no easy ways to address them. Or, rather, there *are* easy ways, but these mostly lead the unwary straight into traps.

The most tempting approach is to equate Shostakovich's supposed words with his supposed sociopolitical attitudes, and then to equate both with the supposed meaning of his music. This gratifies those who come to his music with a ready-made idea of what they would like it to "say," also those who are still in rebellion from the modernist-autonomist view of music so widespread in professional musical circles in the 1950s, 1960s, and 1970s, and those, as well, who seek to counter Shostakovich's disparagement at the hands of the rump avant-garde. It is understandable, too, that this approach should appeal to the nonspecialist, for whom appreciation of music has to be expressed in nonmusical terms. It can even be a useful motivational tool for conductors or teachers confronted with jaded musicians or unimaginative pupils.

As a basis for serious commentary, however, it is wholly inadequate. It is like a tripod, each of whose legs—words, attitudes, and music—is precarious, and whose braces are illusory. Neither Shostakovich's words nor his attitudes nor his music is explicit, still less the relationship between them.

What is the alternative, then, for anyone who finds the music profoundly stirring and who recoils from the sterility of the autonomist approach?

For a composer such as Shostakovich, who grew up in and stayed broadly faithful to the humanist artistic tradition, assumptions about music were inevitably conditioned by German early-romantic aesthetics, even if only through contact with the "mainstream" repertoire that most powerfully embodies them. Expressed most famously by Hegel and Schopenhauer, and given a new spin in the early years of the Soviet Union in the writings of the most influential of Soviet musicologist-critics, Boris Asafyev, this view proposed, essentially, that music, particularly symphonic music, was a language of the soul. To engage seriously with music, in whatever capacity, was therefore to engage in a wordless dialogue with one's soul. It follows that if musical experience were to be translated into words at all, one would do better to draw on concepts from philosophy and psychology rather than on analogies with the world of actions and events. Music in this tradition articulates aspects of the human condition, particularizing them through the infinite variety of its own elements and their interrelationships. Furthermore, whatever goes into any musical work by way of life experiences and conscious intentions is far from the same as what comes out, since the process of musicalization transmutes everything into another communicative medium. If this were not so, we would not encounter so much feeble music by composers with unimpeachable intentions or so much inspiring music by those whose intentions and ideological attitudes we might deplore. This does not stop us from exploring where pieces of music come from (which may even guard against our barking up wrong trees), so long as we realize that this is all we are doing.

It is true, of course, that Marxist, and later Socialist-Realist, critiques muddied the waters considerably, at least concerning the Soviet cultural milieu. And it is a matter for debate to what extent Shostakovich's relationship to the Germanic neo-idealist view of music was modified by such critiques, or by his temperamental predisposition, his life experiences, and his local cultural and political environment. The mix quite obviously comes out differently from work to work. But, to my mind, the modifications, though far-reaching, hardly ever displace the aesthetic foundation. His major works, by and large, transcend their circumstances, which they compel to serve higher ends. It is this contention—more than a wish to counterbalance literalist interpretations, more even than a wish to defend Shostakovich's reputation as a great craftsman—that impels me toward musical analysis. For in highlighting musical significances—such as idiosyncrasies of structure and harmony, surface thematic transformations, generic and intertextual reference—I feel I get as close as I can to understanding Shostakovich's dialogue with the soul, and to reading his comments on the human condition.[1]

It follows that I cannot regard the *Testimony* debate as an issue of paramount importance for understanding Shostakovich's music.

Yet if one chooses, or if one is asked, to embed a musical (i.e., humanistic) commentary on Shostakovich in sociopolitical contexts, and to relate it to ongoing controversies, the debate can hardly be avoided. In this respect I still tend to view the "authenticity" side of *Testimony* as a sideshow. If, as seems to me overwhelmingly probable, Solomon Volkov was less than candid about the origins of the book, that is no reason not to treat its contents as anything less than a fascinating document from the mid-Brezhnev era (provided, of course, that it is referred to as Volkov's reportage rather than as the composer's words). At the very least it offers an insight into Shostakovich's appeal to a significant constituency of the Soviet intelligentsia, which he and Volkov in some unknown proportion were jointly addressing. Unfortunately many readers have become uncritically wedded to the image of the composer presented in

Testimony and various post-glasnost sources, ignoring the contradictions and treating what may have been no more than off-the-cuff remarks as lifelong articles of faith.

In this connection Volkov himself is less fundamentalist than some of his spokespersons, as the statement I quote toward the end of my "Comments at the Panel" indicates:

> What Shostakovich felt and thought at the time of the première of the Fifth Symphony I don't know, you don't know, he didn't know at the time he dictated to me *Testimony*. What is in *Testimony* is an expression of Shostakovich's views and opinions at that time. . . . It summarized his views toward the end of his life and it should be perceived as such.[2]

What Volkov nearly says here is something that has emerged more and more clearly in recent years, namely, that Shostakovich habitually tailored his words to the understanding of whomever he was addressing. This is more or less obvious so far as his official pronouncements are concerned, and the same could be said of many Soviet citizens in the public eye. But it also holds true for his conversations with individuals, of whatever political persuasion, and this trait was evidently sufficiently remarkable for a number of his acquaintances to draw attention to it. Sviatoslav Richter's story shows how ingrained the habit was. Richter's teacher, Heinrich Neuhaus, was sitting next to Shostakovich at a bad performance of a symphony by an unidentified composer:

> Neuhaus leaned over to whisper in Shostakovich's ear: "Dmitri Dmitrievich, this is awful." Whereupon Shostakovich turned to Neuhaus: "You're right, Heinrich Gustavovich! It's splendid! Quite remarkable!" Realizing that he'd been misunderstood, Neuhaus repeated his earlier remark: "Yes," muttered Shostakovich, "it's awful, quite awful."
>
> That was Shostakovich to the life.[3]

This was evidently a personal character trait, as much as it was a defense mechanism to cope with life in a society founded on mendacity. Of course, this does not mean that everything Shostakovich said or wrote has to be regarded as insincere. But it does suggest that whatever the source, and however well authenticated, nothing he said or wrote can be assumed to represent his genuine thoughts.

All this was my starting point for the paper that follows. First of all, in presenting "Testimony" (hot off the press at the time I was speaking) from an East German admirer of Shostakovich, I sought to highlight the inadvisability of taking *anything* Shostakovich said, or is alleged to have said, at face value. Predictably enough, the speakers whom I was addressing dismissed the "evidence" on the grounds that the interlocutor was "obviously" an informer for the Stasi (but, according to the German editor of the volume in which his reminiscences appear, he was not). My point, however, was that we should be just as cautious about the content of all statements attributed to Shostakovich, including—especially including—those we would personally like to believe. This applies no matter what we make of the authenticity or otherwise of *Testimony.* And the point that even a wholly candid and authenticated "Testimony" might have only limited relevance to the music as experienced was one I hardly had time to touch on in a presentation designed to last fifteen minutes.

Comments at the Panel, 31 October 1998[b]

I'd like to start by quoting from a private conversation that [reportedly] took place on 22 March 1975 between Shostakovich and an East German admirer of his music on a visit to Moscow. The subject under discussion is unjust criticism, especially as experienced by Shostakovich at the time of the 1948 Zhdanov crackdown. He mentions jealous colleagues who should be ashamed of what they said, and he continues to the effect that he himself feels no such shame. [The passage quoted below was available to those in attendance as Fanning's Extract 1.]

> I said then what I have always thought and what I still think today: I am a Soviet artist and was brought up in a socialist country. I always wanted and still want today to find the way to the heart of the People. . . . At that time I spoke up several times, spoke up several times. I said unequivocally that it was painful for me to hear, to hear the Central Committee's judgments on my music! But I also said that I knew the Party was right, that the Party wanted the best for me, and that I had to seek out and find definite ways that would lead, would lead me to a socialist, realist, popular mode of creation—do you understand? I also said then that this would not be easy for me, would not be easy for me. But I promised the Party to find, to find the new path. And I did it! I have always tried honestly, tried honestly to write good music, music for my people, for men and women, for men and women. . . . Not Socialism, and certainly not my Party, the great Party of Lenin, is guilty! No, no! Those were distortions of the Party line and distortions of the politics of Socialism.[4]

All this but two years after the rather different views supposedly dictated to Solomon Volkov [and printed in *Testimony*].

As one of Shostakovich's last reported conversations, off the record and so far as he was aware not for publication, this surely qualifies as evidence of the kind Professor Ho invites us to consider. In considering it we take into account the circumstances of the conversation and the credentials of the interlocutor. This was a one-to-one, ninety- to ninety-five-minute meeting in Shostakovich's apartment with one Hans Jung, an official in the "Society for German-Soviet Friendship," which was a mass organization in the German Democratic Republic with about eight million members. The meeting was instigated by Shostakovich to thank Jung for a gift and to find out about reactions to his music in East Germany.

So to what extent, if any, was he speaking the truth? Bear in mind that I've just read out, using my own stresses and inflections, my translation of a German translation of a conversation remembered, transcribed, and edited for publication—already some scope for inauthenticity there. And if Shostakovich's true thoughts at the time were of the dissident kind, he would hardly have been likely to share them with an East German visiting him in a semi-official capacity.[5] Right. So is everything I've quoted just so much hot air? Did he just press the same buttons he'd pressed so often before in his official speeches? Could be, but then couldn't he have made his points just as effectively without going out of his way to endorse the Communist Party, and without saying earlier in the conversation, quite unprompted, "I am a Communist today"?[6]

And so the argument goes back and forth. Ultimately this remains an unwitnessed, un-tape-recorded conversation, and it's up to us what we make of it. But I think it illustrates the kind of difficulty involved with oral history, particularly when it emanates from a climate of fear and disinformation as in the former Soviet Union, where there's no reason to think that written documents or tapes are necessarily any more reliable than hearsay. If you don't like the content of a particular document, you can usually find ways of discrediting it. On the other hand, you can just as easily persuade yourself that views you concur with come from trustworthy sources. What's well nigh impossible is producing hard evidence with which to challenge someone with convictions opposite to your own. And disentangling Shostakovich's "genuine" thoughts from his verbal evasions and cover-ups will always be, surely, a conjectural matter. Did he or did he not try to write Music for the People; did he or did he not exonerate the Party from the victimization he had to endure? The problem lies not with finding the right answers but with the simple-mindedness of the questions, their black-and-white, either-or mentality. And if you prefer to keep an open mind or answer in shades of gray, you risk being accused of "intellectual helplessness"[7] by commentators who take the line "if you're not for us you're against us."

Nor can we just declare a pox on it and pretend that Shostakovich's music somehow "says it all," or that whatever the verbal nonsense he put his signature to he "never lied in his music," to use the language of *Testimony.* The music manifestly doesn't say it all, if by that we include revealing a sociopolitical stance. Even *The Antiformalist Peepshow* [*Antiformalisticheskii rayok*], his most obviously satirical work, doesn't actually tell me that he wasn't a Communist. What it does do is to confirm his contempt for the dogmatic administrators of Soviet artistic policy in the postwar era. And that's not quite the same thing, is it?

I wince when I'm told that "the meaning of Shostakovich's music is crystal clear" (that is from Professor Ho and Mr. Feofanov's book, by the way).[8] Could we just play an extract and ask everyone here for a précis of its meaning? Then maybe we'd discover how crystal clear it is. Or is the implication even more sinister; that only politically competent listeners can grasp the meaning? If so, who is going to set the standard? Maybe Mr. Feofanov is simply proposing that the satirical intent of particular pieces of music seems to be clear. Agreed. But even that doesn't compel us all, politically competent or not, to perceive those pieces in the same way, still less to extrapolate from them the same conclusion about the composer's politics.[9]

I am happy to admire bold statements, but bald ones are another matter, and I find quite a few of those in Professor Ho's and Mr. Feofanov's papers. Not that there aren't things about them and the book on which they're based that I admire. To have researched and presented detailed counterarguments to the various objections to *Testimony* requires tenacity and painstaking work; and, as Professor Ho has indicated, I myself have been sufficiently impressed by some of their arguments to want to put references to Volkov's "dishonesty" on ice.[10]

But I still have a number of worries—some possibly minor, some more fundamental. I do find it hard to reconcile Professor Ho's concluding appeal to open-mindedness with some of his other statements. I'm bothered by his claim that "we discovered . . . that the Shostakovich memoirs are, indeed, authentic and accurate." Would it not be more prudent to say "formed the conclusion" rather than "discovered"? I also find the reference to "Western opinion" disturbing. Western opinion on *Testimony* has never been monolithic; and, insofar as there has been a majority view, I'd have thought it was largely pro; certainly I've found the objections Laurel Fay raised in 1980 to be virtually unknown outside academic circles.[11] Still, on the subject of bald statements, I fail to see how Galina Drubachevskaya's reading of chapters of manuscript reviewed by Shostakovich "vindicates" Volkov, unless she actually witnessed the composer reviewing them.[12] Was that the case? If not, we're still only being told that *Testimony* is authentic because Solomon Volkov says it is.

Tempted though I am to go into detail, I think that it would be more appropriate for Malcolm Brown, Richard Taruskin, and Laurel Fay to respond themselves, in person or in print, to the criticisms leveled at them. The process has already begun, as you can read in the Shostakovich Society Journal *DSCH* (summer 1998).[13] And, personally, I hope that they will continue to react, because if they don't, I fear they may fall under a similar suspicion as Volkov has for the last nineteen years for not answering his critics. Simply for my own information, though, may I ask Mr. Feofanov which *Pravda* editorials Laurel Fay "repeats," and where?[14] And on the possibly contradictory statements in *Testimony* regarding the origins of the "Leningrad" Symphony, I would suggest that Professor Ho has not addressed the main point.[15] Of course, "planning" and "writing" are two different matters, just as "composing" and "writing" apparently were for Rachmaninoff.[16] But the real contradiction is surely elsewhere, somewhere between the statements "I wanted to create the image of our country at war" and "it simply cannot be seen as a reaction to Hitler's attack." Of course, it's fine to speculate that the symphony is at some level "about" both tyrannies, not one or the other; that would be my hunch, too. But that is not what the statements under discussion say.

Now I want to air a more substantial issue not raised in Professor Ho's paper, because, for me, it is crucial to the debate. Extract 2 on my handout is an example of one of the previously published passages that appears almost verbatim in *Testimony*. [Extract 2 reproduced in parallel texts the first page of chapter 6 of *Testimony* (p. 178) and the virtually identical text from Shostakovich's memoirs of Chekhov, "Samyi blizkii" (One of my favorites), first published in 1960.][17]

There are eight such pages in the book, and seven of them appear at chapter beginnings, on the very pages that Shostakovich signed as having read. This issue is addressed in *Shostakovich Reconsidered*, but I do not find the arguments there as persuasive as on other matters of detail. We are asked not only to believe that Shostakovich might have repeated to Volkov nearly verbatim what he said or wrote in some instances decades before, and in addition that Volkov managed to reconstruct such passages with uncanny accuracy from his shorthand notes, but also that these very passages, by a truly spooky coincidence, proved ideally suited to kick off seven out of the eight chapters, as though Shostakovich had somehow "mapped out his memoirs in his mind" in advance of the conversations.[18] Now we all have to tread a line between cynicism and gullibility here, but I personally find all that hard to swallow: at least as hard as the notion that Volkov could have written nine-tenths of the book in his own words (which I also do not swallow, by the way). As I have said in my review of *Shostakovich Reconsidered*, one way for Volkov to lay this to rest would surely be to show the world his shorthand notes from which he says he constructed *Testimony* (for I cannot believe he would have destroyed such a priceless source), have the paper and ink scientifically dated, reveal the shorthand system used, and point out the passages in question and let us see that they run continuous with the rest of the conversations. Ideally someone could then make a verbatim transcript to verify the rest of the text. That would surely be a major step forward.[19]

By the way, I would not mind personally if it did transpire that Volkov was responsible for adding those passages, with or without the composer's agreement. I would not even mind if Volkov had a hand in a good deal more of the book. But if that were the case, I just wish he would be frank about it.

Turning to Mr. Feofanov's paper, I find the opening remarks disconcerting. He writes: "Historians have finally realized that there is not much difference between Communism and Nazism." Well, in terms of the murderous brutality of their respective regimes, maybe so, and I would certainly concur that some historians took far longer to recognize that fact about Stalin's Russia than they should have. But I am worried about equating practice with principles. International Socialism and National Socialism are significantly different as ideologies, are they not?[20]

Mr. Feofanov then asks point-blank whether Shostakovich was or was not a Communist. But do we have to jump only one way or the other? Much as I might want to believe it, I wonder if it is really true to say that in Elizabeth Wilson's book "Shostakovich's friends describe his anticommunism in explicit terms." At the moment I can think of only one, not very explicit instance,[21] whereas the instances of Shostakovich's opposition to the barbarisms of the regime and the crassness of the Party are, of course, numerous. But if I believe that he was revolted by many manifestations of Stalinism and post-Stalinism, certainly from the mid-1930s and maybe from some time before that, do I have to equate that with anticommunism? What evidence is there against the possibility that Shostakovich remained wedded to at least some communist ideals, to the point where he could regard many of the things that happened in its name as indeed "distortions" rather than expressions of it? And how would that in any way diminish his stature as a human being or as a composer?

Surely it should go without saying that adherence to political or religious creeds does not have to be an all-or-nothing affair. It is possible to be broadly for the ethical principles but violently against the application, for example. And something else bothers me: if Shostakovich never made his attitude to the tenets of communism crystal clear, at least not in any trustworthy document I know of, are we happy for any biographer to do so for him, even with reference to his family, friends, and colleagues? Would anyone in this hall care for his or her views to be summed up in this way, posthumously?

I have to say that none of Mr. Feofanov's supposed evidence of anticommunism strikes me as anything of the sort. Shostakovich may have disliked the deification of Lenin. He may have despised some of the crudely agit-prop texts and storylines to which he composed music. He may even have "loathed the Soviet system"—at some points in his life more than others, I would prefer to add. But does that prove he was anticommunist? If you or I are scornful of aspects of political life in our democracies, does that make us antidemocratic? Nor do I believe it helps matters to imply that Shostakovich's views were unchanging—that what he said in 1973 was what he thought in 1937, for instance. Do not take my word for it:

> What Shostakovich felt and thought at the time of the première of the Fifth Symphony I don't know, you don't know, he didn't know at the time he dictated to me *Testimony*. What is in *Testimony* is an expression of Shostakovich's views and opinions at that time. . . . It summarized his views toward the end of his life and it should be perceived as such.[22]

You'll have gathered that the wise words here are those of Solomon Volkov, recorded for the BBC in July of this year [1998].

I said that I would not try to defend writers under attack in these papers. But one point must not be allowed to pass. Mr. Feofanov quotes Richard Taruskin as referring to Shostakovich as "perhaps Soviet Russia's most loyal musical son." The phrase comes from an article about *Ledi Makbet Mtsenskogo uezda* [Lady Macbeth of the Mtsensk District], just after quotation from and comment on the infamous 1936 *Pravda* editorial

"Muddle [better: A Mess] instead of Music." Professor Taruskin's full sentence is as follows: "Thus was Dmitri Shostakovich, perhaps Soviet Russia's most loyal musical son, and certainly her most talented one, made a sacrificial lamb, precisely for his pre-eminence among Soviet artists of his generation." Now I have already begged to differ with Professor Taruskin's views on Shostakovich's opera as expressed in this particular article,[23] nor do I approve his choice of words at this point, not least because the phrase in question echoes *Pravda*'s official obituary notice. But, from the context in which it appears, it is clear to me that this is no bald statement about Shostakovich's entire career. So to suggest that by adding the words *until then* Professor Taruskin was doing anything more than clarifying his point seems to me bizarre, and I am alarmed to see a phrase held up for ridicule when it has been removed from context and thereby had its meaning radically altered.

I am concerned about how this whole debate strikes scholars in related disciplines. I do not just mean the personalized nature of the attacks. I mean the spectacle of a vulgarized concept of musical meaning. Now maybe some of us feel we have been through our years of deconstructionist purgatory, and we are ready to trade in a bit of methodological purity for the sake of making commentaries with some sort of human relevance. Hooray for that. And let us make due allowance for Soviet music not playing the game entirely by Western rules, for occasionally taking on an expanded social role because of surrounding constraints on free speech. But surely the battle for integrating cultural context into Shostakovich commentary has long since been won. Please do not tell me I now have to go and renew my long-lapsed subscription to the intentional fallacy as well. And please do not say Shostakovich is only going to win his rightful place in the history books because he has become a bone of political contention. There is Shostakovich the composer to consider, too, though sadly that is not what this evening's forum is concerned with.

In any case, when we come back to the music, dangerously armed with a little sociopolitical learning, let us not confuse our legitimately passionate commentaries with The Whole Truth, and let us not be tempted into thinking we can somehow correct the outrageous treatment meted out to Shostakovich in his lifetime by creating a posthumous counter-mythology. Let us rather equate our commentaries with performances. These may justifiably be full of conviction and intensity; they may be fashioned partly by dissatisfaction with other performances; and their relative merits can be openly debated. These same performances can never be definitive and are always evolving, they should be aware of having, and proud to have, as much of ourselves and our times in them as of the composer and his times, and they should never seek to lay down the law to other performers.

Three more wishes in conclusion, if I may. Let us all listen respectfully to one another's points of view and see whether we can learn from them. Let us assume that we are all contributing to this debate out of genuine commitment to Shostakovich's music and a belief in its continuing importance. And, above all, let us strive to be worthy of that listening, and that assumption.

Thank you, Professor Shreffler, for the invitation to address this session.

Notes

1. This is the attitude that underpins my book-length studies, *The Breath of the Symphonist: Shostakovich's Tenth* (London: Royal Musical Association, 1988), and *Dmitri Shostakovich: String Quartet No. 8* (Aldershot: Ashgate, 2003).

2. Solomon Volkov, spoken contribution to the documentary feature "Brave Words, Brave Music," BBC Radio 3, broadcast 16 August 1998.

3. Sviatoslav Richter with Bruno Monsaingeon, *Sviatoslav Richter: Notebooks and Conversations* (Princeton, N.J.: Princeton University Press, 2001), p. 126.

4. Hans Jung, "Ausführlicher Bericht über meinen Besuch bei D.S. am 22. März 1975," in Hilmar Schmalenberg, ed., *Schostakowitsch in Deutschland* (Berlin: E. Kuhn, 1998), p. 231, my translation. The omitted passages are Jung's comments on pauses in Shostakovich's statement. The German text is as follows: "Ich habe damals das gesagt, was ich immer gedacht habe und auch heute denke: ich bin ein sowjetischer Künstler und bin in einem sozialistischen Lande erzogen worden. Ich wollte immer und will es auch heute noch, den Weg zum Herzen des Volkes finden. . . . Ich habe damals mehrmals das Wort ergriffen, mehrmals das Wort ergriffen. Ich habe unmißverständlich gesagt, daß es mir sehr schwerfiel, die Urteile über meine Musik und noch mehr die Verurteilung seitens des Zentralkomitees zu hören, zu hören! Aber ich habe auch gesagt, daß ich weiß, daß die Partei recht hat, daß die Partei mein Bestes wünscht, und daß ich konkrete Wege suchen und finden muß, die mich zu einem sozialistischen, realistischen, volkstümlichen Schaffen führen werden, führen werden—verstehen Sie? Ich habe damals auch gesagt, daß dieser [*sic*] für mich nicht leicht sein wird, nicht leicht sein wird. Aber ich habe der Partei versprochen, den neuen Weg zu suchen, zu suchen. Das habe ich gemacht! Ich habe immer ehrlich versucht, ehrlich versucht, eine gute Musik, eine Musik für mein Volk, für die Menschen, für die Menschen zu schreiben. . . . Nicht der Sozialismus und schon gar nicht meine Partei, die Partei des Großen Lenin, trägt die Schuld! Das waren Entstellungen der Parteilinie und Entstellungen der Politik des Sozialismus."

5. Indeed, some have assumed that Jung must have been a member of the Stasi, although in response to follow-up correspondence from Allan Ho, Hilmar Schmalenberg, editor of Jung's reminiscences, replied that he at least never thought so (*DSCH*, no. 12 [January 2000]: 23).

6. Schmalenberg, *Schostakowitsch in Deutschland*, p. 229.

7. Ian MacDonald, "Naive Anti-Revisionism: The Academic Misrepresentation of Dmitri Shostakovich," in Ho and Feofanov, *Shostakovich Reconsidered*, p. 683.

8. Ho and Feofanov, *Shostakovich Reconsidered*, p. 14.

9. This part of my response dealt with a passage near the beginning of Dmitri Feofanov's paper, where he asked the question, "Was he or wasn't he [a Communist]? Let us hear what the composer had to say on this subject." Instead of the verbal statement eagerly awaited in the hall, Feofanov then played Shostakovich and Weinberg's duet recording of the second movement of the Tenth Symphony, in its entirety, following it with the claim that "the meaning of this music is crystal clear. This is not the work of a Party-line Communist." Although I had been sent Professor Ho's and Mr. Feofanov's papers in advance of the meeting and was aware that there would be a musical extract at this point, the specific work was not identified. In the light of Dmitri Feofanov's framing remarks, I had presumed it would be from the *Antiformalist Peepshow*. Precisely which aspects of the second movement of the Tenth Symphony Mr. Feofanov considered could not be the work of a Party-line Communist, and why, he did not explain.

10. In my review of *Shostakovich Reconsidered*, published in the *BBC Music Magazine*, September 1998, pp. 31–33.

11. This is, of course, far less the case now than it was before the appearance of *Shostakovich Reconsidered*.

12. Solomon Volkov's interview with Galina Drubachevskaya appears under Volkov's byline over an articled entitled, "*Zdes' chelovek sgorel*" [A man burned out here], in *Muzykal'naia Akademiia*, March 1992, pp. 3–12. English translation is in Ho and Feofanov, *Shostakovich Reconsidered*, pp. 315–58.

13. And, of course, it has continued since, as the present volume indicates.

14. In the spoken version of his paper Mr. Feofanov changed his written text, substituting the word *reports* for *repeats*, which is, of course, unproblematic.

15. This is in response to the arguments also set out in Ho and Feofanov, *Shostakovich Reconsidered*, pp. 150–59.

16. Having analyzed the layering of musical material found in the autographs of Rachmaninoff's mature scores, David Cannata concludes that the actual process of *composing* had been concluded well before the composer began *writing* a score: "Before he even considered the next step, the laborious task of preparing a legible, exemplar composition for him had finished" (*Rachmaninoff and the Symphony* [Innsbruck: Studien Verlag, 1999], p. 48).

17. Extract 2 was copied from "Comparative Texts—*Testimony* v. Original Articles," prepared by Malcolm Hamrick Brown and published in the journal *DSCH*, no. 9 (summer 1998): 29–34; Extract 2 is reproduced on page 32. The "Comparative Texts" have been retranslated on the basis of the Moscow typescript of *Testimony* and appear as chapter 3 in the present volume. The Chekhov memoirs appear in that chapter on page 76.

18. Ho and Feofanov, *Shostakovich Reconsidered,* p. 213.

19. As Professor Ho explained in subsequent discussion, Volkov left his shorthand notes with his mother-in-law when he left Russia, and they have subsequently eluded his attempts to retrieve them. Mr. Feofanov believes that they are being held by the KGB. It remains to be seen whether the archives will one day disclose this potentially decisive piece of evidence.

20. This point could be greatly elaborated. In Western literature and historiography the equation of Hitler's Germany and Stalin's Russia was already commonplace in the early days of the Cold War; see Sheila Fitzpatrick, *The Russian Revolution,* 2nd ed. (Oxford: Oxford University Press, 1994), p. 6. Moreover, since the 1970s, intense debate has raged on the adequacy of the totalitarian model for understanding the history of the Soviet Union, even in the era of high Stalinism; see idem, *Stalinism: New Directions* (London: Routledge, 2000), pp. 1–11.

21. Elizabeth Wilson, *Shostakovich: A Life Remembered* (Princeton, N.J.: Princeton University Press, 1994), p. 272.

22. See note 2 above.

23. Liner note to Deutsche Grammophon 437 511-2 (1993).

Editor's Notes

a. Quoted from the official abstracts of Ho's and Feofanov's papers submitted to the Program Committee of AMS-Boston.

b. David Fanning's response was commissioned by the session chair, Professor Anne Shreffler, of the University of Basel, Switzerland. Fanning's comments follow, essentially as he read them at the Saturday evening session, 31 October 1998. His comments have since appeared in printed form in the journal *DSCH,* no. 11 (summer 1999): 37–40. For their reprinting in the present volume, the author has added explanatory footnotes and some very minor refinements of substance in square brackets. The volume editor has also introduced a few incidental editorial changes in adapting the original text, which was spoken, to the written text printed here.

21

Whose Shostakovich? (2000)

GERARD MCBURNEY

"Whose Shostakovich?" suggests a small and rather obvious pun. Not just "Whose?" but "Who's?" Not just "To whom does Shostakovich belong?" but "Who *is* he?"

The thought of this gentle wordplay is prompted by what some have come to call in recent years "The Shostakovich Wars." All kinds of people—from musicians and music lovers to historians, journalists, and musicologists—have been sparring in these often intemperate debates, which at times have seemed nothing less than a struggle for the composer's soul. In the course of this dispute, two different questions—"Who is he?" and "To whom does he belong?"—have somehow become entangled, as though the answer to one were also the answer to the other. Both questions, moreover, have come to be seen as fundamentally concerned with the extra-musical significance of Shostakovich's music rather than with what it sounds like. Whether this composer's work is a thing of visionary power and originality, as some maintain, or, as others think, trashy, empty, and secondhand, what matters to the Shostakovich warriors is what his work means. Arguments have raged in recent years about how to uncover its meaning and whether that meaning, once revealed,

---

Presented as a BBC Proms Pre-concert Lecture at the Victoria and Albert Museum, London, 30 July 2000.

is to be understood as tragedy, irony, cynicism, heroism, capitulation, or denunciation.

If the questions that drive these arguments are already only partly musical, beyond them there tends to be a host of decidedly nonmusical queries. Whose side was Shostakovich on? Was it their side or ours? Was he a Communist or a Communist hater,[1] a collaborator or a dissident, a modernist or a reactionary, with history or against it? In short, the question is not only whether he was a good composer or a bad composer but was he a good man or a bad man.

Somewhere behind that last pair of questions—"Good composer/bad composer, good man/bad man"—there lurks an old and disturbing anxiety about the uncertain moral connection between a work of art and the person who made it. It seems increasingly clear that, in Shostakovich's case, this anxiety is provoked not only by the rich undergrowth of anecdotes about his life but by the music itself. The music would actually seem to stir us to question both its meaning and its value; the anxiety is that its value might depend on its meaning.

This special anxiety about Shostakovich makes him notable. With regard to most composers, what we thought of their personal behavior and opinions would not normally affect the answer to the question, "What does their music mean?" Accusations of being a bad man, of thinking or meaning bad things, have been leveled at many—at Wagner, in the first place, but at twentieth-century figures, too: Debussy, Stravinsky, Berg, Webern, Puccini, Richard Strauss, even Britten. The alleged or proven moral failings of these people have sometimes provoked interesting commentaries on particular pieces in their output. But, except in the case of Wagner, they do not usually seem to have caused us to worry about the significance of an entire oeuvre. Whether any of these composers were anti-Semites, fascist sympathizers, untrustworthy, or mendacious, their musical achievements have usually been seen as something separate, even in the case of Prokofiev, parts of whose biography and compositional practice might seem at times quite similar to those of Shostakovich.

At the same time, were any of these other composers suddenly revealed to us as spotless saints or heroes, we would still be unlikely to think more highly of their music. With Shostakovich, however, this is not the case. His music has repeatedly been praised or damned in direct response to how one interprets the meaning of the music as reflecting the role the composer played in life. Through the years he has been characterized, in East and West, as both a cowardly collaborator and as a hero of our times (even a "moral beacon");[2] the point about both the positive and negative descriptions has been to make a case for or against his music. One way or another, something about this composer worries us.

Modern Western anxiety about Shostakovich owes most, of course, to the 1979 publication of *Testimony: The Memoirs of Dmitri Shostakovich*, as related to and edited by Solomon Volkov (New York: Harper & Row, 1979). Whatever anyone might think about the debated authenticity of this book, it would be foolish to deny its impact. In Europe and America, at least, it spawned a culture of interpretation, appearing to change the way many who listened to Shostakovich thought about what they heard.

But though the impact of *Testimony* was great, it must be viewed—like the material of the book itself—in context. It seems clearer now that, by chance or otherwise, *Testimony* was published when it was needed. For one thing, these were the tedious "stagnation" years of the later Brezhnev period, and the book's stories and especially its tone of voice seem to have provided, for certain Western readers, the precise image they wanted to see as a Soviet "intelligent," a "great Russian artist"—mocking, angry, whimsical, and self-justifying, a far cry from the previous public and official Shostakovich. This was a good time to learn that the man who wrote this music was not what he seemed.

Then again, the late 1970s were years of restlessness for all who were tired of the long postwar romance with modernism. Certain gods were felt by many to have failed. As Laurel Fay says at the end of her recent Shostakovich biography, "dissatisfaction had reached a breaking point"[3] and the music of Shostakovich, seen from *Testimony*'s point of view, offered an attractively different way of listening to the noise of our own time.

The Shostakovich of *Testimony* also answered an older need as well, strongly felt by those who had always taken Shostakovich seriously and were frustrated by the refusal to do so of those whom they perceived as the snobs of an exclusive and largely modernist establishment. For such Shostakovich lovers, in the words of a young friend of mine, "the *Testimony* portrait seemed to fit the music," or at any rate, as others have insisted, it was easy enough, when listening, to make the music fit the portrait.[4]

But *Testimony* did not *create* anxiety about the music of Shostakovich (especially not in Russia where that book has never been made available in Russian). It was the music itself that first caused worry, right from the beginning of this composer's career. From the early 1920s on, his teachers and mentors alternated between amazement at the brilliance of the child and doubts about the musical result. An exasperated Maximilian Steinberg complained often that the young man's music was "grotesque"[5] and even referred to it as *krivlian'e*—something twisted, distorted, grimacing, an affectation.[6] Alexander Glazunov, one of the young Shostakovich's greatest supporters, said of the First Symphony op. 10 (1924–25) in 1926 that "it shows great talent, but I don't understand it"[7]—this of a piece that the boy composer himself proudly called not a symphony but "a symphony-grotesque."[8] One year later, the Second Symphony op. 14 (1927), "To October," made Steinberg wonder, "Can this really be the New Art? Or is it only the daring of a naughty boy?"[9] And the same piece provoked a more distinguished figure, Nikolai Miaskovsky, to write:

> I don't much like his music. But he touches something live. You can't admire him and follow his jokes . . . but his music simply and immediately thrills you. I spat at the rehearsals . . . it was as disgusting as the rehearsals of Stravinsky, but at the concert the thing simply astounded me. Everything is so strong, everything in the right place, so laconically and at the same time so interestingly and so consummately well said. He's an unpleasant little boy, but really a major talent.[10]

One of the most interesting reactions to Shostakovich from this early period comes from another Russian, Stravinsky, who at that point had not yet met him and must have known little about him. Stravinsky's defensive attitude toward the success of others is well known. Nonetheless, in a letter to the conductor Ernest Ansermet, written from New York in 1935, he makes some incisive points:

> I heard *Lady Macbeth* [*Ledi Makbet Mtsenskogo uezda* op. 29 (1930–32)] by Shostakovich. . . . A well-organized advertising campaign bore its fruit, exciting all the N.Y. snobs. The work is lamentably provincial, the music plays a miserable role as illustrator, in a very embarrassing realistic style . . . marches brutally hammering in the manner of Prokofiev, and monotonous—and each time the curtains were lowered, the conductor was acclaimed by an audience more than happy to be brutalized by the arrogance of the numerous communist brass instruments. This première (and I hope *dernière*) reminds me of the performances of Kurt Weill two years ago in Paris and all the première-goers and the snobs of my new country [France].

A few lines later Stravinsky adds:

> I regret being so hard on Shostakovich, but he has deeply disappointed me, intellectually and musically. I regret it the more because his [First] Symphony favorably impressed me two years ago, and I expected something very different

> from a man of twenty-seven. *Lady Macbeth* is not the work of a musician, but it is surely the product of a total indifference toward music in the country of the Soviets.[11]

Leaving aside the jibes and resentments, that letter, written sixty-five years ago, already and almost prophetically sums up what were to become, outside Russia, established doubts and reservations about Shostakovich. Words and phrases like "lamentably provincial . . . miserable . . . very embarrassing . . . merely illustrative . . . brutally hammering . . . monotonous . . . arrogant . . . intellectually and musically disappointing"—all these tags and others like them have resonated down the years, especially in the more high-minded traditions of Western commentary, reaction, and criticism. So, too, has the idea that Shostakovich's later music is a betrayal of the brilliant promise of the First Symphony, and the uncomfortable sense that a streak of violence, crudeness, and monotony in the music, possibly something even of the sadomasochistic[12] or malevolent, might appeal in an unpleasantly chic way to a certain kind of Western snobbery.

However, Stravinsky's comments are prophetic not only of Western but of Soviet judgments, too. Consider this famous assault on *Lady Macbeth*, written nearly a year later than Stravinsky's letter:

> From the beginning, the listener is shocked by a deliberately dissonant, confused stream of sound. Fragments of melody, embryonic phrases appear—only to disappear again in the din, the grinding, and the screaming. . . . The music is built on the basis of rejecting opera. . . . Here we have "leftist" confusion. . . . All is coarse, primitive and vulgar. The music quacks, grunts, and growls, and suffocates itself, in order to express the amatory scenes as naturalistically as possible. And "love" is smeared all over the opera in the most "vulgar" manner.

The above comes, of course, from the famous *Pravda* article "Sumbur vmesto muzyki" [Muddle instead of music], published on 28 January 1936 (p. 3), a terrible turning point in Shostakovich's life, and long perceived as written at Stalin's personal behest. It is something of a shock to find in such a classic Soviet text so many words so close to what Stravinsky had already written, from what we suppose to have been a quite different point of view.

In fact, when one examines the two main traditions of criticizing Shostakovich from the 1930s on—the official Socialist-Realist one from inside the Soviet Union and the Western "high-art" tradition from outside—surprisingly one often finds peculiar parallels. In 1943, for example, at the height of the worldwide propaganda triumph of the "Leningrad" Symphony, the Seventh, the British writer on Russian music Gerald Abraham sneered that "Shostakovich cannot write even a moderately good tune,"[13] an opinion he shared, it turned out later, with those repulsive Party hacks unleashed on Shostakovich by Zhdanov in the famous purge of 1948.

Nonetheless, and notwithstanding what amounts at times to an eerie East-West critical consensus, the music of this composer did not go away. On the contrary, and especially since his death, and not only in his homeland but in certain other musical cultures like those of the English-speaking world and Northern Europe, Shostakovich's reputation has continued to grow to the point where he now appears to have found a vastly wider audience than most composers will ever know. But the ancient criticisms have not gone away either. Recently, in the London *Sunday Times*, Pierre Boulez defiantly placed Shostakovich "much lower" than "the second division, where you find Prokofiev and Hindemith." He went on:

> Shostakovich plays with clichés most of the time. . . . It's like olive oil, you have a second and even third pressing, and I think of Shostakovich as the second, or even third pressing of Mahler. . . . [W]ith Shostakovich, people are influenced by the autobiographical dimension of his music.[14]

That last comment brings us back to the central question. In Boulez's mind, it is obvious that the music cannot be validated by the extramusical story it tells, and reactions to that story are not reactions to the music. It is possible, however, to express this in another way, one that argues for Shostakovich and not against him. The American scholar and polemicist, Richard Taruskin, observes that "Shostakovich's works are fraught with horrific subtexts that can never be ignored."[15]

It would be hard to disagree. "Horrific subtexts" cry for our attention. But nonetheless, as time removes us from this composer's historical period, it is worth wondering whether we may not also listen to his music in other ways. Can Shostakovich's works simply not stand without what is supposed to lie behind them? Has what he wrote so little intrinsic substance, apart from the "autobiographical dimension," as Boulez puts it? Is it really as clichéd and cheaply derivative as the Frenchman says it is or as "lamentably provincial" as Stravinsky claims? And if that is indeed how the music sounds, could it not be that Shostakovich wrote it that way on purpose? And could that not be something interesting in itself?

It seems to me that the broadest, most urgent question now about Shostakovich should be not what does or doesn't lie behind his music but what happens when we listen to the sounds and notes that comprise his music and to the way they are composed; or, as the late Alfred Schnittke used to say (speaking specifically of Shostakovich), when we listen to what happens "between the notes" (rather than in some imagined world beyond them).[16] More than twenty-five years have passed since Shostakovich's death, and it is surely time to pay attention to this composer's art as art. For it is his music that we shall have to listen to in the future, as the fearful history of his age begins to slip a little further from us and it becomes less possible and less immediately vivid to hear the notes primarily as a chronicle, a "message in a bottle,"[17] a soundtrack to a nightmare, however moving.

Although I am not primarily a scholar and have read only a few of the flood of books and articles about this man, it seems fairly clear that, as yet, few questions have been asked about the language, the inner structure and coherence of this music, about what it is and how it works and why it is the way it is. There has been plenty of commentary, of course, about the signs and symbols he uses, and some of that is interesting. But it still tells us less about how the music works and more about how we are supposed to read things into it—and Shostakovich's music notoriously seems to require that we read things into it, even to the point, as Taruskin comments, that it might be "too easily read."[18] In particular, his unmistakably distinctive rhetoric and his repertoire of gestures, immediately startling features of his language, frequently distract us, leading us almost like puppets past the sounds and structures of the notes into a looking-glass world where we are mesmerized by what we take the notes to represent.

This in itself is a crucial quality of Shostakovich's language, one that any investigation of his work might well begin with. There is a fascinating question to be asked as to how he makes us listen in this way, especially if it is true, as Boulez would have us think, that what the notes themselves are doing is clichéd and uninteresting. On the other hand, perhaps those qualities that Boulez so dislikes may be exactly how Shostakovich does it, by rendering the surface of the music somehow lacking, so as to force us to imagine something else behind.

When I was a student in Moscow in the 1980s, the most widely repeated "bon mot" or rather "mauvais mot" about Shostakovich to circulate among younger musicians emanated from the venerably waspish figure of Filip Gershkovich (or Hershkovits). He was a Rumanian-Jewish composer and theorist who, in Vienna in the 1930s, studied with Berg and Webern, before being swept by events of war into a long, strange exile in the Soviet Union. For the rich post-Shostakovich generation of Soviet composers and performers, Gershkovich was a crucial influence and inspiration. As one of his pupils put it, he seemed like "an apostle sent by Webern to the barbarians."[19]

Coming from his Middle-European standpoint, and being an unwilling prisoner in Soviet culture, Gershkovich understandably had little time for Shostakovich. But his description of him was memorable: "*khalturshchik v transe.*"[20] This might be translated, more or less, as "a hack in a trance," except that *khalturshchik* is a word with an ancient history, suggesting not just a newspaper "hack" but originally someone like a priest or a monk who chants ritual gibberish in an incomprehensible language,[21] someone cynically going through the motions.

Gershkovich's point, contemptuous though it is, is subtler than Boulez's. It acknowledges that the man who wrote the music is himself entranced, like a shaman. So the issue is not merely, as so many have suggested, that we, the gullible ones, have been taken in by a quack. Rather, by using this loaded word *khalturshchik*, Gershkovich is suggesting that it is precisely because Shostakovich writes like a "hack" that he has fallen into a trance. The trance is induced by his way of writing, by the relentless incantation, by the frantically scribbled repetition of stock ideas that lost their meaning long ago, by the endless "playing" (in Boulez's words) "with clichés."

What Gershkovich must have intended by his remark is close to what we are told Goethe said of epic diction: that the problem with its formulae is that they do your thinking for you.[22] Gershkovich was objecting to the absence in this music of what he understood as musical thought. But however negatively he meant it, his distinctive description of Shostakovich puts its finger on something far from thoughtless at the heart of this composer's way of composition, at the heart of how his music operates.

For what Gershkovich saw and did not like in Shostakovich—art as trance, and the artist in the trance, and the artist's language as trance-inducing babble, or as the delusive parroting of common-stock conventions—are qualities that, however bad he might think them, at different times have been aspired to and embraced by many, not just by Shostakovich—and not so as *not* to think but as *another way* to think. There have been an abundant number who wanted their art to be this way, and this is especially true of many from the place and time Shostakovich came from, the complex, fascinating world of early-twentieth-century Russian modernism, and, more particularly, the immediate postrevolutionary years in Leningrad.

This is important because, insofar as recent writers have tried to describe Shostakovich's language at all, they have tended to concentrate on his more "mature" pieces, from the Fifth Symphony on, often treating the way they work as an Aesopian strategy of codes and implications evolved specifically to deal with the catastrophic circumstances of the Stalinist terror from the mid-1930s on.

Such an approach is troublesome because it treats his later language as though it had sprung from his head at that point in his life and was fully formed that way in response to immediate undeniable needs. It may have done so in part, but it also arose out of what was there before, a seething, restlessly experimental atmosphere that flourished in both Moscow and St. Petersburg/Petrograd/Leningrad. This often self-consciously brave new world was dominated, naturally, by the familiar giants of Russian modernism: not just composers, like the already dead Scriabin and the far-away Stravinsky and Prokofiev, but also those who changed the course of all the other arts, such as Meyerhold, Eisenstein, Mayakovsky, and Malevich.

This was especially true in Leningrad, which was a city with a wealth of complex subcultures, contrasting and shifting networks of artists and theorists, often people of Shostakovich's own age and circles of acquaintance. There were schools of them, writers, musicians, painters and all sorts in between, with manifestos, concerts, magazines, discussion groups, exhibitions, and impromptu happenings on roofs, in cellars, and on street corners. Among those with whom Shostakovich had connections at that time was that rich swathe of writers called the Leningrad absurdists,[23] and a small but important circle of filmmakers who at one point called themselves "the Depot of Eccentrics."[24] Moreover, and this is something that should give thought to anyone considering examining the development of Shostakovich's musical language, this was also the time of that deeply influential school of literary theory, the Formalists.

To understand how Shostakovich's music works, how it first evolved and then how it turned into what it became much later, we must surely begin where the composer himself began, before the period of high Stalinism, in Leningrad in the 1920s and early 1930s, in the artistic and philosophical ferment of that time. For that was where and when key aspects of Shostakovich's art and outlook first took shape, aspects that continued to play a part in his musical thinking right up until the time of his apparently quite different final works in the early 1970s.

The character of the Russian cultural life that the young composer knew is well remembered by his contemporary from student days, the musicologist Mikhail Druskin:

> Life seethed around the young Shostakovich, sucking him into its vortex. Anyone who did not experience those years together with [him] must find it difficult to imagine the intensity of this whirlpool, which threw up an explosion of creative energy and provided the strongest impulse to increased artistic endeavor and innovation.[25]

Shostakovich's detailed connections to this "whirlpool" of artistic life around him in his youth have not yet been mapped in detail,[26] although the lineaments he knew of and associated with are plotted in the opening chapters of Laurel Fay's new biography. It is clear from what she writes that, as Shostakovich himself suggested afterward,[27] his relations with his cultural and intellectual surroundings were mediated to a considerable degree from 1927 on by his close friendship with a prominent figure in Leningrad at that time, Ivan Sollertinsky—critic, linguist, aesthete, polymath, socialite, and wit.[28]

Even a slight acquaintance with the artistic world to which both Shostakovich and Sollertinsky belonged will show there were creative figures all around them fascinated, in different ways and to different degrees, by the kinds of issues touched on by the "bon mot" of Gershkovich. There were those who were interested in language as cliché or as nonsense, language and inarticulate sound as incantation, as a window into a trance, language and rhetoric as strategy; others delighted in the richly subversive possibilities of the absurd, the grotesque, the banal, the alienating, the deformed, and the outrageous; and still others played with the preposterous and simultaneously horrifying effect of long lists, for example, or dreary repetitions. And lurking behind all these enthusiasms was the persistent idea of the surface of the work of art, the stuff of which it was made, as something to be distinguished from the intoxicating realm that was supposed to lie beyond it, whether that realm made sense or nonsense or "trans-sense,"[29] as some called it.

Of course, ideas like these were, in different combinations, part of the dreams of modernists not only in Russia but everywhere; the Russian world Shostakovich knew, however, had its own patterns and striations of these issues, its own favorite formulations. Above all, it had its own heightened and self-consciously excited awareness of the gap between language and meaning, of the schemes and negotiations needed to overcome and dramatize that gap, of the bittersweet and often culturally specific pleasures to be derived from the contradictions inherent within language.

One point is clear, though. At this period, such Russian and Soviet attitudes toward language rarely meant treating language simply as a signifier, a chain of self-explanatory symbols. Symbols in this world were nearly always at least double-freighted, meant to be ambiguous.

This matters for how we hear Shostakovich. First, it reminds us that the instability and haze of paradox that, throughout his life, was such a feature of his music, of the way it sounds and hangs together, was not just a function of his personality or a way of coping with appalling circumstances (though it must have been both those things, at least in part) but also a response to an older, deeper, wider preoccupation with flexibility and change that almost inevitably touched everyone within his time and cultural environment.

This should give us pause at those moments when we long to read fixed and stable messages behind his music. For he came from a world that not only doubted such messages but one that delighted in the assumption that contradictory messages would always be present at the same time. Instinctive to this culture's fascination with the play of language was the simple sense that meaning was impossible to fix with words or notes or daubs of paint.

The music of Shostakovich's early adulthood vividly reflects his engagement with the modernist experiments he encountered. His first symphonies and piano pieces, his scores for Meyerhold's production of Mayakovsky's *Klop* [*The Bedbug*] (1929) and for the epic silent-movie *Novyi Vavilon* [The New Babylon] (1928–29), and, above all, his Gogol-inspired opera, *Nos* [*The Nose*] (1927–28), show him already to be a master manipulator of the currents of invention that swirled around him.

In particular, what preoccupied him in those days were violent degrees of dissonance, atonality, and disruption; the possibilities of instrumental color for its own sake; different varieties of heterophony or what he called "ultra-polyphony";[30] and, most of all, the principle of nonrepetition. Mikhail Druskin especially remembered "the kaleidoscopically shifting episodes in the Third Symphony, where, according to the composer's concept, not one idea was to be repeated."[31]

What happens next in his career, beyond these early and self-consciously "avant-garde" attempts, is more debatable.[32] Commentators have generally paid little attention to the mass of more or less popular film and theater music, including three full-length ballets that he wrote between 1929 and 1935. The received idea, probably first put forth by Shostakovich himself in his manifesto, "A Declaration of a Composer's Responsibilities,"[33] seems to be that these less important theater pieces are merely the unfortunate result of the composer's need to earn a living.

On the other hand, his dramatic masterpiece of that period, the opera

Ledi Makbet Mtsenskogo uezda [Lady Macbeth of the Mtsensk District] op. 29 (1930–32) and the Fourth Symphony op. 43 (1935–36), which followed it, have received much attention, almost, at times, as though they were works that somehow stood alone, and, in the case of the symphony, quite often with the sense that that piece represents a vision of the still modern Shostakovich who might have flourished afterward had he not been so savagely attacked in 1936.

The most attention, of course, has been given to his next "great work," the Fifth Symphony op. 47 (1937), as a triumphant answer to any kind of criticism and for its apparently radical change of stylistic direction, whether that represents an act of political retrenchment or a signing on to the new simplicity or plainness that was such a feature of the work of composers everywhere in the mid-1930s. Viewed from either angle, the Fifth Symphony, to most listeners, evidently seems to have been, for Shostakovich, a "rebirth," a "*vozrozhdenie*," a word borrowed from the title of the Pushkin poem the composer curiously turns out to have hidden in the symphony's finale (by quoting his own setting of the poem, op. 46 no. 1 [1936–37]).[34]

Since I myself have spent time trying to reconstruct various missing theater scores from 1931 and 1932,[35] perhaps not unnaturally I take a slightly different view of the sequence of events at this point in his life. It seems to me important to understand that although the Fifth Symphony sounds like a dramatic change, it is also the culmination of a long period of development, of more than fifteen years spent perfecting a musical language, making a way to write.

In this light it should be obvious that the more than twenty film and theater scores (apart from the opera) from those six years or so to the mid-1930s are worth looking at not only because they are what he wrote at that time, but because they represent a bridge, a line of continuity and evolution between the early works and what came later. They also tell us much about what was going on in Shostakovich's mind at this period of his life. Certainly they are interesting for aesthetic reasons, for they are all marked, like his more "serious" pieces of this period, by what Taruskin calls "the debunking spirit of the 'new objectivity' that had emanated in the 1920s from Germany."[36] But they also have considerable technical and musical importance for the way they were, for their composer, what the conductor Genady Rozhdestvensky calls a "laboratory" for the exploration and development of new techniques and a full-fledged dramatic language. As Shostakovich worked on *Lady Macbeth*, for example, by far his most ambitious theater work, he threw ideas from it into other pieces he was writing at the same time.[37] The ballets also overlap, quote from other pieces, and the ideas expressed in them are in turn recycled in still later music.

In fact, almost his whole output at this period can be seen as a kind of web or tissue of self-quotation and cross-reference. Clearly this was not because he was running out of ideas—ideas were pouring from him at this time—although reusing earlier ideas must have been helpful when he was working at such tremendous speed. Most interesting, however, about this practice of recycling, is how we find Shostakovich trying out in different contexts the various strengths and weaknesses of his musical material, like a tailor with a length of cloth or a potter with his clay, testing all the different ways it works. Often in these pieces Shostakovich tests his material from several points of view: for example, its dramatic effectiveness; the ways in which it has autonomy and identity; its modal two-sidedness; and, most of all, its pulsing rhythmic possibilities, which, at this point in his development, absorbed him more and more.

Much of the strength and character of the raw material he draws on in these theater works, including *Lady Macbeth*, depends on the evocation, loving or parodic, of a whole range of models from the musical past, and from the lighter end of the demotic repertoire, including the hybrid jazz-and-klezmer that was the popular staple of the time, *chastushki* (Russian comic songs), mass songs, pioneer songs, cheap waltzes and marches, and those syrupy tunes that every Russian knows are only sung by drunks.[38]

What matters about this stuff is not just that it is full of energy or funny or aggressive or sarcastic but that it delivered into Shostakovich's hands possibilities, still modernist and of their time, but different from those offered by the experimental, non-repeating, acoustically blurred material he was more often using earlier. In short, he was becoming more interested in another kind of modernism. The shapes of the tunes and corny harmonies that now obsessed him were designed to be not far out but typical and recognizable, even (to paraphrase Taruskin again) "too easily" so. For out of such imagery came opportunities for (often relentless) patterns of contrast, repetition, exaggeration, and the reduction of the surface of the music to banal absurdity and, at times, even to the blank-faced, uncertainly half-mocking, half-ecstatic horror that was the stock-in-trade of contemporary writers of the then "avant-garde."[39]

However, as well as allowing Shostakovich to engage with musical versions of the forms of play that meant so much to his most innovative contemporaries, material like this did something else, something basic and crucial to his craft as a composer: it opened new possibilities for unfolding what he wrote, for creating continuity and form. The problem with the earlier, more obviously "modernistic" material was, as Shostakovich is not the only composer to have found, that it posed massive problems of syntax (making sustained invention very difficult) and of formal articulation (making the construction of any kind of musical architecture problematic). From the beginning, Shostakovich had been someone who yearned to write on a large scale, someone who needed syntax and substantial structural elements with which to engage in formal architecture. This was a young man longing to breathe the air of the symphonic.

Of the several different ways in which we can observe the young Shostakovich using the opportunities his theater work allowed to achieve a growing mastery of large-scale form, perhaps one of the most interesting is his ever expanding grasp of pulse and rhythm. Especially from the end of 1931 on, we can see him concentrating on the vigorous possibilities of middle-ground rhythm, the kind that governs how you move from phrase to phrase and paragraph to paragraph.

Like the tunes and harmonies, the characteristic rhythmic images from this period of Shostakovich are cheap, vulgar, and commonplace, even by the standards of some of the more notorious ideas he used in later life. He was fascinated by "hammering," to use Stravinsky's word, and exaggerating to absurdity and outright aggression, the plainest and silliest patterns of eight and sixteen bars, like those in many kinds of popular music. By latching onto the way such trashy, low-down rhythms inevitably fall and collect themselves into larger groups and phrases, making crude shapes of a kind the previous generation of composers like his teachers loathed, Shostakovich could do several things. He could hold onto some of the more outrageous images from his earlier work, while simplifying them, giving them a dramatic framework and theatrical immediacy. At the same time he could make his music flow in new ways, new spans of time. He could expand his language to build sequences and pulsing paragraphs of sound which, in the old phrase, "rock and roll."

This "rock and roll," so obvious to any music lover swept away by a great performance of almost any of the fifteen symphonies, is probably somewhere near the heart of what annoys all those who have never been able to take this composer seriously, all those who feel cheated or manipulated by him, all those who think his music is a "slap in the face of public taste"[40] and decency, or who hate, as Robin Holloway puts it, Shostakovich "banging on my head."

To put it another way, it is precisely this quality about the music that produces what Gershkovich called the trance. It is this that makes even the thinnest of Shostakovich's later film scores never quite devoid of concentration and endows his greatest concert masterpieces with what seems to be, as time passes, their ever more disturbing force.

This "rock and roll" enables us to make sense of all the other layers of thought and meaning in his music, of what would otherwise be the amorphous shifting of modal and tonal sands, the apparent shapelessness of so many of his melodies, the raucous orchestration, the ciphers and the disrupting gestures toward neo-classicism or romantic film music. Most of all, it is this "rock and roll" that holds together the mighty polyphony of this composer's vision—polyphony not just in the sense of counterpoint, although Shostakovich was one of the natural contrapuntists of his age, but in that other looser sense, once so popular with artists and theorists of the time of Shostakovich's youth, meaning the complex play of different contradictory voices in a drama, in a narrative, what keeps a story going, what makes a piece of music come alive.

This fundamental rhythmic power of Shostakovich has its sources in his early work. There are examples, in the first three symphonies and in *The Nose*, of what one might call long rhythmic "rallies," to use a tennis metaphor, and these were already marked, as was to remain true of this composer to the end, by their striking connection to the physicality of human movement, rather than being, as seems true of the rhythm of some other music of that time, invented and self-conscious. A visceral grasp of pulse and of the patterns that it makes was always part of Shostakovich's gift. You can hear it in surviving schoolboy works and in recordings of his piano playing.

But through the theater years, while he went on working on his opera or later dreamed of starting the Fourth Symphony,[41] he stretched this gift, tightened it and made it stronger. The opera, in particular, is a virtuosic demonstration of his new powers in this field. In *Lady Macbeth*, beats and sequences of different pulses become a vital way of driving the drama forward musically. To make pulse work in this way Shostakovich raided an astonishing range of sources, from Verdi and Offenbach, to what sound like scraps of silent-movie music, dance-hall music, or stuff written for the radio and phonograph.[42]

Stravinsky's reaction to this use of pulse was that it was "brutal" and "monotonous." Presumably, given the nature of the drama, it was meant to be just that—but not only that. It was also a show of eruptive rhythmic impetus, sustained and drawn out for as far as it will go—as far, that is, until it could go further in the next large-scale work, the Fourth Symphony.

The symphony is shorter than the opera. But its rhythmic paragraphs are larger, less segmented, more complex, interlocking, and dependent on one another. The composer's rhythmic language has advanced another stage. On the other hand, there are elements in the melodic and harmonic material of the Fourth that look back to music earlier than the opera—disruptions, contrasts, and non sequiturs that echo the Third Symphony and that symphony's principle of non-repetition. The volcanic character of the Fourth has much to do with tension between the implosive, decay-threatened melodic material of which it is made and the expansive, neo-Mahlerian scale of its rhythmic architecture.

The conversion of this tension into dynamic energy that is less eruptive and more constructive is the work of the composer's next step forward, the Fifth Symphony. The Fifth, more so even than the Seventh (the "Leningrad"), is undoubtedly his piece most charged with history, myth, and expectation. It is probably the one most often played, most often treated as a masterpiece, most mocked by those who hate the very sound of this man's music, most loved by audiences, recorded and chewed over. As Victor Suslin has put it, maddened both by the symphony and its reputation: "Good God! . . . How much ink has been spilt [over it], how many lofty words been spoken!"[43]

Of course, no one can take from the Fifth its frightful context which down through the years has moved so many listeners, just as no one could possibly deny the circumstances of its making—those terrible words printed in *Pravda* in 1936, the unspeakable threat of state-instigated violence, the treachery of erstwhile friends, and the isolation of its composer. No one can or ought to deny the wider engulfing Terror of that time, nor could they ever take away the tears of those who heard the first performances of the Fifth Symphony.

But nonetheless, and in spite of all of this, the Fifth Symphony, so undeniably a triumph of one human spirit, is also a structure, made of sound as well as fury, of notes and images and phrases held together by a will and by technique and by deep musical experience. It was written by someone who had already spent well over a decade forging a language for himself. That language had been tempered in the intense heat of the practical experience of performance. When the young composer came to write this symphony, he was speaking in ways deeply affected by all he had written and heard in the years before. However different this work might first appear from most of the pieces Shostakovich wrote before it, it could only have been written by someone who had traveled on the journey that had led to it, someone who had indeed already written all those other pieces.

This is, at the very least, one reason why anyone who seeks to answer the double question "Whose Shostakovich?/Who is Shostakovich?" should give a thought to where his music came from, how it began, how it developed, and why it came to sound the way it does. For looked at in that way, two things about his art become immediately clear: that he was, and in some very peculiar senses remained to the end of his life, a child of his time, the Soviet 1920s; and that he took the already intriguing inheritance of that age and made it into something utterly his own.

Listening to Shostakovich with this in mind might be a first step in finding what else this music has to offer apart from that extra-musical dimension that Boulez called its "autobiographical dimension." It also does the composer the simple courtesy of giving him credit for being and belonging to himself.

Notes

1. "But what an alien face he has!"—"The face is a mask for one's ideological readiness . . . one's readiness to fight on either side of the front of struggle!" (Andrei Platonov, *Fourteen Little Red Huts* [*14 krasnykh izbushek*], act 4, trans. Robert Chandler and Elizabeth Chandler, in *The Portable Platonov* (Moscow: GLAS, 1999), p. 159.

2. Joseph Horowitz, "A Moral Beacon amid the Darkness of a Tragic Era," *New York Times,* 6 February 2000, pp. AR1, 34.

3. Laurel Fay, *Shostakovich: A Life* (New York: Oxford University Press, 2000), p. 286.

4. For what it is worth, it is my personal experience that my Russian acquaintances who knew Shostakovich in some manner find the idea that Volkov's picture can be taken as an authentic portrait to be ignorant, patronizing, and offensive to the composer's memory. I have yet to encounter exceptions to this pattern.

5. Fay, *Shostakovich: A Life,* p. 24.

6. "Potom slushal simfoniyu Vainberga [Moisei Samuilovich, b. 1919]—uzhasno, sploshnoi Shostakovich perioda krivlian'ii" (15 January 1943) [Afterward I listened to a symphony by Vainberg—horrible, pure Shostakovich from his period of affectation] (L. G. Kovnatskaya, ed., *Shostakovich mezhdy mgnoveniem i vechnost'yu* [Shostakovich between now and eternity] [St. Petersburg: Izdatel'stvo kompozitor, 2000], p. 136).

7. Elizabeth Wilson, *Shostakovich: A Life Remembered* (Princeton, N.J.: Princeton University Press, 1994), p. 9.

8. Fay, *Shostakovich: A Life*, p. 26.

9. Ibid., p. 62.

10. O. P. Lamm, *Stranitsy tvorcheskoi biografii Miaskovskogo* [Pages from Miaskovsky's creative biography] (Moscow: Sovetskii kompozitor, 1989), p. 187.

11. Stravinsky, *Selected Correspondence*, vol. 1, ed. and with commentary by Robert Craft (New York: Knopf, 1982), p. 224.

12. The private comments of Shostakovich's contemporary the musicologist M. S. Druskin include reference to the issue of sadomasochism in a musical context (personal communication from L. G. Kovnatskaya). Very different, but also worth registering, are comments by his brother, Y. S. Druskin, in Yakov Druskin, *Dnevniki* [Diaries] (St. Petersburg: Akademicheskii proekt, 1999), p. 418.

13. Gerald Abraham, *Eight Soviet Composers* (London: Oxford University Press, 1943), p. 30.

14. Interview by Hugh Canning, "A Nice Guy in a World Full of Monsters," *The Sunday Times* (London), 9 January 2000, Section 9, p. 21

15. Richard Taruskin, "Shostakovich and Us," in Rosamund Bartlett, ed., *Shostakovich in Context* (New York: Oxford University Press, 2000), p. 9.

16. I remember this phrase in a conversation between Schnittke and Sir Peter Maxwell Davies, in a small flat near Covent Garden, London, in, I think, 1989 or 1990.

17. Taruskin, "Shostakovich and Us," p. 23.

18. Ibid., p. 25.

19. Victor Suslin in a 1989 interview with the present writer for the BBC TV documentary *Think Today, Speak Tomorrow* (1990), directed by Barrie Gavin.

20. First communicated to me in 1985 by Dmitri Smirnov. Mentioned in a letter from Victor Suslin to Galina Ustvol'skaia of 4 August 1994, published in O. Gladkova, *Galina Ustvol'skaia—muzyka kak navazhdeniie* [Galina Ustvol'skaia—Music as hallucination] (St. Petersburg: Muzyka, 1999), p. 51.

21. See the entry under "khaltura" in Max Vasmer, *Russisches Etymologisches Wörterbuch*, 4 vols. (Heidelberg: C. Winter, Universitätsverlag, 1950–58), translated into Russian as Maks Fasmer, *Etimologicheskii slovar' russkogo iazyka* [Etymological dictionary of the Russian language], 4 vols., trans. O. N. Trubachev, ed. and with an introduction by V. A. Larin (Moscow: Progress, 1973 [1964]; reprinted, 1986–87), 4:218.

22. Mentioned by Jeremy Noel-Tod in his review of Thom Gunn's *Boss Cupid* in the *London Review of Books*, 6 July 2000, p. 31.

23. See Graham Roberts, *The Last Soviet Avant-Garde: OBERIU—Fact, Fiction, Metafiction* (New York: Cambridge University Press, 1997). Through various common acquaintances, such as the Druskin family and the painter Alisa Poret, Shostakovich is reported to have had connections with a number of writers from this group, including Daniil Kharms and Nikolai Oleinikov. According to the composer's widow (personal communication), to his last years and, even at the end of his life, Shostakovich remembered the poetry of Oleinikov with laughter, and he dreamed of setting some of it to music. His connections with other writers (not from the same specific group but from the same world), such as Evgeny Zamyatin and Mikhail Zoshchenko, are quite well documented.

24. See *Eccentric Manifesto* (London: Eccentric, 1992), with an introduction by

Marek Pytel. The "Depot" included three young directors and film theorists for whom Shostakovich later was to write some of his most important film scores: Sergei Yutkevich, Leonid Trauberg, and Grigorii Kozintsev.

25. Wilson, *Shostakovich: A Life Remembered*, p. 43.

26. A start is made, for example, in Tamara Levaya, "Kharms i Shostkaovich: nesostoiavsheisia sotrunichestvo" [Kharms and Shostakovich: An unrealized collaboration], in *Kharmsizdat predstavliaet: issledovaniia, esse, vospominaniia, katolog vystavki, bibliografiia* [Kharms Publishers presents: Research, essays, reminiscences, an exhibition catalog, bibliography] (St. Petersburg: Kharmsizdat, Arsis, 1995), pp. 94–96; Ludmila Mikheeva-Sollertinskaya, "Shostakovich as Reflected in his Letters to Ivan Sollertinsky," in Bartlett, *Shostakovich in Context*, pp. 67–77; and Olga Komok, "Shostakovich and Kruchonykh," in idem, *Shostakovich in Context*, pp. 99–122.

27. Ludmila Mikheeva, *Pamiati I. I. Sollertinskogo. Vospominaniia, materialy, issledovaniia* [In commemoration of I. I. Sollertinsky. Reminiscences, materials, research], comp. Ludmila Vikentievna Sollertinskaya, ed. I. Glikman, M. Druskin, and D. Shostakovich (Moscow: Sovetskii kompozitor, 1974), pp. 91–94.

28. Fay, *Shostakovich: A Life*, pp. 41ff.

29. "Zaum" in Khlebnikov and Kruchonykh's theoretical writings.

30. Fay, *Shostakovich: A Life*, p. 44.

31. Wilson, *Shostakovich: A Life Remembered*, p. 45.

32. Professor Robin Milner-Gulland of Sussex University, United Kingdom (personal conversation, 27 July 2000), points out that the kind of evolutionary journey, out of the avant-garde grotesque, through fragmented popular idioms, toward large-scale, even epic forms, was one traveled by an astonishing number of Shostakovich's artistic contemporaries. He suggests Zabolotsky as an obvious example, though one might equally point to the stylistic changes in the later work of Kharms (especially in his novella, *Starukha* [The old woman], which was allegedly attacked by his friend Vvedensky, with the defensive words, "*A ia eshcho avangardist*" [Well, I am still an avant-gardist]. More obvious comparisons could be made with the development of a number of Shostakovich's filmmaker contemporaries, especially those who had been his colleagues (see note 24 above).

33. Shostakovich, "Deklaratsiia obiazannostei kompozitora" [A declaration of a composer's responsibilities], *Rabochii i teatr* 31 (20 November 1931): 6. See Fay, *Shostakovich: A Life*, pp. 63ff., 301 nn. 63, 64.

34. See Richard Taruskin, *Defining Russia Musically* (Princeton, N.J.: Princeton University Press, 1997), pp. 532ff.

35. Including *Uslovno ubityi* [Declared dead; or, Hypothetically murdered] op. 31 (1931) and movements from *Hamlet* op. 32 (1931–32).

36. Taruskin, "Shostakovich and Us," p. 16.

37. Especially, but not exclusively, in *Declared Dead.*

38. For example, the song "*Son popovny*" [The dream of the priest's daughter], from the 1933 score for the Pushkin-based animated film, *Skazka o pope i o rabotnike ego Balde* [The tale of the priest and his servant Balda] op. 36, parodies *Shumel kamysh* [The rushes sighed], a song associated only, and laughably so, with extreme intoxication.

39. See, for example, Daniil Kharms's 1933–39 cycle, *Sluchai* [Incidences] or Alexander Vvedensky's 1938 play, *Iolka u Ivanovykh* [Christmas at the Ivanovs].

40. *Poshchiochina obshchestvennomu vkusu* [A slap in the face of public taste], the Cubo-Futurist manifesto of 1912, signed by Mayakovsky, Kruchonykh, and others.

41. Note, for example, the 1934 aborted sketch of the opening of the Fourth, performed by the London Symphony Orchestra under Rostropovich at the Barbican Centre, London, on 26 February 1998.

42. David Fanning has pointed out in conversation (21 July 2000) that the ending of the *entr'acte* from act 2 of *The Nose* suggests a 78-rpm phonograph winding down.

43. Gladkova, *Galina Ustvol'skaia*, p. 52.

22

The Shostakovich Variations (2000)

PAUL MITCHINSON

There is something suspicious about music, gentlemen. I insist that she is, by her nature, equivocal. I shall not be going too far in saying at once that she is politically suspect.

—Thomas Mann, *The Magic Mountain*

If the epic tragedy of Soviet history were ever made into a film, the music of Dmitri Shostakovich would undoubtedly be its soundtrack. At the piercing blast of a factory whistle (courtesy of Shostakovich's Second Symphony), peasants and workers would crowd the squares of 1917 Petrograd. The madcap 1920s, when Soviet Russia's last capitalists flaunted their wealth and Western tastes, might be accompanied by the inspired silliness of "Tea for Two" from the ballet *The Golden Age* [*Zolotoi vek*]. And as the bitter night of Stalinism spread its gloom over Soviet Russia in the 1930s, an oboe would sing out in quiet anguish from the Fifth Symphony's Largo. Finally, the Seventh Symphony's "invasion theme"—an insipid scrap of a tune plucked out on hushed strings—would build gradually and inexorably into an earsplitting military march, as Hitler's armies approached and then encircled Leningrad. In fact, with music this powerful, making a film might be superfluous.

Shostakovich speaks a musical language that is familiar as well as evocative. He is heir to Gustav Mahler rather than Arnold Schoenberg. One may not be able to hum his melodies, and his harmonies may be sharp and astringent, but his music remains rooted in the grand symphonic tradition of the nineteenth century. Though he experimented with twelve-tone composition in his later years, he embraced tonality. He was the last great composer to work almost exclusively in the traditional genres of classical music: the symphony, the concerto, the string quartet, the keyboard prelude and fugue. The result is a body of work of both emotional power and technical achievement. Shostakovich is that rarest of breeds, a genuinely popular twentieth-century composer.

Perhaps because the music is so accessible, audiences have wondered about the man—and the troubled age in which he lived. Born in 1906, Shostakovich spent his entire creative life as a citizen of the Soviet Union. When he died in August 1975, his *Pravda* obituary hailed him as a "loyal son of the Communist Party."[1] The London *Times* agreed. Shostakovich was the "greatest figure in Soviet music over the last two decades,"[2] the *Times* wrote, one who "saw himself equally as a Soviet citizen and a composer." Perhaps it was inevitable that his music came to be understood as a faithful reflection of pro-Soviet politics. He composed a song for the Soviet cosmonaut Yuri Gagarin to sing in outer space and signed a letter denouncing Andrei Sakharov. His best-known musical offerings—the fifteen symphonies—were in many cases burdened with dedications that invited such a reading: "October," "The First of May," "The Year 1905," "The Year 1917."

But in October 1979, four years after the composer's death, Harper & Row published a book that cast doubt on his Soviet credentials. A manuscript purporting to be the memoirs of Dmitri Shostakovich had been smuggled out of Russia by a young Soviet music journalist who claimed to have interviewed the aging composer at length. It would become one of the most explosive documents of the Cold War and one of the most influential books on music published in the twentieth century. The Shostakovich who emerged from its pages was not the legendary "loyal son of the Communist Party" but a bitter man who despised Soviet power. Audiences, it seemed, had got the political message in his music exactly wrong.

"The majority of my symphonies are tombstones," this Shostakovich told his interlocutor. "Hitler is a criminal, that's clear, but so is Stalin. . . . I haven't forgotten the terrible prewar years. That is what all my symphonies, beginning with the Fourth, are about, including the Seventh and Eighth."[3]

Testimony, the book's dust jacket read, *The Memoirs of Dmitri Shostakovich, as related to and edited by Solomon Volkov.* But are the memoirs genuine? And, if so, what do they tell us about the music? After more than twenty years of controversy, scholars of Shostakovich seem more bitterly divided than ever.

Solomon Volkov was a sixteen-year-old student at the high school affiliated with the Leningrad Conservatory when he met his idol. In 1960, after writing an enthusiastic review of Shostakovich's Eighth String Quartet, Volkov was introduced to the fifty-four-year-old composer. Shostakovich expressed his gratitude for Volkov's brief article, and their relationship blossomed into one of respect and trust, if not close friendship.

Several years later, in the late 1960s, Shostakovich agreed to contribute a preface to Volkov's first book, a study of Leningrad's young composers. Volkov reports that he interviewed Shostakovich at length about his former composition students, prodding the reluctant and notoriously private composer to reminisce about his youth. Volkov claims he "had to resort to trickery: at every convenient point I drew parallels, awakening associations" in order to overcome Shostakovich's reserve. Unfortunately, Volkov says, the Soviet censor expunged these biographical details when the book was published in 1971.[4]

According to Volkov, this act of censorship provided the "final powerful impetus" for the creation of *Testimony*. The self-effacing and hesitant Shostakovich was transformed into an eager memoirist. " 'I must do this, I must,' [Shostakovich] would say. He wrote me, in one letter: 'You must continue what has been begun.' "[5]

At first, Volkov says, he and Shostakovich met at a retreat belonging to the Union of Composers in Repino, near Leningrad. Later, when Volkov became a senior editor at *Sovetskaia muzyka*, the official journal of the Union of Composers, Shostakovich invited Volkov to his Moscow apartment, which happened to be in the same building as Volkov's office. They did not use a tape recorder, since Shostakovich would "stiffen before a microphone like a rabbit caught in a snake's gaze."[6] Volkov scribbled down the composer's words in his own shorthand.

As the "mound of shorthand notes" grew higher, Volkov says, he "divided up the collected material into sustained sections, combined as seemed appropriate; then I showed these sections to Shostakovich, who approved my work. . . . Gradually I shaped this great array of reminiscence into arbitrary parts and had them typed. Shostakovich read and signed each part."[7] This piecemeal method is reflected in the book's digressive, rambling style. But the composer apparently liked it, for he affixed his signature, along with the Russian word *chital* (read), on the first page of each of the manuscript's eight chapters. According to Volkov, the composer's only demand was that the book be published after his death.

Shortly after Shostakovich died, Volkov emigrated to the West. His precious manuscript had already been smuggled abroad. The original shorthand notes were left behind and have never been located.

Speaking from his New York home almost thirty years later, Solomon Volkov still considers the book a miracle. *Testimony* was "a product of this crazy era, with all the anxieties and all the imbalances that were typical of it," he reflects. "I was nervous because I was a young neophyte music journalist. Before me was a genius who was also under a lot of pressure, and this colored the whole situation irrevocably."*

Western critics greeted *Testimony* with enthusiasm, praising its depiction not just of Shostakovich and his music but also of cultural life in the Soviet Union generally. Harold C. Schonberg raved about it in the *New York Times Book Review*, calling it a "serious indictment of past and present Russia, as well as the recollections of a life apparently spent in fear and despair."[8] The London *Times*'s chief book critic, Michael Ratcliffe, called it the "book of the year."[9]

In the Soviet Union, however, the book was denounced as a fraud. Just two weeks after the book was published, the Moscow weekly *Literaturnaia gazeta* printed a letter signed by six Soviet composers—students and friends of Shostakovich—declaring *Testimony* a "pitiful fake."[10] When a *New York Times* reporter visited the composer's widow, Irina Antonovna, in her Moscow apartment, she claimed that Volkov had only met with her husband "three or maybe four times," clearly not enough to create a book-length manuscript.[11] But Westerners suspected that these public denunciations were coerced—an example of the double life Soviet citizens were compelled to live, and to which *Testimony*'s Shostakovich bore witness.

Westerners would soon have second thoughts, but the most vocal critics of Volkov today began as true believers. One of Volkov's earliest supporters was Richard Taruskin, then a young assistant professor of music at Columbia University. In 1976, after meeting Volkov and dis-

*Quotations marked with an asterisk came from interviews, conducted in late January and early February 2000, with Laurel Fay, Dmitri Feofanov, Allan Ho, Ann Kjellberg, Margarita Mazo, Irina Shostakovich, Richard Taruskin, and Solomon Volkov. My sincere gratitude to them all for agreeing to be interviewed for this essay.

cussing the memoirs, Taruskin wrote a glowing letter of reference to support Volkov's application for a research fellowship at Columbia's Russian Institute. It was a letter Taruskin would come to regret. Now at Berkeley, he insists that his letter proves that he approached *Testimony* with an open mind, eager to accept Volkov's word. "The idea that I was out to get Volkov from the start is simply a fabrication—one of his many fabrications. I was all on his side."*

Laurel Fay was a graduate student in musicology at Cornell University when she heard rumors of *Testimony*'s impending publication. In April 1978, while finishing a dissertation on Shostakovich's late string quartets, Fay eagerly wrote to ask if she could be of any assistance to Volkov. "I understand that you have unique material concerning Shostakovich," she wrote. "Is it possible that you have an autobiography?"

The letter was "very naïve," she now admits, "but it was clear to me that I approached the book with great excitement and enthusiasm, and with *no* idea that it might not be authentic." Shortly after she began reading *Testimony*, her attitude changed. "Something just didn't feel right," she says. "It was all just a little too convenient, both in terms of the explanation of the genesis and the background and then in the actual text itself." The tone also puzzled her. *Testimony* is filled with biting sarcasm, bitter recrimination, and gossipy asides. Apart from a warm tribute to his mentor, Alexander Glazunov, Shostakovich says nothing about his life's happy moments and expresses little gratitude. And why would Shostakovich, a devoted father and husband, recklessly endanger his family by agreeing to publish such a frontal attack on the Soviet system?

But there was something even more troubling. "I began to realize that I'd read some of this material before," Fay says, although at first she could not identify where. The breakthrough came in November 1979, when Simon Karlinsky published a review of *Testimony* in *The Nation.*[12] Karlinsky noted that two substantial passages in *Testimony*—a book said to derive entirely from interviews with the composer—had already appeared in print under Shostakovich's name in Soviet publications. "Then it all began to click for me," Fay says, "and it didn't take me very long then to find another five passages."* She presented her findings in April 1980 at a meeting of the Midwest chapter of the American Musicological Society. Indiana University musicologist Malcolm Hamrick Brown invited her to publish her research in *Russian Review*, an academic journal published by Stanford University's conservative Hoover Institute.

The article, titled "Shostakovich versus Volkov: Whose *Testimony*?"[13]

appeared to deliver a shattering blow to Volkov's credibility. For example, one passage in *Testimony*, the composer's reflections on Stravinsky, reproduced an earlier text verbatim. Paragraph breaks, parentheses, dashes, and quotation marks remained in their original positions—details that even the most repetitive speaker and scrupulous note taker would be unlikely to reproduce. Other passages paraphrased the material they reproduced, but the borrowing was no less egregious: Shostakovich's reflections in *Testimony* on the Russian theater director Vsevolod Meyerhold apparently derived from an article Shostakovich published in *Sovetskaia muzyka* while Volkov had worked there as a senior editor. And as Fay has recently pointed out, the introduction to the original *Sovetskaia muzyka* article was attributed to none other than "S. Volkov."

Incredibly, Volkov claims never to have heard of the original sources of any of the material reproduced in *Testimony*. "No, no," he insists over the phone, "if I did I wouldn't have included it, of course." Asked about Shostakovich's *Sovetskaia muzyka* article about Meyerhold, for which Volkov apparently wrote an introduction, Volkov responds: "I can assure you that there wasn't a single staffer who would read the current issue of the magazine in its entirety. Material dealing with Shostakovich was appearing in almost every issue."*

Adding to the mystery, all the borrowed passages in *Testimony* appear on the first manuscript page of a chapter—on the only pages that Shostakovich actually signed. (The manuscript pages in question were reproduced in the German and Finnish editions of *Testimony*.)[a] In other words, Shostakovich's authentications appear where no authentication was necessary. After the page is turned, the text begins to diverge, sometimes dramatically, from its original source. A striking example occurs in chapter 5, during Shostakovich's discussion of his Seventh Symphony. "I wrote my Seventh Symphony, the 'Leningrad,' very quickly," *Testimony*'s Shostakovich says at the chapter's start, quoting a previously published article. "I couldn't not write it. War was all around. I had to be with the people, I wanted to create the image of our country at war, capture it in music. . . . I wanted to write about our time, about my contemporaries who spared neither strength nor life in the name of Victory Over the Enemy."[14]

On the next page, however, the composer says something radically different: "The Seventh Symphony had been planned before the war and consequently it simply cannot be seen as a reaction to Hitler's attack. The 'invasion theme' has nothing to do with the attack. I was thinking of other enemies of humanity when I composed the theme." As Fay asked in her article, "Is it possible that Volkov misrepresented the nature and contents of the book to Shostakovich just as he may be misrepresenting them to the reader?"[15] Volkov did not reply to an invitation by the editors of *Russian Review* to respond to Fay's questions, and he has tightly controlled access to the manuscript. According to Volkov, it is now in the hands of a private collector.

Although many academics considered *Testimony* discredited, it continued to be a much-cited source throughout the 1980s. Despite its dubious origins, it provided an alternative to the Soviet-sanctioned image of Shostakovich as a "loyal son of the Communist Party." Some of the revelations in the book had been whispered about in the Soviet Union for years: The Fifth Symphony's radiant finale was "forced rejoicing"; the marching and gunshots in the Eleventh Symphony ("The Year 1905") alluded to the Soviet suppression of Hungary in 1956.

Whether or not *Testimony* was the authentic voice of Shostakovich, it seemed true to a widely shared understanding of him. After Maxim Shostakovich, the composer's son and a world-renowned conductor, defected in 1981, he was reluctant to disavow *Testimony*, because of his hatred for the greater distortions imposed on his father's memory by official Soviet biographers such as Sofia Khentova. "I hate, I *khhhate* her book," he told David Fanning in a May 1991 *Gramophone* interview. "She makes him look like a genuine son of the Communist Party."[16]

It became common for writers to acknowledge the inauthenticity of *Testimony*, while vouching for its basic message. For instance, in *The New Shostakovich*, Ian MacDonald, a British journalist, stated outright that Volkov's book was a "dishonest presentation."[17] But MacDonald then offered evidence of political dissidence in Shostakovich's music. An example of MacDonald's style is his description of the Fourth Symphony, which the Party pressured Shostakovich into withdrawing: "A little strutting promenade for bassoons and giggling piccolo leads us into the hall where thrumming harps call the [Party] conference to order. A wan waltz (the composer?) enters and sits dejectedly while flute and piccolo trill the opening remarks in a mood of schoolboy hilarity."[18]

There is little doubt that Shostakovich *could* express dissidence in music. Perhaps the most poignant example is his Eighth String Quartet (1960). Dedicated to the "victims of fascism and war," it opens with and obsessively quotes the composer's musical signature, the four-note sequence D, E-flat, C, and B. (In German musical notation, the names of these notes are D, S, C, and H, which spell out "D. Sch.," the Germanized form of Shostakovich's initials.) Snatches of earlier works by Shostakovich also appear, including his banned opera, *Lady Macbeth of Mtsensk*, and the revolutionary song "Tormented by Grievous Bondage" (one of Lenin's favorites). Shostakovich was telling his listeners, as clearly as he could, that he was fascism's victim, too.

But none of the composer's other published works expressed political ideas so literally, and Shostakovich seems to have resented such easy paraphrase. In the *Slavic Review* in 1993 Taruskin upbraided MacDonald with a 1933 quote from Shostakovich himself: "When a critic . . . writes that in such-and-such a symphony Soviet civil servants are represented by the oboe and the clarinet, and Red Army men by the brass section, you want to scream!"[19]

Is it possible that Shostakovich had intended to embed protest in his music? "Whoever said it was impossible?" says Taruskin. "The only people who ever said it was impossible were Soviet officials, upholding the notion that Shostakovich was a 'loyal son of the Communist Party.' "* (When Taruskin himself resurrected that shopworn Soviet expression in a now notorious 1989 article for the *New Republic*,[20] he assumed that readers would understand it as a reference to Shostakovich's *official* reputation.) But the problem, he continues, is that there is no way of telling just by listening to the music. "A loud noise from an orchestra is just a loud noise from an orchestra," says Taruskin. "It doesn't inherently mean one thing or another. So those who want to hear the Eleventh Symphony as a protest against the Soviet invasion of Hungary will hear it explicitly and unequivocally. Those who want to hear it as what its official program says it was—a memorial to the martyrs of the 1905 Revolution—will hear it just as explicitly and just as concretely."*

A similar ambiguity continues to surround Shostakovich's character. In 1994 the British writer and cellist Elizabeth Wilson published *Shostakovich: A Life Remembered*, a collection of oral and written reminiscences by the composer's friends and colleagues. It is a largely sympathetic portrait of a man tormented by the demands of his political masters. Veniamin Basner, a close friend, argues that we should "discount the articles and statements that Dmitri Dmitrievich [*sic*] 'signed'; we knew that they were meaningless acts to him, but served him as a public shield. His many courageous actions were taken in private."[21] Galina Vishnevskaya, the great Russian soprano and the wife of cellist Mstislav Rostropovich, echoes this justification, and adds that Shostakovich "didn't worry about what people would say of him, because he knew the time would come when the verbiage would fade away, when only his music would remain."[22]

But is it really possible to declare the realm of public behavior—even in a Soviet context—inauthentic and trivial, thus absolving it from moral scrutiny? In fact, one might argue that it is precisely in the *public* realm where true dissidence is shown. This, at any rate, might explain the few notes of criticism that appear among the contributors to Wilson's book. Some felt that Shostakovich crossed the line when his name appeared on a letter denouncing Andrei Sakharov in 1973. Not having the courage to express open disapproval of Soviet power was one thing, but denouncing others who dared to dissent was another altogether.[23] "I felt that he had every right to refuse to write or sign such a letter," the composer Edison Denisov told Wilson; "in fact, he was duty bound *not* to do so. Why he did so is incomprehensible to me."[24] After learning of Sakharov's denunciation, the theater director Yuri Lyubimov refused to shake the elderly Shostakovich's outstretched hand after a concert at the Union of Composers.[25]

By the mid-1990s Volkov's *Testimony* appeared to be destined for oblivion. Shostakovich, it seemed, had not dictated his memoirs, nor had he been much of a dissident. But in 1998 Allan Ho, a professor of musicology at Southern Illinois University, Edwardsville, and Dmitri Feofanov, a pianist and practicing lawyer, published a book whose dedication was a call to arms: "To Solomon Moiseyevich Volkov," it read. Ho and Feofanov's *Shostakovich Reconsidered*[26] brought the controversy over Shostakovich's memoirs back to life.

Ho and Feofanov met at the University of Kentucky in the 1980s. Ho was completing a dissertation on the piano concerto as a genre, and Feofanov was teaching. Their first collaboration was a reference work, *Biographical Dictionary of Russian/Soviet Composers* (Westport, Conn.: Greenwood, 1989). They asked Volkov, then at work on a book of conversations with the choreographer George Balanchine, to write the entry on Shostakovich.

In the early 1990s, when they first began work on *Shostakovich Reconsidered*, Feofanov and Ho again approached Volkov, inviting him to contribute a thirty-page defense of *Testimony*. Volkov declined. "He was not the right person to do it," says Ho, "because people wouldn't believe what he said."*

And so, for the next six years, Ho became the principal researcher and writer for the most controversial part of the book. Ho admits that he has a "terrible time in Russian" and relies on translated material. This has presented some obvious problems. When I spoke to Ho in February 2000, I asked him about an eight-month-old *Izvestiia* letter that challenged a key claim made in his book.[27] Ho had never heard of it. Feofanov apologized on his behalf: "I've been very negligent," he told me. "I haven't translated that stuff for him yet."* But for *Shostakovich Reconsidered*, Ho was forced to rely on his colleague and a team of translators to help research his three-hundred-page "case for the defence."[28]

Ho's article constitutes more than a third of *Shostakovich Reconsidered* and is devoted entirely to refuting Laurel Fay's ten-page article written two decades earlier. The structure of the book parallels that of a trial, and its conclusions are harsh: It convicts Fay and her supporters of "subjective and selective editing of the facts," "inept scholarship," "historical ignorance," and a lack of scholarly integrity. It alleges that Fay has "difficulty reading plain English."[29] Volkov adds a few insults himself. One of the epigraphs to the book includes this quote by Volkov: "Only stupid people couldn't understand [the true meaning of Shostakovich's music.] But there are still a lot of these stupid people around."[30]

In conversation, Ho and Feofanov insist that their book and their argument have not been given proper respect. Both commented bitterly to me that Oxford University Press, which published Laurel Fay's recent *Shostakovich: A Life* (1999), turned down their own manuscript. They are eager to set the record straight. Just hours after I contacted Toccata Press, asking for a review copy of *Shostakovich Reconsidered*, both authors sent e-mail messages announcing their eagerness to talk to me. By the end of the day I had received three messages from Feofanov alone, the last one referring to Taruskin as "Richard the Third . . . or Little Richard . . . depending on one's perspective."[31]

The new evidence uncovered by Ho and Feofanov tends to corroborate the general picture of Shostakovich presented in *Testimony*. Like most Soviet citizens, Shostakovich hid a complex private life behind a mask of Communist loyalty. The composer loved, for instance, to mock the stilted and formalistic language of Soviet bureaucratese in his letters to friends. Other evidence seems to buttress *Testimony*'s claim to authenticity. Ho, Feofanov, and a research assistant in Moscow have collected written and oral statements by several of Volkov's former colleagues who say that they knew of Volkov's Shostakovich project at the time.

Then there is the piece of evidence that Ho calls a "smoking gun." In 1996 Shostakovich's friend Flora Litvinova reported that the composer had once told her he had been meeting "constantly" with an unnamed young Leningrad musicologist who had "dug everything up, even my youthful compositions. . . . I tell him everything I remember about my works and myself. He writes it down, and at a subsequent meeting I look it over."[32] Unfortunately Litvinova states that her final conversation with Shostakovich took place in 1970 or 1971—that is, *before* Volkov claims to have begun meeting with Shostakovich for *Testimony*. It is more likely that Shostakovich was speaking about the autobiographical preface for Volkov's first book.[33]

Responding to Fay's observation that *Testimony* reproduced passages previously published elsewhere, Ho argues that Shostakovich's prodigious memory allowed him to quote himself at length. He points out that Shostakovich often repeated certain stock phrases verbatim. (For instance: "That Sonata of yours is an interesting, good music. I liked it, I would say, a lot.") He also notes that the composer often retold the same stories, though not verbatim. But could an aural memory reproduce texts so exactly and at such length, punctuation and all? Even Ho recognizes the difficulty: "I think I'll always have some doubt," he reflects, "because these recyclings are hard to explain with 100 percent certainty."*

In the case of Dmitri Shostakovich, musicologists have not always debated in a cool, scholarly tone. In fact, both sides have been insulting. Malcolm Hamrick Brown, the Indiana musicologist who encouraged Fay's research back in 1980, has written that he believes Volkov "lied about how he put *Testimony* together."[34] Though she now regrets it, Fay, at an American Musicological Society meeting, referred to MacDonald's book as a "moronic tract." Taruskin, as any reader of the *New York Times* or the *New Republic* knows, is a polemical writer and has compared his opponents to both Stalinists and McCarthyites—sometimes on the same page.

But Ho, Feofanov, and their supporters may be winning this race to the bottom. Insults and invective are scattered on virtually every page of the opening essay of *Shostakovich Reconsidered.* In a fifty-thousand-word review posted on Ho's website, Ian MacDonald has dismissed Fay's recent biography of Shostakovich as a "dismal, devious, and at times dishonest book,"[35] since he believes she methodically erases evidence of the composer's political dissidence. MacDonald even claims to discern in the book "telltale signs of a pro-communist attitude."[36] One of Volkov's supporters has gone even further, hinting that Fay was knowingly accepting information from the KGB.[37]

Feofanov charges that Fay and her supporters are "blatantly lying, and I wonder whether they're just too stupid to know the difference, or whether there is some sort of agenda. I can't imagine that they're that stupid." What sort of agenda? "I hate to sound like one of those Mc-

Carthyites," says Feofanov, referring to Taruskin's accusations against him, "but they were kind of pro-Soviet, and they were caught being professionally incompetent, and now they're really pissed."* In January 2000 the British journalist Norman Lebrecht reached an impressive new low when he compared Laurel Fay to a Holocaust revisionist in the *Daily Telegraph*.[38] When I mention Lebrecht's charge to Ho, he chuckles, then suggests that it was tit for tat: "This name-calling has been going on for some twenty years, coming from them against us."*

In Fay's case, that may be unfair. She rarely mentions her opponents in print. Her 1980 *Russian Review* article raised its questions about *Testimony* in a measured tone. In fact, it is her equanimity that gets on her critics' nerves.

In *Shostakovich: A Life* (New York: Oxford University Press, 2000), Fay coolly presents verifiable details about her subject in a manner that downplays his engagement with politics. Her Shostakovich is a man nearly broken by the political demands imposed on him, but he does not assume the heroic proportions of a Solzhenitsyn. Fay refuses to portray his compromises with authority as secret attempts at political subversion. Her approach has provoked critic Joseph Horowitz to pronounce the book "inordinately dry-eyed."[39]

For example, Fay's opponents have characterized Shostakovich's 1948 song cycle, *Iz evreiskoi narodnoi poezii* [From Jewish folk poetry], as a valiant attempt to denounce the Soviet government's increasingly murderous sponsorship of anti-Semitism. Fay, however, sees it as the composer's good-faith attempt to abide by his pledge to the Composers Congress to write melodies "infused with the essence of folklore." As Fay wrote in the *New York Times* in April 1996, "It was his rotten luck that of all the available nationalities, great and small, he just happened to pick the wrong 'folk' as his inspiration."[40]

Like Fay, many Russians who knew the composer have been doubtful of *Testimony*'s authenticity. Of Shostakovich's close friends and family, his daughter, Galina, has offered the most convincing endorsement. "I am an admirer of Volkov," she told Ho and Feofanov. "There is nothing false in [*Testimony*]. . . . It represents, fairly and accurately, Shostakovich's political views, although there is too much 'kitchen talk' and anecdotes."[41]

Her brother, Maxim, has been far more cautious. Shortly after his 1981 defection he told the London *Sunday Times* that *Testimony* was "not my father's memoirs. It is a book by Solomon Wolkow [*sic*]."[42] He continues to stand by this claim, referring repeatedly to *Testimony* as a book "about my father." As recently as 1998, he told the *Los Angeles Times* that although he liked *Testimony*, "There are a lot of rumors in it, and like all rumors, some are true and some aren't." He singled out *Testimony*'s claim about the scherzo in the Tenth Symphony as an example: "Father never said it was a portrait of Stalin."[43]

Many others have also refused to vouch for *Testimony*, among them Mstislav Rostropovich, Galina Vishnevskaya, Manashir Yakubov (the curator of the Shostakovich Family Archive), and the composer Boris Tishchenko. Tishchenko, who was Shostakovich's most prized pupil, helped to arrange Volkov's interviews with the composer and attended at least one of them. Volkov thanked him in *Testimony* as "my distant friend who must remain nameless." Yet in his recently published correspondence with Shostakovich, Tishchenko condemns *Testimony* as "not the memoirs of Shostakovich, not even a book by Volkov about Shostakovich, but a book by Volkov about Volkov."[44]

Tishchenko was one of the six Soviet composers who denounced *Testimony* in *Literaturnaia gazeta* in 1979, in the letter that most Western observers then believed to have been coerced.[45] Apparently it wasn't. In June 1999 the daughter of another signatory wrote to *Izvestiia* that her father had been familiar with *Testimony* and had firmly believed it was a fake.[46] Ho and Feofanov claim that yet another signatory, the Azerbaijani composer Kara Karaev, had been "undergoing treatment for a heart condition, [and] had been ordered to sign or be kicked out of the hospital."[47] Yet Karaev's son, Faradzh, has emphatically denied this account to Laurel Fay.[48]

Shostakovich's widow, Irina Antonovna, also remains a skeptic. Reached at her Moscow apartment, Irina stands by the story she told more than twenty years ago. "Dmitrich wanted to write his memoirs himself," she says, "but this had nothing to do with Solomon Volkov." Volkov met with her husband three times, she said, and the meetings lasted between ninety minutes and two hours. Since Shostakovich was ill and Irina was acting as his personal secretary and often his nurse, she rarely left him alone. The interviews were supposed to be published in *Sovetskaia muzyka*. "The rest," she insists, "came from Volkov himself."*

Asked about the Russians whose memories contradict Volkov, Feofanov openly ridicules the individuals in question. He says that Irina Antonovna and Boris Tishchenko "don't know what they're talking about." Irina's published interviews, Feofanov says, suggest that she is "primarily concerned about money, so maybe not getting money has something to do with it." About Maxim's guarded comments, Feofanov asked, "Does Maxim read English enough to read the book? I don't think so. I've heard him speak—by the end of his time in the United States he spoke very broken English with very limited vocabulary.[49] I doubt very much that he read [*Testimony*] from cover to cover. I doubt very much that he read *our* book, although I sent it to him and I spoke to him about it. I sent it to him with a kind of in-your-face letter trying to provoke him to respond, because he was always so equivocal about the whole issue." And Rostropovich? "With all due respect to Slava," says Feofanov, "I happen to know that his English is not so hot either."* Competence in English is an issue, because *Testimony* has never been published in Russian.[50]

Shostakovich's widow raises an entirely different concern about Volkov's method. "So many of his books have been published after the deaths of those about whom he is writing," she says. "After the death of Brodsky, after the death of Balanchine, after the death of Mitya—it's a very strange thing. . . . And the dead are unable to respond."[51]

Indeed, Volkov has made a career for himself as amanuensis to Russia's dying cultural elite. He has published books of conversations with Balanchine (*Balanchine's Tchaikovsky* [New York: Simon & Schuster, 1985]), the violinist Nathan Milstein (*From Russia to the West* [New York: H. Holt, 1990]), and the poet Joseph Brodsky (*Conversations with Joseph Brodsky* [New York: Free Press, 1998]).[52] His study, *St. Petersburg: A Cultural History* (New York: Free Press, 1995), relies heavily on these collaborations. Volkov's current project is a book of interviews with the renowned Russian pianist Vladimir Horowitz, who died more than ten years ago. Volkov is likable and well read, and he seems to have an extraordinary ability to win the confidence of interviewees. He attributes this to a "device" he has perfected over the years. If you want "to do a book with a star," Volkov said in 1992, then "tell him to start remembering about his friends. Then inevitably he will tell something about himself as well."[53]

Volkov has admitted that collaboration is not without its tensions. As he wrote in the Russian weekly *Ogonyok* in 1991, "Sometimes something unpleasant happens, cruel failures and wounds. The 'stars' make a fuss and torture you."[54] But Volkov believes he has learned a great deal since his book on Shostakovich. "If I'd known that [*Testimony*] would be such a controversial book for which accounting of day-to-day activities and material would be needed, maybe I would at least have tried to preserve all this material," he said at a press conference in New York City in February 1999. "It was my first big project in this genre. If I'd been wiser by twenty-five-plus years, then probably I would have handled it better.

My book of conversations with Joseph Brodsky—my personal belief is that it's structured better than *Testimony*."[55]

But structure was never the issue with *Testimony*. Authenticity was. And as Irina Antonovna Shostakovich points out, there are unsettling parallels between *Testimony* and *Conversations with Joseph Brodsky*. During the late 1970s and early 1980s Volkov interviewed the Russian poet on several occasions, and Volkov's accounts of the interviews appeared in the émigré Russian press in Paris and New York. As Volkov himself admitted, the texts he published were the result of "long and careful 'montage' and editing."[56] Friends and family claim that Brodsky complained to them about the finished product. When Volkov approached a Russian-language publisher in New Jersey in 1987 about printing his interviews as a book, Brodsky wrote to the publisher about what he called "Volkov's little interviews [*interv'iushek*]." Brodsky insisted that he "look them through before they're printed. THERE IS A MASS of purely stylistic RUBBISH."[57] The deal fell through.

Volkov never showed Brodsky a manuscript of his book. The poet died in January 1996. But just a year later, a Free Press catalog for autumn 1997 announced the impending publication of *Conversations with Joseph Brodsky*, almost half of which consisted of previously unpublished material. In an advance version of the book sent to magazine and newspaper editors in July 1997, Volkov's preface referred to Brodsky as one of his many "collaborators" on book projects. (The word *collaborators* was replaced by *interview subjects* in the published preface, after complaints from Brodsky's literary executor, Ann Kjellberg.) "A completed book project," Volkov wrote, "is sustained by the belief of both parties involved that this particular arrangement is vital."[58] Vital to Volkov, certainly: He is the sole owner of copyright for both *Testimony* and *Conversations with Joseph Brodsky*, and he has never consulted with or offered any compensation to either the composer's or the poet's heirs.

Like the Shostakovich shorthand notes, the tapes of Volkov's conversations with Brodsky remain unavailable. (He plans to donate them to the Anna Akhmatova Museum in St. Petersburg sometime in the future.) Meanwhile Dmitri Feofanov, now acting as Volkov's lawyer, has issued Kjellberg a cease-and-desist order and has threatened to sue her for defamation if she persists in objecting to the book as having been unauthorized by Brodsky.

What is *Testimony*? It is a book based in part on personal interviews with the composer; it is a vivid portrait of a brilliant composer living in difficult times; and it is a collection of rumors and anecdotes, many of which were such common currency in the Soviet Union of the 1970s that Fay and Taruskin heard them when they visited as exchange students. But can it be considered the authentic "memoirs of Dmitri Shostakovich"?

The defenders of *Testimony* commonly portray the dispute as a final skirmish in the Cold War, a last desperate stand by Soviet apologists. "It's a matter of common knowledge," observes Feofanov, "that the last refuge of true Marxists is American academia." Somewhat dramatically, he also declares that the dispute is a "struggle for Shostakovich's soul."*

In fact, the dispute is about a way of listening to Shostakovich's music, and to music in general—a way that *Testimony* encouraged. The book's defenders become most enthusiastic when they discuss music in which they discern a dissident "message in a bottle": the Eighth Quartet, the Tenth and Eleventh Symphonies, and the *Antiformalist Peepshow* [*Antiformalisticheskii rayok*], Shostakovich's vicious (and unpublished) caricature of his Stalinist persecutors, apparently written in the 1950s and 1960s. Feofanov has recently become intrigued by the possibility that the Twelfth Symphony "encoded" Stalin's initials.

But can anything be more impoverishing of music than a search for literal paraphrase? Once, after an evening spent performing his Seventh Symphony on the piano for friends, all of whom understood it to be "about" fascism and the war with Germany, Shostakovich confided to Flora Litvinova: "Of course—fascism. But music, real music, can never be literally tied to a theme. National Socialism is not the only form of fascism; this music is about all forms of terror, slavery, the bondage of the spirit."[59] Ironically Ho and Feofanov have seized on Litvinova's recollection as evidence that the "invasion theme" of the Seventh Symphony "depicts Stalin and his henchmen."[60]

Richard Taruskin is intrigued by how Shostakovich's music has come to embody so many different meanings to so many different people. Ho and Feofanov "need the security of saying that the dissidence that many hear in Shostakovich's music was the composer's intention. I'm more interested in the question of interpretation, and the way interpretation is socially negotiated." The transformation of Shostakovich from loyal Communist to dissident is "the next chapter in this ongoing saga, and a wonderful object lesson in the way meaning is created."*

Others are less philosophical. Although deeply skeptical of *Testimony*, Margarita Mazo, a Russian émigré now teaching at Ohio State University's School of Music, finds the dispute over its authenticity unseemly. "For many of us [in the Soviet Union] listening to a new piece by Shostakovich was a sacred experience," she says, her voice breaking. "Was he a dissident or was he not? Was he a Communist or was he not? He was so much more complex than that." She pauses, and then adds, "Besides, can you tell music with words? Can you say with words what this music is about? If so, then why do you need music?"*

Notes

An earlier version of this article was published in *Lingua franca* 10, no. 4 (May/June 2000): 46–54.

1. *Pravda*, 12 August 1975, p. 3.

2. *The Times* (London), 11 August 1975, p. 12.

3. Solomon Volkov, *Testimony: The Memoirs of Dmitri Shostakovich*, as related to and edited by Solomon Volkov, trans. Antonina W. Bouis (New York: Harper & Row, 1979), p. 155.

4. Volkov, *Testimony*, p. xv.

5. Ibid.

6. Ibid., p. xvi.

7. Ibid., pp. xvi–xvii.

8. Harold C. Schonberg, "Words and Music under Stalin," *New York Times Book Review*, 21 October 1979, pp. 1, 46–47.

9. *The Times* (London), 24 November 1979, Section 2, p. 1.

10. "Zhalkaia poddelka" [A pitiful fake], *Literaturnaia gazeta*, no. 46 (14 November 1979): 8; an English translation is printed in the present volume (selection 4).

11. Craig R. Whitney, "Shostakovich Memoir a Shock to Kin," *New York Times*, 13 November 1979, p. C7.

12. Simon Karlinsky, "Our Destinies Are Bad," *The Nation*, 24 November 1979, pp. 533–36.

13. Laurel E. Fay, "Shostakovich versus Volkov: Whose *Testimony*?" *Russian Review* 39 (July 1980): 484–93. Reprinted in this volume (article 1).

14. Volkov, *Testimony*, pp. 154–55.

15. Fay, "Shostakovich versus Volkov," p. 493.

16. David Fanning, "Always a Great Composer, Not a Papa," *Gramophone*, May 1991, p. 1992.

17. Ian MacDonald, *The New Shostakovich* (Boston: Northeastern University Press, 1990), p. 245.

18. MacDonald, *The New Shostakovich*, p. 115. See also Malcolm Hamrick Brown's review of 1993 in *Notes of the Music Library Association* 49, no. 3 (March 1993): 957; reprinted here, chapter 18.

19. *Slavic Review* 52 (summer 1993): 396.

20. Richard Taruskin, "The Opera and the Dictator," *New Republic*, 20 March 1989, pp. 34–40.

21. Elizabeth Wilson, *Shostakovich: A Life Remembered* (Princeton, N.J.: Princeton University Press, 1994), p. 123.

22. Wilson, *Shostakovich: A Life Remembered*, p. 430.

23. Solzhenitsyn never bothered to ask for Shostakovich's signature on a pe-

tition denouncing the 1968 Warsaw Pact invasion of Czechoslovakia, since he knew that the composer, along with other prominent intellectuals, would not have the courage to sign such an incriminating document. "They wouldn't sign," Solzhenitsyn later wrote. "Their upbringing and their outlook were all wrong. The shackled genius Shostakovich would thrash about like a wounded thing, clasp himself with tightly folded arms so that his fingers could not hold a pen" (Alexander Solzhenitsyn, *The Oak and the Calf: Sketches of Literary Life in the Soviet Union* [*Bodalsia telenok s dubom*], trans. Harry Willetts [New York: Harper & Row, 1980], p. 221).

24. Wilson, *Shostakovich: A Life Remembered*, p. 432.

25. Ibid., p. 433. This version of the incident is related by Edison Denisov. Lyubimov himself describes a somewhat milder version of the same story in ibid., p. 435. But see Irina Shostakovich, selection 9, this volume, pp. 132–33.

26. Allan B. Ho and Dmitri Feofanov, *Shostakovich Reconsidered* (London: Toccata, 1998).

27. Republished in the present volume as "The Regime and Vulgarity," by Elena Basner, daughter of composer Veniamin Basner (chapter 11).

28. See note 33, below, for an example of Feofanov's translation.

29. Ho and Feofanov, *Shostakovich Reconsidered*, p. 287 n. 288, p. 16 n. 81.

30. Ibid., pp. 33, 390.

31. E-mail to author, 19 January 2000.

32. Litvinovna's recollections were published in Russian in their entirety as "Vspominaia Shostakovicha" [Remembering Shostakovich], *Znamia*, no. 12 (December 1996): 156–77. An edited version of the recollections, omitting the contentious passage, was published in English in Wilson's *Shostakovich: A Life Remembered*.

33. In the article "Volkov's *Testimony* Reconsidered," published in the present volume, Fay has outlined some of the problems Litvinova's account raised (chapter 2).

There are other problems as well. Litvinova wrote that her "last conversation (*razgovor*) with Dmitri Dmitrievich took place at the House of Creativity in Ruza in 1970 or 1971. He had returned from having treatment at Dr. Ilizarov's clinic [in Kurgan]." (Her final talk with the composer does not appear to have been the "smoking gun" conversation, which must have taken place even earlier.) But Volkov himself claims to have begun meeting with Shostakovich for *Testimony* only in 1971, assisted by his friend Boris Tishchenko. Tishchenko confirms that this meeting took place in July 1971—sometime after, that is, Flora Litvinova's "last conversation" with Shostakovich, and even long after the "smoking gun" conversation.

Moreover, Volkov's account of *Testimony*'s genesis involves a "mound of shorthand notes . . . growing," with Volkov "read[ing] them over and over," then "dividing up the collected material into sustained sections." Finally, Volkov claims, Shostakovich would look over these sections and give his approval. (This should not be confused with the composer's signature on the typescript, which were allegedly inscribed much later.) The process of creating these "sustained sections" must have taken many months. Yet in Litvinova's account, Shostakovich is already looking over the material that the unnamed "young Leningrad musicologist" had given him.

So what could Shostakovich have been talking about in his conversation with his old friend Flora Litvinova? Based on the likely timing of this conversation—the late 1960s—I speculate that it could have had to do with the preface Shostakovich wrote for Volkov's first book, *Molodye kompozitory Leningrada* [Young Leningrad composers] (Leningrad: Sovetskii kompozitor, 1971). Volkov himself claims that the original preface was autobiographical in nature and based heavily on the composer's recollections of his youth. Litvinova has Shostakovich referring to his "youthful compositions" (*detskie sochinenie*) in his conversations with the unnamed musicologist.

My theory is not airtight. Shostakovich allegedly told Litvinova that they met "constantly" and talked about "everything" (Volkov told me he could not remember how many times he met with Shostakovich while preparing the preface to *Young Leningrad Composers*). But it seems to me a more convincing explanation of Litvinova's account than the alternatives.

Dmitri Feofanov's letter to the editor of *Lingua Franca* disputes my interpretation (see *Lingua Franca* 10, no. 8 [November 2000]: 7, 64):

> In discussing *Shostakovich Reconsidered*, the book I coedited with Allan Ho [Feofanov wrote], Paul Mitchinson delivers what he thinks is a coup de grâce to our "smoking gun" piece of evidence, the statement of Flora Litvinova. In it, she recounts meeting Shostakovich who told her of his meetings with "a young Leningrad musicologist" (Volkov), to whom he tells "everything" he remembers about his life and works. Seems like a firsthand corroboration of the genesis of *Testimony*, which was related to and edited by Solomon Volkov.
>
> "Not so," says Mitchinson. "Litvinova was referring to another collaborative work—a preface Volkov wrote to a book about Leningrad composers, and, besides, she met with Shostakovich much earlier, in 1971, before the work on *Testimony* had begun."
>
> I called Flora Pavlovna Litvinova and asked her whether her statement referred to a conversation with Shostakovich before work on *Testimony* had begun (1971) or after, because her earlier statement that her last "meeting" with the composer was in 1971. Her answer—"I ran into Shostakovich here and there until his death. The conversation in question could have taken place in 1972, or 1973, or 1974." Question: "Do you think Shostakovich was referring to *Testimony* or some other work he did with Volkov?" Answer: "I understood it to be referring to *Testimony*."

Feofanov's letter should be treated with some caution. He has invented a quotation he attributes to me. He has misquoted Flora Litvinova's published account. (She wrote that her last "conversation" [*razgovor*] with Shostakovich was in 1970 or 1971—*not* her last "meeting.") He has falsely suggested that Shostakovich identified the "young Leningrad musicologist" as Volkov. (Litvinova explicitly wrote that Shostakovich "did not tell me his name.") Finally—and rather embarrassingly, given the nature of the controversy—he has attributed the preface of *Young Leningrad Composers* to Volkov rather than to Shostakovich. Nevertheless, there is still the possibility that he has accurately quoted and represented what Litvinova told him over the phone.

If, under Feofanov's cross-examination more than ten years after her initial statement, Flora Pavlovna now remembers additional "conversations" taking place between 1972 and 1974, then what we have is no longer a "smoking gun" but rather, like almost everything having to do with *Testimony*, conflicting and ambiguous "testimony." Lawyers traditionally place greater weight on a witness's earlier testimony, for good reason—witnesses often incorporate what they have heard or read much later into their earlier memories. A case in point: Litvinova allegedly told Feofanov, "I understood it [her conversation with Shostakovich] to be referring to *Testimony.*" This is unlikely, since *Testimony* was not published until 1979—many years after the conversation took place.

In January 2002 Allan Ho suggested on the DSCH-list that I should contact Litvinova to "cross-examine" her myself <http://listserv.uh.edu/cgi-bin/wa?A2=ind0201&L=dsch-l&P=R8146>. Given the vivid and precise character of her published testimony, I find it unnecessary to subject Flora Pavlovna, now eighty-one, to any further "cross-examination."

34. Malcolm Hamrick Brown, "*The New Shostakovich.* By Ian MacDonald," a review-article, *Notes of the Music Library Association* 49, no. 3 (March 1993): 957; reprinted here, chapter 18. See also *DSCH Journal*, no. 9 (summer 1998): 37.

35. <http://www.siue.edu/aho/musov/fay/fayrev6.html>, accessed 9 July 2003.

36. Ibid.

37. See comments by Maya Pritsker at <http://www.siue.edu/aho/musov/man/mannes1.html> (accessed 9 July 2003). Ho and Feofanov have made similar claims: "We trace the *Testimony* controversy to the KGB and query whether Volkov's most prominent critics feasted off the 'Soviet platter' " (*Shostakovich Reconsidered*, p. 17).

38. Norman Lebrecht, "Music Dissident Notes," *Daily Telegraph* [London], 19 January 2000, p. 25

39. "A Moral Beacon amid the Darkness of a Tragic Era," *New York Times*, 6 February 2000, Section 2, p. 1.

40. "The Composer Was Courageous, But Not as Much as in Myth," *New York Times*, 14 April 1996, Section 2, p. 27.

41. Ho and Feofanov, *Shostakovich Reconsidered*, p. 83.

42. Shostakovich: Why I Fled from Russia," interview with Norbert Kuchinke and Felix Schmidt, *Sunday Times* (London), 17 May 1981, p. 35.

43. Quoted by Chris Pasles, "Was He or Wasn't He?" *The Los Angeles Times/Calendar*, 29 November 1998, p. 74.

44. *Pis'ma Dmitria Dmitrievicha Shostakovicha Borisu Tishchenko; s kommentariiami i vospominaniiami adresata* [The letters of Dmitri Dmitrievich Shostakovich to Boris Tishchenko; with the addressee's commentary and reminiscences] (St. Petersburg: Kompozitor, 1997), p. 49.

45. A translation of the letter is included in the present volume. See "A Pitiful Fake: About the So-Called 'Memoirs' of D. D. Shostakovich" (chapter 4).

46. Basner, "The Regime and Vulgarity." See note 27 above.

47. Ho and Feofanov, *Shostakovich Reconsidered*, p. 64.

48. See Fay's "Volkov's *Testimony* Reconsidered," in the present volume, article 2.

49. Nevertheless, as Ho and Feofanov have been eager to point out, Maxim's English was good enough for him to read and publicly praise Ian MacDonald's *The New Shostakovich*. In fact, they argue that this should be considered a "solid

endorsement of the Shostakovich memoirs." See Ho and Feofanov, *Shostakovich Reconsidered*, p. 40.

50. Precisely why is a mystery. Both Volkov and a HarperCollins representative to whom I spoke suggest that market forces in Russia prevent publication of a book that would appeal only to a marginal readership. But in an interview published in *Literaturnaia gazeta* on 2 July 1997, Volkov gave quite a different justification: "I receive many proposals [for publication in Russian]," he told Lili Pann, "but they come from people who haven't heard a note of Shostakovich in their entire lives. In other words, they are primarily interested in political sensation. But I would like to find someone who understands the cultural significance of this book. In such a case, even financial arrangements are immaterial" (quoted by Lili Pann, "Muzyka prosvechivaet vsego cheloveka naskvoz" [Music illuminates the whole man through and through], a conversation with Solomon Volkov, *Literaturnaia gazeta*, 2 July 1997, p. 14). Apparently there is no publisher in today's Russia with sufficient cultural sensitivity to be entrusted with the task.

51. Since my telephone interview with Irina Shostakovich in February 2000 she has published her current perspective on Volkov in an article reprinted in the present volume: "An Answer to Those Who Still Abuse Shostakovich" (selection 9). The version of the article printed here first appeared in the *New York Times*, Sunday, 20 August 2000, pp. AR 27, 31.

52. Volkov objected strenuously to this characterization of his work in a letter to the editor of *Lingua Franca* 10, no. 5 (August 2000): 5.

He points out that not all his books were published after their subject's death—something I never asserted. He also suggests bizarrely that Brodsky "voiced no complaints" about his published interviews with Volkov, a suggestion disproved by the note Brodsky sent to his publisher, which I cite later. Brodsky, Volkov continues, "considered this endeavor my project, not his."

This last phrase is interesting. In my published response to his letter I wondered whether it might shed light on the nature of *Testimony*. "What is *Testimony*? Is it one of Volkov's 'collaborative books'? Is it 'my project, not his,' like *Conversations with Joseph Brodsky*? Or is it, as the dust jacket declares, the 'memoirs of Dmitri Shostakovich'?"

53. Ho and Feofanov, *Shostakovich Reconsidered*, pp. 392–93.

54. Solomon Volkov, "Priznanie pisatel'ia-prizraka" [The confession of a ghostwriter], *Ogonyok*, no. 7 (February 1991 [this is issue no. 7 of 1991, which happens to have been published in February]): 9.

55. A transcript of the remarks can be found at <http://www.siue.edu/aho/musov/man/mannes.html> (accessed 7 July 2003).

56. *Ogonyok*, no. 7 (February 1991): 9.

57. A note from Joseph Brodsky to Igor Yefimov, 1 November 1987. A copy is in the author's possession.

58. Solomon Volkov, *Conversations with Joseph Brodsky: A Poet's Journey through the Twentieth Century*, trans. Marian Schwartz (New York: Free Press, 1998), p. x.

59. Wilson, *Shostakovich: A Life Remembered*, pp. 158–59.

60. Ho and Feofanov, *Shostakovich Reconsidered*, p. 269.

Editor's Note

a. Mitchinson is mistaken here. The Shostakovich signatures that are said to appear on each of the pages of *Testimony* are indeed reproduced in the German and Finnish editions, but without actually showing the "manuscript pages in question," as Mitchinson writes. The individual signatures are extracted, presumably from the corresponding page of the manuscript—in reality, a typescript—and reproduced at the beginning of the printed German or Finnish text.

23

Shostakovich

A Brief Encounter and a Present Perspective (1996, 2002)

MALCOLM HAMRICK BROWN

When I was a student at the Moscow Conservatory in 1962, Shostakovich would occasionally walk past me in the hallway. He was never alone, as I remember, but always flanked by students who clustered around and moved alongside him like a phalanx through the corridors. Shostakovich hardly seemed conscious of where he was or where he was going, his familiar face tensed and concentrated. Still, whenever a passerby spoke to him, he would immediately stop and exchange a few polite formalities. "Maybe this is what I should do, since I want to meet him," I thought to myself. But how could I interrupt him?! After all, he was Shostakovich, and I was just an anomalous American exchange student.[1] So, I only nodded when he passed but hoped that, before the end of my residency in Moscow, I would have a chance to meet him.

I did. An invitation came to attend a buffet supper at the American Embassy on 2 April 1962. The event had been organized to celebrate the close of the Third All-Union Congress of Soviet Composers, which had convened in Moscow during the previous week, 26–31 March 1962. Samuel Barber and Franz Waxman would be honored guests, along with a small but high-powered delegation of Soviet composers.

Barber and Waxman had attended the Soviet Composers Congress at the special invitation of the Union of Composers. Waxman's scores for such films as *Sunset Boulevard* (1950) and *A Place in the Sun* (1951), both Academy Award winners, had attracted many admirers among Soviet musicians, who felt an affinity with his expressive and accessible romantic style, so close in spirit to the ideals of Soviet Socialist Realism.

A comparable affinity also very likely accounted for Barber's invitation to the Congress. His eloquent post-Straussian romanticism showed little evidence of the modernist experimentation anathematized by the Soviet musical establishment. Moreover, by 1962, Barber was numbered among the most distinguished American composers. He was then already at work on his Piano Concerto, commissioned for the inaugural week at New York's Philharmonic Hall (1962), and about to start on *Antony and Cleopatra*, commissioned for the opening of the new Metropolitan Opera House (1966).

The Soviet delegation at the embassy supper was headed by Shostakovich and Aram Khachaturian (with his wife, composer Nina Makarova), and also included Rodion Shchedrin and Andrei Eshpai—the latter two not so well known in the United States but big-time personalities in Soviet music.

Almost the moment I entered the room at the embassy where drinks and snacks were being served, I saw Shostakovich. He was leaning against the wall at the back of the room, puffing on a cigarette held close to his mouth in his right hand. His left arm was folded across his stomach, his left hand cupping his right elbow. He barely moved the cigarette from his lips as he smoked. The corners of his mouth were drawn down slightly, his features fixed in an expression familiar from many photographs. Other guests were milling around nearby, but Shostakovich appeared oblivious, staring blankly into space, unengaged and uninvolved.

Every detail of the image that takes shape now, in my memory, externalizes a classic posture of defensiveness, but it did not deter me at the time. This was the chance I had been hoping for. With no regard for the composer's apparent preference to be left alone, I hesitated only long enough to think about what to say, then walked toward him, my hand held out. Shostakovich started, fumbled with his cigarette, caught it with the fingers of his left hand, and extended a very limp right hand in my direction. I grasped his hand and started to pump it with gusto, American-style, not stopping to remember that Soviets customarily fulfill this formality with a single, quick, up-and-down movement. Shostakovich naturally shook hands in Soviet style, then abruptly withdrew his hand, leaving mine hanging in mid-air. It was my turn to be startled, and, as a consequence, I also stumbled over the conventional greeting I was trying so hard to pronounce correctly. Shostakovich answered in a mumble but nodded politely. And his face seemed to relax just the slightest bit. It was all the encouragement I needed.

I explained that I was an American graduate student based at the Conservatory and that I was in Moscow researching Prokofiev and his music in preparation for writing a Ph.D. dissertation. Shostakovich voiced a few decidedly conventional and essentially noncommittal remarks about Prokofiev, still speaking mostly in a mumble, which I had to strain to understand. I found myself replying in thoroughly stock phrases, in part because I had difficulty hearing him. After a few exchanges of this sort, Shostakovich fell silent, leaving the burden of conversation on me. My attempts to open the subject of his creative plans foundered altogether, whereupon I resorted to more clichés: "What a pleasure it has been to meet you, Dmitri Dmitr'ich. I never thought I'd actually speak with you in person." My platitudes evoked his nearly inaudible repetitions of, "Thank you, thank you. I'm much obliged, much obliged,"[2] his head bobbing all the while in little jerks, the motion begetting slight spasms that ran through his entire body.

I realize now that his twitching must have been a tic that betrayed his impatience with the brash American student who was trying so hard to get him to talk. Still, I continued to blather on for several more minutes, about how popular his music was in the States, how often it was played, and so on. But then private thoughts started to dissent from my hackneyed sweet talk, because I knew very well that Shostakovich's music was not appreciated all that much by a great many professional musicians back home. Prokofiev seemed a much more impressive figure to many. Yet there I stood, intruding on Shostakovich's time and forcing him to talk, when he obviously wanted to be left in peace.

I do not recall exactly how I finally took leave of him, but the memory of that brief encounter embarrasses me to this day. Describing it, however, provides an opportunity to consider just how greatly perspectives have changed over the forty years since. Keep in mind that my meeting with the composer took place in the spring of 1962 at the height of the Cold War. Not two years earlier the Soviet Union had downed an American U-2 spy plane flying surveillance over Soviet territory, which led to the collapse of plans for a summit conference between the USSR, Great Britain, France, and the United States. During the summer and fall of 1961 Soviet engineers aided in building the Berlin Wall. The next summer, of 1962, only months after my brief encounter with Shostakovich, the Soviets started constructing intercontinental ballistic missile sites in Cuba, bringing the United States and the USSR to the brink of nuclear confrontation.

This, then, was the sociopolitical context at the time, and certainly it contributed to the widespread disdain of Shostakovich's music in the United States, especially in academic circles. And as recently as the very week before I met Shostakovich, I had been sitting with Samuel Barber at a concert given in connection with the Composers Congress. Shostakovich's Fourth Symphony was the work Barber and I were hearing, each of us for the first time. As we listened to the music, Barber himself reinforced my personal doubts about the significance of Shostakovich as a composer.

Barber and I had become rather well acquainted during the ten days or so he had been in Moscow for the Composers Congress. Our desks during the daily Congress sessions were side by side. We often had drinks and meals together. And since I could speak Russian, Barber depended more on me than on his official interpreter for informal talks with Russian student composers and fans interested in meeting the famous American musician.

Back to Shostakovich's Fourth Symphony: This was the symphony that had been in rehearsal for its première at the very moment in 1936 when *Pravda* published the notorious official denunciation of Shostakovich's opera, *Ledi Makbet Mtsenskogo uezda* [Lady Macbeth of the Mtsensk District]. In the wake of the scandal, the première of the symphony was canceled. Some twenty-five years would pass before its first performance on 30 December 1961. Samuel Barber and I were listening to its *second* public performance, especially arranged for the delegates to the Composers Congress, in March 1962.

The Shostakovich Fourth is a *long* symphony. It takes a good hour to perform. At some point well along the way, perhaps already in the final movement, Barber leaned over and whispered, "Why can't he get out of C minor? Doesn't he know *how*?!" Throughout the time remaining, I was acutely conscious of Barber shifting in his seat and altering his facial expressions, all suggesting a highly critical commentary on the symphony. When the concert ended and Barber and I were making our way out of the Great Hall of the Conservatory, he shared a few more terse observations under his breath, remarking in particular about the symphony's *formidable* length. He certainly seemed to share Virgil Thomson's aversion to what Thomson had characterized as "the masterpiece tone." I quote Thomson:

> This tone is lugubrious, portentous, world-shaking; and length, as well as heavy instrumentation, is essential to it. Its reduction to absurdity is manifest today through the later symphonies of Shostakovich. . . . Rarely in the history of music has any composer ever spread his substance so thin.[3]

Such condescension toward Shostakovich was typical in the United States during the immediate decades following World War II when I was a student. Even American composers who might have been expected to hold more generous opinions of Shostakovich, because of shared aspirations to reach a wider audience, nevertheless tended to speak slightingly about his music. Aaron Copland, for example, in the 1968 edition of his book *The New Music*, which spans the period from 1900 to 1960, allowed a dismissive evaluation, dating originally from the 1940s, to stand:

> The effectiveness of . . . [Shostakovich's] music on a large public both inside and outside the Soviet [Union] has been proved beyond a doubt. Few people would say that this music is first-rate in quality. But if it seems unnecessarily trite and conventional at times, there is no denying the extraordinary "flair" and sheer musical invention displayed. The man certainly can write music.[4]

Copland himself can scarcely be said to have enjoyed wide acclaim as a "first-rate" composer in music academic circles at the time. This was the period in the United States when prewar "modernist" musical currents were embraced by the academy—the heyday of autonomist, formalist aesthetics, the era of the greatest influence of the Second Viennese School, the post-Webernists, and the proponents of an objectified "New Music."

The first edition of Donald Jay Grout's *History of Western Music*, which was to become the most widely adopted and influential music history textbook ever in the United States, was published in 1960 (New York: Norton). A grand total of twelve lines of text referred to Shostakovich, whereas fourteen *pages* were devoted to "Schoenberg and His Followers"—at once a testament to the canonization within the academy of the Second Viennese School and a catechism for the following generation of students. The value judgment implicit in such a startlingly disproportionate allocation of space in a textbook could scarcely fail to leave traces in the minds of American music students for years to come.

No doubt there were other factors but, as I see it, two played particularly influential roles in the devaluation of Shostakovich and his music within the American intellectual musical world of the period when I was a student. One I just identified: the triumphant authority in Academe of the true believers in Schoenberg's discovery and their whole-hearted acceptance of the mystical historical necessity ascribed to that discovery by its prophet. The rationalized compositional processes involved in the music composed by the adherents to this method could easily be discussed in the lecture hall and lent themselves as readily to student research projects as to learned articles in scholarly journals. Moreover, the intellectualized aesthetics associated with this music resonated with the anti-romantic sensibilities of the time of the New Music and appealed to that ideal of scientific objectivity cultivated within the Ivory Tower. How *could* the music of Shostakovich prosper in an environment such as this?

The other important factor that weighed heavily on attitudes toward Shostakovich when I was a student can be directly related to the appropriation of his music by Soviet officialdom for use as propaganda, along with the composer's apparent acquiescence in this political exploitation of himself and his creative property. At that time in the United States prevailing aesthetic opinions, no less than cultural attitudes in general, were still very much colored by memories of the recent war and the even more recent Iron Curtain. Both the Nazi Fascists and the Soviet Bolsheviks had called for a simplified music with broad popular appeal, and any composer who appeared to support official ideology of either stripe was viewed as a collaborator.

Shostakovich was widely seen in this light. Take, for example, Virgil Thomson's notorious review of the composer's Seventh Symphony dedicated to the City of Leningrad under Nazi siege in 1941. Thomson disdained the score as thin in substance and adapted to "the comprehension of a child of eight," which suggested to Thomson that Shostakovich was "willing to write down to a real or [a] fictitious psychology of mass consumption in a way that may eventually disqualify him for consideration as a serious composer."[5]

Thomson took for granted, as did Ernst Křenek, that Shostakovich had willingly capitulated to Communist Party dictates. If musicians in Nazi-dominated countries were to be held to unequivocal standards of professional ethics, then "Shostakovich ought [also] to be condemned along with . . . [the other] collaborationists," Křenek declared, since "he has acknowledged the right of his government to impose esthetic demands upon art for political purposes."[6]

Attitudes softened somewhat in the wake of the Communist Party's harsh public rebuke of Shostakovich in 1948 for the composer's alleged failure to apply the lessons he should have learned from the Party's 1936 condemnation of *Lady Macbeth*. Shostakovich's much publicized and pathetic kowtowing before the bonzes of Soviet orthodoxy unsettled American academics, who began to express a bit more compassion for the composer's predicament. I remember the more conciliatory, if still patronizing, tone of Homer Ulrich's assessment in his 1952 textbook on symphonic music:

> One may well deplore Shostakovich's adherence to the musical-political formulas that are imposed upon him. His undeniable gifts as an original and powerful composer would, in another cultural atmosphere, lead him into other directions and to a higher place than he now occupies. One senses the fact that he composers out of technical mastery, not out of conviction.[7]

The clearly partisan character of Ulrich's assessment, however sympathetic, typifies evaluations of Shostakovich's music as I remember them from that time. Still, his uncommon prowess as a composer was recognized and acknowledged, sometimes from unexpected quarters. Shortly before Shostakovich was to arrive in New York City as an official representative of the USSR at the 1949 Conference for World Peace, Schoenberg was invited to sign a message welcoming Shostakovich to the United States. Here is what Schoenberg said in response:

> [Myself] being [a] Scapegoat of Russian [i.e., Soviet] restrictions on music I cannot sign. But I am ready to send the following: Disregarding [the] problem of styles and politics I gladly greet a real composer.[8]

That Schoenberg would greet Shostakovich as "a real composer" gains significance in the context of the latter's public declaration, "To be heard and understood by as many new listeners as possible is the cherished dream of every Soviet composer,"[9] in light of Schoenberg's axiom, "If it is art, it is not for all, and if it is for all, it is not art."[10]

The elitist perspective encapsulated in Schoenberg's axiom fused readily with the formalist aesthetics that persisted in the United States up until the time of Shostakovich's death in 1975. If one considers this in the context of a pervasive Cold War rhetoric that subtly infiltrated American patterns of thought during that period, one can better comprehend the concurrent disdain of Shostakovich's music.

The transformation of disdain into judicious esteem was facilitated by a congeries of circumstances, two of which seem to me of particular importance. During the 1970s Minimalism and neo-romanticism captured the attention of both audiences and composers, once again bringing to the fore musical styles that embodied the expressive and communicative powers of music. This swing of the pendulum of musical taste, away from intellectualized music to that which was more frankly emotional, contributed to a revival of serious discussion about what music means and how that meaning is constructed. And, with regard to Shostakovich in particular, a book appeared in 1979 that turned all earlier interpretations of the composer and his music upside down. The book was *Testimony* (New York: Harper & Row), conspicuously pitched on its title page as "the memoirs of Dmitri Shostakovich, as related to and edited by Solomon Volkov."

Volkov's Shostakovich was *not* the Shostakovich exalted in the official obituary issued at the time of the composer's death just four years earlier, an obituary with Brezhnev's name at the top, followed by a list of eighty-four names representing the crème de la crème of Soviet politics and music, an obituary that eulogized Shostakovich in all the old familiar clichés: "Loyal son of the Communist Party, . . . artist-citizen . . . [who] revealed to the whole world the indomitable spirit of the Soviet people, . . . found inspiration in our Soviet reality, . . . [and] affirmed and advanced the art of Socialist Realism."[11]

Volkov's Shostakovich, on the contrary, was a composer embittered, acid-tongued, and pessimistic, who by turns mocked and cursed everything implicated in *his* "Soviet reality." Confronted by this diametrically reconstructed Shostakovich, not only the composer's family and friends but also the cultural world at large, both inside and outside the Soviet Union, reacted with shock. Questions about the authenticity of *Testimony* were raised immediately, with particular vehemence by those in the Soviet Union who were closest to the composer, namely, his wife, Irina Antonovna, his son, Maxim Dmitrievich, and a handful of former students who had become intimate family friends, notably Boris Tishchenko and Veniamin Basner.[12]

A telling commentary on the power of political attitudes shaped by Cold War rhetoric is that a great many people at the time, and many still today, took the Soviet-era disavowals of *Testimony* as certain confirmation of the book's authenticity.

Now, nearly a quarter of a century after its publication, anyone who has conscientiously reviewed the literature on the debate about *Testimony*'s authenticity knows that Volkov's book is a flawed source. Laurel Fay's scrupulously documented essay "Volkov's *Testimony* Reconsidered," chapter 2 in the present volume, should dispel any remaining doubts. She has marshaled unambiguous evidence that the text on every single page of *Testimony* submitted to Shostakovich for his approval, and on which he affixed his signature, was extracted from previously published sources, that is, the text on all the pages Shostakovich signed had already been vetted earlier by the composer for Soviet consumption and printed under his personal byline.

In addition, a close reading of Volkov's preface to *Testimony* suggests the methodology he followed in weaving together the previously published text with whatever information he may have learned in conversation with Shostakovich or with other informants close to the composer—for instance, Lev Lebedensky (see, in the present volume, Manashir Yakubov's interview with Irina Nikolskaya, chapter 13; editor's note p in chapter 13; and Levon Hakobian's "The Latest 'New Shostakovich': Allan Ho and Dmitri Feofanov's *Shostakovich Reconsidered*," chapter 16).

Volkov acknowledges that "Shostakovich had a characteristic way of speaking—in short sentences, very simply, often repetitiously," and Volkov says he had to encourage the composer to reminisce by "asking questions, which he [Shostakovich] answered briefly and, at first reluctantly," while Volkov was "taking notes in . . . shorthand." Volkov also concedes that the composer "often contradicted himself. Then the true meaning of his words had to be guessed, extracted from a box with three false bottoms."

Finally, Volkov "construct[ed] from the penciled scribbles" an uninterrupted monologue—a sustained, pseudo–first-person narrative—which he placed into the mouth of Shostakovich, weaving it together seamlessly with the previously published text authenticated by the composer's signature. Volkov even suggests, in his preface to *Testimony*, where he learned this methodology. He reminds us that Soviet citizens "had all come across articles in the official press with his [Shostakovich's] name at the bottom. No musician took these high-flown, empty declarations seriously. People from a more intimate circle could even tell which 'literary adviser' of the Composers Union had stitched together which article."[13]

Volkov himself, after taking a position in 1972 with the official journal of the Composers Union, *Sovetskaia muzyka*, seems quite easily to have assumed the role of "literary adviser." Indeed, he acknowledges functioning "as his [Shostakovich's] assistant, preparing evaluations, replies, and letters at his request," thus becoming "something of an intermediary between Shostakovich and the journal's editor in chief."[14] Such service could well have encouraged Volkov to feel himself sanctioned to stitch together the composer's memoirs.[15]

No further comment seems necessary, given Laurel Fay's exceedingly thorough analysis included in the present volume. I would offer only a supplement, in the form of an anecdote, to Fay's account of Maxim Shostakovich's curious ambivalence toward *Testimony.* The following story, related to me by Luba Edlina-Dubinsky, pianist and founding member, along with her husband, violinist Rostislav Dubinsky, of the Borodin Piano Trio, provides a bit of personal history that may shed light on why Maxim Shostakovich picks his words so carefully in any reference he makes to what he invariably calls "Mr. Volkov's book," never "my father's memoirs" or "the memoirs of Shostakovich."

Luba and Rosti Dubinsky were well acquainted with Maxim Shostakovich when Maxim was a student at the Moscow Conservatory. He and Luba studied with the same piano teacher, Yakov Flier. Maxim and the Dubinskys reconnected after Maxim had settled in the United States to pursue a career as a conductor. On one occasion in the 1980s, when Maxim was guest conductor of the Indianapolis Symphony Orchestra, he stayed with Luba and Rosti in their home in nearby Bloomington. During Maxim's visit, the Dubinskys asked his opinion of *Testimony:*

> "Maxim was angry," Luba remembers. "He said Volkov's account of the historical situation was entirely accurate. But he said he did not like Volkov, because Volkov put words into his father's mouth."
>
> "My father would *never* have spoken about such things in those words. But what am I supposed to do? Just look at what Volkov's book has done for my father's music."[16]

Undeniably! Consider all that Volkov's book has indeed done for the music of Shostakovich! Prior to the publication of *Testimony*, the sporadic firsthand reports in the United States about the grim vicissitudes of day-to-day Soviet musical life had not really imprinted themselves in the collective consciousness. Volkov, with his bona fide talent as a writer, succeeded in conjuring up those stern realities and in giving them durable emotional force by associating them with Shostakovich. No wonder Maxim Shostakovich might choose his words carefully when speaking about "Mr. Volkov's book." Shostakovich was being discussed more widely and with more sympathy than ever before, and his music was being played everywhere, very often in the 1980s conducted by Maxim Shostakovich.

Given the cultural climate of the United States in the period before the collapse of Soviet communism, "the political context of a Soviet musical work . . . [was] an essential—often the primary—yardstick in the assessment of [its] aesthetic worth. Needless to say, this is a measure we would not dream of applying so broadly to the music of any other nation."[17] Americans at the time, and perhaps still today, found it virtually inconceivable that a composer living under a communist regime might be capable of producing masterworks of universal merit, unless, of course, the composer did so as a conscious protest against his or her repressive surroundings.

This, then, was the context in which Volkov's purported "memoirs of Shostakovich" contributed hugely toward advancing the prestige of the composer's music in the United States. *Testimony*, in portraying Shostakovich as a bitter closet dissident, provided the perfect aesthetic yardstick for measuring the worth of the Soviet composer's music in the time of the Cold War. The voice heard in *Testimony* rants and raves against the Soviet regime and implicitly suggests that his music embodies his protest, ergo the music must be far more worthy than many American critics of the 1940s, 1950s, and 1960s had thought. Moreover, if the music indeed embodies protest against communist repression, then the inference is but a step away that its surface intensity, fraught with vividly drawn contrasts, must seethe with the secret codes of anti-Soviet dissidence.

Writers of popular program notes and concert commentaries have found enough grist in *Testimony* to keep the mills of music criticism running for years. Narrative accounts of works such as the Seventh Symphony, for example, fashioned after the voice heard in *Testimony*, will no doubt survive in the popular imagination for as long and persistently as the perennial legend of Tchaikovsky's suicide.

The most blatant example of sponging off Volkov is Ian MacDonald's *New Shostakovich*, a book now twelve years old but still inspiring undergraduate term papers.[18] MacDonald's approach to Shostakovich and his music amounts to a black-to-white reversal of hard-line Soviet criticism at its most vulgar and reductive. *The New Shostakovich* is chock full of such bizarre descriptive analyses as this interpretation of an episode from the first movement of the Fifth Symphony:

> We are at a political rally, the leader [Stalin] making his entrance through the audience like a boxer flanked by a phalanx of thugs. This passage (the menace theme dissonantly harmonised [*sic*] on grotesquely smirking low brass to the two-note goosestep of timpani and basses) is a shocking intrusion of cartoon satire. Given the time and place in which it was written, the target can only be Stalin—an amazingly bold stroke.[19]

This is what Shostakovich himself thought about musical analysis of this sort:

> When a music critic writes that in such-and-such a symphony the Soviet office-workers are depicted by the oboe and clarinet, and the Red Army soldiers by the brass section, you want to shout, "Not true!"[20]

Simplistic spin-offs aside, *Testimony* also attracted the attention of more serious scholars and prompted them to begin thinking deeply about the complex issues involved in what Shostakovich's music might actually mean and how that meaning was culturally, socially, and subjectively constructed. The questions raised could hardly have been more timely, just when interest in hermeneutic inquiry was regaining respectability among intellectuals in the United States.

Let us approach this subject of meaning in Shostakovich's music indirectly, by another reference to Schoenberg. In his *Style and Idea*, Schoenberg complains that the principles of style sanctioned by many supporters of "new music" are stipulated "even more negatively than the strictest rules of the strictest old counterpoint," and he goes on to list what has been ruled out: "chromaticism, expressive melodies, Wagnerian harmonies, romanticism, private biographical hints, subjectivity, functional harmonic progressions, illustrations, leitmotivs." Then he declares with a flourish: "In other words, all that was good in the preceding period should not occur now."[21]

Musicians need no reminder that a substantial number of the *Verbote* listed by Schoenberg as having been ruled out of the "new music" constitute the very historic conventions adapted by Shostakovich, and imagined anew, for the purpose of marking his music with telling expressive imagery, characteristic topics, and familiar semiotic codes. The communicative power of his music derives precisely from his distinctive deployment of these familiar codes drawn from the tradition of post-Beethoven symphonism. The meaning ascribed to his music, by both the composer himself and his listeners, obtains essentially from them.

Many writers on music who take their departure from the voice that speaks in *Testimony* believe they know what Shostakovich's music means. Or what the composer intended it to mean. Another perspective on the subject is suggested in a second anecdote, this one taken from the fertile repertory of Rosti Dubinsky.

On a social occasion I shared with him some years ago, Rosti began reminiscing about his personal contacts with Shostakovich. He then moved into a story I had heard him tell before, but no matter. He was an enthralling raconteur. Face rapt, eyes wide, as he witnessed his memory replay an event, he often caught details not reported in an earlier account.[22]

The time was late 1960. Not many weeks before, the venerable Beethoven Quartet had played the first performance of Shostakovich's Eighth String Quartet op. 110 (1960). The composer held the "Beethovens" in high regard and had entrusted them with the premières of all his quartets, starting with the Second in 1944. But by the time he composed the Eighth, Shostakovich had also developed a keen appreciation for the "boys" [*rebiata*] of the Borodin Quartet. He habitually referred to them as "boys," because he had known them all as students at the Moscow Conservatory. The Borodin Quartet's performance of his Fourth Quartet had particularly pleased Shostakovich.

The Beethoven Quartet in the 1960s was numbered among the elite in the Soviet musical establishment. They played everything, the Russian and Western classics, in an urbane and cultivated performance style widely understood to emulate, in musical terms, "the great Russian tradition of the Maly Theater," which performed classic drama, both Russian and Western, in a manner *understood* to represent the best of the Russian national cultural tradition. Nothing alien to accepted performance practices, nothing "not ours" [*ne nash*], as Dubinsky carefully characterized their approach. All the players in the Beethoven Quartet were of *ethnic* Russian descent, he took pains to emphasize. All the "boys" of the Borodin Quartet were Jewish, although the cellist, Valentin Berlinsky, was Jewish only on his father's side.

Shostakovich had heard the Beethoven Quartet play the première of his new Eighth Quartet, now he wanted to hear the "Borodins" play it. Would they kindly consent to come to his home and perform the new quartet just for him alone, in private? Of course! The *Borodintsy* could not imagine declining such an invitation.

I wish to say a word about the Eighth Quartet before continuing with Dubinsky's story. The dedication at the top of the first page of the score reads, "In memory of the victims of fascism and the war" [*Pamiati zhertv fashizma i voiny*]. But in a personal letter to his close friend Isaak Glikman, Shostakovich writes that he had a different dedication in mind when he was composing the quartet:

> It occurred to me that should I die, it would be unlikely that anyone would write a piece dedicated to my memory. So I decided to write one myself. . . . My initials are the quartet's main theme, that is, the notes D, Es, C, H [D, E-flat, C, B-natural].[23] I also use other themes from my works in the quartet, as well as the revolutionary song "Tormented by Grievous Bondage." My own themes come from the First Symphony, the Eighth Symphony, the [Second] Piano Trio, the [First] Cello Concerto, and *Lady Macbeth*. I also hint at Wagner's Funeral

> March from *Götterdämmerung* and the second theme from the first movement of Tchaikovsky's Sixth Symphony. I forgot—there is also a theme from my Tenth Symphony. Not too bad, this little potpourri. The pseudo-tragedy of the quartet is such that while composing it my tears flowed as abundantly as urine after downing half a dozen beers.[24]

I return now to Dubinsky's story about Shostakovich's invitation to the *Borodintsy* to play the Eighth Quartet for him privately. On the appointed day, and at precisely the appointed hour—they knew the composer's fanaticism about punctuality—the players knocked on the door, which was opened immediately by Shostakovich. He shook hands all around, in his characteristically abrupt and somewhat spastic style, thanking each one for coming. Then, without further ado, he motioned them toward chairs and music stands already set up. Sensing the composer's eagerness, the musicians quickly took out their instruments, found their places, and prepared to play. Shostakovich seated himself close by, score and pencil at the ready, his head tilted a bit to the side, as if already listening intently to the music, oblivious of the players' presence in the room.

In a moment the music came forth, all five movements without pause: the solemn ricercar-like exploration of the composer's motto theme, recurring amid plaintive thematic reminiscences from earlier works; the harsh furioso scherzo, with "the Jewish theme," from the finale of the Second Piano Trio, the one dedicated to the memory of Shostakovich's closest friend, Ivan Sollertinsky.

Dubinsky looked up from his music and caught a glimpse of the composer. Shostakovich's head had dropped forward, and he was starting to slump in his chair.

The eccentric waltz came next, with its unsettling, ostinato-like iteration of the composer's motto theme, again combined with still more provocative allusions to the composer's earlier works. And after that, three brutal downstrokes—like an ominous knock at the door—followed by a requiem for those "Tormented by Grievous Bondage."

Finally, the return of the ricercar from the beginning of the quartet but now played with mutes, hushed and even more dirge-like. And then the quartet's sustained and muffled unwinding on the composer's four-note motto theme.

The players slowly lifted their bows and looked over expectantly at Shostakovich. He was bent over nearly double, holding his head in his hands, eyes covered, his arms resting on his knees. The players waited. Shostakovich did not move. Finally, the musicians stood up slowly, silently, quietly put their instruments away, and left the apartment without saying a word.

Dubinsky's graphic description of the pathetic Shostakovich, slumped over in his chair, huddled into himself, wasted by the emotions evoked on listening to his quartet played by the *Borodintsy*—the image left me with a sizable lump in my throat. I deeply empathized with how vulnerable I imagined he must have felt, because I, too, often feel emotionally disarmed by the expressive force of music. And Shostakovich had been listening to his own music, conscious of all the emotional associations it had for him.

For my part, aware of the history of the Eighth Quartet as I replayed it in my mind while listening to Dubinsky's story, responding emotionally to its familiar topics and affective codes, I imagined myself sharing the composer's grueling emotional journey.

After Dubinsky finished his tale and the somber mood had lifted a bit, I asked his opinion about Shostakovich's response to the *Borodintsy*'s performance. Why did the composer react in such an astonishing manner? Dubinsky circled around an answer and finally said, "Well, you know, our style of playing differed a lot from that of the Beethovens." He hesitated, and then declared, "We played like Jews!" He gave a short laugh. "We emphasized everything in the music that Socialist Realism wanted hidden."

"What do you mean?" I said. "How did you do that?"

"We tried our best to bring out *everything* in the music. *Everything* Shostakovich himself wanted to express."

I wondered to myself if Dubinsky and the other three players, back in 1960, had actually discussed what they thought Shostakovich wanted to express in the Eighth Quartet, if they in fact shared some common understanding of the expressive meaning of the work that they might have been able to put into words, as well as into their performance style. And, I wondered, too, what Dubinsky and his colleagues might have to say about the many other Soviet listeners at the time who, when listening to Shostakovich's music, perceived it as fraught with Aesopian meanings that Socialist Realism would rather suppress.

Certainly the Eighth Quartet is a work rife with invitations to read it as the composer's reflections on more than thirty years of personal, compositional, and political history. Yet to study and appreciate the quartet only from this standpoint limits its relevance as a work of art and yields a narrow interpretive perspective. However "autobiographical" the selection of thematic material and however suggestive the imagery may be in evoking potent emotional associations, both for the composer and for his listeners, these are the *subjects* of the artistic discourse, not the work of art itself. By analogy, Rembrandt's aged and sober face peering from his 1669 self-portrait in London's National Gallery represents an autobiographical perspective that invites commentary on the painter's life experience and, for the viewer acquainted with Rembrandt's biography, may elicit a more powerful affective response. Still, the viewer, like the listener, can only surmise what the autobiographical subject meant to the artist who used it in creating his self-portrait; in both cases, the pictorial one and the musical one, the subject of artistic discourse is not the artwork itself in its capacity as artwork.

No debate about authenticity or questions about methodology tarnish the thirty-odd memoirs by the composer's friends and associates that comprise Elizabeth Wilson's *Shostakovich: A Life Remembered* (Princeton, N.J.: Princeton University Press, 1994).[25] The complicated, contradictory, and sometimes exasperating Shostakovich revived in the memories of people who knew him well resurrects a full-blooded personality very different from the cardboard Scrooge encountered in Volkov's *Testimony*. When the composer speaks here, we know that it is his personal friends and colleagues who are placing the words in his mouth, recounting them in the context of their own personal histories and explaining what prompted them, and we take for granted the fickleness of the best-intentioned human memory.

In the course of reading through these recollections, one repeatedly encounters remarks and intimations about how the music of Shostakovich spoke solace to Soviet listeners, how it helped to make tolerable, conditions that often verged on the intolerable, how it offered spiritual consolation for the accumulated indignities of lives degraded by political propaganda and corrupt officialdom.

This special quality of Shostakovich's music so intrigued Igor Shafarevich, noted Soviet mathematician, that it inspired him to make a "study of that tragic genius, that pitiful wreck Shostakovich, who had always fascinated him," because, as fellow dissident Alexander Solzhenitsyn put it, Shafarevich wanted "to understand how Shostakovich steals into our souls and what it is he promises them—a task that cried out to be done, but that no Soviet musicologist had carried out."[26]

How, indeed, was Shostakovich's music able to steal into the souls of his Soviet listeners, and what did they understand it to promise them? These questions simply cannot be answered without addressing the fundamental critical issue of how meaning in music is socially, culturally, and subjectively constructed. It is well to remember that these meanings are not inherent in the music itself but change continuously, evolving along with changes in culture and society, all the while assuming idiosyncratic shapes peculiar to every individual in every time. This is the perspective often neglected by interpreters of Shostakovich who read his music as "notes in a bottle."

It is also well to remember that questions of meaning have enduring force and validity only in association with artworks that reveal themselves as masterfully wrought in a technical sense. Shostakovich's music as it manifests itself qua music ought never to be disengaged from hermeneutic discourse about what it means. The composer himself has implied exactly this in the very same letter to Isaak Glikman, quoted earlier:

> The pseudo-tragedy of the quartet is such that while composing it my tears flowed as abundantly as urine after half a dozen beers. Since arriving back home, I've tried playing it through a couple of times, and again the tears flowed. But this time not only on account of the pseudo-tragedy but also from surprise at the work's remarkable formal integrity.[27]

The composer's own words would seem to make clear that the meaning he gleans from the Eighth Quartet, in its capacity as an artistic expression, had transcended those personalized and more limited meanings associated with the autobiographical subject matter he had employed in its compositional process.

Beware interpretations of Shostakovich's music that decode its "pseudo-tragedies" as analogues of the composer's personal life or as glosses on the history of Soviet repression. The reception of Shostakovich's music and its aftereffects are facts in the social and political life of the composer himself and his time, and they are inseparable from any responsible attempt to interpret the meaning of his music. But an honest interpretation concedes the innate capacity of an artwork to elude efforts at confining its boundless potential for giving rise to meaning. Solomon Volkov, whose work has spawned so many reductive interpretations of the composer's music, once reported the following information relevant to the issue:

> Shostakovich has always reacted with the most extreme reluctance to attempts to make direct—and simplistic!—correlations between his music and this or that event in the life of the composer Dmitri Shostakovich as "a private individual."[28]

May those who would stake claim to the meaning of Shostakovich's music pay close attention!

Notes

The earliest version of this article was presented as the keynote address for the festival Dmitri Shostakovich on the 90th Anniversary of His Birth, at California State University, Long Beach, on 17 February 1996. Later variants and developments of it were presented on 1 November 1996 at Indiana University, Bloomington, as part of the Commemoration of the 90th Anniversary of the Birth of Shostakovich; on 19 March 1997 at The Florida State University; on 24 January 1997 at the College-Conservatory of Music, University of Cincinnati, as part of the series Thinking About Music; on 14 April 2000 at the University of Tennessee–Martin, as the keynote address for the spring meeting of the South-Central Chapter, American Musicological Society; and on 21 July 2001 at the Staunton Music Festival in Staunton, Virginia. The revised version presented here is published for the first time.

1. I was truly "anomalous." Only one other American exchange student had ever attended the Moscow Conservatory before I arrived in early January and remained through June 1962. Composer and musicologist Stanley Dale Krebs had preceded me during a residency of about a year and a half in 1958–59. Krebs's book, *Soviet Composers and the Development of Soviet Music* (London: Allen and Unwin, 1970; New York: Norton, 1970), grew out of his studies at the Conservatory and represented the first wide-ranging scholarly book on the subject, antedating Boris Schwarz's *Music and Musical Life in Soviet Russia* by some two years (the first edition of Schwarz's book was published in 1972, also by Allen and Unwin in London and Norton in New York; an enlarged edition was published in 1983 by Indiana University Press, Bloomington).

2. "Spasibo, spasibo. Blagodariu, blagodar*iu.*"

3. From a review dated 15 June 1944; reprinted in Virgil Thomson, *The Musical Scene* (New York: Knopf, 1945), p. 278.

4. Copland, *Our New Music 1900–1960*, rev. and enl. ed. (New York: Norton, 1968), pp. 83–84.

5. From a review of 18 October 1942; reprinted in Thomson, *The Musical Scene*, p. 104.

6. Křenek, "On Artists and Collaboration: A Symposium," *Modern Music* 22, no. 1 (November–December 1944): 8.

7. Ulrich, *Symphonic Music* (New York: Columbia University Press, 1952), p. 308.

8. Schoenberg to Olin Downes, night letter of 11 March 1949, in *Arnold Schoenberg Correspondence*, compiled and annotated by Egbert Ennulat (Metuchen, N.J.: Scarecrow, 1991), p. 259.

9. Shostakovich quoted in *Pravda*, 17 June 1956; reprinted in D. Shostakovich, *O vremeni i o sebe 1926–1975* [About the times and about myself], comp. M. Iakovlev, ed. G. Pribegina (Moscow: Sovetskii kompozitor, 1980), p. 190.

10. Schoenberg, *Style and Idea*, ed. Leonard Stein, trans. Leo Black (New York: St. Martin's, 1975), p. 124.

11. "Verny syn Kommunisticheskoi partii, . . . khudozhnik-grazhdanin. . . . [povedavshii] vsemu miru o nesgibaemoi sile sovetskikh liudei. . . . On cherpal

vdokhnovenie v nashei sovetskoi deistvitel'nosti, . . . utverzhdal i razvival iskusstvo sotsialisticheskogo-realizma." Phrases selected from the composer's obituary issued by the leadership of the Communist Party and the Union of Soviet Composers, Brezhnev's and Andropov's names in the first two positions, as published in *Sovetskaia muzyka*, no. 9 (September 1975): 6–7.

12. See Craig R. Whitney, "Shostakovich Memoir Shock to Kin," *New York Times*, 13 November 1979, p. C7. See also "Zhalkaia poddelka: O tak nazyvaemykh memuarakh D. D. Shostakovicha" [A pitiful fake: About the so-called memoirs of D. D. Shostakovich], a letter to the editor signed by V. Basner, M. Vainberg, K. Karaev, Yu. Levitin, B. Tishchenko, and K. Khachaturian, in *Literaturnaia gazeta*, no. 47 (14 November 1979): 8. A complete English translation of this letter is published as selection 4 in the present volume. See also Norbert Kuchinke and Felix Schmidt, an interview with Maxim Shostakovich, "Why I Fled from Russia," trans. Gillian Macdonald, *Sunday Times* (London), 17 May 1981, p. 35.

13. All of these quotations are from the preface to *Testimony*, pp. xiv–xvii. See also Fay, "Volkov's *Testimony* Reconsidered," chapter 2 in the present volume.

14. Quote is in Volkov's preface to *Testimony*, footnote, p. xvii.

15. Volkov writes that he became a senior editor at *Sovetskaia muzyka* after he moved to Moscow in 1972. I have looked through every issue of the journal, starting in 1965 and continuing through 1976, the year of Volkov's emigration, and found his name only as a byline to nine items. The first item appeared in 1970, the remaining eight in 1973 and 1974. There follows a complete listing of news items and articles associated with the name Solomon Volkov found in *Sovetskaia muzyka* 1970 through 1974; all issues in the period from 1965 to 1976 were searched:

- S. Volkov, a report on "the week of musical Leningrad in Riga," dedicated to the one-hundredth birthday of Lenin, published in the section headed "Pis'ma iz gorodov" [Letters from the cities], under the subheading, "Riga," *Sovetskaia muzyka*, no. 8 (August 1970): 61–62.
- S. Volkov, "Interv'iu s Bernkhardom Biuttnerom" [An interview with Bernhard Büttner], *Sovetskaia muzyka*, no. 10 (October 1973): 130–31.
- S. Volkov, a short review of two German song collections, Inge Lammel's *Das Arbeitlied* and Lammel's *Lieder der Partei*, published under the general heading, "Na muzykal'noi orbite" [In musical orbit], *Sovetskaia muzyka*, no. 10 (October 1973): 133.
- S. Volkov, "Vospominanie o 'Leningradskoi Vesne' " [A recollection of the "Leningrad Spring (Festival)"], *Sovetskaia muzyka*, no. 1 (January 1974): 14–22.
- S. Volkov, an introductory essay under the general heading, "K 100-letiiu so dnia rozhdeniia Vs. E. Meierkhol'da" [To the 100th anniversary of the birth of Vs(evolod) E(mil'evich) Meyerhold], preceding D. Shostakovich, "Iz vospominanii" [From my recollections], *Sovetskaia muzyka*, no. 3 (March 1974): 53–54. Paragraphs 2–6 at the beginning of chapter 3 of *Testimony*, pp. 77–78, are derived from this issue of *Sovetskaia muzyka*, p. 54, paragraphs 1–4.
- S. V., "Krizis ISCM" [A crisis in ISCM], *Sovetskaia muzyka*, no. 4 (April 1974): 30–31. Note at the bottom of page 30: "Material translated and reworked by P. Veis, S. Volkov, M. Volodina, and I. Medvedeva.
- S. Volkov, "Avtorskii vecher D. Shostakovicha" [A composer's soirée for D. Shostakovich], a review of the first performance in Leningrad, in the Small

Hall of the Conservatory, 30 October 1973, of Shostakovich's *Shest' stikhotvorenii Mariny Tsvetaevoi* op. 143a [Six verses of Marina Tsvetaeva op. 143; orchestrated as op. 143a], *Sovetskaia muzyka,* no. 5 (May 1974): 88–89.

- S. Volkov, "Muzykanty Estonii v gostiakh u tvorcheskoi molodiozhi Moskvy" [Estonian musicians as guests of Moscow's gifted young musicians], *Sovetskaia muzyka,* no. 6 (June 1974): 77–78.
- S. Volkov, "Glinka v Augsburge, ili 100 let spustia; replik" [Glinka in Augsburg, or 100 years later; a rejoinder], *Sovetskaia muzyka,* no. 11 (November 1974): 127–28.

Volkov's name could not be found in the 1975 or 1976 issues of *Sovetskaia muzyka.* He emigrated from the USSR in 1976.

16. Luba Edlina-Dubinsky recounted this anecdote to me and to a group of colleagues and friends, including Marina Rytsareva, Leslie Kearney, Eric Onore, and John Clower, on the evening of 26 February 1999. She granted permission to publish it here.

17. Laurel Fay, "Soviet Music and the Gorbachev Thaw," *Keynote* 11, no. 6 (August 1987): 13.

18. Ian MacDonald, *The New Shostakovich* (Boston: Northeastern University Press, 1990).

19. Ibid., p. 129.

20. Shostakovich in *Sovetskaia muzyka* 1, no. 3 (1933); reprinted in *O vremeni i o sebe 1926–1975* [About the times and about myself, 1926–1975], comp. M. Yakovlev, ed. G. Pribegina (Moscow: Sovetskii kompozitor, 1980), p. 34. I am grateful to Richard Taruskin for calling this passage to my attention.

21. Schoenberg, *Style and Idea,* ed. Leonard Stein, trans. Leo Black (New York: St. Martin's, 1975), p. 124.

22. Dubinsky gives an account of this same story that differs in some details in his published memoir, *Stormy Applause: Making Music in a Worker's State* (New York: Hill and Wang, 1980), pp. 282–84. Valentin Berlinsky also recalls the same event, but with much less detail; see Elizabeth Wilson's *Shostakovich: A Life Remembered* (Princeton, N.J.: Princeton University Press, 1994), p. 246.

23. D, Es, C, H are the German pitch names corresponding to the German transliteration of Shostakovich's initials, that is, D. Sch.

24. Shostakovich to Glikman, 19 July 1960, *Pis'ma k drugu: Pis'ma D. D. Shostakovicha k I.D. Glikmanu* [Letters to a friend: The letters of Dmitri Shostakovich to Isaak Glikman], edited, and with commentary, by Isaak Davydovich Glikman (Moscow: Izdatel'stvo "DSCH," 1993)], p. 159. I quote from the Russian edition in my own translation. An English edition of the letters has been published: *Story of a Friendship: The Letters of Dmitri Shostakovich to Isaak Glikman, 1941–1975,* trans. Anthony Phillips, with commentary by Isaak Glikman (London: Faber, 2001).

25. My review of Wilson's book appeared in the *Slavic and East European Journal* 40, no. 1 (spring 1996): 192–93. It is reprinted in the present volume, selection 19.

26. Solzhenitsyn, *Bodalsia telionok s dubom* [The calf butted with the oak tree] (Paris: YMCA Press, 1975), pp. 433–34; English translation here from *The Oak and the Calf,* trans. Harry Willetts (New York: Harper & Row, 1980), p. 405.

27. See note 23, above. Immediately following on this uncharacteristically im-

modest statement, the composer writes, “Still and all, regarding the latter, some degree of self-satisfaction may be involved, which will probably pass quickly and I’ll suffer a hangover of self-criticism.”

28. S. Volkov, “Avtorskii vecher D. Shostakovicha” [A soirée devoted to the music of D. Shostakovich], *Sovetskaia muzyka*, no. 5 (May 1974): 88–89.

24

Laurel Fay's *Shostakovich: A Life* (2000)

SIMON MORRISON

One of the most provocative sentiments expressed in *Shostakovich: A Life* concerns not the biography of the composer but his music. In the concluding chapter Laurel Fay ascribes the popularity of Shostakovich's scores to their accessibility, their "audible links to the traditions of the past" (pp. 286–87). Though her biography necessarily addresses Soviet *Realpolitik*, Fay intimates that, whereas the memory of the Soviet Union will mercifully fade, the composer's music will undoubtedly endure. In a marked improvement over the current state of affairs, in which the evaluation of Shostakovich's music is fettered by lingering Cold War biases, over time fewer and fewer people will associate it with totalitarian politics, and more attention will be paid to the traditions behind it.

In accord with this sentiment, Fay's biography offers a multifaceted portrait of its subject, arguably the sole compositional genius to emerge from the Soviet Union. The conventional interpretation of his life posits that he alternately mollified and enraged the *apparatchiki*, alternately maneuvered and stood his ground. Fay, the leading anglophone scholar of

---

The original review appeared as "*Shostakovich: A Life*, by Laurel E. Fay. Oxford and New York: Oxford University Press, 2000. xxii, 458 pp.," *Journal of the American Musicological Society* 53, no. 2 (summer 2000): 426–36. The review has been subject to minor editing and updating. Reprinted with permission.

Soviet music, complicates this assertion, demonstrating that Shostakovich was an inconstant artist, at once brave and timid, self-confident and self-doubting, who found the boundary between conformity and resistance tenuous in the extreme. Moreover, she shows that, just as "people, ideas, and facts that became unpalatable were routinely 'airbrushed' out of existence in the later Soviet sources" in order to demonstrate the composer's loyalty to the regime (p. 5), post-Soviet sources show an equally problematic tendency to suppress inconvenient details in order to demonstrate his dissidence. In this regard, her biography nuances the assertion of such senior Russian musicologists as Mark Aranovsky, who recently declared that the composer "actively *resisted* the totalitarian regime" throughout his career, with the performance of music offering a "*moment of truth*" to Soviet audiences.[1] Skeptical of the post–Cold War rush toward exculpatory revisionism, Fay endeavors to foreground the ambiguities of Shostakovich's public and private personae. One of the challenges she faced in writing the biography is articulated on page 216, where she reports that the composer's unexpected application for membership in the Communist Party in 1960 led to an emotional breakdown and contemplation of suicide. The explanations he gave to his colleagues about these events, Fay points out, are contradictory.

The biography took fifteen years to write but, given the level of detail, it could have taken longer. Supplementing the core narrative—fifteen chapters covering 287 pages—are 57 pages of notes (many of which contain revisionist historical minutiae), an accurate work list, a useful annotated glossary of names, and a comprehensive bibliography. Fay relies extensively on primary sources collected in the *glasnost'* era and on secondary sources published after the fall of the Soviet Union. Had the book been conceived more recently, one could have interpreted it as a non-polemical refutation of the highly polemical writings of Dmitri Feofanov, Allan Ho, and Ian MacDonald in support of an anti-Soviet Shostakovich. These authors aspire primarily to exonerate the 1979 publication *Testimony: The Memoirs of Dmitri Shostakovich*, as related to and edited by Solomon Volkov. In a 1980 review article in the *Russian Review*, Fay (relying in part on the findings of Simon Karlinsky) challenged the authenticity and veracity of the memoirs. Her argument constituted a powerful indictment of the book as at least a partial forgery, and has found support in a recent article written by Shostakovich's widow.[2] Volkov has not directly refuted Fay's findings, though a "case for the defense" has been presented by Allen Ho and Dmitri Feofanov in their militant publication titled *Shostakovich Reconsidered*, to which Ian MacDonald has contributed a preponderance of the essays.[3] In their attacks against not only Fay but also Richard Taruskin and, to a lesser extent, Malcolm Brown, they exhibit a similar thinking. To cite the scathing satire of the Stalinist judicial system by the émigré writer Abram Tertz, *The Trial Begins* [*Sud idët*], they "took up [their] spades as one man."[4]

Rather than engage with this group, Fay remains resolutely above the fray. In *Shostakovich: A Life* she only indirectly addresses her opponents. In the introduction she comments that,

> writing about Shostakovich remains laced with political and moral subtexts. At its most extreme, it simply replaces one orthodoxy with another, reversing the polarities of the old, shopworn Soviet clichés: the true-believing Communist citizen-composer is inverted into an equally unconvincing caricature of a lifelong closet dissident. (p. 2)

Of *Testimony*, she simply notes that,

> even were its claim to authenticity not in doubt, [it] would still furnish a poor source for the serious biographer. The embittered, "death-bed" disclosures of someone ravaged by illness, with festering psychological wounds and scores to settle, are not to be relied upon for accuracy, fairness, or balance when re-creating the impact of the events of a lifetime as they actually occurred. (p. 4)

Fay does not belabor the point. Having expressed her aversion to polarities, she turns to her chief concern: reviewing the available facts—double-, triple-, and cross-checked—of Shostakovich's existence. Through judicious citation, she subsequently demonstrates that the recently published diaries and reminiscences of Flora Litvinova and Daniel Zhitomirsky, as well as the letters from the composer to Isaak Glikman and Boris Tishchenko, superseded *Testimony* as a biographical source, both by supplying greater detail and by calling into question several of its narratives. Thus the hotly debated issue of its "authenticity" and "veracity" in effect becomes moot: whoever actually authored *Testimony*, whatever the relationship between its voice and Shostakovich's private and unknowable psychology, it is comparatively uninformative.[5]

Fay's narrative is devoid of hyperbole. She clearly has no intention of writing an NKVD or KGB thriller[6] or to engage in the arguably disingenuous exercise of trying to represent what most of us, thankfully, cannot imagine: the tremendous psychological pressure under which Shostakovich and his compatriots at times had to live and work. Instead, her prose is a model of concision, the arrangement of sentences and paragraphs offering different angles on events, the sober, lapidary reportage foregrounding the irrational, abnormal nature of the historical facts. Sensitive to the fact that memoirs, in their re-animation of the past through later experiences, invent as well as recall, Fay attempts, whenever possible, to compare and contrast multiple contemporaneous narratives. For example, in a seemingly innocuous passage concerning the earliest manifestation of Shostakovich's musical talent, Fay first quotes from a transcription of a 1941 discussion between the composer and his librettist Victor Smirnov, printed in *Teatral'naia nedelia;* qualifies it with a reference to an interview by Sofia Khentova, printed in 1996 in *V mire Shostakovicha* [In Shostakovich's world]; reinterprets it with a quotation from the reminiscences of his mother, "Moi syn" [My son], printed in 1976 in *Smena;* and then embellishes it with information taken from the composer's 1956 essay, "Dumy o proidyonnom puti" [Thoughts about the path traversed], printed in *Sovetskaia muzyka,* cross-referenced with a related essay from 1981. One paragraph—five references (p. 9). This is exceptionally thorough—and exceptionally patient—research.

Her attention to detail allows her to isolate conflicting recollections, rectify attributions, and correct dates. (Fay not only identifies numerous mistakes in Khentova's two-volume Russian-language biography of the composer,[7] she isolates several instances where Shostakovich bought time to fulfill official commissions by delaying and canceling promised premières, or diverted the funds from such hack work to the scores he really wanted to write.) More pertinent, the attention to detail offers the reader insights into the inner workings of Soviet society during the cultural battles of the 1920s, the Stalinist purges of the 1930s, and the Khrushchev thaw of the 1960s.[8] Fay tacks swiftly between descriptions of Shostakovich's creative labors and bureaucratic chores, his public and private life. Among the novelties of the biography are the revelations about the composer's public service: Fay reports that Shostakovich was elected a deputy of Leningrad's October District in 1934 (pp. 78–79), a representative to the Leningrad City Council in 1939 (p. 111), and a deputy to the RSFSR Supreme Soviet from Leningrad's Dzerzhinsky District in 1951 (p. 181). It is quite startling to learn that, during the most trying years of his life, he devoted his spare time to neighborhood apartment upkeep and pension disbursements. Her descriptions of Shostakovich's home life and personal foibles—morbid self-criticism, verbal tics, chain smoking, and occasional binge drinking—are mediated by chilling, estranging reminders of the psychological traumas, "the terror," in her words, "that had warped his life" (p. 219). However, like the leading Russian historian Katerina Clark, Fay recognizes that the story of Stalin's repressions "has been told many times before."[9] Her work aims to build on such accounts while affording them greater cultural and historical complexity. Her biography is a search for texture.

This point is perhaps best illustrated by Fay's description of the central event, the peripeteia, of Shostakovich's career: the publication on 28 January and 6 February 1936 of the unsigned editorials "Muddle instead of Music" [*Sumbur vmesto muzyki*] and "Balletic Falsehood" [*Baletnaia fal'sh*] in *Pravda*, the official Communist Party newspaper. The first of these articles condemned the opera *Ledi Makbet Mtsenskogo uezda* [Lady Macbeth of the Mtsensk District] op. 29 (1930–32) for "leftist deviation" and "Meyerholditis," and the second attacked the ballet *The Sparkling Stream* [*Svetlyi ruchei*] op. 39 (1934–35) for its inaccurate portrayals of collective farm workers and its recycled music. Fay reveals that Shostakovich was at first less worried by the *Pravda* scandal than is often assumed; in other words, people commonly perceived his immediate reaction to the scandal based on hindsight, on knowing what followed. He was in the northern port city of Arkhangelsk when the first editorial appeared, and he responded sedately, by asking the musicologist Ivan Sollertinsky, his closest friend, to register him for a newspaper clipping service. As a supplement to the eyewitness accounts of the *Pravda* scandal compiled by Elizabeth Wilson in *Shostakovich: A Life Remembered*[10]—another first-rate English-language book on the composer—Fay observes that it "exacted a predictable toll on the number of performances of his works" and that "at times he was reduced to living in debt, reminiscent of his poverty-stricken student days" (p. 94). Shostakovich's anxieties, she continues, were increased by the burdens of fatherhood: his first wife Nina had just given birth to their daughter. In one of many excerpts that illustrate the composer's gallows humor, the reader is also told that, by the beginning of June 1936, he had recovered sufficiently from the *Pravda* scandal to be "able to joke with Sollertinsky and a group of his Leningrad compatriots about whether he should name his daughter 'Sumburina' or 'Falshetta' (feminine names derived from the key words in the titles of the two *Pravda* editorials)" (p. 92).

The focus on the specific details of the *Pravda* scandal does not obscure the big picture. Fay asserts that, whereas the attack against *Lady Macbeth* "was by no means the first time the debate over formalism had been engaged" (p. 87), it followed directly on the heels of the establishment of the All-Union Committee for Arts Affairs, whose function was to ensure that Soviet artists upheld the official doctrine of Socialist Realism. Not only the composer but also those critics who had championed his works came under fire, and one can only marvel at the boldness of the novelist Maxim Gorky—one of the architects of Socialist Realism—and of the theater director Vsevolod Meyerhold for speaking out on the composer's behalf. Meyerhold's subsequent arrest and execution emblematize the senseless tragedy of the Stalinist period. One underutilized source in Fay's summary of the *Pravda* scandal is the recent findings of Leonid Maximenkov, who maintains that Shostakovich had been an unwitting instigator of the bureaucratic restructuring that led to the public condemnation of his own opera. Shostakovich, Maximenkov argues, had been one of several artists who had advocated the dissolution in 1932 of the "proletariat" musical establishments of Soviet Russia—the Moscow Conservatory Production Collective, the Organization of Revolutionary Composers and Musical Activists, and especially the Russian Association of Proletarian Musicians—which had become bureaucratic thorns in more than one side.[11] In summarizing the Kremlin intrigue that preceded and succeeded the dissolution, Maximenkov reports that Platon Kerzhentsev, a high-ranking cultural official, decided to mount an attack on formalism in the arts. His "personal priority" had initially been dramatic theater, but "for several reasons Shostakovich's opera seemed a convenient target" for him.[12] Thus, rather than weakening the anti-Western and anti-modernist currents in Soviet musical life, the bureaucratic restructuring that Shostakovich had supported actually strengthened them.

Fay, as noted, does not provide this information in her discussion of *Lady Macbeth*, though, to be sure, she refers to Maximenkov in her comments about the possible authorship of the *Pravda* editorials (p. 304 n. 67). Evidently his claims could not be verified. She instead turns her attention to the complex history of the Fourth Symphony in C Minor op. 43 (1934/35–36), the composition that suffered most from the *Pravda* scandal. Shostakovich began writing the symphony in 1934, abandoned it, and then began it again in 1935. His progress on the second version was interrupted by the *Pravda* scandal, but he managed to complete it two months later. Fay provides solid critique of the conflicting accounts as to why he withdrew the score from public performance but, to her, "the more intriguing question is not why it was withdrawn but how it came as close to public performance as it did" (p. 96). Despite being "jam-packed with formalism,"[13] the Fourth Symphony had been extensively rehearsed for an 11 December 1936 performance.

Most scholars contend that, following the condemnation of *Lady Macbeth*, Shostakovich's career became a juggling act. In Marina Sabinina's view, "the composer often, as it were, made amends for presumed boldness with a lethargic and insipid 'Socialist Realist' composition. For example, *Loyalty* [*Vernost'* op. 137 (1970)], a cycle of choral ballads to verses by Evgeny Dolmatovsky, was written after the Fourteenth Symphony op. 135 (1969)."[14] Through deft detective work, Fay illuminates the comic and tragic events behind this and other odd juxtapositions in Shostakovich's oeuvre. These include the pairings of the oratorio *Song of the Forests* [*Pesn' o lesakh*] op. 81 (1949) with the Twenty-Four Preludes and Fugues op. 87 (1951), and the cantata *Nad rodinoi nashei solntse siiaet* [The sun shines over our motherland] op. 90 (1952) with the *Chetyre monologa na stikhi A. Pushkina* [Four monologues on texts by A. Pushkin] op. 91 (1952). Most striking, perhaps, is the proximity of the Party-line operetta *Moskva, Cheryomushki* [Moscow, the "Bird-Cherry" Precinct] op. 105 (1958)—referring to the "heroic" construction of apartment blocks in the southwest of the capital in the Cheryomushki Precinct[15]—and the more politically elusive Eleventh Symphony in G Minor, "The Year 1905" [*1905 god*] op. 103 (1957). Fay concludes her assessment of this last score by positing that it deals neither with the 1905 workers' uprising against Tsar Nicholas II, as its subtitle suggests, nor with the brutal Soviet quelling of the 1956 Hungarian uprising, as its date suggests, but instead with the "timeless and universal" theme of "the evils of tyranny and oppression" (p. 202). The distinction is significant: in Fay's reading, the Eleventh Symphony deals with pacifism, not militarism. Devoid of the intonations that would certify it as pro- or anti-Soviet, it depicts war as a natural phenomenon, beyond individual human governance.[16] Though it cannot be proven that Shostakovich was not in some way reacting to the events of 1956 (or, for that matter, 1905), the symphony appears to take and condemn all sides in all struggles. The music's ambiguities serve as an object lesson, explaining why Shostakovich, throughout his career, was at once commended by the Soviet government and badgered as a threat to its stability.

In amending the historical record, Fay stresses that, rather than avoiding operatic composition after 1937, Shostakovich sought to regain his former footing on the lyric stage. The reader learns, for example, that after successfully rehabilitating *Lady Macbeth* in 1963 (in a politically palatable version entitled *Katerina Izmailova*), he immediately decided to compose a new opera. "In February 1964," Fay points out, he "confirmed rumors that the opera he was planning was based on Mikhail Sholokhov's *Quiet Don* [*Tikhii Don*]." The novel had served as the source text for the 1934 "song opera" of the same name by Ivan Dzerzhinsky, "the very one that had profited from the banishment of *Ledi Makbet Mtsenskogo uezda*

[Lady Macbeth of the Mtsensk District] from the stage in 1936" (p. 242). Why would he make such a perverse choice to mark his operatic rehabilitation? Fay does not provide an answer, but this episode almost cries out for creative speculation. Sholokhov's novel, it turns out, is a highly unusual example of Socialist-Realist fiction (that is, Socialist-Realist fiction of the Stalinist period). Rather than preordained, the ending is unexpected; rather than tracking the Marxist-Leninist reeducation of a "positive" hero, the novel explores romantic themes and probes psychology.[17] *Quiet Don*, to crudely paraphrase the last line of text in the Thirteenth Symphony, arguably provided Shostakovich with the means to "pursue" his operatic career by "not pursuing it." Fay herself comes close to making this very claim when she explains why the composer, on the advice of the one-time Central Committee member Dmitri Shepilov, eventually shelved the project: "His dilemma was that he was supposed to be writing an opera to celebrate the anniversary of Soviet power about a hero who did not embrace Soviet power!" (pp. 242–43).

If Shostakovich ever resorted to subterfuge, it perhaps manifested itself in his willingness to allow the Russian musical past to oversee the Soviet musical present. His most introspective symphonic movements allude to Russian Orthodox Church music, to folk music, and to such composers as Tchaikovsky and Musorgsky (whose *Boris Godunov* and *Khovanshchina* he re-orchestrated). Furthermore, his use of the motto secretly referring to his own name (DS [E-flat] CH [B-natural]) in the Eighth String Quartet in C Minor op. 110 (1960) has been interpreted as a personal protest. Only one of his compositions explicitly critiques the regime: the cantata *The Antiformalist Peepshow* [*Antiformalisticheskii rayok*], without opus number (?1948–?68). Before describing its contents, Fay considers the political events that inspired it. Of these, the principal event was the 10 February 1948 Central Committee resolution that condemned Vano Muradeli's opera, *The Great Friendship* [*Velikaia druzhba*] (1947) for ideological deficiencies and that allowed Andrei Zhdanov, the Soviet Minister of Culture, to launch a massive crackdown on Soviet musical activity. Nicknamed the *Zhdanovshchina*, this crackdown resulted in the prohibition of performances of the music of Shostakovich, Prokofiev, Aram Khachaturian, and others; deprived them of income; and removed them from positions of power. Fay offers the reader unsettling new details about the crisis. She reports, for example, that the "lessons" of the 1948 resolution "were subsequently simplified and reinforced by the publication and production at the Moscow Art Theater in 1949 of a contemporary play about the downfall and eventual redemption of a 'formalist' composer; the protagonist was widely perceived to represent Shostakovich" (p. 161). To the familiar accounts of the composer's abject public acts of contrition, moreover, Fay adds a painful detail: "his ten-year-old son was made to vilify his father during a music school exam" (p. 162).

Fay then considers the cantata itself and its genesis. A peepshow, or *rayok*,[a] is an example of "home theater" [*domashnyi teatr*], a private work performed by friends and family. The libretto makes wicked fun of the locution of Shostakovich's bureaucratic tormentors, especially that of Shepilov, who had trouble pronouncing the names of even such familiar composers as Nikolai Rimsky-Korsakov (in one of his soporific speeches on music and ideology, he placed the stress in the surname on the *a*). Fay indicates where details are fuzzy and evidence suspect in the eyewitness accounts of the creation of the score. Though, as usual, her narrative includes suggestions for further research; she cautions that, in the case of *Peepshow*, fact-finding missions might prove counterproductive:

> Contemplating [*Peepshow*] primarily as a "composed" work, with fixed dates of composition, may not be the most helpful approach. The spoof bears all the hallmarks of the Russian genre of *kapustnik*, a party skit, a diversion that might have been improvised, expanded, and embellished through many private "performances" over a long period of time. (p. 165)

The composer, Fay implies, neither conceived the cantata in direct response to the formalist purge of 1948 nor intended it for posterity. Herein lies the central thesis of her biography: Shostakovich actively resented, rather than actively resisted, the Soviet regime. He wanted to be left alone to work. His were neither the politics of conformity nor the politics of resistance but rather the politics of artistic and personal survival.

Biographies of artists are not necessarily biographies of their works: Fay discusses in detail neither Shostakovich's scores nor his aesthetic theories (such as biomechanics and montage, aligned with Proletkult and Constructivist Theater) that had influenced them. However, by stressing caricature and the grotesque as integral features of Shostakovich's compositional persona—features stamped into his consciousness like genetic codes—she alludes to something crucial to the evaluation of his scores: their resistance to analytical and interpretive paradigms. Fay declares that, during the 1920s and 1930s, Shostakovich "remained aloof from the intrigues and the cliques that plagued Leningrad's musical life" (p. 57).

In *The Nose* [*Nos*] op. 15 (1927–28), a three-act opera based on Nikolai Gogol's 1836 short story, Shostakovich satirized the ideological platforms of the two rival musical institutions in the city: the Association of Contemporary Music and the aforementioned Russian Association of Proletarian Musicians. As affirmed by the rancorous press debate that followed its première, *The Nose* rejected accepted dramaturgical principle by including unusual instruments in the orchestra, using recitative patterns derived from vernacular speech, and replacing serious acting with pantomime. To an extent, the dismantling and downgrading of conventional forms in the opera capture the spirit of the source text, an absurdist morality tale set in a world in decay.[18] The assertion is not so much that Shostakovich combined "high" and "low" musical genres in the opera, but that he brought grotesque caricature into the realm of social—rather than socialist—realism.

A comparable practice is found in a composition at the end of Shostakovich's oeuvre: the Fifteenth Symphony in A Major op. 141 (1971). Owing to its allusions to his earlier scores and quotations from such disparate works as Rossini's *William Tell Overture* and Wagner's *Ring* cycle, this work has puzzled commentators since its first performance. Fay comments that,

> while Shostakovich vouchsafed no program for the symphony, after [it] was screened at the Composers' Union in the fall of 1971, he inflamed speculation by describing the first movement by means of metaphors of childhood, likening it to "a toy store." At least one critic [Matias Sokolsky] found the implication of carefree innocence here deceptive, concluding that if this was a toy store, at the very least it was one that had been locked up for the night and whose toys were clearly inclined to mutiny against the tyranny of the evil store owner. (p. 272)

The symphony beguiled Sokolsky and others because it was not internally consistent with Shostakovich's corpus as a whole—at least as Soviet music critics had assessed that corpus. The quotation of the Rossini galop in the first movement, like the quotation of the *Ring*'s "Fate" motif in the fourth movement, is a gesture that disrupts the overall system of musical representation. Through their collusion, and through the interlocking of tonal and post-tonal passages, Shostakovich not only denies symphonic norms, he also denies deviations from those norms.[19] Owing to the obfuscation of the borders between genres and syntaxes, the Fifteenth Symphony cannot be heard as an artifact of a single time and place, that is, as an artifact of a monological political system. Rather, it leaves future audiences to append their own idiosyncratic interpretations to its content—a catharsis that the symphony, and its composer, doubtless warrants.

But such points are, sadly, lost on Fay's detractors. For amending the factual record of Shostakovich's life, for straightening ideological slants, she has suffered a storm of invective in the mainstream press. Some reviews of *Shostakovich: A Life* have denounced the book's emphasis on research findings over titillating political intrigue.[20] (Post–)Cold Warrior protestations aside, Fay has produced a biography that, for the first time, places Shostakovich in accurate historical and cultural context. Her documentary work is of value precisely because questions of intention will probably continue to inform audience experiences of the composer's music, and because of the troubling and perplexing nature of his career. Beyond maintaining the highest scholarly standards, Fay affirms what Elena Basner, the widow of one of the composer's protégés, wrote about the anglophone Shostakovich debate:

> I feel sorry for those people—musicians and non-musicians—for whom, given a phenomenon such as Shostakovich, the most important question is whether he was "pro-Soviet" or "anti-Soviet." . . . I am sorry for those who are told that "the finale of Shostakovich's Fifth Symphony is not a hymn to the triumph of good over evil, but, in fact, the exact opposite," and that "the scherzo of the Tenth Symphony was conceived as a musical portrait of Stalin!" What a primitive, protozoan level of understanding! And how vulgar.[21]

Notes

1. Mark Aranovskii, "Inakomysliashchii" [The nonconformist], *Muzykal'naia akademiia*, no. 4 (1997): 3.

2. Laurel E. Fay, "Shostakovich versus Volkov: Whose *Testimony*?" *Russian Review* 39, no. 4 (1980): 484–93 (reprinted in the present volume, chapter 1. Irina Shostakovich, the composer's third wife, discusses the limited contacts between Volkov and Shostakovich in "An Answer to Those Who Still Abuse Shostakovich," *New York Times*, 20 August 2000, pp. AR 27 & 31 (reprinted in the present volume, chapter 9).

3. Allan B. Ho and Dmitri Feofanov, *Shostakovich Reconsidered* ([London]: Toccata, 1998). The book includes an "Overture" by Vladimir Ashkenazy, an interview with Volkov, a pre-*Testimony* interview from 1978 with Mstislav Rostropovich, a transcription of a Shostakovich symposium, transcriptions of lectures by Maxim Shostakovich concerning his father's symphonies, and thirteen articles, five of which are by Ian MacDonald. Ho and Feofanov's written contribution, occupying pages 33 to 311, is a hostile polemic contra Fay, Richard Taruskin, and Malcolm

Brown. Incredibly Ho and Feofanov cite a single phrase by Taruskin—"perhaps Soviet Russia's most loyal musical son" ("The Opera and the Dictator: The Peculiar Martyrdom of Dmitri Shostakovich," *New Republic*, no. 12 [20 March 1989]: 40)—nine times, albeit in two cases, on pages 172 and 532, without the "perhaps." The indexical heading "Fay, Laurel E." refers the reader to sixteen different pages of *Shostakovich Reconsidered;* the indexical subheading "Fay, Laurel E./lack of perspective" refers to ninety-six (!) pages. Now *that* is lack of perspective. Irrespective of the book's length, Ho and Feofanov do not disprove the allegation of Fay's 1980 review article, namely, that Volkov asked the ailing composer to autograph the first pages of some of his previously published articles and speeches (perhaps under the pretext that he was editing a collection of them) and then used these pages to vouchsafe the authenticity of at least partly inauthentic memoirs. Their defense of *Testimony* rests on the hard-to-swallow premise that Shostakovich, during his purportedly clandestine meetings with Volkov, dictated the pages in question from memory without alteration. Levon Akopian [Hakobian] observes that the central issue here "is not the authenticity of Shostakovich's memoirs, but that [*Testimony*] is, to a great extent, a rather primitive, empty document. The Israeli scholar Joachim Braun . . . characterizes it as a collection of lobby gossip" ("Ocherednoi 'Novyi Shostakovich' ") [The latest "new Shostakovich"], *Muzykal'naia akademiia*, no. 2 [2000]: 133; the complete text of Hakobian's article is reprinted, in translation, in the present volume, chapter 16). For a balanced overview of the entire *Testimony* debate, see Paul Mitchinson, "The Shostakovich Variations," *Lingua franca* 10, no. 4 (May/June 2000): 46–54 (an updated version of this article is printed in the present volume, selection 22).

4. Abram Tertz [Andrei Siniavskii], "*The Trial Begins*" and "*On Socialist Realism*" [*Sud idët* and *Chto takoe sotsialisticheskii realizm*], trans. Max Hayward and George Dennis, intro. Czesław Miłosz (Berkeley: University of California Press, 1960), p. 126.

5. Flora Litvinova, "Vospominaia Shostakovicha" [Remembering Shostakovich], *Znamia*, no. 12 (December 1996): 156–77; Daniel' Zhitomirsky, "Shostakovich ofitsial'nyi i podlinnyi" [Shostakovich official and genuine], *Daugava*, no. 3 (1990): 88–100, and no. 4 (1990): 97–108; *Pis'ma k drugu: Pis'ma D. D. Shostakovicha k I.D. Glikmanu* [Letters to a friend: The Letters of Dmitri Shostakovich to Isaak Glikman], edited, and with commentary, by Isaak Davydovich Glikman (Moscow: Izdatel'stvo "DSCH," 1993); *Pis'ma Dmitriia Dmitrievicha Shostakovicha Borisu Tishchenko: s kommentariiami i vospominaniiami adresata* [Letters from Dmitri Dmitrievich Shostakovich to Boris Tishchenko: with the addressee's commentaries and reminiscences] (St. Petersburg: Kompozitor, 1997).

6. The NKVD (Narodnyi kommissariat vnutrennikh del [The People's Commissariat of Internal Affairs]) was created in early 1918 to handle policing and internal affairs. In March 1954—one year after Stalin's death—the KGB (Komitet gosudarstvennoi bezopasnosti [The Committee on State Security]) replaced the NKVD.

7. Sofia Khentova, *Shostakovich: Zhizn' i tvorchestvo* [Shostakovich: Life and works], 2 vols. (Leningrad: Sovetskii kompozitor, 1985–86).

8. For example, concerning the premiére of the Thirteenth Symphony in B-flat Minor (*Babyi Yar* op. 113 [1962]), a setting of five poems by Evgeny Yev-

tushenko that decried the absence of humanity in Soviet society, Fay states that "the principals withstood all the pressures put to bear on them to cancel the performance voluntarily. Tactics of repression had changed significantly since the death of Stalin; cultural bureaucrats shrewdly calculated that the consequences of banning the performance would be more damaging than of letting it proceed" (p. 234).

9. Katerina Clark, *Petersburg, Crucible of Cultural Revolution* (Cambridge, Mass.: Harvard University Press, 1995), p. x.

10. Elizabeth Wilson, *Shostakovich: A Life Remembered* (Princeton, N.J.: Princeton University Press, 1994), pp. 108–47. Fay cites the interviews and reminiscences collected in this book throughout her biography, but, whenever possible, she independently verifies their content.

11. To support this assertion, he cites a 9 January 1936 letter from Shostakovich to Sollertinsky, in which the composer states that the two of them "would be working together for the restructuring of the musical front in Leningrad, if only on the basis of my conversations with [the Bolshevik cultural official Victor] Gorodinsky, [S.] Dinamov, and several other comrades" (Leonid Maximenkov, *Sumbur vmesto muzyki: Stalinskaia kul'turnaia revoliutsiia, 1936–1938* [A muddle instead of music: The Stalinist cultural revolution, 1936–1938] [Moscow: Yuridicheskaia Kniga, 1997], p. 76).

12. Ibid., p. 81.

13. *Pis'ma k drugu: Pis'ma D. D. Shostakovicha k I.D. Glikmanu*, p. 12, as quoted in Fay, *Shostakovich: A Life*, p. 95.

14. Marina Sabinina, "Bylo li dva Shostakovicha?" [Were there two Shostakoviches?], *Muzykal'naia akademiia*, no. 4 (1997): 236. The recently deceased author, a member of the Russian State Research Institute for Arts History in Moscow, knew Shostakovich personally.

15. "Cheryomushki," the name of a residential precinct of the city of Moscow, derives from the plural diminutive of the Russian word for the bird-cherry tree, *cheryomukha* (the *prunus padus*).

16. That Shostakovich provided subtitles for the four movements of the symphony, and imbued them with quotations from revolutionary songs, does not scuttle this interpretation. The songs date from the nineteenth century, before the events the symphony purports to represent. One of them, the marching song "Varshavianka," is of Polish, not Russian, origin; another, "You Fell a Victim" [*Vy zhertvoiu pali*], is a funeral dirge that Shostakovich quoted in different contexts in his film scores. The quotations function less to represent specific events than to create ambience.

17. On this point, Gary Saul Morson comments that *Quiet Don* "resembles [Lev] Tolstoy's *Cossacks* [*Kazaki* (1863)] more than [Nikolai] Ostrovsky's [archetypal Socialist-Realist novel], *How the Steel Was Tempered* [*Kak zakalialas' stal'* (1934)]" (in "Socialist Realism and Literary Theory," *Journal of Aesthetics and Art Criticism*, no. 38 [1979]: 122). With respect to *How the Steel Was Tempered*, Fay notes that, in 1937, Shostakovich opted out of the contract to compose the incidental music for the play version (p. 114).

18. As Alla Bretanitskaya remarks, the dramaturgical structure is composed "primarily of domestic genres, crude and utilitarian, which create strong connec-

tions between the representatives of middle-class, bureaucratic Petersburg: a galop aligns [the hero] Kovalyov and the Police Commissioner, a polka the Police Commissioner and the Doctor, a waltz rhythm unites Kovalyov and Podtochina . . . and so forth" ("O muzykal'noi dramaturgii opery 'Nos' " [On the musical dramaturgy of the opera, "The Nose"], *Sovetskaia muzyka,* no. 9 [1974]: 48).

19. On this point, see Edward Murphy, "A Programme for the First Movement of Shostakovich's Fifteenth Symphony: 'A Debate about Four Musical Styles,' " *Music Review* 53, no. 1 (1992): 47–62.

20. See, for example, Sudip Bose, "Subversive Symphonies," *Washington Post Book World,* 28 November 1999, p. X03; and Harlow Robinson, "A Bitter Music," *New York Times Book Review,* 2 January 2000, p. 22. For a critical response to these and two other writers, Joseph Horowitz and Norman Lebrecht, see Richard Taruskin, "Casting a Great Composer as a Fictional Hero," *New York Times,* 5 March 2000, p. AR 43.

21. Elena Basner, "Vlast' i poshlost' " [The regime and vulgarity], *Izvestiia,* 8 June 1999, p. 5; reprinted in the present volume, chapter 11. Basner loosely paraphrases two passages from Volkov's *Testimony,* as cited in Ho and Feofanov, *Shostakovich Reconsidered,* pp. 165, 168.

Editor's Note

a. For an explanation of the Russian word *rayok,* see the Nikolskaya interviews in the current volume, chapter 13, editor's note r.

25

When Serious Music Mattered

On Shostakovich and Three Recent Books (2001)

RICHARD TARUSKIN

I

The big signal fact of Dmitri Shostakovich's career was his eventual status as the one and only Soviet artist to be claimed equally, and equally ardently, by the official establishment and the rising counterculture alike. The achievement was not his alone. It was the convoluted result of the enormous talent he was dealt, the all-too-interesting times in which he lived, the nature of the art in which he worked, and his capacity to maintain a poker face. His music was at once an irresistible expressive conveyance and a tabula rasa on which all and sundry could inscribe their various messages with a minimum of resistance.

Shostakovich became, in sum, the very embodiment of existential doubleness, a distinction that magnified his significance far beyond the frontiers of the society he served, and far beyond the confines of the aesthetic. The enormous burgeoning of worldwide interest in him since his death in 1975 has been a token of the twentieth century's anxious

---

Originally published as "Double Trouble," *New Republic*, 24 December 2001, pp. 26–34. Updated and reprinted with permission.

efforts to come to terms with its ghastly historical legacy—efforts that will inevitably continue far into the twenty-first. As they do so, Shostakovich will surely overtake Schoenberg and Stravinsky for recognition as "the most consequential composer of the twentieth century," which is what Susan McClary, a leader in postmodernist (or "new") musicology, somewhat surprisingly persisted in calling Schoenberg at a recent symposium organized in his honor by the Los Angeles Philharmonic. Schoenberg's and Stravinsky's consequences were of course immense. But they were felt mainly within the world of music composition—the world treated as the entire subject of music history only by "old" musicologists. Shostakovich was consequential within far more consequential domains, those of music's meaning and its social reception. These have become the subject matter of a newer, far more consequential musicology.

Stravinsky tried to insulate his art from questions about its meaning. Those famous, and for a long time hugely influential, fighting words from his 1936 autobiography—"music is, by its very nature, essentially powerless to *express* anything at all"—are no longer taken seriously by any serious musician. They can serve now as a memento of their time, when artists—especially uprooted aristocrats like Stravinsky—were frantic to protect their creative autonomy from totalitarian threat. Schoenberg, believing that art had a history separable from that of the social world, and believing that that history imposed inexorable obligations on serious artists, tried to insulate his art from social reception. He organized the Society for Private Performances in Vienna, where significant works of new music were disseminated among musicians so as to further the stylistic and technical evolution that history mandated in an atmosphere uncontaminated by publicity. It provided the conceptual model and inspiration for the retreat of advanced musical composition into universities and think tanks after the Second World War. It was a self-deluded, self-defeating mission. "Autonomy" (which was not only guaranteed but enforced) metamorphosed into sheer irrelevance.

Like most members of my generation, I was reared musically and musicologically in this atmosphere. I was taught to disdain the artistic products of societies in which the creative autonomy of artists was not guaranteed. The only time I recall hearing the music of Shostakovich in the classroom during my undergraduate years and those when I attended graduate seminars (roughly the 1960s) was when the "invasion" episode from his Seventh ("Leningrad") Symphony was juxtaposed with Bartók's mockery of it in his Concerto for Orchestra, and we were all invited to mock along. Then, I suppose, we went back to analyzing Schoenberg's technical innovations.

Soon afterward I was forced to revise my opinion, not only about Shostakovich but also about my own education in music. I spent the academic year 1971–72 as an exchange student at the Moscow Conservatory, researching a dissertation on Russian opera in the 1860s. The better part of my time, in every sense of the word, was spent socializing with my Soviet counterparts and attending concert and opera performances. Naturally many of those events were devoted to the works of Shostakovich. At one concert I heard the Seventh Symphony, performed under Kirill Kondrashin in the Conservatory's fabled Great Hall. I knew the work not only as the butt of Bartók's sarcasm but also as the object of one of Virgil Thomson's snottiest reviews. Connoisseurs of musical invective knew Thomson's text almost by heart. It opened with the remark that "whether one is able to listen without mind-wandering to the Seventh Symphony of Dmitri Shostakovich probably depends on the rapidity of one's musical perceptions; it seems to have been written for the slow-witted, the not very musical and the distracted"; and it ended with an immortal insult: "That he has so deliberately diluted his matter, adapted it, by both excessive simplification and excessive repetition, to the comprehension of a child of eight, indicates that he is willing to write down to a real or fictitious psychology of mass consumption in a way that may eventually disqualify him for consideration as a serious composer."[1]

Since deriding this symphony was a badge of musical sophistication where I came from, I glanced at appropriate moments at my Soviet companions, hoping to exchange a wink. But, no. My friends, who were at least as learned and intelligent as I, and who were normally just as irreverent about everything students were supposed to be irreverent about, were mesmerized. I glanced around the hall and noticed my scholarly adviser, a deeply erudite musicologist, and also some composition students I knew from the dormitory who were studying with Denisov and Schnittke, the touted nonconformists of the day, and even (privately) with Filip Gershkovich, the shadowy ex-Webernite who was keeping the sputtering flame of modernism alive somewhere in darkest Moscow. They, too, were in a trance.

These were not eight-year-olds. There was nothing wrong with their musical perceptions. For their quick wits and musicality I could certainly vouch. The awful thought struck me that they valued this music, which

I had been taught to despise, more highly than I valued any music, and that Shostakovich meant more to his (and their) society than any composer meant to mine. For the first time there occurred to me, half-formed, the unbearable suspicion that the ways of listening to and thinking about music that had been instilled in me and all my peers at home were impoverished.

In the case of the Seventh, the thought could be somewhat allayed by recalling its special historical circumstances. The audience around me, I told myself, was not responding to the symphony but rather to memories of, or propaganda about, the war. The war, not Shostakovich, was the artist who was working such an uncanny effect on them. It was a relatively benign example, or so I let myself think, of Soviet brainwashing. But soon after, I attended two concerts in the Great Hall at which later works of Shostakovich were played that carried no such ready-made associations, and at which the composer appeared on stage to receive applause.

At one of them, Mstislav Rostropovich, already under a gathering cloud for sheltering Solzhenitsyn (who was in attendance and much gawked at), played the Second Cello Concerto, which had been written for and dedicated to him five years earlier. The same electric atmosphere pervaded the hall, but this time it was an atmosphere not of patriotic nostalgia but of risk. The idea of Shostakovich's doubleness struck me then for the first time, and with tremendous force. It was not only Shostakovich's unique stature among Soviet composers that struck me but also his unique stature among all the artists I could name. It was a backhanded fulfillment of the old Socialist-Realist—and the even older Tolstoyan—ideal of an art that spoke with equal directness and equal consequence to all levels of society, from the least to the most educated. Obviously that fulfillment was not to be credited in this case to Socialist Realism. By the time he wrote the Second Cello Concerto in 1966, Shostakovich had made a *reprise de contact* with his modernist youth. His new works were regarded as "difficult"—a difficulty that members of the audience acknowledged but that did not faze them in the way new music put off audiences in the West. Still less, of course, was the universality of Shostakovich's appeal a matter of Christian fellowship à la Tolstoy. So what was its source?

The first glimmer of an answer came on the other occasion where I saw Shostakovich: the première of the Fifteenth Symphony, his last, led by his son Maxim in the Great Hall on 8 January 1972. The work, with its jolly quotation from Rossini in the first movement and its ravaged quotation from Wagner in the last, was puzzling, as everyone I conversed with agreed. It was not much liked, actually. But the outpouring of love that greeted the gray, stumbling, begoggled figure of the author, then sixty-five and beset by a multitude of infirmities, was not just an obeisance to the Soviet composer laureate. It was a grateful, emotional salute to a cherished life companion, a fellow citizen and fellow sufferer, who had forged a mutually sustaining relationship with his public that was altogether outside the experience of any musician in my part of the world. I was shaken that night in a way that no concert before or since has shaken me.

If the overall effect of a year lived in the USSR during its Brezhnevite "stagnation" was to rattle me out of my complacency regarding the inhumanity of the Soviet regime, the effect of this particular evening was to rattle me out of my complacency regarding the inhumanity of the musical aesthetic in which I had been raised—one that nurtured self-regard and social indifference, and placed the highest value on *l'audace, toujours l'audace*. That aesthetic reached its farcical apogee with Karlheinz Stockhausen's enviously admiring response to the destruction of the World Trade Center. But long before Stockhausen turned it into a grim laughingstock, the avant-garde position—in effect the aesthetic of spoiled brats—had become a cultural leftover, emptied of appeal not just for audiences but for artists as well. What it lacked, precisely, is the resonance that comes from doubleness. And the source of doubleness is social engagement.

II

Shostakovich's doubleness was something he never sought. It was thrust upon him on 28 January 1936 (the very year Stravinsky published his autobiography, with its formalist credo), when the twenty-nine-year-old composer was not only attacked but mortally threatened ("It could end very badly")[2] in the pages of *Pravda* by what everyone was soon calling the "Historic Document," namely, the famous and ominously unsigned editorial "Muddle Instead of Music" that ended the brilliant two-year career of his opera *Ledi Makbet Mtsenskogo uezda* [Lady Macbeth of the Mtsensk District], during which time it had gone round the world.

Up to that point Shostakovich had himself been a spoiled brat of sorts. His preeminence among the first generation of Soviet-educated composers was assured by the première of his First Symphony, when he was nineteen. After Bruno Walter played the work in Berlin in February

1928, the composer, twenty-one years old at the time, became a world celebrity and would remain one for the rest of his life. In 1927 Shostakovich received a state commission for a large choral-orchestral composition to mark the tenth anniversary of the Bolshevik Revolution. Originally titled "To October," it entered his catalog as his Second Symphony. In 1929 Vladimir Mayakovsky asked him to furnish incidental music for the play *The Bedbug* [*Klop*], after which Shostakovich became the most sought-after composer for the Soviet stage and the fledgling Soviet film industry. Between 1929 and the date of the *Pravda* denunciation, he composed seven incidental scores (including one for Nikolai Akimov's sarcastically "revisionist" staging of *Hamlet* at the Vakhtangov Theater) and three ballets. *Lady Macbeth* was Shostakovich's second opera. The first was the wildly surrealistic *The Nose* [*Nos*] (1930), after Gogol, with its all-percussion entr'actes, its snoring and gargling cavatinas, and its mock-castrato constables. During the first decade of his creative career, Shostakovich was the musical spokesman and darling of the young Soviet state, thriving in the din of industrialization and social experiment, giving interviews to foreign correspondents, and sending his works all over Europe and America for performance.

His musical style during this period is often called satirical. It owed a lot to the Weimar Republic's we-won't-be-fooled-again aesthetic of *Neue Sachlichkeit* or "New Objectivity," musically exemplified by the young Hindemith, whom Shostakovich idolized. Its satire arose out of a play of incongruities—a rhetorical doubleness—that undermined eloquence and "seriosity." The most primitive (and popular) examples were "wrong note" pieces like the Polka from Shostakovich's ballet *Golden Age* [*Zolotoi vek*] (1930), in which dissonance, normally an expressive device, is used pervasively within a trivial dance genre where expressive dissonance is rarely, if ever, employed. The incongruity calls both components into question. If a polka, why dissonant? If dissonant, why a polka? In its original context a third incongruous element was introduced in the form of top-hatted *burzhuis* [bourgeoisie] on stage, canting in Geneva on behalf of disarmament and world peace. The hypocritical rhetoric of the League of Nations (from which the Soviet Union was then excluded) may have been the original target of satire, the polka mocking its pretension, the dissonance its absurdity. In a concert performance, the venue itself could become the butt, as Shostakovich implied when he arranged the Polka a year later for string quartet, the quintessentially *burzhui* medium (and one for which he had not yet composed seriously).

In Shostakovich's early symphonies and concertos, the *lyogkii zhanr* [light genre] itself became the incongruous marker, with or without wrong notes. The cabaret waltz that assumes the role of "second theme" in the first movement of the First Symphony, or the madcap galops in the second and fourth movements (in which a solo piano unexpectedly participates, recalling the fledgling composer's employment in silent-movie theaters), suggested a brash, good-humored skepticism toward canonical genres that was easily correlated with the brashness and healthy cynicism of the limber, fast-moving young Soviet state in its time of (as yet relatively uncoerced) optimism. That happy iconoclasm acted as a preservative through which a high professional culture that might have seemed outmoded, along with the class system that supported it—and did so seem to the many clamoring proletarian factions who called for its dismantling—could be adapted to the new order and thus have a Soviet future.

The same techniques, adapted to the purposes of characterization, found their most trenchant application in *Lady Macbeth* (1930–32). Nikolai Leskov, the author of the eponymous horror story on which the opera was based, had cast the title character, a multiple murderess, as a she-devil pure and simple. Shostakovich took it upon himself, in a move all too characteristic of the high-Stalinist onrush then in progress, to rehabilitate her, even to make her a class heroine, by dehumanizing all her victims and potential judges through admixtures of low genre. In taking his famous umbrage at the graphic sex scenes, Stalin missed the Stalinist message of the work (not that there was any real message in "Muddle Instead of Music" beyond the warning that no one was safe). Others at home read it loud and clear; but abroad, the stylistic incongruities tended to baffle and offend. Elliott Carter, who caught the opera in a very late staging in East Berlin, dismissed it on the high-modernist grounds of stylistic disunity, and found "unaccountable" the opera's capital sociopolitical stroke: the mitigation of the innocent husband's murder by accompanying it with a typically trivializing galop that deprived him of his humanity.

It was the banning of this inhumane opera that humanized its composer and turned him into an emblem of doubleness—a doubleness that ineluctably colored the reception of his works from then on (and was later read back, inevitably, into his early works as well). Shostakovich was now a marked man, in every sense of the word. His victimization by the regime effectively transformed him into a semiotic marker. Every one of his subsequent compositions now had a subtext. That subtext, ironically enough, was first foisted upon the composer by the regime itself, when it commissioned from Shostakovich (or from somebody) a newspaper article published under the composer's byline that characterized his Fifth Symphony (1937) as "a Soviet artist's creative response to just criticism" and described the work as a record of "all that I have thought and felt"[3] since being attacked in *Pravda*.

That opened up the floodgates to the Babel—or at least the babble—of conflicting interpretations that has since swirled around every single one of his works. Everything was read as a creative response to the totalitarian state, all the more so after the next bout of victimization: the so-called *Zhdanovshchina*, a series of musical show trials convened by Andrei Zhdanov, Stalin's de facto cultural commissar, at which all the major Soviet composers were forced to make groveling recantations of their "formalist" misdeeds, and which culminated in the promulgation, on 10 February 1948, of the infamous Resolution on Music of the Central Committee of the All-Union Soviet Communist Party (Bolshevik).

For a long time, only the official interpretations had access to the Soviet public media; but even the published reviews and analyses were subjected to Aesopian examination, and a counter-literature of private diary entries, word of mouth, émigré publications, and samizdat began to gather around Shostakovich. One of the earliest examples to see print came in 1951 with the publication of *Taming of the Arts*,[4] a memoir by Juri Jelagin (that is, Yury Elagin), a postwar émigré who had been a violinist at the Vakhtangov Theater and had attended one of the early Leningrad performances of the Fifth. "Later," he wrote,

> when I tried to analyze the reason for the devastating impression the Fifth Symphony made on me and on the entire audience I came to the conclusion that its musical qualities, no matter how great, were by themselves not enough to create that effect. . . . The Soviet government had set the stage for the incredible triumph of the gifted composer with long months of persecution and with the senseless attacks on his works. The educated Russians who had gathered in the auditorium that night had staged a demonstration expressing their love for his music, as well as their indignation at the pressure that had been exerted in the field of art and their sympathy and understanding for the victim.[5]

Shostakovich managed to maintain his doubleness, and the consequent social value of his reception, first, by maintaining a near-perfect silence, rarely if ever offering any interpretive commentary on his work except the kind that, by appearing under fully controlled government auspices, guaranteed an Aesopian reading; and, second, by profoundly altering his stylistic manner after the watershed of 1936. This was indeed a creative response. It could be read as conformism, but it also managed vastly to stimulate the unofficial interpretive pluralism that turned Shostakovich's music—or, rather, the reception of it—into the secret diary of a nation.

III

In the aftermath of "Muddle," Shostakovich renounced his older satirical manner and replaced it with what might best be called heroic classicism. Seemingly in keeping with official demands, he adopted a suitably exalted "high style" for the properly reverential positive treatment of Soviet reality. Following the example of Beethoven—particularly the Ninth Symphony, which shared his own Fifth Symphony's key of D minor—but also following the Socialist-Realist precepts then being worked out for music (particularly by the musicologist Boris Asafyev, who codified the theoretical categories of "musical imagery" and "intonation"), Shostakovich began loading his work, especially his large instrumental compositions, with what musicologists in the West now call "topics" (from the Greek *topoi*). These are musical morphemes, basic semantic units that are marked by associations of various kinds—ecclesiastical, martial, pastoral, and so forth. They can refer to everyday musical genres or to specific musical works or to the phenomenal world through onomatopoeia (or through metonymy, as when a sudden rapid scale in a high "bright" register evokes lightning or when an up-and-down contour suggests water). They can be "iconic," suggesting modes of human behavior indicative of affect. They can be straightforward or they can be distorted—in rhythm, in harmony, in tempo, in timbre, in contour.

The naïve or ideal view of musical topics, the view espoused by Asafyev, is that they render the content of music more explicit and hence more accessible (and more susceptible to censorship and control). In actual practice they easily lead to a Bakhtinian "carnivalism," especially when they are as brusquely contrasted, or as violently exaggerated, as they often are in Shostakovich. Above all, they are transferable, through the listener's own repertoire of associations. A vivid example is the reception of Shostakovich's Eleventh Symphony (1957), somewhat belatedly commemorating the semi-centennial of the "first" Russian revolution of 1905. The movements carry titles that ostensibly specify (that is, limit) the referential significance of the topics and images, which include old revolutionary songs and lots of violent percussion.

The music is perfectly adequate to the program. Indeed, Anna Akhmatova, no paragon of conformism, straightforwardly praised the imagery of the first movement ("The Palace Square") for the way it conjured up the vast, quiet expanse of the Winter Palace grounds and the atmosphere of foreboding that she remembered from having lived through the events depicted. In May 1958 Shostakovich was sent on a goodwill tour of Italy and France, the two Western European countries with the strongest communist parties. The Eleventh Symphony, which had been awarded a Lenin Prize, was given its foreign premières at this time (and recorded in Paris under André Cluytens), and it was effusively praised for its vivid embodiment of the hopes of progressive humanity. The French composer Georges Auric sang it a paean (*Dmitri Chostakovitch, j'écoute, nous écoutons!*) precisely for its Socialist-Realist virtues of accessibility and clarity of expression:

> It is "as an open book" that our composer is to be deciphered. From night to full sunlight, he avoids having any "secret," and does not seek to keep for himself and a few chosen ones the keys to his language and his heart. We are here in an authentically "public" domain, and—let it immediately be added—in the highest meaning of such a term. Anyone who wishes may enter into it and share in the special radiance of such music.[6]

Meanwhile, back home, as numerous memoirs now attest, the second movement of the symphony ("January Ninth"), with its big bangs, was being widely read by audiences primed to Shostakovich's endemic doubleness not as a depiction of "Bloody Sunday," the massacre of peaceful petitioners by tsarist troops, but as a principled protest against the Soviet suppression of the Hungarian revolt of 1956.

Which was it? Silly question! Guns go bang whether wielded by Tsarists or Soviets, and all that Shostakovich had put into his score (that is, into "the music itself") was the bang. One could argue at any length and any heat that the subtitle favored the one view, but no argument could prevent an audience from assembling in a concert hall and deriving from the other view an elating (and risk-free!) sense of solidarity in protest that was otherwise beyond its reach. One chose the reading that suited one's needs, and in the Soviet Union there was an enormous need for that choice. Never were the special nature and the special value of music so nobly affirmed as it was by the sheer interpretive opportunism Shostakovich offered listeners, thanks to the inherent polysemy of the medium in which he worked, and the invitation to double reading that his personal circumstances extended.

That huge social value is what I witnessed in Moscow when I caught my glimpses of the precious, infirm composer and was so greatly moved. I did not know how to name it at the time. And there are very many who cannot see it even now. For strange to say, there seems to be less understanding abroad of Shostakovich's doubleness now, especially in the uncomprehending West, than there was during Soviet power. Most of the late- and post-Soviet literature has been an attempt to reduce that doubleness to singleness, albeit the opposite singleness to what the Party had once tried to enforce. The new party line traces its origin to *Testimony*,[7] the volume of "Memoirs of Dmitri Shostakovich, as related to and edited by Solomon Volkov," that appeared in 1979, when the Cold War was about to enter its final phase (the Reagan presidency, the Afghan adventure). It portrays the composer as an implacable enemy of the Evil Empire, who used his music to send explicitly dissident, explicitly anti-communist messages. This is the model according to which Shostakovich has been marketed for the last two decades, very successfully, in the West.

Scholars have easily exposed *Testimony* as a fraud within only a year of its publication, and evidence has been mounting ever since. (Laurel Fay, Volkov's most persistent and effective critic and herself the author of the one factually reliable biography of Shostakovich in English,[8] delivers the coup de grâce in the present volume, "Volkov's *Testimony* Reconsidered," chapter 2.) *Testimony* has been published by now in some thirty languages, but Volkov, who owns the rights to it, has never allowed publication of the original Russian text, which speaks for itself.

Still, the scholarly objections have been dependably shouted down by a host of political and commercial exploiters (and a few timorous or dull-witted academics), and there is no reason to expect them to stop. Francis Maes, the Belgian impresario who directs the Flanders Festival, and who himself, in that capacity, has participated in the commercial exploitation of the dissidence myth, atones by unsparingly setting out its motives and strategies in a section of his recent *History of Russian Music* called "Shostakovich and the Modern Music Market."[9] One of the ugliest phases of this exploitation has been the systematic vilification of Laurel Fay in a fashion that farcically replays the tragic tactics of the *Zhdanovshchina*.

IV

That is why one extends such a hopeful welcome to Esti Sheinberg's *Irony, Satire, Parody and the Grotesque in the Music of Shostakovich*.[10] It is a study that not only accepts the doubleness of Shostakovich's creative persona but also sets out to analyze it. The author is a semiotician by training rather than a Shostakovich specialist. She was attracted to Shostakovich precisely by the interpretive conflicts that surround his legacy, which seemed to promise a rich field for the study of music as a sign system and, in particular, as a means of approaching "the overall semantic structure of ambiguity" in a nonverbal medium. "Rather than focusing on ways 'to get to correct solutions' and decide which element of a certain ambiguity is to be preferred," Sheinberg writes, "this study examines the various ways in which musical correlations of semantic ambiguities are created and how they work as artistic expressions" (p. 15). Instead of replaying the behavior of Shostakovich's audiences and invoking semiotics opportunistically to support arbitrary or tendentious interpretations, she purports to take a distanced view, setting Shostakovich's works within the broad context of structuralist semiotics and the history of its applications, within the history of artistic irony in all media, and in light of its various philosophical and political critiques.

Building on the work of linguists and music semioticians such as Algirdas Greimas, Edwin Battistella, Eero Tarasti, Robert Hatten, and Raymond Monelle, Sheinberg shows how the topics that Shostakovich manipulates are often deployed as "contrarieties," contradictory pairs that are defined not in absolute terms but within a given cultural context. Normally one member of a contrariety is taken as a norm or default mode, the other as a "marked" deviation. To boil down her central claim to a single (and, of course, oversimplified) sentence, she contends—and succeeds in demonstrating—that musical irony is achieved when a marked element is treated as if unmarked.

This is a useful model. I have been tacitly applying it in my descriptions of such pieces as the *Golden Age* Polka and the First Symphony. It works best when the contrarieties are simple binaries (consonance versus dissonance, high culture versus low). This is the level at which satire operates. Sheinberg is well aware that this simple level does not exhaust the possibilities for musical ambiguity or its interpretation. She astutely associates the watershed in Shostakovich's career in 1936 with a shift in the nature of his ironic practice. Once a (mere) satirist, for whom irony was a means toward a debunking end (irony as stimulus, in Kierkegaard's terminology), the composer became, in the battered latter half of his career, an existential ironist for whom irony was a detached and melancholy worldview (irony as terminus). "Like a half-smiling, resigned Pierrot," she writes, "Shostakovich's music seems to dance on a tightrope, letting its unresolvable incongruities express the infinite provisionality of existential irony" (p. 319).

In a brief historical survey Sheinberg recounts the ethical objections that melioristic or progressive thinkers like Hegel and Marx have leveled at half-smiling existential irony, regarding it as nihilistic, alienating, degenerate. That already begins to account for the official suspicion that always dogged Shostakovich under the high-Stalinist regime, and the fear of the uncontainable that his powerful music has always inspired in authoritarians (Soviet or anti-Soviet), leading to all the attempts at containment, whether by denunciation or adulation, coercion or cajolery, censorship or co-option, but never to neglect or indifference. Shostakovich was perhaps the most pestered composer who ever lived, and surely the most posthumously pestered. Better than any previous writer, Esti Sheinberg shows why.

Unfortunately her practice falls rather short of her theory. Even when dealing with the later work she tries "to get to correct solutions," subjecting works like the Thirteenth Symphony, and especially the song cycle *Iz evreiskoi narodnoi poezii* [From Jewish folk poetry] (everybody's favorite hobbyhorse), to readings just as opportunistic and limiting as anyone else's, often relying for evidence, it pains me to report, on *Testimony*. Elsewhere she ventures to isolate as many as four layers of definite, mutually exclusive meaning in the tiny Prelude for piano op. 34 no. 2, usually heard as an innocently humorous "wrong note" parody of the "Canto gitano" from Rimsky-Korsakov's *Cappriccio espagnol* (itself a parody). Arbitrary segmentation, the great bane of ordinary musical analysis, becomes even more of an encumbrance here than usual, because the stakes have been raised.

Like other semioticians who have tackled music, Sheinberg relies heavily on analogies to literature (or literary criticism) and painting, where semantics are presumed to be more stable. That presumption having been so damagingly challenged by poststructuralist theory, it would have been much more useful to let music dictate the semantic terms for a change and provide a model for literature. But even if one grants her premises, Sheinberg's literary analogies can be naïvely literalistic. She seems to imply that Shostakovich learned his rhetorical strategies from the Russian Formalists and Bakhtin, wasting many pages attempting to show that it was not unlikely that Shostakovich was not unaware of this critic or that one, or that he knew someone who knew someone who knew someone else. At one point she even proposes that

Shostakovich's topical allusiveness "might be the result of an attempt to apply Bakhtin's ideas about literary plurivocality to music" (pp. 197–98). But it is critics, in this case Sheinberg, who "apply" such things, not composers.

The source of all these difficulties is Sheinberg's unwillingness to shed the notion that musical meaning, simple or complex, is something vested in it by the creator. Shostakovich's doubleness, in her view, is entirely of his making. Her reluctance to acknowledge that irony is as much a way of reading as of writing is a dated prejudice that greatly limits the explanatory reach of her theory. Her treatment of Shostakovich's doubleness finally remains univocal and misses at least half the story. It will be surpassed, and soon. But whoever surpasses Sheinberg's treatment will have to take her work onboard. Despite its limitations, she has made an indispensable contribution to the analysis of Shostakovich's creative potency, and to understanding how his meanings were constructed.

V

Two books of letters also reinforce, albeit unintentionally, the great watershed of 1936. Those in *Story of a Friendship: The Letters of Dmitri Shostakovich to Isaak Glikman, 1941–1975*, addressed to and edited by Glikman, a theater historian, were originally published in Russia in 1993.[11] By now they have been well assimilated into the scholarly and, to a lesser extent, even the popular literature about the composer. Glikman was not only a confidant of Shostakovich but was also a frequent factotum who served as unpaid secretary, occasional ghostwriter, and ever-ready errand runner. His portrayal of Shostakovich, reflexively aping the manner of Soviet biography, is hagiographical, although the canonizing authority is now more anti- than pro-Soviet. His book shares with Soviet publications some other annoying habits, including frequent and obtuse editorial interventions (some of them consolidated, abridged, or omitted by the capable translator) to control the reader's response. I have strong suspicions, too, that the texts it transmits—which Glikman reportedly dictated to a stenographer—have been silently "corrected" like those published in Soviet times.

The most noteworthy news item in the collection concerns the poignant Eighth Quartet (1960), dedicated to "the victims of Fascism and the war" but almost universally read as a rueful musical autobiography because all its themes are derived from the composer's musical monogram—DSCH, which equals D, E-flat, C, B, as named in German—and placed in counterpoint with a web of self-quotations, and also with a famous revolutionary prison song. In his letter to Glikman of 19 July 1960 Shostakovich remarked that the work was dedicated to his own memory, and Glikman's commentary explains that it was composed in a fit of self-loathing after Shostakovich had allowed himself to be recruited for membership in the Communist Party as part of a campaign to validate Khrushchev's liberalizing moves by mobilizing the support of the intelligentsia. (The clinching argument was the reminder that Khrushchev had authorized the partial rescinding of the 1948 Resolution on Music.) The juxtaposition of the monogram and the prison song was, in effect, the composer's apology for his craven behavior, a reminder that he was "tortured by grievous unfreedom," as the words of the song declare.

The story is plausible, and it answers a frequently asked question: Why did Shostakovich join up as a Communist just as the dissident movement, with which so many now want to associate him, was getting under way? And yet the actual circumstances of the quartet's composition (assuming that they indeed are these) did not prevent audiences from being deeply moved by it when it was interpreted, and promoted by the cultural bureaucracy, in accordance with its stated dedication. The actual musical content—construed as sonic gestures, topics, and "intonations"—supports either reading, or both. There is no reason, apart from political bias, to regard them as contradictory.

Those looking for corroboration of Shostakovich's political dissidence will think that they have found it when they read the many letters to Glikman that express the composer's resentment at his mistreatment or that skillfully parody Soviet officialese or poke guarded fun at the "cult of personality." The one that most moved me was a letter in which Shostakovich quietly but staunchly expressed his wonder at the quality of one of his compositions (Glikman speculates that it was the Eighth Symphony, banned by the *Zhdanovshchina*) and his joy in being its author. What makes the letter moving is not its content but its date, 21 December 1949—Stalin's seventieth birthday, manically celebrated throughout the Soviet Union in a manner unforgettably satirized by Solzhenitsyn in *The First Circle* [*V kruge pervom*]. Strangely enough, Glikman, elsewhere so keen to point out the most trivial and transparent ironies, failed to notice this one. Shostakovich may have overestimated his friend's perspicacity.

But none of this is dissidence. It is, rather, the old "fig in the pocket,"[a] the self-consoling recourse of the disaffected. Another example was Shostakovich's incorporation of a greatly distorted and disguised version of

Suliko, a Georgian popular tune known to be Stalin's favorite, in his First Cello Concerto. He asked Rostropovich one day whether he had noticed. Rostropovich had not. Shostakovich's pocket could be rather deep. A dissident did not use pockets. It is the open fig that marks—no, makes—the dissident.

Shostakovich's holy human hatred of his oppressors was vehement and profound. It is hilariously expressed in his *Antiformalist Peepshow* [*Antiformalisticheskii rayok*], a cantata that ridiculed the *Zhdanovshchina*, which he wrote "for the drawer" (the composer's version of the pocket), possibly in 1948, and revised around 1968. Glikman shared his friend's love of parodies of this sort and wrote a few himself (included in an appendix to the volume of letters). But to jump from such expressions of disaffection to blunt anticommunism (or pro-Westernism), as so many reviewers of the Glikman letters have done, is a gross misstep. It amounts to equating a critic, say, of Sen. Joseph McCarthy with an enemy of America (or a friend of Russia)—that is to say, it amounts to adopting the viewpoint and the values of a Zhdanov or a McCarthy. And it casts the composer's many civic acts and duties—not only as a Party member but also as a deputy to the Supreme Soviet who met regularly with his "constituents," a Soviet representative to several international peace conferences, and the president of the Russian branch of the Union of Soviet Composers—not to mention his acceptance of as many official honors and medals as any Politburo member—as so much hypocrisy. It was by participating in the life of his society—the only society he had a chance to participate in—rather than by holding himself above it in holy alienation, that he achieved the unique public stature that so distinguished him both from the Party hacks at home and from his sadly marginalized Western counterparts.

In a large, comprehensive, fabulously informative but not yet translated publication of documents from the museum's own collection called *Dmitri Shostakovich v pis'makh i dokumentakh* [Dmitri Shostakovich in letters and documents],[12] the Glinka Museum of Musical Art in Moscow has provided hair-raising evidence that Shostakovich could play the Soviet political game as well as anybody, and that he used his newly powerful position as Party member and Union president (and, possibly, accepted it) with an eye toward payback. At the first Union meeting at which he presided, in February 1960, Shostakovich delivered a blistering attack on the repertoire of the Pyatnitsky Choir, the Soviet Union's preeminent "fakelore" ensemble, and in particular on the work of its director, Marian Koval, a hack composer who had published, during the

Zhdanovshchina, a slanderous trio of essays in *Sovetskaia muzyka* (February, March, and April 1948), the official organ of the all-Soviet Composers' Union, collectively titled "Tvorcheskii put' D. Shostakovicha" [D. Shostakovich's creative path]. To V. V. Khvatov, one of the choir's staff arrangers, Shostakovich wrote in his official capacity that Khvatov's arrangement of the folk dance *Kamarinskaya* "has nothing in common with the art of music" (p. 425 n. 4), repeating practically verbatim the humiliating words uttered by Vladimir Zakharov, Koval's predecessor as choir director, about Shostakovich's Eighth Symphony from the very rostrum of the Central Committee in 1948. No, Shostakovich was not a saint.

Perhaps the least palatable passage in Glikman's volume to those who need to see a heroic resister in Shostakovich will be the letter of 21 March 1955, in which he discusses with Glikman the revisions he wished to make in *Lady Macbeth* before submitting it for rehabilitation (something not achieved until December 1962). The new version, retitled *Katerina Izmailova* and so extensively revised as to merit a new opus number, was significantly softened along lines that were consistent with the harsh criticism the opera had received in "Muddle instead of Music." Some of the most blatant "pornophony" (to use the pretty term coined in 1935 by the reviewer for the *New York Sun*) was removed from the score, and the text was bowdlerized. The letter leaves no doubt that at least the textual softening was voluntary, motivated by civil consideration, altogether at variance with the composer's younger self, for the sensibilities of the audience. Performing the opera in the form that was banned in 1936 has become the standard practice in the West (often incorporating the revised and expanded version of the final scene, which depicts a convoy en route to Siberia), and it is usually thought of as an act of solidarity with the composer against the prudery of the totalitarian state. But in fact Shostakovich disagreed, and even moved to suppress the opera in its original form once the new version was ready. Today's producers and audiences have every right to prefer what they prefer, but they cannot claim to be vindicating the composer's intentions, still less claim a moral justification for indulging a profitable taste for pornophony. The composer of *Katerina Izmailova*, the subject of Glikman's book, was evidently a far different composer from that of *Lady Macbeth*.

VI

It is the great merit of the Glinka Museum anthology that it finally gives that younger composer a voice. Roughly half its nearly six hundred pages contain material from the mid- to late 1920s, the period of his first fame. The voice of Shostakovich in those days was the voice of a young Siegfried, a cocky voice and a happy one despite periods of real material privation. (In one letter he apologizes for a late reply by explaining that in the past couple of weeks he did not have the price of a postage stamp.) It is the voice of a young man reveling in his strength and, above all, the voice of one who has not yet learned to live in fear. At the same time it is the voice of a spoiled mama's boy (drolly accompanied at times by Mama herself, writing to some of her son's eminent correspondents to make sure Mitya was drinking his kefir and wearing his jacket) and of an inveterate joker. It is much assisted in its present reincarnation by the editors' factual annotations, and it is only occasionally saddled with their interpretive intrusions. Although one can never be sure, one is given no reason a priori to suspect bowdlerization of the texts one is reading. In a fashion no previous Russian publication has approached concerning Shostakovich, readers are invited to lower their well-exercised strategic defenses and indulge the illusion that they are for once seeing Shelley plain, even if it is a Shelley who loved to pose and prevaricate. To say as much brings all the defenses rushing back, of course, and that is only as it should be. But I take pleasure in quoting some plums.

"The trrrragic style makes me laugh out loud" (p. 109), writes Mitya in 1927 in one of the sixty-six letters collected here addressed to Boleslav Yavorsky (1877–1942), one of the great *éminences grises* in the history of Russian and Soviet music. Trained as a mathematician, Yavorsky was a minor pianist and composer, but a dazzlingly original music theorist who published little but had an enormous influence on his many pupils, as well as on those who, like the young Shostakovich, sought him out as a mentor. I would be failing in my duty to the new musicology not to report, as well, that Yavorsky lived openly with a male lover, his former pupil Sergei Protopopov (1893–1954), with whom Shostakovich was also close, and that there has been a fair amount of post-Soviet speculation on the nature of Yavorsky's relationship with his protégé, the golden boy of early-Soviet music.

Considering Shostakovich's reputation now as the twentieth century's prime musical tragedian, the flip remark to Yavorsky is arresting, and it has many echoes. A few months after writing the letter that contains the comment, Shostakovich submitted to a mammoth interview cum questionnaire administered by the music historian Roman Gruber as part of a research project on "the psychology of the creative process." As to the stated subject, Shostakovich reported that "when composing I always suffer from insomnia; I smoke even more than usual; I take long walks, which helps me mull things over; I pace around the room, write standing, can't stay put in one place" (p. 477).

But the interview covered much more. Asked about his tastes in the other arts, Shostakovich replied that he had no interest or response at all to painting ("I am repelled mainly by its static quality" [p. 474]) or poetry—but that if he had to name a couple of poets he liked "relatively," he would name Derzhavin and Mayakovsky (p. 473). This is a great joke. Gavrila Derzhavin (1743–1816), a neoclassical panegyrist and the official "great poet" of the age of Pushkin, was the gold standard of empty orotundity. So, by implication, was the stentorian Mayakovsky, soon to be officially proclaimed the Soviet poet laureate. (Shostakovich's own collaboration with Mayakovsky on *The Bedbug* was still more than a year away.) Asked about his taste in composers, Shostakovich went after the foghorns (Bruckner, Scriabin) and the long faces (Medtner, Miaskovsky)—"hedgehog" composers (to recall the famous comparison Isaiah Berlin adapted from Archilochus) who purveyed univocal messages. His list of favorites is a gallery of foxes: Mahler, Richard Strauss, Alban Berg, Musorgsky, Stravinsky, and Prokofiev (p. 475).

Two letters to Yavorsky from December 1926, already summarized and commented on in Fay's excellent biography, contain priceless descriptions of the Conservatory exam in "Marxist methodology" that twenty-year-old Mitya almost failed with potentially serious consequences for his career (pp. 90, 95). He and another student laughed boisterously when a third was asked to explain the difference between Chopin's music and Liszt's in sociological and economic terms. After thus attracting unfavorable notice from the examiner, Shostakovich was asked which of the required books he had read. Arrogantly answering that he had read none of them, he was ejected from the room. (He petitioned for a re-exam and easily passed it.) Fay comments that Shostakovich's behavior, in retrospect, "seems an ominous prescription for early martyrdom."[13] But more striking is that Shostakovich (naïvely, in Fay's judgment) was not at all chastened by the experience and recounted it to Yavorsky with undisguised merriment in a letter sent through the mail.

Was this political (or "apolitical") naïveté? Does it give evidence of actual or future political dissidence? Or was it just young Siegfried's high spirits and irreverence, expressed during the relatively low-pressure years of the New Economic Policy, when he was not just a bright student but an already famous composer counting on the protection of his burgeoning reputation, and all within what he took to be a closed and cosseted circle of friends and teachers? The Conservatory students I lived with in Moscow during the Brezhnevite stagnation had a similar attitude toward their "historical materialism" courses and the teachers who staffed them. By then, of course, they would have behaved more circumspectly than Shostakovich did, and would not have written letters about it; but their attitude implied no political opinion and neither did his. It is well summed up by a lovely quip in one of the letters to Yavorsky, where, before writing "Marxist methodology," Shostakovich wrote "God's Law" (*Zakon Bozhii*) and lined it through so that it remained legible (p. 90), recalling the equivalent prerevolutionary course requirement, which students had treated with comparable respect.

In any case, no political qualms prevented Shostakovich from eagerly accepting the honor of a commission from the Musical Sector of the Soviet government's publishing arm for the Second Symphony ("To October") or from working on it with great enthusiasm, as we may now read in a whole sheaf of letters to the functionary who was responsible for the commission, one Lev Shulgin, a respectable pianist who had trained as a composer with some of the same teachers who taught Shostakovich. The work was to be a showpiece of Soviet "industrial" modernism. Shostakovich's twenty-minute single movement replays in highly compressed form the dramaturgy of Beethoven's Ninth Symphony, beginning with indistinct rumblings and ending with a choral paean to "October! Herald of the Desired Dawn!" on words by the fittingly monikered Alexander Bezymensky (literally, "No-name"), one of the many sub-Mayakovskys of the period. It was Shulgin, it turns out, who came up with what is now the Symphony's best-remembered idea—a factory whistle blast to cap a bustling polytonal fugue and usher in the choral apotheosis.

Shostakovich, carried away with the task, sent Shulgin ebullient if inveterately leg-pulling progress reports. In one, he described early reactions to the piece:

> I showed it to a few musicians. They approve. But that is unimportant. What is important is that a few days ago I played it over to a few acquaintances, among whom were four workers from a metallurgical plant and one peasant who had come in from the far countryside. They got less out of the instrumental part but went into ecstasies over the chorus and, although they could not read the music, tried to sing along. That filled me with joy. (p. 172)

In later life Shostakovich repudiated both the Second Symphony and the Third (1929), dedicated to the First of May. The reason was their immature modernism, as he came to judge it, rather than their overt political content (which, after all, was no different from that of the Eleventh or Twelfth Symphonies). But Gruber's interview notes give startling evidence of what the Second Symphony meant to Shostakovich at the time. He complained that upon finishing his Conservatory studies he felt unable to compose. Only by "squeezing them out of myself" was he able to write such early pieces as the famous First Symphony, the Octet for strings, and so on. Later, he reported, he went utterly dry for a while, his "creative imagination being unable to get past the boundaries set by classroom rules." This situation persisted until the autumn of 1926, when "I turned to the study of contemporary Western European composers (Schoenberg, Béla Bartók, Hindemith, Křenek), which apparently provided the stimulus I needed to 'emancipate' my creative imagination; the first works of this new period were written in a great burst: the [first] piano sonata, the Aphorisms for piano, the Symphonic Poem for the Tenth Anniversary of the October Revolution (Second Symphony) and the first act of *The Nose*" (p. 472).

These are indeed inspired works, every one. Having heard a magnificent performance of the Second Symphony last year by the Royal Scottish National Orchestra under Alexander Lazarev, I can attest to its stunning effect. An ex-Soviet musicologist seated next to me, an embittered refugee from the tyrannical state her homeland had become, was almost in tears at its conclusion. It reminded her, she said, of the idealism and the unfeigned revolutionary ardor of her parents' generation, as yet unclouded by the tragedies to come. It gave her (and even me, who only knew that idealism and ardor at a scholarly remove) a poignant case of the might-have-beens.

The tragedies that came were what made a tragedian of Shostakovich. They were already looming on the horizon in 1931, when, appalled by the rise of the Russian Association of Proletarian Musicians (RAPM), which had lobbied against him (and ended the run of *The Nose*), taken over the conservatories, and threatened to reduce Soviet music to a rubble of marches and mass songs, he published a "Declaration of a Composer's Obligations" (reprinted in the Glinka Museum anthology, pp. 493–96) in which he repudiated the *lyogkii zhanr* as inartistic, singling out for special excoriation his own theatrical and music-hall scores, especially the most recent one, the "bad and shameful" *Declared Dead* (*Uslovno ubityi* [1931]). Ironically enough, this is the very score that, reconstructed from sketches and orchestrated by Gerard McBurney, has been lately performed and recorded (under the title *Hypothetically Murdered*) to wide acclaim.

After RAPM was dissolved in 1932, in accordance with the decree that created the Union of Soviet Composers, Shostakovich made a characteristic comment: "All I hope is that, if RAPM couldn't manage to grind me to a powder, neither will the Union" (p. 218). He wrote this to his close friend Levon Atovmyan (1901–1973), a minor composer and a career bureaucrat who held various administrative posts within the cultural establishment, eventually (after a two-year stint in the GULAG) rising to the directorship of the Muzfond, the Union office that managed commissions and disbursements. The two-hundred-odd short letters and telegrams from Shostakovich to Atovmyan in the Glinka Museum collection are at times a surrealistic chronicle of musical life during the most stringent phase of Soviet history.

One of the few correspondents with whom he was on familiar second-person terms, Atovmyan was also one of the very few whom the post-1936 Shostakovich could trust with irony, for example, in a letter addressed to Atovmyan in his capacity as administrator in charge of commissions, dated 15 January 1940, while Shostakovich was at work on his orchestration of Musorgsky's *Boris Godunov:* "Unfortunately I fear that I will not be able to write a Triumphal Overture just now, since I am very busy with Boris. Besides, I do not feel it in my power to create a portrait of Comrade Molotov in music, since such a complex task would require enormous labor, mastery, and, above all, time" (p. 245).

Among the weirder commissions Atovmyan successfully brokered for Shostakovich was a series of snappy numbers for the NKVD's own Song and Dance Ensemble, composed between 1942 and 1946. The notion of a hall full of secret police operatives—perhaps including those who interrogated Shostakovich's imprisoned brother-in-law—or the imprisoned composer Alexander Mosolov (whose ballet suite *Steel* [*Stal'*], including the famous "Foundry" movement, shared the program with the Second Symphony's Moscow première) or Atovmyan or even (if a story spread by his friend Veniamin Basner is true) Shostakovich himself—being regaled by a stage full of dancers and prancers all kicking up their heels to the strains of Shostakovich's "Victorious Spring" . . . well, that is a scene worthy of Bulgakov. How is that for a creative response to just criticism?

I cannot keep from chuckling at the thought, but finally its inevitable doubleness disquiets, and shames. By the 1940s there was no innocent humor in the Soviet Union, and one can only shudder at the pressures

Shostakovich must have faced—pressures we cannot comprehend or truly empathize with now, no matter how many books we read. In the end, the relentless opportunistic speculation over Shostakovich's legacy, the dueling exegeses, the triumphant claims and counterclaims, the charges and countercharges, amount to little more than political prurience. A quarter-century past the end of his tormented life, we are still tormenting his ghost, appropriating his authority, seeking his support to bolster new Party lines.

So let us give him the last word. One of the newly published letters, sent on 24 June 1959 to Yury Keldysh, the editor of *Sovetskaia muzyka*, protests the airing there of a nasty memoir by Sol Hurok about Alexander Glazunov, one of Shostakovich's revered early mentors. "We all know that F. Schubert died of syphilis," he wrote. "But that doesn't mean we need to print scholarly articles about it. Musorgsky died of drink. About this there is also no need to write articles and studies, just as there is no need to keep reprinting that insulting portrait of Musorgsky by Repin. It seems to me that this principle is clear enough" (p. 422).

I may not exactly agree with this "principle." (What scholar would?) But the miseries of peoples' lives ought not, perhaps, to be exploited *ad libitum* in the furtherance of our profits or our careers, and in the vain conviction that we understand everything. By turning Shostakovich into a saint, a hero, or a martyr to gratify our hatred of the evil that surrounded him, we grant him no posthumous victory. All we do is reduce him to the level of our imperfect comprehension and our biases. Better let the contradictions stand. They are what have made Shostakovich so consequential.

Notes

1. From a review of 18 October 1942; reprinted in Virgil Thomson, *The Musical Scene* (New York: Knopf, 1947), p. 104.

2. "Sumbur vmesto muzyki" [A muddle instead of music], *Pravda*, 28 January 1936, p. 6.

3. "Moi tvorcheskii otvet" [My creative answer], *Vecherniaia Moskva*, 25 January 1938, p. 30.

4. Juri Jelagin, *Taming of the Arts*, trans. Nicholas Wreden (New York: Dutton, 1951). The original Russian text was published a year later (Yuri Elagin, *Ukroshchenie iskusstv* [The taming of the arts] [New York: Izdatel'stvo imeni Chekhova, 1952]).

5. Jelagin, *Taming of the Arts*, pp. 167–68.

6. G. Auric, "Dimitri Chostakovitch," in "XI[me] Symphony 1905" (booklet accompanying Angel Records 3586 S/L [1958]).

7. Volkov, *Testimony: The Memoirs of Dmitri Shostakovich*, as related to and edited by Solomon Volkov, trans. Antonina W. Bouis (New York: Harper & Row, 1979).

8. Laurel E. Fay, *Shostakovich: A Life* (New York: Oxford University Press, 2000).

9. Francis Maes, *A History of Russian Music from Kamarinskaya to Babyi Yar*, trans. Arnold J. Pomerans and Erica Pomerans (Berkeley: University of California Press, 2002), pp. 345–48.

10. Esti Sheinberg, *Irony, Satire, Parody and the Grotesque in the Music of Shostakovich: A Theory of Musical Incongruities* (Burlington, Vt.: Ashgate, c. 2000).

11. *The Story of a Friendship: The Letters of Dmitri Shostakovich to Isaak Glikman, 1941–1975*, with commentary by Isaak Glikman, trans. Anthony Phillips (Ithaca, N.Y.: Cornell University Press, 2001); *Pis'ma k drugu: Dmitri Shostakovich—Isaaku Glikmanu* [Letters to a friend: Dmitri Shostakovich to Isaak Glikman] (Moscow: "DSCH," 1993).

12. *Dmitri Shostakovich v pis'makh i dokumentakh* [Dmitri Shostakovich in letters and documents], ed. and comp. I. A. Bobykina (Moscow: RIF "Antikva," 2000).

13. Fay's comments on the episode and the quoted passage appear in her *Shostakovich: A Life*, pp. 35–36.

Editor's Note

a. For an explanation of the phrase "fig in the pocket," see chapter 15, editor's note b.

Selected Bibliography

Abraham, Gerald. *Eight Soviet Composers.* London: Oxford University Press, 1943.

Bartlett, Rosamund, ed. *Shostakovich in Context.* New York: Oxford University Press, 2000.

Berger, L., comp. and ed. *Cherty stilia D. Shostakovicha* [Traits of Shostakovich's style]. Moscow: Sovetskii kompozitor, 1962.

Bobrovsky, Victor. "Shostakovich v moei zhizni; Lichnye zametki" [Shostakovich in my life; Personal observations]. *Sovetskaia muzyka,* no. 9 (September 1991): 23–30.

Bobykina, I. A., comp. and ed. *Dmitri Shostakovich v pis'makh i dokumentakh* [Dmitri Shostakovich in letters and documents]. Moscow: RIF "Antikva," 2000.

Braun, Joachim. *Shostakovich's Jewish Songs: From Jewish Folk Poetry* op. 79. Introductory essay with original Yiddish text underlay. Tel-Aviv: World Council for Yiddish and Jewish Culture, Institute Yud Lezlilei Hashoa, 1989.

Danilevich, Lev. *Dmitrii Shostakovich.* Moscow: Sovetskii kompozitor, 1967.

———. *Dmitrii Shostakovich: Zhizn' i tvorchestvo* [Dmitri Shostakovich: Life and works]. Moscow: Sovetskii kompozitor, 1980.

Di Vanni, Jacques. *1953–1983: Trente ans de musique soviétique.* Arles: Actes Sud, 1987.

Dmitrin, Iurii. *"Nam ne dano predugadat' . . .": razmyshleniia o libretto opery D. Shostakovicha "Ledi Makbet Mtsenskogo uezda," o ego pervonachal'nom tekste i posleduiushchikh versiiakh* ["It is not ours to venture a guess . . . ": Thoughts about the libretto of Shostakovich's opera *Lady Macbeth of the Mtsensk District,* about the original text and the subsequent versions]. Summary in English. Printed under the auspices of Vsemirnyi klub peterburzhtsev. St. Petersburg, 1997.

Dolinskaya, Elena Borisovna, comp. *Shostakovichu posviashchaetsia: sbornik statei k 90-letiiu kompozitora (1906–1996)* [Dedicated to Shostakovich: A collection of articles for the composer's 90th anniversary (1906–1996)]. Moscow: Kompozitor, 1997.

Dubinsky, Rostislav. *Stormy Applause, Making Music in a Worker's State.* New York: Hill and Wang, 1989.

"Dusha i maska: pis'ma D. D. Shostakovicha k L. N. Lebedinskomu" [Soul and mask: The Letters of D. D. Shostakovich to L. N. Lebedinsky]. *Muzykal'naia zhizn',* nos. 23–24 (1993).

Fanning, David. *The Breath of the Symphonist: Shostakovich's Tenth.* London: Royal Musical Association, 1988.

———. *Dmitri Shostakovich: String Quartet No. 8.* Aldershot, England: Ashgate, 2003.

———, ed. *Shostakovich Studies.* Cambridge: Cambridge University Press, 1995.

Fay, Laurel E. *Shostakovich: A Life.* New York: Oxford University Press, 2000.

Feuchtner, Bernd. *"Und Kunst geknebelt von der groben Macht": Dimitri Schostakowitsch, künstlerische Identität und staatliche Repression.* Frankfurt am Main: Sendler, 1986.

Frei, Marco F., Günter Wolter, and Ernst Kuhn. *Dmitri Schostakowitsch, Komponist und Zeitzeuge.* With an introduction by Hilmar Schmalenberg. Berlin: E. Kuhn, 2000.

Fromme, Jürgen, ed. *Dmitri Schostakowitsch und Seine Zeit: Mensch und Werk.* Translated by Gundula Bahro and Vally Heikkonen. A catalog of an exhibition held 16 September through 28 October 1984 at the Niederrheinisches Museum der Stadt Duisburg, sponsored by the Museum and by Ministerium für Kultur der UdSSR. Articles, materials borrowed from the Shostakovich Family Archives, and a list of the books in Shostakovich's personal library.

Fuchs, Martina. *Ledi Makbet Mcenskogo uezda: vergleichende Analyse der Erzählung N.S. Leskovs und der gleichnamigen Oper D.D. Šostakovics.* Heidelberg: J. Groos, 1992.

Gladkova, Olga. *Galina Ustvol'skaia—muzyka kak navazhdeniie* [Galina Ustvol'skaia—music as hallucination]. St. Petersburg: Muzyka, 1999. German translation: Olga Gldakowa, *Galina Ustwolskaja: Musik als magische Kraft.* Translated by Jürgen Köchel and Dorothea Redepenning. Berlin: E. Kuhn, 2001.

Gojowy, Detlef. *Schostakowitsch in Deutschland.* Berlin: E. Kuhn, 1998.

Hakobian, Levon. *Music of the Soviet Age, 1917–1987.* Stockholm: Melos Music Literature Kantat HB, 1998.

Ho, Allen B., and Dmitry Feofanov. *Shostakovich Reconsidered.* With an "Overture" by Vladimir Ashkenazy. [London]: Toccata, 1998.

Hulme, Derek C. *Dmitri Shostakovich: A Catalogue, Bibliography, and Discography.* 2nd ed. Oxford: Clarendon, 1991.

Iakovlev, M., comp. *D. Shostakovich o vremeni i o sebe, 1926–1975* [D. Shostakovich about himself and the times, 1926–1975]. Edited by G. Pribegina. Moscow: Sovetskii kompozitor, 1980. English translation: *About Himself and His Times.* Compiled by L. Grigoryev and Ya. Platek. Translated by Angus and Neilian Roxburgh. Moscow: Progress, 1981.

Jelagin, Juri. *The Taming of the Arts.* Translated by Nicholas Wreden. New York: Dutton, 1951. Original Russian text: Iurii Elagin, *Ukroshchenie iskusstv* [The taming of the arts]. New York: Izdatel'stvo imeni Chekhova, 1952.

Khentova, Sofia. *D. D. Shostakovich v gody Velikoi Otechestvennoi voiny* [D. D. Shostakovich during the years of the Great Patriotic War]. Leningrad: Sovetskii kompozitor, 1979.

———. *Molodye gody Shostakovicha* [Shostakovich's youthful years]. 2 vols. Leningrad: Sovetskii kompozitor, 1975, 1980.

———. *Plamia Bab'ego Iara: trinadtsataia simfoniia D. D. Shostakovicha* [The flames of Babyi Yar: D. D. Shostakovich's Thirteenth Symphony]. St. Petersburg: (s.n.) Tipografiia VIR, 1997.

———. *Shostakovich: Tridtsatiletie 1945–1975* [Shostakovich: The thirty years 1945–1975]. Leningrad: Sovetskii kompozitor, 1983.

———. *Shostakovich: Zhizn' i tvorchestvo* [Shostakovich: Life and works]. 2 vols. 2nd ed. Moscow: Kompozitor, 1996 [1985–86].

———. *Udivitel'nyi Shostakovich* [The astonishing Shostakovich]. St. Petersburg: Variant, 1993.

———. *V mire Shostakovicha: zapis' besed s D.D. Shostakovichem* [In Shostakovich's world: Notes of conversations with D. D. Shostakovich]. Moscow: Kompozitor, 1996.

Klemm, Sebastian. *Dmitri Schostakowitsch, das zeitlose Spätwerk.* Berlin: E. Kuhn, 2001.

Koball, Michael. *Pathos und Groteske: die deutsche Tradition im symphonischen Schaffen von Dmitri Schostakowitsch.* Berlin: E. Kuhn, 1997. Originally presented as the author's thesis at the Universität Dortmund, 1997, under the title *Die deutsche Tradition im symphonischen Schaffen von Dmitri Schostakowitsch.*

Kopp, Karen. *Form und Gehalt der Symphonien des Dmitrij Schostakowitsch.* Bonn: Verlag für Musikwissenschaft, 1990.

Kovnatskaia, Ludmila, comp. *Shostakovich: mezhdu mgnoveniem i vechnost'iu* [Shostakovich: Between now and eternity]. St. Petersburg: Kompozitor, 2000.

Krebs, Stanley Dale. *Soviet Composers and the Development of Soviet Music.* London: Allen and Unwin, 1970.

Kuhn, Ernst, Andreas Wehrmeyer, and Günter Wolter, eds. *Dmitri Schostakowitsch und das jüdische musikalische Erbe.* Berlin: E. Kuhn, 2001.

Lebedinskii, Lev. *Sed'maia i odinnadtsataia simfonii D. Shostakovicha* [The Seventh and Eleventh Symphonies of D. Shostakovich]. *B pomoshch' slushateliam narodnykh universitetov kul'tury: Besedy o muzyke* [Aids to listeners at People's Universities of Culture: Conversations about music]. Moscow: Sovetskii kompozitor, 1960.

Levaia, Tamara. "Kharms i Shostakovich: nesostoiavsheisia sotrunichestvo" [Kharms and Shostakovich: An unrealized collaboration]. In *Kharmsizdat predstavliaet: issledovaniia, esse, vospominaniia, katolog vystavki, bibliografiia* [Kharms Publishers presents: Research, essays, reminiscences, an Exhibition Catalog, bibliography]. St. Petersburg: Kharmsizdat, Arsis, 1995.

Litvinova, Flora. "Vspominaia Shostakovicha" [Remembering Shostakovich], *Znamia,* no. 12 (December 1996): 156–77.

Luk'ianova, Natalia. *Dmitrii Dmitrievich Shostakovich.* Moscow: Muzyka, 1980.

MacDonald, Ian. *The New Shostakovich.* Boston: Northeastern University Press, 1990.

Makarov, Evgenii. *Dnevnik: vospominaniia o moem uchitele D.D. Shostakoviche* [Diary: Memories of my teacher D. D. Shostakovich]. Moscow: Kompozitor, 2001.

Maksimenkov, Leonid. *Sumbur vmesto muzyki: Stalinskaia kul'turnaia revoliutsiia, 1936–1938* [A muddle instead of music: The Stalinist cultural revolution, 1936–1938]. Moscow: Iuridicheskaia Kniga, 1997.

Martynov, Ivan. *D. Shostakovich.* Moscow-Leningrad: Muzgiz, 1946. English translation: *Dmitri Shostakovich, the Man and His Work.* Translated by T. Guaralsky. New York: Philosophical Library, 1947.

melos nr 4-5/93 (Sommaren 1993). "Special issue on Dmitri Shostakovich." Editor, Vahid Salehieh. Kantat HB, Box 27278, 102 53 Stockholm, Sweden.

Meskhishvili, Erna, comp. *Dmitrii Shostakovich: notograficheskii spravochnik* [Dmitri Shostakovich: A guide to the scores]. Moscow: Orekhovo-Zuevskaia tipografiia, 1995.

Meyer, Krzysztof. *Shostakovich: zhizn', tvorchestvo, vremia* [Shostakovich: Life, works, and times]. St. Petersburg: "DSCH" and Kompozitor, 1998. German language edition: *Dmitri Schostakowitsch: sein Leben, sein Werk, seine Zeit.* [Zürich]: Atlantis Musikbuch-Verlag, 1998.

Mikheeva, Liudmila. *Pamiati I. I. Sollertinskogo. Vospominaniia, materialy, issledovaniia* [In commemoration of I. I. Sollertinsky. Reminiscences, materials, research]. Compiled by Ludmila Vikentievna Sollertinskaya. Edited by I. Glikman, M. Druskin, and D. Shostakovich. Moscow: Sovetskii kompozitor, 1974.

———. *Zhizn' Dmitriia Shostakovicha* [Dmitri Shostakovich's life]. Moscow: Terra, 1997.

Niemöller, Klaus Wolfgang, Vsevolod Vsevolodovich Zaderatskii, and Manuel Gervink, eds. *Bericht über das Internationale Dmitri-Schostakowitsch-Symposion, Köln 1985 [Soobshchenie o mezhdunarodnom simpoziume, posviashchennom Dmitriiu Shostakovichu, Keln 1985*]. Regensburg: G. Bosse, 1986.

Norris, Christopher, ed. *Shostakovich, the Man and His Music.* London: M. Boyars, 1982.

Orlov, Genrikh. *Dmitrii Dmitrievich Shostakovich: kratkii ocherk zhizni i tvorchestva* [Dmitri Dmitrievich Shostakovich: A brief essay on his life and work]. Moscow: Muzyka, 1966.

———. *Simfonii Shostakovicha* [The symphonies of Shostakovich]. Leningrad: Muzgiz, 1961.

Pis'ma Dmitriia Dmitrievicha Shostakovicha Borisu Tishchenko: s kommentariiami i vospominaniiami adresata [Letters from Dmitri Dmitrievich Shostakovich to Boris Tishchenko: With the addressee's commentaries and reminiscences]. St. Petersburg: Kompozitor, 1997.

Pis'ma k drugu: Pis'ma D. D. Shostakovicha k I. D. Glikmanu [Letters to a friend: The letters of Dmitri Shostakovich to Isaak Glikman]. Edited and with commentary by Isaak Davydovich Glikman. Moscow: Izdatel'stvo "DSCH," 1993. English translation: *Story of a Friendship: The Letters of Dmitri Shostakovich to Isaak Glikman, 1941–1975* (*Chronicle of the Friendship*, in some copies of the Faber edition). With commentary by Isaak Glikman. Translated by Anthony Phillips. Ithaca, N.Y.: Cornell University Press, 2001.

Razhnikov, Vladimir. *Kirill Kondrashin rasskazyvaet o muzyke i zhizni* [Kondrashin speaks about music and life]. Moscow: Sovetskii kompozitor, 1989.

Richter, Sviatoslav, with Bruno Monsaingeon. *Sviatoslav Richter: Notebooks and Conversations.* Princeton, N.J.: Princeton University Press, 2001.

Sabinina, Marina. *Schostakowitsch in Deutschland.* Edited by Hilmar Schmalenberg. Berlin: E. Kuhn, 1998.

———. *Shostakovich—Simfonist: Dramaturgiia, estetika, stil'* [Shostakovich as symphonist: Dramaturgy, aesthetics, style]. Moscow: Muzyka, 1976.

———. *Simfonizm Shostakovicha: Put' k zrelosti* [The symphonism of Shostakovich: The path to maturity]. Moscow: Nauka, 1965.

Schwarz, Boris. *Music and Musical Life in Soviet Russia, 1917–1981.* 2nd. enl. ed. Bloomington: Indiana University Press, 1983 [1972].

Seehaus, Lothar. *Dmitrij Schostakowitsch, Leben und Werk.* Wilhelmshaven: F. Noetzel, 1986.

Sheinberg, Esti. *Irony, Satire, Parody, and the Grotesque in the Music of Shostakovich: A Theory of Musical Incongruities.* Burlington, Vt.: Ashgate, c. 2000.

Shneerson, Grigorii Mikhailovich, comp. and ed. *D. Shostakovich: Stat'i, materialy* [D. Shostakovich: Articles, materials]. Moscow: Sovetskii kompozitor, 1976.

Shostakovich, Dmitrii Dmitrievich. *Erfahrungen: Aufsätze, Erinnerungen, Reden, Diskussionsbeiträge, Interviews, Briefe.* Edited and translated by Christoph Hellmundt and Krzysztof Meyer. Leipzig: Reclam, 1983.

Sollertinsky, Dmitri, and Ludmilla Sollertinsky. *Pages from the Life of Dmitri Shostakovich.* Translated by Graham Hobbs and Charles Midgley. New York: Harcourt Brace Jovanovich, 1980.

Stetina, Edmund. *Die vierte Symphonie von Dmitrij Šostakovic: ein zurückbehaltenes Bekenntnis.* Aachen: Shaker, 1997.

Taruskin, Richard. *Defining Russia Musically.* Princeton, N.J.: Princeton University Press, 1997.

Tosser, Grégoire. *Les dernières oeuvres de Dimitri Chostakovitch: une esthétique musicale de la mort, 1969–1975.* Paris: Harmattan, 2000.

Vishnevskaya, Galina. *Galina. A Russian Story.* Translated by Guy Daniels. New York: Harcourt Brace Jovanovich, 1984.

Volkov, Solomon. *Testimony: The Memoirs of Dmitri Shostakovich,* as related to and edited by Solomon Volkov. Translated by Antonina W. Bouis. New York: Harper & Row, 1979.

Wilson, Elizabeth. *Shostakovich: A Life Remembered.* Princeton, N.J.: Princeton University Press, 1994.

Wolter, Günter. *Dmitri Schostakowitsch, eine sowjetische Tragödie: Rezeptionsgeschichte.* Frankfurt am Main: P. Lang, 1991.

———. *Volksfeind Dmitri Schostakowitsch.* "Eine Dokumentation der öffentlichen Angriffe gegen den Komponisten in der ehemaligen Sowjetunion ; mit einem Originalbeitrag von Günter Wolter und einer Systematischen Auswahl-Bibliographie der internationalen Literatur über Schostakowitsch bis 1996." Translated by Ernst Kuhn. Berlin: E. Kuhn, 1997.

Zak, Vladimir Il'ich. *Shostakovich i evrei?* [Shostakovich and the Jews?]. New York: Izdatel'stvo "Kiev," 1997.

Zhitomirskii, Daniil. "Shostakovich," *Muzykal'naia akademiia,* no. 3 (1993).

———. "Shostakovich ofitsial'nyi i podlinnyi: vospominaniia, materialy, nabliudeniia" [The official Shostakovich and the real one: Reminiscences, materials, observations], *Daugava,* nos. 3–4 (1990).

Contributors

Elena Veniaminovna Basner, daughter of composer Veniamin Basner, one of Shostakovich's most trusted friends, was herself closely acquainted with the composer. An art historian, she is Senior Research Curator [*Vedushchii nauchnyi sotrudnik*] in the Late Nineteenth- and Twentieth-Century Painting Department at the Russian State Museum [*Gosudarstvennyi Russkii muzei*] in St. Petersburg. Her recent essays have appeared in *Nataliia Goncharova: Gody v Rossii* [Nataliia Goncharova: The years in Russia] (2002); *Kazimir Malevich v Russkom muzee* [Kazimir Malevich in Russian music] (2000); *V kruge Malevicha: soratniki, ucheniki, posledovateli v Rossii, 1920–1950-kh* [In Malevich's circle: Companions, students, followers in Russia, 1920s–1950s] (2000); *David Burliuk, 1882–1967: Vystavka proizvedenii iz Gosudarstvennogo Russkogo muzeia, muzeev i chastnykh kollektsii Rossii, SShA, Germanii* [David Burliuk, 1882–1967: An exhibition of works from the Russian State Museum, museums, and private collections in Russia, the USA, Germany] (1995).

Alla Vladimirovna Bogdanova has published a number of books on the music of Shostakovich, among them *"Katerina Izmailova" Shostakovicha* [Shostakovich's *Katerina Izmailova*] (1968); *Sochineniia Shostakovicha konservatorskikh let* [Shostakovich's works from the conservatory years] (1971); and *Opery i balety Shostakovicha* [Shostakovich's operas and ballets] (1979). Other books include the biography *Andrei Eshpai*, 2nd edition, revised and enlarged (1986); *Pamiati pogibshikh kompozitorov i muzykovedov, 1941–1945: Sbornik statei* [In memory of the composers and musicologists who perished, 1941–1945: A collection of articles], vol. 1 (1985); and *Ran'she i teper': Besedy Borisa Pokrovskogo s Alloi Bogdanovoi* [Then and now: Conversations of Boris Pokrovsky with Alla Bogdanova] (2001).

Malcolm Hamrick Brown is the founding editor of the scholarly series Russian Music Studies, published by Indiana University Press since 1990 (UMI Research Press, 1981–88). From the time of Brown's first extended stay in Moscow in 1962, when he was doing research for his dissertation on Prokofiev's symphonies, he has been continuously involved in teaching, researching, lecturing, writing, and publishing on Russian and Soviet music.

David Fanning is Senior Lecturer in Music at the University of Manchester, author of *The Breath of the Symphonist: Shostakovich's Tenth* (1988), and editor of and contributor to *Shostakovich Studies* (1995). He wrote the entry on Shostakovich for the revised edition of *The New Grove Dictionary of Music and Musicians*, and his monograph on Shostakovich's Eighth String Quartet was published by Ashgate Press in 2003. Fanning has also published *Nielsen, Symphony no. 5*, Cambridge Music Handbooks (1997).

Laurel E. Fay's scholarly biography, *Shostakovich: A Life* (2000), received the Otto Kinkeldey Award in 2001 from the American Musicological Society. The award is made to an American or Canadian scholar for a "work of musicological scholarship deemed by a committee of scholars to be the most distinguished of those published during the previous year in any language and in any country." Fay, who is an independent scholar, also serves as Consultant on Russian Music to the music publisher G. Schirmer, Inc. Her articles have appeared in the *New York Times*, *Musical America*, *Opera News*, *Stagebill*, and *Keynote*, as well as in many scholarly publications. She was a contributing editor for the *New Grove Dictionary of Opera*.

Levon Hakobian (Lev Oganesovich Akopian) holds a position as Senior Research Fellow [*Vedushchii nauchnyi sotrudnik*] at the Russian State Institute for Art Studies [*Gosudarstvennyi institut iskusstvoznaniia Ministerstva kul'tury Rossiiskoi Federatsii*] in Moscow. His *Music of the Soviet Age, 1917–1987*, in English (1998), is the first synoptic, post–Soviet-era, insider account of the subject. Other research publications include the book *Analiz glubinnoi struktury muzykal'nogo teksta* [The analysis of deep structure in music] (1995), as well as the major articles "Šaraknoc'i ergerieta nakner ew wranc' stora bažanumner" [The melodic structure of Armenian Sarakan hymns and their variants], in Armenian, *Echmiadzin* 49, nos. 4/5 (1992): 63–86; and "The Versification of the Sarakan Hymns," in English, *Revue des études arméniennes*, new ser., 24 (1993): 113–27. Hakobian was the editor, translator, and author of supplemental articles for the concise edition of *New Grove* in Russian: *Muzykal'nyi slovar' Grouva* (2001). He expects to publish, in the near future, his book *Dmitrii Shostakovich: Opyt fenomenologii tvorchestva* [Dmitri Shostakovich: An attempt at (analyzing) the phenomenology of his creative work].

Ludmila Grigorievna Kovnatskaya teaches at the Rimsky-Korsakov State Conservatory in St. Petersburg and holds the title Senior Research Fellow [*Vedushchii nauchnyi sotrudnik*] at the Russian Institute of Fine Arts History in St. Petersburg [*Rossiiskii institut istorii iskusstv, SPb*]. Her publications include *D. D. Shostakovich: Sbornik statey k 90-letiyu so dnya rozhdeniya* [D. D. Shostakovich: A collection of articles commemorating his 90th birthday] (1996) and *Shostakovich: Mezhdu mgnoveniem i vechnost'iu* [Shostakovich: Between now and eternity] (2000), both of which she compiled, edited, and contributed to. She has also published a monograph on the music of Benjamin Britten, *Bendzhamin Britten* (1974), and the study *Angliiskaia muzyka XX veka: istoki i etapy razvitiia* [English music of the twentieth century: Sources and stages of development] (1986).

Gerard McBurney composes, arranges, teaches, and writes about music. He has specialized in reinventing the music of Shostakovich, having devised performing editions from sketches of Shostakovich's 1931 music-hall show *Uslovno ubityi* op. 31 [Hypothetically murdered, as translated by the writer Grigory Gerenstein] and the lost 1938 three-movement Suite for Jazz Orchestra no. 2, without opus. His reorchestration of Shostakovich's 1958 musical comedy, *Moskva Cheryomushki*, op. 105 [Moscow, the "Bird-Cherry" Precinct], was recently given a new production by Opera North as *Paradise Moscow*. He has composed dramatic scores for the English National Theatre and for the theater company Complicite. *Letter to Paradise*, his setting for baritone and orchestra of a text by Daniil Kharms, was a BBC commission for the 1998 Royal Albert Hall Proms.

Paul Mitchinson is a Canadian writer and historian. He completed a doctorate in Russian history at Harvard, where he wrote his dissertation on music and politics in the early Bolshevik period. His work has appeared in the *National Post*, *Lingua Franca*, *Queen's Quarterly*, *East European Quarterly*, the *Canadian Journal of History*, and *Left History*.

Simon Morrison teaches music history at Princeton University. Author of *Russian Opera and the Symbolist Movement* (2002), he is now working on a collection of essays with the provisional title *Ballet Imaginaire*. Last year he received an American Council of Learned Societies grant, which supported research in Paris, London, and St. Petersburg. Other recent and current writing projects include a study of Rimsky-Korsakov's *Sadko* for *Cambridge Opera Journal;* an article (coauthored by Lesley-Anne Sayers) on Prokofiev's *Le Pas d'Acier* [*Stal'noi skok*] for the collection *Soviet Music and Society under Lenin and Stalin;* an essay on Shostakovich's ballet *The Bolt* [*Bolt*]; and an essay-review of the *Prokofiev Diaries (1907–33)*.

Irina Nikolaevna Nikolskaya specializes in twentieth-century Polish music. A student of Zofia Lissa's, her publications include *Conversations with Witold Lutosławski, 1987–92*, in English, translated from the Russian by Valeri Yerokbin (1994); *Ot Shimanovskogo do Liutoslavskogo i Penderetskogo: Ocherki razvitiia simfonicheskoi muzyki v Pol'she XX veka* [From Szymanowski to Penderecki: Essays on the development of symphonic music in twentieth-century Poland] (1990); *Karol' Shimanovskii: vospominaniia, stat'i, publikatsii* [Karol Szymanowski: Reminiscences, articles, publications], with Yulia Kreininaia (1984); and *Sovremennoe pol'skoe iskusstvo i literatura: ot simvolizma k avangardizmu* [Contemporary Polish art and literature: From symbolism to the avant-garde], with G. Kovalenko (1998).

Henry Orlov (Genrikh Aleksandrovich Orlov) formerly served as Senior Research Fellow [*Starshii nauchnyi sotrudnik*] at the Leningrad State Scientific Research Institute for Theater, Music, and Film [*Leningradskii gosudarstvennyi nauchno-issledovatel'skii institut teatra, muzyki i kinematografii*]. After settling in the United States he held appointments at Cornell, Harvard, and Wesleyan (Connecticut) universities. Three of his books are devoted to Shostakovich: *Dmitrii Dmitrievich Shostakovich: kratkii ocherk zhizni i tvorchestva* [Dmitri Dmitrievich Shostakovich: A brief essay on his life and works] (1966); *Simfonii Shostakovicha*

[The symphonies of Shostakovich] (1961); and *Muzyka, rozhdyonnaia zhizn'iu* [Music born of life] (1963). The composer also figures prominently in the book *Russkii sovetskii simfonizm: puti, problemy, dostizheniia* [Soviet Russian symphonism: The paths, the problems, the achievements] (1966), as well as in contributions to various collective publications and periodicals. Orlov has also published *Drevo muzyki* [The tree of music] (1992) and the biography *Vladimir Vladimirovich Shcherbachëv: ocherk zhizni i tvorchestva* [Vladimir Vladimirovich Shcherbachov: An essay on his life and works] (1959).

Irina Antonovna Shostakovich (née Supinskaya), Shostakovich's third wife, married the composer in 1962. "Irina finally brought stability and tranquility back into his life, relieving him of the domestic cares that he found so burdensome. And as his physical condition and health steadily deteriorated during the remaining years of his life, Irina was his indispensable companion and helpmate" (Laurel E. Fay, *Shostakovich: A Life* [Oxford: Oxford University Press, 2000], pp. 227–28). As Shostakovich's direct heir, she has remained involved in all aspects of managing his heritage and matters related to his copyright. Together with the composer's children, Galina and Maxim, she founded the *Association Internationale "Dimitri Chostakovitch"* in Paris (http://www.devinci.fr/chostakovitch/VF/assfr.htm) and the "DSCH" publishing house in Moscow.

Richard Taruskin, the single academic to be included in BBC *Music Magazine*'s recent list of the sixty most powerful figures in the musical world today, is recognized internationally for his scholarship on Russian music. His books on the subject include *Defining Russia Musically: Historical and Hermeneutical Essays* (1997); *Stravinsky and the Russian Traditions: A Biography of Works through Mavra* (2 vols., 1996); *Musorgsky: Eight Essays and an Epilogue* (1993); and *Opera and Drama in Russia as Preached and Practiced in the 1860s* (2nd ed., 1993). Some 160 of his articles on Russian composers and their works are found in the *New Grove Dictionary of Opera.*

Boris Ivanovich Tishchenko, noted Russian composer, studied as a youngster with Shostakovich's student Galina Ustvolskaya, and many years later with the master himself. Tishchenko's close friendship with the composer is reflected in letters he received from Shostakovich during the latter's final years, published as *Pis'ma Dmitriia Dmitrievicha Shostakovich Borisu Tishchenko* [The letters of Dmitri Dmitrievich Shostakovich to Boris Tishchenko], with commentary and reminiscences by the addressee (1997). Musical reminiscences of his teacher can also be perceived in Tishchenko's grandly realized Symphony No. 5.

Manashir Abramovich Yakubov, curator of the Shostakovich Family Archive in Moscow, has devoted his scholarly attention largely to Shostakovich over the past twenty years. In 1993 he became editor-in-chief of the "DSCH" publishing house and has since prepared all the scholarly works issued, including the satirical *Antiformalisticheskii rayok* [The antiformalist peepshow] (1995). He has reconstructed and edited the piano scores of the ballets *Zolotoy vek* [The Golden Age]

(1995); *Bolt* [The bolt] (1996); and *Svetlyi ruchei* [The sparkling stream] (1997). Yakubov also prepared the editorial prefaces to some twenty-five scores published in *Shostakovich: Sobranie sochinenii v soroka dvukh tomakh* [Shostakovich: Collected works in forty-two volumes] (1980–87), although, for Soviet-era political reasons, he was not given credit for doing so.

Index

Abraham, Gerald, 227*n*11, 228n17, 288
Absurdists, Leningrad, 291
Aesthetics, 194, 196, 209, 270–71, 294, 330, 334, 364; formalist, 329, 331; and ideology, 12, 242–43; Socialist-Realist, 245
Akhmatova, Anna Andreevna (1889–1966), 50–51, 108, 134, 173, 177, 369; Museum, 317
Akimov, Nikolai Pavlovich (1901–68), 365
Aksiuk, Sergei Vasilievich [Vasil'evich] (1901–94), 238, 241–42
Alienation, 198
Allegories, 207, 214
All-Union Copyright Agency (VAAP), 53, 90–91, 92–94, 132
Allusions, musical, 194, 196, 353, 355
Ambiguity, 262, 277–78, 347, 371; musical, 310, 352, 371
Ambivalence, 249, 286, 334
Analogies, literary, 372
Analysis, 371; descriptive, 335–36; musical, 224, 258, 270–71, 293–96, 298, 352, 372; theoretical, 239, 242–43
Anecdotes, 1, 260, 334; contained in *Testimony*, 45, 97, 138, 261, 314, 317; of Shostakovich's life, 196, 284, 336
Antiformalisticheskii rayok [*raëk;* The Antiformalist peepshow], for four bass soloists, mixed chorus, piano, and narrator, without opus number (?1948–?68), 174, 233, 275, 281*n*9, 318, 353–54, 375
Anti-Semitism, 157, 158, 166, 172, 207, 284, 314
Anxiety, 284–85, 350, 360–61
Apollinaire, Guillaume, 148, 211–13
Apostolov, Pavel Ivanovich (1905–69), 266
Aranovsky [Aranovskii], Mark Genrikhovich (b. 1928), 347
Arnshtam, Leo [Lev] Oskarovich (1905–79), 128, 132, 178
Art, 200, 217, 219, 222, 363; and propaganda, 201–202
Artists, Soviet, 249, 273, 291
Asafyev [Asaf'ev], Boris Vladimirovich (1884–1949), 270, 368
Ashkenazy [Ashkenazii], Vladimir Davidovich (b. 1937), 45, 233, 356*n*3
Association of Contemporary Music, 355
Atmosphere, 198, 217, 291–92, 331. *See also* Context
Atovmyan [Atovm'ian], Levon Tadevosovich (1901–73), 381
Attacks, critical, 161, 175, 197, 294, 364, 367. *See also* Criticism; *Pravda*, editorials in
Attitudes: changes in, 165, 175; political, 332; of Shostakovich, 270; toward Shostakovich, 128–29, 168, 279, 329–30, 334, 350
Audience, 87, 245, 339, 340, 347, 368, 376
Auric, Georges, 369
Authenticity, of *Testimony*, 1–2, 12–13, 21*n*16, 46, 272–74; and ambiguity, 107–108; attempts to prove, 122; debate over, 44–45, 97–99, 257, 285, 317, 347–48; determination of, 86, 98, 179, 231–32; evidence for, 13–14, 18–19, 86, 258, 274–76, 312, 332, 357*n*3, 370; guarantees of, 118; and KGB, 55–57; opinions on, 52, 54, 101, 117, 171, 223, 234, 271, 314; and reception of *Testimony*, 48–49. *See also Testimony* debate
Autonomy, 361
Avant-garde, 123, 130, 151, 176, 220, 222, 225, 270, 293, 295; supremacy of, 49

Babyi yar [*Babii iar*] (Yevtushenko), 156–57, 181, 208. *See also* Symphony No. 13
Bach, 70, 160, 173–74, 199, 201
Bakhtin, 368, 372–73
Balanchine, George, 311, 316
Barber, Samuel, 325–326, 328
Barshai, Nina Grigorieva [Grigor'eva], 163
Barshai, Rudolf [Rudol'f] Borisovich (b. 1924), 163, 166
Bartók, Béla, 380; music of, 361–62
Basner, Elena Veniaminovna, 55, 137–40, 356
Basner, Veniamin Efimovich (1925–96), 4, 55, 80, 83, 137–40, 310, 332, 381
BBC (British Broadcasting Company), 86, 120–21, 278
Beethoven, 164, 174, 245, 228*n*14, 368; biography of, 225; borrowings from, 201; comparisons with, 211, 379
Beethoven Quartet, 159, 162, 337, 339
Bench, Robert E., 90, 93
Berg, Alban, 179, 200, 284, 289, 378
Beria, Lavrenty [Lavrentii] Pavlovich (1899–1953), 207
Berlin Wall, 327
Berlinguer, Enrico, 131
Berlinsky [Berlinskii], Valentin Alexandrovich [Aleksandrovich] (b. 1925), 162–67, 337

Bezymensky [Bezymenskii], Alexander [Aleksandr] Il'ich (1898–1973), 379
Biography, 257–58, 263, 265, 267, 278, 346–47, 354, 356. *See also* Scholarship
Bloch, Jean-Richard, 88
Blockade, Leningrad, 159
Blok, 144, 148
Bobrovsky [Bobrovskii], Victor [Viktor] Petrovich (1906–79), 238–41, 242, 243, 249–50
Bolero (Ravel), 159
Bolsheviks, 330
Bolt [The bolt], 167, 201
Boris Godunov (Musorgsky), 77–78, 109, 381
Borodin, Aleksandr Profir'evich (1833–87), 109
Borodin Quartet (Moscow Philharmonic Quartet), 154, 337–39; performances by, 124, 162–65, 166
Boulez, Pierre, 288–90, 299
Braun, Joachim, 232
Brezhnev, Leonid Il'ich (1906–82), 193, 234, 332
Brezhnev era, 220–21, 271, 285, 364, 379
Britten, Benjamin, 151, 173, 199, 266, 284
Brodsky [Brodskii] Joseph [Iosip] Aleksandrovich (1940–96), 316–17, 323*n*52
Brown, Malcolm Hamrick, 276, 307, 313; criticism of, 233, 348, 356–57*n*3
Bruckner, 378
Bulgakov, Mikhail Afans'evich (1891–1940), 234, 237*n*i, 381

Capitulation, 284, 330
Cappriccio espagnol (Rimsky-Korsakov), 372
Caricature, 201, 259, 318, 348, 354–55
Carter, Elliott, 366
Cello Concerto, 211; First, 145–46, 147, 375; Second, 363
Censorship, 198, 249, 305, 368, 372
Central Committee of the Communist Party, 81, 94, 166, 168, 186*n*m, 273, 376; archives of, 92–93, 95; Cultural Department of, 94, 166; and reaction to *Testimony*, 3, 93; and *Sovetskaia muzyka*, 154–55
Character. *See* Personality, cult of; Personality, of Shostakovich
Chekhov, Anton Pavlovich (1860–1904), 30, 14, 76–77, 110, 155, 171, 174, 196
Chërnyi monakh [The black monk] (Chekhov), 155, 174
Chetyre monologa na stikhi A. Pushkina [Four Monologues on texts by A. Pushkin], for bass and piano, Op. 91 (1952), 352
Chigaryova, Evgenia [Chigarëva, Evgeniia], 239
Chopin, 245
Chorny [Chërnyi], Sasha, 148, 209
Class struggle, 245
Classicism, 368
Clichés, 249, 288–90, 292
Climate, 128, 151, 208; cultural, 334–35
Codes, musical, 336, 354
Coercion, 46, 55, 306, 315
Cold War, 48, 55, 58, 304, 318, 327, 331–32, 335, 346, 370
Collaboration. *See* Interviews
Collaborator, Shostakovich as, 262–63, 284, 330
Collected Works, 182
Commentary, musical, 271, 367
Commissions, 201, 365, 379, 381
Committee for Arts Affairs, 350
Communism, 144, 226, 277, 334
Communist, Shostakovich as, 275, 277, 284, 319, 332
Communist Party, 176–77, 217, 219, 241, 262, 273–74, 277; and criticism of Shostakovich, 203, 330; French, 205; Italian, 131, 205; membership in, 85, 154–55, 223, 229*n*c, 261–62, 347, 374; and *Testimony*, 122; and Thaw, 206. *See also* Central Committee of the Communist Party
Composers, Soviet, 86, 94, 170, 220, 284
Composers Union, 50, 94, 135, 166, 174, 187*n*n, 305, 333, 381; conference, 258, 326; expulsions from, 220; and *Lady Macbeth*, 167–68; leadership of, 13, 89, 138, 169–70, 178–79, 186–87*n*m, 241, 261; meetings of, 119, 242, 262; performances at, 18, 311, 355
Composition, 123, 199–200, 204, 259, 276, 352; musical, 75, 220, 361, 376; operatic, 352–53; process of, 70, 75, 330, 341. *See also* Music; Techniques, compositional
Compromises, 160, 195–96, 225–26, 263, 278, 314; artistic, 153, 155–56; personal, 154, 157
Concentration camps, 158, 218
Concepts, musical, 204, 205
Concerto for Orchestra (Bartók), 361–62
Concerto for Piano, Trumpet, and String Orchestra (1933), 201
Conformists, 5, 217
Conformity, 225, 226, 245, 347, 354, 367, 369
Congress for World Peace, 161, 195, 331
Congress of Soviet Composers, 314; First, 195; Second, 86, 245–46; Sixth, 12, 121; Third, 325, 328
Conscience, 206, 249, 257
Content, 245; musical, 221, 243–44, 245–46, 368, 374; political, 176, 380
Context, 156, 158, 257, 290, 298, 348; cultural, 200, 279, 331, 355, 366, 371; historical, 6–7, 350; sociopolitical, 271, 311, 327, 334
Contradictions, 262–63, 278, 333, 382. *See also* Personality, of Shostakovich
Convictions, 196, 223
Copland, Aaron, 329
Copyright, 3; ownership of *Testimony*, 53, 91, 177, 317, 370; protection of, 90–91, 93. *See also Testimony*
Correspondence, 56–57, 238; of Dolzhansky and Bobrovsky, 240–41, 243, 249; with Glikman, 225, 337, 341, 373; with Krem-

lyov, 247–48; of Kremlyov and Aksiuk, 241–42; of Orlov and Volkov, 118; of Shostakovich, 13, 41–42, 51, 132, 174, 312, 315, 377–82
Cosmopolitanism, 154
Craft, Robert, 123, 196, 232, 236*n*b, 260
Creativity, artistic, 150, 170, 217–19, 220, 223
Criticism, 241–42, 286–87, 335; and ideology, 231, 249, 271; official, 161, 206, 330; responses to, 12, 161–62, 184, 271, 273, 350, 367, 376; self, 109, 374; of Shostakovich, 81, 85, 195, 203, 242, 247–49, 286–88, 311
Cuban Missile Crisis, 327
Cultural life, Soviet, 12, 150, 291, 306
Culture: Soviet, 82, 85, 87–89, 169, 267, 271, 290, 337; musical, 86, 220–22; Shostakovich's role in, 88, 248
Cynicism, 82, 277, 284
Czechoslovakia, invasion of, 320*n*23

Davidenko, Alexander Alexandrovich [Aleksandr Aleksandrovich] (1899–1934), 234
Death, image of, 172, 210, 212, 214, 266
Debussy, 241, 284
Declaration of a Composer's Obligations, 293, 380
Dedyukhin, Alexander [Dediukhin, Aleksandr] Aleksandrovich (1907–2002), 145–46
Deineka, Alexander [Aleksandr] Aleksandrovich (1899–1969), 245
Delvig [Del'vig], Anton Antonovich (1798–1831), 215*n*h
Denisov, Edison Vasilievich [Vasil'evich] (1929–96), 31, 166, 261, 266, 362
Denunciations, 132–33, 284; by Shostakovich, 225, 261, 266; of Shostakovich, 127–28, 202; of *Testimony*, 97, 306. *See also* Signature, of Shostakovich
Derzhavin, Gavrila Romanovich (1743–1816), 378
Development, musical, 291–99
Diaghilev [Diagilev], Sergei Pavlovich (1872–1929), 173
Dialogue, 238–39, 242, 270–71; about Shostakovich, 241, 242–43
Dignity, 128, 196, 206
Discourse, 340–41
Dissidence, 311, 318, 335; and music, 223, 261, 309; political, 309, 313, 374, 378
Dissident, 5, 182, 187*n*q, 217, 240, 248; art, 217; movement, 207; Shostakovich as, 51, 53, 122, 135, 175–76, 231, 233, 262, 274, 284, 311, 319, 335, 347, 370, 375; works as, 223
Dolmatovsky [Domatovskii], Evgeny [Evgenii] Aronovich (1915–94), 148, 175, 352
Dolzhansky [Dolzhanskii], Alexander [Aleksandr] Naumovich (1908–66), 238–41, 242, 243, 249
Dostoevsky [Dostoevskii], Fydor [Fëdor] Mikhailovich (1821–81), 109, 148, 151, 171, 196, 223
Doubleness, 198, 312, 360, 363–67, 369–71, 373, 381
Druskin, Mikhail Semyonovich [Semënovich] (1905–91), 99, 291–92, 300*n*23
Dualism, 194, 216–17, 220, 223, 226, 312
Dubinsky [Dubinskii], Rostislav (1923–97), 163, 165–66, 260, 334, 336, 338–39
Duty, civic. *See* Responsibility, civic
Dzerzhinsky [Dzerzhinskii], Ivan Ivanovich (1909–78), 352

Edlina-Dubinsky, Luba, 334
Ehrenburg [Erenburg], Ilya [Il'ia] Grigorievich (1891–1967), 258
Eisenstein [Eisenshtein], Sergei Mikhailovich (1898–1948), 200, 291
Elagin, Yuri [Iurii] Borisovich (b. 1910) (Juri Jelagin), 367
Emigration, 100, 119, 121–22, 166, 259, 309
Émigrés, 28, 44–45
Energy, creative, 292
England, 94
Environment, 271, 293, 297, 299
Eshpai [Èshpai], Andrei Yakovlevich [Iakovlevich] (b. 1925), 326
Evolution, musical, 294–95, 279, 301*n*32, 361
Executions, mass, 156
Exile, 144, 156, 176, 290
Existence, human, 203, 218
Existentialism, elemental, 218–21
Experience, 260, 270, 298
Experimentation, 293, 304, 326, 365
Exploitation, 294, 330, 382
Expression, 207, 369; artistic, 341, 371; personal, 194–95, 201, 203, 209–14
Ezhov, Nikolai Ivanovich (1895–1940), 160

Fanning, David, 48
Fascism, 85, 87, 205, 206, 284, 318, 337; victims of, 310
Favorsky [Favorskii], Vladimir Andreevich (1886–1964), 245
Fay, Laurel E., 2, 20, 22, 177, 307–309, 313–15, 318, 332; criticism of, 6, 233, 276, 312, 370; scholarship of, 257–58, 346–59, 378
Fear, 198, 207, 274, 372
Fears (Yevtushenko), 207–208
Feofanov, Dmitri, 33–34, 39–40, 42–43, 59*n*14, 230–31, 277–78, 281*n*9, 282*n*19, 311–18, 321*n*33, 347
Feuchtwangler, Leon, 85, 108
The First Circle (Solzhenitsyn), 374
Fleishman, Veniamin Iosifovich (1913–41), 18, 51
Folklore, 196, 314; Jewish, 158; musicological, 249
Formalism, 81, 128, 189*n*cc, 204, 245, 350–51, 367; accusations of, 151, 206, 220; and *Sovetskaia muzyka*, 154; war on, 152–53, 351

Formalists, 291, 372
Freedom, creative, 151, 200, 203
Frid, Grigory [Grigorii] Samuilovich (b. 1915), 262

Gagarin, Yuri [Iurii] Alekseevich (1934–68), 304
Galina (memoirs of Galina Vishnevskaya), 44–45, 96
Gasparov, Mikhail Leonovich (b. 1935), 238–39
Genina, Liana Solomonovna (b. 1931), 43
Genre, 304, 365–66
German Democratic Republic, 274
Gershkovich, Filip Moiseevich (Herşcovici, Philipp) (b. 1906), 289–90, 292, 297, 362
Gilels, Emil Grigorievich [Gilel's, Èmil' Grigor'evich] (1916–85), 154
Ginzburg, Eugenia Semyonovna [Evgeniia Semënovna], 258
Glasnost, 49–50, 347
Glazunov, Alexander [Aleksandr] Konstantinovich (1865–1936), 18, 48, 52, 56–57, 109, 130, 178, 286, 307, 382
Gliasser, Ignaty Albertovich (1850–1925), 60*n*29, 70
Glière, Reinhold Moritsevich [Glièr, Reingol'd] (1875–1956), 85
Glikman, Isaak Davidovich, 41–42, 128, 146; correspondence with, 132, 225, 337, 341, 348, 373–76
Glinka, Mikhail Ivanovich (1804–57), 73, 245
Glinka State Museum of Musical Art, 183, 375, 376
Gmyrya [Gmyria], Boris Romanovich (1903–69), 181
Goethe, 196, 290
Gogol [Gogol'], Nikolai Vasilievich [Vasil'evich] (1809–52), 148, 170–71, 179, 355
Golovanov, Nikolai Semyonovich [Semënovich] (1891–1953), 167
Gopak, Georgian, 224–25
Gorky [Gor'kii], Maxim [Maksim] [Aleksei Maksimovich Peshkov] (1868–1936), 74, 350
Gosman, Lazar [Lazar'], 260
Gossip, 222, 232
The Great Friendship (Muradeli, Vano), 353
Grotesque, 201, 286, 354–55
Gruber, Roman Il'ich (1895–1962), interview by, 377–78, 380
GULAG, 156, 216, 220

Handel, 160
Harper & Row, 3, 29, 80, 84, 90–94, 128, 304; and review of *Testimony*, 99, 100, 103, 121. *See also* Publication, of *Testimony*
Harris, Ann, 100–106
Haydn, 70, 174, 201
Hegel, 218, 270, 372
Hindemith, 200, 288, 365, 380
Hitler, 205, 304; invasion of, 16, 107, 262, 276, 303, 308
Ho, Allan B., 33–34, 39–40, 42–43, 59*n*14, 230–31, 274–76, 311–15, 318, 347
Holocaust, 158
Honegger, 200
Honesty, musical, 196–98
Horowitz, Joseph, 314
Horowitz [Gorovits], Vladimir (Samoilovich) (1904–89), 316
Humanism, 87, 151, 270–71
Humanity, 89, 165, 358*n*8, 366, 369; enemies of, 308
Humor, 201, 203, 207, 209, 381; sense of, 152–53, 350
Hungarian uprising, 194, 233, 352, 369, 309–10
Hurok, Sol, 56–57, 382

Idealism, 204, 380
Ideals, 81, 199, 206, 266, 278
Identity, 218, 239
Ideology, 86, 117, 199, 249; depravity of, 246; and music, 176; official, 203, 219, 330
Idioms, musical, 201, 202
Imagery, musical, 156–59, 168, 172, 200–201, 205, 207, 212–13, 295–96, 318, 336, 339, 368; nature of, 153; revolutionary, 200
Images, 201, 216, 296; of Shostakovich, 87, 109–10, 122, 138, 151, 223–24, 309, 312; in *Testimony*, 11, 44–49, 81–83, 85–86, 225–26, 231, 234, 261, 267, 271–72, 285, 304, 306, 340; of Volkov, 86–87
Imagination, creative, 205, 380
Immortality, 214
Innovation, musical, 85, 88, 159–60, 199, 292–95, 336; and Revolution, 200–201; and Schoenberg, 362
Inscription. *See* Signature, of Shostakovich
Inspector General (Meyerhold), 73
Inspiration, 156, 380; revolutionary, 200–201
Intelligentsia, 166, 176, 185*n*c, 195, 217, 374; and denunciations, 132; images of, 285; life of, 97, 198; and Shostakovich, 160, 271
International Socialism, 277
Interpretations, 1, 171, 194, 285, 341, 346, 355–56, 371, 380; critical, 221, 267; criticism of, 224–25; ideological, 175, 245; literalist, 258, 271, 310, 335–36; limits of, 339, 341; meanings of, 284–85, 368; of music, 6, 162–64, 172, 174, 212, 221, 231, 244–45, 258–59, 263, 289, 310, 318, 347, 353, 369; official, 367. *See also* Meaning, musical
Interviews, 266–67, 315, 317, 378; between Shostakovich and Volkov, 4, 23, 25, 34, 42, 51–55, 92–93, 130, 134–35, 138, 178, 225, 305, 313, 321*n*33
Iron Curtain, 207, 330
Irony, 201, 225, 284, 370–74
Isolation, 298

Istoriia stikhotvortsa [Story of a Versifier] (Pushkin), 209
Iz evreiskoi narodnoi poesii [From Jewish folk poetry], for soprano, contralto, tenor, and piano, Op. 79 (1948), 153–54, 158, 183, 206, 314, 372

Jelagin, Juri. *See* Elagin, Yuri Borisovich
Jews, 158
Jolivet, André, 88
Jung, Hans, 274

Karaev, Faradzh Karaevich, 55, 315
Karaev, Kara Abul'fazogly (1918–82), 55, 80, 83, 315
Karlinksy, Simon, 14, 307, 347
Katerina Izmailova. See *Ledi Makbet Mtsenskogo uezda*
Kazn' Stepana Razina [Execution of Stepan Razin], Op. 119 (1964), 210
Keldysh, Georgy (Yuri) [Georgii (Iurii)] Vsevolodovich (1907–95), 56–57, 382
KGB (*Komitet gosudarstvennoi bezopasnosti* [The Committee on State Security]), 43, 53, 55–56, 216, 282*n*19; and *Testimony*, 97, 122, 124, 313
Khachaturian, Aram Ilich [Il'ich] (1903–78), 222, 225, 245, 248, 326, 353
Khachaturian, Karen Surenovich (b. 1920), 80, 83, 153
Khentova, Sofia [Sof'ia] Mikhailovna (b. 1922), 309, 349
Khrennikov, Tikhon Nikolaevich (b. 1913), 12–13, 119, 121, 138, 168–69, 178–79, 186–87*n*m, 245
Khrushchev, Nikita Sergeevich (1894–1971), 208, 234, 262, 374
Kjellberg, Ann, 317
Klop [The Bedbug], 365, 378; Mayakovsky version of, 84, 293; Meyerhold version of, 73, 79
Køenek, Ernst, 200, 330, 380
Kommunist, 87
Kondrashin, Kirill Petrovich (1914–81), 44, 157, 181, 362
Koval [Koval'] (Kovalëv), Marian Viktorovich (1907–71), 375–76
Kozlovsky [Kozlovskii], Vladimir, 120–21
Kremlyov, Yuli Anatolievich [Kremlëv, Iulii Anatol'evich] (1908–71), 56–57, 228*n*14, 238, 241–49
Küchelbecker, Wilhelm, 183, 148, 213, 215*n*h
Kukharsky, Vasily Feodosievich [Kukharskii, Vasilii Feodos'evich] (1918–95), 246, 253*n*42

Language, 17, 223, 209, 290–94, 312, 369, 371; Aesopian, 194, 208, 231, 240, 267, 291; of the Eighth Symphony, 168–69; musical, 143, 151, 194, 240, 270, 289, 298, 296, 303
League of Nations, 365
Lebedinsky [Lebedinskii], Lev Nikolaevich (1904–92), 41–42, 49, 128, 132, 151, 234, 333; and dissidence, 176; and music of Shostakovich, 154, 171–72, 183; and personality of Shostakovich, 172–73; and *Testimony*, 171, 178, 180
Lebrecht, Norman, 314
Ledi Makbet Mtsenskogo uezda [*Lady Macbeth of the Mtsensk District*], Opera, Op. 29 (1930–32); rev. *Katerina Izmailova*, Op. 114 (1954–64), 146, 174, 202, 211, 294, 295, 297, 310, 365–66; book about, 183–84; and Central Committee Resolution, 168; criticism of, 81, 85, 127, 203, 278–79, 328, 330, 350–53, 364; performances of, 142, 240; reactions to, 160–61, 167, 286–87; recording of, 131; reminiscences about, 14, 16, 30, 73–74, 75; revisions to, 168, 184, 352, 376
Legacy, 3, 110, 371, 382; creative, 151, 164, 173; historical, 361; literary, 195; musical, 203, 221, 223, 310
Lenin, Vladimir Ilich [Vladimir Il'ich Ulianov] (1870–1924), 143, 156, 175, 203, 213, 278, 310; commemoration of, 156
Lenin Prize, 89, 182
Leninism, 172
Lermontov, Mikhail Iurevich (1814–41), 148
Leskov, Nikolai Semyonovich [Semënovich]; pseud., Stebnitsky [Stebnitskii] (1831–95), 73–74, 148, 226, 232
Letter writing, 238–39
Letters. *See* Correspondence
Levitin, Yuri [Iurii] Abramovich (1912–93), 80, 83
Literature, 219, 220, 245, 372
Literaturnaia gazeta, 84, 87, 135; letter to the editor of, 3, 4, 12, 50, 55, 80–83, 90, 138–39, 306, 315
Litvinova, Flora Pavlovna (b. 1920), 43, 312–13, 318, 320–22*n*33; reminiscences of, 54–55, 348
Lokshin, Alexander [Aleksandr] Lazarevich (b. 1920), 174
Lyogkii [*lëgkii*] *zhanr*, 380, 365
Lyubimov [Liubimov], Yuri [Iurii] Petrovich (b. 1917), 266, 311

MacDonald, Ian, 48, 224–26, 230–31, 233–34, 257–59, 263, 309–10, 313, 335, 347
Maes, Francis, 370
Mahler, Gustav, 160, 173, 196, 200, 303, 378; comparison with, 158–59, 199, 204, 288
Makarova, Nina Vladimirovna (1908–76), 326
Malevich, Kazimir Severinovich (1878–1935), 291
Malraux, Andrei, 108
The Man with a Gun, Op. 53 (1938), 203
Mandelshtam [Mandel'shtam], Osip Emil'evich (1891–1938), 176–77
Mandelstam [Mandel'shtam] (née Khazina), Nadezhda Yakovlevna [Iakovlevna] (1899–1980), 258

March of the Defenders of Peace, for tenor, chorus, and piano (?1950), 206
Marsh sovetskoi militsii [March of the Soviet Militia], Op. 139 (1970), 209
Martynov, Ivan Ivanovich (b. 1908), 151, 167–71
Marx, 372
Marxism-Leninism, 139, 176, 217, 218, 353
Materialism, 218
Maximenkov, Leonid Valentinovich (b. 1960), 351
Maxim's Return, Op. 45 (1936–37), 203
Maxim's Youth (The Bolshevik), Op. 41 (1934), 203
Mayakovsky [Maiakovskii], Vladimir Vladimirovich (1893–1930), 144, 200–201, 291, 378; reminiscences about, 14, 30, 79, 85; works of, 84, 218, 242, 365
Mazo, Margarita, 318
McCarthy, Joseph, 375
McCarthyites, 313–14
Meaning, musical, 159, 223, 269–70, 279, 283–84, 361; ambiguities of, 246, 293; clarity of, 275; construction of, 332, 336, 340–41, 373; context for, 207; evolution of, 341; hidden, 194–95, 267, 293, 339, 367; layers of, 240, 297; and metaphors, 196; social, 363; universality of, 318, 352
Medvedev, Roy Aleksandrovich (b. 1925), 258
Memoirs, 14, 19, 57, 80, 94, 258, 267; nature of, 97, 107, 165–67, 349. *See also Testimony*
Memory, 196, 261, 266, 340; immortalization of, 94; of Shostakovich, 91, 129, 140, 156, 309, 337
Meyerhold [Meierkhol'd], Vsevolod Emilievich [Èmil'evich] (1874–1940), 18, 48, 52, 130, 144, 197, 200, 291, 350; family of, 33, 50, 134; fate of, 161, 178; reminiscences about, 14, 42, 23, 32, 34, 72–73, 79, 308; works of, 73
Miaskovsky, Nikolai Iakovlevich (1881–1950), 286, 378
Michelangelo, 148, 182
Miller, Edward A., 91
Miłosz, Czesław, 258
Milstein [Mil'shtein], Nathan [Natan] Mironovich (1904–92), 316
Minimalism, 331
Ministry of Culture, 94, 166, 168
Ministry of Internal Affairs (MVD), 209. *See also* KGB
Mistakes, 203–204, 206
Models, 295, 372
Modernism, 242, 270, 284–85, 290–93, 295, 362, 380
Morality, 87, 130, 158, 207, 284, 311
Moscow Art Theater, 353
Moscow Conservatory, 71, 152–53, 162, 325, 334, 337, 362
Moscow Conservatory Production Collective, 351
Moskva, Cheryomushki [*Cherëmushki;* The Cheryomushki Precinct, Moscow], Operetta, Op. 105 (1958), 208–209, 352
Mosolov, Alexander [Aleksandr] Vasil'evich, 381
Motsart i sal'eri [Mozart and Salieri] (Pushkin), 179
Mozart, 70, 174, 199
Mravinsky, Evgeny Alexandrovich [Mravinskii, Evgenii Aleksandrovich] (1903–88), 85, 154, 157, 162, 169; and relations with Shostakovich, 172, 174, 179, 180–82, 185*n*b
Muddle instead of Music editorial, 81, 279, 350, 364, 366, 368, 387, 376. *See also* Criticism; *Ledi Makbet Mtsenskogo uezda; Pravda*, editorials in
Music, 83, 139–40, 151, 154–57, 159–60, 183–84, 233; accessibility of, 196, 304, 346, 369; appeal of, 128, 142–43, 271, 330, 346; appreciation for, 98, 270, 289; approaches to, 201, 206, 270–71, 288–90, 318, 363; appropriation of, 330; autobiographical dimensions of, 258, 288, 299; complexity of, 196, 298; currents in, 329–31; emotional response to, 197, 246, 267, 334, 339–40; evaluation of, 122, 284, 318, 331, 354; evolution of, 164, 199, 291, 294–95; fate of, 219–20, 353; festivals of, 51, 124, 142, 156, 158, 162; importance of, 137, 145, 206, 257, 279, 369; influences on, 291–92, 380; and innovation, 85, 88; intentions of, 164–65, 262, 270, 376; interest in, 49, 58, 98, 122–24; nature of, 6, 203, 219–20, 289, 293, 354, 360, 369; perceptions of, 158, 275; and politics, 304, 335, 367; popular, 293, 296, 297; power of, 148; reactions to, 161, 244–45, 274, 286–87; reception of, 5–6, 242, 304, 327, 329–32, 341, 363, 364, 367, 368; recordings of, 165, 182; recycling in, 295, 298, 310, 350; revision of, 156–57, 168, 184, 376; significance of, 175, 267, 283; study of, 69–72, 75, 239, 271, 291, 329–30, 361; universality of, 205, 335
Music, ballet, 293
Music, film, 153, 156, 203, 293, 294, 297, 365
Music, Soviet, 82, 94, 195, 242, 245, 260, 279, 326
Music, theater, 293, 294, 296
Music, vocal, 210
Musical life: Soviet, 5, 12, 230, 238, 260, 267, 334, 351, 381; American, 329–32, 361–62, 364
Musicians, Soviet, 362
Musicologists, 107, 242
Musicology, 123, 124–25, 239, 243, 249; approaches to, 242, 361, 364, 377; Soviet, 99, 239–40
Musorgsky [Musorgskii], Modest Petrovich (1839–81), 56, 77–78, 109, 196, 242, 378, 382; allusions to, 353; comparisons with,

153; reminiscences about, 14; works of, 77–78, 109, 169, 188*n*r, 212, 235*n*6, 266, 381
Mythology, 279

Nad rodinoi nashei solntse siiaet [The Sun shines over our Motherland], for boys' choir, chorus, and orchestra, Op. 90 (1952), 156, 175, 206, 352
Naiman, Anatoly [Anatolii], 118
National Socialism, 277, 318
Nazism, 159, 277, 330
Nemirovich-Danchenko, Vladimir Ivanovich (1858–1943), 161
Neo-romanticism, 331
Nestyev [Nest'ev], Israel [Izrail'] Vladimirovich (1911–93), 159–62, 246
Neuhaus [Neigauz], Heinrich [Genrikh] Gustavovich (1888–1964), 154, 272
New Economic Policy, 378
New Music, 330, 336
The New Music, 329
New Objectivity, 365
The New Shostakovich, 6, 48, 230, 257–59, 263, 309, 322*n*49, 335
Nezabyvaemyi 1919 [The Unforgettable year 1919], 153
Nezhdanova, Antonina Vasilievna [Vasil'evna] (1873–1950), 167
Nightingale (Stravinsky), 71–72
Nikolskaya [Nikol'skaia], Irina, 49
NKVD (Peoples' Commissariat of Internal Affairs), 161. *See also* KGB
Nomenklatura, 240, 241, 246
Nos [The Nose], Opera, Op. 15 (1927–28), 73, 174, 201, 293, 297, 355, 365, 380
Novyi Vavilon [The New Babylon] (1928–29), 293

Obituary, 193, 279, 304, 332
Offenbach, 174, 201, 297
Oistrakh, David Fyodorovich [Fëdorovich] (1908–74), 157
Opinion, 110, 129, 198, 249, 261, 275, 284, 330
Opportunism, 207–208, 369
Order of Lenin, 181
Organization of Revolutionary Composers and Musical Activists, 351
Orlov, Genrikh (Henry) Alexandrovich, 3, 29, 60*n*28, 99–100, 177–78, 260; and BBC interview, 120–21; and music of Shostakovich, 121–24; and opinion on *Testimony*, 107–10, 111–16, 117; and relationship with Volkov, 117–19; and review commission, 100–106, 119–20, 125
Orwell, George, 232
Our Song, for bass, mixed chorus, and piano (1950), 206

Pacifism, 352
Padenie Berlina [The Fall of Berlin], 153
Palata No. 6 [Ward No. 6] (Chekhov), 155
Pasternak, Boris Leonidovich (1890–1960), 172, 177, 187*n*q
Pateticheskaia oratoriia [Oratorio patètico], comp. Svidirov; text, Mayakovsky (1959), 242
Peiko, Nikolai Ivanovich (b. 1916), 161
Perestroika, 260–61
Performances, 128, 148, 162–63, 165, 174, 279–80, 338, 347; banning of, 153, 166, 220, 250–51, 353, 358*n*8; by Shostakovich, 71, 73, 159, 168–69; style of, 337; of symphonies, 94, 169, 180–82, 298, 363
Persecution, 150–51, 175, 184
Personality, cult of, 197, 206, 262, 374
Personality, of Shostakovich, 85–86, 108, 117, 196, 197, 259, 290, 293; and ambivalence, 122; and compassion, 82, 145–46, 162, 331; complexities of, 154, 176, 224, 262–63, 267, 319, 340, 347, 350; conflicts in, 123, 177; creativity of, 202, 370; and cynicism, 261; mannerism of, 40–41, 195, 272, 333; and memory, 41, 70, 107, 109, 313; and moral standards, 57, 167; and punctuality, 163, 170, 182, 338; and relations with others, 157, 172–73, 364; stubbornness of, 164, 175; traits of, 110; and weaknesses of character, 120, 165–66, 195, 261, 265, 311
Perspectives, 1–2, 331; changes in, 327
Pesn' o lesakh [The Song of the forests], Oratorio, for tenor and bass soloists, boys' choir, chorus, and orchestra, Op. 81 (1949), 151, 156, 175, 206, 242, 352
Pesni i pliaski smerti [*Songs and Dances of Death*] (Musorgsky), 169, 212, 235*n*6, 266
Petrushka (Stravinsky), 71, 188*n*r
Philistinism, 160, 209
Philosophy, 218, 270
Photographs, 13, 18–19, 52, 130–31, 178
Piano Concerto No. 1 in C Minor with solo trumpet, Op. 35 (1935), 153
Piano Quintet op. 57 (1940), 159, 162–63
Piano Trio No. 2, Op. 67 (1944), 45, 158, 211
Picasso, 265–66
Platonov, Andrei Andreevich [Andrei Platonovich Klimentov] (1899–1951), 219
Politics, 47–48, 157, 275, 304, 346; cultural, 12
Polyphony, 251*n*9, 293, 297
Polystylistics, 159
Pornophony, 376
Portrayal, of Shostakovich, 139, 225, 346–47, 373; in *Testimony*, 11, 85, 98, 109, 124, 135, 138, 150–51, 225, 309, 317, 332, 370
Poskrebyshev, Alexander [Aleksandr] Nikolaevich (1891–65), 178–79
Prague Spring Festival, 169
Pravda, editorials in (1936), 161, 197, 203, 219, 278–79, 287, 294, 298, 328, 330, 350–51, 364, 371; response to, 195, 367

Predislovie k polnomu sobraniiu moikh sochinenii i kratkoe razmyshlenie po povodu etogo predisloviia [Preface to the Complete Edition of My Works and a Brief Reflection apropos to the Preface], for bass and piano, Op. 123 (1966), 209
Pressures, 200, 261, 348, 367, 382
Primitivism, 225
Principles, ethical, 278
Prison, Stalinist, 172
Production, artistic, 219, 221, 226
Professionalism, 245
Prokofiev [Prokof'ev], Sergei Sergeevich (1891–1953), 142, 177, 199, 222, 259, 288, 291, 378; comparisons with, 284, 286; music of, 147; popularity of, 123, 167, 196, 248, 327; prohibition of, 353; and relations with Rostropovich, 46; and relations with Shostakovich, 48, 147–48, 173; *Testimony* portrait of, 4, 45, 47, 85
Proletarian music organizations, 351
Proletarskii muzykant, 234
Proletkult, 354
Propaganda, 86, 95, 201, 216, 223, 243, 330; agitation, 202, 278; anti-Soviet, 13, 93–94; political, 340
Property, intellectual, 132
Protest, 158, 199, 200, 223, 369; courage to, 128, 260; lack of, 195, 161; music as, 153–54, 160, 172, 197, 205, 310, 335; personal, 353; voice of, 213
Protopopov, Sergei Vladimirovich (1893–1954), 377
Psychology, 175, 218, 270
Publication, of *Testimony*, 3, 19, 25, 28, 56, 90–93, 98–99, 106, 121, 307; Russian-language, 19, 28, 92–93, 98, 132, 138–39, 177–79, 316, 323*n*50, 370
Publications, 157, 225
Publicity, 95
Puccini, 284
Purges, 197, 203, 349
Pushkin, Alexander [Aleksandr] Sergeevich (1799–1837), 148, 179, 194, 209, 236*n*c, 294
Pyatnitsky Choir, 375

Quotations, 355, 363–64; self, 295, 374

Rachmaninoff [Rakhmaninov], Sergei Vasilievich [Vasil'evich] (1873–1943), 142, 276
Radlov, Nikolai E. (1889–1942), 197
Rationality, 223
Rayok [*Raëk*] (Musorgsky), 188*n*r
Realism, 242
Reality, 204; Soviet, 124, 129, 152, 176, 223, 260, 332, 368
Realization, artistic, 259
Regime, Soviet, 226, 250, 364; conflicts with, 122–23, 144, 222–24, 335, 354; loyalty to, 241, 347; opposition to, 93, 233–34, 277–78; relationship with, 12, 88–89, 108–109, 127, 139–40, 160–61, 167–68, 231, 263; Stalinist, 160, 171
Rembrandt, 320
Reminiscences, 14–17, 19, 135; about Shostakovich, 24, 39, 151
Repin, Il'ia Efimovich (1844–1930), 56, 382
Repino, 52, 54, 305
Repression, 150, 178, 207, 341; and anti-Semitism, 166; Stalinist, 156
Requiem (Tishchenko), 50–51
Resistance, 347, 354
Resolution on Music (1948) of the Central Committee of the Communist Party, 152–53, 166, 168, 204, 206, 220, 330, 353, 367, 374; and public confession, 265; and purges, 240, 288, 354
Response, creative, 194, 367, 381
Responsibility, 89, 158, 349; civic, 86, 155, 196, 200, 240, 375. *See also* Service, public
Revolution (1905), 177, 310, 352, 369
Revolution (1917), 199, 200, 203, 218, 365; appeal of, 144; ideals of, 176, 199, 204; musical portrayal of, 156, 176, 201–204, 234, 235*n*7
Rhetoric, 289, 292, 365; Cold War, 331, 332
Rhythm, 296, 297, 298
Richter [Rikhter], Sviatoslav Teofilovich (1915–97), 154, 272
Rilke, Rainer Maria, 148, 213
Rimsky-Korsakov [Rimskii-Korsakov], Nikolai Andreevich (1844–1908), 77–78, 196; music of, 372
Rolland, Romain, 85, 88, 108, 225
Romanticism, 160, 326
Rossini, 172, 355, 363
Rostropovich, Mstislav Leopoldovich [Leopol'dovich] (b. 1927), 44–46, 142, 260, 310, 356*n*3, 363, 375; education of, 146; letter of, 95–96; and music of Shostakovich, 131, 143–44, 148–49; and relationship with Shostakovich, 145–47; and *Testimony*, 315–16
Rozhdestvensky [Rozhdestvenskii], Genady [Genadii] Nikolaevich (b. 1931), 177, 294
Rumors, 11, 47–48, 63*n*58, 307, 315, 317
Russian Association of Proletarian Musicians (RAPM), 168, 186*n*k, 233–34, 351, 355, 380–81
The Russian Review, 20, 22, 307, 309, 315, 347
Russian State Archive of Literature and Art, 183
Russkaia mysl' o muzyke [Russian thoughts about music], 241
Russkii sovetskii simfonizm [Russian Soviet symphonism], 99
Ryzhkin, Josif Yakovlevich [Iosif Iakovlevich] (b. 1907), 228*n*14

Sabinina, Marina Dmitrievna (1917–2000), 152–58, 351
Sacrifice, 210

Sakharov, Andrei Dmitrievich (1921–89), 172; and letter of denunciation, 128, 132, 166, 225, 266, 304, 311
Sartre, Jean-Paul, 218, 222
Satire, 209, 225, 365, 371; social, 217
Satiry [Satires], Op. 109 (1960), 209
Scandal, 45, 86, 124, 129–30, 153, 221
Schnittke, Alfred [Al'fred] Garrievich (1934–98), 166, 289, 362
Schoenberg, Arnold, 123, 200, 303, 329–31, 380; and separation of art from history, 361–62; and *Style and Idea*, 336
Scholarship, 5–7, 13, 224–26, 232, 249, 258, 267, 276, 347–50, 354, 356; contributions to, 223; integrity of, 120, 263, 312; musicological, 239–40
Schonberg, Harold C., 11, 86, 306
Schopenhauer, 270
Schubert, 56, 382
Schwarz, Boris, 124, 222, 342*n*1
Scriabin [Skriabin], Alexander [Aleksandr] Nikolaevich (1871/72–1915), 142, 167, 199, 291, 378
Second Viennese School, 329
Semiotics, 371–72
Semyonov [Semënov], Sergei Aleksandrovich (b. 1893), 41
Sensationalism, 124
Serenade in A (Stravinsky), 71
Service, public, 89, 170–71, 195, 203, 206, 349. *See also* Responsibility, civic
Shafarevich, Igor [Igor'] Rostislavovich (b. 1923), 340
Shakespeare, 148
Shaw, Bernard, 85, 88, 108
Shchedrin, Rodion Konstantinovich (b. 1932), 55, 225, 326
Shchelokov, Nikolai Anisimovich, 210
Shebalin, Vissarion Yakovlevich [Iakovlevich] (1902–63), 235*n*5
Sheinberg, Esti, 370–73
Shepilov, Dmitri Trofimovich (1905–95), 189*n*cc, 353–54
Sholokhov, Mikhail Alexandrovich [Aleksandrovich] (1905–84), 174, 352–53
Shostakovich: A Life, 2, 6, 312, 314, 346, 356
Shostakovich: A Life Remembered, 6, 310, 340, 350; reviews of, 265–68
Shostakovich, Dmitri Dmitrievich (1906–75), 143, 325–27, 337–39; conduct of, 226; conversations with, 273–74; death of, 14, 193, 289; defense of, 240, 271; evaluation of, 12, 44–45, 284–85, 329; exploitation of, 129, 370; fate of, 117, 194; genius of, 144, 148, 163, 166, 172, 196, 286, 346; health of, 52, 108, 131, 153, 155, 175, 211, 315; intelligence of, 148; international recognition of, 87–88, 150–51, 196, 360; life of, 58, 150, 224; literary interests of, 79, 174, 179; morality of, 225; musical interests of, 174, 295, 297; in photograph, 18, 52; and politics, 242, 278, 284; psychological state of, 108, 110, 161, 155, 347; and public statements, 95; reinterpretation of, 257–58; reputation of, 201, 288, 377; significance of, 144–45, 173, 174, 176, 196, 221, 284, 328, 360; stature of, 48–49, 122, 137, 160, 167, 194, 196, 199, 206, 221, 233, 248, 261, 278, 288, 304, 363–65, 375; as storyteller, 41, 46, 54; as tragic figure, 151, 153, 157, 173, 260, 380; voice of, 98, 109, 195, 377; youth of, 79, 200, 202, 286, 293, 364–66, 377–78. *See also* Personality, of Shostakovich
Shostakovich, Galina Dmitrievna (daughter; b. 1936), 43, 52, 93, 314
Shostakovich, Irina Antonovna, née Supinskaia (3rd wife; b. 1934), 3–4, 18, 94, 138, 182, 332; and defense of Shostakovich, 128–30, 132–33; and *Testimony*, 12, 17, 52–53, 90, 92–93, 119, 130–32, 306, 317, 315; and Volkov, 135, 155
Shostakovich, Maxim [Maksim] Dmitrievich (son; b. 1938), 52, 259, 260, 261, 314–16, 332; as conductor, 363; and *Testimony*, 46–48, 93, 121, 135–36, 309, 334
Shostakovich, Nina Vasilievna [Vasil'evna], (1st wife; see Varzar, Nina Vasileievna [Vasil'evna])
Shostakovich, Sofia Vasilievna [Sof'ia Vasil'evna], née Kokoúlina (mother; 1878–1955), 69–70
Shostakovich Family, 3, 53, 90–94
Shostakovich Family Archive, 28–30, 182–83
Shostakovich Reconsidered, 1–2, 6, 46, 122, 276, 311–12, 347; reviews of, 5, 230–35, 277
Shostakovich Wars, 2, 6, 283
Signature, of Shostakovich: on articles, 195, 261, 310; and denunciations, 132–33, 187*n*q, 198, 261, 266, 311; musical, 199, 309, 373–74; on photograph, 13, 52, 60*n*25, 65*n*89, 130; on *Testimony* manuscript, 3, 14, 17, 19, 23, 25, 28–30, 32, 39, 43–44, 45, 55, 69, 89, 101, 108, 131, 132, 147, 276, 305–306, 308, 320*n*33, 324*n*a, 332–33, 357*n*3 (*see also* Authenticity, of *Testimony; Testimony* debate); and willingness to sign, 43, 56–57, 120, 132, 166, 262
Simfonii Shostakovicha [The symphonies of Shostakovich] 3, 99, 124
Sinfonia Concertante (Prokofiev), 147
Skrebkov, Sergei Sergeevich (1905–67), 246, 253*n*43
Skripka Rotshil'da [Rothschild's violin] (Fleishman), 18, 51
Slavery, 266
Socialism, 273
Socialist Realism, 5, 87, 176, 217, 221, 222, 287, 332, 339; and American composers, 326; and fiction, 353; ideals of, 152, 169, 350; and Shostakovich, 175, 243, 363
Society, Soviet, 85, 88, 198, 216, 224, 349, 375

Society for Private Performances, 361
Sokolsky [Sokol'skii], Matias, 355
Solidarity, 376
Sollertinsky [Sollertinskii], Ivan Ivanovich (1902–44), 158, 292, 338, 350
Sologub, Fyodor [Fëdor Kuzmich Ternikov] (1863–1927), 89
Solzhenitsyn, Alexander [Aleksandr] Isaevich (b. 1918), 172, 182, 187*n*q, 258, 314, 319*n*23, 340, 363; and denunciation letter, 261, 266; and satire, 374
Songs: prison, 194, 374; revolutionary, 204, 211, 310, 337
Soul, 218, 270, 271, 283, 318, 340
Sovetskaia muzyka, 47, 57, 93, 246, 248; editorial board of, 154–55, 247; reminiscences published in, 24, 33, 39, 308; and Shostakovich, 132; and Volkov, 23, 46, 52, 92, 130, 305, 333, 343*n*15
Sovetskoe isskustvo [Soviet art], 159
Soviet power, 226, 265, 353
Soviet Union, 143–44. *See also* Regime, Soviet; Society, Soviet; System, Soviet
Spirit, human, 222, 298
Spirituality, 225, 340
St. Petersburg: A Cultural History (Volkov), 50–51, 52, 316
Stagnation, 220
Stalin, Joseph [Iosif] Vissarionovich [Iosif Vissarionovich Dzhugashvili] (1879–1953), 16, 109, 186*n*m, 219, 222, 226, 304, 374; and Composers Union, 178–79; death of, 128, 206, 358*n*8; and *Lady Macbeth*, 160–61, 366; and personality cult, 262; and portrayal in music, 175, 189*n*cc, 224–25, 318, 335, 356; praise of, 177; and Tenth Symphony, 139
Stalin era, 109, 353, 372
Stalin prize, 175
Stalin regime, 48, 220, 277
Stalinism, 108, 172, 222, 234, 277, 282*n*20, 291, 303, 313
Stanislavsky, Konstantin Sergeevich [Konstantin Sergeevich Alekseev] (1863–1938), 85
Stasi, 273
Steinberg [Shteinberg], Maximilian [Maksimilian] Oseevich (1883–1946), 286
Stockhausen, Karlheinz, 364
Stoicism, moral, 206
Story of a Friendship; The Letters of Dmitri Shostakovich to Isaak Glikman, 1941–1975, 373
Strauss, Richard, 284, 378
Stravinsky, Igor Fyodorovich [Stravinskii, Igor' Fëdorovich] (1882–1971), 109, 200, 284, 291, 296, 378; memoirs of, 196, 232, 236*n*b; music of, 45, 71–72, 188*n*r, 361; perceptions of, 123; reminiscences about, 14, 23, 25, 27, 29, 40, 42, 48, 308; and Shostakovich, 45, 173, 286–88, 297
String Quartet No. 1 in C Major, Op. 49 (1938), 153, 163
String Quartet No. 3 in F Major, Op. 73 (1946), 154, 162–64, 186*n*g
String Quartet No. 8 in C Minor, Op. 110 (1960), 211, 318, 339; imagery in, 309; interpretation of, 373–374; meaning of to Shostakovich, 337–39, 341; performances of, 337–38; reviews of, 51, 305; signature in, 353
String quartets, 163–65, 210–11, 240, 266, 337
Structure, musical, 204, 205, 239, 240, 246, 271, 289, 296, 298
Struggle, dramatic, 171
Stukach, 219, 222
Style, musical, 159–60, 164–65, 201–202, 224, 293, 331, 367; compositional, 240, 290, 295–98, 304, 336, 354–55, 365–66; dramatic, 205; evolution of, 200, 371, 368, 376; individual, 199; performance, 337, 339. *See also* Analysis; Music; Structure, musical; Techniques, compositional
Subtexts, musical, 231, 288, 366
Suffering, human, 177, 196
Suicide, 212
Svetlyi ruchei [The Sparkling Stream], Ballet, Op. 39 (1934–35), 350
Sviridov, Georgy (Yurii) Vasilievich [Georgii (Yurii) Vasil'evich] (1915–98), 161, 222, 225, 248
Symbolism, musical, 156, 172, 205, 206, 223–24, 289, 293. *See also* Imagery, musical
Symphonies, 41, 117, 123, 155–56, 158, 204–207, 240, 304; and drama, 200; early, 297; and ideology, 246; later, 329; meaning of, 160, 171, 212, 233, 276; study of, 99
Symphonism, 336
Symphony No. 1, Op. 10 (1924–25), 167, 172, 199, 200, 227*n*11, 233; analysis of, 366, 371; quotations from, 211; reception of, 364; responses to, 286–87; symbolism of, 205
Symphony No. 2, "Dedication to October" (*Posviashchenie Oktiabriu*), Op. 14 (1927), 176, 201, 286, 303, 365, 379–80
Symphony No. 3 in E-flat Major, "The First of May," Op. 20 (1929), 181, 201, 228*n*17, 293, 298, 380
Symphony No. 4 in C Minor, Op. 43 (1934/35–36), 12, 181, 202–204, 240, 294, 297–98, 304; compared to Mahler, 158; history of, 351; interpretations of, 258–59, 309; performance of, 328, 351; tone of, 329
Symphony No. 5 (1937), 127, 139, 160, 272, 291, 298, 303, 309; descriptive analysis of, 335; interpretations of, 356; parallels to Beethoven's Ninth, 368; reception of, 168, 367; as response to criticism, 294
Symphony No. 7, "Leningrad," Op. 60 (1941), 262, 276, 298, 303, 304, 361; composition of, 16, 75, 107; facsimile edition of, 183; interpretations of, 85, 233, 335; performances of, 94, 318, 362;

reception of, 159, 168–69, 205, 287–88, 362–63; review of, 330; in *Testimony*, 308
Symphony No. 8, Op. 65 (1943), 107, 123, 148, 151, 167–68, 171, 205, 304, 374; criticisms of, 169, 376; quotations from, 211; review of, 154, 169
Symphony No. 10 (1953), 63*n*58, 139–40, 151, 171, 206, 224, 281*n*9, 315, 318; interpretations of, 356; reactions to, 241–42, 243–48
Symphony No. 11 in G Minor, "The Year 1905" (*1905 god*), Op. 103 (1956–57), 143, 151, 156, 171, 176–77, 194, 204, 233, 240, 309, 318, 380; imagery of, 172, 368–369; interpretations of, 310, 369; quotations from, 211; reception of, 247, 352, 369
Symphony No. 12, "The Year 1917" (*1917 god*) (1959–61), 155–56, 160, 172, 175, 203, 233, 240, 380; artistic value of, 177; critique of, 157; interpretations of, 176; meaning of, 318
Symphony No. 13 in B-flat Minor, *Babyi Yar* [*Babii iar*], for bass soloist, chorus of basses, and orchestra, Op. 113 (1962), 151, 155–58, 172, 176, 207, 210, 240, 357*n*8, 372; criticism of, 208; and Mravinsky, 180–82, 185*n*b
Symphony No. 14, for soprano, bass, string orchestra, and percussion, Op. 135 (1969), 54, 172, 176, 181–82, 211–13, 266
Symphony No. 15 in A Major, Op. 141 (1971), 54, 172, 174, 181–82, 355; performance of, 363–64
System, Soviet, 87–88, 94, 220, 241, 265, 307. *See also* Regime, Soviet

Talent, 199, 360
Taruskin, Richard, 233, 276, 278–79, 288–89, 294–95, 310, 312, 318; criticism of, 348, 356–57*n*3; and reception of *Testimony*, 306–307; and *Testimony* debate, 313–14
Tchaikovsky, Pyotr Ilich [Chaikovskii, Pëtr Il'ich] (1840–93), 48, 199, 242, 245, 259, 353; music of, 70, 152
Techniques, compositional, 200, 202, 220, 296, 366. *See also* Style, musical: compositional
Ten Poems on Texts by Revolutionary Poets of the Late-Nineteenth and Early-Twentieth Centuries, for *a cappella* chorus, Op. 88 (1951), 204
Terror, 144, 197, 207, 298; Stalinist, 160, 291
Tertz, Abram [Andrei Donatovich Siniavskii] (b. 1925), 348
Testimony: The Memoirs of Dmitri Shostakovich, as related to and edited by Solomon Volkov (1979), 84, 128, 150, 275, 347; compilation process for, 14, 17, 18–19, 25, 42, 51, 98, 101, 107, 119, 257–58, 277, 305–307, 317, 320*n*33, 333, 357*n*3; contents of, 14, 46–48, 50, 52–53, 65*n*89, 134–35, 138, 178, 180; context of, 285; criticism of, 44–46, 47–48, 50–51, 55, 57–58, 85, 122, 139, 223, 306; defense of, 45–46, 49, 54, 97, 122, 312; errors in, 12–13, 16–18, 46, 81, 108–10, 177–80; fate of, 121–22, 311; impact of, 48–49, 53, 98, 124, 222, 260, 285, 304, 332, 334; impetus for, 305; nature of, 93, 107, 110, 120, 134, 138, 259, 317; and previously published materials, 3, 13–17, 22, 23, 28–30, 33–34, 39–40, 42–43, 46, 69–79, 81, 109, 178, 262, 276–77, 307–308, 313, 332–33; reception of, 14, 44–47, 86, 97–98, 151, 180, 232, 306, 370; relevance of, 273; reviews of, 2, 11, 12, 22–23, 307; veracity of, 347–48. *See also* Authenticity, of *Testimony;* Publication, of *Testimony;* Signature, of Shostakovich; *Testimony* debate; Volkov, Solomon Moiseyevich
Testimony debate, 2, 124, 222, 271, 279, 283, 305, 311, 313, 318, 348, 356. *See also* Authenticity, of *Testimony;* Textual comparison
Testimony manuscript, 90, 107, 131, 179, 306, 308; access to, 309; expert evaluation of, 99–110, 111–16, 118, 119, 121; layout of, 28–29, 30, 32–34, 39–40, 42–43; Moscow version of, 30–40, 60*n*22, 69, 74; original, 17, 23, 26, 28–29, 34, 39, 42–44, 59*n*14. *See also* Authenticity, of *Testimony;* Signature, of Shostakovich; Textual comparison
Textual comparison: of *Testimony*, 3, 14–16, 23, 29–30, 32–33, 39–40, 69–79, 179, 308, 332; of Shostakovich correspondence, 42
Thaw, 206, 207, 262, 349
Theater, 204–205, 297; Constructivist, 354; influence of, 294–96
Themes, musical, 159–160, 171, 172, 177, 214, 233, 337–38; revolutionary, 200
Theodorakis, Mikis, 128, 133
Theorists, 240, 291
Theory: literary, 291; musicological, 239, 372
Thompson, Virgil, 328–29, 330, 362
Tikhii Don [*Quiet Don*] (Sholokhov), 174, 352–53
Tishchenko, Boris Ivanovich (b. 1930), 63*n*63, 80, 83, 151, 175, 320*n*33, 332; correspondence with, 348; and influence of Shostakovich, 173–74; and *Literaturnaia gazeta* letter, 55, 138, 139; and relations with Volkov, 51–54, 130, 134–36, 178; and *Testimony*, 4, 18, 50–51, 52, 315
Tonality, 304
Tone, 195, 329
Topics, musical, 336, 368, 371
Toscanini, 47, 48, 109, 259
Totalitarianism, 144, 176, 196, 199, 223, 232, 282*n*20
Tragedy, 144, 160, 214, 225, 284; in music, 164–65, 169
Trance, 290, 292, 297

Tree of Music, 99, 124
Truth, 48–49, 207, 239, 258–59, 274, 279, 315, 347; essential, 223, 231, 260, 263; scholarly, 249; universal, 204
Tsvetaeva, Marina Ivanovna (1892–1941), 148, 183, 193–94
Tukhachevsky [Tukhachevskii], Mikhail Nikolaevich (1893–1937), 197
Twentieth Party Congress, 208, 262
Twenty-Four Preludes and Fugues, for piano, Op. 87 (1951), 161, 206, 243, 352

Ulrich, Homer, 331
Union of Composers. *See* Composers Union
United Nations, 202
Uslovno ubityi [Declared Dead] (1931), 380–81
Ussachevsky [Usachevskii], Vladimir (Alexis) (1911–90), 119
Ustvolskaya [Ustvol'skaia], Galina Ivanovna (b. 1919), 174

Vainberg, Moisei. *See* Weinberg, Moisei Samuilovich
Vainkop, Yulian Yakovlevich [Iulian Iakovlevich] (b. 1901), 244
Varzar, Nina Vasileievna [Vasil'evna] (Shostakovich's 1st wife; 1909–54), 54
Verdi, 297
Vernost' [Loyalty], eight ballads for unaccompanied male chorus, Op. 136 (1970), 175, 352
Victims, 156, 160, 176, 204, 219, 233, 310, 366–67; of terror, 197–98
Vintik, 219, 222
Violence, 177, 212, 298
Violin Concerto No. 1 in A Minor, Op. 77 (1947–48), 152, 157, 206, 245
Vishnevskaya [Vishnevskaia], Galina Pavlovna (b. 1926), 44–45, 96, 310, 315; memoirs of, 139, 140; performance in *Katerina Izmailova*, 168
Voina i mir [*War and peace*] (Prokofiev), 146–47
Volkov, Solomon Moiseyevich [Moiseevich] (b. 1944?), 3, 131, 140, 232, 272, 278, 305, 316–17; as author, 47–48, 81–82, 109–10, 138, 259–60; claims of, 1, 23, 25, 34, 271, 341, 343*n*15; credibility of, 45, 86–87, 89, 120, 177, 276–77, 307–308; and defense of *Testimony*, 22, 311; and emigration, 17, 56, 282*n*19, 306; integrity of, 14, 19, 42–44, 46–48, 53, 120, 134, 258, 260; intentions of, 57–58, 138, 235*n*3; in photograph, 18, 52; portrayal of Shostakovich by, 93, 151, 155; and prepublication review of *Testimony*, 100, 103, 117–19; and publication of *Testimony*, 28, 132, 177–79; and relationship with Shostakovich, 51, 84–85; and response to criticism, 13–14, 22, 50–51, 53, 309, 347; scholarship of, 12–13, 223–24. *See also* Interviews
Vonnegut, Kurt, 232
Vstrecha na El'be [Meeting at the Elba], 153
Vstrechnyi [The counterplan] (1932), 202
Vulgarity, 139–40, 160
The Vyborg District, Op. 50 (1938), 203

Wagner, 199, 284, 355, 364
Walter, Bruno, 364
War, 181, 200, 289, 337; First World, 143; Second World (Great Patriotic War), 16, 18, 75–76, 87, 107, 183, 205, 329, 361; and Seventh Symphony, 262, 276, 308, 318, 363; theme of, 243, 352. *See also* Cold War
Waxman, Frank, 325–26
Weber, 201
Webern, 123, 284, 289–90
Weill, Kurt, 286
Weinberg [Vainberg], Moisei [also called Mechislav] Samuilovich (1919–96), 80, 83, 168, 174; and *Literaturnaia gazeta* letter, 55, 137–38, 139
William Tell (Rossini), 172, 355
Wilson, Elizabeth, 265, 266, 277, 310–11, 340, 350
Work, creative, 82, 97, 151, 220, 241–42, 270, 284, 304; and politics, 310; reception of, 366; and regime, 177; and *Testimony*, 231; tragic element in, 153
World of Art, 173
Worldview, 197, 371
Wozzek (Berg), 179

Yakubov [Iakubov], Manashir Abramovich (b. 1936), 175–84, 315
Yastrebstev (Iastrebtsev; also spelled Iastretsov), Vasily Vasilievich [Vasilii Vasil'evich] (1866–1934), 196, 260
Yavorsky [Iavorskii] Boleslav Leopoldovich [Leopol'dovich] (1877–1942), 377–79
Yevtushenko, Evgeny [Evtushenko, Evgenii] (b. 1933), 148, 156–57, 183, 210, 221, 358*n*8; poetry of, 156–57, 181, 207–208. *See also* Symphony No. 13
Yudina [Iudina], Maria [Mariia] Veniaminovna (1899–1970), 108, 161
Yurodivy [*iurodivyi*], 224, 225, 263

Zamyatin, Evgeny [Zamiatin, Evgenii] Ivanovich (1884–1937), 197, 300*n*23
Zhdanov, Andrei Aleksandrovich (1896–1948), 189*n*cc, 273, 288, 353, 367, 375
Zhdanovshchina, 353, 367, 370, 374–76
Zhitomirsky [Zhitormirskii], Daniel [Daniël'] Vladimirovich (1906–92), 41, 49, 176, 348
Zhlob, 219, 222
Zhurbin, Alexander, 137–38, 140
Zionism, 18
Zolotoi telyonok [The golden calf] (Ilf and Petrov), 234
Zolotoi vek [The Golden Age], 167, 201, 303, 365, 371
Zoshchenko, Mikhail Mikhailovich (1894–1958), 18, 48, 52, 108, 130, 178, 300*n*23